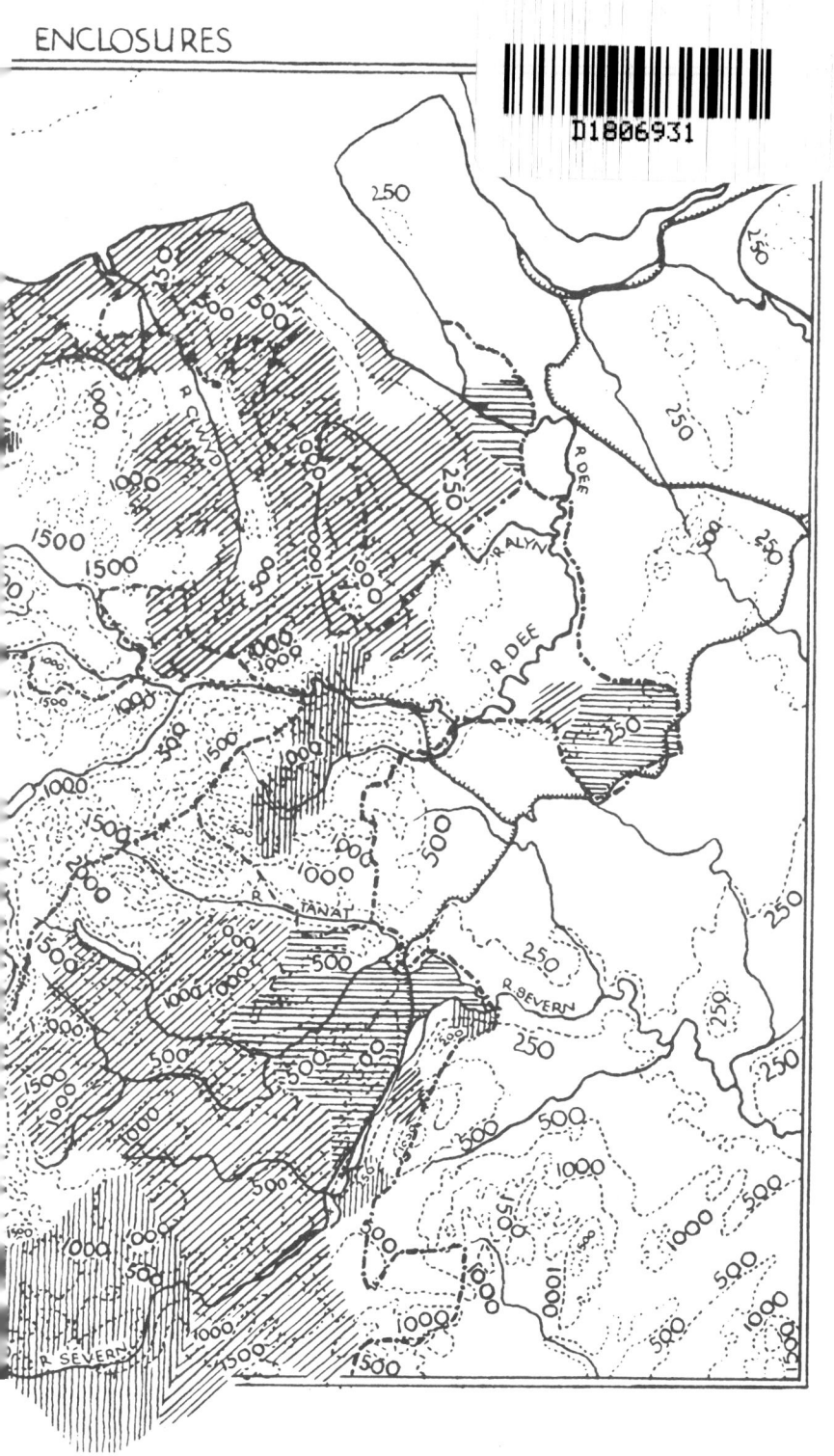

THE
INDUSTRIAL REVOLUTION
IN
NORTH WALES

THE
INDUSTRIAL REVOLUTION
IN
NORTH WALES

A. H. DODD

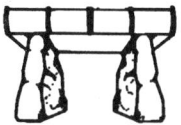

BRIDGE BOOKS, WREXHAM, CLWYD

First Edition 1933
Second Edition 1951
Third Edition 1971

© University of Wales, 1971

First published by the
University of Wales Press.
Bridge Books Edition published 1990.

Published in Great Britain by
BRIDGE BOOKS
61, Park Avenue,
Wrexham, Clwyd.
LL12 7AW

British Library Cataloguing in Publication Data
Dodd, Arthur Herbert 1891 - 1975
The industrial Revolution in North Wales. - 4th. ed.
1. Wales. North Wales. Industrialisation, history
I. Title
338. 094291
ISBN 1-872424-06-6

Printed by
Longdunn Press
Bristol

To the Memory of
My Father.

PREFACE.

THE term "Industrial Revolution," with its many misleading associations, is a legacy of which the modern economic historian would gladly disembarrass himself, if it were not forced on him by the usage of nearly half a century, and if any other brief and convenient label could be found for the period of history and the phase of development which it so imperfectly indicates.[1] The impression created by Toynbee's unfinished sketch, which first gave general currency to the term, has been deepened by the focussing of attention on what has become, *par excellence*, Industrial England, and especially on the highly unrepresentative Lancashire cotton and Yorkshire worsted industries. Mantoux, for instance, intent on tracing the évolution of a set of phenomena rather than on writing the history of a period, restricts his survey to "the midland and northern counties, the chief home of the events which are the objects of our study;" and he is not concerned to carry the story beyond the point where "the stage was ready set" for the full-fledged system of modern industry—a point which he fixes in "the first years of the nineteenth century."[2] Such a treatment, however, almost inevitably lends colour to the legend of a rapid victory for steam power and big industry, accompanied by a hasty concentration of manufactures on the coalfields, and involving the summary demise of scattered trades and handicrafts.

To counteract this impression it is necessary to study other regions—especially regions which do not to-day form part of Industrial Britain, but which nevertheless shared in the wide diffusion of industrial enterprise, the general quickening of economic life, that constituted the first phase of the Industrial Revolution, before the era of concentration set in. To contemporary observers it was by no means as obvious as it is to-day—or rather as it seemed before the

[1] *See* an excellent summary of current views by H. L. Beales in *History*, XIV, p. 125. On the origins of the term *see* Mantoux : *Industrial Revolution*, p. 25 *n*.
[2] *Op. cit.*, p. 43.

War—where the economic centre of gravity of Britain was ultimately to lie.   Hardly a district, however backward or remote, but could, in the early years of George the Third, show signs of change startling enough to give some substance to the wildest visions of material progress.

North Wales, as the following pages will show, was no exception.   Here the leeway to be made up was abnormally heavy, for the country had long been cut off by a geographical and cultural barrier from the main streams of economic development, and its history had not favoured the accumulation or the profitable investment of capital.   Earlier economic upheavals, it is true, had prepared the ground to some extent, and the effects of the most recent—that which followed the Revolution of 1688—had not wholly spent themselves when the Peace of 1763 brought victory in the long commercial struggle with France.   But the mood of optimism and buoyant self-confidence inspired by the victories of Wolfe and Clive had a far more penetrating effect on the economic life of Wales than anything that had gone before.   For now the securing of those world markets for which British inventive skill and stored-up capital had so long been hungering bred boundless confidence in the future, and induced men of substance and enterprise not merely to scoop off the surface wealth of the land, as former prospectors had done, but to sow in faith for a more distant harvest.

And so the long-delayed "development" of the country was taken in hand.   Its economic backwardness and its difficult physical geography were no deterrents in that age of miracles, for they spelt cheap labour, untapped ores, and rapid mountain torrents.   It seemed as though a few short bounds would bring North Wales to a level with regions where industry had been firmly established for centuries.   The village of Bersham, one of the first places where coke iron was made, vied with the Midland ironworks in turning out cannon in the 'sixties and cylinders for Watt's steam engine in the 'seventies.   In the 'eighties Anglesey almost dominated the world market for copper ore, and Holywell was formidable enough for its brass works to arouse the jealous suspicion of Boulton, and its cotton mills that of the Arkwrights.   Even after the turn of the century, we find at Llangollen one of the earliest power looms to be successfully worked south of the Tweed, and mills in Montgomeryshire that still carried on a precarious rivalry with the North of England in one branch of the woollen industry. This phase came to an end when the "Giant-Power" of steam laid "his hard hands" on industry and drew it ruthlessly to the main coalfields—a process for the completion of which Dr. Clapham has taught us to look "some rather long way down the [nineteenth] century"[1] rather than to its early years. There were still those who believed, on the eve of the repeal of the coal tax in 1831, that with this obstacle removed, the industries of the North Wales coalfield could hold their own with the Black Country ; others, as late as the middle of the century, who thought that only a railway was needed to complete the triumph of Montgomeryshire woollens. Such hopes were delusive, for Nature had not been so bountiful as men thought. The coal seams were thin and broken ; the veins of ore petered out or were submerged ; water power fell out of fashion. The harbours kept silting up, and the districts richest in natural products often proved the poorest in natural outlets and the most intractable to transport : the iron district of Denbighshire had to do without its canal, and the lie of the country prescribed to the main railway lines a course which precluded them from serving the chief national industries. Where the hostility of Nature conspired with the long neglect of Man to impose such heavy pioneering work, for so uncertain a reward, there is small wonder that capital should withdraw to regions of less forbidding contours, more forward in development, richer in coal, and with harbours to which the steamship could bring, from every quarter of the globe, such raw materials as were not to hand. These were the factors which brought the Industrial Revolution in North Wales to an untimely close, at a time when, in the richer coalfield of the South (which had started almost level in the race), the "real Industrial Revolution"[2] was just beginning. · It was a gradual process, almost unnoticed at the time. At first, developments in transport promised to be a further stimulus to local industry,

[1] *Early Railway Age*, p. 74.
[2] Rees : *Industrial Revolution in South Wales*, p. 30.

and each successive trade boom brought with it a fresh crop of investors and prospectors ; but as each tide receded it washed away some of the shakier outworks of industry, narrowing the area of successful production to a few more fortunate centres—the Wrexham and Holywell districts (after the crisis of 1826) for the heavy industries ; Newtown and Llanidloes (after that of 1837) for textiles—till, after the Hungry 'Forties had carried the process of elimination a stage further, these too had to give way, the first to South Wales and the Midlands, the second to Lancashire and Yorkshire. As the locomotive penetrated further and further into the heart of the country, the products of these better-equipped regions ousted one local manufacture after another from the home market, and brought North Wales into ever closer dependence on the great industrial centres.

The difficulty of fixing exact chronological limits for the subject in hand will appear from what has been said ; the neatly-sliced "periods" of the political historian are wholly inapplicable to the treatment of social and economic affairs. The core of the story lies in the years 1760 to 1840, but it has often been found necessary to extend these limits in one direction or the other. The first chapter gives a survey of conditions in 1760, and traces briefly the development of the main industries before that date. The next three deal with preparatory changes in agriculture and transport. The former is treated in some detail for the War period (when the greatest changes took place), and in the barest outline from then till the Repeal of the Corn Laws ; the coming of the railway marks the natural limit for the latter. Chapters V to VIII carry forward the account of the main industries—mining, quarrying, smelting, and textiles—from 1760 to the decade 1840–50, when the railway penetrated the North Wales coalfield; and to the following decade for central Wales, where the railway came later. When important stages of the Industrial Revolution (such as the adoption of steam power in the woollen industry) were delayed here till the second half of the century, the range of the book has been widened to include them ; otherwise only the briefest indication has been given of developments subsequent to what Dr. Clapham has christened the Early Railway Age. The concluding two chapters survey the whole period 1760–1850 from two points of view : the organization of production and exchange, and the condition of the "labouring poor."

The book has been written with a twofold object : on the one hand to throw new light on a neglected aspect of the Industrial Revolution ; on the other to sketch a chapter, an important one in many ways, in the history of modern Wales. For the changes here described not only brought with them a new set of anglicizing influences and a fresh cleavage between North and South ; they also form the economic background to those better-known religious and political movements which transmuted Cavalier and Tory Wales, the Wales of the *anterliwt* and the *gwylmabsant*, into the Radical and Puritan Wales of the last generation. The treatment of the subject makes no claim to exhaustiveness : to have utilized the vast stores of available manuscript material—records of estates, of enclosures, of industrial undertakings, of local government —which are daily being saved from the scrap heap by watchful librarians, or to have included the story of the South, with its separate sources and its distinct problems, would have immoderately swollen the bulk of the book and held it up almost indefinitely. If, by provoking some future researcher to correct its errors and to fill in its outlines, it helps to stimulate the production of more detailed monographs, and so brings nearer the day when the history of modern Wales can be definitively written ; if even it induces some student of the Industrial Revolution to turn his gaze awhile from Lancashire, Yorkshire, and the Midlands, it will have served its purpose.

The text was in the publishers' hands nearly three years ago, but the expensiveness of setting it up delayed publication until the Trustees of the Thomas Ellis Memorial Fund and the Board of Celtic Studies came to the rescue with generous grants, which are hereby gratefully acknowledged. So far as possible, material which has subsequently come to light has been referred to in footnotes, but the latest Census figures included are those of 1921. It is my pleasant duty to acknowledge many favours received while the work was in preparation. I have been allowed by the late Sir George Meyrick and by Simon Yorke, Esq., of Erthig, to make use of their family papers ;

by the proprietors of *Archaeologia Cambrensis* and of *Economica*, by the Board of Celtic Studies and the Anglesey Antiquarian Society, to draw from articles which I had previously published under their auspices ; by Messrs. G. W. Bacon and Co. to use their outline relief map of North Wales (10 miles to the inch) as the basis of maps II and IV in the text.   I have also received much generous help from the officials of the   National Library of Wales and of my own College Library.   To all of these, and to the many collaborators whose services are acknowledged from time to time in footnotes, my warmest thanks are due.   I cannot conclude without expressing also my more general indebtedness to Dr. R. H. Tawney, who first awakened my interest in economic history when I attended his Tutorial Class at Wrexham, twenty-one years ago, and who has been unstinting with advice and encouragement at every stage of the work ; to my friend and colleague Mr. R. T. Jenkins, who offered to undertake the laborious task of reading the whole book in proof, and who has made many valuable suggestions ; and finally to my wife, whose constant help has immeasurably lessened the labour of preparing for press.   I need hardly add that the responsibility for any mistakes and omissions is mine alone.

A. H. DODD.

University College of North Wales,
Bangor,
August 16, 1932.

PREFACE TO SECOND EDITION

THIS book has now been out of print for some time. During the twenty years since the writing of it was completed, our knowledge of the subject has expanded in several directions, but the main conclusions have not been seriously challenged. To incorporate into a new edition the results of all this subsequent research would have involved a measure of rewriting to which the author, whose interests have meanwhile shifted to other fields of Welsh history, could not now devote the necessary time, and which under present conditions would have involved the publishers in prohibitive expense. But since the work is still in demand in colleges, schools and extra-mural classes, as well as among the general public, it was decided to reproduce the original edition by a photographic process which has permitted summary correction of errors but not the insertion of any substantial amount of new matter or the discussion of points that have aroused controversy.

To fill this gap, a supplement has been added to the bibliography, containing lists of books and articles published and of manuscripts made available to the public since 1930, of dissertations in this field accepted for university degrees, and of reviews of the first edition, some of which raised issues to which it has not been possible to do justice in the present revision. A few works of earlier date, to which attention has been called by reviewers or correspondents, have also been included; but it must be understood that while the original bibliography was designed merely to indicate the sources actually used, the aim of the supplement is to give some guidance to readers who wish to keep abreast (as the author cannot claim to have done) of the latest developments in the subject. Unfortunately the high cost of colour printing has precluded the reproduction of the physical map of North Wales which formed the original frontispiece, but the other maps have been retained.

In preparing this edition I have had the advantage of many helpful suggestions and much valuable information from friends, colleagues and reviewers. Probably the most substantial advance during the past twenty years in the study of the industrial development of North Wales has been in relation to the peculiarly Welsh industry of slate quarrying. The tragically early death this summer of my late colleague and former pupil, David Dylan Pritchard, put an untimely end to researches which were leading up to a standard work on this subject. Before his last illness he had given me lists of the most recent works in his own field, and of statements in my own work that called for revision in the light of what he had discovered in quarry documents. The necessary corrections have been made on pp. 208–21 and 310–17 herein. I only wish it were still possible for me to let him know how greatly I value this and many other kindnesses I have received from him.

I gladly take this chance too of acknowledging my indebtedness to Professors David Williams and Henry Lewis (then both plain "Mr.") for drawing my attention, soon after the book appeared, to lapses that had escaped my vigilance in proof-correcting, and which I have now been able to put right. Others wrote to send me information for which I am none the less grateful although it has not always been possible to fit it into the text. In a letter from North Wembley, Mr. F. Wynn Jones gave me the benefit of some of his researches in Home Office papers, showing (for example) how when David Davies resolved to introduce mule spinning at Llanidloes in 1835 (*infra*, pp. 269–70) he was threatened with violence, though there is no record of rioting when the mules were actually installed; how the threats were also directed against the power looms which he was believed to be ordering, but which had not appeared when the parliamentary census of these machines was drawn up next year; how during the earlier disturbances of 1830–32 (*infra*, p. 403) bloodthirsty placards appeared in the town threatening to "clear the looms out to the streets and burn them if we were sent to Land Demains [Van Diemen's] Land for it," and ending with the cry "Blood or Bread, my Boys;" and finally how the Mold riots of the following July against Anglesey "knobsticks" (*infra*, p. 407) were started by four or five hundred men swarming in from Holywell. Mr. Wynn Jones also cites contemporary issues of *Y Faner* to show that trade unionism among the leather workers of Denbigh survived the strike which John Williams believed to have dealt it a *coup de grâce* (*infra*, p. 303), and organised another strike two years after his book was written.

From Mrs. L. B. Voge, of Edinburgh, I received some very interesting family reminiscences about Hugh Roberts's ribbon-weaving concern at Holywell (*infra*, pp. 291–92). Mrs. Voge's great-grandfather and great-great-grandfather (both named Thomas Bothwell) worked with Roberts, and the former told his daughter (my informant's grandmother) how the mill was twice burnt down by the local mob—once in protest against the importation of "foreign" (English) labour, and a second time because of the replacement of most of the male operatives by women. It was on this second occasion that the Bothwells left Holywell for Liverpool.

For much of the information contained in the supplement to the bibliography I am greatly indebted to Sir William Ll. Davies and Mr. B. G. Owens of the National Library of Wales; to Mr. Emyr Gwynne Jones, Librarian to the University College of North Wales; to Mr. W. Ogwen Williams, county archivist, Caernarvon; and to Messrs. Norman Tucker and Ian T. Fleming of the Llandudno and Dyserth Field Clubs respectively. That there is no lack of material for future workers in this field appears in the very bulk of these lists; and I re-echo the hope expressed seventeen years ago by Mr. Ambrose Bebb, in a friendly review in *Y Ddraig Goch*, that the day is not far distant when one of our historians (or a group of them) will incorporate in a comprehensive economic history of the whole country the conclusions arrived at in this and other surveys of portions of the field, with such corrections and additions as may be suggested by the growing volume of manuscript material available. Sir Ben Bowen Thomas has mapped out the field in his *Braslun o Hanes Economaidd Cymru;* perhaps further advance must await the results of Professor Jones-Pierce's studies in the evolution of the Welsh land system. Until then, it is hoped that the present volume will continue to serve its day and generation; and I welcome the opportunity offered by re-publication to express my very warm thanks to the readers and fellow-workers who have received it so kindly and have helped to remove some of its imperfections. For those that remain I alone must bear the responsibility.

A. H. DODD.

Bangor,
October, 1950.

PREFACE TO THIRD EDITION

This book, first published in 1933, was reprinted with corrections and a few additions in 1951. The revised edition is now exhausted, and in view of the continuing demand it has been decided to reissue it with corrections of any factual errors which have since come to light. The last twenty years have produced much new work, notably in the field of transport history; but except where fresh research seems to modify or invalidate conclusions embodied in former editions, no new material has been included here. Instead, a list is appended (as in the second edition) of relevant works which have appeared, and manuscript material which has become available, since 1951. This list is found on page xl *et sqq.*

Bangor   A. H. DODD
January, 1971

CONTENTS.

xxii   INDUSTRIAL REVOLUTION IN NORTH WALES

APPENDIX :

MAPS :

BIBLIOGRAPHY.

[NOTE.—No attempt has been made to construct a complete bibliography. The list which follows is meant primarily as a key to the references made in footnotes. Place of publication, unless otherwise stated, is London.]

A. MANUSCRIPTS.

Family papers of the Meyricks of Bodorgan (Anglesey). By kind permission of the late Sir George Meyrick.
Family papers of the Yorkes of Erthig (Wrexham). By kind permission of Simon Yorke, Esq.
Palmer, A. N. : History of Ruabon (unpublished MS., kindly lent by Edward Owen, Esq., F.S.A.).
University College Library, Bangor :—

(a) BANGOR MSS.

31. A tour in North Wales, by Rev. I. Poole,· A.M., and Charles Joseph Harford, F.A.S. 1793.
81. Ledger of J. I. Williams, Esq.. Pentremawr. Denbigh, 1827.
82. Llyfr Siop Penmorfa, 1792–1800.
118. Map of new allotments on Malldraeth and Corsddaugau Marsh, 1790.
400. Report on the various lines by which a railway could be carried from London to Porth Dynllaen (in North Wales), by Charles Vignoles, Civil Engineer, F.R.A.S., M.R.I.A., 1837.
405. Correspondence on Mynydd Parys boundaries, 1832–33.
406. Mynydd Parys accounts, 1863–69.
419–20. Carriers' accounts, Glynrhonwy slate quarry, Llanberis, 1835–36.
454–7. Account book, Abererch Factory, Pwllheli, 1823, 1839–47.
481. Gwyddelwern Vestry Book, 1787–1806.
484. North Wales Port Book, 1725–30.

Manuscript diary of William Bulkeley of Brynddu, Anglesey, 1734–43.[1]

(b) PORTH YR AUR MSS.

This valuable collection of documents from a lawyer's office at Caernarvon (mainly eighteenth and early nineteenth century) is a mine of information on such subjects as enclosures, land tenure, slate quarries, shipping, local government, etc., especially for Caernarvonshire. It has not yet been completely calendared, and it has only been possible to skim the surface of it for the purpose of this book.

[1] Portions of this have now been published in *Trans. Ang. Ant. Soc.* (1931, pp. 22–102).

(c) SPECIAL COLLECTIONS.

Amlwch 3-64, 83-99. Letters, diaries, accounts, and surveys of
 John Matthews of Mold.
Gaianydd 2. Churchwardens' book, Caerhun, 1785–1825.
Henblas 11. Account books of Henblas estate, 1732–75.
Nantlle 19. Quarry accounts, 1816–24.
Searell 3. Documents of a Caernarvonshire quarry
 and copper mine, c. 1840–60.
Yale 20. Madryn rent book, 1823–25.
Yale 21. Madryn workmen's accounts, 1819–21.
Yale 24. Madryn workmen's accounts, 1841–44.
Yale 29–35. Porthdinllaen harbour.

CALENDARS OF MANUSCRIPTS.

HISTORICAL MANUSCRIPTS COMMISSION.
 8th Rept., pp. 353 ff. (Chester Corporation.)
 14th Rept., App., Pt. IV. (Kenyon.)
 15th Rept., App., Pt. VII. (Puleston of Worthenbury.)

NATIONAL LIBRARY OF WALES.
 Deeds and Documents : I. The Coleman Deeds (ed. Francis
 Green), 1921.
 II. The Crosswood Deeds (id.), 1927.

B. PRINTED WORKS.

I. BOOKS AND ARTICLES BEARING ON ECONOMIC AND
 INDUSTRIAL HISTORY.

(a) GENERAL.

[For general bibliography of the Industrial Revolution see Power,
Eileen : The Industrial Revolution (Economic History Society,
Bibliographies, No. 1) 1927.]

Clapham, J. H. : An Economic History of Modern Britain. The
 Early Railway Age. Cambridge, 1926.
Craik, G. L. : The History of British Commerce. (Reprinted from
 The Pictorial History of England.) Three vols. in one. 1844.
Edwards, Ness : The Industrial Revolution in South Wales. 1924.
Jenkins, R. T., and Rees, W. (ed.) : A Bibliography of the History
 of Wales. University of Wales Press. Cardiff, 1931.
Jones, E. J. : Some Contributions to the Economic History of Wales.
 1928.
Lord, J. : Capital and Steam Power. 1923.
Mantoux, P. : The Industrial Revolution in the Eighteenth Century.
 Trans. M. Vernon. 1928.
Rees, J. M. : An Introduction to the Industrial Revolution in South
 Wales. Traethodau'r Deyrnas, English series, No. 4. Wrexham,
 1927.

(b) Special Topics.

(1) Agriculture and Rural Industries.

Bowen, Ivor : *The Great Enclosures of Common Land in Wales*. 1914.
Curtler, W. H. R. : *The Enclosure and Redistribution of our Land*. Oxford 1920.
Davies, Rev. W. (*See* under II (a)).
Dodd, A. H. : "The Enclosure Movement in North Wales." (*Bull. of Board of Celtic Studies*, III, 3, 1926.)
Ernle, Lord [Protheroe, R. E.] : *English Farming, Past and Present*. Second ed., 1919.
Hasbach, W. : *A History of the English Agricultural Labourer*. Trans. Ruth Kenyon. 1910.
Jones, Anna M. : *Rural Industries of England and Wales*. IV, *Wales*. Oxford, 1927.
Jones, E. J. : "The Enclosure Movement in Anglesey." (*Trans. Anglesey Antiquarian Society and Field Club*, 1925 and 1926.)
Kay, G. (*See* under II (a).)
"M. C. J." : "The Enclosure of Common Lands in Montgomeryshire." (*Mont. Coll.*, XII and XV.)
Roberts, R. A. : *Welsh Homespun*. Newtown, 1930.
Skeel, C. A. J. : "The Cattle Trade between England and Wales." (*Trans. Royal Hist. Soc.*, 1926.)

(2) Mining and Metallurgy.

Ashton, T. S.: *Iron and Steel in the Industrial Revolution*. Manchester, 1924.
Ashton, T. S., and Sykes, J. : *The Coal Industry of the Eighteenth Century*. Manchester, 1929.
Dodd, A. H. : "The North Wales Coal Industry during the Industrial Revolution." (*Arch. Camb.*, 1929.)
Galloway, R. L. *The History of Coal Mining*. 1882.
Id.: *The Annals of Coal Mining*. 1904.
Grant-Francis, Col. : *The Smelting of Copper in the Swansea District*. Second ed. 1881.
Griffith, O. : *Mynydd Parys*. Carnarvon, 1897.
Hamilton, H. : *The English Brass and Copper Industries to* 1800. 1926.
Hunt, R. : *British Mining*. 1887.
Mushet, D. : *Papers on Iron and Steel*. 1840.
North, F. J. : *Coal, and the Coalfields of Wales*. (National Museum of Wales.) Cardiff, 1926.
Palmer, A. N. (*See* under V.)
Scrivenor, H. : *A Comprehensive History of the Iron Trade throughout the World*. 1841. Second ed., 1852.

(3) Quarrying.

Davies, D. C. : *A Treatise on Slates and Slate Quarrying*. 1878.
North, F. J. : *The Slates of Wales*. (National Museum of Wales.) Cardiff, 1925.
Owen, Rev. Elias : "The Penrhyn Slate Quarry." (*Red Dragon*, VII, 1885.)
Parry, W. J. : *Chwareli a Chwarelwyr*. Caernarfon, 1897.

(4) *Textiles.*

" Ap Gwilym " : "The Manufacture of Flannels and Tweeds."
(*Red Dragon*, VI, 1884.)
Clapham, J. H. : *The Woollen and Worsted Industries.* 1907.
Dodd, A. H.: "The Story of an Elizabethan Monopoly." (*Economica*,
1929.)
Lipson, E. : *The History of the English Woollen and Worsted
Industries.* 1921.
Skeel, C. A. J. : "The Welsh Woollen Industry in the Eighteenth
and Nineteenth Centuries." (*Arch. Camb.*, 1924. *See also*
corrections, *ibid.*, pp. 391 ff., and 1925, pp. 228 ff.)

(5) *Transport.*

Churton, E. : *The Railway Book of England.* 1851.
Dodd, A. H. : "The Roads of North Wales, 1750–1850." (*Arch.
Camb.*, 1925.)
Harper, C. G. : *The Holyhead Road.* 1902. (Welsh section,
Vol. II.)
Howell, A. : "Roads, Bridges, and Canals of Montgomeryshire."
(*Mont. Coll.*, VIII, IX, XIV, XV, and XVI.)
Parry, E. : *Railway Companion for Chester to Holyhead.* 1848.
Second ed., 1849.
Priestley, J. : *Historical Account of the Navigable Rivers, Canals,
and Railways through Great Britain.* 1831.
Scrivenor, H. : *Railways of the United Kingdom.* 1849.
Webb, S. and B. : *The Story of the King's Highway.* 1920.

(6) *Banking.*

Dodd, A. H. : "The Beginnings of Banking in North Wales."
(*Economica*, 1926.)
Green, F. : "Early Banks in West Wales." (*West Wales Historical
Records*, VI, 1916.)

(7) *Labour Conditions.*

Davies, D. (*See* under IV.)
Dodd, A. H. : "The Old Poor Law in North Wales." (*Arch. Camb.*,
1926.)
Eden, Sir F. M. (*See* under IV.)
Thomas, D. Ll. : *Labour Unions in Wales: their early struggle for
existence.* Swansea, 1901.
Webb, S. and B. : *English Poor Law Policy.* 1910.

II.   TOPOGRAPHICAL WORKS.

(a) GENERAL.

[*See* bibliographies in Anderson, J P. : *The Book of British
Topography.* 1881. (pp. 334 ff.) ; Fordham, Sir H. G. : *The Road-
Books and Itineraries of Great Britain.* 1924. Hughes, W. J. :
Wales and the Welsh in English Literature. 1924. (pp. 189 ff.)]

Aikin, A.: *England Described.* 1818.

Brayley, E. W., and Britton, J.: *The Beauties of England and Wales.* Vol. XVII. Pt. I: North Wales, by Rev. J. Evans, 1812.

Cathrall, W.: *The History of North Wales.* Manchester, 1828. (Vol. II contains a topographical description, based largely on information from Rev. P. B. Williams, Rector of Llanrûg and Llanbeblig. *See* also under (*d*).)

Cooke, G. A.: *Topographical and Statistical Description of North Wales.* c. 1830.

Cundall, L. B. and Landman, T.: *Wales. An Economic Geography.* 1925.

Davies, Rev. W. (Gwallter Mechain): *A General View of the Agriculture and Domestic Economy of North Wales.* 1810. (Begun 1799, *see* p. 38.)

Evans, Rev. J. (*See* under Brayley and Britton.)

Greenly, E.: *The Geology of Anglesey.* Geological Survey, 1919.

Hughes, H., and North, H. L.: *The Old Cottages of Snowdonia.* Bangor, 1908.

Kay, G.: *A General View of the Agriculture of North Wales.* (Paged separately for each of the six counties.) Edinburgh, 1794.

Leigh, S.: *Guide to Wales and Monmouthshire.* Fourth ed., 1839.

Lhuyd, E.: *Parochialia.* c. 1699. Suppt. to *Arch. Camb.:* Part I, 1909; Part II, 1910; Part III, 1911.

Nicholson, G.: *The Cambrian Traveller's Guide.* First ed., 1808; second ed., 1813; third ed., 1840.

North, F. J. (*See* under I (*b*), (2) and (3).)

Sproule, J.: *The Official Handbook to North Wales.* 1859.

Williams, W.[1]: *Observations on the Snowdon Mountains.* 1802. (Mostly written 1798.)

(*b*) DIRECTORIES, GAZETTEERS, ETC. (chronologically arranged).

Barfoot, P., and Wilkes, J.: *Universal British Directory of Trade, Commerce, and Manufacture.* 1790. (Although 1790 is the imprint on the first vol., the later vols. contain information as late as 1796. The descriptions are based largely on the last edition of Defoe's *Tours*. *See* under II (*c*).)

Imperial and County Register. 1810. Part IV: North Wales.

Carlisle, N.: *A Topographical Dictionary of the Dominion of Wales.* 1811.

London and Provincial Directory. Pigot and Sons, 1822–23.

National and Commercial Directory. Id., 1828–29.

Lewis, S.: *Topographical Dictionary of Wales.* First ed., 1833; second ed., 1838; third ed., 1843.

Parliamentary Gazetteer of England and Wales. Fullarton, 1840–44.

(*c*) TOURS.

[NOTE.—Where two dates are given, the first (in brackets) is that of the actual tour or of the first edition, the second that of the edition used in the text.]

Aikin, A.: *A Journal of a Tour through North Wales* (1796). 1797.

___

[1] Agent and "slate reeve" to Lord Penrhyn.

Bingley, Rev. W. : *A Tour round North Wales, performed during the Summer of 1798*. 1800.

Id.: *North Wales . . . delineated from Two Excursions . . . during the Summers of 1798 and 1801*. 1804 ; second ed. 1814. (An expansion of the above. Except where otherwise stated, all references to Bingley in the text are to the 1804 ed.)

Id.: *Excursions in North Wales*. Third ed., with corrections and additions made during excursions in the year 1838 by his son W. R. Bingley. 1839.

Borrow, G. : *Wild Wales*. 1854. Everyman's Library, 1906.

Cradock, J. : *An Account of the most Romantic Parts of North Wales*. 1777.

Id.: (?) : *Letters from Snowdon*. 1770.

[Defoe, D.] : *A Tour thro' the Whole Island of Great Britain*. 1724–25. Third ed., 1742 ; fifth ed., 1753 ; sixth ed., 1761 ; eighth ed., 1778. (All editions after the first contain numerous additions by Samuel Richardson and others. For North Wales these additions are for the most part copied from books of travel which appeared after the first edition.)

Evans, Rev. J. : *Letters written during a Tour through North Wales, in the year 1798 and at other times*. Third ed., 1804.

Evans, T. : *Walks through Wales*. 1819. (A re-issue of the author's *Cambrian Itinerary, or Welsh Tourist*, 1801.)

Fenton, R. : *Tours in Wales*. (1804–13.) Ed. Rev. J. Fisher. Camb. Arch. Ass. 1917.

Hicklin, J. : *Excursions in North Wales*. First ed., 1847. Fifth thousand. 1851.

Hucks, J. : *A Pedestrian Tour through North Wales*, 1795.

Johnson, S. : *Diary of a Journey into North Wales* (1774). Ed. R. Duppen. 1816.

Leland, J. : *Itinerary in Wales* (1563–9). Ed. Lucy Toulmin-Smith. 1908.

Louis, M. L.[1] : *Gleanings of a Tour in North Wales*. Liverpool, 1824.

Id.: *Sketches of Some Parts of Denbighshire and Flintshire*. Liverpool, 1831.

Lyttleton, George, Lord : *An Account of a Journey into Wales*. 1756.

[Mavor, Rev. W. F.][2]: *A Tour in Wales, and through several Counties of England* (1805). 1806.

Pennant, T. : *Tours in Wales*. Ed. John Rhys. Caernarvon, 1883. First tour 1773, pub. 1778 ; second tour 1773, pub. 1781 ; third tour 1776, pub. 1781. First complete ed., 1784. Posthumous ed., with notes and appendices by David Pennant, 1810—the basis of Rhys' ed., which is used in the text.

Pococke, R. : *Travels through England*, 1734–64. Camden Society, 1888–89.

Pratt, S. J. : *Gleanings through Wales, Holland, and Westphalia*. First ed., 1766 ; fifth ed., 1800.

[1] Schoolmaster at Abergele. Also known as Lewis.

[2] J. G. Barnard, to whom Mr. W. J. Hughes (*Wales and the Welsh*, p. 198) attributes this interesting work, was actually the printer. On Mavor's authorship, *see D.N.B.*

Pugh, E.: *Cambria Depicta*. 1816. (Written *c*. 1807.)
Skinner, Rev. J.: *A Ten Days' Tour through the Isle of Anglesey* (1802). (*Arch. Camb*. suppt., 1908.)
Warner, Rev. R.: *A Walk through Wales, in August* 1797. 1798.
Id.: *A Second Walk through Wales . . . in August and September* 1798. 1799.
Wigstead, H.: *Remarks on a Tour to North and South Wales in the year* 1797. 1800.
[Wyndham, H. P.]: *A Gentleman's Tour through Monmouthshire and Wales in the months of June and July*, 1774. First ed., anon., 1775 ; second ed., incorporating tour of 1777, 1781 ; later eds. 1794, 1795, etc. 1781 and 1794 eds. used in the text.
Young, A.: *A Six Weeks' Tour through the Southern Counties of England and Wales*. 1768.

(d) Local Histories, Records, and Guides.

General.

Blackwell, H. (New York) : "Bibliography of Local and County Histories." (*Old Welsh Chips*, Brecon, 1888, pp. 138–45, 171–81, 198–216, 224–30.)

Anglesey.

Hughes, Rev. O.: *Hanes Plwyf Trefdraeth*. Bangor, *c*. 1903.
Llwyd, Angharad : *A History of the Island of Mona*. Ruthin, 1833.
Owen, N.: *History of the Island of Anglesey*. 1775.
Williams, J.: *History of Berw*. 1861. (*Trans. Ang. Ant. Soc.* suppt., 1915.)

Caernarvonshire.

"Alltud Eifion " (R. I. Jones) : *Y Gestiana, sef Hanes Tre'r Gêst*. Tremadog, 1892.
Lloyd, J. E.: *Carnarvonshire*. Cambridge, 1914.
Parry, Rev. G. T.: *Llanberis, ei Hanes, ei Phobl, a'i Phethau*. Caernarfon, 1908.
Williams, Rev. P. B.: *Tourist's Guide through the County of Caernarvon*. Caernarvon, 1821.
Williams, Rev. R.: *History and Antiquities of the Town of Aberconwy*. Denbigh, 1835.

Denbighshire.

Mahler, M.: *Chirk Castle and Chirkland*. 1912.
Palmer, A. N.: *History of the Town of Wrexham*. Wrexham, 1893.
Id.: *History of the Thirteen Country Townships of the Old Parish of Wrexham*. Id., 1903.
Id.: *History of the Parish Church of Wrexham*. Id., 1886.
Id.: *History of the Older Nonconformity of Wrexham and its Neighbourhood*. Id., 1888.
(*See* also under A and under B, V.)
Simpson, W. T.: *An Account of Llangollen*. Birmingham, 1827.
Williams, J.: *Ancient and Modern Denbigh*. Denbigh, 1856.
Id.: *Records of Denbigh and its Lordship*. Wrexham, 1860.

Flintshire.

Anon. : *A Short Account of the Town of Holywell.* Holywell, 1850.
Edwards, J. M. : *Flintshire.* (Cambridge County Geographies.) Cambridge, 1914.
Pennant, T. : *History of the Parishes of Whiteford and Holywell.* 1796.
Poole, J. : *Gleanings of the Histories of Holywell, Flint, St. Asaph, Rhuddlan* [etc.]. Holywell, 1831.
Taylor, H. : *Historic Notices of Flint.* 1883.
[Willett, R.] : *Memoir of the Parish of Hawarden.* Chester, 1822.

Merioneth.

Jones, Rosalie : *History of Barmouth.* Barmouth, 1909.
Morris, A. : *Merionethshire.* (Cambridge County Geographies.) Cambridge, 1913.
Morris, R. P. : *Cantref Meirionydd.* Dolgellau, 1890.
Williams, G. J. : *Hanes Plwyf Ffestiniog.* Wrexham, 1882.

Montgomeryshire.

Davies, Rev. W. (Gwallter Mechain) : "A Statistical Account of the Parish of Llan-y-myneich." (*Camb. Reg.*, I, 1795, pp. 265–83.)
Horsfall-Turner, E. R. : *Municipal History of Llanidloes.* Llanidloes, 1908.
Jones, W. : "Statistical Accounts of the Parishes of Llanervul, Llangadvan, and Garth-Beibio." 1792. (*Camb. Reg.*, II, 1796, pp. 366–85.)
Montgomeryshire Collections. (*See* under VII.) Contain numerous parochial histories.
Roberts, J. E., and Owen, R. : *The Story of Montgomeryshire.* Cardiff, 1916.

Shropshire.

Leighton, S. : *Records of the Corporation of Oswestry.* (Reprinted from *Trans. Shrops. Arch. Soc.*, 1879–83.)
Owen, H., and Blakeway, Rev. J. B. : *History of Shrewsbury.* 1825.
Page, W. (ed.) : *Shropshire.* (Victoria County Histories. Vol. I only published.) 1908.
Phillips, T. : *History and Antiquities of Shrewsbury.* Shrewsbury, 1779.

(*e*) MAPS (chronologically arranged).

Owen, J. and Bowen, E. : *Britannia Depicta, or Ogilby Improved.* Fourth ed., 1724.
Badeslade and Toms : *Chorographia Britanniae.* 1742.
Morris, L. : *Plans of Harbours. Bars, Bays, and Roads in St. George's-Channel,* 1748 ; second ed., 1801. (*See* p. 119.)
Anon. : *An Accurate Map of North Wales.* Bowles. *c.* 1760.
Cary, J. : *New Map of England and Wales.* 1794.
Evans, J. : *North Wales.* 1797.
Furnival, J. and E. : *North Wales.* Llanymynech, 1814, 1820.
Laurie, R. H. : *New Map of North Wales.* 1826.
Greenwood, C. and J. : *Map of the North Eastern Counties of the Principality of Wales, from an Actual Survey made in the years 1831 and 1832.* 1834.

III. BIOGRAPHIES, MEMOIRS, AND LETTERS.

Cust, L. A. : *Chronicles of Erthig on the Dyke.* 1914.
Davies, J. H. (ed.) : *Letters of Lewis, Richard, William and John Morris* (1728-66). Aberystwyth, 1909. [*Morris Letters.*]
Id. (ed.) : *Life and Opinions of Robert Roberts, by Himself.* Cardiff, 1923.
"Nimrod" (Apperley, C. J.) : "My Life and Times." (*Frazer's Magazine,* 1842.)
Owen, R. : *Life of Robert Owen.* (1857-58.) Bohn's Popular Library, 1920.
Palmer, A. N. : *John Wilkinson and the Old Bersham Ironworks.* (Reprinted from *Trans. Cym. Soc.,* 1897-98.) Wrexham, 1899.
Roberts, A. : *Wynnstay and the Wynns.* Oswestry, 1876.
Roberts, T. R. : *Eminent Welshmen.* Cardiff, 1908.
Smiles, S. : *Industrial Biography: Iron Workers and Tool Makers.* 1863.
Id.: *Lives of the Engineers.* 1874. Boulton and Watt. Metcalfe and Telford. Smeaton and Rennie. George and Robert Stephenson.
Williams, R. : *Montgomeryshire Worthies.* Newtown, 1884. Second ed. (used in text), 1894.
Williams, R. : *A Biographical Dictionary of Eminent Welshmen.* Llandovery, 1853.

IV. CONTEMPORARY TRACTS, TREATISES, AND PAMPHLETS.

Anon. : *History of the Chartists, and the Bloodless Wars of Montgomeryshire.* Welsh-Pool, 1840. (*See* pp. 229n., 410.)
Anon. : *Observations on the Comparative Merits of the Eastern and Western Canals.* n.d. (*See* p. 103 n.)
Anon. : *Sketch of a Plan for Building a Timber Bridge across the River Menai.* 1786.
Davies, D. : *The Case of Labourers in Husbandry stated and considered.* 1795.
Eden, Sir F. M. : *The State of the Poor.* 1797.
Phillips, Sir T. : *Wales: the Language, Social Condition, Moral Character, and Religious Opinions of the People.* 1849.
Report to the General Assembly of the Ellesmere Canal Proprietors. Shrewsbury, 1805.
[Roberts, Rev. S. ("S.R.")] : *Letters on Improvements, addressed to the Landlords and Road Commissioners, by a Llanbrynmair Farmer.* Llanbrynmair and Newtown, 1852.
Ure, A.: *The Philosophy of Manufactures,* 1835.

V. CONTEMPORARY NEWSPAPERS AND PERIODICALS.

Cambrian Register. (1796–1818.)
Cambrian Quarterly Magazine. (1829–33.)
Cambro-Briton. (1819–22.)
Chester Chronicle. (1775 ff.)
North Wales Gazette. (1808–27.)

North Wales Chronicle. (1827 ff.)
Oswestry Herald. (1820 ff.)
Salopian Journal. (1794 ff.)
Shrewsbury Chronicle. (1772 ff.)
Wrexham Recorder. (1848-49.)
Wrexham Registrar. (1848.)

VI. PARLIAMENTARY REPORTS AND PAPERS
(Chronologically arranged).

Reports of Committees on Poor Relief and Settlement, 1775–78, 1787. *(Reports from Committees of House of Commons,* IX.) Overseers' returns, Wales, pp. 519–39, 546–7, 715 ff.
Report of Select Committee on the Cultivation and Improvement of Waste, Unenclosed, and Unproductive Lands, 1795. (Id, pp. 201 ff.) Denbighshire, pp. 212–13.
Report of Select Committee on Copper Mines and Copper Trade, 1799. (Id., X, pp. 653–728.)
Census of England and Wales, 1801–1921.
Reports relating to Penrhyn Quarries, 1819–23. (1819, XVI and XVII ; 1821, XXI ; 1822, XXI ; 1823, XII and XV.)
Reports from Committees on Holyhead Roads, Harbour, etc., 1810–22. (1822).
Reports from Holyhead Road Commissioners, 1816–45. (1816, VIII ; 1820, VI ; 1821, X ; 1822, VI ; 1823, X ; 1824, IX ; 1825, XV ; 1826, XI ; 1827, VII ; 1828, IX ; 1829, V ; 1830, XV ; 1831, IV and XII ; 1832, XXIII ; 1833, XVII ; 1834, XL ; 1835, XXXVI ; 1837, XXXIII ; 1838, XXXV ; 1839, XXXIX ; 1840, XXVII ; 1841, XII ; 1842, XXV ; 1843, XXIX ; 1844. XXI ; 1845, XXVII.) *See* indexes to *Reports of Commissioners,* 1800–46 *(Roads and Bridges),* 1847.
Report of Royal Commission on the Administration and Operation of the Poor Laws, 1834. Appendix A, Pt. 88, No. 27 : Report on North Wales, by Stephen Walcott (XXIX, pp. 167a–192a). Answers to Rural Queries (XXX–XXXV). *[P.L.R.]*
Factory Inspectors' Returns, North Wales (1835, XL ; 1836, XLV, 77–8, 138 ; 1837, L, 97, 122 ; 1839, XLII ; 1840, XXIII).
Report of Royal Commission on Municipal Corporations, 1835–8. Appendix to First Report, Pts. IV and V : Reports on Boroughs of N. Wales, by T. J. Hogg and G. H. Wilkinson (1835, XXVI). Reports upon Certain Boroughs, by T. J. Hogg (1837–38, XXXV). *[M.C.R.]*
Report of Royal Commission on Hand-Loom Weavers, 1840. Pt. IV : Reports from Assistant Commissioners : Wales, by W. A. Miles (XXIV, pp. 553–71). *[H.L.W.]*
Report of Royal Commission on the State of the Roads, 1840, XXVII. North Wales, pp. 565–600, 645–6.
Report of Royal Commission on Children's Employment, 1842–43. First Report (Mines) 1842, XV. App. to First Report., Pt. II : Report on Employment of Children and Young Persons in Mines and Mineral Works of North Wales, by H. Herbert Jones. 1842, XVII. (pp. 367–467). Appendix to Second Report (Trade and

Manufactures), Pt. II : Reports and Evidence from Sub-Commissioners : Evidence collected by H. H. Jones, North Wales District. 1843, XV. (pp. 767–72). [*C.E.R.*]

Report of Select Committee on Commons' Inclosure, 1844, V. North Wales, pp. 371–8.

Report of Commissioners of Inquiry into the state of Education in Wales, 1846–47. Pt. III : North Wales.

Report of Royal Commission on Land in Wales and Monmouthshire, 1896. (C–8221.) Appendix (C–8242) contains abstracts of Parliamentary Papers relating to Welsh agriculture, useful bibliographies, etc.

VII. ARCHAEOLOGICAL JOURNALS.

Archaeologia Cambrensis.
Bulletin of the Board of Celtic Studies.
Bye-gones relating to Wales and the Border Counties.
The Cheshire Sheaf.
Cymru Fu.
Journal of the Chester and North Wales Archaeological and Natural History Society.
Journal of the Flintshire Historical Society.
Powys-Land Club: Collections Historical and Archaeological relating to Montgomeryshire. [*Mont. Coll.*]
Transactions of the Anglesey Antiquarian Society and Field Club.
Transactions of the Honourable Society of Cymmrodorion. [*Trans. Cym. Soc.*]
Transactions of the Shropshire Archaeological Society.
West Wales Historical Records. (Transactions of the Historical Society of West Wales.)
Y Cymmrodor.

SUPPLEMENT TO BIBLIOGRAPHY

(*a*) MSS. ACQUIRED SINCE 1930.

(1) *National Library of Wales*

[The items listed below are those which have some direct bearing on the contents of the book. No attempt has been made to enumerate the many sets of parochial records—invaluable on such questions as Poor Law administration, highways, etc.—which have been deposited in the Library, nor the mass of estate papers and other agricultural records to be found there. For fuller details see *Handlist of Manuscripts* published 1940–47, *National Library of Wales Journal*, and *Annual Reports.*]

N.L.W. MSS.

Brewing accounts, Caernarvon (?), 1760–63 [*infra*, p. 330], (1243).
Blacksmiths' accounts: Merioneth, 1829–81 (14136–8); Caernarvonshire, 1847-55 (12110).
Chartism in Montgomeryshire, draft history by E. R. Horsfall-Turner [*infra*, pp. 409–14], (12888–9).
Coal mines: Chirk (6372, 6386, 6392, 6397 = W. M. Myddleton 10, 24, 30, 35); Flintshire, 1824-42 (12476, 12513 = Wigfair 76, 113).

Copper mines: Llandudno, 1773–1831 [infra, p. 167], (12506–12512 = Wigfair 106–12); Trawsfynydd [infra, p. 167], (12513=Wigfair 113).

Crown rents, Caernarvonshire, 1815–56 (10842).

Enclosure, Rhuddlan, 1807 (8971).

Ironworks, Brymbo, 1834–41 (14830), [see also under Wilkinson].

Lead mines: Flintshire, 1718–33 (12491=Wigfair 91); c. 1790–1820 (10345); 1816 (4849); 1825–52 (6296=Henry Taylor 30); 1845–48 (12874). Merioneth, 1828 (10574).

Lead works: Mold, 1810–45 (12430=Wigfair 30); Flint, 1813–54 (9649).

Leather: skinner's accounts, Llanuwchllyn, 1815–19 (8370).

Paper mill, Caerwys [infra, p. 247n.], (10345).

Ports and shipping: Llanelltyd and Barmouth, 1787–1841 (14903–4); Portmadoc, Criccieth and Pwllheli, 1829–62 (12105–9).

Quarrying, Penrhyn (8733–8864 and 10605).

Railways (9745–9857, 14376).

Roads: Caernarvonshire, overseer's accounts, 1842–43 (10941); turnpike trust accounts, 1846-66 (10844). Denbighshire, overseer s accounts, 1828–35 (13890). Flintshire, turnpike tolls, 1814–21 (10436). Holyhead Road, Telford's note on improvements needed, 1822 (10885).

Sankey, Richard [infra, p. 316], letter book (6294=Henry Taylor 29).

Tour in North Wales, 1810 (7344–5=D. Salmon 1–2).

Wilkinson, John [infra, pp. 134–41], estate papers, balance sheets, 1820–23, abstract of will, 1806, etc. (10821–3).

Woollen factory, Bala, accounts, 1845–48 [infra, p. 251], (12063).

Special and Deposited Collections

Bettisfield (Flintshire collieries, 1794–1846).

British Records Assn. (Frere, Cholmeley and Co., 1949) deeds and documents (Hanmer enclosure, 1777, and drainage schemes, 1790–1890; Bagillt collieries, 1840–90).

Broom Hall (Abererch embankment, 1828; Porthdinllaen turnpike, 1802, 1862; Llanaber enclosure, 1810).

Buckley-Jones (Western branch Montgomeryshire canal [infra, pp. 107–8]; Welshpool railway, 1818 [infra, p. 112]).

Glansevern (Montgomeryshire enclosures, 1796–1874; Welshpool Old Bank [infra, p. 316]; Montgomeryshire roads, canals, bridges and railways).

Glynnllifon (Caernarvonshire slate quarries; shipping; railways; Caernarvon Poor Law Union, 1837–42; harbours at Porthdinllaen, 1726, Caernarvon, 1793–1874, Portmadoc, 1807-26; Holyhead, 1846–47; Menai Bridge proposal, 1785 [infra, p. 95]; roads including Nevin-Pwllheli, 1725, Caernarvon-Aberglaslyn, 1796, Caernarvonshire turnpike, 1813, 1828–67, Porthdinllaen turnpike, 1815; 1834–62, quarry roads, 1827–29, proposed Ffestiniog-Llanrwst road, 1846, county surveyor's accounts, 1834). [See Vol. II of typescript schedule and Nat. Lib. of Wales Journ., VI, 179–81.

Glynne of Hawarden (Flintshire collieries, 1746–77, Nos. 83–7, 92, 95).

Gwrych castle (lead mines, Abergele, 1807–19, enclosures, Llanarmon, etc., 1811, Eglwysfach, etc., 1812, Eglwys rhos, etc., 1843; Abergele embankment, 1794; report on St. George's Harbour Bill [*infra*, p. 114], 1853).

Humphreys-Owen (Castle Caereinion turnpike, 1789–93).

L.M.S. records (including Welsh railways and canals incorporated in the system).

Millward (Chester-Holyhead railway, 1846).

Plas Machynlleth (Van lead mines [*infra*, pp. 182–83], Nos. 21–82; Corris quarries.) [See *Mont. Coll.*, L, 1947, pp. 49–55).

Plas yn cefn (lead mines, Abergele and Flintshire, *c.* 1700–1800).

Powis castle (Montgomeryshire and Caernarvonshire lead and copper mining, Montgomeryshire enclosures, transport, etc.). [See *Nat. Lib. of Wales Journ.*, III, 145–50].

Shipping records: Barmouth Harbour Trust, 1797–1929; Account book of J. T. Daniel, master of sloop *Amity*, of Aberdovey, 1803–9; Wharfage book of Jones and Morgan, Machynlleth, in respect of Derwen las [*infra*, p. 122], 1839–62.

Adrian Stokes (memorandum books of W. A. Maddocks and correspondence with his agent John Williams [*infra*, pp. 42–4]; Portmadoc Harbour records, 1825–1916).

R. R. Williams, Chester (Dolgelley tannery, 1767-1830).

(2) *University College of North Wales Bangor MSS.*

Enclosure award: Henllan, 1814 (2530).

Farm accounts: Aberffraw, 1801-62 (7051–3); Beddgelert, 1842–57 (1500); Bryncroes, 1790–1821 (1540); Guilsfield, 1834–81 (1415–9).

Farmers' diaries: Anglesey, 1839–47 (1483); Amlwch, 1821 (2638).

Parish records (including Poor Law, highways, etc.): Bangor, 1837–38 (6838–9); Beddgelert, 1813–18 (1486), 1829–45 (8170); Bodferin, 1826–48 (6462); Clynnog, 1829–48 (1482); Guilsfield, 1822–71 (1414); Holyhead, 1816–81 (6459–60); Llanbedr y cenin, 1658–1816 (8171–93); Llandegai, 1825–30 (6461); Llandwrog (1065–1101); Llantair isgaer (1142-1215); Llanfair mathafarn eithaf, 1821 (1595); Merioneth (western parishes), 1785–1848 (1485); Penmorfa, 1832–36 (1518); Pentrefoelas, 1842–94 (1581).

Ports: Trefriw "port book," 1835–47, and wharfage account, 1855–62 (7057–8).

Quarries: Holland, Ffestiniog (slate), records 1839–47 (2532, 2541, 2546); Llanddeiniolen (limestone), records 1827–47 (8278–8433); Penmorfa (setts), history, 1827–88 (2531).

Special and Deposited Collections

Glanaethwy (parish records, Llandysilio, Ang., and Llandegfan).

Llugwy (Anglesey coal and railways).

Plas newydd (Anglesey coal and limestone quarries, Gallt y llan slate quarry, Llanberis, Penrhyn du lead mine [*infra*, pp. 154, 164–5, 170, *N.L.W. Journ.*, III, 148]).

(3) *Caernarvon County Record Office*

Enclosure Act, Rhoshirwaun, 1803.

Enclosure Awards and maps [see list in *First Rept. of County Records Sub-committee*, 1934, pp. 13–14].

Gas and water undertakings, 1821 ff. [*id.*, pp. 29–31].

Madocks, W. A., Correspondence with John Williams, 1805 ff. [cf. N.L.W., Adrian Stokes MSS.].

Ports: Porthdinllaen Harbour Act, 1803; Portmadoc, minutes of subcommissioners of pilotage, 1849–1936; Plans of harbours, piers and docks, Aberdovey, Bangor, Caernarvon, Criccieth, Deganwy, Llanfairfechan, Llandrillo yn Rhos, Llyfni Vale, Ormeshead, Penmaenmawr, Porthdinllaen, Portmadoc, Pwllheli, St. George's Llandudno), 1824–1907 [see *Rept.*, as above, p. 22]; Railway plans, 1824–1925 [*id.*, pp. 23–8].

Roads and bridges: Porthdinllaen turnpike, 1803, 1805–24, 1852 [cf. N.L.W., Broom Hall and Glynllifon]; Caernarvon old turnpike, 1840–75, 1879–82 [cf. N.L.W., 10844]; Plans of bridges, 1745–1878, and of road diversions, 1797–1929, contractors' bonds for bridges, 1774–1882. [See *Rept.*, as above, pp. 14–22.]

(*b*) PRINTED BOOKS AND ARTICLES (mainly 1930–50)

Bowen, E. G.: *Wales, a Study in Geography and History*. Cardiff, 1941.

Brown, Kenneth : "Anglesey's ghost railway." *Railway Mag.*, July, 1940 [reprinted without map, *Trans. Ang. Ant. Soc.*, 1941, pp. 39–42; cf. *infra*, p. 111].

Calvert, J. : *The Gold Rocks of Great Britain and Ireland*. 1853. [Chap. vi, on Merioneth, *infra*, p. 168].

Cropper, Thomas : *Buckley and District*. Buckley, 1923 [Chap. vi. on Jonathan Catherall, *infra*, p. 192].

Chaloner, W. H. : "New light on John Wilkinson's token coinage." *Seaby's Coin and Medal Bulletin*, July, 1948 [*infra*, pp. 139–40].

Crick, W. F. and Wadsworth, J. E.: *A Hundred Years of Joint Stock Banking*. 1936 [Chap. vi, on "The 'Wales Bank'" trans. by R. T. Jenkins as *Canrif o Hanes Banc Gogledd a Deheudir Cymru* and published separately, 1936].

Davies, A. Stanley : "The river trade of Montgomeryshire." *Mont. Coll.*, XLIII (1933), pp. 33–46, XLIV (1934), pp. 198–211.

Id. : "The navigation of the upper Severn." *Trans. Caradog and Severn Valley Field Club*, IX (1935), pp. 198–211.

Id.: *The Early Banks of Mid-Wales*. Welshpool, 1935.

Davies, D. J. : *The Economic History of South Wales prior to 1800*. Cardiff, 1933.

Id.: *Diwidiant a Masnach. Cyfres Pobun*, Lerpwl, 1946.

Davies, H. R. : *The Conway and the Menai Ferries*. Cardiff, 1942 [pp. 199–315 on phase dealt with *infra*, chap. iv A].

Davies, Ifor E. : "The old turnpike, Penmaenmawr." *Proc. Llandudno . . . Field Club*, XVI (1930), pp. 71–85.

Id. : "A master mariner's 'A Count Book'" (Conway, 1838–53). Id., XX (1939–47), pp. 30–40.

Id. · "Copper mining on the Great Orme". *Id.*, XXII (1949, pp. 11–15), [*infra*. p. 167].

Davies, J. Glyn : Reviews of books on North Wales shipping [with much first-hand information]. *Trans. Cym Soc.*, 1945, pp. 205–14, 1948, pp. 475–94.

Davies, W. Lloyd : "The Henllan enclosure award." *Bull. Bd. of Celtic Studies*, IX (1948), pp. 7–10.

Dunn, J. M. : "The Conway Tubular Bridge." *Proc. Llandudno . .'. Field Club*, XXI (1948), pp. 7–10.

Evans, G. Nesta : "The artisan and the small farmer in mid-eighteenth-century Anglesey." *Trans. Ang. Ant. Soc.*, 1933, pp. 81–96.

Id. : *Social Life in Mid-Eighteenth-Century Anglesey.* Cardiff, 1936.

Evans, Thomas : *The Background of Modern Welsh Politics.* Cardiff, 1936.

Gray, H. L. : *English Field Systems.* 1915.

Gresham, Colin A. : "William Fairbairn and the Conway Tubular Bridge." *Trans. Caerns. Hist. Soc.*, IX (1948), pp. 46–58.

Grundy, J. H. : "The geology of Prestatyn and district." *Proc. Dyserth Field Club*, 1917, pp. 4–17.

Griffith, John : *Chwarelau Dyffryn Nantlle a Chymdogaeth Moeltryfan* [to 1869]. Conway, 1934.

Hamer, F. E. : *History of the Chartist Outbreak in Llanidloes.* Llanidloes, 1867 [*infra*, pp. 409–14].

Hughes, Cledwyn Flynn- : "The Bangor workhouse." *Trans. Caerns. Hist. Soc.*, V (1944), pp. 88–100.

Id. : "The workhouses of Caernarvonshire, 1760–1914." *Id.*, VII (1946), pp. 88–100.

Hughes, Henry : *Immortal Sails.* 1946 [Portmadoc and its shipping].

Hughes, P. G. : *Wales and the Drovers.* 1943.

Ingman, J. : "Early Bangor banks." *Trans. Caerns. Hist. Soc.*, VIII (1947), pp. 35–43.

Jenkins, R. T. : "A drover's account book." *Id.*, VI (1945), pp. 46–57.

Jones, Emyr G. : "Hanes bore chwarel Dinorwig." *Lleufer*, V (1949), pp. 9–16.

Jones, Francis : "A squire of Anglesey." *Trans. Ang. Ant. Soc.*, 1940, pp. 76–92 [Edward Wynn, Bodewryd, 1681–1755].

Jones, H. Gwynne : "The charcoal-iron industry." *Journ. Royal Soc. of Arts*, LXXXVIII (1939), pp. 41–57.

Id. : "The Llandudno copper mines in the eighteenth century." *Bull. Bd. of Celtic Studies*, X (1939), pp. 94–101.

Jones, Moses J. : "The Merioneth woollen industry, 1758–1820." *Trans. Cym. Soc.*, 1939, pp. 181–208.

Klapper, C. F. : "The Shropshire and Montgomeryshire Railway." *Railway Mag.*, LXXV (1934), pp. 199–203, 341–45.

Lee, Charles E. : *Narrow-gauge Railways in Wales.* 1945.

Lerry, G. G. : *The Collieries of Denbighshire.* Wrexham and Oswestry, 1946.

Morgan, D. W. : *Brief Glory.* Liverpool, 1948 [Cardigan Bay shipping].

North, F. J. : *The Slates of Wales* (third ed.) Cardiff, 1946.

O[wen], H[ugh] (ed.) : "Observations on the application to Parliament for an Act for building a timber bridge over the Streights of Menai, 1786." (*Trans. Ang. Ant. Soc.*, 1936, pp. 129–34.) [*infra*, p. 95].

Panton, Paul : Contributions to *Annals of Agriculture*, IX, 647–50, XII, 151–52; XIV, 407–10; XXIV, 260; XXVI, 11–12. 1784–1815.

Parry, Owen : "The financing of the Welsh cattle trade in the eighteenth century." *Bull. Bd. of Celtic Studies*, VIII (1936), pp. 46–51.

Parry, Thomas: *Baledi Ddeudawfed Ganrif.* Cardiff, 1935.

Peate, Iorwerth T. : "Some aspects of agrarian transport in Wales." *Arch. Camb.*, XC (1935), pp. 219–38.

Pritchard, D. Dylan : "The early days of the slate industry." *Quarry Managers' Journal*, July, 1942.

Id. : "New light on the history of the Penrhyn quarries in the eighteenth century." *Id.*, Sept., 1942.

Id. : "Financial structure of the slate industry of North Wales, 1780–1830." *Id.*, Dec., 1942.

Id. : "Investment in the slate industry, 1830–1930." *Id.*, Jan.–Apr., 1943.

Id. : "Aspects of the slate industry: the expansionist period, 1790–1877." *Id.*, March, 1944 – Feb., 1945.

Id.: "The industrial activities of Snowdonia." Chap. xii of H.R.C.Carr and G. A. Lister: *The Mountains of Snowdonia*, second ed., 1948.

Rees, J. F. and Rees, W. : "A select bibliography of the economic history of Wales." *Econ. Hist. Rev.*, II (1930), pp. 320–26.

Richards, Thomas : "Mona mine letters." *Trans. Ang. Ant. Soc.*, 1946, pp. 80–91.

Richards, W. M. : "Some aspects of the Industrial Revolution in south-east Caernarvonshire : I. Y Traeth Mawr." *Trans. Caerns. Hist. Soc.*, IV (1942–43), pp. 67–85; "II. Portmadoc." *Id.*, V (1944), pp. 71–87.

Roberts, O. Glynne : "The Britannia Bridge." *Trans. Ang. Ant. Soc.*, 1946, pp. 92–112.

Rogers, Emlyn : "Helyntion glowyr Dinbych a Fflint yn 1830-31." *Lleufer*, II (1946), 75–9, 121–4; III (1947), 15–20.

Senogles, Harold : "Llandysilio in 1815." *Id.*, pp. 60–79 [Enclosure award and map].

Thomas, B. B. : "The old poor law in Ardudwy uwch Artro." *Bull. of Bd. of Celtic Studies*, VII (1935), pp. 153–91.

Id. : *Braslun o Hanes Economaidd Cymru.* Caerdydd, 1941.

Thomas, David : "Anglesey shipbuilding down to 1840." *Trans. Ang. Ant. Soc.*, 1932, pp. 107–18.

Id.: "Llechi a llongau." *Trans. Caerns. Hist. Soc.*, I (1939), pp. 68–84.

Id. : *Hên Longau a Llongwyr.* Cardiff, 1949.

Williams, Caradoc : "Mines and miners in Flintshire." *Proc. Dyserth Field Club*, 1932, pp. 70–73.

Williams, David : "Some figures relating to emigration from Wales." *Bull. Bd. of Celtic Studies*, VII (1935), pp. 396–415; VIII (1936), p. 160 [*infra*, pp. 381–82, 386, 395, 397–98].

Id. : "A note on the population of Wales, 1536–1801." *Id.*, VIII (1937), pp. 359–63.

Id. : *History of Modern Wales.* 1950 [Chaps. xii–xv].

Williams, Deiniol : "An eye-witness account of agrarian conditions in Caernarvonshire during the Napoleonic era." *Trans. Caerns. Hist. Soc.*, III (1941), pp. 72–84.

Williams, E. A. : *Hanes Môn yn y Bedwaredd Ganrif a Bymtheg.* Llangefni, 1927.

Williams, Robert : "Hunangofiant Chwarelwr." *Cymru*, XVI (1899), XVIII (1901), XIX (1902), [N.L.W. MS. 8412].

(c) DISSERTATIONS ACCEPTED FOR UNIVERSITY DEGREES

[Copies may normally be consulted in the library of the writer's university or college, which is given in parenthesis after his name. Duplicates of theses presented in the University of Wales are available in the National Library at Aberystwyth].

Andrews, L. S. : Changes in land utilisation in the upper Severn valley, Montgomeryshire, 1750–1936 (Aberystwyth, 1940).

Ellis, Gweirydd : A history of the slate quarryman in Caernarvonshire in the nineteenth century (Bangor, 1931).

Hughes, Cledwyn Flynn- : The development of the Poor Law in Caernarvonshire and Anglesey, 1815–1914 (Bangor, 1945).

Jones, Moses, J. : The industrial development of Merioneth, 1750–1820 (Cardiff, 1937).

Parry, R. Ivor : The attitude of the Welsh Independents towards working-class movements from 1815 to 1870 (Bangor, 1931).

Plume, Gertrude A. : The enclosure movement in Caernarvonshire, with special reference to the Porth yr aur papers (Bangor, 1935).

Pritchard, D. Dylan : The slate industry of North Wales : a study of changes in economic organisation from 1780 to the present day (Bangor, 1935).

Richards, W. M. : The history of Traeth Mawr and the industrial results of the formation of the embankment (Aberystwyth, 1925).

Rogers, Emlyn : The history of trade unionism in the coal mining industry of North Wales up to 1914 (Bangor, 1928).

Thomas, David : A study of a rural and maritime community in the nineteenth century, with special reference to the relation between agriculture and shipping (Liverpool, 1928).

Williams, C. R. : The industrialisation of Flintshire in the nineteenth century (Aberystwyth, 1950).

Williams, P. T. : The industrial history of Flintshire in the nineteenth century (Liverpool, 1928).

(d) CRITICAL NOTICES OF FIRST EDITION
(1) *Reviews and Journals*

Archæologia Cambrensis, LXXXVIII (1933). pp. 132–36 (the late H. Harold Hughes).

Arrows (Univ. of Sheffield), 1933, p. 29 (Professor G. P. Jones).

Economica, n.s., I (1934), pp. 113–14 (C. R. Fay).

Economic History Review, IV (1933), pp. 367–69 (Professor A. Redford).

Economic Journal, XLIII (1933), pp. 690–92 (Professor G. N. Clark).

English Historical Review, XLIX (1934), pp. 547–48 (the late Sir John Clapham).

Geographical Journal, LXXXII (1933), p. 542 (G. R. Crone).

Geographica, XVIII (1933), p. 330 (Professor E. G. Bowen).

Llenor, XII (1933), pp. 126–28 (Professor David Williams).

Montgomeryshire Collections, XLIII (1934), p. 181 (A. Stanley Davies).

Times Literary Supplement, May 11, 1933.

Welsh Outlook, XX (1933), pp. 199–200 (Sir Ben Bowen Thomas).

xl INDUSTRIAL REVOLUTION IN NORTH WALES

(2) *Newspapers*

Baner, Mai 16, 1933.
Brython, Mai 4, 1933.
Ddraig Goch, Mai, 1933 (W. Ambrose Bebb).
Ford Gron, Awst, 1933 (W. Eames).
Goleuad, Mai 24, 1933.
Liverpool Post, April 24, 1933 ("Celt").
Liverpool Weekly Post, May 6, 1933.
Manchester Guardian, June 13, 1933.
News Chronicle, March 31, 1933 (English), June 3, 1933 (Welsh).
Times, May 2, 1933.
Tyst, Mehefin, 1933.
Western Mail, April 6, 1933 (Sir Frederick Rees).

SUPPLEMENTARY BIBLIOGRAPHY 1970

A. BOOKS

Beazley, Elizabeth: *Madocks and the Wonder of Wales.* 1957.
Boyde, J. I. C.: *The Ffestiniog Railway*, i (2nd ed.), 1961, ii, 1959.
Bradley, V. J. and Hindley, P. H.: *Industrial and Independent Railways in North Wales.* 1968.
Cozens, L.: *The Welshpool and Llanfair Light Railway.* 1951.
id.: *The Llanfyllin Railway.* 1959.
Christiansen, R. and Miller, R. W.: *The Cambrian Railway* (2 vols.), 1967-8.
Davies, D. Ll.: *The Glyn Valley Tramway.* 1962.
Dodd, A. H.: *The character of Early Welsh Emigration to the U.S.* 2nd ed., 1957.
id.: (ed.) *Hist. of Wrexham.* 1957 (ch. viia).
id.: *History of Caernarvonshire.* 1968 (chaps. ixB and xi).
Hadfield, E. C. R.: *English Canals* (revised ed.). 1959.
Harris, J. R.: *The Copper King. A Biography of Thomas Williams of Llanidan.* 1964.
Holland, Samuel: *Memoirs* (ed. Davies, W. Ll.). 1952.
Hughes, D. Ll. and Williams, D. M.: *Holyhead: the Story of a Port.* 1957. (chs. vi and vii).
Jenkins, J. Geraint: *The Welsh Woollen Industry.* 1969.
Jones, Emrys: *Canrif y Chwarelwr.* 1963.
Lee, C. E.: *The Welsh Highland Railway* (new ed.). 1962.
Lewis, M. J. T.: *How Ffestiniog got its Railways.* 1968.
Rolt, L. T. C.: *Talyllyn Centenary.* 1965.
Rowlands, J.: *Copper Mountain.* 1966.
Thomas, David: *Cau'r Tiroedd Comin.* 1954.

B. ARTICLES

Bevan-Evans, M.: "Gadlys and Flintshire lead-mining in the eighteenth century." *Flints. Hist. Soc. Publns.*, xviii, 1960.

Chaloner, W. H.: "Charles Roe of Macclesfield." *Trans. Lancs. and Ches. Antiq. Soc.*, lxii-lxiii, 1950-3.

id.: "John Wilkinson, ironmaster." *History Today*, i, 1951.

id.: "Gilbert Gilpin, chief clerk at Bersham iron-works, 1786-96." *Nat. Lib. of Wales Jnl.*, xi, 1960.

Clarke, M. L.: "Britannia Park (Bangor)". *Trans. Caerns. Hist. Soc.*, xix, 1958.

Cockshutt, E.: "The Parys Mountain Copper Mines." *Arch. Camb.*, 1965.

Dodd, J. P.: "The Denbighshire crop returns for 1854." *Trans. Denbs. Hist. Soc.*, viii, 1959.

Dunn, J. M.: "The Anglesey Central Railway." *Railway Mag.*, 1960.

Davies, Alun E.: "Sir Hugh Owen and the New Poor Law." *Bull Bd. of Celtic Studies*, xxi, 1964-6.

id.: "Paper-mills and paper-makers in Wales, 1700:1900." *N.L.W. Jnl.*, xv, 1967-8.

Edwards, Ifor: "The charcoal iron industry of east Denbighshire, 1690-1770." *Trans. Denbs. Hist. Soc.*, x, 1961.

id.: "Iron founders in North Wales: the canal era, 1775-1830."

id.: xiv, 1965.

Flinn, M. W.: "The Lloyds in the early English iron industry." *Business Hist.*, ii, 1959.

Griffiths, W. A.: "An early eighteenth-century account book." *Mont. Coll.*, lii, 1951-2.

Hughes, Mairwen: "The marram grass industry of Newborough." *Trans. Ang. Antiq. Soc.*, 1956.

Jones, D. V. J.: "The corn riots in Wales, 1793-1801." *Welsh Hist. Rev.*, ii, 1964-5.

Jones, Emrys: "Casgliad o dermau chwarel." *Bull. Bd. of Celtic Studies*, xx, 1962-4.

Jones, G. R. J.: "The Llanynys quillets: a measure of landscape transformation in North Wales." *Trans. Denbs. Hist. Soc.*, xiii, 1964.

Lloyd, George: "The canalization of the river Dee in 1737." *Flints. Hist. Soc. Pubns.*, xxiii, 1967-8.

Lerry, G. G.: "The industries of Denbighshire from Tudor times to the present day." *Trans. Denbs. Hist. Soc.*, vi-xi (1957-60), xiii (1964).

Morris, E. R.: "The Dolobran family in religion and industry in Montgomeryshire." *Mont. Coll.*, lvi, 1960.

id.: "Who were the Montgomeryshire Chartists?" id.: lviii, 1963.

Owen, Bob: "Yr ymfudo o Sir Gaernarfon i'r Unol Daleithiau." *Trans. Caerns. Hist. Soc.*, xiii-xv, 1952-4.

Owen, G. W. and Davies, V. C.: "The gold mines of Merioneth." *Jnl. Mer. Hist. and Rec. Soc.*, iv, 1961-4.

Pritchard, R. T.: "The post road in Caernarvonshire." *Trans. Caerns. Hist. Soc.*, xiii, 1952.

id.: "The post road in Anglesey." *Trans. Ang. Ant. Soc.*, 1954.

id.: "The turnpike trusts of Caernarvonshire." *Trans. Caerns. Hist. Soc.*, xix-xx (1958-9), xxii (1961).

id.: "The Beaumaris-Menai Bridge turnpike." *Trans. Ang. Ant. Soc.*, 1959.
id.: "Merioneth roads and turnpike trusts." *Jnl. Mer. Hist. and Rec. Soc.*, vi, 1961.
id.: "Montgomeryshire turnpike trusts." *Mont. Coll.*, lvii, 1961-2.
id.: "Denbighshire roads and turnpike trusts." *Trans. Denbs. Hist. Soc.*, xii, 1963.
Rees, D. M.: "Copper mining in North Wales." *Arch. Camb.*, 1968.
Rhodes, J. N.: "The London (Quaker) Company and the Prestatyn mines scandal." *Flints. Hist. Soc. Pubns.*, xxiii, 1967-8.
Richards, Gwynfryn: "Chwareli Dyffryn Nantlle." *Trans. Caerns. Hist. Soc.*, xxix, 1968.
Roberts, J. L.: "Early railway controversies at Llangollen." *Trans. Denbs. Hist. Soc.*, ix, 1960.
Roberts, R. O. "Copper and economic growth in Britain, 1729-1824." *N.L.W. Jnl.*, x, 1957-8.
id.: "The mills of Anglesey." *Trans. Ang. Ant. Soc.*, 1958.
Rogers, Emlyn: "The history of trade unionism in the coal mining industry of North Wales." *Trans. Denbs. Hist. Soc.*, xi-xix, (1963-70). Continuing.
Rowlands, J.: "Cornishmen at the Amlwch copper mines." *Trans. Ang. Ant. Soc.*, 1963.
Thomas, Brinley: "Robert Owen of Newtown." *Trans. Cymm. Soc.*, 1961.
Vallance, H. A.: "The mid-Wales line." *Railway Mag.*, 1963.
Williams, David: "Some figures relating to emigration from Wales." *Bull. Bd. of Celtic Studies*, vi-vii, 1935-6.
id.: "The crop returns of 1801 for Wales." id., xiv, 1950-1.
Williams, J. Roose: "Quarryman's champion." *Trans. Caerns. Hist. Soc.*, xxiii-xxvii, xxix-xxx (1962-6, 1968-9).
Wynne, R. F.: "Llandudno and the N.P. Bank." id.: xxiii, 1962.

C. MANUSCRIPTS

(a) NATIONAL LIBRARY OF WALES

(i) *Slate and stone quarrying*

NLW 11081, 16877, 18365-18418, 18760-1, 18870, 19515, 19652-5; Brogyntyn (Caernarvonshire 1840); Londonderry estate papers (Mer. 1834-44); C. E. Vaughan Owen (Mer. 1738 ff.); H. T. Elwes (Caerns. 1824-5); North Wales Quarrymen's Union.

(ii) *Lead*

NLW 16046, 17743, 19674; NLW Deeds 665-9; Dolgaradog (Mont. 1830-7); Garn (Denbs. 1751-7); Cefnronydd (Mer. 1759); Wynnstay, 1952 Deposit (Denbs. 1814 ff.); H. T. Elwes (Mer. 1826-8): Oldfield (Flints. 1757-1806); Llidiardau (Mer. and Flints. 1743-5); Berth-lwyd and Dol-llys (Montgom. 1848 ff.); Plas Power (Denbs. 1692-1822); Longueville, Whitehall-Davies (Flints. 1813).

(iii) *Copper*

NLW 18466, 19223; Druid Inn (Flints. and Caerns., 1828-58); H. T. Elwes (Mer. 1826).

(iv) *Coal and iron*

NLW 18959-60; NLW Deposit 690B (Denbs. 1839); Brogyntyn (Denbs. 1670, 1684); H. T. Elwes (Flints. 1723-36); Plas Power (Denbs. 1671-96); Longueville, Chirk Castle (Denbs. 1634-88); id., Whitehall-Davies (Flints. 1804); Dolgaradog (Flints. 1820).

(v) *Woollens*

NLW 19271; Thomas, Machynlleth (Mont. 1839-46).

(vi) *Drovers*

NLW 17927 (Mer. 1821-2).

(vii) *Enclosures*

Maesmawr (Montgom.); Oldfield (Flints. 1809-53); Montgom. County Council (1785-1879); H. T. Elwes (Mer. 1822-4); Voelas (Denbs. 1812); Longueville (5 counties, 1789-1854); and a number of separate Acts, awards, maps, etc.

(viii) *Communications (inland)*

NLW 18317; Brogyntyn (Montgom. 1807); E. Francis Davies (Denbs. and Montgom. 1779); Wynnstay, 1952 Deposit (Denbs. 1773-1850); Garn (Denbs. 1784); Llwyn, Llanfyllin (Mer. and Mont. 1769-1808); Maesmawr Hall (Mont. 1711-74, 1833); Powysland Club (Mont. 1756-1873); W. J. Morris, Barmouth (Mont. 1827-85); Glyn Davies, Newtown (Montgom.); Longueville (Mont. and Denbs. 1717-1812); Montgom. County Council (1813 ff.).

(ix) *Shipping and ports*

NLW 18608-11; Miss Judith Williams (Caerns. 1830-48); Longueville (Conway port bk. 1800-2).

(x) *Trade Unions*

NLW 18957, 18961; Mrs. A. M. Rogers, Marchwiel (Denbs.).

(xi) *Poor Law*

Dolgaradog (Flints. 1743-1820); Montgom. County Council (1830 ff.).

(b) U.C.N.W., BANGOR

(i) *General Collections* ('Bangor MSS')

Many individual items such as parish records, enclosure awards, and a few relating to industrial undertakings and banks, have been added to these since 1951. They relate principally to Caernarvonshire and Anglesey, but are too numerous to list separately.

(ii) *Special and deposited collections*

Gwysanau 557-85 (coal, lead and other mineral enterprises, mainly Flintshire); *Kinmel* 480-1 (lime and minerals, Flints.); 485-7 (enclosures, Flints.); 531-5 (Anglesey copper). *Mostyn* 6935-7198 (coal, lead and other minerals and stone quarries, mainly Flintshire); 7199-7258 (inland transport and communications);

7259-92 (ports and shipping). *Plas Newydd* i. 2311-2466, ii. 2450-2470, iii. 5039-5058, iv. 8610-20 (transport and communications); ii. 2943-3004, iii. 4474, vii. 1-142 (copper and lead, Caerns. and Ang., 1765-1872); iii. 4444, 4446, 4453, 4457-8, 4967-4991, 5133-60, vi. 566-7 (stone quarries, Caerns. and Ang.); iii. 4652-3, 5059-5132 (coal mines, Ang.).

(c) FLINTSHIRE RECORD OFFICE, HAWARDEN

(i) *Coal, lead and copper*

Keene and Kelly MSS: Manor of Mold, Richardson of Greenfield (incl. plan of Parys Mountain, Ang., 1764), and Douglas of Gyrn (incl. Llandudno copper mine 1842-6); Birch Cullimore; Records of Halkyn United Mines (Milwr lead mine 1822-48); Mostyn of Talacre; Trevalyn Hall; Panton (incl. copper and coal mines, Ang. and Caerns., 1694 ff.); Mostyn.

(ii) *Enclosures*

Flints.   Quarter Sessions records.

(iii) *Transport and communications*

Id.;   Birch Cullimore (Aston Rly. 1837-57).

(iv) *Potteries*

Catherall and Hancock MSS.

(v) *Cotton*

Rhual MSS.   (Mold cotton mill 1871).

(d) CAERNARVONSHIRE RECORD OFFICE, CAERNARVON

(i) *Quarries.*

Slate. Dinorwic 1810 ff. (Special coll.) and 1842-74 (M/1236); Dorothea 1848 ff., Penrhyn 1800 ff. (Special colls.); Llechwedd 1838 ff. (J. W. Greaves); Betws Garmon 1810 ff. (Garreg Fawr). *Stone.* Vaynol (Ang. and Caerns. 1826 ff.).

(ii) *Lead, copper, etc.*

Trefriw 1754 (Wern MSS.), 1818-56 (M/1001); Cwm Dyli 1857 ff. M/297); Drws y coed 1760 ff. (Vaynol), 1845 (M/298).

(iii) *Coal*

M/342 (Ang.).

(iv) *Woollens*

M/1266 (Penmachno).

(v) *Railways*

M/1441 (Holyhead Railway and harbour 1844 ff.); Wern (Britannia Bridge 1844-8).

(vi) *Shipping and Harbours*

M/321 (Pwllheli 1818 ff.); M/511, 531 (Portmadoc); M/756 (Porthdinllaen 1846-7), and Porthdinllaen Harbour Co. records 1808-1911; M/658, 804, 911 (Barmouth harbour and Caernarvonshire shipping 1818-49).

(vii) *Miscellaneous trading and farming accts*

M/902 (Glyn estate); M/303 (Nanhoron); M/1331 (Abererch).

(viii) *Parish records*

(inc. Poor Law, highways, etc.) of eleven Caernarvonshire parishes.

(ix) *Banks*

M/923 (Caernarvonshire Old Bank, letter bk. etc., 1855-85).

For the information on which the foregoing lists of MSS are based the author is indebted to the Keeper of MSS and Records, and Miss Nia Lewis (NLW, Aberystwyth), the Librarian and Archivist, UCNW (Bangor), the County Archivist and Mr. Christopher Williams (Hawarden) and the County Archivist, Caernarvon.

CHAPTER I

THE OLD ORDER.

They [though] that londe be luyte [little],
Hit is ful of corne and fruyte ;
And hath grete plente i-wis
Bothe of flesche, and of fische ;
Of bestes, tame and wylde,
Of hors, schepe and oxen mylde ; . . .
Valeyes bryngeth forth food,
And hilles metal right good,
Col groweth under lond,
And gras above at the hond ;
There lyme is copious,
And sclattes also for hous. . . .
The manere levynge of that lond
Is wel dyvers from Engelond,
In mete and drynk and clothing,
And many other doyng . . .
With oute hodes, hatte or cappes,
Thus arraied gooth the geggis [clowns],
And alle with bare legges ; . . .
They eteth brede, colde and hote,
Of barliche and of oote ; . . .
They haveth growel to potage,
And a leke is skyn to compernage ;
Also butter, melk and chese
I-schape euelong [oblong] and cornered wise.

—Higden : *Polychronicon* (*De Wallia*).[1]

If some Rip van Winkle of North Wales had been put to sleep by a magic draught on the top of Snowdon (let us say) in the year of Queen Elizabeth's coronation, to wake again at George the Third's accession, he would have seen less to gape at in his new surroundings than his American counterpart found after a mere nap of twenty years. If the gentry lived in better-furnished houses, fared more sumptuously, dressed more soberly, spoke less Welsh, and spent more of their time in England, the mass of the people—peasants and fishermen, shepherds and drovers—lived much as their

---

[1] Trevisa's translation, Lib. I, cap. XXXVIII (Rolls series, 1865, I, pp. 395 ff.).

1

ancestors had done in Shakespeare's time.   Indeed, if we allow for the fact that

> Drede of losse of here good
> Maketh hem now stille of mood,

they were still essentially the Welshmen described by Higden (in the lines quoted above) in the fourteenth century, or even by his informant, Giraldus Cambrensis, in the twelfth.

Their dress was made of the same rude homespun.   The poorest of all wore hempen cloth ; those in better circumstances made themselves woollen hose and suits of undressed greyish cloth (*brethyn cartref*) from wool purchased of a neighbouring farmer—eked out, it might be, by what they could gather from brambles or beg at the shearing.   Only well-to-do farmers would rise to the extravagance of buying broadcloth at the fair.   Shoes and stockings were worn with strict economy ; linen and hats were a luxury of the rich ;   even the Welshwoman's "chimney hat," dear to the hearts of the sentimentalists, had only just come in— from England.   The same traditional diet served them : oat cakes, rye or barley bread and *llymru* (flummery) ; bacon and dried goat's flesh in some parts ;   fish in the coast villages ;   butcher's meat only in the richer lowlands of Denbigh and Flint.   Buttermilk and mead were the common beverages.   Beer was a specific for illness and a fair-day extravagance.   Tea was a rarity, and its devotees were the butt of all ballad-mongers ;   De Quincey found the cottagers of Merioneth still innocent of the habit as late as 1802.[1]

Nor had domestic architecture made much progress. The cottages of the peasantry were low cabins rudely built of the materials nearest to hand :   timber frames filled in with wattle and daub in wooded Montgomeryshire, unmortared stones in the upland parishes of Snowdonia. The floors were unpaved, the roofs of straw or rush thatch ;

---

[1] Pococke : *Travels*, I, p. 238, II, p. 178 ;   Cradock : *Letters from Snowdon*, p. 37 ;   Davies : *Labourers in Husbandry*, pp. 189, 191 ;   letters in *North Wales Gazette*, May 7, July 9 and 23, 1812, describing changes of last 40 or 50 years; Davies, J. H. : *Bibliography of Welsh Ballads* (Cymrodorion Society, 1911), No. 304 ; De Quincey : *Opium Eater* ("Everyman" edition), p. 131.

slates—thick, small, and irregular in size and surface—were used in those districts where they could be had for the picking up. The smoke from the peat fire (for outside the coalfield of Denbighshire and Flintshire none but the gentry used coal) went through a gaping hole in the roof, and windows and even doors were sometimes lacking. The living room was not infrequently shared by the farm animals ; and sleeping accommodation was primitive in the extreme. Among the more prosperous farmers and in the market towns, of course, things were different. A century before the time of which we are speaking, Fuller (writing on second-hand information) had observed that though Welsh cottages were worse than English, Welsh market towns were better built, "the gentry, it seems, having many of their habitations there," and so raising the general standard of amenities.[1]

The civil and religious storms of the seventeenth century had passed over the face of the country without uprooting any familiar landmarks, and Methodism had hardly yet begun to transform the national character. The Welshman of the mid-eighteenth century, as English travellers saw him, was still the Welshman of tradition—suspicious of strangers, yet given to hospitality ; frugal and parsimonious in daily life, but apt to break loose at fair-times ; passionately wedded to the ancient ways ; fond of pranks and practical jokes ; devoted to spectacles and stage-plays. From time to time a band of "hempen homespuns" would give an open-air rendering of some traditional theme, much as a Welsh Bottom and his friends might have acted it two centuries earlier—and with as great a freedom of language and allusion. It was this, indeed, that brought the *anterliwt* under the frown of the Methodists : early in the next century the rustic players found themselves in the courts on charges of indecency.[2] The Wakes, too, were

[1] *Report on Land*, 1896, pp. 690 ff. ; Hughes and North : *Old Cottages of Snowdonia* ; Evans : *Tour*, pp. 31, 39, 86, 115, 160–2, 312 ; *Mont. Coll.* XXVI, p. 161 ; Wigstead : *Tour*, pp. 20–21 ; Fuller : *Worthies*, 1662 (Nuttall's edition 1840), III, p. 488.

[2] Pococke : *Travels*, II, p. 18 ; Cradock : *Letters from Snowdon*, pp. 64–6, and *Account of North Wales*, pp. 14–15 ; *Bye-gones*, 1871, p. 2, 1903–04, p. 366 ; *Bull. of Bd. of Celtic Studies*, IV, ii (1927). *Cf.* sketches of Welsh character in Aikin : *Journal*, chap. VII ; Fenton : *Tours*, p. 186.

soon to be shorn of their glory ; so far they held their own
as times of licensed roystering, marked by semi-pagan rites
which were already hoary with age when our hypothetical
Rip van Winkle began his slumbers.[1]

If travellers about to cross the Welsh border no longer
had need to go in bands, well armed and fortified beforehand by prayers for safety from highwaymen, it still needed
a measure of courage to encounter "a Welsh journey."[2]
For since the Romans no one had *made* roads ; they had
"just growed," at the whim of man and beast, tackling
hills and mountains "more by a spirit of· daringness
than by craft or circumvention." There were, in short,
"but few travellable roads in the whole district."[3] A
family coach, a post-chaise, or even in some parts a
waggon or farm-cart, was rarely to be met with. Men
travelled on horseback, goods in horse or ass panniers, and
it needed a sledge to negotiate the more mountainous
regions. In the immediate neighbourhood of the English
border, some two or three turnpike trusts had been set up
since the middle of the century, and another had taken over
a small portion of the route to Holyhead and Ireland.
Otherwise the roads were a parochial concern, repaired (if
at all) by statute labour under the supervision of amateur
surveyors.

The uplands of Snowdonia and of Mid-Wales remained,
as they had always been, regions of scattered farmsteads,
where the shepherds followed their flocks in summer to the
boundless mountain commons, bringing them back to the
valleys in winter.[4] Many of these hillside pastures were
still open and unfenced, and customary rights of use were

---

[1] *See*, e.g., account of Holyhead Wakes and their decline in *N.W.
Gaz.*, Aug. 3, 1809, Aug. 9, 1810, and picture of them in Pugh's
Cambria Depicta (1806), opp. p. 53 ; *cf*. Lewis : *Top. Dict.* under
Llanvihangel yn nhowyn, Meivod, Llaneilian, etc., and accounts of
various superstitions in *Letters from Snowdon*, p. 66, Williams :
Observations on Snowdon Mountains, pp. 9–18, *Cambro-Briton*, I
(1819), pp. 349–51.

[2] Phillips : *History and Antiquities of Shrewsbury*, pp. 135–8 ;
cf. Cust : *Chronicles of Erthig*, I, p. 46.

[3] Davies : *General View*, pp. 372–80.

[4] Pennant : *Tours*, II, p. 325 ; Williams : *Snowdon Mountains*,
p. 22.

of more vital import than legal claims to ownership. Here and there they had been divided into "stints" among the neighbouring sheep-owners by formal or informal agreement ;[1] and cultivation had crept slowly up the mountainside as squatters carved new holdings out of the waste ;[2] but Enclosure Acts were still unknown in North Wales. A little wheat was grown, more barley and rye, but the mainstay of the peasant was his sheep and goats (though the latter were said to be falling out of fashion); in Merioneth and Montgomeryshire there were also the wild mountain ponies to be caught and sold.[3] The village, save on fair-days, played but small part in the life of these regions ; the centre of social activities was the bigger farmhouse. There scattered households would meet for song and tale after mutual aid in the harvest or the sheep-shearing, and for communal knitting or hemp-dressing, rush-peeling or wool-carding, in the long winter evenings—tame relics of the lawless mediaeval *cymorth* (still bearing the dread name) and forerunners of the chapel tea-meeting and Dorcas Society.[4]

In the lowlands, and especially along the English border, arable farming was the staple occupation, and genuine village communities had flourished from an early date. The "open field" system, however, had for generations been slowly breaking down through the purchase and consolidation of scattered quillets by the more prosperous freeholders, and their consequent detachment from tenements in the village.[5] The valleys of the Severn and the Clwyd produced good wheat crops—Flintshire even helped to victual Liverpool—and the woodlands of eastern

---

[1] E.g. Deythur (Montgomery), 1585 (*Y Cymmrodor*, XXXVIII, pp. 35–6); Allt Dolgelley (Merioneth), 1654 (*Mont. Coll.*, XV, pp. 420–2 ; *Bye-gones*, 1897–8, pp. 248, 254–5) ; Cardiganshire *c.* 1756 (*Y Cymmrodor*, XV, p. 9).

[2] *Rept. on Land*, 1896, pp. 210–14, 578 ; *infra*, chap. III.

[3] *Britannia Depicta*, pp. 50, 109, 182, 185, 233, 265, 313 ; Evans : *Tour*, p. 205 *n.*

[4] Pennant : *Tours*, II, pp. 210–11, III, pp. 355–6 ; Evans : *Tour*, p. 68 ; *Y Cymmrodor*, V, pp. 49–50 ; Williams : *Hanes Plwyf Ffestiniog*, p. 76.

[5] On the consolidation of holdings in the seventeenth century *see* Palmer, A. N. : *Town, Fields and Folk of Wrexham in the time of James the First* (Wrexham, 1883).

Montgomeryshire had from early in the century been supplying the navy with timber.[1]

Outside these few districts, subsistence farming was the aim, and an aim very imperfectly realized. Despite some imposing figures of corn exports from Anglesey and Caernarvonshire given by local topographers in the latter half of the eighteenth century,[2] it is clear that both counties were largely dependent on imported English grain, and Merioneth still more. Little progress, indeed, had been made in the yield of the soil since Elizabeth's time. It is true that the new-born scientific curiosity of the late seventeenth century had produced some impulse towards agricultural improvement even in the remoter parts of Wales, but the impulse soon spent itself. Henry Rowlands, the antiquary, who was Vicar of Llanidan in Anglesey from 1696 to 1723, wrote with pride in his *Idea Agriculturæ* of the many experiments in the treatment of soils made by his neighbours ; but a full generation after his death, when his essay was still unpublished, a traveller described the island as "a naked and unpleasant country . . . uncultivated still . . . so that I am told it does not produce a tenth of what the land is capable of."[3] On the very eve of the Napoleonic Wars, less than a tenth of its enclosed lands were under crops. Yet Anglesey had once been the granary of Wales—*Môn, Mam Cymru* ; it produced twice as much as Caernarvonshire, and five times as much as Merioneth, where less than 14,000 acres out of 400,000 were under tillage.[4]

Here and there "buildings [had been] enlarged, hedges or ditches made or repaired, and some drainage attempted,"[5] but that was all. Turnips had not yet become a regular field crop, and potatoes were almost as rare. The old-fashioned cumbrous plough, drawn by its team of oxen, was

---

[1] *Britannia Depicta*, pp. 182, 265 : Pennant : *Tours*, I. p. 5 : Defoe: *Tour* (sixth ed., 1761), pp. 364–5, 372 ; Lewis : *Top. Dict.*, under *Montgomeryshire* ; *Mont. Coll.*, XXVI, p. 328, XLIII, p. 43.

[2] Caernarvonshire, 20–30,000 bushels a year (Morris : *Plans of Harbours*, p. 6) ; Anglesey, 90,000 bushels (*Hist. of Anglesey*, pp. 6, 7).

[3] Lyttleton, pp. 239–40.

[4] Davies : *General View*, pp. 139–40 ; Lewis : *Top. Dict.*, under *Merioneth*.

[5] *Report on Land*, 1896, p. 663.

still in general use ; the lowland counties were only just beginning to substitute lighter and more up-to-date models. Threshing machines were unknown. Even the farm carts were clumsy in pattern, and many farms had none at all ; the scanty produce taken to market could easily be carried on horseback. The use of scientific methods in manuring and fallowing, in the care of pastures, and in the feeding and breeding of stock, was confined to a few faddists.[1] In the more backward parts

> oats and barley were alternately sown ; and during seven months of the year the best soil was ravaged by flocks of sheep. . . . When seed time was finished, the plough and harrow were laid aside till autumn, and the sole employment of the farmer consisted in weeding his cornfields or digging and conveying home peat, turf, and heath for winter fuel. The produce of the farm. . . was barely sufficient to pay the trifling rent and the servants' wages, and to procure the family a scanty subsistence."[2]

Since the disappearance of tribal law and custom under the Tudors, land tenure had changed but little. Farms were still small ; even at the end of the century, after there had been a movement towards larger holdings, not more than a dozen farms of six hundred acres were to be found in the whole of North Wales. Only at busy seasons like the harvest was it necessary to hire supplementary labour to help the family and the handful of permanent servants who boarded with them.[3]

The principal wealth of the country was in its livestock, and cattle were the chief item in its export trade. In the more fertile valleys they could be fattened for sale or for home consumption ; elsewhere they were bought by drovers and driven in herds to the Midlands and London, where English farmers bought and fattened them. The interruption of this trade had been one of the greatest hardships felt by the country during the Civil Wars of the seventeenth century.[4] Anglesey was then said to be sending three thousand head of cattle every year to swim the Straits and

[1] Davies : *op. cit.*, chaps. V and VII.
[2] Letter in *N. W. Gaz.*, July 9, 1812, recalling conditions "fifty or sixty years ago."
[3] Davies : *op. cit.*, pp. 92–5 ; *Report on Land*, pp. 136–49.
[4] *See* petitions quoted in Williams : *Ancient and Modern Denbigh*, pp. 220–1, and in *Arch. Camb.*, 1846, pp. 332–3 ; 1922, pp. 249–50; *cf. Trans. Royal Hist. Soc.*, 1926, pp. 135 ff.

then to make their way by easy stages through the pastures of Denbighshire to the English markets. "I have seen yearly great droves of fair beasts brought thence and sold in Essex itself. The mother of Wales is in some sort a nurse to England." So wrote Fuller in 1662 ; a century later there was a popular belief, apparently without much foundation, that these exports had increased fourfold or fivefold ; but the trade at least continued and flourished. Nor was it confined to Anglesey. The uplands of Caernarvonshire, Montgomeryshire, and West Denbighshire all added their quotas, and Merioneth, which produced fewer cattle itself, supplied its neighbours with professional feeders.[1]

Beside the life of the farms, town life was of very minor importance. In the later Middle Ages Welshmen had been nominally excluded from municipal status, and when at last the rule of the Tudors removed these disabilities, the towns were too undeveloped to offer many attractions to men of ambition ; better far to enrich one's self with monastic spoils, or to seek one's fortune in London, where all was "ripe for exploits and mighty enterprises." And so Wales was left without an industrial middle class.[2] The gilds that had been sanctioned in ancient boroughs by royal or seigneurial charter had generally little more than a formal existence. Their trade was trifling and purely local ; they never exerted over the surrounding countryside the influence that was typical of so many English boroughs. It is said of the gilds of Denbigh, in the seventeenth century, that they "monopolized the trade of the country from the Dee to the Conway and far into the interior of Merioneth and Caernarvon";[3] and the local gentry, and even families from across the border, did not scorn the honour of membership. This, however, was exceptional. The Denbigh glovers and cordwainers might send their wares all over North Wales and to the English markets for export abroad ; but in most towns

[1] Roberts, Lewes : *Merchant's Map of Commerce* (1638) ; Fuller : *Worthies*, III, p. 508 ; Owen : *Hist. of Anglesey*, p. 8 ; Pennant : *Tours*, III, p. 22 and *n* ; Davies : *General View*, p. 310 ; Lewis : *Top. Dict.*, under *Merioneth*.
[2] *Welsh in Education and Life* (Report of Departmental Committee on Welsh Language, 1927), p. 27.
[3] Williams : *Ancient and Modern Denbigh*, pp. 126 ff.

the craftsman did not aspire beyond the custom of his next-door neighbours, and in the country his place was taken by the parish tailor, shoemaker or saddler, cooper, weaver or sieve-maker, wandering with his apprentice from farm to farm, working on his temporary employer's materials, and boarding with the family till his job was finished. Even in an old borough like Llanidloes—the centre, as we shall see, of a busy weaving district—shops opened only on market days, and the shopkeepers mostly came in from Newtown.[1] In other parts of the country, especially in Snowdonia, boroughs had been created as English garrisons rather than on economic grounds, and many of them had sunk by now to their natural condition of sleepy villages.

So far as the town had any influence on the economic life of the surrounding country, it was not through its skilled craftsmen or its gilds, but rather through its fairs and markets. Here the surplus produce of the countryside—corn and wool, livestock and dairy produce—found purchasers both from the district around and among English merchants who thought it worth while to come. Here, too, might be obtained domestic luxuries or farming necessaries which could not be produced at home : tea, coffee and sugar, porter, wine and spirits, hemp and flax, fine linen and broadcloth, superior pottery and ironware, tallow, pitch and tar. Wrexham is the only town likely at this time to have attained a population of four thousand ; its markets had long put it in the front rank as a distributing centre for rural produce, and its great March Fair was soon to be the chief means of supplying all North Wales with Lancashire, Yorkshire, and Sheffield wares for the whole year. In 1724 Anglesey had two market towns, Caernarvonshire and Montgomeryshire six apiece, Denbighshire four, and Flintshire and Merioneth three each. Since then a few markets had been added and a few discontinued. In addition there were the periodic fairs for wool, livestock, and dairy produce, at dates fixed by local custom or varying with the convenience of the moment.[2]

[1] Pococke : *Travels*, II, p. 20 ; *cf.* Wyndham : *Gentleman's Tour of Wales* (1794 ed.), p. 96, *Hanes Plwyf Ffestiniog*, p. 72.

[2] *See* lists in *Llyfer Plygain* 1612 (1931 rep.), pp. 35–46, and *Britannia Depicta; cf.* Pococke : *Travels*, I, p. 234, II, pp. 19, 20, 178 ; Defoe : *Tour* (1761 ed.), II, pp. 371, 373, 374 ; Willett : *Memoir of Hawarden*, p. 112; Palmer: *Wrexham*, pp. 4–6, 19, 82–3, 96.

Agriculture and town handicrafts were not the only occupations of the people. The tanning of hides and the weaving of woollens were among the most ancient and widespread of rural arts.[1] For the tanner there was plenty of oak-bark and of good streams ; for the weaver an abundant supply of fleecy wool. Much of the best wool in the country went to enrich the manufacturers of Yorkshire, East Anglia, and the South-west of England[2], but some was kept at home, or dispersed at fairs among the neighbouring farms and cottages, or sold in small parcels by the landlords to their tenantry. Many of the bigger farmhouses had their looms and weaving-sheds ; hardly even the poorest cottage was without its hand-cards and spinning-wheel ; and the woven cloth could be taken for fulling to one of the little *pandai* that had long abounded on Welsh streams, much as corn was taken to the corn mill.[3]

In addition to these widely-diffused cottage industries, there had grown up in the counties of Denbigh, Montgomery and Merioneth an organized woollen manufacture, producing for the market. Its origins are difficult to trace, Even in the Middle Ages Wales was exporting a little cloth ;[4] but, as in other phases of Welsh life, it was the peace of the Tudors that hastened development, especially in these three counties of the North. They now began to attract to themselves the wool of South Wales, and to appear alongside the English clothing counties in Acts of Parliament and Privy Council decrees for regulating the quality of woollens.[5] From these and other sources we can form some idea of the nature of the industry. It was not a townsman's craft like the ancient clothing trades of

---

[1] *Y Cymmrodor*, XXIV, p. 96.

[2] Dyer : *The Fleece*, III, 60–88.

[3] Early references to fulling mills abound in wills and other family documents, and the frequency of the name *pandy* (fulling mill) in old maps of North Wales tells its own tale. *Cf.* also *Bye-gones*, 1886, p. 83 ; 1905–6, p. 32 ; *Mont. Coll.* XVII, pp. 65–80, XXIV, pp. 60, 84 ; Mantoux : *Industrial Revolution*, p. 58.

[4] Lewis, E. A. : *Mediaeval Boroughs of Snowdonia* (1912), pp. 180, 189, 200 ; *Y Cymmrodor*, XXIV, pp. 96–7, 126, 129, 170 ff. ; *Arch. Camb.*, 1922, pp. 220–3.

[5] E.g. 32 and 33 Hen. VIII, cap. 3 ; 34 and 35 Hen. VIII, cap. 26 ; 5 and 6 Edw. VI, cap. 6 ; 4 and 5 Phil. and Mar., cap. 5 ; 1 Jac. I, cap. 25 ; 3 Jac. I, cap. 17.

Norwich, nor was it so fully specialized as the country industries of the West Riding and the Cotswolds. But a growing number of weavers had come to depend on the profits of the loom as their chief means of livelihood, though they mig..t also have a small farm, or at least a few sheep on the common. Those who were without this source of supply bought their wool at a fair, or from a travelling woolman; or again it might be supplied by their customers. For those who could not do their own spinning there were yarn markets at Dolgelley, Machynlleth and elsewhere ; but in general, of course, spinning was part of the daily routine of a woman's life in any well-regulated family.[1] A prosperous "clothier" might even have several looms and spinning wheels under his roof, and keep a number of his servants busy at them most of their time.[2]

By the end of the sixteenth century the wage assessments of the county justices, in Merioneth at least, extended to weavers as well as to farm servants,[3] and during the Civil Wars the industry was extensive enough to prove a hindrance to recruiting on the one hand, and to suffer from looting and general interruption of trade on the other.[4] It was at this time, too, that it received the form of organization which it retained until the end of the eighteenth century. At first the Welsh clothiers had sold their wares freely in fairs and markets at home, or shipped them abroad by vessels which called at the ports with cargoes of grain ;[5] but the Shrewsbury Drapers' Company,

[1] Leighton : *Records of Oswestry*, p. 97 ; Pennant : *Tours*, III, p. 184.

[2] The term "clothier" (usually qualified by "poor") occurs frequently in references to the Welsh woollen industry in seventeenth century State Papers ; "draper" also appears sometimes (e.g. *Cal. S. P. Dom.* 1622, CXXXI, Nos. 20, 22, 77 ; *Records of Oswestry*, p. 98). No doubt the terms were used without any very precise significance ; the Welsh clothiers can rarely have been trained gildsmen like those of Norwich or large employers like those of the South-West.

[3] *See* assessment quoted in Davies : *op. cit.*, pp. 500–1, and criticism of it in *Bye-gones*, 1874, p. 70.

[4] Phillips, J. R. : *Civil War in Wales and the Marches* (second ed., 1878), p. 171 ; Williams : *Ancient and Modern Denbigh*, pp. 220–1 ; Penbedw MSS. (*Camb. Quart. Mag.*, I, p. 66) ; Roberts, Lewes : *Map of Commerce*, pp. 226–7.

[5] *See*, e.g., *Cal. S. P. Dom.*, 1622, CXXXI, No. 22 (p. 404); *Y Cymmrodor*, XXIV (1913), pp. 126, 129, 170–88.

ever since it received its charter in 1462, had always been an important customer.[1]   In Elizabeth's time this powerful corporation employed some 600 shearmen on the "finishing" processes which were beyond the skill of the Welsh. Jealous of any "interlopers" in such a profitable trade, it now began to claim that all Welsh cloth should be bought and sold in the Drapers' Hall at Shrewsbury, and there only.   An Act of 1565[2] laid the foundations of their monopoly, round which a furious struggle raged for nearly a century.

The monopoly was fought tooth and nail by London merchants trading with France and Spain. Strongly entrenched in the House of Commons, they refused to surrender their right to buy cloth at the markets, fairs, and seaports of North Wales.   Some even got themselves made free of boroughs like Oswestry (a Welsh town in all but name) in order to purchase there.   And the Welshmen, for their part, were nothing loth to dispense with the services of middlemen whom they suspected of pocketing the lion's share of the profits.   Against them the Shrewsbury men could plead public policy as well as local interests ; for were not these exporters of unfinished wares traitorously taking bread out of the mouths of English skilled workers, and comforting their rivals abroad ?   Again and again, in the Star Chamber, the Privy Council and the Council of Wales, harassed statesmen issued orders on the petition of one party and rescinded them after hearing the other ; till in 1624 Parliament cut the Gordian knot by declaring the trade open to all.[3]   But to no purpose ;   Shrewsbury was too strong for her foes, and by simply persisting in her refusal to buy cloth outside her own markets she got.her way more effectively than by any Act of Parliament or decree of Council..   In the middle of the eighteenth century the Shrewsbury Drapers' monopoly was still intact.[4]

Like agriculture, then, the woollen industries of North Wales remained till the very eve of the Industrial Revolution in the stage of economic development they had reached

---

[1] *Victoria County Histories: Shropshire*, p. 429.
[2] 8 Eliz., cap. 7.
[3] 24 Jac. I, cap. 28.
[4] On the details of this struggle, *see Economica*, June, 1929, pp. 197–212, and *cf. History*, XXII, p. 166.

under the Tudors. The poet Dyer, writing about 1757, tells how

> The Northern Cambrians, an industrious tribe,
> Carry their labours on pygmean steeds

(the mountain ponies of Montgomery and Merioneth) and "lay their bales in Salop's street." Here every Thursday the Drapers hold their market over the Town Hall, making their purchases in order of seniority, sending them out to be "finished," and whisking them off in waggons to where

> Pearly Sabrina waits them with her barks,
> And spreads the swelling sheet,

till at last they reach "great Augusta's mart." In London they find their way to Blackwell Hall, or to the special Welsh Hall in Leadenhall, and the foreign merchants disperse them far and wide in France, Spain and Portugal, Hamburg and Italy, Turkey, Archangel, and even Africa and the two Indies. But little of the resultant wealth found its way to Wales. Only the rough cloth dyed and kept for home use was sold in the local markets and fairs.[1]

This form of economic domination, of course, was by no means unknown in the English clothing districts, but nowhere did it survive the "age of monopolies" in so pronounced a form. Moreover, in other regions the dominant market was a local one, whereas here "the Welsh have the labour, and strangers the profit." Much of the money gained by sales was spent outside the country, and the road to advancement for an ambitious weaver lay through Shrewsbury, by apprenticeship with the all-powerful Company, and not at home. It was whispered, too, that the profits of the middlemen were swollen by frauds in measurement. However that may be, the total annual value of the woollen manufactures of North Wales can hardly have exceeded £100,000 in the middle of the eighteenth century, while Yorkshire, a little later, was selling two millions' worth, all in her own markets.[2]

[1] Dyer : *The Fleece*, III, 581 ff. ; Pennant : *Tours*, III, pp. 168, 202, 224–5 ; Phillips : *Shrewsbury*, pp. 135–8.
[2] *Arch. Camb.*, 1922, p. 255 n. The estimate in Lansdown MSS., 1215, f. 172B (£100,000), includes South Wales. That of Lewis Morris, a year later (£50,000), does not seem to include flannels, and only allows £160 for webs made for home use (*Plans of Harbours*, 1748, Addenda).

Among many local varieties, two sorts of Welsh woollens were now gaining wider fame: the "webs" or "cottons" of Denbighshire and Merioneth ("a thick sort of flannel of which soldiers' clothing is chiefly made"[1]) and the flannels of Montgomery. The latter was the characteristic Welsh manufacture ; its very name may be Welsh in origin. It was less dependent on the skill of the Shrewsbury shearmen and dyers, and—as we shall see later—it was the first branch of the industry to assert its independence. In Montgomeryshire "nearly every farm had its weaving contingent, and rents were half made from the making of flannel " ; steady young men waited to be married till they could afford "a set of linen, a wedding dinner, and a weaving loom."[2] Merioneth in 1748 had sixteen fulling mills in constant employ, each turning out an average of four webs a week (the web being a piece of cloth 34 inches by 120 yards, and worth £10 or so). But for such accidents as failures in the water supply and the shortage of hands at harvest time (so our informant declares), it might have been possible to produce seven webs a week.[3]

In Denbighshire, parish registers from the sixteenth century onwards indicate an abundance of weavers of webs, friezes, and flannels in the Vale of Clwyd and the neighbourhood of Wrexham.[4] For these products Wrexham served as principal mart, and it seems somehow to have escaped the jealous watchfulness of the Shrewsbury Drapers. In 1680 we find the steward at Eaton Hall going there for "one yeard and a quarter of Wilsh cloth to make ye swyne lad Waller, a peare of breeches on." Sixty years later, if we may believe the continuators of Defoe, "factors" used to buy flannel at Wrexham of the "poor Welsh people who manufacture it," and carry it off to London.[5] In 1749 an experiment was made in producing

[1] Pococke : *Travels*, II, pp. 15, 179. The name "cottons," which has misled many writers, refers to the process of "cottoning," i.e. raising the nap by teazels. The fabrics were all wool.

[2] *Mont. Coll.*, XXVI, p. 161 ; Pratt : *Gleanings through Wales*, I, p. 253 ; *cf. Report on Land*, 1896, p. 699.

[3] Morris : *Plans of Harbours*, Addenda.

[4] *See*, e.g., extracts from Wrexham parish registers in Palmer : *Parish Church*, chaps. V and VI, and his *Wrexham*, pp. 9–10, and from those of the Vale of Clwyd in *Arch. Camb.*, 1906, p. 131.

[5] Gatty, C. T. : *Mary Davies and the Manor of Ebury* (1921), I, p. 276 ; Defoe : *Tour* (third ed., 1742), II, p. 374.

broadcloth at Denbigh. The originator was Mr. John Mostyn of Segrwyd—one of the local gentry—who formed a company under the name of Mostyn, Pigot and Company (otherwise John Mostyn, Esq., and Co.), and built a factory in the town for the accommodation of the weavers. A Denbigh tradition even asserts that carding was done by water power, but as Arkwright's patent was not taken out till 1775, by which time the business was dead or dying, this seems improbable. In its palmy days, it is said to have employed 800 people ; but an expensive lawsuit (or, according to another account, the loss of a valuable cargo at sea) ruined it, and many of the weavers enlisted to fight George Washington.[1]

In some districts of Denbighshire, Caernarvonshire and Merioneth, both men and women knitted vast quantities of woollen stockings, and gloves from wool procured at Llanrwst fair, and sold them in Bala market to the extent of about £200 worth a week. Felt hats, too, were made from local wool in one or two places, and a certain amount of flax was grown and dressed—or, more often of late, imported from Ireland—and woven into linen on domestic looms.[2] Every country house of any standing would keep replenishing its stock of sheets and blankets by the labours of skilled household servants or occasional "helps," and from the later years of the seventeenth century, when the silk industry began to spread in England, we find stray references to silk weavers and throwsters in North Wales.[3] In all their varied phases, these rural industries, primitive in organization and stunted in development though they might be, must have kept starvation from many a peasant's cottage.

Another breach in the monotony of rural life was made by mining and quarrying. Like the woollen industry, these occupations had been more or less fitfully carried on in

---

[1] Davies, *General View*, p. 408 ; Williams : *Ancient and Modern Denbigh*, p. 128 ; Palmer : *Parish Church*, p. 164.

[2] Morris : *Plans of Harbours* ; Williams : *Ancient and Modern Denbigh*, p. 129, and *Records of Denbigh*, p. 147 ; Pococke : *Travels*, II, p. 178 ; Palmer : *Wrexham*, p. 10.

[3] Meyrick papers (1754 ff.) ; Palmer : *op. cit.*, p. 10 ; *Morris Letters*, I, p. 78.

North Wales from a remote past. The country had always been able to supply its own building material; only for millstones did it need to supplement its resources from abroad.[1] Cottages were usually built from whatever material lay loose about; when necessary, stone would be quarried for the purpose, either under some vague right of common, or by payment of toll to the owner of the soil; and the erection of a big country house would keep several little quarries busy for years.[2] Slates seem to have been used for roofing in Caernarvonshire since the Middle Ages. Cilgwyn quarry, near Nantlle, is usually awarded the palm of seniority; but by Tudor times there is good evidence that slate was being procured, "to kyver houses" (as Leland puts it), from somewhere near the present Penrhyn quarry, from the Berwyns in Denbighshire and from southern Merioneth.[3] Churchwarden's accounts point to quarrying at Glynceiriog in the seventeenth century and at Llansannan (also in Denbighshire) early in the eighteenth.[4] By 1748 about four million slates were being exported from Caernarvon to Ireland and other places every year; but except for the introduction of larger sizes and rough classifications, the industry remained primitive and unorganized. Partnerships of two or three quarrymen, without any capital to speak of, would work a bed superficially, and then leave it when the particular demand was satisfied or when working became too expensive.[5]

The mining and working of metals was also an ancient occupation. In early days it seems to have been confined, for the most part, to "foreigners" imported by English Kings or Lords Marcher. We find Edward I authorizing

---

[1] *Y Cymmrodor*, XIV, p. 100.

[2] " Quarries of freestone" are frequently included among the rights of common in manorial surveys; *cf.* Hughes and North: *op. cit.*, p. 28; Gatty: *op. cit.*, I, p. 212.

[3] *The Red Dragon*, VII (1885), p. 319; Davies, D. C.: *Slates and Slate Quarrying* (1878), pp. 32, 162, 163; Leland: *Itinerary in Wales*, p. 94.

[4] *Bye-gones*, 1895–96, p. 203; 1899–1900, p. 16; Lhuyd: *Parochialia*, I, p. 124.

[5] Morris: *Plans of Harbours*, p. 6; Williams: *Snowdon Mountains*, pp. 126–7. The North Wales Port Book for 1730 (Bangor MS. 484) shows that as early as that year over a million slates were sent to Ireland, and nearly a million more exported coastwise, from Caernarvon only. Beaumaris accounted for nearly half a million.

the removal of Derbyshire miners to work (under strict supervision) in the lead mines of Flint, and near Wrexham a colony of Englishmen who worked some iron mines and a forge in the same period have left themselves a permanent memorial in the name of the township (Moreton Anglicorum).[1] There was, in fact, a continual interchange of population between Cornwall, Derby, and Wales, as the tide of industry ebbed and flowed. Lead miners from the Wrexham district were being pressed into the service of the Cornish mines in 1295 ;[2] and we shall find Cornish and Derbyshire miners swarming into North Wales at several later periods. Coal, too, had been mined in Flintshire at least as early as the thirteenth century, and in the fifteenth the right to "dig for coals" in some of the wastes of the lordship of Bromfield (where the main coal seams of Denbighshire lie) had been granted by the lord to his new borough of Holt. There was even a trifling export of coal at times ; but generally home production was insufficient for home demand, and the mediaeval Welshman had to import what little iron, lead and coal he needed from outside.

Mining, indeed, made but little headway till the time of the Tudors. Then it was that needy monarchs began the practice of selling to projectors the right to search in Crown and other lands in Wales for the precious metals and those found in association with them. The Company for the Mines Royal—largely financed by German capital—scoured the country for silver and gold, smelted Cornish copper ore at Neath, and opened up those lead and silver mines in the counties of Cardigan and Montgomery which later enabled Sir Hugh Myddleton to bring the New River to London, and helped to equip King Charles' army. Probably, too, it was responsible for the first search for copper on Parys Mountain, in Anglesey, and the first use of the precipitation process there. In Denbighshire and Flintshire, grant after grant of coal-bearing and lead-

---

[1] *Journal of Chester and North Wales Archaeological and Historical Society*, New Ser., VIII, p. 112 ; Wrexham Free Library : *Ancient Local Records* (transcribed by Palmer, A. N.). Court of the Bailiwick of Wrexham, 1339–40.

[2] Salzman, L. F. : *English Industries of the Middle Ages* (1923), p. 64. The Lordship of Bromfield became part of Denbighshire, not (as he says) of Shropshire.

bearing lands (including the ancient preserves of the burgesses of Holt, now Crown land) was made to the family of
Grosvenor, till in Pope's time "Grosvenor's mines" had
become a synonym for wealth along with "Townshend's
turnips." Even in Anglesey, trials for coal were made on
Crown lands. The earliest known adventurer there was a
Tudor of Penmynydd, who received his grant in 1450—
thirty-five years before his· kinsman became King of
England.[1]

By the time of the Civil Wars there was a brisk traffic in
coal between Flintshire and Ireland, and Chester had
become so dependent on Flintshire coal as to feel the pinch
severely when trade was interrupted by the Parliamentary.
siege. Sir Roger Mostyn's mines, which worked for the
Irish market, were already troubled with fire-damp. Daily
the "fireman" had to discharge· his perilous duty of des-
cending the shaft in early morning, covered with damp
sacking, to explode the accumulated gas. Before the end
of the century these mines had reached a sufficient depth to
require an elaborate pumping engine "with Wheels and
Pinions" to drain the water. The Denbighshire coalfield,
cut off from the best markets by execrable roads, developed
more slowly. The Myddletons began mining for coal at
Chirk when Elizabeth was Queen, and under the Protec-
torate we find the Roundhead general, Sir Thomas Myddleton—fresh from his victories in the field—spending £2 4s.
on "a newe engine at blacke parke." Further developments took place in Anglesey also under Charles II, when
the coal under Malldraeth Marsh was first used by the
neighbouring gentry for burning lime.[2]

The same period saw some progress in the mining and
working of metals. In the Conway valley the Wynns of
Gwydir made persevering search for lead and copper on
their estate,[3] and on the Flintshire coast, which had been
lurid with smelting hearths since the later Middle Ages
Sir Roger Mostyn was in Charles II's day reducing the

[1] Greenly : *Geology of Anglesey*, II, p. 812.
[2] *Arch. Camb.*, 1929, p. 197 ; M. Mahler : *Chirk Castle and Chirkland* (1912), pp. 158–9 ; N.L.W., Chirk Castle *MSS*. E. 3293, 3299, 3301 ; Rowlands : *Idea Agriculturæ* (1769), p. xxv
[3] Wynn, Sir J. : *History of the Gwydir Family* (1878 ed.), p. ix, nos. 1 and 2 ; Nat. Lib. of Wales : *Calendar of Wynn (of Gwydir) Papers*, nos. 455, 456, 460, 466, 467; *Trans. Ang. An. Soc.*, 1920, p. 90.

produce of his extensive lead mines in a large furnace with a water wheel to work the bellows.[1] By this time the old Roman workings at Minera (near Wrexham) had been re-opened, and small quantities of lead ore were sent to be worked up in the town.[2] At least three iron forges which continued producing (after reconstruction) right into the nineteenth century, go back to the Stuart period. These were the Abenbury forge, which must have supplied material for the numerous smiths and nailers of Wrexham;[3] further south the Pont y blew forge, near Chirk ; and finally the Mathrafal forge, in the heart of Montgomery-shire. This last was built, near his ancestral home, by Charles Lloyd of Dolobran—the much-persecuted leader of the Montgomeryshire Quakers—whose brother became Penn's right-hand man in Pennsylvania, and who was him-self to found a dynasty of Quaker ironmasters and bankers. The forge appears to have been used at one time by Sir Thomas Myddleton for refining silver.[4]

In mining and smelting alike, however, there was one serious obstacle to further progress. "There were mines of lead sometimes also in Wales," wrote Harrison in 1577, "which endured so long till the people had consumed all their wood by melting of the same." Time and again there arose a panic that all the woods and forests would soon be devoured, and smelting received a check, if not from actual legislation, at least from the soaring price of charcoal, till insistent demand for the metal made it worth while to start again. In spite of long and painful researches, no progress had yet been made in the application of coal to the smelting of metals, save in the copper industry, and that remained in a state of arrested development.[5]

Until this barrier should be removed, a definite limit was set to mining both for coal and for metals. In a region like

[1] *Bye-gones*, 1913–15, p. 26; *Official Progress of Duke of Beaufort*, 1684 (facsimile, 1888), pp. 95–6 ; Pennant : *Whiteford and Holywell*, p. 281.

[2] *Y Cymmrodor*, VI, p. 44 ; Palmer, *Parish Church*, p. 134.

[3] Palmer: *Wrexham*, p. 11, and *Old Parish of Wrexham*, pp. 149-50.

[4] *Hist. MSS. Com.*, 7th Rept., App., p. 86 ; Myddleton, W. M. : *Chirk Castle Accounts* (1908), pp. 123, 128 ; *Bye-gones*, 1888, p. 78 ; Williams : *Montgomeryshire Worthies*, pp. 169–71; *Mont. Coll.*, IX. pp. 333ff., XLIII, pp. 41–2 ; *N. L. W. Journ.*, III, pp. 41, 48–9 ; N. L. W., Chirk Castle MS. E. 558.

[5] Ashton : *Iron and Steel*, pp. 9–12 ; Hamilton : *Brass and Copper Inaustries*, chap. IV ; Galloway : *Annals of Coal Mining*, pp. 85 124, 195, 228.

North Wales the domestic use of coal, except on the coalfields themselves, was virtually confined to the big country
houses ; for the brew-house, dye-vat, kiln, and smithy
demand was trifling. Only in districts so fortunately
situated as to be able to supply populous markets, like those
of Chester and Dublin, could the industry advance beyond
the stage of superficial "digging for coals." Elsewhere the
typical coalmine was a shallow pit, worked spasmodically
by adventurers on payment of royalty, or else by the landlord himself through his steward, with nothing more elaborate by way of machinery than a horse-whimsey to wind
the coal or a horse-pump to drain the pit.[1]   And the other
branches of mining were in the same state.

It may be plausibly argued that the first chapter of the
Industrial Revolution opens in Elizabeth's reign ; and as
good a case could be made for dating the second chapter
from the years when the Revolution of 1688 created an
atmosphere of confidence at home and wars abroad in which
companies and patents sprang up like mushrooms.[2]   The
mining industries all boomed ; the revival of the copper
and brass trades was accompanied by the successful
application of coal to the smelting of lead and the separation
of silver, and followed, early in the next century, by
Abraham Darby's twin discovery in the smelting of iron.[3]
The results of these discoveries were quickly felt in North
Wales.

The "Governor and Company for smelting down Lead
with Pit Coale and Sea Coale" began operations in Flintshire before the end of the seventeenth century, and in the
course of the next fifty years, up-to-date furnaces using coal
were set up, by this and other companies or private partnerships, in the neighbourhoods of Whitford, Holywell, Bagillt,
Flint, Mold, Hawarden, and elsewhere.[4]   By the use of

---

[1] *See* description, from contemporary records, of the working
of a small pit on the Erthig estate near Wrexham, 1715–21, in *Arch.
Camb.*, 1929, pp. 201–2.

[2] Macaulay : *History of England* (Firth's edition, 1914), Vol. V,
ch. xix, pp. 2275–80 ; Scott, W. P. : *Constitution and Finance of
English Joint-Stock Companies*, II, pp. 438–9 ; *Ec. Journ.*, XLIII
p. 691.

[3] Galloway : *op. cit.*, p. 228 ; Ashton, *op. cit.*, p. 37.

[4] Pennant : *Whiteford and Holywell*, pp. 156, 201–3, 260–2, 275,
281–2 ; *Memoir of Hawarden*, p. 107 ; *cf.* ma   in *Britannia Depicta*,
1724, pp. 175, 267.

Lydall's patent, over 400,000 ounces of silver are said to have been recovered in Flintshire between 1704 and 1744 ; zinc and calamine were also separated and worked.[1] All this meant a busy time for the lead mines, and speculators of every degree were tempted to dabble in them.[2]

Particularly rich were the discoveries on Halkin Mountain. "The process of extracting lead from flint," in the playful phrase of a later topographer, "has turned out so profitable as to create a baronet, give rise to esquires, and add grandeur to the equipages of noblemen." The baronet was Sir George Wynne, M.P., of Leeswood—patron and distant connection of Richard Wilson, the landscape painter—who attained the honour in 1731, probably as a reward for his service in wresting Flint boroughs from the Jacobite interest. In 1703 he had inherited a small freehold on Halkin Mountain, worth about £30 a year ; a quarter of a century later it was yielding lead to the annual value of £22,000, enabling the owner to build the stately mansion of Leeswood, at a cost of £40,000, and to fight three hotly-contested elections, in one of which he appears to have used his miners for purposes of intimidation. But his expenses, swollen by a ruinous lawsuit with his father over the ownership of the lead, swallowed up the diminishing income from the mines, and he died an insolvent debtor in 1756.[3] The leading county families—Grosvenors, Pennants, Mostyns, Hanmers—all had their share in the lead boom, and the coal mines profited equally. The export trade was just beginning to suffer from changes in the Dee channel, but ample compensation was found in the home market. Round Hawarden the mines were reaching a depth which made drainage problems acute, and the Newcomen "atmospheric" engine was adopted there soon after its invention in 1712.[4]

Progress was not confined to this one county. In Denbighshire the systematic working of the Minera lead

[1] Evans : *Beauties*, p. 97 ; Pennant : *op. cit.*, pp. 261–2.
[2] Scott : *Joint-Stock Companies*, II, p. 449 ; Palmer : *Old Parish of Wrexham*, p. 230 ; Cust : *Chronicles of Erthig*, I, p. 259.
[3] Pennant : *Tours*, II, p. 68 ; Davies : *General View*, p. 55 ; *Cheshire Sheaf*, 1883–85, pp. 75, 79 ; *Journ. Flints. Hist. Soc.*, IX, pp. 1–29 ; *Journals of the House of Commons*, XXI, p. 175.
[4] *Memoir of Hawarden*, pp. 100 ff.

mines began early in the eighteenth century, and about
fifty years later a private partnership opened up the
neighbouring mines of Nant y ffrith.[1]   The rich vein at
Llangynog, in northern Montgomeryshire, which had
possibly been worked in Elizabeth's time, was seriously
attacked in 1692, and yielded excellent results till the influx
of water brought operations to a standstill, about 1730.[2]
At the same time the southern parts of the county and the
Dovey valley were stirred into activity by the revival of the
old works of the Mines Royal Company by Sir Humphrey
Mackworth and the Mine Adventurers ; but litigation has
been the curse of mining in mid-Wales, and the Adventurers
were soon snowed under with recriminatory pamphlets and
lawyers' bills of costs.[3]

The Glorious Revolution also brought about developments in the copper industry.   The abandonment of the
Crown monopoly of copper mining in 1689 encouraged the
private prospector, and smelting, which had languished
since the Civil War, was soon in full vigour again.   South
Wales became dotted over with smelting works, many of
them in the hands of the Mine Adventurers.   In the North
the effects were not felt till past the middle of the century ;
another attack seems to have been made on Parys Mountain, but in 1748 its sole product was an "okery earth"
used for paints.   The copper and brass industries of
Holywell did not begin their career till about 1750, and
then the ores came from Warrington.[4]

The smelting of iron stood in a more favoured position,
thanks largely to the friendship between the two Quaker
ironmasters, Darby of Coalbrookdale and Lloyd of
Dolobran.   In 1698 Charles Lloyd (the second) succeeded
to the family estate in Montgomeryshire ; his younger
brother thereupon migrated to Birmingham, there to
accumulate the capital which ultimately created Lloyds
Bank.   It was in the following year (1699) that Abraham

[1] Hunt : British Mining, p. 439 ; Palmer : Old Parish of Wrexham,
pp. 129–30.
[2] Pennant : Tours, III, p. 162 ; Davies : General View, pp. 58–9 ;
Chirk Castle MSS., Bye-gones, 1889–90, p. 524 ; Lewis : Top. Dict.,
under Montgomeryshire.
[3] Scott : Joint-Stock Companies, II, pp. 443–58 ; Hamer, E., and
Lloyd, H. W. : Parochial History of Llangurig (1875), pp. 9–10.
[4] Infra, p. 153; Davies, D. J. : Econ. Hist. of S. Wales (1933), p. 74.

Darby made his first experiments in cast-iron manufacture at Bristol with the aid of a former shepherd from Dolobran, whom Lloyd had recommended to his notice ; and ten years later, in his new works at Coalbrookdale, he solved the problem of smelting with coke. This did not mean, however, that the older methods were abandoned. In 1715 we find Darby smelting the iron ore of Cader Idris—doubtless with charcoal—in a little furnace at Dolgûn,[1] near Dolgelley ; in 1717 his friend Lloyd was deep in negotiations with the squire of Erthig (near Wrexham) for the supply of cordwood to the neighbouring furnace at Bersham, where he was now a tenant.[2] But Bersham, unlike Dolgelley, had coal near to hand. Southward lay the rich seams of Ruabon parish, already exploited on a scale large enough to make Sir Watkin Williams Wynn's colliers a redoubtable asset to local Jacobitism, as Sir George Wynne's lead miners were to the loyalist cause. Within a few years of his acquisition of the Bersham furnace, Charles Lloyd began to substitute coal for charcoal as his reducing agent. We may fairly assume that it was Darby who taught him the Coalbrookdale methods ; for there were no other works, outside Shropshire, where coke-smelting came in till another generation had passed.

This year (1721) was an important date for both the coal and the iron industries of Denbighshire ; but its importance was not yet obvious. Lloyd failed to make his furnace pay, and gave it up in 1726. Fortunately, there were other Quaker acquaintances of the Darbys ready to take it in hand, until in 1753 it came into the possession of Isaac Wilkinson, whose son was to make it one of the most famous in the land. Another furnace at Ruabon, which was worked for a time in connection with Bersham, was abandoned as a complete failure. The general quickening

---

[1] The 6¼ tons of British iron sent from Aberdovey to Pwllheli in October, 1729 (as recorded in the North Wales Port Book for that year), may have come from this furnace.

[2] Richard Jones (steward) to John Meller of Erthig, Dec. 28, 1717 : "I could not see lloyd the quaker since receipt of your letter, but sent for his friend Davies who is . . . either partner or agent for Mr. Lloyd . . . I doubt they will have ocasion for abbundance of timber besids what gose to build the furnese for they talk of raising a large Pile for Char Cole almost as bigg as Pentre Clawdd barn." (Erthig papers).

of the industry extended in some degree to the manufacture of malleable iron. Charles Lloyd rebuilt the Mathrafal forge in 1719, and after he had failed at Bersham, his agent there, Edward Davies, set up a new forge at Abenbury, replacing the older one. The Chirk forge seems to have been reconstructed in 1710, and there was a fourth in Flintshire—probably at Holywell. None of these used coal (its employment in this branch of the industry belongs to a later date) and their output was only about 100 to 150 tons a year—rather below the average for the times.[1] It met the needs, however, of two famous gatesmiths—the brothers Robert and Thomas Davies—who lived near Bersham, and whose superb workmanship is to be seen in the gates of Eaton Hall and Malpas Church in Cheshire, Leeswood and Emral in Flintshire, Chirk Castle in Denbighshire, and the screens of Ruthin, Oswestry, and Wrexham Churches.[2]

It will be seen that even mining and smelting were only partial exceptions to the general economic stagnation. The new developments were confined to a small group of industries in a limited area ; there was no general transformation of the country, no wholesale shifting of population, no creation of mushroom towns and villages. The powers of coal were but dimly realized, and there seemed no reason why this wave of enterprise should not recede as so many of its predecessors had done, leaving nothing but a few waste heaps and derelict buildings to mark the scenes of former activity. In fact the Dee collieries had already fallen on slack times again before the middle of the century.[3] Not till the development of the copper and brass industries of Holywell, and the reorganization of the Bersham ironworks by the great John Wilkinson, did the real Industrial Revolution begin in the mining and metal industries of North Wales. In the middle years of the eighteenth century Lewis Morris, a pioneer of economic advance as well as a collector of ancient lore, was declaring that "the art of mining is but in its infancy." "We choose

[1] Ashton : *op. cit.*, chaps. II and IX, and App. B ; Palmer : *John Wilkinson*, pp. 1–6, 40–44 ; Lewis : *Top. Dict.*, under *Chirk;* Pennant : *Whiteford and Holywell*, p. 201 ; Mushet : *Iron and Steel*, pp. 42–3, 390.

[2] *Journ. Flints. Hist. Soc.*, IX (1922), pp. 19–20.

[3] Pennant : *Whiteford and Holywell*, pp. 133–4.

to rummage the East and West for money," he grumbled, "rather than to go fifty or a hundred yards under ground in our own island."[1]

Like every other form of economic activity which has come under our notice, mining and smelting were held back by the general condition of the country. The state of the roads made it impossible to reach a wide market except in districts fortunate enough to have seaports within easy call, and the seaports themselves were silting up from want of capital to keep them open. In the Middle Ages men had talked with pride of "the lawyers of Carnarvon, the merchands of Beawmares, and the gentlemen of Conway";[2] but the port of Beaumaris had made way, first for Chester, then for Liverpool, and its subordinate "creek" of Caernarvon, in proportion as its burgesses deserted litigation for the shipping of slates, was fast outstripping the parent port. In 1760 the sea-going traffic of North Wales amounted to little more than a trifling coasting trade in such small vessels as her harbours could accommodate.[3]

Everywhere the prime obstacle to advance was lack of capital, and this, as we have seen, was the legacy of the turbulent past. In the days of Charles the First, Welsh counties often had to beg for a remission of taxes till after the cattle sales—otherwise the money simply could not be found ; and any interruption of trade with England meant a shortage of specie.[4] After the lapse of more than a century things were still much the same. Weavers came back from the Drapers' Hall at Shrewsbury with enough money jingling in their saddle-bags to tide them over till their next sale ; miners depended on the proceeds of a "lucky strike" to provide them with funds for pursuing the seam or vein to the next stage. On a country gentleman's

[1] *Morris Letters*, I, p. iii ; Morris : *Plans of Harbours.*
[2] Wynn, Sir J. : *History of the Gwedir Family* (1773 ed.), p. 128.
[3] In the North Wales Port Book for 1725–30 (including the ports of Beaumaris, Caernarvon, Conway, Pwllheli and Holyhead) only the first two can show any volume of trade, and this does not extend further than Dublin, Drogheda, and Dumfries. The exports consist almost exclusively of livestock, timber, produce, and slates ; coal and groceries are the chief imports. But of course Barmouth and the Dee ports are not accounted for here.
[4] *See*, e.g., *Wynn Papers*, 2186 (1659).

estate, moneys received for rent and sales of produce were kept in the steward's hand and doled out by him in wages to servants and tradesmen, in purchases for the estate, and in petty cash to members of the family. Sometimes cattle from the estate might be paid for by a bill on a London banking house, obtained by the drover when he sold them at Smithfield ; this would save a hunt for some merchant, with a "bill on London" to dispose of, before the squire's next annual visit to town. The "bill on London" was, in fact, the only credit instrument in general vogue, and that was often hard to negotiate ; for names to conjure with in Wales might well be unknown to the great world of finance. "I have had above £8,000 in money in ye house at ye same time, where the meanest shepherd might have come at them"; so writes Lewis Morris, busy on the derelict workings of the Mine Adventurers in Cardiganshire, in 1757. At another time we find him drawing bills on Childs for £100 or so, or writing post haste to beg his brother in London to stop payment of a bill over which there has been some· error.[1]

Such financial methods as these sufficed for the small-scale economy which then prevailed. Tillage and tanning, spinning and weaving, superficial mining and quarrying, primitive smelting—none of these called for elaborate tools ; and machinery, as distinct from tools, hardly existed. It is true that water power had been used for the corn mill and the *pandy* since the Middle Ages, and for working the bellows of forge and furnace since Stuart times, if not earlier ; a water-driven paper mill at Esclusham (near the Bersham furnace) dates back to the Restoration, and the Tudor invention for drawing wire by water power was in use at Holywell before 1740.[2] But no great outlay of capital was needed for any of them, and few of the industries they served involved a wage-bill of any magnitude. With ordinary luck and economy, men (or groups of men) of the lowliest fortune could set up even in trades like these, employing the tiny staff of journeymen

[1] *Morris Letters*, I, pp. 447, 464, II, pp. 109, 137–8. For other references in the foregoing paragraph *see Economica*, March, 1926, pp. 17–19.
[2] Palmer : *Wrexham*, p. 11 ; Pennant : *Whiteford and Holywell*, p. 201 ; *cf.* Levy, H. : *Monopoly and Competition* (1911), p. 6.

and apprentices that then sufficed for almost any undertaking in which it was necessary to go outside the family at all. It was only the control of natural resources and, when sales were protracted, the disposal of the finished product, that required men of capital : the landlord and the mineral prospector on the one hand, the substantial drover and the merchant draper on the other. The draper's capital was invested outside Wales ; the drover, useful as a financial intermediary, never developed here (as he did in some parts of Wales) into a banker ;[1] the mineral prospector—almost invariably a "foreigner"—came, made or marred his fortune, and departed again ; the landlord, with a few noteworthy exceptions, did not invest, but spent. And so the economic development of the country awaited the time when fashion, or patriotism, or enlightened self-interest should spread the belief—at home or across the border—that the country was worth sinking money in : and this not merely for immediate returns, but on such enterprises as the building of roads and harbours, the permanent improvement of the soil, the pursuit of mineral veins beyond the superficial outcrops, the organization of manufactures and markets, and the provision of financial machinery. These are the matters which will concern us in the following chapters.

One other point remains to be touched upon before we conclude this preliminary survey. Economic change was to introduce the country to many evils unknown before ; but to represent it as reducing to misery a land of prosperous and contented peasants would be the merest travesty of the truth. We shall find that one of the chief inducements to English capitalists to set up works in North Wales was the low standard of living there. How low that standard was we have already seen, but the real conditions are apt to be obscured by the fact that pauperism, in the technical sense, had not yet become an acute problem. In 1729 the only Deanery in the whole diocese of St. Asaph

[1] *Hist. Soc. of West Wales Trans.*, VI (1916), p. 131. Drovers had perforce to be men of substance ; since Elizabeth's time their trade had required a licence, and licences were granted only to independent householders of responsible age. They were also excluded from the benefits of the bankruptcy laws. (*Trans. Royal Hist. Soc.*, 1926. p. 150.)

where compulsory poor rates were levied was the one which included the populous mining district of Wrexham. In Montgomeryshire, excepting the busy market town of Welshpool, none were raised till after 1740; and forty years later most of the parishes of Caernarvonshire and Anglesey were in the blissful state of being able to report "no poor," or "no assessments." Where poor rates were levied, they rarely exceeded fourpence to sevenpence in the pound (on very low assessments) in the middle of the eighteenth century ; a shilling was exceptional.

An English land reformer in 1781[1] drew attention to the fact that Wales had not shared in the general rise in poor rates since the time of Charles II, and he attributed this to the multiplicity of small holdings there. The argument is specious, but it will scarcely hold water. For if there was little pauperism, there was much poverty. In those days of primitive and self-contained agriculture, a bad harvest meant a general famine, a failure in the wool clip caused widespread distress among the weavers, and corn dealers suspected of an intention to corner the market, or to export foodstuffs needed at home, went about in peril of their lives. In May, 1740, the mining districts of Denbighshire and Flintshire, along with many other parts of England and Wales, were disturbed by corn riots of a very alarming character ; a similar uprising on a smaller scale had caused panic in the Wrexham district more than forty years earlier. Hunger was assuredly no invention of the machine age.[2] What made compulsory rates unnecessary was simply the fact that population was still small enough for all men to be neighbours. When times were exceptionally bad, relief would take the form of family charity, or the bounty of the great, or "briefs . . . read in churches for the relief of the poor,"[3] in the best traditions of the *cymorth*.

The tramp and the beggar, too, were familiar figures long before the Industrial Revolution. From time immemorial the harvest season had seen an influx of Welsh labourers into the border counties, and at a later date women and girls

[1] Ogilvie, W. : *An Essay on the Right of Property in Land* (*Pioneers of Land Reform*, Bohn's Popular Library, 1920), p. 73 *n.*

[2] Ashton and Sykes : *Coal Industry*, pp. 119–21 ; Cust : *Chronicles of Erthig*, I, p. 131.

[3] *Letters from Snowdon*, p. 74 ; *cf. Y Cymmrodor*, XXXVIII, p. 56 (Llanfair Caereinion, 1775).

even tramped as far as Kent and Middlesex for temporary employment in fruit-picking, weeding and haymaking. Lancashire parish registers in the first half of the eighteenth century show us Welsh vagrants of both sexes on the road there in quest of work. Even at home begging had become a serious nuisance. Early in the nineteenth century, men called to mind how in rural parishes "fifty years ago it was common for upwards of twenty young people . . . to go begging for want of employment"; mendicancy, we are told, was "an old-established trade."[1]

To discourage reliance on charity, several parishes had adopted the practice of forcing those in receipt of relief to wear a special badge—a relic of Tudor paternalism which survived, in some districts, right up to the nineteenth century. Exceptional energy on the part of vicar or wardens might secure the expenditure of parish funds on stocks of hemp, flax, or wool to "set the poor on work" in their own houses, or on apprenticing their children to a "useful trade," in the true spirit of the Elizabethan Acts. Efforts were also made, here and there, to prevent the extension of charity to those who refused badges or work, and the "settlement" in the parish of outsiders likely to fall on the rates. Finally, under the Act of 1723, which permitted the establishment of the "workhouse test," cottages were sometimes hired or built for use as workhouses, poorhouses, or houses of correction—for the terms seem to have been used quite interchangeably, with an airy disregard of the distinction, so carefully maintained in the Tudor Acts, between employment, charity and punishment. Seven such institutions at least were established in the course of the next forty years : most of them by public subscription, but one at least by "borrowing" a number of small legacies to the poor (which were never repaid). Many, of course, were but temporary expedients and had disappeared or been diverted to other uses before the Commission of 1834.

Such were the steps taken to meet special distress ; but many a self-supporting peasant lived constantly below what later ages would have defined as the "poverty line." If pauperism increased during the next century, it was largely because men had extended their notions of a bare

[1] Letter in *N. W. Gaz.*, June 25, 1812 (*cf.* July 7 and Aug. 13) ; Davies : *Labourers in Husbandry*, pp. 189, 191.

livelihood. Whenever the "good old times" may have been, in North Wales at least they were not the days immediately preceding the Industrial Revolution.[1]

[1] The substance of the foregoing paragraphs is taken from an article by the present writer in *Arch. Camb.*, 1926, pp. 111 ff., where full references are given.

CHAPTER II.

" SPIRITED PROPRIETORS."

> Whose care confined the rapid torrent ?   Whò
> Like Appius, stretch'd the public road ?   Who drain'd
> The deep morass ?   And clothed the naked hill
> With pendant woods ?   Who taught the barren heath
> To smile ? [1]

During the last forty years of the eighteenth century, "improvement" was everywhere in the air.   In Wales it was a time of spiritual and intellectual revival, of which the story has often been told.   But Welsh Methodism owed far less to outside influences than did the movement we are about to trace.   Spiritual revival and material development together broke up the old order ; but it would be difficult to establish any other connection between them.   Industry, by creating new centres of population, provided Methodism with its big congregations ; Methodism gave to industry a body of labour disciplined to suffer hardships and forego rewards in this world by the thought of spiritual glories to come ; and each had its share in undermining the social and political supremacy of the landlords.   Otherwise the two movements worked separately, under different leaders, and often in hostility towards each other ; the one intensified national feeling, the other moved towards assimilation with England.

We have seen that economic advance in North Wales awaited the sinking of capital in ventures where the return was necessarily distant or dubious.   At home such capital could only come from the land, and if the industrial movement, like the spiritual awakening, was to remain under local leadership, it was necessary that Wales should produce a race of "spirited proprietors" like those beloved of Arthur Young in England : men who were prepared to sacrifice in some degree the lustre of hospitality and of sport, of domestic show and of seasons in town, for the sake of developing their estates ; men who preferred a

[1] Roberts, Richard :   *A Poem, Sacred to the Memory of the late Sir Watkin Williams Wynn, Bart.*   London, 1749.

good farmer to a good flunkey, who put roads above race-meetings, and who would turn their backs on the seductions of State lotteries and East India bonds for a humdrum investment in their native soil. Failing this, the capital for development would have to come from outside, and the control of big industrial undertakings would thus pass into the hands of strangers.

We shall find both these processes at work. The gentry of North Wales, rubbing shoulders with their neighbours across the border, began to catch from them the passion for improvement which had inspired such men as "Turnip" Townshend and Jethro Tull. They drained their lands, introduced new crops and better rotation, looked to the breed of their stock, imported new manures and new farm implements, and tried by penalty, precept and example to break down the stubborn conservatism of their tenantry. To give themselves a freer hand, they fought for the extinction of common rights in village fields and mountain pastures, and put their hands deeply in their pockets to finance the passing of Enclosure Acts. They turned their attention to the roads, and either built them independently on their own estates, or joined with their neighbours to form turnpike trusts. They put money into ca als. They scoured their estates for minerals, and (if they could not exploit them directly) entered into a regular contract with some capable capitalist, instead of letting the first comer try his hand on condition of paying a traditional share of the produce, such as the eighth "pytch" of coal, the eighth ton of slate, the seventh ton of marketable ore, or the tenth millstone.[1] They helped to provide the woollen industry with modern machinery.

English aristocrats who settled in Wales were often quite as keen. The Honourable Thomas Fitzmaurice— brother of Chatham's colleague the Earl of Shelburne, and like him a reforming Whig—eschewed public life (save for a turn as Sheriff of Flintshire), and lived "with the affected humility of a tradesman and the pomp of a lord" at Llewenni Hall, near Denbigh. Here he busied himself with all

---

[1] On traditional royalties, *see* Palmer : *Old Parish of Wrexham*, p. 78 (coal) ; Ashton and Sykes : *Coal Industry* (do.) ; *Calendar of Crosswood Deeds*, p. 143 *et passim* (general) ; *infra*, pp. 205, 208-9 (slate), 225 (millstone).

manner of economic enterprises till his death in 1793. One day he would be planning a canal for the Vale of Clwyd ; the next, driving to Chester in a coach and six to sell the linens woven by his Irish tenants and bleached in his own bleacheries at Llewenni. He would stand (so tradition has it) behind a counter inscribed "Ballymote Manufacture" (a device from which he "thought he derived more true honour . . . than from the most pompous motto in French or Latin, upon his escutcheon"), and then return to regale his neighbours with a "grand illumination of the Bleach Works in a Vauxhall style"—or else to deal out pills and plasters to the poor in his own private dispensary.[1]

In a Caernarvonshire paper for 1810, the grievances of a country gentleman's wife are set forth at large in a mock letter to the editor. She hardly sees her husband from breakfast to bedtime : first he is off to the Agricultural Society, then to a meeting of the turnpike trustees, and after that to a Dispensary committee or a political club, or to deliberate on the establishment of Sunday Schools or the revival of national antiquities.[2] In truth the turbulence of the Ap Rhaiaders was giving place to the improving conversations and beneficent projects of Headlong Hall.

Yet at this same time a Welsh artist who knew his country well was saying some very hard things about the supineness of the gentry. Edward Pugh wrote the text of his *Cambria Depicta* about 1807, but the work was published posthumously in 1816—the very year of Peacock's *Headlong Hall*. "These gentlemen," Pugh complains, "seem to leave to others . . . the chance of amassing large fortunes which from locality of situation more properly belong to themselves."[3] There was a measure of truth in the accusation, as we shall see. Perhaps, as some critics suggested, the attraction of a fixed income from the funds was responsible ; perhaps the gentry were deterred by

---

[1] Nicholson : *Cambrian Traveller's Guide* (second ed., 1813), p. 150 ; Davies : *General View*, pp. 409–10 ; Robert Wynn's diary, *Bye-gones*, 1903–04, p. 152 ; *Chester Chron.*, Sept. 9, 1777, May 31, 1782 ; *infra*, chaps. IV and VIII.

[2] *N. W. Gaz.*, Oct. 4, 1810.

[3] *Camb. Dep.*, pp. viii, 443, etc. ; *see* review in *Cambrian Register*, III, pp. 391–2, and *cf.* similar complaints, *ibid.*, pp. 495–6 (Lewis Morris, 1757), and in Williams : *Ancient and Modern Denbigh*, pp. 139–40 (1856).

that solicitude they so often expressed for the amenities of the countryside and the pristine purity of its morals[1] ; but—whatever the reason—having done so much of the spade-work themselves, they left the more speculative developments to outsiders, who swarmed in from regions where the trades had long been firmly established, in quest of richer veins of ore or seams of coal, of cheaper man-power or more plentiful water-power.

Even road-making in North Wales owes something to the Englishman's zest for travel and his untiring eagerness for new worlds to colonize. It was in the latter half of the eighteenth century that England discovered Wales. Again and again the continent was closed to tourists by the outbreak of war ; and in poetry and landscape-painting alike the "picturesque" and the "horrid" were coming into vogue. So travellers turned their horses towards Wales, where they could enjoy—or, what was just as good, say they enjoyed—Nature unspoiled by Man and Man unspoiled by Civilization. Some even adopted the "silly and ridiculous whim of converting pleasure into toil" by travelling there on foot.[2] Before the end of the century, too, Abergele, Caernarvon, Barmouth, Towyn, Aberystwyth, and (save the mark !) Flint, had all become favourite bathing-places.[3] Then in 1800 came the Union with Ireland, entailing a vast increase in the traffic between the two countries. This made the roads of the land through which Irish travellers had to pass a matter of interest, not merely to private individuals, but to the Government itself ; and so it led to the first—and for long the only— grant of public money for the development of Wales.[4]

From about 1770 there was a steadily-rising flood of books on travel in Wales: journals of tours, road-books, guides, itineraries, topographical dictionaries, *et hoc genus*

[1] E.g., *N. W. Gaz.*, April 8, 1813 ; Evans : *Beauties*, pp. 236–8.
[2] *Cambrian Register*, II, p. 421 ; *cf.* the progress of "romanticism" shown in the descriptions of Wales revised, amended and expanded in each successive edition of Defoe's *Tours*.
[3] Cust : *Chronicles of Erthig*, II, pp. 83, 217 ; Barfoot and Wilkes: *Directory* (1790), II, p. 532 ; *Chester Chron.*, June 14, 1782 ; Davies : *General View*, p. 448 ; *Salop. Journ.*, March 30, 1796.
[4] *Times*, Dec. 7, 1843.

omne. Some of the authors show genuine first-hand knowledge and a spirit of intelligent inquiry ; on the other hand—to quote a critic who himself published (anonymously) a well-informed and judicious *Tour*—"some are indolent, some inattentive, some credulous, and some write only to amuse."[1] Such writers are generally content to copy earlier descriptions—now manifestly out of date— of places they themselves may never have seen, seasoning them with the current *clichés* of admiration, tit-bits of history in the style of Geoffrey of Monmouth, and startling commentaries on the habits and customs of the "natives." Of those who managed to get the Druids (the King Charles' head of Welsh history) out of their minds, some were able to give expert accounts of the natural products of the land, others drew graphic and convincing pictures of the prevailing poverty. It is an interesting speculation how far these popular works (and some of them ran into many editions) helped to invite the attention of English capitalists to the possibilities of this "undeveloped land." Travellers who intended to publish accounts of their journeys, it is worth noting, sometimes asked prospective clients for instructions before setting out.[2] At any rate, the prospector and the speculator followed close on the heels of the traveller, and advertisements of business sites in North Wales began to find their way into the English newspapers. The following portion of an advertisement of a mill at Ruthin, which appeared in a Manchester paper of 1787, tells its own tale :—

> . . . The Manufacturer may be supplied with plenty of Hands at low wages, as there are a great number of grown Women, Boys and Girls in the Town of Ruthin that are out of Employ, no manufactory whatever being carried on there at present, and the wages paid out to women in hay harvest do not exceed Eightpence a day upon their own Meat.[3]

"Spirited proprietors" and immigrant adventurers : these were the agents of economic advance in North Wales. As time goes on, the second class gains upon the first, and

[1] [Mavor, F. S.] : *Tour*, p. 85.
[2] E.g., Wyndham's second tour in 1777 was preceded by an announcement of this character (*see* editorial note of 1811 in P. B. Nuttall's edition of Fuller's *Worthies*, 1840, III, p. 505 *n*).
[3] *Manchester Mercury*, Feb. 6, 1787, quoted in Unwin, G., Hulme, A., and Taylor, G. : *Samuel Oldknow and the Arkwrights* (1924), p. 118.

the local gentry fall into the background as pioneers of industry. Indeed, when they set their hands to encouraging it they were preparing, all unawares, their own political and social eclipse. It was a sign of the times when, at a Flintshire county meeting called in 1830 to attack the East India Company's monopoly of trade with India and China, a prominent lead smelter had to call attention to the general absence of the landed gentry.[1]

Our survey will naturally start with the industry most deeply rooted in national life and offering the clearest field for native leadership—the cultivation of the soil. From about 1760 onwards, increasing contact with the more developed agriculture of England began to influence farming in North Wales; in the border counties by the simple fact of contiguity, in remoter regions through the services of landlords who had imbibed advanced ideas. Then came the Napoleonic Wars, when the threat of famine and the stimulus of high prices created a novel interest in agricultural experiment and a widespread optimism about the future of farming. But with the slump that followed the Peace, enthusiasm was damped and optimism languished. Neither in agriculture nor in any other branch of economic enterprise have the dreams of those years of rapid growth been fully realized.

When "improvement" was at its height and elderly men were pausing to take stock of the changes they had witnessed, it was to the early years of George III's reign that they looked back for the first beginnings.[2] Already by 1770 travellers were noticing that along the English border "they have in some degree adopted the English manner of tillage," whereas "the remoter they are from the English counties the less is there of the spirit of industry and improvement among the inhabitants."[3] The landlords were beginning to show their tenantry how to make the most of the land. "I was not out of my saddle or the dirt of the overflowed fields, for 3 days," writes a young Denbighshire heir in 1768, in the throes of "improving" an

[1] *Shrewsbury Chron.*, June 25, 1830.
[2] *See*, e.g., letter in *N. W. Gaz.*, July 9, 1812; Davies: *General View*, pp. 140–1.
[3] *Letters from Snowdon*, p. 97.

estate that had just fallen to him. "Every feild" [*sic*], he adds with unction, "will be kept to the Culture I shall dictate."[1] Such was the spirit of the hour. In Montgomeryshire, Arthur Blayney of Gregynog was trying to force his tenants to adopt a systematic rotation of crops by laying down the order of cultivation in the agreements by which the farms were let ; and he made it his constant business to demonstrate the qualities of the turnip as a farm crop.[2] Richard Pennant (afterwards Baron Penrhyn), on succeeding through marriage to his Caernarvonshire estates in 1765, set the pace for agricultural advance in one of the most backward counties by building roads, planting waste lands with good timber, and putting up better farmhouses for his tenants. When he died, over forty years later, it was claimed that he had been responsible for "greater improvements than during several preceding centuries."[3]

Anglesey began to feel the breath of change about the same time as Caernarvonshire. In 1764 an anonymous editor dug out the sixty-year-old manuscript of Henry Rowlands' *Idea Agriculturæ*, and had it published with a dedication to Paul Panton of Plasgwyn, "an Encourager and Admirer of the no less *pleasing* than *useful* Art of Husbandry."· It was in Rowlands' parish of Llanidan, a year or two later, that Thomas Williams—a small farmer's son whose success in the law had enabled him to buy Lord Boston's old seat of Plas Llanidan, and was soon to make him virtual dictator of the copper industry— carried out the first experiments in turnip culture in the island. Another twenty years passed before the fashion spread to Merioneth, where one proprietor wrung a profit out of the peaty soils round Towyn by extensive draining (an enterprise which gained him the gold medal of the

[1] Cust : *Chronicles of Erthig*, II, pp. 40–1.

[2] *Mont. Coll.*, XXX, pp. 14–17, 110–16 ; *Bye-gones*, 1901–02, p. 55 ; *Salop. Journ.*, Oct. 7, 1795.

[3] *N. W. Gaz.*, Jan. 26, Feb. 18, 1808 ; Evans : *Beauties*, pp. 322–3. He represented Petersfield, and subsequently Liverpool, in Parliament (Pennant : *Whiteford and Holywell*, p. 272).

[4] The date on the title page is 1764, but the dedication is dated 1766. On Rowlands and other Welsh agricultural pioneers *see* Evans, Ven. A. O. : "Some Welsh Agricultural Writers" (*Welsh Journal of Agriculture*, VIII, 1931).

Society for the Encouragement of Arts, Manufactures and Commerce) ; another tried to induce his reluctant tenants to take up turnip husbandry ; and a third demonstrated its advantages by sowing a piece of worthless land with turnips and thereby saving £100 in hay the next winter.[1]

In 1793 the Board of Agriculture, a voluntary society with a Government subvention, was founded in London ; in the same year began the struggle with France which lasted, with one short breathing-space, till 1815. Both these events were of the greatest moment for the development of Welsh husbandry. By its collection and diffusion of agricultural knowledge, the newly-formed Board helped to bring remote and backward regions into touch with the best thought and experience of the day. In the year after its foundation, a report on the agriculture of North Wales was drawn up under its auspices by a Scotsman named George Kay. This report was circulated among practical agriculturists of the district with the following note : "It is requested that this paper may be returned to the Board of Agriculture . . . with any additional remarks . . . written on the margin . . . The report is . . . circulated for the purpose merely of procuring farther information respecting the husbandry of the district." As a stranger whose knowledge of the country was only gained from a hurried visit, Kay could not be expected to give a very sympathetic or understanding report. But the resentment aroused by the harshness of his comments had an excellent result, for it provoked a much more competent observer to undertake a thorough investigation which should supersede Kay's. The Rev. Walter Davies, Rector of Manafon in Montgomeryshire (better known by his bardic name, Gwallter Mechain) took over ten years instead of a few months to collect his information, and he had the great advantage of being able to supplement his own observations by the reports of his many friends up and down the country.[2] The resulting work—*A General View of the Agriculture and Domestic Economy of North Wales*—was published in 1810 ; two companion volumes on South Wales

[1] Davies : *op. cit.*, pp. 201–2, 282–4 ; Evans : *Beauties*, pp. 273–6 ; *see* also later, pp. 132–3, 155 ff.
[2] *See*, e.g., letter by Iolo Morgannwg (1805) in *Bye-gones*, 1891–92, p. 326.

followed. They are a mine of information, not only on agriculture, but on the general economic condition of the land at a critical period in its history. The information they give is generally trustworthy, and although Davies' criticisms are often as severe as Kay's their immediate practical value was infinitely greater, because the author's local knowledge enabled him to trace the vices of Welsh farming to their geographical and historical origins, and to distinguish between practicable advice and counsels of perfection. Unfortunately for the historian, he does not always distinguish so clearly between the successive strata of his report on North Wales, most of which was written in 1799.

It would be difficult to overestimate the effects of publications like these in stimulating interest and diffusing knowledge. The spirited proprietor became the social lion, and all the best society talked crops. In 1808 there appeared the opening number of the *North Wales Gazette*—the first weekly newspaper to be published in this part of the Principality—and for the next six years, general discussions and district reports on agricultural progress formed almost a quarter of its contents. When Kay wrote his survey he complained that there was not a single agricultural society, *eo nomine*, in North Wales.[1] He seems, indeed, to have overlooked the Ancient Druids of Anglesey, an old-established society which concerned itself with philanthropic schemes and literary lore as well as with husbandry :[2] but all the other agricultural societies in the district were of later foundation. Brecknockshire had set the example soon after the middle of the century—thanks to the efforts of Howel Harris, one of the founders of the Methodist movement.[3] It was not till 1796 that the two leading agricultural counties of North Wales followed suit : in that year were founded the Wrexham and the Montgomeryshire Agricultural Societies.[4] In Merioneth—the most backward county of all—a county society was established in 1801, to be followed seven years later by a local organization for the Upper Dee Valley.[5] Caernarvonshire

[1] *Op. cit.*, Denbighshire, p. 40.
[2] *Cambro-Briton*, 1819, pp. 79–80 ; *Bye-gones*, 1903–4, p. 151.
[3] Jones, M. H. : *Trevecka Letters* (Caernarvon, 1932), pp. 185–206.
[4] *Chester Chron.*, Dec. 2, 1796 ; *Mont. Coll.*, XI, p. 395 ; *Bye-gones*, 1888, p. 21.
[5] *N. W. Gaz.*, April 21, 1808 ; *Bye-gones*, 1876, p. 30.

came into line in 1807, Anglesey and the Vale of Clwyd in 1808 ; Flintshire, strangely enough, had no agricultural society till 1817.[1]

These new associations organized ploughing matches and sheep-shearing competitions, introduced new types of agricultural implements, distributed seeds, imported skilled workers ; offered premiums to farmers for success in particular crops or in general husbandry, to farm servants for faithful service, and to cottagers for bringing up large families without parish relief. They petitioned Parliament on the needs of agriculture, took into consideration the state of the roads, and arranged new fairs for farm produce. Their work was supplemented by "agricultural meetings" held by some of the bigger landowners in imitation of the Holkham sheep-shearings, which had become famous throughout the land since their inception in 1778. The Wynnstay agricultural meetings provide a useful example. The Wynns of Wynnstay had long ago laid the foundation of that extensive local influence which was summed up in the title of a well-known "Spy" cartoon of a later representative : "The King of Wales." The way in which that influence was exercised in successive generations aptly illustrates the changes in taste and fashion.[2]

The first Sir Watkin Williams Wynn (1692–1749) was a pillar of Welsh Jacobitism, a doughty opponent of Walpole both in the House and in the country, and an intrepid fox-hunter : something of a Squire Western, in fact.[3] His successor, who came of age in 1770, was of a different complexion. His hobby was the stage, and he built at Wynnstay a theatre in which he and his neighbours and his household servants (some of them chosen for their histrionic talent) performed to select audiences of the neighbouring gentry. The supreme moment of his life came when David Garrick himself paid a visit to one of the performances.[4] The third Sir Watkin succeeded to the estate at the beginning of the French Revolution, and once again

[1] N. W. Gaz., Jan. 5, May 5 and 12, June 2, 1808; Shrewsbury Chron., Oct. 30, 1818.

[2] Wynnstay and the Wynns, pp. 9–24.

[3] Bye-gones, 1874, pp. 27–8 ; 1886, pp. 73–4 ; Hist. MSS. Com., XV, App. 7, pp. 321–4.

[4] Pennant : Tours, I, p. 371 ; Chester Chron., Jan. 22, 1776 ; " Nimrod " (Fraser's Mag.) 1842, pp. 294, 298.

a new order was inaugurated. In 1796 he was instrumental
in founding the Wrexham Agricultural Society, and ten
years later the Wynnstay theatre was dismantled and
appropriated to the uses of an agricultural meeting.
Henceforth a great show of sheep and cattle was held each
year at Wynnstay, with prizes for good farming, and a
Gargantuan feast where five or six hundred guests discussed crops and manures and drank appropriate toasts.[1]
Only when Sir Watkin was away on military service, and
on a few later occasions when circumstances proved
unfavourable, was this popular institution suspended;
and the presence of Coke of Holkham at one of the meetings
made the baronet as happy as his father had been when he
inveigled Garrick to Wynnstay.[2] He was less successful
in his attempt to introduce the culture of hops into Denbighshire, and his efforts to improve the breed of Merioneth
cattle by the introduction of Highland bulls were defeated
by the refusal of the beasts to take kindly to farm life ; but
his extensive afforestation of lands round Llangollen gained
him the gold medal of the Society of Arts.[3]

We have dwelt at some length on Sir Watkin as the
typical landlord of the new era ; but a host of others had
now caught the fashion. An agricultural meeting, similar
to that at Wynnstay, was held on the Gwydir estate in
Caernarvonshire,[4] and afforestation of waste lands in North
Wales became a popular pastime of the well-to-do. Dr.
William Makepeace Thackeray, of Chester, planted extensively in the four counties of Denbigh, Flint, Merioneth,
and Montgomery, and during the time when his more
famous namesake and second cousin, the novelist, was
spending his early boyhood in Calcutta, the Doctor was
perseveringly adding to his collection of medals from the
Society of Arts.[5] In Flintshire Sir Stephen Glynne offered
premiums to his tenants for successful drainage, manage-

---

[1] N. W. Gaz., 1808 ff., passim.
[2] Id., Sept. 1, 1814 ; Shrewsbury Chron., Aug. 28, 1818, Sept. 24,
1819, Aug. 17, 1821.
[3] Shrewsbury Chron., May 11, 1821 ; N. W. Chron., July 29, 1830 ;
Cambro-Briton, I (1819–20), p. 278.
[4] N. W. Gaz., Sept. 27, 1821.
[5] Id., May 4, 1809, July 1, 1813 ; Shrewsbury Chron., April 23,
1819 ; Cambro-Briton, I, pp. 183–4 ; Lewis : Top. Dict., under
Bala; Dict. Nat. Biog.

ment of fallows, and cultivation of turnips, and his leadership in agricultural improvement is indicated by the sale, on his death in 1815, of numbers of Devon cattle, South Devon sheep, and threshing machines, among the effects of his estate.[1]   Another pioneer of improved machinery was a landowner of a different type : John Wilkinson, the famous ironmaster, who on purchasing the Brymbo Hall estate (near Wrexham) for his new ironworks, not only farmed part of the land on improved principles, but used on it the first steam threshing machine in North Wales.[2] Everywhere, too, there was a growing habit of letting farms by written agreement, which stipulated the rotation of crops to be followed and laid down general rules for the management of the land.[3]

In northern Merioneth Mr. W. G. Oakley, of Tan y bwlch, gained the usual honours from the Society of Arts for his success in winning some good corn-lands from periodic inundation by the sea.   But this feat was completely eclipsed by a later one in the same neighbourhood.   The embankment of the Traeth Mawr—the arm of the sea which once flowed between Merioneth and Caernarvonshire—had been discussed as early as James I's reign, when Sir John Wynne of Gwydir vainly tried to enlist on behalf of the project the wealth of Sir Hugh Myddleton, who had just brought the New River to London.   In the course of the eighteenth century some further attempts were made by Dutch adventurers and enterprising landowners ;[4] but the crowning achievement was left for William Alexander Madocks, a Denbighshire man who was educated at Oxford, inherited a considerable fortune from his father, and acquired some notoriety in Parliament (where he sat for Boston) as a member of the dwindling group of Foxites. Madocks was a man of versatile talents.   He was in great demand at house parties as an amateur actor and singer ; and one of his youthful admirers declared in later life that he "possessed a master mind, and wanted nothing but a mine of wealth to render him equal to any undertaking

[1] *Memoir of Hawarden*, p. 153 ; *N. W. Gaz.*, Feb. 9, Aug. 24, 1815.
[2] Davies, pp. 281–2.
[3] *Id.*, pp. 102 ff. ; *Report on Land*, 1896, pp. 448 ff.
[4] Warner : *Second Walk*, p. 117 ; Davies, pp. 256–7, 284, 486–95 ; Kay : *op. cit.*, Merioneth, p. 9 ; *Bye-gones*, 1885–6, p. 170 ; 1900, p. 359.

within the power of man to fulfil."[1] His fame, however, rests neither on political prowess nor on social accomplishments, but on public works, of which he had his first taste, at the age of twenty-three, as trustee under the Barmouth Harbour Act of 1797. In the following year he acquired the estate of Tan yr allt, where—fired, it is said, by reading of Sir John Wynne's old project—he embarked on schemes of drainage which culminated in the embanking and reclaiming of the whole of the Traeth. The embankment itself was entrusted in 1805 to Thomas Paine, of Fenny Compton ; and, to secure his legal position, Madocks shortly afterwards procured an Act vesting in himself and his heirs the whole of the sands between Aberglaslyn (the head of the tidal waters) and Gêst : 2,000 acres in fee, and one-fifth of the lands reclaimed from the sea, the remainder being allotted to the freeholders possessing rights over the salt marshes.[2]

The task kept three or four hundred men employed for nearly six years ; but the sea did not give in without a struggle. No sooner was the embankment finished than a high tide made a breach in it that threatened to bring the whole work to nought, and Madocks had to appeal to the generosity of his neighbours to repair the damage. One of those who came to the rescue was Percy Bysshe Shelley, then living in retirement close to the spot. Inspired by a generous Corporation dinner at Beaumaris, the poet pledged himself "to spend the last shilling of my fortune and devote the last breath of my life to this great, this glorious cause"—a work which "will give to no less than three thousand souls the means of competence." The report of proceedings, it is true, was carefully qualified in the next week's issue of the *North Wales Gazette*, and it is not known whether his promise of £100 (or, according to another account, £50) from a somewhat embarrassed "fortune" was ever fulfilled ; but at least his eloquence is believed to have been effective in drawing subscriptions from others.[3]

[1] "Nimrod" (*Fraser's Mag.*), 1842, p. 295 ; *N. W. Gaz.*, Feb. 2, May 12, Aug. 4, 1808, March 14, 1811, Sept. 8, 1814.
[2] *Chester Chron.*, Sept. 12, 1806 ; *N. W. Gaz.*, May 26, 1808 ; *Bye-gones*, 1889, p. 192 ; 47 Geo. III, cap. 36.
[3] *N. W. Gaz.*, Oct. 1 and 8, 1812 ; *cf.* July 25, Sept. 26, 1811, June 25, 1812 ; Fenton, *Tours*, p. 234.

Not all Shelley's contemporaries looked with equal favour on Madocks and his works.   Four years after the Beaumaris dinner Thomas Love Peacock was lamenting, in *Headlong Hall*, the disappearance of

> a scene which no other country can parallel, and which admirers of the magnificence of nature will ever remember with regret, whatever consolation may be derived from the probable utility of the works which have excluded the waters from their ancient receptacle. . . . The mountain-frame remains unchanged, unchangeable ; but the liquid mirror it enclosed is gone.[1]

Madocks himself exhausted his whole fortune over these public works, and left the fruits to others.   Apart from the heavy expense of the embankment (estimated at £100,000) and the litigation it entailed,[2] he had spent lavishly on his toy village of Tremadoc—built on a barren sandhill, and endowed with church and chapel, market place and woollen factory—on his new harbour of Portmadoc, and on a network of roads to serve the newly-opened territory.   One after another, his estates were mortgaged to his creditors, and in 1827 he had to flee, heavily embarrassed, to France, where he died next year.[3]

While all these changes were taking place, Britain was in the throes of the greatest war she had known.   The Napoleonic struggle stands out from earlier wars, not only in extent and duration, but from the fact that this phenomenal interruption of peaceful traffic took place just at the time when the very existence of the country was becoming dependent on foreign trade.   The effects upon wheat prices of the Seven Years' War and the American struggle had been negligible, because trade had suffered only partial interruption, and also because England still normally grew enough to supply her own needs.   But since then a balance of imports from abroad had become

[1] Chap. VII.
[2] *See*, e.g., *N. W. Gaz.*, April 9, 1812, April 7, 1814.   The original Act had to be amended twice (*ibid.*, Sept. 29, 1825).
[3] *N. W. Chron.*, Sept. 25, 1828 ; Williams : *Eminent Welshmen*, pp. 305–6 ; *Gestiana*, pp. 168–76.   There is a mass of material on Traeth Mawr in the U.C.N.W. Library, Bangor : the Porth yr Aur collection contains a bundle of legal documents *in re* Madocks, and the Amlwch collection contains the following papers of John Matthews, commissioner under the Act of 1821 : accounts, 1821 (4, xxiii), assessments, 1824 (4, xxiv), surveys (61–4).

the general rule, and when the country was cut off for long periods from the wheatfields of central and eastern Europe the land was soon threatened with famine. In 1795 the price of wheat rose, for the first time since the Civil Wars, above 70s. a quarter. At the opening of the nineteenth century it was over 100s. The Peace of Amiens gave a brief respite, but by 1812 the unprecedented figure of 126s. had been reached—almost three times what the price had been before the outbreak of war.[1]

A generation earlier this might not have produced much effect in a district like North Wales, where the mass of the people still lived on home-grown barley and oats ; but by this time the improvement of communications had begun to open up to the Welsh farmer the hungry English market, and the abnormal prices were an irresistible temptation to grow more for sale.[2] On the stony slopes of the Welsh hills, as on the wilds of Dartmoor, the repose of centuries was rudely broken by the plough ; and wheat-crops were wrung out of soils which in ordinary times would never have repaid the outlay.[3] To farmers who were in a position to take advantage of the boom, these were indeed golden days. Even in the 'seventies their tea-drinking habits had been satirized in popular ballads, but now luxury rose to the pitch of pianos for their daughters and a classical education for their sons.[4]

The small holder was not so fortunate. He had been accustomed to grow mainly for the subsistence of his own household, and he was not equipped with the capital for competing in distant markets. To him war meant only higher prices for farming and household necessaries, heavier burdens in taxation and local rates, and often bigger rents.[5] Many small farmers were thus crushed out of existence, and their holdings added to another farm, or kept to increase the personal demesne of the landlord ; and the process, as we shall see later, was accentuated by Enclosure Acts.[6] If the finger of scorn was pointed

---

[1] *See* tables in Ernle : *English Farming*, pp. 440–1.
[2] *Report on Land*, 1896, p. 626.
[3] *See*, e.g., letter in *N. W. Gaz.*, March 3, 1808.
[4] *Bibliography of Welsh Ballads*, No. 218 ; imaginary dialogue in *N. W. Gaz.*, May 18, 1815, *cf.* Jan. 16, 1812.
[5] *Bibliography of Welsh Ballads*, No. 339 (time of American War).
[6] *N. W. Gaz.*, Aug. 15, Oct. 3, 1811. *See* also chap. III.

at the farmer's piano and tea-caddy, his retort was ready to hand : what of the landlord's seasons in town and his devotion to state lotteries ?[1] The growing habit of letting farms by auction over the head of the sitting tenant meant that any exceptional gains were soon transferred to the landlord's pocket.[2] Davies calculated that during the decade which elapsed between the commencement of his survey of North Wales and the publication of the finished work, rents had gone up about sixpence in the pound ; and an old man complains to the local paper in 1816 that he has seen them raised three and even four times in the last fifty years.[3] Writers of ballads tell the same tale, and ample confirmation may be found in the statistics of particular holdings.[4]

War-profits, then, provided a more sordid spur to the enthusiasm of spirited proprietors. The atmosphere to which Welsh agriculture awoke after its long spell of stagnation was not altogether a healthy one. The temptation to unnatural "forcing" was too strong, and even agricultural societies were apt to injure their good work by excessive eagerness for quick results.[5] Yet much that was of lasting value was accomplished during these years. Not only had the stimulus of war improved the yield of rich corn-lands like those of Flintshire and the Vale of Clwyd—where it was frequently doubled and even trebled in twenty years—but Merioneth itself was outgrowing the stage of dependence on its neighbours for corn, till soon it contained "scarcely an upland farm that [did] not grow enough oats and barley for the needs of the farmer."[6] Draining and afforestation had permanently improved the value of lands that formerly lay idle. At the end of the War, sportsmen who had been accustomed to shoot snipe and wild duck in Anglesey found that

[1] *Bibliography of Welsh Ballads*, No. 281.

[2] Evans : *Beauties*, pp. 337–9 ; *N. W. Gaz.*, Sept. 13, 1810.

[3] Davies, p. 94 and *n;* *N. W. Gaz.*, April 11, 1816, *cf.* July 23, 1812.

[4] *Bibliography of Welsh Ballads*, No. 365 ; *Report on Land*, 1896, pp. 435, 438, 450, 459.

[5] *See* charges made in *N. W. Gaz.*, May 10, 1821, and in *Cambro-Briton*, I (1819–20), p. 156.

[6] *N. W. Gaz.*, Aug. 13, 1812 ; Cathrall : *History of North Wales*, II, p. 193 ; Lewis : *Top. Dict.*, under *Merioneth*.

agricultural improvement had robbed them of their quarry.[1] The rocky soils of Caernarvonshire had been cleaned, often by the blasting away of great boulders which obstructed cultivation. Ploughing matches had demonstrated the advantages of newer types of plough, and advertisements of these, as well as of harrows, turnip-slicers, horse hoes and the like, had begun to appear in the local press.[2] When Kay wrote his report there was not a single threshing machine in North Wales; since then Wilkinson's steam thresher had set the example, and models worked by water or by horse power had been adopted on one estate after another, while the use of the winnowing machine, long familiar in the more northerly counties, had extended to Merioneth and Montgomery.[3] In the counties of Denbigh, Flint and Montgomery, the landlords were learning to put up cleaner and more commodious farm houses and buildings; but a Merioneth man, writing to the local paper in 1815, does not scruple to call those of his district "as bad as the huts of Indians on the St. Lawrence." Even in the rich Vale of Clwyd the absence of granaries often forced the farmer to bring to market grain which he had intended for sowing.[4]

The first effects of industrial advance had been disastrous to farming. Not only were the farmer's best hands lured away from him by higher wages and more exciting occupations,[5] but farming operations themselves were interrupted by the all-absorbing claims of industry. In the mineral parts of Flintshire there were in Pennant's time many small farms where the tenants spent the greater part of their time carrying coal or lead ore; tillage was neglected, and in the service of industry the horses devoured good grasslands which might have produced cheese and butter in plenty.[6] The same tale could be told of the slate regions of Bethesda, Llanberis, and Ffestiniog. Industry suffered as well as farming, for all transport had to be held up during the bustle of the harvest. On the other hand,

[1] Davies, chap. X, and pp. 287–90; *Sportsman's Mag.*, Feb., 1815, quoted *Bye-gones*, 1878, p. 46.

[2] Evans : *Beauties*, p. 324 ; *N. W. Gaz.*, March 11, Nov. 18, 1813.

[3] Davies, chap. V.

[4] *Id.*, pp. 80–82 ; *N. W. Gaz.*, Sept. 9, 1813, Feb. 17, 1814.

[5] *See*, e.g., Evans: *Beauties*, pp. 236–8 ; Owen: *Anglesey*, p. 52.

[6] Pennant : *Whiteford and Holywell*, pp. 167–8, and *Tours*, I, p. 22.

of course, this subsidiary source of income was invaluable
to the farmer in times of depression.[1]   But the building of
mineral railways in all these regions released the horses for
the service of the farm.   In other respects, too, the
improvement of communications was a gain to husbandry.
It meant access to better markets, and an increased
capacity for taking produce there.   The light one-horse
farm cart was now coming into general use—except,
indeed, in out-of-the-world hill parishes, where the clumsy
wheel-less "drag-car" or sledge still carried its loads of
produce, peat, or manure, till past the middle of the
century.[2]   It meant also access to lime and to coal for
burning it ;   for although advanced farmers had been
using lime since the seventeenth century,[3] it was only with
the cheapening of fuel and transport that it became general
for farmers to have their own kilns, or for private adventurers to build them (for sale or hire) on main roads and
canal banks or near the limestone quarries.   Towards the
end of the eighteenth century, a fair-sized kiln would bring
in a yearly revenue of £50 and upwards, and the lime-
burner, earning about 9d. or 10d. a day, was in as great
demand as the charcoal-burner had been in an earlier
generation.   The 1831 Census records 52 of them in
Anglesey alone.[4]

Along with improved methods of farming and a better
yield of the traditional crops, new types of produce had

---

[1] *The Red Dragon*, VII (1885), p. 327 ; Fenton : *Tours, 1804–13*,
p. 249 ; *Hanes Plwyf Ffestiniog*, p. 128.   During the bad season of
1822 Mr. Assheton Smith reduced the rents of his farmers by 20 per
cent, but only by 10 per cent to those engaged in carrying slates from
the Llanberis quarries (*N. W. Gaz.*, Feb. 6, 1823).   The Porth yr aur
collection (U.C.N.W. Library, Bangor) contains carriers' accounts
for a number of Caernarvonshire quarries, and a bundle of printed
carriers' notes issued by the Cilgwyn New Company.   Payments
seem to have ranged from 4s. to 8s. a ton, but were sometimes made
in kind, and sometimes by tale instead of weight.   (*Cf.* Parry :
Llanberis, p. 73 ; *N. W. Gaz.*, April 22, 1813.)

[2] Davies, pp. 119–21 ; *Mont. Coll.*, XXVI, pp. 161–2 ; *Red
Dragon*, VII, p. 318.

[3] Rowlands : *Idea Agriculturae*, p. xxv.

[4] Davies, pp. 140–1, 293–302 ; Pennant : *Tours*, I, p. 23 ; *N. W.
Gaz.*, July 28, Sept. 8, 1808, Aug. 15, 1816 ; *Salop. Journ.*, May 2,
1798 ; Meyrick Papers, 1767 ff.   The names of three lime-burners
appear among the creditors of a bankrupt Anglesey landlord in
N. W. Gaz., Dec. 1, 1814.

found a permanent footing in the farmer's scheme of tillage. During the time of scarcity, when harvests at home were bad and foreign supplies were cut off by the War, the growing of potatoes increased enormously. In Anglesey they were first cultivated on a large scale in the last quarter of the eighteenth century, when the herring fisheries fell off ; and during the same period considerable quantities were shipped from Conway.[1] Landlords and farmers gradually acquired the habit of planting them as a regular field crop and not merely to supply their own tables. Labourers who were lucky enough to own a garden, or who could get permission, for a trifling payment, to plant in the farmers' fallows, found in their potato crops a useful supplement to wages and a stand-by in time of unemployment. As we shall see, the curtailment of these opportunities—or at least the failure to extend them —was one of the gravest sins of enclosure commissioners.[2] The prejudice of farmers against the turnip, too, was breaking down everywhere during the period when Davies was engaged on his survey, and advertisements for farm bailiffs were beginning to insist that the applicant should be "acquainted with the turnip and green crop system," as well as with draining and irrigation.[3] This, together with experiments in breeding, was producing some improvement in the quality of stock ; and the need for richer feeding grounds than the thin and often over-stocked mountain pastures was met by the growing practice among landowners of setting aside portions of their parks or demesnes as "summer leys" for the accommodation of a fixed number of cattle at definite prices.[4] Finally, there was the widespread movement for the enclosure and allotment of common and waste lands ; this, however, must be held over for discussion in the next chapter.

[1] Owen: *Anglesey*, p. 8 ; Pennant: *Tours*, III, p. 405.

[2] Davies, pp. 206–8 ; Pennant: *Tours*, I, p. 22, and *Whiteford and Holywell*, pp. 160–1 ; *Parl. Pap.*, 1834, XXIX, p. 187 ; 1840, XXIV, pp. 556 ff. ; 1842, XV, pp. 374, 415, 432–3.

[3] Davies, p. 203 ; *N. W. Gaz.*, Oct. 6, 1814, *cf.* Nov. 12, 1810.

[4] Advertisements offering such accommodation in the counties of Denbigh, Flint, and Montgomery frequently appear in local newspapers from 1777 onwards, and in Caernarvon and Merioneth from 1808. *Cf.* Davies, chap. XIII and p. 84, and for a similar practice in Lancashire *see* Unwin, Hulme and Taylor: *Samuel Oldknow and the Arkwrights*, p. 142.

Much had been accomplished, but more remained to be done if Welsh farming was to catch up with English. "Wales in a general view may be considered a century, at least, behind England as to its state of agriculture" : this was the opinion expressed by a patriotic Welshman in 1812, when the process of "improvement" was in full swing ; and he followed up his general charge by a veritable Newgate Calendar of the crimes of the farmer.[1] Equally harsh are the strictures of agricultural correspondents in the *North Wales Gazette* upon their neighbours. But these criticisms bear the mark of the impatient optimist ; their very severity is a measure of the rising standard of agricultural practice and the growing expectations of agricultural reformers. There was a general impression that if only the relations between landlord and tenant could be put on a satisfactory footing all would soon be well with Welsh farming. Everyone knew that what the farmer needed was more capital, more enterprise, and greater security for the fruits of his outlay of capital and enterprise. But how were these desirable ends to be attained ? By long leases or by yearly tenancies ? By small farms or by big farms ? These were the points round which discussion ranged. Yearly tenancies gave better opportunity for the adjustment of rents to the state of the market ; long leases gave the farmer greater security. Big farms were more economical to work, but to the man of small capital they were nothing but a snare ; small farms saved the poor rates and fought monopoly in the corn markets, but they were the preserve of the incompetent cultivator who resisted all innovations.[2]

Into the midst of these debates, the slump which followed the end of the War fell like a thunder-bolt. Even during the interval of peace preceding Waterloo there had been an ominous fall in the price of stock and of crops,[3] and early in 1816 discussions of agricultural distress began to take the place, in the columns of the local press, of schemes for improvement. Those farmers who had taken long leases hoping (like Mr. Punch's Irish farmer in our own

[1] Evans : *Beauties*, p. 97.
[2] *See* discussions in *N. W. Gaz.*, 1811–13, *passim;* Kay : *op. cit.,* Denbighshire, pp. 18, 37 ; Davies, pp. 92–5, 98–109, and chap. XVI.
[3] Foulkes MSS., in *Bye-gones*, 1905–6, p. 118.

time) that the War would "hould," found themselves unable to meet their rents now that they could only get a half to a third of the former prices for their produce. Many of them, to procure the bare necessities of life, had to sell off stock for what it would fetch. Notices of sales (under distress) of farms and farming stock, and references to compassionate reductions of rent by landlords, became a weekly feature in the newspapers. Nothing but the obstinate devotion of a race of peasants to their native soil prevented a wholesale desertion of the countryside.

In the early months of 1816 the Board of Agriculture issued a *questionnaire* to its local correspondents on the state of agriculture in their respective districts. The replies sent on behalf of North Wales by Gwallter Mechain and two other ministers of religion indicate an alarming state of affairs. "Sheriff's officers," says one of them, "are the only class of men who in these days are fully employed and make their fortunes." Three years later financial deflation, with its usual disturbing effects, came to aggravate the farmers' worries. When the House of Commons Committee on Agriculture made its report in 1821, Welsh conditions had improved a little, but wheat cultivation was on the down grade, and much land had gone out of tillage altogether.[1] The country fairs were almost deserted in 1822, and bankruptcies among farmers were still distressingly frequent.[2] There was a ray of returning prosperity during the next few years,[3] but the financial crash of 1826 brought agriculture down with the other industries of the country, and Parliamentary blue books of the 'thirties report that Welsh farming capital is steadily declining.[4] If North Wales was mercifully free from the attentions of Captain Swing (whose field of campaign extended as far as the Cardiff district) it was largely because the plight of the farmer was little better than that of the labourer himself.[5]

---

[1] *Report on Land*, 1896, App., pp. 22, 25–6 ; *N. W. Gaz.*, July 3, 1822.

[2] *N. W. Gaz.*, March 14, June 13 *et passim*, 1822; *Oswestry Her.*, March 26, Oct. 1, 1822.

[3] Reports of fairs, *N. W. Gaz.*, 1824, *passim; cf.* July 28, 1825.

[4] E.g., Poor Law Report (1834, XXIX), p. 190 *n; cf. Report on Land*, 1896, p. 153.

[5] *P.L.R.* (1834, XXXIV) ; *Shrewsbury Chron.*, Dec. 24, 1830.

This long period of depression simply killed the enthusiasm for agriculture which had begun to bud during the opening years of the century. It is highly significant that when the *North Wales Chronicle* resumed in 1829 the agricultural columns which had been such a prominent feature of its predecessor the *Gazette*, hardly any local correspondents could be induced to contribute, and the page had to be padded out with borrowings from the English journals. Now and again the Welsh farmer would stir himself from his apathy to attend a county meeting on agricultural distress—the papers are filled with reports of them—and to sign a petition urging the Government to "do something" for agriculture ; but his practical suggestions usually did not go beyond an exhortation to Ministers to be less extravagant and to keep out foreign corn. Even in this latter remedy he came at last to lose faith. He was learning now to take his politics from the Nonconformist pulpit and the denominational press, where influential voices were already trying to persuade him that his landlord was the only gainer by the Corn Laws. *Seren Gomer* began the agitation in 1819—soon after, having failed as a weekly newspaper (the first to be printed in Welsh), it had come to life again as a Baptist periodical. The *Seren* was long a lone star, but during the 'thirties its editor found some support among his brother ministers.[1] By this time corn growing had long ceased to be a prime concern with the Welsh farmer, and scientific interest in agriculture had receded before the absorbing claims of political and sectarian strife. On the very eve of Repeal, reports on Welsh agriculture still echoed the old complaints of bad fallowing, unscientific rotation, and unsatisfactory leases, and the old charge that the land did not produce half as much as it might.[2] The gulf between landlord and farmer had widened,[3] and the abolition of the Corn Laws knocked yet another nail into the coffin of the landed gentry as national leaders. The day of the "spirited proprietor" was over, the bright promise of the war years belonged to a forgotten past, and the agriculture of North Wales remained in a state of arrested development.

[1] *Report on Land*, 1896, p. 152 ; *id.*, App., pp. 188–9.
[2] Fullarton's *Parl. Gaz.*, 1840–44, IV, p. 405 ; *Life and Opinions of Robert Roberts*, p. 12.
[3] *See*, e.g., *Letters on Improvements*, 1852.

CHAPTER III.
ENCLOSURES.

Inclose, inclose, ye swains !
Why will you joy in common field, where pitch,
Noxious to wool, must stain your motley flock
To mark your property ? . . . Besides, in fields
Promiscuous held all culture languishes ;
The glebe, exhausted, thin supplies receives ;
Dull waters rest upon the rushy flats
And barren furrows ; none the rising grove
There plants for late posterity, nor hedge
To shield the flock, nor copse for cheering fire ;
And in the distant village every hearth
Devours the grassy sward, the verdant food
Of injur'd herds and flocks, or what the plough
Should turn and moulder for the bearded grain . . .
Add too, the idle pilf'rer easier there
Eludes detection, when a lamb or ewe
From intermingled flocks he steals ; or when,
With loosen'd tether of his horse or cow,
The milky stalk of the tall green-ear'd corn,
The year's slow rip'ning fruit, the anxious hope
Of his laborious neighbour, he destroys.

—The Fleece, II, 109–33.

In these lines, written about 1757, the Carmarthenshire painter-poet, John Dyer, gives us the gist of the case for enclosure. Dyer was a much-travelled man, and one of his objects in writing his didactic poem, *The Fleece*, was to give his slow-going countrymen the benefit of his wider experience. Across the border the gradual process of reclaiming waste lands, and straightening out the "mingle-mangle" of the common fields, had never wholly ceased since the days when More and Latimer made their eloquent protests. But with the Glorious Revolution came the triumph of individualism, the birth of scientific agriculture, and the replacement of a national monarchy by a parliament of landlords and all this had given a new aspect to the enclosure of commons and wastes. No longer was it the act of "insatiable cormorants" who must be repressed by the might of an even-handed law ; it now appeared in the guise of a patriotic policy to be fostered by the legislature in the teeth of obstructive small holders and cottagers. There had been talk of a General Enclosure Act as early as 1681 ; and, although this came to nothing, a *pis aller* was found in the development of procedure by Private Act, which placed in the hands of wealthy and "advanced" landlords a trusty weapon for breaking down the factiousness of local opposition. By the time Dyer wrote, well over two hundred of these Acts had been passed. But it was under George III that the real mania for enclosure began ; before he died, the number of Acts had risen to between four and five thousand.[1]

In North Wales too (as we saw in the first chapter) the area of common field and waste had been slowly reduced, generation after generation—sometimes by fair and open purchase or exchange, sometimes by illegal encroachment on the part of powerful landlords on the one hand and obscure squatters on the other. These early enclosures did not always pass unchallenged. In Queen Elizabeth's reign there had been litigation before the Star Chamber about enclosures at Chirk in Denbighshire, Penmon in Anglesey, Leighton in Montgomeryshire, and elsewhere ; at Llangollen, in Denbigh, and Strata Marcella, in Montgomery, aggrieved parties had taken the law into their own hands by forming "confederacies" to break down enclosures. This crime became still commoner under the early Stuarts : at least six cases (four from Merioneth, the rest from Flint and Montgomery) were tried before the Star Chamber, and another (concerning certain " audatious persons " of "insolent and Rietous carriage" at Ewloe in Flint) before the Council of Wales.[2] There were further legal disputes arising out of enclosures at Denbigh in 1691 and near Berriew, Montgomeryshire, about a generation later.[3]

---

[1] Curtler : *The Enclosure and Redistribution of our Land*, pp. 136–7, 148. The figures given on the latter page seem to exhibit some strange inconsistencies.

[2] Edwards, I. ab Owen : *Star Chamber Proceedings relating to Wales* (Cardiff, 1929), pp. 21, 61, 68, 119, 125, 174, 183–5, 187, 200 ; Skeel, C. A. J. : *The Council in the Marches of Wales* (1904), pp. 263-4; Mahler : *Chirk Castle and Chirkland*, p. 159 ; Cust : *Chronicles of Erthig*, I, p. 57. Merioneth family archives show that enclosures there "commenced in the reign of Elizabeth and continued uninterrupted until completed by the Enclosure Acts" (*Y Cymmrodor*, XXXVIII, p. 3).

[3] Williams : *Ancient and Modern Denbigh*, pp. 196–7 ; *Mont. Coll.*, XXIV, pp. 157–8.

Sometimes the object of the landlords was purely benevolent : we have at least one instance from South Wales where the lord of the manor and the freeholders enclosed part of the common to build and endow a free school.[1] But the author of the *Bardd Cwsc*, writing in Queen Anne's time, talks with bitterness of the "Great Man who steals from the mountain half a parish" and "robs the poor man of a living for his beast, and thereby of a living for himself and his household."[2]

These, however, were merely cases of local enterprise or local rapacity. In Wales there was no deliberate, concerted movement towards enclosure till the reign of George III, and the remoter parts of the country remained untouched till the time of the Napoleonic Wars. The neighbouring counties of Cheshire, Shropshire, Gloucester, and Hereford had been pretty thoroughly enclosed for dairy-farms or orchards, stock-raising or grain-growing, before 1700 ; but a century later a quarter of the soil of Wales was "either true common or waste and unenclosed land."[3]

What were these common and waste lands ? In the first place there were the arable strips in villages where the "open-field" system had taken root. The extent to which this form of land tenure had penetrated North Wales is a subject still awaiting investigation. That it was early acclimatized, if not indigenous, in the Marches, has been abundantly proved ; and if the recurrence of the word "quillets" in notices of land-sales in early newspapers may be taken as an indication, it was common in all the less hilly counties.[4] But there were vast stretches of mountain

[1] *Trans. Cym. Soc.*, 1904–05, p. 142.

[2] Wynne, Ellis : *Gweledigaetheu y Bardd Cwsc*, 1703 (ed. Morris-Jones, J., Bangor, 1898), p. 21.

[3] *History*, VI, p. 80 ; *Report on Land*, 1896, p. 587.

[4] *See* Palmer, A. N., and Owen, E. : *History of Ancient Tenures of Land in North Wales and the Marches* (1910) ; Palmer : *Town, Fields, and Folk of Wrexham in the Reign of James I* (1883) ; *Trans. Ang. Ant. Soc.*, 1925, pp. 21–32 ; *Y Cymmrodor*, XXXVIII, p. 3 ; Rees, W. : *South Wales and the March* (1924), pp. 39, 131 ; Fleure, H. J. : *Wales and her People* (1926), p. 17 ; Davies, D. J. : *Econ. Hist. of S. Wales*, p. 19. References to quillets are numerous in estate papers and newspaper advertisements of the late eighteenth and early nineteenth centuries, especially in valley and coastal areas ; but the late Sir John Clapham expressed the opinion to me that most of these would be intakes from the waste.

pasture and extensive marshy wastes to which the system, as it existed in the English lowlands, was wholly unsuited, and these it was that formed the main objective of the apostles of enclosure. Common rights in the village fields were extinguished by a silent and gradual process which had begun centuries before the great enclosure movement, and which continued, for the most part, without exciting comment or arousing opposition, till a witness could tell the Committee on Inclosures in 1844 that he knew of no commonable or common field lands in the whole of Cheshire and North Wales.[1]

The mountain pastures were to have a much stormier history. In legal theory, of course, the waste lands of a manor were the property of the lord, subject only to any common rights over it for which the freeholders and copyholders could show legal title. But in Wales there were special historical conditions which had complicated the issue. For one thing the manorial system, and the whole complex of law and custom which governed it, were not indigenous growths. They had been, not introduced, but rather assumed to exist, when Welsh law and administration were assimilated to those of England. So long as the waste lands remained unimportant, ownership was left conveniently vague, but when suddenly they rose to the rank of a national asset, the community was rudely awakened to the existence of these alien legal theories. Then again, in most of North Wales, with the single exception of Montgomeryshire, the lord of the manor was the King. In the Principality he had stepped into the shoes of the dispossessed Welsh prince, and in Denbighshire and Flintshire many of the most extensive Lordships Marcher had eventually passed to the Crown. Now the Crown was a distant and impersonal landlord; moreover, since the Stuart dream of a strong centralized executive and an independent Crown revenue had been finally dispelled, its only agents were other local landowners with axes of their

---

[1] *Parl. Pap.*, 1844, V, p. 371.

own to grind. The result was that Crown claims fell into oblivion, and Crown wastes came to be looked upon as a sort of no-man's land which

> . . . they should take who have the power,
> And they should keep who can.

Add to this the growing prejudice among the governing classes against anything that savoured of public or communal ownership, and the almost idolatrous belief in the magic of private property (in the right hands, of course), and we are in a position to understand the problem presented by the unenclosed lands of North Wales.

In the first place these mountain pastures were invaluable —indispensable, indeed—to the neighbouring freeholders, who had been accustomed, "time out of mind," to use them as *arosfeydd* or summer "staying places" for their flocks and those of their tenantry. For generations these freeholders, tenants of the manor, had ceased to think of the lordship of the Crown as anything but a shadowy survival. Even an attempt to hold a manorial court was sometimes resented and obstructed by them as an outrage. Their quit-rents (when they remembered to pay them at all) had become merely nominal with changes in the value of money, and the sheep walks which they and their fathers and their fathers' fathers had used without let or hindrance they had come to regard as unfettered freehold property. The ill-determined boundaries of many tracts of former Crown land which had been alienated, for ready cash, by the ever-needy Stuarts, helped to increase the confusion.[1]

In the middle years of the eighteenth century, Lewis Morris, attempting in his capacity of deputy steward of Crown lands in Cardiganshire to work the minerals on the wastes, had to encounter the strenuous and turbulent opposition of those who claimed them as sheep-walks. "If some care be not immediately taken about the King's rights in Wales," he writes in 1750, "it will be all sunk in a few years. I wish His Majesty knew as well as I do the consequence this loss will be to him."[2] Soon after the accession of George III some attempt was made to cope with the situation. Vigorous Crown agents and surveyors

[1] *Report on Land*, 1896, pp. 194 ff.
[2] *Y Cymmrodor*, XV, p. 11.

were appointed to track down illegal encroachments and to
collect arrears of rent ; indeed, the making out of Crown
titles to usurped domains in Wales became a much-prized
job of place and pension hunters.[1] The indignation of the
local squires knew no bounds. Tories almost to a man, they
did not shrink from adorning their speeches at county
meetings with tags about "alarming invasions . . . of our
undoubted rights and liberties," such as Hampden might
have used to harangue the Buckinghamshire freeholders ;
and for a time they won the day.[2] In 1787 Crown rents
from North Wales were still some £32,000 in arrear.[3] Just
over thirty years later, the struggle was re-opened by the
appointment to the Receivership of Crown lands in Wales
of another vigorous jack-in-office, who proceeded to set the
country ablaze by demanding arrears of rent and granting
to mineral prospectors (including, among others, Nathan
Meyer Rothschild) leases of waste land which had long been
claimed as sheepwalks by the surrounding estates. Fulmi-
nations against this "feudal tyranny" mingled in the air
with pained reproofs to cottagers who were pulling down
enclosures, and they had hardly died down before country
gentlemen had to ransack their vocabularies afresh for
imprecations on the lawlessness of Chartism. The question
of the Crown lands was not really settled till 1845.[4]

It was not only by the landlords that possession of the
waste lands was disputed. It has already been pointed out
that the gradual reclamation of the wastes had been largely
the work of squatters—humble landless peasants who had
built themselves hovels there and cleared patches of ground
to plant potatoes. There seems to have been no foundation
in either Welsh or English law for the widely-accepted
theory that the man who could build a cottage on *terra*

[1] Winstanley, D. A. : *Lord Chatham and the Whig Opposition*
(1912), p. 207.
[2] *Chester Chron.*, Jan. 15, 1779 ; *cf.* Dec. 25, 1778, Jan. 8, 22, 29,
March 19, April 2, Oct. 17, 1779, March 24, 1780 ; *Bye-gones*,
1882–3, pp. 6, 10 ; *Mont. Coll.*, V, p. 226.
[3] *Report on Land*, 1896, App., p. 4.
[4] *Id.*, pp. 199 ff. ; *Shrewsbury Chron.*, Aug. 7, 1818, Nov. 19,
1819, July 14, 1826, Aug. 10, 1827, Aug. 28, 1829 ; *N. W. Gaz.*,
Sept. 14, 1826 ; *N. W. Chron.*, Nov. 22, 1827, etc. ; *cf. infra*,
pp. 215–16. There is much correspondence about Crown lands
(especially concerning arrears of debt) in the Porth yr Aur
collection, Bangor.

nullius in a day and a night—a *caban un nos*—became legal
owner of it, but until the ownership of the wastes became a
burning question this belief was sufficient to leave the
squatter in undisturbed possession ; and in later days the
desire to keep "the poor" off the rates often led to positive
encouragement of the practice by parish authorities.[1] If
the waste lands were nobody's property—so the squatter
might argue—the first comer had the best right.

But conditions were rapidly changing. When once the
question of legal rights had been raised, the Welsh landlord
began to envy the unfettered ownership which enclosure
was conferring on his English neighbours. If the Crown
challenged his "encroachments," he would no longer
connive at the squatter's *caban un nos*. There must be a
definite determination of rights, leaving each legal claimant
(including the Crown) with his separate, fenced-in share
of the mountain lands in exclusive and unchallenged
property. And the needs of agricultural improvement
pointed in the same direction. At a time when war conditions called for every ounce of foodstuffs the land could
bear, the Welsh pastures were certainly failing to "do their
bit." Some of them, it was thought, were suited to corn-
growing ; others could treble their value, and at the same
time help to win the War, by growing timber for the Navy ;
and even those retained as sheep-runs might be made to
produce a greater weight and a better quality of mutton
and wool. The expansion of the woollen industry, the
increased consumption of butcher's meat, and the growing
use of horses on the farms, all strengthened the case for a
more economical use of grazing lands.[2] On the majority
of the mountain wastes the sheep of the neighbouring
farms grazed at will : "unlimited rights of pasture" on such
and such a mountain were a frequent inducement held out
to purchasers of farms advertised for sale in the local press.
Gross over-stocking and underfeeding were the inevitable
results. Occasionally, however, a specific number of sheep
is mentioned, from which we may gather that an agreement
had been made to limit the rights of each farm according to
its size. Even then, we are told, "the richer sort always

---

[1] E.g., *N. W. Gaz.*, Feb. 1, June 7, etc., 1827.
[2] *See* letter in *N. W. Gaz.*, May 17, 1810.

overstock, and the poorer sell the privilege for fourpence per head."[1]. In the richer lowlands, the pasture lands were so mismanaged that they did not carry a third of the number of sheep they could be made to support.[2]   And such was the danger from the "idle pilf'rer" in "intermingled flocks" that the sheep had not infrequently to be kept tethered, to the detriment of their feeding and their health.[3]

On the mere ground of productivity, then, a case could be made out for a repartition of the commons and wastes. "The magic of property," Arthur Young was preaching, "turns sand into gold."   A sermon so well according with the private interests of his hearers did not fall on stony ground ; for "property," of course, meant exclusive individual ownership, and not intermingled rights of common or quasi-public domain like the Crown lands. "Let the Crown lands be sold to private proprietors with a personal stake in their efficient management," urged some.[4]   "If the ownership of a piece of waste land is indeterminate, and it is good for nothing else, let the Government plant trees on it for the Navy," said others.[5]   "Fence in the commons and divide them up," was the general chorus.[6]   As for the cottager who had built on the waste, or who kept a few half-starved sheep there, or "devoured the grassy sward" for household fuel—would he not be more industrious and better off in the discipline of regular employment ?[7]   English landowners added their patronizing applause : one of the patriotic toasts drunk at the Holkham sheep-shearing in 1819 was "The Inclosure of Lands in Wales."[8]   So did public policy come to the aid of private selfishness.

[1] N. W. Gaz., April 4, 1811, Aug. 13, 1812, Feb. 4, 1813 ; Evans : Beauties, p. 325 ; Report of S. C. on Waste Lands (1795), p. 213 ; Davies, chap. VIII ; Observations on Snowdon Mountains, p. 133 ; Evans : Tour, pp. 378–9.   Complaints of "surcharging" the common pastures go back at least to the reign of James I (Edwards : Star Chamber Proceedings, p. 174).
[2] Letters from Snowdon, p. 98 ; N. W. Gaz., March 26, 1812.
[3] Evans : Tour, p. 371 n.
[4] E.g., Evans : Beauties, pp. 334–7.
[5] E.g., letter in N. W. Gaz., Dec. 23, 1813.
[6] Davies, pp. 268–9 ; Evans : Tour, pp. 371 ff. ; N. W. Gaz., Sept. 29, 1808, Dec. 14, 1809, May 17, June 28, July 26, Sept. 27, Oct. 4, 18, 25, 1810, April 25, June 27, 1811.
[7] N. W. Gaz., March 26, 1812.
[8] Shrewsbury Chron., July 16, 1819.

As usual, it was the counties bordering on England that led the way. Before 1790 Flint and Montgomery were the only two counties in North Wales where enclosure by Private Act had made any headway. In the former a company formed early in the century to improve the navigation of the Dee found it necessary to procure several Acts for the enclosure of marshy lands, and a number of Flintshire parishes felt the benefit. Saltney Marsh, a stretch of waste land some two thousand acres in extent, on which inhabitants of Hawarden parish had found meagre pasturage for their cattle, was enclosed by Private Act in 1778 (after the failure of an earlier project in 1770). Good crops were grown on the reclaimed lands, a thousand acres or so were added to the estates of the Glynnes (lords of the manor and chief promoters), and "the spirit of industry" was awakened in the whole neighbourhood. Three years earlier, Sir Walden Hanmer had procured the enclosure of three thousand acres of fenny heath in the parish of Hanmer—politically in Flintshire, though belonging geographically to Denbighshire or Shropshire.[1]

About this time, too, Montgomeryshire was making its first acquaintance with Parliamentary enclosure. After a minor Act of 1761 dealing with the municipal commons of Welshpool, a series of three big enclosures took place during the decade 1780–90, affecting in all nearly 9,000 acres of land in the valleys of the lower Severn and Vyrnwy, the rivers being embanked at great expense, though not at first with corresponding success. In describing the effects on cultivation, Gwallter Mechain is moved to quote the words of the "Asiatic bard" about valleys standing so thick with corn that they laugh and sing. The county was beginning to live down the reproach that half its lands lay waste.[2] Outside Flint and Montgomery little was done as yet. In Denbighshire the Clwyd was surveyed by a professional engineer in 1778, with a view to embanking it against floods, but nothing further is heard of the application for an Act of Parliament.[3] In Anglesey the drainage

---

[1] *Memoir of Hawarden*, pp. 96, 107–9 ; Davies, p. 260 ; Hanmer, Lord : *Memorials of the Parish and Family of Hanmer* (1876), pp. 277–8 ; Pennant : *Whiteford and Holywell*, p. 186.

[2] Davies, pp. 262–6 ; *N.L.W. Journ.*, III, p. 150.

[3] *Chester Chron.*, April 17, Aug. 14, 1778.

of Malldraeth Marsh was taken in hand under Acts of 1788 and 1790, but some of the proprietors took fright at the accumulating expenses, and withdrew their support when the embankments were within an ace of completion.[1]   In Caernarvonshire there was nothing but a tiny enclosure of marsh-land by the Caernarvon Corporation, and in Merioneth a projected enclosure of lands near the head-waters of the Clwyd was abandoned in 1778.[2]

After 1790, and especially after the outbreak of the Napoleonic Wars, waste lands began to bulk more largely than common fields in the national movement towards enclosure, and it was now that the counties of North Wales felt its full effects.   Before 1790, according to a calculation made by Gwallter Mechain only about 13,000 acres had been enclosed ; before he completed his survey 80,000 more had been added.[3]

In Flintshire the valley of the Alyn in the south, and the boggy regions round the mouth of the Clwyd in the north, were enclosed by 1800 ; between then and the end of the War almost all the rest of the county was brought into line, excepting only the lead-bearing Halkin Mountain and the industrial neighbourhood of Holywell and Bagillt, most of which had been enclosed long before.   Some of these Acts extended also to the Denbighshire moorlands lying south-west of the Flintshire border, where further progress was made in 1808–11.   The Vale of Clwyd and the neighbouring highlands were enclosed piecemeal between 1800 and 1814 ;   most of the northern plain, from the coast to the Elwy, in 1808–9 ; and portions of the Conway valley in 1812.   A proposal for enclosing the south-west corner of Denbighshire, with the adjacent parts of Merioneth, was considered and dropped in 1808.   In Montgomeryshire, enclosure was pushed gradually westward until the heart of the county was reached in 1815. In 1802 the first assault was made on the rocky wastes of the Lleyn peninsula, which became the scene of extensive enclosures during the next ten years.   The marsh of Dinas Dinlle, south-west of Caernarvon, was enclosed and

[1] Davies, pp. 252–4.

[2] *Chester Chron.*, March 30, 1781, Oct. 16, 1778.

[3] Johnson, A. H. : *The Disappearance of the Small Landowner* (1909), p. 94 ; Davies, p. 274.

drained under an Act of 1806; in the same year the northern spurs of Snowdon were attacked, and the reclamation of Traeth Mawr was immediately followed by the enclosure of the flat lands lying north-west of it.

Anglesey and Merioneth, as always, lagged in the rear. In Merioneth, parts of the coastal marshes, the Mawddach valley, and the neighbourhood of Cader Idris were enclosed between 1805 and 1811; and at the north-eastern extremity of the county the abortive project of 1778 was brought to fruition in 1810; but powerful local interests defeated a proposal for enclosure on the Caernarvonshire border, and the whole of the mountainous interior was left untouched. The "friends of improvement" in Anglesey met at Beaumaris in 1809 to discuss plans for "the regulation and improvement of the waste lands."[1] Two years later the Act was passed under which the drainage of Malldraeth Marsh (some 3,000 acres) was at last completed, and between then and the end of the War three more Acts were added, affecting about 4,000 acres of land, mostly in the middle of the island.

Altogether, between 1790 and 1815, seventeen Acts were passed for Flintshire, thirteen for Denbighshire, ten for Caernarvonshire, seven for Merioneth, six for Montgomery, and five for Anglesey. These totals include a small proportion of mere amendments of earlier Acts; but to balance this, each of the six counties saw during these years a number of enclosures by private agreement, of which, in the absence of official records, it is impossible to offer even the roughest statistics.

During the generation between Waterloo and the General Enclosure Act of 1845 the movement slackened off. No further Acts were passed relating to Anglesey or Merioneth. In Caernarvonshire the Creuddyn peninsula was added. Flintshire had hardly any waste lands left, but one small enclosure was made in 1826. The south-western portion of Montgomeryshire, including the head-waters of the Severn, was enclosed in 1816; the Long Mountain (east of the Severn, along the Shropshire border) in 1821; and there was another minor Act ten years later. For Denbighshire five Acts were passed, and enclosure was extended in the opening years of Queen Victoria's reign to the Ceiriog

[1] *N. W. Gaz.*, Oct. 26, 1809.

valley, the borders of Montgomeryshire, and—at the opposite end—to the upper waters of the Elwy.[1] By this time the proportion of common and waste lands in Anglesey had been reduced, since 1795, from one thirty-sixth to one sixtieth, in Caernarvonshire from a third to an eighth, in Flintshire from a quarter to one twenty-third, and in Montgomeryshire from half to an eighth ; but Merioneth had only brought its proportion down from half to a third.[2]

A land-valuer told the Select Committee on Inclosures in 1844 that there was still much to be done in North Wales : the higher hilltops, where sheep were still depastured, should, he thought, be enclosed and cultivated : this, too, at a time when tillage was receding even in the valleys ![3] But although enclosure, on a smaller scale and by different methods, has never wholly ceased, it may safely be said that the movement had done its work, for good or ill, before the Repeal of the Corn Laws. It remains to consider the methods by which it was carried out, and to estimate its effect on the social and economic life of North Wales.

The frequent notices about enclosures, pending or in progress, which are scattered through the pages of the local press from about 1775 onwards, enable us to reconstruct the usual course of procedure.[4] The first step was the calling of a meeting of gentry, clergy, and freeholders, to discuss the question of applying for a Private Act. The meeting was usually summoned, on behalf of the promoters, by a local solicitor, to whom it was proposed to entrust the legal formalities of application. The interested parties were not always able to agree on the scope of the projected measure or even on its general advisability. Not infre-

---

[1] For details *see* my article in *Bull. of Board of Celtic Studies*, III, iii (1926).
[2] *Report on Land*, 1896, App., pp. 214–17.
[3] *Parl. Pap.*, 1844, V, pp. 371–9.
[4] The earliest notice I have seen is one in the *Chester Chronicle* announcing a meeting of the Hanmer Enclosure Commissioners for July 13, 1775. From about 1796 they become a regular feature.

quently meetings were held year after year before the application was finally agreed upon : sometimes the whole project was abandoned at this stage.[1] To convince the House of Commons, the applicants had to show that the owners of a definite proportion (usually three-fourths or four-fifths) of the acreage or value of the lands concerned had given their consent, and the procuring of these "consents" was often a costly business. In one enclosure a lawyer was paid £100 by the promoters for this service.[2] If agreement was reached, a draft bill was drawn up by the solicitor, discussed at further meetings, and then entrusted to the local Member for introduction in the next session of Parliament. Under the terms of a Standing Order of the House of Commons in 1774, due notice of application for an Enclosure Act had to be given. In addition to notices in the Church porch, such announcements were usually made, for North Wales, in the *Shrewsbury Chronicle*, the *Salopian Journal*, the *Chester Chronicle*, and the *Chester Courant*, until the foundation of the *North Wales Gazette* in 1808 and its successor the *North Wales Chronicle* in 1827.

The scene of activities was now transferred to the House of Commons. The Bill was not likely to meet with serious opposition there. The prevailing economic theories, and the natural readiness of a body of landowners to do each other neighbourly services, generally ensured a smooth passage. Occasionally, it is true, some technical flaw in the Bill would hold up progress and necessitate a re-introduction the following session ; sometimes, too, the local opponents of the measure were able to get up a petition backed by signatures of sufficient weight to

---

[1] E.g., Llandisilio and Llaneilian enclosure (Anglesey) : attempt at enclosure (of Llandisilio) by consent, Aug. 11, 1809 ; meetings held to promote Act, Sept. 8, 1812, Aug. 25, 1813 ; Act not passed till July 17, 1814. Cerrig y drudion : meeting held, Jan. 27, 1808, but no enclosure till 1863. Trawsfynydd : draft bill Dec. 2, 1813 ; protest on Dec. 8 by eleven freeholders including W. G. Oakley, Tan y bwlch, Sir Watkin Williams Wynn, and Sir Thomas Mostyn ; project dropped (*N. W. Gaz.*).

[2] Williams : *Records of Denbigh*, p. 156 ; *cf.* Hammond, J. L. and B. : *The Village Labourer* (1919), p. 49.

procure its rejection.[1] But in general this stage in proceedings was got through with almost indecent haste ; provided the requisite "consents" could be shown, the rest of the process was automatic. The interval between the drawing up of the draft Bill and the first sitting of the Commissioners was not often more than three to six months;[2] it was after this that the law's delays began in earnest.

The commissioners who were to carry out the enclosure were usually named in the Act. This means that their names had been agreed upon in the draft Bill, and that they were persons on whose judgment the promoters of the enclosure felt they could safely rely. In the earliest Enclosure Acts for our district, the commissioners were chosen, as a rule, from among the gentry and clergy of the neighbourhood, who presumably acted without fee ;[3] sometimes an arbitrator or a local committee was appointed to act in case the commissioners should disagree.[4] But as procedure became stereotyped, and especially after the consolidating Act of 1801, genuine efforts were made to prevent the possibility of adjudication by interested parties. It became customary to appoint professional men as paid commissioners, and they were made to take an oath of impartiality, and forbidden to purchase any part of the lands in question till five years after the award. From the commissioners the only appeal was to Quarter Sessions, that is, to the principal landed gentry of the shire. How far this "professionalizing" of enclosure succeeded in promoting fairness, speed and economy can best be judged, first by considering some of the commissioners who most frequently acted in North Wales, and then by looking into the actual working of a few sample Acts.

[1] E.g., petition for enclosure of waste lands of Wrexham parish presented by Mr. W. Wynn and Mr. Griffith, Feb., 1819 ; counter-petition referred to Committee, May ; Bill rejected, June (*Shrewsbury Chron.*, Feb. 5, May 7, June 18, 1819). *Cf.* notices of unsuccessful petitions against Llanaber and Caereinion Iscoed Bills, 1810, in *Imperial and County Register* (1810), North Wales, p. 7.

[2] E.g., Henllan enclosure : draft bill read Feb. 22, 1802 ; Commissioner begins sitting June 29, 1802 (*Chester Chron.*). Llangefni enclosure : draft bill read Jan. 6, 1812 ; Commissioners begin sitting Aug. 29, 1812 (*N. W. Gaz.*).

[3] E.g., Pool and Guilsfield, 1761 (*Mont. Coll.*, XII, p. 269).

[4] E.g., Kerry, 1797 ; Caereinion Uwchcoed, 1815 (*ibid.*, pp. 272–3, 277).

Walter Jones, of Cefn Rûg, near Corwen, a Commissioner of Militia, clerk to an Agricultural Society, trustee of Barmouth Harbour, and engaged in many public activities of a similar character, acted as commissioner under at least one Act for Anglesey, four for Caernarvonshire, two for Denbighshire and two for Merioneth, all between 1806 and his death in 1819. On two occasions he is known to have declined to act. By profession he was agent to Sir Robert Williames Vaughan, owner of a large estate in Merioneth, and one of the chief beneficiaries under the Llanaber enclosure, for which Jones served as commissioner.[1] John Maughan, of Luton, Bedfordshire, and subsequently of Oswestry, was commissioner under two Acts in Anglesey, and four in Denbighshire. He described himself before the Committee on Agriculture in 1821 as "engaged in the superintendence of property in Wales, in Cheshire, Warwickshire and Worcestershire," and he appears also to have had property near Holywell. Josiah Boydell, commissioner under two Acts in Flintshire, two in Merioneth, and one in Denbighshire, is described variously as of Cilhendre, Salop, and of Rossett, Denbighshire ; he acted as agent to estates in both counties, and his family had long served the Glynnes of Hawarden in this capacity. Incidently he was a nephew of the famous engraver Alderman John Boydell, and joint publisher of some of his works. Thomas Colley, of Cefngwifed, "best known . . . from his work in connection with the inclosure of waste lands . . . which engaged most of his time during the last twelve years of his life" (1800–1812), was agent to the Blayneys of Gregynog, Montgomeryshire, in which county most, if not all, of his work as Commissioner was carried on. Benjamin Wyatt, commissioner under at least two local Acts and referee in several private agreements as well, was an architect, clerk to a number of turnpike trusts and an Agricultural Society, and agent to Lord Penrhyn. John Matthews of Mold (later of Llanidloes and Aberystwyth) was one of the most successful land surveyors of his day in North Wales. Although an ardent pioneer of Methodism he won his way so completely into the confidence of the gentry—even of staunch Tory and Anglican houses like those of Wynn of Gwydir, Lloyd of Pengwern and Clough of

[1] 37 Geo. III, cap. 50 ; 50 Geo. III, cap. 56.

Bathafarn—by his skill in mapping their estates and in reporting on waste lands, that he was frequently called in as surveyor, and occasionally as commissioner, under Enclosure Acts.[1] Valentine Vickers, a Shropshire man, Robert Williams, of Llandegai, and Richard Jebb, of Oswestry, who served respectively under four, three and two Acts, are all described as land agents or surveyors.[2]

These were the principal commissioners who acted in North Wales. We are left with the conclusion that they were generally men of wide professional experience, but that their connection with the owners of large estates (for a small proprietor would hardly need the services of an agent) was too close to fit them for the delicate task of adjusting the claims of the big man and the small man in the allocation of commons and wastes. It was more a question of unconscious bias than of deliberate sharp practice, though there are occasional indications even of this. For example, in the year after the Hope Enclosure Act was passed, lands in the area to be enclosed were leased by Josiah Boydell and his fellow commissioners to another Boydell: "this, I say, hath an ill savour." Far more questionable, however, were the dealings of Richard Ellis, of Pwllheli, who served under four Acts, all in Caernarvonshire. A member of a firm of solicitors, he held various maritime offices such as Commissioner of Customs and Principal Coast Surveyor; he also farmed on his own account. In 1833 he was called as a witness before the Royal Commission on Municipal Corporations, and the Report describes him (somewhat sweepingly) as "ignorant of the nature of titles [and] of all laws." In two enclosures where Ellis had served—at Nevin and Pwllheli—no formal

[1] The name of John Matthews appears at least ten times as commissioner in Enclosure Acts for North Wales; but it is not always the same John Matthews. The Amlwch MSS. at Bangor contain the diaries of John Matthews of Mold for 1812–37 (nos. 5–22, 83–99), two volumes of his letters (3–4), his ledger of surveying accounts (23), and many of his maps (24–64). They all throw an interesting light on his surveying activities, but they also show that he sometimes worked as surveyor for another enclosure commissioner of the same name, about whom I have found nothing beyond the fact that he lived at Plas yn Llysfaen. (*See Chester Chron.*, Feb. 1807, *cf.* Dec. 1, 1809.)

[2] For references to this section *see* my article in *Bull. of Celtic Studies*, cited above.

award had been made and no accounts passed in 1833, though the Acts passed twenty-one years earlier had stipulated for an award within ten years. In one case he excused himself by saying (only too truly) that he had known instances where the award had been delayed for an even longer period ; in the other he tried to deny that he had been a commissioner at all. By other witnesses he was flatly accused of illegally feathering his own nest.[1]

There is happily no reason to believe that such dealings as these were at all common ; but that the commissioners had other interests to serve besides those of pure agrarian justice can hardly be denied. Even apart from any question of class bias, the commissioner had his fees to think of. He was paid, as a rule, two guineas (in addition to travelling expenses) for each day during which he was attending upon, or travelling to and from, enclosure business. The temptation to a policy of " ca' canny" in order to "make the job last" must have been almost as strong—if the excuse was less cogent—to the enclosure commissioner as to the modern bricklayer. Frequently the Act laid down that an award must be made within ten years ; but there seems to have been no means of enforcing compliance. There were one or two enclosures where the whole business was completed within twelve months, and perhaps half-a-dozen where the commissioners made their award in less than two years after the first sitting. But at the other end of the scale we have (in addition to the examples quoted above) Morfa Dinas Dinlle Enclosure, where the process took twenty-three years ; Llandanwg, where the final statement of accounts was not rendered till nineteen years after the first sitting ; and many instances where the total period amounted to fourteen years and upwards. Sometimes, of course, the situation was complicated by the necessity of overcoming local obstruction or of obtaining a fresh Act to remedy some flaw in the original measure ;[2] and the fact that a

[1] My friend Mr. David Thomas, who has examined the Custom house correspondence at Caernarvon, tells me that Ellis was accused of neglecting his official duties for his enclosure work and his farm ; in the subsequent enquiry, however, he "came off very well."

[2] E.g., Rhoshirwaun : first meeting, 1802 ; lapse between 1806 and 1810 owing to opposition of cottagers ; final award 1814. Llanrwst : first Act 1812, second 1821.

popular commissioner might have half-a-dozen enclosures on his hands at once did not make for speed.

Every delay meant an increase in costs. In addition to the commissioners' fees there would usually be expenditure on clerk, surveyors (paid as a rule by the acre, with a lump sum for a "fair plan on vellum"), a banker or treasurer, and possibly an assistant commissioner to watch the interests of the Crown.[1] In the matter of these minor officials, practice varied from one Act to another. When the necessary appointments had been made, the first task was to determine the boundaries of the manor, township or parish in question, and of the common lands it contained, with appropriate legal and surveying fees when disputes arose. When the area of land to be enclosed had been determined, it was all vested in the commissioners till the award should be made. Then came the hearing of claims on the part of those who desired to participate in the re-allotment, followed by objections and counter-objections. As a rule, claims had to be entered in writing, with plans when necessary, and the cost of the surveying and legal advice fell upon the claimant. Attempts were sometimes made to cut down both time and expenses at this stage in proceedings by agreeing to some general principle in the presentation of claims. In the Kerry Enclosure (1797) it was suggested that, to avoid lawsuits, all pretensions to exclusive rights of pasture should be dropped ; freeholders with common rights in the townships where their tenements lay should claim in proportion to the size of their holdings, and those whose claims lay outside in proportion to the number of cattle commonly depastured by them.[2]

In spite of all such efforts, the determination of claims was of necessity a long and costly business, often dragging through several years. When at last it had been settled, the commissioner had to decide (usually in consultation with the claimants) on what principle the ultimate division should be conducted ; to draw up schemes for roads, embankments and other public works, to hear objections to them, and to receive tenders for their construction ; and finally to take appropriate measures for meeting all expenses. For this there

[1] *See*, e.g., Llangefni Act, 52 Geo. III, cap. 169.
[2] *Salop. Journ.*, Oct. 22, 1797.

were two alternative methods : sometimes portions of the land under survey were sold, from time to time, to meet the costs as they arose ; sometimes graduated assessments were levied on all who were due to receive allotments and in default of payment their shares were disposed of by auction. In the draining of Saltney Marsh, expenses were met by the sale of annuities, but this was by special arrangement between the commissioners and the River Dee Company.[1]

Last of all came the reading of the award. Even at this stage objections might be raised, and this would necessitate fresh hearings, further legal advice, new surveys, and a general re-allotment. In the Nevin Enclosure the Crown and other parties objected to the allotments made on their behalf in December, 1814, and new plans were drawn up and laid open for inspection. Then in May, 1815, came counter-claims from cottagers who had built on the waste. In the following August a meeting was held to announce the "Final settlement"; notwithstanding which, further objections were heard in May, 1816, a draft award was prepared in March, 1817, and finally four years later the commissioners summoned a special meeting to "read and execute their award"; this seems to have been really the end.[2] When the award had been made, there still remained a few loose ends to pick up. The allotments of those who had not paid their assessments must be sold ; where the King was lord of the manor he usually directed that the same course should be taken with the Crown allotments ; where there were embankments and other works requiring constant attention, surveyors or engineers must be appointed.

We can hardly wonder at the constant complaints of the costliness of enclosure, even though we may suspect exaggeration in the contemporary charge that allotments sometimes cost thirty per cent more than the fee simple of the land was worth. "If the present rage for enclosing can be deemed a sort of fashionable delirium," wrote Gwallter Mechain (a warm sympathizer with the movement) in 1810, "these expenses are drugs that must act as powerful

[1] *Chester Chron.*, 1779–80, *passim.*
[2] *N. W. Gaz.*, Dec. 22, 1814, May 8, Aug. 3, 1815, May 16, 1816, Sept. 27, 1821.

correctives."[1] It is true that we have record of one enclosure (at Rhayader in Radnorshire) where the total expenses fell short of £1,000, while the sale of allot-ments brought in nearly £1,250. The chief items were as follows :—

	£	s.	d.
Act	.. 337	5	6
Solicitor	.. 84	14	10
Commissioner	.. 186	17	0
Clerk	.. 55	2	6
Stationery, etc.	.. 22	1	0
Printing, etc.	.. 15	3	3
Fencing, roads, etc.	.. 68	2	1

Here, however, the job was completed in record time—within twelve months of the first sitting of the commis-sioners. To estimate the cost of enclosures which dragged on through a whole generation we must multiply many of these items by twenty or thirty.[2]

We now come to the real crux of the matter—the principle on which the allotments themselves were made. First came the claim of the lord of the manor as owner of the soil ; this was generally recognized as a first call on the ·estate, and the proportion allotted varied from one-twentieth to one-fourteenth. This did not necessarily extinguish all his claims in the soil. Davies complains that a host of semi-feudal rights remained to him, including the ownership of coal and metallic ores under all allotments of former waste land. In the Cedewain and Kerry Enclosures, he points out, the lord's allotment was increased to one-thirteenth on condition of his relinquishing these mineral rights—an illusory concession, since men were about as likely to work minerals there as to fish for lobster on Plynlimon.[3] Where minerals were prolific, the lord's

---

[1] Letters in *Shrewsbury Chron.*, Aug. 8, Sept. 14, 1827 ; *cf.* answer to such charges by a land surveyor in *N. W. Gaz.*, May 17, 1810 ; Davies, p. 272.

[2] *Shrewsbury Chron.*, Aug. 14, Oct. 23, 1829. The items as recorded here only add up to £769 6s. 2d., but the total is given as £914 4s. 2d., leaving nearly £145 unaccounted for.

[3] *General View*, p. 267.

rights in them, as a rule, were specifically reserved in the Act, and on one occasion at least an amending Act was rushed through to remedy the omission of this clause.[1]

The tithe-owners had next to be considered. Little or no tithe had been paid on the common pastures, but the impropriator now claimed his share in the added value created by enclosure. Sometimes this claim was extinguished by an allotment of land proportional to the amount of tithe which could justly be claimed; sometimes the Act provided that the newly-enclosed lands should go free for seven years or so, and then pay their full quota to the tithe-owner. The whole question was a subject of much heart-burning and not infrequent litigation; for it was felt that parsons and lay rectors, more than all the other beneficiaries of enclosure, were reaping where they had not sown.[2]

Finally there came the general mass of proprietors— including, of course, both lord of the manor and tithe-owner in their capacity of ordinary landowners. The normal method was to distribute allotments in proportion to the incidence of the land-tax on the respective claimants.[3] The first expense of fencing was charged, in most enclosures, on the fund created by assessments or sales, but of course the new owner was responsible for all subsequent costs. Sometimes, when a large area of mountain common was enclosed, only a portion of it was actually fenced off, the rest being left open as limited sheep-walks to the several proprietors.[4] On the enclosed lands it was frequently enjoined by the Act that no sheep should be kept for seven years, unless effectual measures were taken to prevent them from straying on to other allotments.[5]

How did the small landowner fare under these conditions? He might, in the first place, find himself shut out by the

[1] Minera (Palmer: *Wrexham*, p. 56).
[2] Bowen: *The Great Enclosures of Common Lands in Wales*, pp. 26–8, 38–9; *N. W. Gaz.*, March 5, 1812; *Shrewsbury Chron.*, Aug. 8, 1823.
[3] *Report on Land*, 1896, p. 330.
[4] E.g., Kerry, 1797 (Lewis: *Top. Dict.*, 1833, *sub loc.*); cf. *Parl. Pap.*, 1844, V, pp. 371–9. In the Llanaber Act (50 Geo. III, cap. 56) it was provided that any group of proprietors who so desired might have a common pasture allotted to them in place of individual shares.
[5] E.g., Llanddeiniolen Act (46 Geo. III, cap. 29).

fact that he was not assessed to the land-tax. The expensiveness of the services of lawyers and surveyors, again, placed him at a disadvantage in pressing his claims, as they had debarred him from an effective hearing when the scheme was first mooted. Even if he got a fair allotment, the burden of the assessments, and the subsequent cost of upkeep, might well outweigh the advantage of exchanging vague rights of common for a compact piece of land in exclusive ownership. Hence it is not surprising that many of the smaller proprietors sold their allotments for ready cash, and—having no longer the means of grazing their animals—went out of farming altogether.[1]

Far worse was the lot of the man who could not strictly be called a landowner at all : the cottager who had "encroached" (often with the connivance or encouragement of parochial authorities) on the common land. In strict law he had no claim to an allotment, or, if he had, it was out of his power to press it save by lawless methods of obstruction. In justice to the legislators of the time it must be observed that most Enclosure Acts, from the beginning of the nineteenth century, contained provisions for dealing with this defenceless class. Squatters who had been in occupation of their cottages and holdings for twenty years before the passing of the Act were to be allowed to retain them ; if they had encroached subsequently, they were to have the option of buying their encroachments. To indemnify those who had enjoyed customary rights of gathering turf, furze, or brushwood on the commons, of watering their cattle there or quarrying stones, provision was made in several Acts for the setting aside of a public turbary,[2] quarry,[3] or watering ground[4] in a convenient position ; others merely gave vague injunctions to the commissioners that compensation (in money or otherwise) should be found for cottagers who were injured by the enclosure.[5]

How did these provisions work out in practice ? That the cottagers felt themselves aggrieved is clear from many

[1] Davies, pp. 266–7 ; *Report on Land*, 1896, pp. 384 ff., 589 ff.

[2] E.g., Llangefni, Llan y mynech, Caereinion Uwchcoed.

[3] E.g., Llanddeiniolen, Minera, Llangefni, Llan y mynech, Caereinion Uwchcoed.

[4] E.g., Minera, Llan y mynech, Ystrad Marchell.

[5] E.g., Cedewain, Kerry, Teirtref, Caereinion Iscoed, Caereinion Uwchcoed.

instances. They were too ignorant to understand the legal position and too poor to avail themselves of legal advice ; and when they found themselves evicted from cottages they had built with their own hands, or patches of land they had laborious.y cleared for crops in their spare time, they failed to appreciate the subtle distinction which made these evictions meritorious while the trapping of a hare might be punished with death. Sometimes they even went on building *cabanau un nos* after the Act had been passed, hoping —in spite of warnings they could not read in newspapers they could not buy—that it was still not too late to secure themselves behind a *fait accompli*.[1] The commissioners had rarely gone far with their duties before the question of the squatters cropped up. The Penmorfa Enclosure Act was passed in 1812 ; in 1814 the commissioners were selling encroachments on the waste to defray their expenses. The Llanbedrog Commissioners, two years after the passing of the Act, were considering proposals made by cottagers and others for purchasing parcels of common and waste land already enclosed. In 1815—three years after their sittings began—the commissioners for the Nevin Enclosure met to investigate the claims of some who declared they had built on the wastes of Clynnog and Llanllyfni, twenty years before the Act was passed, cottages which were now being awarded to others. The Forden Enclosure Act (1821) described in a schedule a number of cottages adjacent to the common which were to be allotted to the lords of the manor —the Archdeacon of Salop and Panton Corbett, Esquire— in exchange for their rights in the soil of the commons.[2]

"There be manie thousand Cottagers in england," wrote the author of the Tudor *Discourse of the Commonweal,*

> which, haveing no landes to live of their oune but their handie labours and some refreshinge uppon the said commons, yf they weare sodenly thrust out from that commoditie might make a great tumult and discord in the comon wealth.[3]

[1] *See,* e.g., notices to cottagers by Cedewain commissioners, in *Salop. Journ.,* Oct. 10, 1798.
[2] *N. W. Gaz.,* Feb. 3, 1814, March 1, 1810, May 18, 1815 ; Bowen : *op. cit.,* p. 37.
[3] Ed. Elizabeth Lamond, 1893, pp. 49–50.

The words might have been written with equal truth of Wales, and especially of Snowdonia, two centuries later, But the Snowdonian squires were not versed in Tudor lore. In 1808 they met at Caernarvon and passed a resolution full of those exalted sentiments of which such liberal use had been made in obstructing the claims of the Crown. They would oppose to the utmost of their power all manner of "encroachments"; they would "enforce the different enclosure acts which have lately been obtained, the carrying into effect of which has in many cases been violently opposed"; they pledged themselves "to bring to justice all those who shall be guilty of such . . . attacks on the fair and indisputable rights of the freeholders of the county."[1] Already there had been a deadlock over one enclosure, and worse was to follow.

On the Crown common of Rhoshirwaun, in Lleyn, scores of fishermen had "squatted," and when an Act was passed in 1802 for its enclosure and allotment, their claims to ownership had to be investigated.   At the second meeting of the commissioners (August 2, 1802) plans were submitted "for the relief of cottagers whose length of possession does not entitle them to property in the common or allotments under the Act."   Whatever these plans were, they evidently did not satisfy the cottagers, who for some time successfully resisted the execution of the Act.   In 1806 it was resolved that all encroachments made within twenty years before the Act should be sold, the encroachers to have the first option of purchase ; those who possessed encroachments of more than twenty years' standing were to prove their claims before the commissioners on the day before the sale.   Even after this, no progress seems to have been made with the enclosure till the beginning of 1810, and the final award was not given till 1814.[2]

In the meanwhile, trouble had arisen in another quarter. The parish of Llanddeiniolen stretches south-eastward from near the Strait, between Bangor and Caernarvon, to the eastern shore of Llyn Padarn and the northern slopes of Elidir Fawr.   It is part of the old Crown manor of Dinorwic, which William III had alienated—subject to a nominal

---

[1] *N. W. Gaz.*, Sept. 8, 1808.

[2] *Chester Chron.*, July 30, 1802, Aug. 8, 1806 ; *N. W. Gaz.*, Dec. 28, 1809, June 23, 1814 ; Bowen : *op. cit.*, pp. 42–3.

rent and other reservations—to a Hampshire gentleman who served as commissioner of the Salt Office, and whose descendant, Thomas Assheton Smith, was now lord of the manor.[1] The southern part of the parish consisted in rocky wastes, valueless except to groups of obscure quarrymen who had been allowed to "dig" for slates there on consideration of a small acknowledgment to the lord. But when, in the last decade of the eighteenth century, the high profits of the slate industry induced the lord to start working his own slates,[2] he was naturally anxious to secure his title to the manorial wastes. In 1806 he obtained an Act for the enclosure of the parish, and a second, to "amend and explain" it, was passed in 1808. The lord's rights to exploit the minerals of the waste (save only those which were the special preserve of the Crown), and to the ownership of all existing shafts and machinery, were expressly reserved.[3] Numbers of quarrymen who had built cottages or opened little quarries on the common thus found their living threatened. In August, 1809, the claims of these cottagers to compensation were being "considered" by the commissioners. At the beginning of the next month some of them, growing impatient of delay, "met on the common in Llanddeiniolen and continued together in a riotous and tumultuous manner after the Riot Act had been read, and committed several violent assaults." A reward of five guineas was offered for information leading to their arrest. Among the ringleaders were William Evan Shôn Foulk, Foulk Evan Shôn Foulk, and Ellis Evan Shôn Foulk, quarrymen, Richard Jones, son of Mary Werglodd Goch, Margaret Owen, wife of Rowland David, and Margaret Hughes, wife of David John Pryse. By the end of the month all but three were in Caernarvon gaol, but they were released, it appears, under the comprehensive amnesty by which the Jubilee of George III was celebrated shortly

[1] Pennant : *Tours*, III, p. 21 ; *Report on Land*, 1896, App., p. 447.
[2] *Infra*, chap. VI.
[3] But some quarries on the waste lands of Llanddeiniolen, advertised in *N. W. Gaz.*, May 28, 1812, are described as "held under the Crown."

afterwards. Resistance, at any rate, was at an end, and the execution of the Act went forward.[1]

There was further rioting in connection with the Llanaelhaiarn enclosure, as a result of which two men were sentenced to death, though for one at least the sentence was commuted to penal servitude.[2] But Caernarvonshire provides one instance of successful resistance to an enclosure project. Once more quarrymen were the culprits—this time from the Tryfan and Cilgwyn quarries, south of Caernarvon ; and the dispute was about extensive barren wastes in the parishes of Llanwnda and Llandwrog, within the domain of the Crown. About the time of the Llanddeiniolen Enclosure Act the quarrymen, encouraged by their Parish Vestries, were assembling by moonlight after their day's work to level the ground, clear away boulders, and build themselves cottages with gardens. By 1826 a straggling community of 140 houses and three chapels—the village of Rhostryfan—had grown up on the common. About 700 persons were thus provided with rent-free dwellings and enabled to keep a garden and a cow—a great saving to the poor rates. But Lord Newborough and the neighbouring proprietors determined to put a stop to these illegal encroachments on the customary sheepwalks of the freeholders. A formal enclosure had been considered in 1813, and in October, 1826, they resolved to apply for an Act. In the meanwhile they forced matters to an issue by summoning as trespassers all who cut peat on the commons, and demanding rent from the occupiers of cottages—under cover, it seems, of a recent statute[3] which permitted ejectment even before an enclosure award had been made. The squatters made ready to resist, by violence if necessary.

Their cause was taken up by an influential group of Welshmen in London, and one local proprietor—Colonel

---

[1] *N. W. Gaz.*, July 27, Sept. 28, 1809. Mr. R. T. Jenkins has drawn my attention to a graphic but somewhat confused account of these events (based on local tradition) in Jones, J. O. : *Cofiant a Gweithiau Robert Ellis, Ysgoldy* (Caernarfon, 1883), pp. 4–6, 8, from which it appears that Ellis Evans (or Ellis Evan Shôn Foulk), who was Robert Ellis' father, fled to Merthyr—the contemporary Cave of Adullam—and returned home when the storm had blown over.

[2] *N. W. Gaz.*, April 22, 1813, and information from Mr. David Thomas.

[3] 1 Geo. IV (*see N. W. Gaz.*, April 6, 1826).

Hughes, afterwards Lord Dinorben—spoke up for them in Parliament. Thanks to these efforts, the Bill was modified to the extent of allowing compensation for any money spent in building houses on the common ; but this did not remove the real grievance. What had been spent was not money but labour, and the proposed palliative did nothing to compensate the squatter for the increased value which his toil had given to the land. "Whatsoever, then, he removes out of the state that Nature left it in, he hath mixed his labour with it, and joined to it something that is his own, and thereby makes it his property."[1] That was the case for the cottagers ; but as they were unable to meet their opponents with arguments from Locke, they had recourse to the cruder dialectic of laming any unfortunate sheep that were turned out on the common by the promoters of enclosure. More effective were the services of their educated friends in London, who contrived, in July, 1827, to get the Bill rejected root and branch. The villagers showed their gratitude by brewing a special cask of ale, which they sent for consumption at a triumphal dinner in London. But angry feelings in the neighbourhood did not die down for some time ; recriminations in the press, libel actions, and lawsuits against those who had tried to disturb the commoners, continued into the next year, and Lord Newborough, by a successful action at the local assizes, seems to have prevented further building on the commons. The big proprietors were careful to point out that their efforts had been purely disinterested : "if this was permitted to go on, we should soon be reduced to the miserable condition of the sister kingdom by being overrun with cottages built on common land by encroachment, and universal poverty would be the consequence."[2]

Here we see the cloven hoof of Malthusianism. It was doubtless by the same process of reasoning that the promoters of enclosure, and their agents the commissioners, justified to themselves the whittling down of even such

---

[1] Locke : *Two Treatises of Civil Government*, Bk. II, chap. V.
[2] *N. W. Gaz.*, Sept. 8, 1813, Oct. 19, Nov. 11, 1826, Feb. 1, April 26, June 7 and 21, 1827 ; *N. W. Chron.*, March 13, 1828 ; *Shrewsbury Chron.*, Jan. 27, March 23, April 27, June 1 and 29, July 13, Sept. 14, 1827 ; Carlisle : *Top. Dict.* under *Llanllyfni; Report on Land*, 1896, p. 592 ; *id.*, App., p. 186.

concessions as were made in the Acts to the "admitted, but vague, interests of the inhabitants . . . who were neither owners nor [in strict law] commoners." There were many leaders of Welsh opinion who, while they hated common rights, nevertheless thought no harm would come of setting aside a few acres to the poor—even those who could show no legal claim—as potato patches.[1] *Dominis aliter visum.* Sir Watkin Williams Wynn, whose services as a "spirited proprietor" have already come under our notice, was one of the chief opponents in 1800 of a Bill, backed by the powerful pleading of Wilberforce himself, for encouraging the planting of potatoes in waste grounds. Such a "violation of private property" (*sic !*) he believed to be "big with the greatest mischiefs."[2]

This theory, on the whole, prevailed. Here and there a little land was set apart for the cottagers ; under the Henllan Enclosure Act cottages were built on the waste lands at a cost of £450, and let out rent free to 22 poor persons ;[3] but these were rare concessions. Where public turbaries or quarries were provided for in the Act, it was frequently complained that the allotments actually made were grossly inadequate and inconveniently placed. In the Nevin Enclosure some four or five hundred acres were earmarked as a turbary for those who had relied on the commons for their supplies of fuel ; but the ground in question was claimed as belonging to a contiguous estate, and twenty years later the poor of Nevin were shivering for want of peat.[4] In Llanddeiniolen less than a hundred acres (out of over three thousand) were allotted to the poor in the form of two small fuel grounds, and even these were later encroached upon by the neighbouring owners till they vanished altogether. Without an exhaustive survey of all the enclosure awards, it is impossible to generalize about the extent to which the Acts were complied with in this respect ; one can only say that at the present time the shares of "the poor" in enclosed parishes are generally hard to find.[5] Not till after the Act of 1845 was any serious effort made to

---

[1] E.g., *N. W. Gaz.*, May 17, 1810, Dec. 31, 1812.
[2] *Chester Chron.*, March 28, 1800.
[3] Fullarton's *Parl. Gaz,.* II, p. 316.
[4] *N. W. Gaz.*, Oct. 6, 1814, Nov. 23, 1815 ; *M.C.R.*, 1837–38, XXX, pp. 326–7, XXXV, p. 346.
[5] *Report on Land*, 1896, pp. 214–18.

provide public recreation grounds out of the enclosed lands,[1] and only two cases have been noted where free schools were endowed out of the proceeds of enclosure.[2]

A word must be said about the municipal commons of North Wales. They present a somewhat peculiar problem because of the large number of tiny boroughs, first created for purely military or political purposes, where the burgesses were too poor to resist any encroachments on their claims or even too ignorant to understand what claims they had. Most of these boroughs had commons of some sort, but legal ownership was even more uncertain here than on the mountain sheep-runs. Sometimes the soil was the property of the lord of the manor, the burgesses enjoying only rights of common on the surface ; sometimes the fee simple was vested in the corporation. The rights of common themselves were equally indeterminate : in some boroughs only freemen could use them, all "strange" beasts being driven off or impounded by corporation officials ; in others they were open to all inhabitants, with or without a fee to the corporation.

The fate of these municipal commons engaged the attention of the Municipal Corporations Commissioners in that era of feverish "tidying-up" which followed the passing of the Reform Bill. A few corporations had retained their rights intact and exercised them with vigilance. At Machynlleth, though the soil belonged to the lord of the manor, the body of burgesses exercised common rights over two pieces of land. One they used as a racecourse ; on the other they grazed their cattle in common, and for the last ten years all "strangers" had been rigidly excluded.[3] The common wood of the burgesses of Holt (in Denbighshire)—long cleared of trees and used as a borough pasture—shrank under continuous encroachment until the Corporation awoke to its rights at the beginning of the nineteenth century. A proposal for complete enclosure in 1815 came to nothing, but in 1846, after a few acres had been sold and a due proportion allotted to the Crown as lord of the manor,

---

[1] *Id.*, App., pp. 212–3 ; Bowen : *op. cit.*, p. 43.
[2] Bettws Abergele, and Newchapel (Mont.) ; *see* Lewis : *Top. Dict.* under these headings.
[3] *M.C.R.* (1837–38, XXXV), p. 305.

the remainder was divided between the existing burgesses in 64 several allotments.[1]

Montgomeryshire provides two examples of amicable adjustment of rights between the Corporation and the lord of the manor : at Welshpool under a Private Act of 1761, and at Montgomery by a voluntary agreement of 1782. In both places, after the rights of the lord (the Earl of Powis) had been bought out, the burgesses were left with a piece of land in exclusive property. At Welshpool this was let out at rents which went to the relief of the poor and the upkeep of public buildings ; at Montgomery only a third was used for this purpose, the remainder being kept as a common pasture for the burgesses.[2] Denbigh Green—long the cause of expensive litigation—was brought under an Enclosure Act in 1802. The allotments of the Crown, as lord of the manor, were sold as usual ; but difficulties arose when the Corporation proposed to deal with its own share after the manner of Welshpool. Each individual burgess, they were advised, was entitled to his separate portion of the spoils in hard cash ; to put enclosed property to communal uses was in flat opposition to the prevailing legal theories. By the time of the Municipal Corporations Commission, however, the lands were being used as the borough fathers desired.[3] The Corporation of Ruthin, which had been in the habit of spending the proceeds of enclosed borough lands in annual junketings, was fired to emulate the example of Denbigh ; it also received allotments under the Llanfwrog Act of 1800.[4] At Caernarvon less tenderness was shown for the interests of the burgesses. In 1781 the Corporation aroused great resentment by enclosing (apparently on its own authority) a marsh hitherto used as a pasture and watering ground for cattle by occupiers of land in the borough, and letting it out for rent.[5]

[1] Palmer, A. N. : "History of Holt" (*Arch. Camb.*, 1908, pp. 169–72).

[2] *Mont. Coll.*, XIII, pp. 276–81, XV, pp. 318–19, XXXVI, pp. 53–78 ; M.C.R. (1837–38, XXXV), pp. 369–70.

[3] *Salop. Journ.*, April 8, 1795 ; *N. W. Gaz.*, Sept. 26, 1815 ; Williams : *Records of Denbigh*, p. 156 ; M.C.R. (1835, XXVI), pp. 593–5.

[4] *Arch. Camb.*, 1921, p. 442 ; M.C.R. (1835, XXVI), p. 778.

[5] *Chester Chron.*, March 30 1781.

We have dealt so far with instances where municipal rights were at least recognized ; but all too frequently enclosure commissioners simply ignored the existence of boroughs which happened to lie within their area. When the manor of Arustley was enclosed in 1816, the charter of Llanidloes mysteriously disappeared, and the burgesses, unable to prove their claims, lost their immemorial rights of common.[1] The Corporations of Nevin and Pwllheli, as we have already seen, were introduced to the blessings of enclosure by that egregious commissioner, Mr. Richard Ellis. However ignorant of the law Ellis may have been, he was well versed in the art of bluffing a corporation more ignorant than himself. Either he or his father induced the bailiffs of Nevin to sign away their claims on some three or four hundred acres of common land—used at large by all the inhabitants as a sheep run—under the impression that they were putting their hands to an indenture of apprenticeship ; at Pwllheli the corporation received, in exchange for lands worth about £500 a year, a few square yards of barren rock. Ellis told the Municipal Corporations Commissioners, first that the borough officials had raised no objections, then that their objections were invalid and had been overruled.[2] When the tiny borough of Newborough, in Anglesey, was enclosed in 1815, a hundred acres were allotted to "the poor"; but as the allottees could not pay their assessments it was directed that the land should be sold. And so the inhabitants got no compensation whatever for the loss of a rabbit warren which had brought in an annual rent of £23, a common on which (irrespective of tenure) they had enjoyed unlimited rights of pasturage and turbary, and the means of collecting *moresg* for the manufacture of ropes and matting—the only local industry.[3]

In the Enclosure Acts concerning Rhuddlan, Flint, and Caerwys, municipal rights were not so much as mentioned, although at Caerwys the burgesses were probably not mere

---

[1] *Mont. Coll.;* IV, pp. 415–96 ; XII, pp. 279–80.

[2] *M.C.R.* (1837–38, XXXV), pp. 326–8, 345. Gimlet Rock, which is supposed to have been allotted to the Corporation, was offered for sale by the Commissioners, except one small portion, in 1814 (*N. W. Gaz.*, March 3, 1814).

[3] *P. L. R.* (1835, XXVI), pp. 738–9 ; Carlisle : *Top. Dict.* ; *infra*, pp. 299–300.

commoners, but owners of the soil of the commons.[1] "The beggarly burgesses of Harlech," as a traveller politely calls them, felt as a grievance the loss by enclosure of their common rights in the adjacent marsh, failing to appreciate the argument that the "loss to a beggarly individual" might mean "a great accession of wealth to the Country."[2] The Corporation of Conway was more fortunate, for it jealously and successfully defended against an enclosure project of the 'twenties its two hundred acres of "fertile sandy loam," for the use of which it used to receive trifling rents from the commoners. "In such cases," as the Municipal Corporations Commissioners observe, "the loss to smaller farmers is considerable, and the expense enormous." Llanfyllin, a petty borough of Montgomeryshire, affords a rare instance of positively generous treatment. It seems to have had no common lands of its own, but in 1789 the lord and freeholders of the surrounding manor sold some of their waste lands, and devoted the proceeds to rebuilding the borough market house.[3]

Our picture would not be complete without some reference to the enclosures which were carried out by private agreement, without recourse to Parliament. Where a sufficient measure of unanimity could be secured, an umpire or arbitrator (frequently a man with experience as a Parliamentary Commissioner) was chosen to re-allot the lands ; his award, of course, lacked the binding force of law, but otherwise the usual procedure of Parliamentary enclosure was closely followed. Sometimes it was merely a matter of permission by the lord of the manor for the users of sheep-walks to fence off their customary "stints" without prejudice to his ultimate rights as owner of the soil, or for squatters to purchase their encroachments on the waste.[4] Of this kind of enclosure, naturally, but few records have survived.

What is the verdict of history upon the enclosure movement in North Wales ? We must remember, in the first

[1] *P.L.R.* (1835, XXVI), pp. 539, 611.
[2] Fenton : *Tours*, p. 105.
[3] Davies, pp. 255, 262 ; *M.C.R.* (1837–38, XXXV), pp. 20, 262.
[4] *See*, e.g., *Mont. Coll.*, XV, pp. 195–6 ; *Report on Land*, 1896 : Evidence, IV (C–7757), pp. 188–9.

place, that we are concerned, not with the general subject of the reclamation of waste and uncultivated lands, but with a particular method of creating and redistributing proprietary claims. It was primarily a question of ownership—a lawyers' question. Economists gave it their blessing because they believed that ownership of a certain kind promoted cultivation, but the effects of enclosure on tillage were secondary and derivative ; all that happened immediately was a change or a re-definition of ownership. "Enclosûre" might be merely a redistribution of lands already enclosed, and it was not necessarily followed by cultivation. We frequently meet with notices in the newspapers about lands "now built on and enclosed and *to be* divided under an Inclosure Act" ;[1] and Gwallter Mechain says of his own day that "thousands of enclosed acres have never been cultivated."[2] "We have been fully employed," writes a Denbighshire landowner in 1846, "in restoring enclosed farms that might be called waste, but which have been long enclosed."[3] The following is the unanimous conclusion of the Royal Commissioners—by no means a body of extremists—who investigated the Welsh land question in 1893–6 :—

> It would be idle to suppose that the main motive of the Welsh landowners who eagerly used the facilities given by Parliament was to extend the margin of cultivation. They saw clearly enough that the movement gave them the opportunity of acquiring the sheep-walks and pasture lands till then unenclosed as their own in severalty under the title of an Act of Parliament, while the prospect of costs gave the family solicitors of the Principality a sufficient inducement to use their best endeavours to secure the passing of an Inclosure Act wherever a waste was extensive enough to make the process appear profitable all round.[4]

The question for us then is : did this creation of private property "turn sand into gold " ? That it would do so was the belief, not merely of the big proprietors, but of

---

[1] E.g., *N. W. Gaz.*, Aug. 23, 1810 (Waunfawr) ; *cf.* Hasbach : *English Agricultural Labourer*, p. 58 *n*.
[2] Davies, p. 270. At Llanerful (Mont.), 4,000 acres allotted under an Act of 1815 were still used as unenclosed sheepwalks in 1833 (Lewis : *Top. Dict; P.L.R.*, 1834, XXX, p. 653a).
[3] *Report on Land*, 1896, pp. 440–1.
[4] *Id.*, p. 214.

many farmers and small owners who shared the general passion for improvement.[1] Undoubtedly the market value of landed property was enhanced by enclosure ; a glance at the announcements of sales of land in the local press is enough to convince us of that.[2] The gross assessments of land for income tax purposes in the six counties of North Wales increased between the Napoleonic War and the Repeal of the Corn Laws, on an average, to the extent of thirty per cent—almost twice the average for England and Wales as a whole. Anglesey came highest, with nearly seventy per cent. This was largely due to the Holyhead Road ; but it is noteworthy that in Merioneth, the most backward county in enclosure, the increase was only a little over twelve per cent.[3] But do these increases in market value necessarily mean a genuine advance in productivity ? In part they certainly do. There can be no doubt about the value of improvements which made it possible to grow crops on the once drowned lands of Traeth Mawr, to drain the marshes of Malldraeth, Dinas Dinlle, Saltney, and Towyn, to make better harbours at Rhuddlan and Pwllheli, or to bring under cultivation hilltops which had hitherto produced nothing but scraggy mutton and inferior wool. By means of embankments erected under Enclosure Acts, twelve hundred acres were reclaimed from the tides on the Flintshire coast and as many as three thousand near Pwllheli, and the farmers of Montgomeryshire were relieved from the periodic depredations of the Severn and the Vyrnwy.[4] The laying out of roads, again, was a regular part of the work of Enclosure Commissioners —as many as fifteen miles are said to have been constructed under a single Act in Denbighshire[5]—and these were a definite asset both to the farmer and to his customers. Even where enclosed land was still used for sheep-walks, there was clear gain in the limitation of the number of sheep to be depastured, and exclusive control gave a needed incentive to care and vigilance.

[1] E.g., *N. W. Gaz.*, Sept. 27, Oct. 4 and 18, 1810, April 25, Dec. 12, 1811.
[2] *Id.*, Jan. 5, Nov. 17, 1808, April 12, Aug. 2, 1810.
[3] *Infra*, p. 96 ; *Report on Land*, 1896, p. 371.
[4] Lewis : *Top. Dict.*, under *Montgomeryshire, Llanasa*, and *Pwllheli;* Cathrall : *History of North Wales*, II, p. 307.
[5] Lewis : *Top. Dict.*, under *Henllan*.

Yet, as we saw in the preceding chapter, the stimulus to production during the great European War—the zenith of the enclosure movement—was largely factitious, and there was a disastrous collapse when the stimulus was removed. Under war conditions money was sunk in the enclosure of lands that could not possibly repay the capital expenditure in peace time. Even while the movement was at its height, a Flintshire gentleman told Gwallter Mechain that he was beginning to regret the active part he had taken in promoting it ; the mania for growing crops on land enclosed from the common pasture, he declared, was becoming a positive hindrance to the breeding of sheep. Davies himself is much more critical of the movement in the pages he added to his survey in 1810 than in the original draft of 1799. Like Arthur Young, he found enclosure less idyllic in practice than it had seemed on paper.[1]

But the most serious criticism of enclosures comes from the side of the small holder and the cottager. The former found that his hopes of gain were dashed by extravagant costs which either stopped him from claiming his share at all, or else saddled him with a burden too heavy to be borne when the abnormal conditions had passed.[2] The Commissioners on the Poor Law in 1834 refer to a Montgomeryshire enclosure where a number of small farmers had obtained leases for lives on recently-enclosed lands, in hopes of fanciful profits. Burdened with rents which were calculated on the "improved" value of the land, they found themselves in bad years unable even to supply their own tables. As holders of property they could not apply for poor relief ; they were worse off than the very paupers.[3]

To the poor labourer the chief effects of enclosure were to reduce the number of cheap cottages at a time when population was increasing,[4] to restrict the supply of cheap fuel at a time when war taxation was making the price of coal prohibitive,[5] and to deprive him of his resources for a rainy day—a cow, a pig, or a potato patch—at a time

[1] Davies, pp. 270–1, and chap. XI, *passim*.
[2] *Id.*, pp. 266–7.
[3] *P.L.R.* (1834, XXIX), p. 187ᵃ.
[4] E.g., Forden (see below).
[5] *Infra*, pp. 199–201.

when unemployment was rife.[1] Small wonder that the poor rates went up. Not that any direct correspondence can be established between the increase of the rates and the progress of enclosures over the country at large : too many other factors come in to complicate the issue. But in glaring cases of local spoliation the effects were felt at once. At Newborough, for example, the poor could no longer obtain *moresg* for plaiting unless they paid ; many of them could not pay, and fell on the rates, which were doubled in the course of a few years. Even in Montgomeryshire, the Directors of the Forden House of Industry claimed that their institution had saved the parishes pounds in house rents which would otherwise have had to be paid for destitute cottagers ; in other words the poor who had lived, without expense to the community, in cottages now claimed by the lords of the manor had henceforth to be supported in a costly public institution.[2]

A Ffestiniog shepherd—so at least he signed himself—wrote to the *Shrewsbury Chronicle* in 1827 suggesting that before another Enclosure Act was passed for Wales, attempts should be made to discover the costs of enclosures already completed ; the extent to which the commissioners carried out the Acts in letter and in spirit ; how far cultivation had been improved, justice done to poor claimants, and the rights of the Crown recognized ; and whether sheep-walks were really improved by the process of parcelling out.[3] The modern inquirer will probably agree that these questions are pertinent ; perhaps he will also agree that such answers as can be supplied to them leave the case for the enclosure movement in North Wales "not proven."[4]

---

[1] *See* evidence of Vicar of Meifod in *P.L.R.* (1834, XXXII), p. 656ᵉ.
[2] *Supra.* p. 75 ; *infra*, pp. 389–91.
[3] Aug. 10, 1827.
[4] The Porth yr aur MSS. contain almost complete materials (surveys, petitions, minutes, correspondence, balance sheets, maps, etc.) for the following enclosures : Llanrûg and Llanbeblig, Nevin, Llanddeiniolen, Aberdaron and Rhoshirwaun, Morfa Dinas Dinlle, Llandanwg and Llanfihangel, Newborough, and the projects for Llanwnda and Llandwrog and for Llanllechid. When they have been sifted, it may be necessary to rewrite the whole history of Welsh enclosures, but a hasty examination did not bring to light any points in which they made necessary a modification of the conclusions presented here.

CHAPTER IV.
COMMUNICATIONS.

> The foot-path faintly marked, the horse-track wild,
> And formidable length of plashy lane,
> (Prized avenues ere others had been shaped
> Or easier links connecting place with place)
> Have vanished—swallowed up by stately roads
> Easy and bold, that penetrate the gloom
> Of Britain's farthest glens. The Earth has lent
> Her waters, Air her breezes ; and the sail
> Of traffic glides with ceaseless intercourse,
> Glistening along the low and woody dale ;
> Or, in its progress, on the lofty side
> Of some bare hill, with wonder kenned from far.
> —Wordsworth : *The Excursion* (1814), Book VIII.

A. ROADS.

When Arthur Young visited France in 1787, he found "circulation" stagnant upon excellent roads.[1] If he had visited North Wales at the same time he would have seen a fast-increasing traffic desperately trying to accommodate to its uses the "untracked heaths and narrow lanes"[2] which for centuries had been churned into mud by droves of cattle and trains of pack-animals ; twenty years earlier, indeed, the worst thing he had found to say about some of the roads of south-eastern England was that they forced him "to move as slow as in any unmended lane in *Wales.*"[3] The contrast is significant. France had a military monarchy strong enough to plan its communications nationally, and oppressive enough to smother enterprise in those who should have used them. England since the Glorious Revolution had been the home of a freedom in local affairs which increased in direct ratio to the distance from the capital : freedom for the landlord or the manufacturer in the disposition of his property and his human assets ; freedom to the parochial surveyor of roads to

[1] *Travels in France and Italy* ("Everyman" ed.), pp. 8, 9, 39, 48, etc.
[2] Letter in *N. W. Gaz.*, May 17, 1810, describing conditions fifty years earlier.
[3] *Southern Counties*, p. 250.

scamp his job with the aid of the notoriously inefficient
statute labour and team duty of the parishioners.   North
Wales was far from the seat of government ; no great
highway passed through it, for it led nowhere but to
stagnant Ireland ; and Welsh Jacobitism[1] had been too
feeble a growth to frighten the Government into providing
Wales, as it provided the Highlands, with military roads.

But if the claims of travel in North Wales were not yet
strong enough to pierce the plate-armour of *laisser-faire* in
which the Government had encased itself, local interests
were slowly but steadily awakening to the condition of the
roads.   The country gentleman wished to be able to visit
his neighbours when he chose, and not to be deterred by
the "uncertainty . . . occasioned by deluges, tides, rocks,
and precipices."[2]   Or, if he had caught the spirit of the
age and desired to develop his estate, he looked for more
efficient means of conveying his crops to market, procuring
lime, or exploiting and disposing of his minerals.   Then
there was the growing body of English tourists to be
catered for.   Welsh watering places were deploring
"malicious rumours of want of conveyance,"[3] and even
English innkeepers on the chief routes into North Wales
began to ask themselves how they might temper for the
parting guest the discomforts of a Welsh journey.   Last of
all the Government was stirred out of its lethargy.   In
1800 the Act of Union with Ireland helped to swell the
volume of traffic along the Holyhead Road ; and there is
a certain irony in the fact that the first Government grant
towards the improvement of this highway was made in
the very year of Waterloo—just after we had successfully
"bashed the baggonets" of the French, as Mr. Chesterton
puts it,

> because they came arrayed
> To straighten out the crooked road an English drunkard made.

The earliest attempts at reform, however, were of a much
less far-reaching character.   Country gentlemen bent on
improvement would try to infuse some vigour into

---

[1] *See*, e.g., *Trans. Cym. Soc.*, 1920–21, pp. 11–39 ; *Y Cymmrodor*,
1901, pp. 136 ff.

[2] Letter from Sir Thomas Hanmer, 1721, in *Memorials of the
Parish and Family of Hanmer* (1876), pp. 234–5.

[3] *Salop. Journ.*, Aug. 30, 1797.

parochial maladministration by " presenting " before the quarter sessions some patch of specially ill-kept road—an expedient which even the General Post Office did not find beneath its dignity. Or, again, a public-spirited landowner might volunteer to act as surveyor himself. Here and there, too, statute labour—unkind critics called it "statute knavery and indolence "[1]—was commuted for money payments, and a fund was thus formed for the hiring of skilled navvies. In Anglesey an ambitious scheme for transferring the whole duty of maintaining the highways from the parishes and townships to the county, with an adequate salaried staff paid out of the rates, excited much discussion in 1824-5, but it all ended in smoke. Meanwhile the more energetic landlords were taking matters into their own hands. Even before the middle of the eighteenth century, the first Sir Watkin Williams Wynn was able to spare time from fox hunting and politics for road-making. Early in the second half the Glynnes of Hawarden built a causeway over Saltney Marsh to Chester, and an active Montgomeryshire vicar endowed his extensive mountain parish with carriage roads and milestones. Lord Penrhyn, as we have seen, was a road-builder as well as an agricultural improver ; and in the provision of highways for the carriage of his slates to the sea he was imitated, early in the next century, by the other big quarry-owners of Caernarvonshire and Merioneth. Nor were landowners the only pioneers. It was the owner of the Dublin packet who in 1752 equipped the main road across Anglesey to Holyhead with milestones, and twenty years later the improvement of the road over Penmaenmawr—another section of the usual Irish mail route—was largely financed from Dublin. About the same time, the initiative in improving the main highways through North Wales, from Chester and Shrewsbury respectively, to Bangor, was taken by innkeepers of these two English towns.

More ambitious than these occasional displays of private generosity and enterprise were the efforts of the turnpike trusts, which were empowered under Act of Parliament to take charge of a whole system of roads, widening, straightening or diverting them as need arose, adding new roads

[1] Davies, p. 378.

and stopping up obsolete ways, and meeting their expenses by the erection of toll-gates. In England, Turnpike Acts had been gradually widening the area of road-administration since the beginning of the eighteenth century. From 1750, we are told by Mr. and Mrs. Webb,[1] there arose a " perfect mania " for them, and this was the time when they began to appear in North Wales. The earliest Acts aimed at improving communications across the English border. In 1752 the road between Shrewsbury and Wrexham, and four years later those radiating from Chester to Wrexham and Mold, were placed under turnpike trusts. About the same time, the system was extended to Montgomeryshire by Acts regulating the roads between Shrewsbury, Welshpool and Oswestry—the main artery of the Welsh woollen industry. Under Acts of 1757 and 1759, trusts were set up to deal with what was then the principal route to Ireland—through Flintshire and along the coasts of Denbigh and Caernarvon towards Holyhead ; and the Anglesey Turnpike Act of 1765 brought the last lap of the Holyhead Road under control. The Acts for Denbighshire and Flintshire also began the process of road improvement in the mining areas, which was continued under the Wrexham and Oswestry Trust of 1762 and under a succession of local Acts in the early nineteenth century.

All the main roads through Montgomeryshire were placed under a comprehensive trust in 1769, and a county meeting at Dolgelley procured a similar Act for Merioneth in 1775. Two years after this, communications with Caernarvonshire from the east were further improved by the establishment of trusts to manage the roads from Corwen to Llanrwst and down the Conway Valley to Conway ; at the same time the existing Caernarvonshire turnpike was extended through Caernarvon to Pwllheli. It was this, we are told by a writer of the next generation,[2] that first opened the remoter regions of Lleyn to " itinerant trade," and so " roused the long dormant spirit of local amelioration " which was, during the first thirty years of the nineteenth century, to push the turnpike system into the very heart of Snowdonia. In 1802 the completion of the road from

[1] *Story of the King's Highway*, p. 124.
[2] Evans : *Beauties*, pp. 341–2.

Capel Curig to Bangor enabled passengers to Ireland from the direction of Shrewsbury to take this more direct route instead of the coastal road. During the ensuing years it was extended from Capel Curig along the Pen y gwryd Pass, northwards to Llanberis and Caernarvon and southwards to Aberglaslyn and Tremadoc, from which point the draining of Traeth Mawr had provided a short and easy way into Merioneth. Finally, direct communication between North and South Wales was facilitated by the construction in 1825 of a new road linking up the turnpike systems of Montgomeryshire and Radnorshire.

Turnpike trusts were usually established for a period of twenty-one years, during which time the trustees were expected to make the existing roads fit for traffic and to provide new ones where necessary. But the trusts had a way of being an unconscionable while a-dying. From time to time they were given a fresh lease of life under a new Act—sometimes in order to enable the trustees to complete a task held up for lack of resources ; sometimes to place additional " cross-roads " under their care or to subdivide the duties of an overgrown trust. Most of the turnpike trusts of North Wales were renewed in this fashion up to within fifty or sixty years of the present day ; the Anglesey new turnpike—last survivor of all— did not expire till 1895.[1]

The passing of a Turnpike Act did not effect an immediate and magical improvement in the state of the roads, nor did it necessarily do away with the obligation of statute labour. The burden of the tolls was severely felt by the farmers, despite the preferential treatment so frequently given to agricultural produce ; and the leisurely rate of progress, the monotonous tale of financial mismanagement, and the irresponsibility of the trustees might well make the toll-payer pause to ask whether he was getting value for his money. But undoubtedly the gravest defect of the turnpikes lay in the nature of their origin. Their primary purpose was to co-ordinate the network of roads serving a single market or parish church, or (though this was naturally not avowed) the country house of a powerful

---

[1] There is a good deal of material bearing on turnpikes (especially of Caernarvonshire) in the Porth yr aur collection.

trustee.[1] Such a system did not readily adapt itself to the needs of through routes and long-distance traffic.

This difficulty is most clearly seen in the successive measures taken for expediting the Irish mails through North Wales. After vainly trying to extort, by the antiquated weapon of indictment, impossible labours from the poor and thinly-populated Welsh townships through which the main highway passed, the General Post Office nerved itself to ask for a Parliamentary Committee to take into consideration the whole of the road from London to Holyhead. The first Committee was appointed in 1810, and from that time fresh Committees sat each session of Parliament, and presented regular reports, sometimes as many as six in a year. In these reports we can trace the gradual breakdown, under stress of stubborn necessity, of the stolid British prejudice against state control, until at last the country found itself, in its own despite, possessed of a genuine *route nationale*—one of the very few which came into existence before the days of motor traffic. On the recommendation of the Parliamentary Committees, a survey of the entire road was made in 1811 by Thomas Telford, the rising engineer of the day. In 1815, as we have seen, the House of Commons authorized a grant of £20,000 for repairs.[2] This sum of money, the first of a long series of public grants, was placed in the hands of ten Parliamentary Commissioners, who, with Telford as their chief adviser, were given considerable powers of " gingering up " the twenty-three local trusts with which they had to deal.

Here, of course, we are concerned only with the Welsh section of the road. The route adopted for the Irish mails since 1808 had been through Shrewsbury, Corwen, and Capel Curig, and to this part of the road—described by the Committee of 1817 as " in the worst possible condition "—the Commissioners devoted their chief attention ; but the repair of the northern route (through Chester and along the coast) was also undertaken, as a subsidiary enterprise. On each of these routes a considerable feat of bridge-building was called for, in order to

---

[1] *See*, e.g., complaints about second Anglesey Turnpike Act in *Chester Chron.*, April 4, 1776.

[2] 55 Geo. III, cap. 152.

dispense with the slow and often dangerous ferries over the Menai Straits near Bangor and over the Conway River at Conway. The idea of bridging the Straits had long been " in the air." Plans had been drawn up in 1776 ; the question was reconsidered by a committee of local gentry in 1785 ; and new specifications had been exhibited by John Rennie in 1801.[1] " God knows," wrote a traveller on the last occasion " whether this plan will ever be brought to perfection, but in this mechanical age we can scarcely wonder at the projection of any enterprise, however vast or difficult."[2] After the appointment of the Committee of 1811, it became a live issue in local politics. Caernarvon thought its trade would be injured, and petitioned against the project ; Bangor and Beaumaris were favourable.[3] The recommendations of the Parliamentary Committee carried the day ; in 1818 the House of Commons made a grant of £20,000, and in the next year an Act was passed to authorize the building of a suspension bridge on plans submitted by Telford.[4] Two years later it was decided to build a similar bridge at Conway, and an extra duty was put on Irish letters to contribute to the expenses.[5]

One of the chief difficulties with which Telford had to contend was the incompetence and obstructiveness of the six small trusts which mismanaged the Welsh portion of the main line. The drastic step was taken, in 1819, of removing from their control all but the less important " cross-roads." To take charge of the Irish Road an entirely new trust—the Shrewsbury-Holyhead Turnpike —was set up by Act of Parliament. The fifteen trustees named in the Act were granted an initial sum of £15,000 (to be followed by many supplementary grants) for improvements, and with this assistance they were required to employ a professional engineer and to give an annual

---

[1] *Sketch of a Plan for Building a Timber Bridge across the River Menai* . . . London, 1786 ; Smiles : *Metcalfe and Telford*, p. 263, *Smeaton and Rennie*, p. 264 ; *N. W. Gaz.*, Aug. 23, 1810, Nov. 19. 1812 ; Davies, H. R. : *The Menai and the Conway Ferries* (1942), pp. 252–60.

[2] Skinner : *Ten Days' Tour*, p. 52.

[3] *N. W. Gaz.*, March 8, 22, May 24, 31, June 14, 1810 ; *Camb. Quart. Mag.*, I, p. 222.

[4] 58 Geo. III, cap. 101 ; 59 Geo. III, cap. 48.

[5] 1 and 2 Geo. IV, cap. 35.

report of his activities.[1]   Another body of Parliamentary
Commissioners was charged with the building of Menai
Bridge and of a new and more direct road across Anglesey,
with a new coaching inn to take the place of those which
would now be left side-tracked.[2]   This road was completed
and placed under the Holyhead Turnpike in 1823, the
old Anglesey trust being dissolved ; four years later the
two suspension bridges were opened.[3]

By 1830 the reconstruction of the Holyhead Road was
virtually complete.   Its services to North Wales were
considerable.   Not only did it directly promote inland
trade in parts of five out of the six counties, but it
influenced the other turnpike trusts by giving them
a model of scientific road making and management.
Among other things they learned the habit—common
in England since the middle of the eighteenth
century—of appointing salaried surveyors instead of
" setting " the roads to contractors for a period of years.[4]
In 1840 the Royal Commission on the State of the Roads
was able to report favourably on almost all the turnpikes
of North Wales.   Some few were described as " excellent "
or " very good ; " none were condemned out and out.
Most of them had learned to do without statute labour,
though a few received voluntary assistance from the
parishes.   The total mileage covered by the trusts was
over 1,200 ; of this the Holyhead Road accounted for
nearly 107, Caernarvonshire for 160, Denbigh and Flint
for nearly 300, Merioneth nearly 240 and Montgomery
over 400.   Anglesey had only four miles, apart from the
Holyhead Turnpike.   The bulk of the pioneering work
had been done before the beginning of the nineteenth
century.[5]   When we read the impatient (and not un-
merited) diatribes of Telford against the turnpike trusts,

[1] 59 Geo. III, cap. 30.
[2] 4 Geo. IV, cap. 74.
[3] The chief authorities for the development of the Holyhead Road
are the successive reports of the Parliamentary Committees and
Commissions from 1810 to 1845.   *See* also Webb : *King's Highway*,
chap. VIII, and Harper : *Holyhead Road*.
[4] *See*, e.g., *N. W. Gaz.*, Aug. 24, 1815 (Capel Curig Turnpike) ;
Third Rept. of Ctte. on Holyhead Roads, 1822.
[5] *Report on Roads* (1840, XXVII), pp. 565–8, 577–87, 595–600,
645–6 ; *cf.* Davies, p. 372.

or the reports of trustees meeting "to consider the propriety of examining and adjusting the Treasurer's accounts, which have long remained unexamined,"[1] we must remember the other side of the picture: the public-spirited services of men like William Pugh of Brynllywarch, a Radical squire of Montgomeryshire who took under his wing the local branch of Brougham's Society for the Diffusion of Useful Knowledge, squandered a considerable fortune in county works, and (like W. A. Madocks) died in comparative poverty before he could reap his reward; his investments are said to have included £7,000 in county road bonds and another £10,000 in the Newtown-Builth road.[2]

Freed from the menace of ruts, deadly angles and impossible gradients, the highways began to swarm with wheeled vehicles. The pack-horse, pack-mule and sledge gave place to the waggon,[3] and degenerate travellers sought the idle discomfort of the stage-coach or post-chaise instead of riding their own horses. Everywhere there were speedier and more punctual facilities for transport. " The country may be traversed in every direction," boasted a local topographer in 1810, " and few towns are devoid of the accommodating vehicle, a post-chaise."[4] It was on the Holyhead Road that regular coaching services began. As far back as the Civil Wars there seems to have been a brief period when a coach ran periodically from Birmingham through Shrewsbury as far as Holywell. No further developments occurred for over a century. There was talk of a Chester-Holyhead coach in 1752, but it was not till 1776 that the enterprising landlord of the White Lion, Chester, turned dreams into sober reality by putting a " flying post-chaise " on the road to carry passengers daily (Sundays excepted) to Holyhead, for the sum of two guineas each. Three years later a Shrewsbury innkeeper—Robert Lawrence, of the Raven and Bell—set up a rival service. His coaches ran daily to Holyhead by Wrexham and Mold ; and in 1780

---

[1] *N. W. Gaz.*, Oct. 7, 1812.
[2] Williams : *Montgomeryshire Worthies*, pp. 266–75 ; *Penny Mag.*, 1832 ff.
[3] *See*, e.g. *N. W. Gaz.*, May 7, 1812 ; *Red Dragon*, VII, pp. 324 ff. ; Warner : *Second Walk*, p. 184.
[4] Evans : *Beauties*, p. 100.

he was collaborating with the metropolitan inns to provide a service all the way from London. It was four years after this that the General Post Office took up the scheme of Mr. Palmer of Bath, and began to run its own mail coaches. The Irish mails were naturally among the first to reap the benefit ; in 1785 the mail bags ceased to be carried by post-boys on horseback, and were transferred to a mail coach travelling daily through Chester. Lawrence, however, continued to urge the advantages of the Shrewsbury route, and in 1808, after the opening of the Capel Curig road, he gained his point. Henceforth the mail coach to Holyhead left Shrewsbury every night to travel along the new route. Even before it was put on the road, travellers had been flocking to the new Capel Curig hotel (built by Lord Penrhyn) in such numbers as to necessitate a hasty increase of accommodation ; and not all the sneers, protests, and alternative schemes of the men of Chester were able to divert the route again until the railway came to supersede the highway.

This was, for North Wales, the beginning of the coaching age. The coaching services of the Holyhead Road were soon imitated on the other main highways. In 1788 Chester and Shrewsbury were connected by a post-coach, which ran three times a week through Wrexham and Ellesmere, continuing to Bath and Bristol. Ten years later was "launched" the first coach from Shrewsbury through Welshpool, Newtown, and Llanidloes to Aberystwyth. At first the service was a weekly one ; within the next twenty years it was increased, during the bathing season, to twice a week, and supplemented by a second coach which ran through Llanfair and Mallwyd. But these were mainly for the convenience of summer visitors ; it was not till about 1823 that a daily " Royal Mail " began plying between Shrewsbury, Welshpool, and Newtown, nor till 1840 that its circuit was extended to include Machynlleth and Aberystwyth. In 1816 Merioneth obtained its first coaching service—from Barmouth to Corwen in connection with the Holyhead coaches, and to Dolgelley and Mallwyd to meet those running between Aberystwyth and Shrewsbury. These were followed in 1827 by a coach twice weekly from Welshpool and Newtown to Machynlleth, Aberdovey and Towyn, along the newly-made coastal road. Denbighshire and Flintshire had services three times a week from Chester to Mold, Ruthin, and Denbigh by 1812, and daily to Wrexham and Welshpool by 1829. In Caernarvonshire a coach to accommodate the "gentlemen and clergy of Lleyn and Evionydd" began plying between Bangor, Caernarvon, and Pwllheli in 1822.

By these means regular postal deliveries gradually came to be established in place of the casual services—usually dependent on the weather—of old women, shopkeepers and obliging neighbours ; and the traveller, instead of waiting for days with his luggage packed in hopes of a passing post-chaise, could rely on conveyances which ran to time-table. Mailcarts and postboys on horseback connected the main routes with the remoter towns and villages, and the ordinary goods traffic, with which the coaches could not satisfactorily cope, was speeded up. In 1780 we find the tradesmen of Caernarvon arranging for public carriers to Bangor and Chester, and within the next decade most of the principal market towns were similarly served. Not only so, but long-distance stage or " fly " waggons—common in England since about 1750—began to radiate through Chester and through Shrewsbury into North Wales. Chester at first had the bulk of the traffic. At least as early as 1790 a stage waggon from London to Holyhead went through weekly, carrying goods at a penny a pound on each side of Chester. There were also periodic fly waggons to Oswestry by 1802 and to Pwllheli by 1817. But Shrewsbury also had its share. By 1790 the flannel trade kept as many as three stage waggons busy with weekly journeys to and from Welshpool, and the *wagen fawr* from Llanidloes to Welshpool was a familiar institution till 1859. About the beginning of the nineteenth century, too, the web manufacturers of Merioneth began to discard Dyer's " pygmean steeds " and to take their goods to Shrewsbury by waggon.[1] There was a Shrewsbury waggon " flying " to Holyhead in four days (soon reduced to two) by 1809, and another to Aberystwyth by 1816, which seven years later was doing the journey in twenty-eight hours. In 1818 a Welsh waggon from London through Shrewsbury

[1] Morris : *Cantref Meirionydd*, p. 115.

was in contemplation ; and, finally, the opening of the Newtown-Builth road in 1825 made it possible, for the first time, to carry goods through Central Wales from the manufacturing districts of the North of England to South Wales.

Meanwhile the coaches were steadily increasing both in number and in speed, though as late as 1839 travellers found Wales " not so well furnished with stage coaches as other parts of the kingdom."[1]   Rival proprietors were metaphorically cutting each other's throats, and literally breaking the passenger's necks, in quest of record speeds, and the battle of advertisements was carried on with vigour in the local press.   The following announcement of a coach on the Holyhead Road, which was trying to outbid the night mail in 1815, will serve as a sample :—

> Every day, *not round about*,
> As is the boasted *Mail Coach route*,
> And *better road* at length is found ;
> Travels all day by *solar* light
> Every *Morning, Noon* (NOT NIGHT!).[2]

Accidents were as frequent as in the early days of the railway.   " Once you crawled, and were overset gently ; now you gallop and are dashed to atoms," grumbled a querulous passenger in this same year.[3]   The *North Wales Gazette*, during the whole of its career from 1808 to 1827, rarely passed a year without reporting one or more coaching accidents.

But if you were lucky enough to reach your destination with a whole skin, you did at least get there more speedily. The journey from London to Holyhead was shortened by gradual stages, between 1784 and 1836, from 48 hours to 27, though in 1815 the rate of travel on the Welsh roads still had to be a mile an hour slower than on the English.   On minor roads the rate of acceleration was naturally not so sensational.   It took 8 hours to get from Chester to Shrewsbury in 1806, 5½ from Chester to Denbigh in 1812, 4 from Bangor to Pwllheli in 1822 ; and it was only within the next few years that the time between Shrewsbury and Newtown was reduced from 5½ to 4 hours.

[1] Leigh's *Guide*, p. 6.
[2] *N. W. Gaz.*, Sept. 28, 1815.
[3] Letter in *Monthly Mag.*, quoted *N. W. Gaz.*, Nov. 23, 1815.

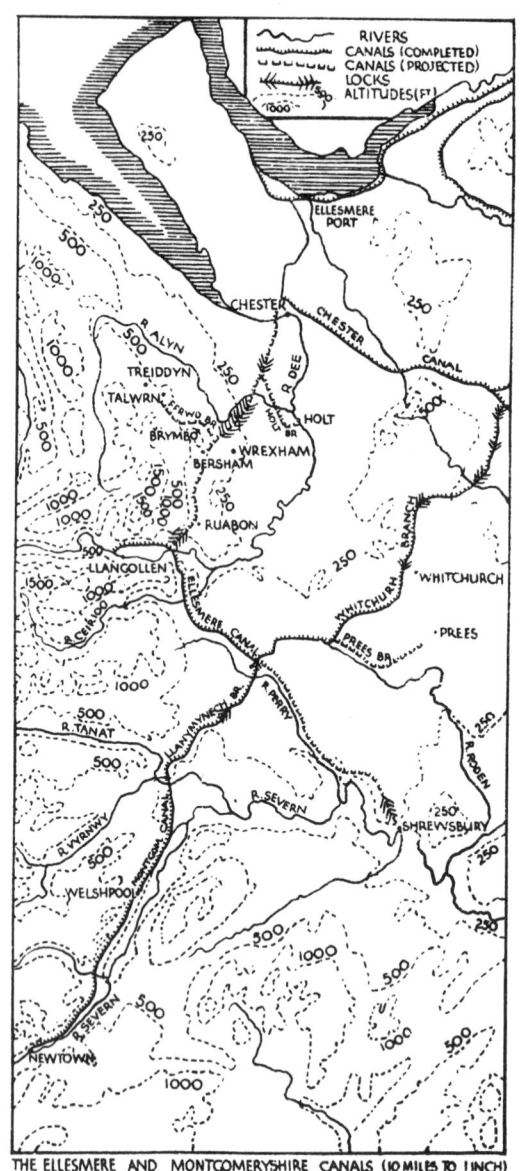

THE ELLESMERE AND MONTGOMERYSHIRE CANALS (10 MILES TO 1 INCH)

Most striking of all is the fact that the journey from Shrewsbury to Aberystwyth, which took 16 hours in 1818, was hardly any quicker in 1864. For when once the railway came, the efforts at speeding up the mail coach slackened off even in those regions which, like Aberystwyth, still depended wholly on this means of conveyance. The " Wonder " coach, which had done so much to increase the rate of travel on the Holyhead Road (it was the first to do a hundred miles in a day), gave up the struggle after a gallant race with a railway train in 1842. By the middle of the century the great days of coaching were over.[1]

B. CANALS.

Before the railway came, some regions of North Wales had begun to benefit from another device for expediting traffic. Ever since the first sod of the Duke of Bridgewater's canal was cut, in 1759, the " rage for hydraulics," as detractors called it,[2] had been rapidly spreading over industrial England a network of artificial rivers. The first canal in North Wales was a short one dug across Saltney Marsh by Sir John Glynne in 1768 for the conveyance of Hawarden coals to the Dee. For a few years the coal was taken by punts from the hamlet of Bretton, where the canal started, to the river, and there re-loaded into barges. Naturally this frequent handling proved wasteful and expensive, and the canal was soon abandoned and partially filled in.[3] Before it was finally given up, another canal had been projected in a different part of the country by the versatile Fitzmaurice of Llewenni. Convinced that coal could be worked in the Vale of Clwyd, and that only a canal was needed to turn the whole valley into a hive of industry and a source of boundless wealth, he tried (about 1770) to interest some Liverpool merchants in a scheme for a canal from Rhuddlan (the point where the Clwyd ceased to be navigable) to Ruthin. An engineer had reported favourably on the course some

---

[1] On the whole subject of roads and coaching in North Wales *see* my article in *Arch. Camb.*, June, 1925, pp. 121–48, from which several of the foregoing paragraphs have been taken or adapted, and where full references are given.

[2] Davies, p. 385.

[3] *Memoir of Hawarden*, pp. 102–3.

years before ; but opposition from the neighbouring estates killed the project, and nothing came of an attempt to revive it in 1807.[1]   In 1782, the course of a proposed canal to cónvey coal in the neighbourhood of Holywell and Flint was surveyed and declared practicable ; but nothing had been done when the outbreak of war tightened the purse-strings of speculators, and though a start seems to have been made later on, the project eventually fell through.[2]   A navigable cut for the conveyance of hypothetical coal in Merioneth—or, alternatively, a canalization of the River Dovey—was contemplated in the early years of the nineteenth century,[3] and the construction of a similar outlet for Anglesey coal was also under discussion.[4]

Meanwhile, more ambitious schemes than these were afoot.   In 1779 the Chester Canal had been opened as far as Nantwich.   While it was still in course of construction, proposals were made to open up inland navigation between Chester, Warrington, and Liverpool.   By these means, it was urged, Chester could be supplied with Lancashire coal at cheaper rates than those it had to pay for Welsh coal ; at the same time the projectors were careful to point out that the industries of Denbigh and Flint could not fail to benefit from a canal near enough to provide an outlet for the produce of the " grand foundery at Bersham."[5]   But Welshmen were not satisfied with this.   On June 28th, 1791, three Welsh landowners met at Overton and decided to summon by advertisements in the Chester, Shropshire and Liverpool papers a meeting at Ellesmere " to consider the propriety of making a canal to connect the Severn, Dee and Mersey."   The result of the meeting was the formation of the Ellesmere Canal Company, with the Duke of Bridgewater as chairman and the principal landowners of Shropshire, Denbighshire, and the adjacent counties, as well as ironmasters and coal-owners like John Wilkinson and Richard Kyrke, among the leading shareholders.   For some time discussion raged fiercely about the appropriate route for the canal.

[1] Pugh : *Cambria Depicta*, p. 442 ; Davies, p. 385 and *n*.
[2] Pennant : *Whiteford and Holywell*, p. 189 ; *Cambrian Traveller's Guide* (1813), p. 602.
[3] *Infra*, p. 201 ; Pugh : *Cambria Depicta*, p. 221.
[4] Carlisle : *Top. Dict.; N. W. Gaz.*, Oct. 21, 1813.
[5] *Chester Chron.*, May 21, 1779, *et seq*.

One party advocated a line from the Chester Canal, east of the Dee, to Welshpool and Shrewsbury, with a branch to Ruabon and the Dee to meet the industrial needs of East Denbighshire ; others were convinced that it would be practicable, and more convenient, to follow the line of the present Great Western Railway from Chester to Wrexham (with a branch to Brymbo) and thence by Bersham, Ruabon and Chirk to Shrewsbury.[1] It was this " westernizing " party—representing, as it did, the interests of the great industrialists—that carried the day when the Act was passed in 1793. The Company as originally constituted had 1,238 shareholders, with an authorized capital of £400,000 ; if necessary, further shares to the value of £50,000 might be issued, and another £50,000 raised by mortgage on the tolls.[2]

The general agent, once again, was Thomas Telford. A branch line across the Wirral, from Chester to Ellesmere Port, was begun at once and completed in the next year. The Pontcysyllte aqueduct, by means of which the canal was to be carried over the Dee, was also taken in hand in 1795, and the line from Chirk towards Shrewsbury was completed as far as Weston in 1797, with a branch to the Vyrnwy at Llan y mynech ; Shrewsbury itself was never reached. As soon as this section had been opened, work was commenced on another branch, past Whitchurch and Ellesmere (with short connecting cuts to each of the two towns) to join the Chester Canal north of Nantwich. But meanwhile difficulties had arisen over the western section. In 1796 a start was made with a short branch intended to connect the Chester-Ruabon line with the collieries and ironworks belonging to Messrs. Kyrke and Wilkinson (two influential shareholders) in the neighbourhood of Brymbo. A reservoir was dug by Telford near to Mr. Kyrke's colliery at Ffrwd, and another basin near Gwersyllt, the spot intended for the junction with the main line. The water supplies were tapped ; but in a short time the canal was dry again, and all work had to be stopped in

[1] The respective merits of the two routes are discussed in an undated pamphlet preserved in the library of Erthig Hall (*Observations on the comparative merits of the Eastern and Western Canals*), which I have been allowed to consult through the kindness of the present proprietor.

[2] 33 Geo. III, cap. 91.

1798.[1] The whole of the Chester-Ruabon section soon
went the way of the Ffrwd branch ; one scheme after
another for dealing with this difficult bit of country was
considered and rejected, and eventually the plan was
given up as hopeless.[2] This source of water supplies
having failed, powers were obtained in 1802 for tapping
the Dee by means of a water-line to Llangollen from
Pontcysyllte—an enterprise not completed for some
years.[3] The directors naturally did not emphasize the
fact that nearly £9,000 had been spent on a scheme which
proved—as many had foreseen at the outset—quite
impracticable, and for long the Ellesmere Canal was
still referred to in advertisements, maps, and guide books
as if the original plan of 1793 had been carried out : even
Gwallter Mechain is guilty of thus misleading his readers.[4]
As some compensation for the failure to penetrate the
busiest colliery district, the Company was authorized to
build a short railway connecting some of the nearer mines
with the canal.[5]

The branch to the Chester Canal now became the main
line, and the completed portions were opened to navigation
on November 26, 1805.   A procession of boats containing
officials and other notabilities crossed the Pontcysyllte
aqueduct to the sound of salutes from the artillery of
the Shropshire Volunteers, and Mr. Rowland Hunt, M.P.,
delivered a florid oration. He told how, while " our
honest friends the workmen . . . . were being regaled
in their favourite manner, and were hailing our approach
with honest jollity," their betters were filled with thoughts
of the golden future in store for local industry, and of how

generous Commerce binds
The round of Nations in a golden chain.

[1] *See* an interesting article on this abandoned enterprise in *Brymbo
Works Mag.*, Vol. II, No. 6 (Sept., 1923), pp. 164–70.
[2] 36 Geo. III, cap. 96 ; *cf.* notices in *Salop. Journ.*, Sept. 16,
Oct. 7, 1795.
[3] 42 Geo. III, cap. 20 ; 44 Geo. III, cap. 54 ; *cf. Shrewsbury
Chron.*, May 25, 1821.
[4] E.g., advts. in *Chester Chron.*, Nov. 2, 1798, and *Salop. Journ.*,
June 4, 1800 ; Barfoot and Wilkes' *Directory*, V, pp. 280–1 ;
Davies, pp. 380–2 ; Evans : *Beauties*, pp. 105–6, *cf.* 511–12 ;
Cambrian Traveller's Guide (1840 ed.), p. 483 ; and maps by John
Evans (1797), Laurie and Whittle (1811), etc.
[5] 44 Geo. III, cap. 54.

The proprietors might, indeed, justly pride themselves on the fact that a work begun in " a year of unbounded prosperity " had been brought to a successful issue despite the " singular and not infrequently alarming state of public a. airs " which followed.[1] Yet the delays and the financial stringency of the war years had frightened investors ; shares started at a premium of 20 per cent ; by 1803 they were selling at a 50 per cent discount, and even after the canal was opened they were quoted at as low a figure as £55, as compared with £174 for Leeds and Liverpool Canal shares. " Thanks to its ambitious lay-out," as Dr. Clapham remarks, " the Ellesmere and Chester [Canal] had a capital of £500,000, as much as that of the Forth and Clyde." Small wonder that it was difficult to get an adequate return on this outlay.[2] But soon after the end of the War the Company's finances were sufficiently recovered not only to afford regular dividends to the shareholders, but to set the directors thinking of fresh developments. A hare-brained scheme for carrying a water-line down to Bala Lake and thence locking down to Dolgelley and Barmouth, so as to promote direct transport between mid-Wales and the industrial North, came to nothing, as one might expect ;[3] but in 1813 the Ellesmere and Chester Canal Companies were consolidated,[4] and the joint concern later obtained powers for linking up with the Trent and Mersey Canal.[5]

Far more important for Wales, however, were the developments which brought the Ellesmere canal system into touch with Montgomeryshire. In 1794, the year after the passing of the Ellesmere Canal Act, a committee of Montgomeryshire gentlemen procured an " Act for making a Navigable Canal from or near Porthywain Lime Rocks in the Parish of Llanyblodwel in the County of Salop to or near Newtown in the County of Montgomery, and also certain collateral cuts from the said canal."

[1] *Report to General Assembly*, 1805.
[2] *Salop. Journ.*, Feb. 16, 1803, April 24, 1818 ; *Chester Chron.*, Oct. 17, 1806, May 15, 1807 ; Clapham : *Early Railway Age*, p. 81.
[3] *N. W. Gaz.*, Jan. 4, 1810.
[4] 52 Geo. III, cap. 80.
[5] 7 and 8 Geo. IV, cap. 102 ; *Shrewsbury Chron.*, Aug. 31, 1827. On the Ellesmere Canal, *see Report to the General Assembly*, 1805 ; Priestley : *Navigable Rivers, Canals and Railways*, pp. 233 ff.

The original proprietors included the Earl of Powis, Lord Clive, Sir Watkin Williams Wynn, and most of the principal landed gentry of the district (some of whom were also interested in the woollen industry), as well as one or two local bankers and the clerk to the Forden House of Industry. All owners of land to the value of £40 a year and upwards in the counties of Denbigh, Montgomery, and Salop were placed on the list of commissioners for the canal. The Company was authorized to issue 72 shares of £100 each, bearing 5 per cent interest till the canal should be completed. If necessary, a further sum not exceeding £20,000 might be raised among the existing proprietors or by mortgage. Compensation was to be made for any diminution of tolls on the chief turnpike roads from which traffic was likely to be diverted.[1]

Work was begun at once. The first meeting of the proprietors to put the Act into execution took place at the beginning of July; the commissioners met in the same month, and tenders were invited for the building of an aqueduct over the Vyrnwy and other necessary works.[2] During the summer of 1795 about 700 men were employed on the section from Llan y mynech to Welshpool; next year the work was sufficiently advanced to permit the launching of a boat, and operations were commenced south of Welshpool. It was hoped that the whole work would now be finished within three years.[3] And, indeed, by the August of 1797 the section from Llan y mynech to Garthmyl—a mile or so south of Berriew—was in a condition to allow the conveyance of lime, limestone and coal to the wharves and limekilns which had been constructed at Welshpool, Berriew and Garthmyl.[4] But now a hitch occurred, and the work was hung up for a time. According to one contemporary writer, there was a strong local prejudice against the undertaking, and the smaller landowners offered opposition " at every step "; but then he was a scoffer at " artificial rivers " and complained bitterly

---

[1] 34 Geo. III, cap. 39.
[2] *Salop. Journ.*, July 2, 9, 23, Aug. 20, Nov. 12, 1794.
[3] *Cambrian Register*, I (1795, pub. 1796), p. 269 ; *Salop. Journ.*, Jan. 14, April 8, Nov. 11, Dec. 2, 16, 1795 ; Feb. 24, March 8, May 18, 1796.
[4] *Salop. Journ.*, Aug. 16, 1797.

that "because one set of speculators have discovered a new mode to acquire wealth, the whole country must be laid under tribute to support the vanity or rashness of future speculators."[1] War and its effects on the money market, at any rate, are sufficient to account for the delay.

In 1805 the proprietors, in a Special General Assembly, declared a dividend of 2½ per cent, and considered the question of continuing the work to Newtown,[2] but nothing was done till after the War. In 1815 an Act was passed incorporating a new Company, with a share capital of £40,000, to complete the Western Branch of the canal.[3] The moving spirit in this concern was William Pugh, Brynllywarch, whose acquaintance we have already made as a turnpike enthusiast, and whom we shall encounter again as a pioneer of machinery in the woollen industry. He is said to have held over half the shares and to have lent a further £25,000 on mortgage, in addition to which he bore the expenses of the Act (another £1,700) and advanced money for salaries and purchase of land.[4] Thanks to these efforts, the canal was completed to Newtown in 1819.[5] Immediately after this an Act was obtained for continuing the Eastern Branch (as it now came to be called) from Llan y mynech to join the Ellesmere Canal near Hordley.[6] Both branches were now apparently paying their way. On the Western Branch dividends had risen from 2½ to 4 per cent even before Newtown was reached ; and the same improvement took place on the Eastern Branch between 1825 and 1827 ;[7] yet all was not well financially. The proprietors of the Western Branch made a handsome presentation to William Pugh on its completion, but kind words and pieces of plate did not go far towards paying the Company's debts to him, which were estimated in 1833 at nearly £40,000.

[1] Evans : *Tour*, pp. 8–11 ; *cf*. Davies, pp. 383–4.
[2] *Salop. Journ.*, July 3, 1805.
[3] *Mont. Coll.*, XV, p. 91 ; *N. W. Gaz.*, May 26, 1814.
[4] *Montgomeryshire Worthies*, p. 267 ; *Mont. Coll.*, XV, pp. 93–7.
[5] *Shrewsbury Chron.*, March 5, 1819.
[6] Evans: *Walks through Wales*, p. 220, *cf*. pp. 61–2 ; *Oswestry Her.*, Sept. 19, Oct. 3, 1820 ; *Shrewsbury Chron.*, March 23, 1821.
[7] *Shrewsbury Chron.*, July 10, 1818, Aug. 12, 1825, Aug. 10, 1827.

Attempts to introduce legislation enabling the proprietors to discharge these liabilities by. means of higher tolls seem to have failed ; Pugh got into deep waters and had to take refuge from his creditors abroad.[1]

The completion of the Ellesmere and Montgomery Canals' opened up direct communication between the woollen and farming districts of Montgomeryshire, the coal and iron of Denbighshire, and the industrial North of England, at rates far cheaper than those charged for road transport. By 1825 goods were being conveyed regularly by canal between Manchester and Newtown at 2s. 11d. a hundredweight, the journey taking six days. At Newtown they were met by the " fly vans " arriving from South Wales along the newly-opened road.[2] A trade directory for 1828 announces canal services from Llangollen to Chester once a week, from Newtown to Chester twice a week, from Welshpool to London, Birmingham, Wolverhampton, Gloucester, and Bristol twice a week ; two services (once and twice a week respectively) from Welshpool to Chester, Liverpool, Manchester, Ellesmere and Nantwich ; and three (once, twice, and three times a week) from Welshpool to Newtown and South Wales.[3] It may be assumed that, although the canal barge proprietors made themselves responsible for delivery, the goods did not travel all the way by canal ; in fact a canal service between Welshpool and Ellesmere had been announced as early as 1802, before ever the Ellesmere and Montgomery canals were connected.[4] But in June, 1839, the first boat direct from London arrived at the canal basin in Newtown ; it left again the next evening and was expected to complete the return journey in four days.[5] When George Borrow was in Llangollen he met a bargee who had frequently carried slates all the way to Paddington, sometimes taking as long as three weeks over the job.[6]

---

[1] *Shrewsbury Chron.*, Aug. 10, 1821 ; *Montgomeryshire Worthies*, p. 115 ; *Calendar of Coleman Deeds*, No. 1150. There is a good account of the Montgomeryshire Canal in *Mont. Coll.*, XV, pp. 91–116.

[2] *Shrewsbury Chron.*, April 29, 1825.

[3] Pigot's *Directory*, 1828–29.

[4] *Chester Chron.*, April 23, 1802.

[5] *Bye-gones*, 1913–15, pp. 177, 182.

[6] *Wild Wales*, pp. 38–9.

It would be difficult to over-estimate the effects on North Wales of the improved communications brought about by canals and turnpike roads. Agriculturists were the first and perhaps the principal gainers. It was the landed interest that took the lead in the turnpike trusts, and the Montgomeryshire Canal was primarily an agricultural concern throughout. Both turnpike trusts and canal companies were tender to the farmer in respect of tolls—unfairly so, to the mind of the manufacturers, who saw manures go free, while loads of flannels or of ores had to pay.[1] To the farmer, speedier and cheaper transport meant access to supplies of lime and coal. In Merioneth and the south-west of Montgomeryshire it had sometimes taken four days, and the labour of two men and five horses, to get a cartload ; the construction of the canal is said to have caused a twenty per cent. reduction in the costs of coal and lime in districts like these. But to agriculture and industry alike, the chief gain lay in the extension of markets. Nowhere is this more evident than in the Montgomeryshire woollen industry. At last, as we shall see more fully later on, its long subservience to the Shrewsbury market was brought to an end. For a brief period after the completion of the canal, Newtown became a flourishing and independent centre of manufacture, finding its outlet on the Mersey instead of the Severn.[2] Finally, the way was opened for that influx of outside capital which was to provide the country with new industrial leaders. The Ellesmere canal affords a striking example. A Shrewsbury ironmaster, William Hazeldine, secured the contract for the ironwork of Pontcysyllte aqueduct, and came to the district to set up his foundry. Within a few years we find him acquiring coal mines and slate quarries, and establishing, all along the line of the canal, depôts for the sale of coal and slate and the burning of lime.[3]

---

[1] *See*, e.g., Montgomeryshire Canal Act, §§ XLI to XLV ; *cf. Arch. Camb.*, 1925, p. 140, and *Letters on Improvements*, pp. 36–9.

[2] *Cambrian Register*, I, p. 269 ; *Montgomeryshire Worthies*, pp. 113–4 ; Cundall and Landman : *Wales: an Economic Geography*, p. 227 ; *infra.*, chap. VII.

[3] *Report to General Assembly*, 1806 ; *Chester Chron.*, Aug. 4, 1797 ; *Salop. Journ.*, May 2, 1798 ; *infra*, pp. 144, 190, 213, 326.

Yet there is another side to the picture. If better communications opened a wider market for Welsh goods in England, they also attracted English goods to Wales, and the English manufacturing centres had all the advantages of age and accumulated wealth. As early as 1839 Rochdale imitation " Welsh flannels " were beginning to oust the genuine article from its own markets; and the copper, iron, wool and other raw products of North Wales gravitated by insensible degrees towards the large-scale manufactories across the border or in the South. The current of trade turned eastward more definitely than ever, and outlets like the Dovey fell out of use.[1]

C. Railways.

This process was completed by the railway. Both roads and canals in North Wales were reaching the height of their development when their supplanter arrived—just in time to rob those pioneers whose faith, almost literally, had removed mountains, of what the older economists would have called the reward of their enterprise and abstinence. Already at the beginning of the nineteenth century—when the days of steam locomotion were yet to come—Gwallter Mechain ventured on the prophecy that " the iron age [had] commenced " and that the future lay with the railroad. A line from the Brymbo collieries to Ruthin, he thought, would be more useful than any canal to the farmers of the Vale of Clwyd.[2] In the collieries of South Wales, wooden tramways had been in use since the end of the seventeenth century; iron had been substituted for wood, after the example of Coalbrookdale, in the later years of the eighteenth, and at the beginning of the nineteenth Trevethick was experimenting there with steam locomotives.[3] North Wales seems to have been content with horse-trams till the great age of railway construction; but these at least were becoming common in the mining and quarrying districts. In the Hawarden district a wooden tramway had been built about 1770

---

[1] *Mont. Coll.*, XIV, p. 106.
[2] Davies, p. 385.
[3] Galloway : *History of Coal Mining*, pp. 65–6 ; Williams, F. S. : *Our Iron Roads* (1883), pp. 4–5 ; Trevethick, F. : *Life of Richard Trevethick* (1872), I, p. 222.

to convey coals from the Ewloe Hills to the short-lived canal ; and numerous iron tramways appeared there from 1790.[1] Between that date and the beginning of steam locomotion the Ruabon, Flint and Holywell districts became covered with a network of short mineral lines. The Ellesmere Canal Company built railways to the Ruabon collieries and the Porth y waun lime rocks.[2] Even in Anglesey a company was formed in 1811 to construct, for the purpose of clearing coal from the little pits along Malldraeth Marsh, a tramway which would have anticipated by a century the present branch railway from Holland Arms to Red Wharf Bay ; but nothing came of it.[3]

A similar tale could be told of the quarries of Caernarvonshire and Merioneth. To convey the produce of his quarries to the newly-constructed Port Penrhyn, near Bangor, Lord Penrhyn built in 1800 a horse tramway along which a pair of horses could draw thirty or forty trucks, each of a ton weight, three times a day ; in its early days traffic had sometimes to be suspended because—as foremen, struggling with an unfamiliar tongue, have left on record— " it was a Large Wint."[4] During the mineral boom of 1824-5, when as many as 48 railway projects were sanctioned by Parliament,[5] a seven-mile line was built by Mr. Assheton Smith (at a cost of £25,000) from his Llanberis quarries to Port Dinorwic, another (by a joint-stock company) from Nantlle quarries to Caernarvon,[6] and two projects for a railway from Ffestiniog quarries to Portmadoc were afoot. One was sponsored by W. A. Madocks

[1] *Memoir of Hawarden*, pp. 103–5 ; *Cambrian Traveller's Guide* (1812), p. 602.

[2] First Rept. of Ctte. on Holyhead Roads, 1815 ; *N. W. Gaz.*, May 5, 1825 ; *Shrewsbury Chron.*, April 15, 1825 ; *Camb. Quart Mag.*, IV (1831), p. 351 ; Lewis : *Top. Dict.*, under *Holywell, Flint*, and *Ruabon.*

[3] 52 Geo. III ; *N. W. Gaz.*, Sept. 12, 1811 ; Lewis : *Top. Dict.* (1833 and 1843) under *Llanvihangel Ysceiviog.* Dr. Clapham (*Early Railway Age*, p. 88) writes as if this line had actually been built.

[4] Fenton : *Tours*, pp. 210, 238 ; *Red Dragon*, VII, p. 327 ; Hobson, W. D. : *The Penrhyn Quarries* (Bangor, 1913).

[5] Craik : *History of British Commerce*, III, p. 246.

[6] Lewis : *Top. Dict.* (1833) under *Llanberis*; *N. W. Gaz.*, Oct. 21, 1824, March 31, June 30, 1825 ; *N. W. Chron.*, Nov. 5, 1827, April 10, July 17, 1828 ; Parry : *Llanberis*, p. 73. The Nantlle railway had been projected as early as 1813. There is a good collection of documents bearing on it among the Porth yr aur MSS.

(who had conceived the idea when he first completed his embankment), the other by Nathan Meyer Rothschild. Their rivalry, combined with the opposition of the local farmers (trembling for the revenue they got from slate-transport), procured the rejection of successive Bills in Parliament till 1832. In the following year, however, the first stone was laid, and the first load of slates was carried in 1836. Four years later the trustees of the Ffestiniog-Maentwrog turnpike estimated that their securities had depreciated fifty per cent in consequence of the competition of the railway. But it was not till the 'sixties that it was opened to passenger traffic, and that a steam engine was substituted for horses.[1] The latter change had been made on the Nantlle line in 1848, and was imitated on the Penrhyn tramway in 1874. There was also, before 1833, an eight-mile line for the conveyance of copper ore from Beddgelert to Caernarvon, and in Montgomeryshire short railroads carried limestone from the Llan y mynech quarries to the canal.[2]

In North Wales, as elsewhere, it was the opening of the Stockton and Darlington line that aroused interest in railway development on a large scale. On September 2nd, 1824, while work was still in progress there, and while the respective merits of horses, locomotives and stationary engines for railway traction were in hot dispute,[3] the *North Wales Gazette* contained an article drawing the attention of its readers to the possibilities of " Rail-Roads and Loco-Motive Engines."

> Hitherto [the writer observes] rail-roads have been used for very limited purposes, and whenever they are spoken of it is in connection with Coal Pits and Stone Quarries ; but they are now about to be applied for the purpose of conveying merchandise over very extended lines of country. . . . By the Loco-Motive Engine fifty tons of goods may be conveyed by a ten horse power engine on à level road at the rate of six miles an

[1] Williams : *Hanes Plwyf Ffestiniog*, pp. 128–30 ; *Gestiana*, pp. 83, 178–9 ; *N. W. Gaz.*, May 26, 1808, Nov. 11, 1824, March 10, Oct. 13, 27, 1825, March, 2, July 13, 1826 ; *Report on Roads* (1840, XXVII), p. 597.

[2] Lewis : *Top. Dict.* (1833) under *Beddgelert; ·id.* (1843), II, p. 171 ; Cathrall : *History of North Wales*, II, p. 312 ; *Shrewsbury Chron.*, June 5, 1818.

[3] Clapham : *Early Railway Age*, pp. 381–2.

hour, [and] carriages for the conveyance of passengers at the rate of twelve or fourteen miles an hour. The discovery of the Loco-Motive engine will be almost as important to the trade and commerce of the country as the discovery of the steam engine itself.

Early in the next year the trustees of the Holywell, Flint, Wrexham-Mold and Mold-Denbigh turnpikes were meeting to discuss the menace to their interests in the proposed railway from Treiddyn (where colliery development was proceeding apace under the Welsh Coal and Iron Company) to the ' Dee estuary at Flint.[1] Turnpike opposition to railway projects, indeed, was sometimes as serious an obstacle as the exalted ideas held by land-owners of their claims to compensation.[2] But such schemes hung fire during the lean years that followed, and the supremacy of the stage coach and the canal barge remained unchallenged in North Wales for another decade.

As trade improved, enthusiasm for railways revived ; towards 1836 a question of vital moment to North Wales became the subject of acute and even acrimonious controversy—the choice of a locomotive route for the Irish mails. The old fight between Shrewsbury and Chester for the traffic through Wales—dating back to the time when the Post Office first turned its attention to the Holyhead Road—now broke out afresh. The Capel Curig route presented obvious engineering difficulties ; yet Shrewsbury was naturally unwilling to forego its hard-earned victory of forty years back, and as late as 1847 the *Shrewsbury Chronicle* was still urging the advantages of taking the mails this way.[3] Another possibility was to discard Holyhead and to bring them through Oswestry, up the Tanat valley to Bala, and thence by Ffestiniog, Tremadoc and Pwllheli to a new packet station at Porthdinllaen. This project had first been broached in the early 'seventies—before loco-motives, or even a *route nationale* to Holyhead, had ever been dreamt of. With this end in view, improvements had been undertaken in Porthdinllaen harbour, and several new turnpikes created ; but Government assistance

---

[1] *N. W. Gaz.*, Jan. 13 and Nov. 3, 1825.
[2] *N. W. Gaz.*, Jan. 13, Nov. 3, 1825 ; Cundall and Landman : *op. cit.*, p. 240.
[3] Oct. 22, 1847.

could not be obtained, and the scheme slumbered for more than sixty years.[1] In its new form it found a strong backer in William Pugh of Brynllywarch—now an exile in France, but ever mindful of the interests of his beloved Montgomeryshire ; his idea, however, was to carry the line further south even than Shrewsbury, and to take the Irish mails along the present Great Western route to Worcester, and thence by Ludlow, Newtown, and Dolgelley to Porthdinllaen.[2]

But Mid-Wales is a difficult country. A line along the Dee estuary and the north coast might be longer, but it would at least be simpler ; and if a harbour were made under the Orme to serve as the packet station for Ireland, long tunnels and difficult gradients could be avoided altogether. A prospectus setting forth the advantages of the proposed harbour—to be called St. George's Harbour, or (since it could serve as an outlet for the mineral produce of the Wrexham district) Port Wrexham—was issued by the St. George's Harbour and Railway Company as early as 1836.[3] In the following year the advocates of Porthdinllaen and the Mid-Wales line were heartened by a favourable report from Charles Blacker Vignoles, the Irish engineer who had already been employed on many English and Irish railways. The coastal route, he reported, involved a longer journey and a greater mileage of new permanent way ; and

> in place of affording access . . . to the very heart of North Wales, serving as a grand artery to accommodate the distribution North and South, and extending to them the advantages and facilities of a Railway communication, such a route would be a coast line for nearly 90 miles, bounded by the sea on one hand, and by almost inaccessible hills on the other, having no connexion or means of connexion but with the places it may actually pass.

Further, if Holyhead remained the packet station, it would be necessary (a second bridge over the Straits having been ruled out as impracticable) to " horse " the

---

[1] For references *see Arch. Camb.*, 1925, pp. 134–5.
[2] *Montgomeryshire Worthies*, pp. 273–4 ; *Camb. Trav. Guide* (1840), p. 91 ; *Y Gestiana*, p. 98.
[3] Parry : *Railway Companion.*

railway carriages one by one over the existing suspension bridge.[1]

Vignoles' report did not long remain unchallenged. His more famous rival, George Stephenson, employed by the Irish Railway Commissioners to make a fresh survey of the two routes, presented his conclusions in 1838, and they were emphatically in favour of the northern line. His prestige decided the issue. Meetings held at Chester and in London took up Stephenson's project with enthusiasm. A provisional committee was formed, including the Mayor of Chester, Sir Richard Bulkeley, of Beaumaris, and a number of gentlemen whose estates lay along the proposed route.[2]

Meanwhile the progress of railways in England was taking the sting out of Vignoles' argument that the adoption of the Holyhead line would mean a prohibitive expenditure on new permanent way. By 1839 the London-Birmingham and Birmingham-Liverpool railways were open for traffic, and the mail coach from London to Holyhead, which had just achieved the feat of performing the whole journey in less than 27 hours, disappeared from the English part of the road. The Irish mails were now taken by rail as far as Hartford station (midway between Crewe and Runcorn), and thence by coach to Holyhead *via* Chester.[3] Investors in turnpike bonds were seriously alarmed. The tolls between Shrewsbury and Holyhead were dwindling rapidly, and a further extension of the railway threatened them with ruin. Since the onset of steam seemed irresistible, it was proposed to put a steam

[1] Vignoles' *Report*, 1837 (Bangor MS. 400). The estimated distances and times from London to Dublin are as follows :—

Port.	Railway (miles).	Sea (miles).	Total time (hours).
Porthdinllaen ..	260	69	16
Holyhead ..	272	62½	17
Orme	230	96½	18
Liverpool ..	200	130½	19

[2] Smiles : *George and Robert Stephenson*, chap. XVII ; Parry : *op. cit.*, p. 1.
[3] Harper : *Holyhead Road*, I, p. 17 ; *Cheshire Sheaf*, 1878–9, p. 241.

coach on the road itself. Sir Henry Parnell, the Irish baronet who had done such yeoman service in Parliament and on committees while the road was in progress, took part in the preliminary discussions, and Telford was called in as consulting engineer ; but there the matter ended.[1]

The crisis of 1837, while it did not seriously hinder the prosecution of lines already under construction, made it difficult to get new projects floated, and little progress was made by the Chester-Holyhead committee till the opening of the Chester and Birkenhead Railway in 1840, and the rapid extension of the Great Western line in the following years, threatened the diversion of the Irish traffic to Liverpool on the one hand or to South Wales on the other.[2]   At last, in 1844—when the great railway mania was just beginning—the Act for the Chester and Holyhead railway received the Royal assent. Of the authorized capital, a million pounds were subscribed by the London and North Western Railway Company. The first sod was cut in the same year, and the work was carried through by the younger Stephenson, with Thomas Jackson as contractor.

It presented some knotty problems in engineering. The section from Chester to Conway is said to have cost £22,000 a mile. The sea-wall at Penmaenmawr was destroyed by a storm in its first winter, and had to be rebuilt at an alarming expense. The idea of using the suspension bridges for railway transport was abandoned, and the foundations of the two tubular bridges were laid in 1846. The Britannia Bridge alone afforded employment for some time for 1,500 men, who were housed in wooden huts at Bangor ; luckier than most navvies of that day, they got their pay regularly every week. On June 18, 1849, the Irish mails were for the first time taken all the way to Holyhead by rail. A further Act of 1848 authorized the Company (which had contributed £299,000 towards the new harbour and pier at Holyhead) to purchase, hire or use steam boats. The extension to Caernarvon took place in 1852 ; it was at first proposed

---

[1] *Report on Roads* (1840, XXVII), pp. 567, 568, 581 ; Clapham : *op. cit.*, p. 386.
[2] *See*, e.g., Fullarton's *Parl. Gaz.*, II, p. 101.

to carry a branch to Ffestiniog, but this project remained unfulfilled till 1874.[1]

The choice of the coast route had important consequences. A railway so placed, as Vignoles had foreseen, could be of little service to the main industries of the country ; what he did not foresee was the creation, through the tourist traffic, of a new industry (on which North Wales is coming more and more to depend for its subsistence) and a new belt of population, largely of English origin and speech. More than half the people of Snowdonia now live in the coastal resorts.[2] It was urgently necessary, however, that something should be done for the mineral products of Denbighshire and Flintshire. For such heavy merchandise, road and canal transport were terribly expensive. £5,000 a year were believed to be spent on carrying minerals along the five miles of road between Flint and Greenfield, and—in consequence of the failure to carry out the original plan of the Ellesmere Canal—coal from the pits round Wrexham had to be carried to Chester by a roundabout route of sixty miles. Ever since 1836 the principal owners of mines and ironworks had been addressing meetings and organizing petitions in favour of a railway to serve this region.[3] As usual, there were many rival schemes ; and it was not till 1844 that the North Wales Mineral Railway Company was floated, with an authorized share capital of £120,000 (increased within the next two years to £276,000) to build a railway from Wrexham to Chester, with a mineral branch from Wrexham to Brymbo. Next year there followed the Shrewsbury, Oswestry, and Cheshire Junction Railway Company, with a capital more than twice as great, and in 1846 the two Companies were amalgamated into the Shrewsbury and Chester Railway Company, with power (under a further Act) to make a branch to Llangollen. The beautiful viaduct at Cefn, with its nineteen slender arches, was completed in September, 1848—a fitting companion to its neighbour

[1] Scrivenor : *Railways of the United Kingdom*, pp. 414–19 ; Smiles and Parry : *loc. cit.; Hanes Plwyf Ffestiniog*, p. 132 ; Clapham : *op. cit.*, pp. 407, 409–10.

[2] Cundall and Landman : *op. cit.*, p. 10.

[3] *Chester Chron.*, Jan. 15, 29, May 6, 1836, Jan. 8, Feb. 3, June 19, 1837 ; Fullarton's *Parl. Gaz., loc. cit.* I owe some of these references to Mr. Emlyn Rogers.

the aqueduct ; by November the line was partially open
to traffic and the remaining sections were finished in the
course of the next year. The railway from Chester to
Mold (built by a separate company) was also opened
in 1849.[1]

Central Wales fared much worse. The future of the Welsh
flannel industry might have been different if support had been
forthcoming for William Pugh's scheme, or for the later
project of a Grand Welsh Junction Railway from Shrewsbury through Welshpool and Dolgelley to Porthdinllaen,
with connections to South Wales by Ludlow and Hereford.
As it was, Montgomeryshire and Merioneth were still
dependent on the stage coach long after the great trunk
lines had been completed. " Because of the difficulty
in obtaining the necessary capital outside the coal-fields,"
as the authors of a recent Economic Geography of Wales
remark, " many schemes for railways in Wales were either
abandoned or postponed and the general poverty of the
upland districts prevented any great undertakings being
attempted."[2] In 1846 was floated the Shropshire Union
Canal and Railway Company, which took over the Ellesmere and Chester Canals, the Birmingham and Liverpool
Junction Canal, and the Eastern (and subsequently the
Western) Branch of the Montgomeryshire Canal—a transfer
of property which involved Pugh of Brynllywarch in
further losses. One of the objects of the new Company
(which had an authorized capital of over £3,000,000)
was to drain the whole length of the Ellesmere and Montgomery Canals, and to construct a railway along the
canal bed from Newtown to Crewe. In 1847, however,
it leased its property in perpetuity to the London and North
Western Railway Company ; and the original project
soon vanished into thin air.[3] Among the many bogus
prospectuses issued in the late 'forties was one for a
railway from Ruthin to Bala.[4] During the 'fifties the air
was thick with plans for the railway development of

[1] Scrivenor : *op. cit.*, pp. 419, 513–21 ; *Wrexham Recorder*, I
(1848), Nos. 7 and 9 ; Palmer : *Wrexham*, p. 77 ; Fullarton's *Parl.
Gaz.*, I., p. 420.
[2] Cundall and Landman, p. 236 ; pp. 233–4 give an account (not
very helpful) of Welsh railway development as a whole.
[3] *Mont. Coll.*, XIV, p. 106, XV, pp. 97–100.
[4] *Wrexham Recorder* II (1849), No. 1.

Montgomeryshire,[1] but not till the very end of the decade did the first solid achievement—the completion of the Llanidloes-Newtown Railway—take place ; and the stage coach remained the only means of communication between Newtown and Shrewsbury until the Cambrian line was carried through to the west coast in the 'sixties.[2]

The old difficulties—lack of capital and the awkward lie of the country—had prevented North Wales, at the critical moment, from devising a railway system suited to her economic needs ; while she was still struggling forward, the industrial centres of the North and Midlands were steadily consolidating their position. The railway, which elsewhere brought with it a period of feverish expansion, in North Wales helped to nip the Industrial Revolution in the bud.[3]

NOTE.

RAILWAY FINANCE.[4]

Railway.	Date.	Authorized Share Capital.	Loans Authorized.
Chester— Holyhead	1844 1847 1848	£2,100,000 £400,000 £250,000	£700,000 £133,332 £83,000
Shrewsbury— Chester	1844 1845 1846	£120,000 £150,000 £6,000	£40,000 £50,000 £2,000
Shrewsbury, Oswestry, and Cheshire Jct.	1845 1846 1846	£410,000 £240,000 £30,000	£136,666/13/4 £80,000 £10,000

D. SHIPPING.

In the year 1737, Lewis Morris, customs officer at Beaumaris and Holyhead, was engaged by the Admiralty

[1] *Letters on Improvements*, pp. 33–6, 40–4.

[2] *See* an article on Montgomeryshire Railways in *Mont. Coll.*, XXX, pp. 282–90.

[3] There is a not very informative article on Welsh railways in *The Red Dragon*, IV (1883), pp. 489–94.

[4] Scrivenor : *op. cit.*

to make a survey of the Welsh coast from Anglesey to
Pembrokeshire. The results of his survey were published
eleven years later under the title: *Plans of Harbours,
Bars, Bays and Roads in St. George's Channel . . . Together*
*with a Short Account of the Trade and Manufactures on
that Coast.* All the chief ports and creeks were mapped,
with notes on their commerce, and suggestions for their
improvement. Morris draws a gloomy enough picture
of the existing situation, but of the future possibilities of
Welsh commerce he speaks with an enthusiasm which was
doubtless inspired, in part, by the hope of enlisting the
practical sympathy of the Admiralty. In 1801 a second
edition, based on a new survey, and extended to Liverpool
on the one hand and Cardiff on the other, was issued by his
son William. A comparison between the two editions shows
that not many of the dreams of 1748 had been realized.
With a few exceptions the silting-up of the harbours
was allowed to go on unchecked until the nineteenth
century ; and by that time the economic domination
of Lancashire and Liverpool was making it hopeless
to expect that North Wales, by competing directly in
world markets, would be able to provide a profitable
return on capital sunk in improving them.

Yet the later years of the eighteenth century saw a
considerable advance in shipping. Beaumaris, once the
nursery of seamen and merchants, was credited in 1701
with a single ship, and that of only fourteen tons. But
it still remained the premier port of North Wales, with
control over the customs of the whole coast from the
Conway to the Mawddach, including the subordinate
" creeks " of Amlwch, Holyhead, Caernarvon, Pwllheli,
and Barmouth. Before the end of the century this little
zollverein boasted 360 vessels, with a tonnage of nearly
14,000. This may be taken as the total shipping of North
Wales, excepting only that of a few small creeks included
in the port of Chester. By the end of the Napoleonic
Wars the figures had risen to 538 ships and over 25,000
tons.[1] But Beaumaris itself was being outclassed by
some of its subordinate creeks. Caernarvon, thanks
to the development of the slate industry, was in Pennant's
time doing a thriving trade with London, Bristol, Liverpool,

[1] *Cambrian Register*, I, p. 319 ; II, p. 418 ; III, p. 340.

and Ireland, and before the end of the century she was sending vessels direct to America and the West Indies. In 1792 there were 61 ships, with a tonnage of 2,240, belonging to the port ; in 1790 the trade in slates alone was reputed to reach £50,000 ; and during the following decade a total of over a thousand foreign and nearly two thousand coasting vessels were reported " cleared out " of the harbour.[1] Barmouth, which became for a short time the port for the woollen trade of Mid-Wales, was trading with Leghorn for lambswool and sending its " webs " to Spain and Portugal, and even as far as South America. The port was said to possess a hundred vessels in 1813.[2] There seems to be no foundation, however, for the tradition that the English name (a corruption of the original Abermaw) was deliberately adopted by a meeting of masters of vessels for the convenience of English traders at this time of increasing traffic.[3]

> The commerce of Wales [wrote an observer shortly before 1810] may justly be considered at present in its infancy . . . Few of the Welsh ports possess vessels of very considerable tonnage, though no part of the island contains a greater proportion of harbours and roads, some of which are safe and good, and more might be made so by the building of piers and other improvements . . . Were the public attention paid to this manifest scheme for enriching the principality, . . . it would be found very practicable . . . to render several of the Welsh harbours—now barred by choaking sands, capable of receiving ships of burthen . . . When the benefits arising from industry shall be thoroughly understood by the higher, and properly encouraged in the lower classes, of the Welsh, the spirit of improvement will be rapidly diffused ; the present coast-trade be despised ; and the fruits of trade and commerce exalt places, now scarcely known, in a scale of rank, equal with Chester, Bristol and Liverpool.[4]

The bulk of the shipping of North Wales, as the foregoing extract indicates, was engaged in the coasting trade —between Beaumaris and Caernarvon and the Dee, the Mersey and Ireland on the one hand, and between the

---

[1] Pennant : *Tours*, II, pp. 397–8 ; *Camb. Reg.*, I, p. 319 ; Evans : *Beauties*, pp. 366, 385–6 ; Barfoot and Wilkes' *Directory*, II, p. 532.
[2] Pennant : *Tours*, III, p. 253 ; *Camb. Trav. Guide* (1813), p. 97.
[3] Lewis : *Top. Dict.* (1833) under *Barmouth; Camb. Quart. Mag.*, II, p. 9 ; *Bye-gones*, 1895–6, p. 340.
[4] Evans : *Beauties*, p. 113 ; *cf. N. W. Gaz.*, Sept. 13, 1810.

Cardigan Bay ports and Swansea and Bristol on the other.[1]
To this we must add the river traffic. Corn vessels plied
down the Dee from Holt to Chester.[2] The Severn was
regularly navigated as far as Pool Quay until the construction of the Montgomeryshire Canal ;[3] and the volume of
shipping was swollen by barges of Llangynog slates coming
down the Vyrnwy from Llan y mynech.[4] Of the smaller
rivers, the Clwyd was extensively used for the conveyance
of corn to Rhuddlan, and considerable improvements in
navigation were brought about under the Rhuddlan
Enclosure Acts of 1807 and 1811. The Conway carried
slates and copper ore from Llanrwst and Trefriw ; in
1797 a meeting of all interested in the navigation of the
river was called to consider the question of cutting a
channel through some dangerous rocks which impeded
shipping.[5] On the Mawddach, ships frequently sailed
past Barmouth and unloaded at Penmaenpool or Llanelltyd,
which served as ports for Dolgelley.[6] Derwen lâs, on the
Dovey, stood in a similar relation to Machynlleth until
the completion of the Montgomeryshire Canal, which
had the same effect on Derwen lâs as on Pool Quay ;
after the opening of the Machynlleth and Aberystwyth
Railway in 1863-4 the port was "physically obliterated."[7]

Shipping was by no means confined, however, to these
short voyages. In the account books of an Anglesey
family during the latter half of the eighteenth century,
we find frequent notices of payments to masters of coasting
vessels for goods shipped from London to Caernarvon,
and *vice versa*.[8] The *North Wales Gazette* advertises in
1810 :—" THE CAMBRIA of Carnarvon, is now in the

[1] Cundall and Landman : *op. cit.*, p. 245.
[2] *N. W. Gaz.*, Sept. 27, 1812.
[3] *Mont. Coll.*, XIV, pp. 106, 211–12, XV, pp. 197 ff. ; *Cambria Depicta*, pp. 246–7 ; *Oswestry Her.*, May 7, 1822.
[4] Carlisle : *Top. Dict.*, under *Llanymynech; Bye-gones*, 1871–73, pp. 140, 149.
[5] Lewis : *Top. Dict.*, under *Rhuddlan* and *Carnarvonshire; Chester Chron.*, June 23, 1797 ; Davies, p. 280.
[6] Fenton : *Tours*, p. 107 ; Pigot's *Directory* (1828–29) ; Lewis : *Top. Dict.*, under *Llanelltyd.*
[7] *Mont. Coll.*, XXV, p. 113, IX, p. 192, XIV, p. 106, XLIII, pp. 33 ff ; *N.W. Chron.*, May 22, 1828 ; Lewis : *Top. Dict.*, under *Machynlleth* ; H.L.W. (1840, XXIV), p. 565.
[8] Meyrick Papers, 1755–98.

Thames, and will begin to load immediately for Carnarvon and ports adjacent. Any Gentleman having goods to ship, will do well to give their immediate orders." To balance, we have the following notice " To Masters of Vessels in the Coasting Trade " in 1818 :—" Wanted : conveyance for ten tons of goods from London to Pwllheli"; and in 1816 the same paper announces a " new and fast sailing-brig," with accommodation for passengers, from Caernarvon to Charlestown in South Carolina.[1]

Pari passu with the increase of shipping went improved devices for the safety and convenience of mariners. In 1810 the merchants of Liverpool set up a signalling station on Holyhead Mountain, and this was supplemented, between 1826 and 1829, by a complete chain of signals to carry messages by way of Point Lynas, Puffin Island, the Great Orme, Llysfaen and Point of Air to Chester and Liverpool. By means of these " telegraphs " (each consisting of a mast with six arms, working a system of code signals) news of the arrival and departure of vessels could be sent from one end of the chain to the other, on clear days, in less than a minute.[2] Life-saving apparatus was first provided on the coast of North Wales (at Point Lynas, the Great Orme and Point of Air) by order of the House of Commons in 1815.[3] The first lighthouse in the district had been built (thanks, again, to the efforts of Liverpool merchants) in Queen Anne's time, on the Skerries, north-west of the Anglesey coast. It was maintained by private individuals, who were allowed by Parliament, first a pension from the Post Office revenue, and subsequently the right to collect a small toll towards their expenses from passing vessels.[4] There followed lighthouses at Point of Air in 1777, Holyhead in 1808, Bardsey in 1821—a project which was opposed by Sir John Gladstone (father of the statesman) and other Liverpool

[1] *N. W. Gaz.*, April 5, 1810, Aug. 1, 1818, April 11, 1816.
[2] *Imperial and County Register*, 1810, Pt. V, pp. 17–18 ; *N. W. Gaz.*, Oct. 11, 1827 ; *Shrewsbury Chron.*, May 22, 1829 ; *Trans. Ang. Ant. Soc.*, 1921, pp. 53–4 ; *Bye-gones*, 1909–10, p. 53..
[3] *N. W. Gaz.*, Sept. 21, 1815, *cf.* Aug. 30, 1810.
[4] *Hist., MSS. Com.*, 8th Rept., App., p. 395 ; Lewins, W. : *Her Majesty's Mails* (1865), p. 115 ; Pennant : *Tours*, III, pp. 66–7; *Cambria Depicta*, p. 50 : *Trans. Ang. Ant. Soc.*, 1924, pp. 54–76.

merchants—Amlwch by 1831 and Penmon in 1835. These later erections, of course, were the work of Trinity House.[1]

Finally, some progress was made with the long-desired improvement of the principal harbours. The first to benefit were naturally those in which the increase of shipping had been most marked. The development of the trade in woollens from Barmouth impelled a number of the local merchants and gentry to procure in 1797 an Act for enlarging the harbour. The preamble recites how Barmouth " is a place of very considerable and increasing Resort for Ships and Vessels trading to and from the same, which are now more numerous and of larger Dimensions than heretofore " ; and the trustees —160 of the chief men of the county—are empowered to undertake any necessary works on the harbour, paying for them by means of tonnage dues (with specially low rates for coal) and public loans. But times were bad : the War impoverished the investing public, and in the very year after the Harbour Act was passed, a traveller described how "a paralyzing damp" had been cast on the port, till the "spirit of adventure" was "almost extinguished." He saw

> numerous vessels lying heeled upon their sides, or moored in the mud, their sails laid up ; and their owners out of employment, or earning a scanty pittance . . . by the precarious profits of an uncertain fishery.

Eventually a sum of about £1,600 was laid out ; but the hopes of a post-war revival of trade were disappointed. Foreign shipping did not come back to Barmouth ; its trade was reduced once more to the ordinary coastwise traffic, and this in turn was ruined by the railway.[2]

Before the Act of Union, Holyhead is said to have had "neither pier nor jetty." Almost immediately after the Act was passed, John Rennie the engineer was sent by Government to report on the condition of the harbour. In consequence of his report a grant of £10,000 towards improvements was made in 1808, and further grants followed. The work was not actually taken in hand

[1] *The British Pharos* (second ed., Leith, 1831), pp. 44–7 ; *Chester Chron.*, Sept. 19, 1777 ; *N. W. Gaz.*, Feb. 23, 1809, Dec. 11, 1821 ; *Shrewsbury Chron.*, Nov. 26, Dec. 31, 1819.

[2] 37 Geo. III, cap. 50 ; Evans : *Tour*, pp. 89, 112–4 ; Lewis : *Top. Dict.*, under *Barmouth; Bye-gones,* 1916–18, p. 83.

till 1810, and not finished till 1824. Once again the prime movers had been Sir John Gladstone (then plain Mr. Gladstone) and his fellow merchants of Liverpool. A further enlargement of the harbour took place when the Holyhead Railway was built, and these undertakings did much to relieve the widespread unemployment from which the rest of Anglesey was then suffering.[1]

Several new ports were created by the slate and copper industries of Caernarvonshire and Anglesey. To cope with the growing output of his quarries, Lord Penrhyn constructed in 1790 the harbour of Port Penrhyn, near Bangor, which, after enlargement in 1800, could accommodate fifty vessels. A little later the smaller quay at Felin Heli (re-named Port Dinorwic) was adapted to receive the produce of Mr. Assheton Smith's quarries.[2] Portmadoc was another slate port. Mr. Madocks began his harbour there while he was embanking the Traeth. He procured an Act of Parliament for it in 1821, and it was completed three years later.[3] He was also largely responsible for the improvements (never finished) in the harbour of Porthdinllaen, by means of which it was hoped to equip it for capturing the Irish traffic.[4] When copper mining began in earnest on Parys Mountain, the neighbouring harbour at Amlwch was "no more than a cove between two steep rocks, where a vessel hath not room to wind even at high water." But in 1793 the mining companies obtained an Act under which it was made capable of sheltering thirty sloops of 50 to 100 tons.[5]

Some of the older ports in this district were also adapted to meet the needs of increasing trade. Improvements in Caernarvon harbour and the navigation of the Straits were begun about 1808, and were still in progress in 1830.

[1] Smiles : *Smeaton and Rennie*, pp. 313–8 ; Reports of Committees on Holyhead Roads, 1810–29, *passim;* Census of 1851 ; *N. W. Gaz.*, Feb. 20, 1823.

[2] Lewis : *Top. Dict.*, under *Llandegai* and *Port Dinorwig; Oswestry Her.*, Dec. 19, 1820.

[3] *N.W. Gaz.*, May 26, 1808; *Gestiana*, pp. 175–6; *cf. supra*, pp. 42–4.

[4] The Jones Parry family of Madryn were also prominent supporters. They had not abandoned hope as late as the 'sixties and 'seventies. *See* Yale MSS. 31, 32, 33, 35; *cf. supra*, p. 114.

[5] Evans : *Beauties*, pp. 250, 378 ; Morris : *Plans of Harbours* (second ed., 1801), pp. 3, 6 ; Lewis : *Top. Dict.*, under *Nevin* and *Amlwch.*

Under Act of Parliament, the Corporation was allowed to raise money for the purpose by means of a port tax on tea and coals. With this assistance the harbour was greatly enlarged, and a neighbouring landowner and a sea captain equipped it with a pier in 1827 ; further down the Straits the dangerous rocks known as the Swillies were blasted. It was on the score of this outlay of capital that the inhabitants of Caernarvon opposed the building of the suspension bridge, which threatened to injure their shipping.[1] At Beaumaris the Corporation undertook in 1815–16 the placing of buoys, and other measures for the safety of navigation. Pwllheli harbour, like Rhuddlan and the Clwyd, benefited from an Enclosure Act, passed in 1811. At Conway, where the port was spoiled by shifting sandbanks, nothing was done till 1840.[2]

The industrial regions of the north-east were less fortunate. It has been a great drawback to the development of North Wales that one of her coalfields is landlocked, and the other depends for its outlet by sea on the changing channel of the Dee estuary. Mostyn, once of considerable importance as a quay for the export of Flintshire coal to Ireland, was gradually deserted by the tide in the course of the eighteenth century, in spite of spirited efforts on the part of the family whose name it shares to fight the accumulating silt.[3] The work of nature was aided and abetted from 1732 by the Dee Navigation Company, which took in hand the deepening of the channel towards Chester—at the expense of creeks like Bagillt and Flint.[4] Bagillt, indeed, contrived to hold its own for a century or more as a depôt for passenger and goods traffic with Liverpool and for the coastal trade in lead and coal ; but Flint, although fresh changes in the channel led to a brief revival of coal exports in the early nineteenth

[1] Evans : *Beauties*, pp. 364–7 ; *N. W. Gaz.*, March 8, 1810, May 12 *et seq.*, 1814 ; *N. W. Chron.*, June 3, 1824, May 5, 1825, Dec. 20, 1827.

[2] *N. W. Gaz.*, Dec. 7, 1815, May 30, 1816, Aug. 26, 1813 ; Evans : *Tour*, p. 260 ; Fullarton's *Parl. Gaz.*, I, p. 497.

[3] Pennant : *Tours*, I, p. 23 and *n*, *Whiteford and Holywell*, p. 134 ; *Shrewsbury Chron.*, July 25, 1823 ; Lewis : *Top. Dict.*, under *Whitford*.

[4] Lhwyd : *Parochialia* (*Arch. Camb.* suppt., 1909), p. 86 ; Pugh: *Camb. Dep.*, p. 354 ; Priestley : *Navigable Rivers*, pp. 189–93.

century, was found by the Municipal Corporations Commissioners in 1835 to be "of very little importance from a commercial point of view."[1] On the other hand, the deepened channel to the south had brought into existence the new creek of Connah's Quay, which was developed by the Irish Coal Company in the early nineteenth century, and flourished greatly after the railway reached it in 1849, making it a maritime depôt for the produce of a wide area.[2]

For many years it was a shipbuilding centre as well as a port. The Scottish firm of Ferguson, McCallum and Baird first set up at Flint in 1840, but in 1859 the land they occupied was required for an extension of the chemical works, and they opened out on a larger scale at Connah's Quay. Steamers and three-masted sailing vessels of about 300 tons were built for the brick trade then carried on between Connah's Quay and London, and the firm "did very well" till the War forced them to close down in 1917. Their ships were all of wood, but iron vessels were also made in Flintshire before the end of the century.[3] Vessels for coasting and fishing were also made at other ports. At Holyhead the firm of Grayson and Howson, from Liverpool, set up in the trade during the boom of 1825, and, although they had to sell out during the ensuing depression, the industry continued for some time to give employment to "numerous workmen."[4] Small cutters and vessels up to 200 tons were made in the shipyard of Messrs. Trewick at Amlwch and Mr. Samuel Samuel built similar craft at Caernarvon till his death in 1821.[5] At Pwllheli

---

[1] *M.C.R.* (1835, XXVI), p. 612 ; Fullarton's *Parl. Gaz.* II, p. 103 ; Churton : *Railway Book of England*, p. 529 ; Edwards : *Flintshire*, pp. 87–9.

[2] *Chester Chron.*, March 12, 1802 ; Lewis : *Top. Dict.*, under *Northop; Camb. Quart. Mag.*, IV, p. 351 ; Parry : *Railway Companion*, pp. 27, 35–6.

[3] Information kindly supplied by Mr. Walter Baird, late of Connah's Quay. The Census gives the following statistics of shipbuilding in Flintshire : 1861 : 34 shipbuilders and shipwrights ; 1891 : 37 shipbuilders (wood), 11 (iron) ; 1901 : 71 (wood), 5 (iron) ; 1911 : 41 (wood), 230 (iron) ; 1921 : 99 in all.

[4] *N. W. Gaz.*, April 14, 1825, Aug. 10, Nov. 9, 1826 ; Lewis : *Top. Dict.*

[5] *Id.*, Oct. 10, 1828, Oct. 12, 1815, March 29, May 17, 1821.

shipbuilding was long the principal industry,[1] and in the early nineteenth century it was also carried on to a small extent at Bangor, Conway and Barmouth,[2] as well as at a few inland creeks on navigable rivers, such as those at Trefriw, Llanelltyd and Welshpool.[3]

But the hope that North Wales would now be able to take a direct and active part in world commerce was never realized. Holyhead retained its position as long as it kept the Irish traffic. In 1801 it had only 2,000 inhabitants; in 1921 it had five times as many, and the most rapid increase took place during the decade 1841-51. But symptoms of decline began to appear soon after the Free State was formed. Similarly the slate trade brought about a growth in the population of Caernarvon from less than 4,000 in 1801 to nearly 10,000 in 1851 —though since then it has decreased somewhat. But Beaumaris is rapidly declining, Barmouth holds its own only as a seaside resort, and Rhuddlan—the grain port of former days—has been ruined by the railway.

The only important development in shipping during the period which followed the Napoleonic Wars was the introduction of the steamship. Here again it was the Irish traffic that set the pace. The old sailing boats from Holyhead to Dublin, which had been increased in number from three to six during the latter half of the eighteenth century, normally did the voyage in twelve to fifteen hours; in exceptionally favourable conditions the time might be reduced by half, but in a storm the traveller could expect to be held up for two or three days. This uncertainty led the Parliamentary Committee of 1815 on the Holyhead Roads and Harbour to explore the possibilities of steam navigation, which had just been tried with success on the Clyde. The first experiments were made in 1819, when the *Talbot*, a privately-owned vessel of 150 tons with two engines of 30 horse-power

[1] Fenton : *Tours* (1804), p. 47 ; Pugh: *Camb. Dep.*, p. 142 ; Leigh : *Guide to Wales* (1839), p. 297.

[2] *N. W. Chron.*, April 23, 1829 (Bangor) ; *N. W. Gaz.*, Oct. 13, 1808 (Conway) ; *Shrewsbury Chron.*, April 23, 1827 (Barmouth).

[3] Carlisle : *Top. Dict.* (Trefriw) ; Lewis : *Top. Dict.* (Llanelltyd) ; *Bye-gones*, 1903–04, pp. 289–90.   Pigot's *Directory* (1828–29) mentions three ship and boat builders at Caernarvon, one at Bangor, three at Pwllheli, and one at Welshpool.

each, started plying daily between Holyhead and Dublin during the summer and autumn. A second was added in the following year, and in 1821 the General Post Office, having with difficulty overcome the prejudices of the commanders of the sailing vessels in its service, began to carry the Irish mails in steam packets. The average length of the voyage was thus cut down to $7\frac{1}{2}$, and shortly afterwards to 6 hours. It is characteristic of the time that a suggestion for compelling every steam packet, in the interests of safety, to carry a certain number of boats, was scouted by the Parliamentary Committee on the ground of "the policy of avoiding to do anything that could by possibility check the spirit of improvement ;" for "individual security . . . will always be sufficiently provided for by the interests of the proprietors." By 1828 there were six Irish boats, some of them sailing twice daily.[1]

The steamer was also beginning to oust the sailing-boat on other routes. There had long been regular packets crossing the Dee estuary, from Holywell and Flint to Chester and Parkgate, and so to Liverpool.[2] In 1821 the *Cambria* steam packet was launched at Liverpool, and henceforth she made daily voyages to Bagillt during the summer, returning the same afternoon. Next year the service was extended once a week to Beaumaris, Bangor and Caernarvon ; and soon there were three or four boats, providing between them, from April to October, a daily service from Liverpool to the Menai Straits.[3] "Formerly," wrote a traveller in 1830, "a winter journey from Caernarvonshire to Liverpool was an era in a man's life, and the Cambrian who was necessitated to make it set his house in order and made his will ;" whereas now steamboats were running throughout the year, covering the whole distance in six hours or less, and providing meals on board. By this date, too, the whole of the northern coast of Wales, as far as Porthdinllaen and

[1] Morris : *Plans of Harbours*, p. 4 ; Owen : *History of Anglesey*, p. 26 ; Reports of Committees on Holyhead Roads, etc., 1815 (second), 1822 (fifth) ; Pigot's *Directory* (1828–29) and Lewis' *Top. Dict.* (1833), under *Holyhead*.

[2] *Chester Chron.*, April 30, 1802 ; Pugh : *Camb. Dep.*, p. 354.

[3] *N. W. Gaz.*, Feb. 22, May 10, Sept. 20 and 27, 1821, Jan. 17, June 13 and 20, 1822, Feb. 27, 1823.

Amlwch, was in constant communication with Liverpool ; from 1822 steamboats left at stated intervals for London,[1] and from 1829 for Dublin, Belfast and Glasgow. In the latter year the Corporation of Pwllheli was considering a scheme for establishing a steam service to South Wales, and in 1830 a steamboat left Tremadoc for New York.[2]

Speedy and regular communication with Liverpool was a great boon to Welsh shopkeepers, and at the same time a heavy blow to the local fairs. Anglesey cattle-breeders, again, found it a convenience to be able to ship their beasts direct to Liverpool, where there was a ready market, instead of having to drive them across the Straits and along the weary roads of Caernarvonshire and Denbighshire ; unfortunately for them, the steamboat also served the cause of their Irish rivals, so the gain was largely neutralized.[3] By 1840, thanks to the competition of the locomotive, steamboat services to the Welsh ports were growing less frequent.[4] In either form, however, the steam engine had the same effects : to push English sales in Wales rather than Welsh sales in England, and to turn the North Wales coast into a playground of Lancashire.[5]

[1] *N. W. Chron.*, Jan. 7, April 8, May 20, 1830 ; *N. W. Gaz.*, Sept. 5, 1822.
[2] *N. W. Chron.*, July 23, 1829, July 29, 1830, Nov. 1 and 29, 1827, Aug. 5, 1830.
[3] *Id.*, June 24, Oct. 7, 1830.
[4] Lewis : *Top. Dict.* (1843), under *Bagillt*.
[5] There is abundant material on shipping (especially for Caernarvonshire) in the Porth yr aur collection. The complete history of many vessels could be written from it.

On the trade of the N. Wales ports in mid-eighteenth century *see* B.M., Lansdowne MS 1215, fos. 169–72, and figures for 1742–6 printed in Owen, E. : *Catalogue of MSS relating to Wales in the British Museum* (Cym. Rec. Ser. lv) i, p. 98.

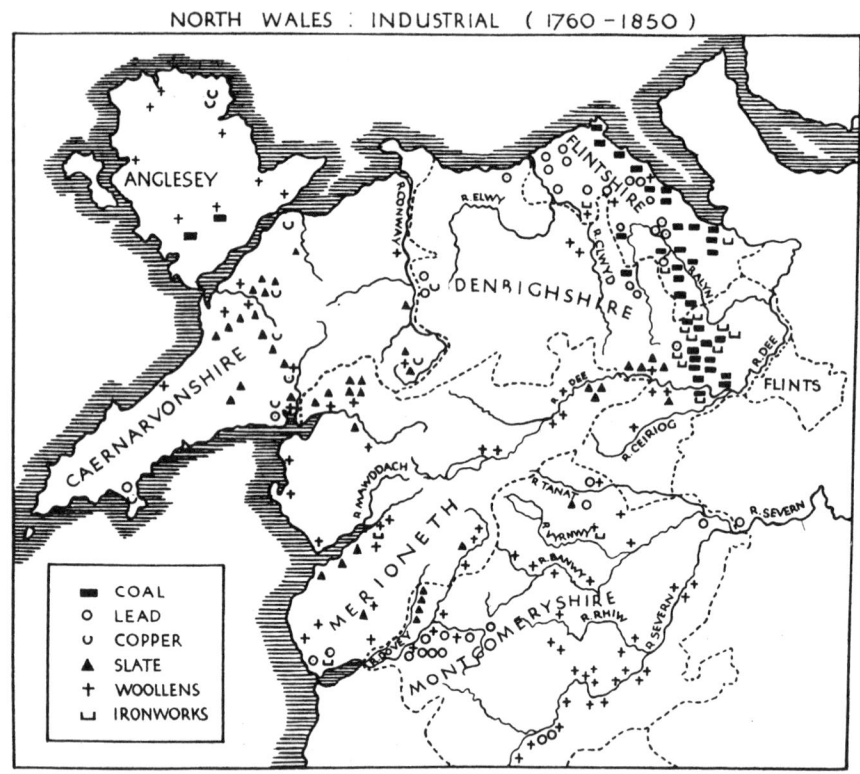

NORTH WALES : INDUSTRIAL (1760 - 1850)

ANGLESEY

CAERNARVONSHIRE

DENBIGHSHIRE

FLINTSHIRE

FLINTS

MERIONETH

MONTGOMERYSHIRE

R. CONWAY
R. ELWY
R. CLWYD
R. ALWYN
R. DEE
R. CEIRIOG
R. TANAT
R. VYRNWY
R. BANWY
R. RHIW
R. SEVERN
R. MAWDDACH

COAL
LEAD
COPPER
SLATE
WOOLLENS
IRONWORKS

CHAPTER V.
METALS.

About five-and-thirty years ago . . . a cry went through the north country that a great deal of money might be made by opening Wales, that is, by mining Wales in the proper fashion . . . There had long been mines in Wales, but they had always been worked in a poor, weak, languid manner, very different from that of the north country.[1]

So Borrow was told by the old Durham miner whom he met near Devil's Bridge in 1854. His informant probably referred to the days when Cobbett's *bête noire*, "Prosperity" Robinson, was at the Exchequer, and when Canning called the New World into existence to extend the markets of the Old. It may or may not be true that tropical ports in South America were then plied with cargoes of skates from Sheffield and warming-pans from Birmingham,[2] but it is certain that the spirit of speculation had never been busier since the South Sea Bubble. In particular it seized hold of mining ; 34 mining companies are recorded among the projects of the boom years 1824-5. The gold and silver of Mexico and Peru were the first objective, but—the fashion once set—speculators began to look nearer home, and to brood over the uncharted resources of the Welsh mountains. Company after company was floated to work the minerals of Wales ; great financiers like Nathan Rothschild, sporting peers like Lord Palmerston, and a host of less reputable speculators all took a hand in it ; and English newspapers hastened to point out what a field there was here for English capital and English skill.[3] The sequel is well known. The crisis that wrecked the fortunes of Sir Walter Scott spread distress throughout the mining districts of North

[1] *Wild Wales*, chap. LXXXIII.

[2] Martineau, Harriet : *History of England during the Thirty Years' Peace* (1849), I, p. 357. A marginal note by Reynolds the ironmaster in his copy of this work (now in the University College Library, Bangor) gives the surprising information that the warming-pans "sold well."

[3] Craik : *History of British Commerce*, III, pp. 240 ff. ; *Shrewsbury Chron.*, Jan. 28, Feb. 4, Aug. 12, 1825 ; *infra*, pp. 146–7, 167, 175, 214–16.

Wales. Few of the mushroom growths survived, and industry paid as dear for this artificial forcing as agriculture had paid for the fictitious prosperity of the Napoleonic era.

The mining boom of 1825 probably did more to injure than to help the group of industries most deeply affected by it. Actually the "opening up" of North Wales had begun —less spectacularly, but more solidly—years before. Mining and smelting inevitably go hand in hand, and it was the progress of the smelting industries, at the very beginning of the eighteenth century, that brought the first great incursion of outside capital into the working of mines.[1] Then the American and Napoleonic Wars, with their heavy demand for iron and copper, helped to complete the displacement of the landowner by the capitalist adventurer. A letter in a local newspaper for 1822 speaks with enthusiasm of the rapid development of copper, slate, lead and iron mining in North Wales during the last thirty years, and of the possibilities of further progress—especially by increased use of steam engines—if only oppressive duties could be removed and the knowledge of geology extended ; and the following advertisement in a Chester newspaper of 1807 is characteristic of the times :

> Several gentlemen interested in the mineralogy of Wales have determined to have the mountains in that country examined by a practical mineralogist, in order that the various veins of metallic ores may be worked if sufficiently valuable.[2]

The opening of communications had done its work, and the spirited proprietors who were foremost in promoting it ceased to exploit their own minerals, and became content with the passive rôle of leasing them out to smelters and other men of humbler origin—frequently immigrants from England.

Among these industrial pioneers two names stand out—those of John Wilkinson the ironmaster and Thomas Williams the "copper king." They both came of farming stock, and prudent parents had equipped them with a good education. Both, too, belong to English as well as to Welsh industrial history ; but one started his

[1] *Supra*, pp. 20–24.
[2] *Caernarvonshire Advertiser*, Feb. 23, 1822 ; *Chester Chron.*, Dec. 11, 1807.

operations in England and later extended them to Wales, while the other started in Anglesey, and from Anglesey came to dominate the copper market of England, if not of the world. They entered industry by different routes : Wilkinson through apprenticeship to his enterprising but unlucky father, Williams by means of legal services to the Anglesey gentry just at the time when they were finding copper on their lands and looking for someone to manage it for them. Both extended their financial activities far beyond the industries with which they were directly concerned, and both amassed great fortunes and aroused great hatreds. Williams became a country gentleman in Anglesey and a borough-owner in Buckinghamshire ; Wilkinson rose to be High Sheriff of Denbighshire, and bore his own coat of arms with the device *Labore et honore*. We have seen, too, how each of them played his part in improving agriculture, and Wilkinson in extending canals.[1] Williams left his fortune to a son who, having married (like the industrious apprentice) the daughter of his father's first employer, used it to push his way into other fields of business. Wilkinson founded no dynasty, and his estates melted away in litigation between relatives who, whatever their title to his effects, had certainly inherited none of his abilities. Each, then, was in his way a typical *entrepreneur* of the new era, and their stories form a natural starting-point for any attempt to describe the "revolution" in mining and metallurgy.

A. JOHN WILKINSON AND THE IRON INDUSTRY.

Ye workmen of Bersham and Brymbo, draw near,
Sit down, take your pipes, and my song you shall hear . . .
Fill up, and without any further parade,
"John Wilkinson," boys, "that supporter of trade,"
Derry Down, Down, Derry Down . . .

That the wood of old England would fail did appear,
And [though][2] iron was scarce, because charcoal was dear,

[1] *Supra*, pp. 37, 42, 102 ; Roberts : *Eminent Welshmen* ; Palmer : *John Wilkinson; see* also Trevelyan, G. M. : *Lord Grey of the Reform Bill*, p. 267 *n*, where Williams is misleadingly described as "a Welsh attorney who [had] speculated in coal mines."
[2] *Hough* in text used by Palmer. He would amend to *tough*.

> By puddling and stamping he prevented that evil,
> So the Swedes and the Russians may go to the devil.
>   Derry Down, etc.
>
> Our thundering cannon too frequently burst ;
> A mischief so great he prevented the first,
> And now 'tis well known, they never miscarry,
> But drive all our foes with a blast to Old Harry.
>   Derry Down, etc.[1]

This was the ditty in which Wilkinson's exploits were commemorated in the district he did most to develop. His father had come from Furness (in North Lancashire) in 1753, to take over the old Bersham ironworks—one of the cradles, as we have seen, of the coke-smelting process. Starting, probably, as a small farmer, Isaac Wilkinson had early found part-time employment in the little haematite furnaces of Cumbria, till at last he came to abandon farming altogether for iron-founding. The Bersham site attracted him by the resources it offered in water-power, as well as in coal and ironstone, which he leased on an extensive scale. The works were adapted to the casting of all manner of iron goods, from box-heaters to water pipes and cannon. Isaac Wilkinson also took shares in an iron furnace in South Wales.[2] But his abilities were not equal to his ambitions ; after about eight years he failed, and gave place to a new company floated by his two sons John and William. John, the elder brother, was from the first the moving spirit. He had widened his experience in the great ironworks of the Midlands—later to be the scene of his most important undertakings—while William had only been his father's right-hand man at Bersham.

The state of the iron industry when John Wilkinson began to extend his operations is not misrepresented in the verses we have quoted above. The discoveries at Coalbrookdale in the beginning of the century had only transformed one branch of manufacture. The employment of coke in the blast-furnaces had led to an enormous extension in the use of cast-iron goods ; but no means had yet been found of adapting mineral fuel to the forging of malleable iron, and the forge declined as the foundry increased in

---

[1] Palmer : *Wilkinson*, pp. 22–3.
[2] Edwards, Ness : *The Industrial Revolution in South Wales*, p. 24.

importance. "Because charcoal was dear," manufacturers who needed as their raw material something tougher and more resistant of shocks than the brittle and often defective castings of the coke-furnace were tempted by the cheaper bar-iron of Sweden and Russia. It needed the series of inventions culminating in Cort's puddling patents of 1783–4 to bring coal into use in the finery and forge ; and even in the blast-furnace charcoal was not completely displaced—especially in the manufacture of ordnance—until the application of steam provided a more effective blast than could be got from bellows worked by horses or by water. These new processes, which revolutionized the iron industry in the 'eighties, were most of them invented by others,[1] but it was to the Wilkinsons, and to those Midland immigrants who were at the same time building up the ironworks of South Wales, that their successful application was chiefly due ; and Bersham had a great part to play in it all.

The closing struggle of the Seven Years' War gave Wilkinson the opportunity to push ahead with the munitions side of his business. The works were reconstructed, and cannon, grenades, and shells of 4-inch calibre were turned out in unheard-of quantities, as well as cylinders and pipes of all sorts. In the Company's ledgers for 1764 the Office of Ordnance stands debited with thirty-two guns ; but by this time the War was over. It might have been expected that the New Bersham Company, like so many ironfounding firms that had been busily turning ploughshares into swords in anticipation of a longer struggle, would have succumbed to the post-war crisis, when even the Darbys at Coalbrookdale were having to "make work" by substituting iron for wooden railways. But Wilkinson employed these slack years in preparations for the next boom : taking over new furnaces, buying up corn and fulling mills with a view to controlling the river that supplied him with his power, making his first ventures in lead-mining, and experimenting in improved methods for the boring of cannon.[2]

[1] The invention of the cupola is attributed to William Wilkinson (Ashton : *Iron and Steel*, p. 102).

[2] Ashton : *op. cit.*, chaps. II, III, and IV ; Smiles : *Iron Workers and Tool Makers* (1863) ; Palmer : *op. cit.* ; *Mont. Coll.*, XXVI, p. 329.

When war broke out between the Russians and the Turks in 1768, he was ready to supply both sides with armaments, and by the commencement of the American War he had taken out his patent for boring cannon, and was zealously guarding it against interlopers.   Throughout the War the foundry was working at full pressure.[1]   There were malicious rumours, indeed, that munitions from Bersham found their way to other armies besides our own. For Wilkinson's brother William had gone out to France, where he secured a contract for supplying iron pipes to the Paris Waterworks Company ; and it was alleged that

> under so coulerable a pretext [he] exported Cannon Balls, Cylinders, of most unusual Thickness, and . . . Ball to the amount of twenty-four thousand tons in six weeks supposed for France [America's ally] as all were put on board those Vessels employed by Wilkinson for exporting iron pipes.

The charge was investigated at the Chester Customs-house in 1782, but the issue is unknown.[2]   At any rate, if Wilkinson did not smuggle munitions out to the enemy, he set up establishments for manufacturing them on enemy soil.   When Arthur Young visited France six years after the War, he found two such factories owned by "Monsieur Wielkainsong," and the people told him that the English ironmaster, who was brother-in-law to Dr. Priestley, "and therefore a friend of mankind," had "taught them to bore cannon in order to give liberty to America."[3]

By this time, however, the plant at Bersham was being turned to more peaceful uses.   In 1775, James Watt took out his second patent for making steam-engines ; and he and Matthew Boulton, his partner at the Soho works, soon found in Wilkinson's cannon-lathe the only "proper apparatus" which could produce the cylinders and some of

[1] Pennant : *Tours*, I, p. 377 ; Ashton : *op. cit.*, pp. 63, 68, 136.
[2] Extracts from the Customs-house correspondence at Caernarvon, for which I am indebted to my friend Mr. David Thomas of Bangor. In Shropshire, at least, Wilkinson's manufacture of pipes was stopped, and a number of his castings littered his warehouse at Willey for many years (Victoria County Histories : *Shropshire*, I, pp. 473–4).
[3] Young : *Travels in France* ("Everyman" ed.), pp. 109, 183 ; *cf*. Boulton to Watt, Feb. 11, 1783 (Lord : *Capital and Steam Power*, p. 213 *n*).

the fittings "with that truth and exactness we require."[1]
For twenty years all but three or four of the engines
supplied by Boulton and Watt had their cylinders made at
one or other of Wilkinson's works. Bersham itself was
now only one among many undertakings, for the two
brothers were manufacturing on an even bigger scale in the
Midlands. Wilkinson was also an important customer of
the Soho firm. Not only did he want steam engines for
pumping his many mines, but he was the first to use them
for other industrial processes. In 1776 he set one up at
Snedshill to operate his blast ; six years later the newly-
patented rotary engine was employed to work the forge
hammers at another of his establishments, and in 1786 he
used it to drive a slitting and rolling mill. All these
processes came to be extended to his Welsh works ; and
the connection between Bersham and Soho was close and
intimate. But Wilkinson was not an easy man to deal
with. His temper was overbearing, his terms exacting,
and his business methods not above suspicion. At last
an open rupture was brought about by the discovery
that he had been infringing the patent by making Boulton
and Watt engines not only for his own use, but for others
(both in England and abroad), without paying the
stipulated premium.

It was John's own brother and partner who revealed
the fraud ; for William Wilkinson had his own grievances
to avenge. John was growing dissatisfied with the
Bersham works. There had been complaints from Watt
of defective material turned out from it ; besides, the
land was only held on lease, and most of his coal and ironstone came from other people's property. In 1792 he
negotiated—not without financial embarrassment—the
purchase of the Brymbo Hall estate, a few miles away.
Here he would have coal resources, almost untapped, at
his command—and coal was becoming daily more vital to
his work ; water-power no longer counted. From this
new enterprise William was excluded, and the estrange-
ment between the two issued in a violent quarrel a couple
of years later. The Bersham works were closed down ;
tradition adds that the brothers hired rival gangs of

[1] Ashton, p. 65. (Boulton to a customer, Dec., 1778.)

Wrexham roughs to smash up the machinery. Three or
four hundred men were thus thrown out of work. Some
of them found employment under Boulton and Watt ;
others went out to fight the French. Fortunately for
the district, the distress caused by this grand act of
sabotage was only temporary. Towards the end of 1795
the works were sold by order of arbitrators, and they were
bought back by John, who by this clever move had got
rid of his unwanted partner both at Bersham and at
Brymbo.[1]

Within a few years two blast-furnaces and an improved
boring mill were built on the new site, and coal was being
sunk for in every part of the estate.[2] Wilkinson's
business, in fact, was extending in all directions. Like
most of the new-fashioned ironmasters, he had his eggs in
many baskets—and they were all capacious baskets. He
was at once mine-owner, coal-merchant, smelter and
founder, and for some time he had also been "in the forge
way." In its early days the Bersham Company had
rented the forge at Abenbury (further down the river) for
the purpose of turning its pig-iron into bars, but later on
forges and mills for slitting, rolling and stamping were set
up at Bersham itself and also (though possibly not in
Wilkinson's time) at Brymbo.[3]

His trade was European in scope, and his goods were
in demand for every kind of manufactory. A newspaper
of 1801 records as a nine-days' wonder the conveyance—on
a specially-constructed vehicle, drawn by eight horses—of
a huge iron plate, weighing $18\frac{1}{2}$ tons, from the Bersham
foundry to the glass works at St. Helens ; it was believed
to be the largest weight ever carried over land in England.[4]
And he had interests in other industries as well. To
ensure a sale for his cylinders, he had become a shareholder,
along with Boulton and Watt, in Cornish copper mines,

---

[1] Palmer : *op. cit.;* Ashton, chap. III ; Smiles : *Boulton and Watt,* pp. 161–2, 252, 285 ; Eden : *State of the Poor,* III, pp. 891 ff.
[2] *Chester Chron.,* May 2, 1800 ; *N. W. Gaz.,* Nov. 9, 1815 ; Ashton, p. 103 and *n.*
[3] Ashton, p. 72 ; Palmer, *op. cit.,* pp. 13–14, and *Old Parish of Wrexham,* p. 150 ; *Camb. Trav. Guide* (1813), pp. 1162–3, 1349 : Lewis : *Top. Dict.* (1833), under *Broughton.*
[4] *Salop. Journ.,* Sept. 23, 1801.

where pumping engines were in great demand. Nearer home, he worked lead mines at Minera and Mold, and smelted some of the produce on the spot. This provided yet another market for Boulton and Watt engines. It was to pump the Minera mine that he made the "pirated" engine which began the quarrel with the Soho partners ; the mine near Mold had eventually six of them at work. What with the crippling expense of drainage and his eternal quarrels with partners and lessors, Wilkinson never managed to make much of his lead-mining ventures.[1] As a canal proprietor, too, he was doomed to disappointment. It was just at the time when he bought Brymbo Hall estate that the respective merits of the eastern and western routes for the Ellesmere canal were under discussion, and it must have been a bitter disappointment to him when engineering difficulties wrecked the project which would have carried the canal past his Bersham works and within easy reach of those at Brymbo.[2]

The Napoleonic Wars created once more an unlimited demand for munitions, of which Wilkinson took full advantage. The old story was revived of secret supplies of cannon and shot finding their way from Bersham to the French, and on top of it came a new accusation. Since 1787 the workmen at Bersham and the sister establishments had been paid in the firms' own copper and silver tokens and guinea notes.[3] In 1790 came Burke's thunders against the "philosophick financiers" of France ; two years later Chief Justice Kenyon received a letter from a Flintshire correspondent denouncing John Wilkinson as a distributor of *assignats*.

> The Presbyterian tradesmen [he was assured] receive them in payment for goods, by which intercourse they have frequent opportunities to corrupt the principles of that description of men by infusing into their minds the pernicious tenets of Paine's *Rights of Man*.[4]

[1] Lord, p. 118 ; Ashton, pp. 44–6, 75 ; *infra*, pp. 172, 174, 185.
[2] *Supra*, pp. 103–4.
[3] Boulton to a London bank director, Aug. 12, 1787 (Lord, p. 207 *n*); *Gentleman's Mag.*, 1787, p. 1161 and plate ; illustrations in Dalton, R., and Hamer, S. H. : *Provincial Token-Coinage of the Eighteenth Century* (1915), vol. II, and in Palmer : *Wilkinson*.
[4] Peter Whitehall Davies to Lord Kenyon, Dec. 19, 1792 (*Hist. MSS. Com.*, 14th Rept., App., Pt. IV, p. 543).

Colour was given to the charge by the fact that the
Wilkinsons were themselves Presbyterians by upbringing,
both the brothers having been educated at Dissenting
Academies. William was still an occasional chapel-goer,
and he shocked his acquaintance among the local gentry
by his heterodox views on Church and State. His brother,
laxer both in morals and in religious observance, was at
any rate enough of a Radical to provide Joseph Priestley,
his brother-in-law, with an income from the French funds
when his library and laboratory were wrecked by "Church
and King" rioters; but one can hardly imagine him going
to the pains of unsettling the political principles of his
own workpeople.[1] Whatever the reason, his *assignats* were
not allowed to remain in circulation, and "the evolution of
John Wilkinson from ironmaster to banker" (a not
infrequent phenomenon) "was thus arrested."[2]

Neither of the Wilkinsons lived to see the end of the War.
John died at his home near Wellington (latterly the chief
scene of his activities) in July, 1808.[3] William had pre-
deceased him by four months, at Plas Grono, his father's
old home, which had once belonged to the great Elihu Yale.
They had both made many enemies. "Owing to his
arbitrary disposition generally," wrote a Wrexham diarist
on the younger brother's death, "few men went to the
grave more generally despised"; yet those who knew him
best found him "a most entertaining companion." Of
the elder, Matthew Boulton himself was constrained to
write: "I can't say but that I admire John Wilkinson
for his decisive, clear and distinct character, which is,
I think, a first-rate one of its kind."[4] He was a good

[1] Palmer, pp. 7, 33–4 ; Cust : *Chronicles of Erthig*, II, p. 263.
[2] Ashton, p. 229. But can he have been a partner in the
firm of Eyton, Reynolds, and Wilkinson, which was banking at
Shrewsbury by 1794, and which acted for both the Coalbrookdale Co.
and the Ellesmere Canal Co. ? (*Salop. Journ.*, Dec. 10, 1794).
Ashton (p. 230 and *n*) thinks the Reynolds may have been the
famous ironmaster of that name. But I have been unable to obtain
further information about the bank, which is not mentioned either
in Barfoot and Wilkes' *Directory* of 1790 ff., or in Owen and Blakeway's *History of Shrewsbury*.
[3] Brymbo Hall itself had been offered for sale in the preceding
year (*Chester Chron.*, June 12, 1807).
[4] Foulkes MS. (*Bye-gones*, 1905–06, p. 114) ; "Nimrod" (*Fraser's
Mag.*, 1842) p. 411 ; Smiles : *Boulton and Watt*, p. 379.

employer, too, after his lights—but one who was fully determined to stand no nonsense from his men.[1] William's grave, in the Dissenters' Burial Ground at Wrexham, can no longer be identified ; John, more careful for posterity, had provided himself beforehand with a pious epitaph, which his executors thought well to tone down a little. But his most serious concern had been for the future of the works. He left behind him three illegitimate children (two daughters and a son) for whom he had obtained permission to bear their father's name. The son, the child of his old age, was sent up to Cambridge ; but even before his father's death he had begun to display what was to be his only distinction—a facility for getting into debt.

It was between these children (his only direct descendants) that John Wilkinson intended his estates to be divided ; failing them there was a nephew, Thomas Jones, who was also to take the name of Wilkinson. Till 1827 the property was to be left in the hands of trustees— the mother of the children and four others. But he had reckoned without the lawyers. Before the trust expired, trustees and nephew, son and sons-in-law were all deluging the Court of Chancery with claims and counter-claims.[2] The nephew, who seems to have tried to play the rôle of ironmaster-banker, ruined himself over the litigation.[3] The son's attempt to re-start Brymbo works in 1829 (a bad time for the iron trade everywhere) ended in his ignominious flight abroad. Bit by bit, the whole estate was disposed of to meet the legal costs. The Bersham works were put up for sale in 1812 ; sixteen years later they lay in ruins. The village has reverted to rural, and the remains of the great cannon-foundry must now be sought in the walls of farm buildings.[4] Brymbo has fared differently. The trustees for a while kept the works going themselves ; then from 1815 they began letting them out on lease ; but there was no permanent revival till in 1841 the concern was bought out of Chancery by a joint-stock company. The chief shareholders in the new

---

[1] *See*, e.g., Ashton, pp. 206–7, 226, and Palmer, p. 33.
[2] *Shrewsbury Chron.*, Sept. 2, Oct. 14, 1825.
[3] *N. W. Gaz.*, June 3, 1813 ; *cf. infra*, p. 316.
[4] *N. W. Gaz.*, Jan. 9, 1812 ; Pigot's *Directory* (1828–9), p. 1178.

concern, and eventually the sole proprietors, were the Darbys and the Robertsons—the former, descendants of the great Quaker of Coalbrookdale, the latter, pioneers of railway enterprise in North Wales ; and it was in the demand for iron rails and locomotive boilers that the works now found their chief market. In 1885 they were taken over by the Brymbo Steel Company, and adapted to the open-hearth process of steel manufacture.[1]

The Brymbo works are Wilkinson's only remaining monument in North Wales, but from the outset his operations served as a stimulus and an example to the surrounding district. The Ruabon furnace, which went with the Bersham property, was re-started after lying idle for a generation, and in 1765 it was disposed of for £6,050 to the owner of the Llannerchrugog estate, where Bersham got most of its coal.[2] Wrexham and Holywell, the two marketing centres of the coalfield—both blessed with abundance of running water—naturally became the resorts of a great variety of workers in metal, but all on a small scale as yet. Wrexham had its locksmiths and scythesmiths, its spurriers and needle makers, and at Gwersyllt (a few miles outside the town) wire mills and forges were erected some time before 1782, and carried on by John Hayton and his son till the middle of the next century.[3] When Dr. Johnson visited Holywell in 1774, the great man was shown a tilting mill, out at Greenfield, where water-driven machinery would slit iron bars and hammer them out "as quick as by the hand" ; a little further along the stream he "saw wire drawn and gave a shilling." An excise officer who went to search these wire-works for contraband a few years later (during the American War) had a rather different reception : he was pushed into the oven while the smuggled goods were spirited away ! Both the works were of long standing,

[1] N. W. Gaz., Nov. 9, 1815 ; Shrewsbury Chron., March 13, 1829 ; Report on Education, 1847, III, p. 82 ; Palmer : Old Parish of Wrexham, p. 115.
[2] Palmer : Wilkinson, pp. 6, 11–13.
[3] Ibid.: History of Wrexham, p. 11 ; Chester Chron., Dec. 27, 1782, March 14, 1845 ; Pigot's Directories, 1822–23 and 1828 ; C.E.R. (1842, XVII), pp. 421–3. Thomas Ainsworth, a Warrington brazier, seems to have been at first associated with Hayton.

and they remained at Greenfield till they and the corn mills and paper mills which flanked them were elbowed out by the growing crowd of copper, brass and cotton works.[1]

From the time when the steam engine was patented, the iron industry throughout North Wales enjoyed a period of fifty years' unprecedented growth, culminating in the great boom of 1824–5. "The year 1775," as a recent writer has observed,[2] "marks more clearly than most dates selected as boundary-stones the end of one economic period and the beginning of another." Among the many enquiries received by Boulton and Watt about the newly-patented "reciprocating engine" was one which came in October, 1776, from the engineer at a foundry near Hawarden, which had just been extended by its owner, Mr. Rigby, so as to produce "all manner of stoves, ovens, boilers, furnaces, cast iron work for cranes, machines, locks, forges, smelting works and collieries." The enquiry was not pursued, and no steam engine was installed till after Watt's patent had expired ; but early in the next century Rigby's son was boring cannon, casting iron bridges, and making engine boilers for locomotives and steamships.[3] The American War produced a widespread revival in iron working ;[4] but far more important in its effects was the long struggle with France which began in 1793. When once the first years of financial panic were over, the effect of the new inventions was quickly felt ; Russian and Swedish iron ceased to come in, and if foreign markets were lost, there was ample compensation at home in the overwhelming demand for munitions and the rapid advance of cast iron machinery and bridges. In East Denbighshire the opening of the Ellesmere canal provided a further stimulus, and the district round Ruabon soon became thickly studded with ironworks.

[1] Johnson : *Diary of a Journey into North Wales*, p. 74 ; Pennant : *Whiteford and Holywell*, pp. 201, 203 ; *Cal. of Coleman Deeds*, No. 1351 ; *Chester Chron.*, Sept. 20, 1776, July 28, 1780 ; Barfoot and Wilkes' *Directory*, III, p. 285.
[2] Ashton, p. 60.
[3] Lord, p. 236 ; *Chester Chron.*, April 11, 1776, Oct. 25, 1816 ; *Memoir of Hawarden*, pp. 106–7.
[4] E.g., a furnace at Eglwysfach, in the Conway valley, is advertised in *Chester Chron.*, May 21, 1779.

We have already seen how William Hazeldine came from Shrewsbury to make the iron work for Pontcysyllte aqueduct. The foundry which he erected near the spot was used by Telford again in 1812 for casting a bridge to connect the counties of Ross and Sutherland. But Hazeldine did no smelting there, and much of his work, including the superstructures of the Menai and Conway suspension bridges, seems still to have been done in Shropshire.[1] Other Ruabon ironmasters were mainly concerned with the production of pig-iron. Two at least of these were of local origin—Thomas Jones and Edward Lloyd Rowland.[2] The former (not to be confused with Wilkinson's nephew) was the son of William Jones (of Llannerchrugog Hall, Ruabon, and Old Marton Hall, Salop), who is described as an ironmaster in 1796. After the death of the Wilkinsons, Thomas Jones for a time worked both Bersham furnace and Abenbury forge, and he later came to live at Plas Grono, the former home of Isaac and of William ; but his chief activities were in Ruabon parish. About 1807 he started the Ponkey furnace near the old workings which had long provided coal for the owners of Bersham. A little later, probably in partnership with Rigby of Hawarden, he opened another at Llwyn Einion—a farm, belonging to Plas Grono, where Isaac Wilkinson had got his iron ore ; and a third followed soon after the Peace. All three were within a stone's throw of Llannerchrugog Hall.[3]

Mr. Rowland was another ironmaster whose capital came from landed property in the neighbourhood. His

<hr/>

[1] *Supra*, p. 109 ; *N. W. Gaz.*, June 18, 1812 ; Telford's Reports on Holyhead Road, 1819 (App. to 6th Report of Parliamentary Ctte.) and 1824 (Rept. to Road Commissioners) ; Victoria County Histories : *Shropshire*, I, pp. 466, 468, 475.

[2] Palmer : *Ruabon*, pp. 52–4, 61, 107–8, *Wilkinson*, p. 37, *Parish Church*, p. 114 *n*, *Old Parish of Wrexham*, pp. 30–31, 150, 256; Pigot's *Directories*, 1822–23 and 1828–29.

[3] *See* advertisments of sales of these various works (from which date of original lease may be gathered) in *N. W. Gaz.*, Feb. 6, 1812, May 5, 1825 ; *Shrewsbury Chron.*, May 8, 1829 ; *Chester Chron.*, May 1, 1840. It is difficult to disentangle all the Thomas Joneses who were engaged in iron work round Wrexham. In addition to the one mentioned above, we have Wilkinson's nephew (*supra*, p. 141) ; another who entered into an ironfounding partnership at Wrexham about 1812, dissolved it, and set up again at Brymbo (*Chester Chron.*, Nov. 12, 1802 ; *Salop. Journ.*, Nov. 21, 1803 ; *Evans* :

father had devoted a long life to the accumulation of estates in Ruabon parish, and his elder brother served as High Sheriff in the year of Waterloo. Some time before this, the younger son launched out as owner of two large blast furnaces at Acrefair (in the southern part of the parish) in which, an admiring traveller noted, "almost everything is done by the aid of a most powerful steam engine." Rowland went bankrupt in 1823, but before this he had added to his original establishment a rolling mill and eighteen puddling furnaces.[1]

The general advance in the industry is seen in other departments besides that of the blast furnace. The puddling process was introduced in the Pont y blew forge, near Chirk, at the commencement of the War—long before Rowland used it at Acrefair—and at Abenbury before 1827.[2] Puddled iron was a boon to wire-drawers, and there was great activity in this branch of the industry, especially in the districts of Wrexham and Holywell. In 1803, for example, the owners of a wire mill at Bersham were advertising for "a good hand who has been accustomed to puddle pig and scrap iron."[3] Wire was also made, before the end of the War, at Llwyn On, near Abenbury forge ; the mill survived the failure of its proprietor, James Hammerton, during the post-war slump, and continued producing for some years under his successors.[4] The tilting mill and wire works that Johnson admired at Holywell had been removed by 1795 to the banks of the River Wheeler at Caerwys, six miles away. There they were worked by W. and J. Smalley (relatives, perhaps, of the Smalleys who had covered the original site at Holywell with cotton mills) till the Orders in Council drove them out of business in 1807.[5] The Wheeler valley was thus

Beauties, pp. 514, 586) ; and possibly yet a fourth who appears as ironfounder at Wrexham in 1822 and subsequently at the Llwyn On wire mills also (Pigot's Directories, 1822–23 and 1828–29).
    [1] Evans : Beauties, p. 585 ; Shrewsbury Chron., Oct. 24, 1823 ; Palmer : Ruabon, pp. 52 ff.
    [2] Lewis : Top. Dict., under Chirk; Shrewsbury Chron., Aug. 24, 1827, Feb. 29, 1828.
    [3] Salop. Journ., Aug. 15, 1803.
    [4] Chester Chron., Feb. 28, 1817 ; Oswestry Her., July 18, 1820 ; Shrewsbury Chron., Jan. 25, 1828.
    [5] Pennant : Whiteford and Holywell, p. 213 ; Chester Chron., March 10, 1797, Aug. 22, 1806, May 1, 1807:

added to the iron districts of North Wales, but it was never of much importance, despite the wealth of the district in haematite ores.[1]

The conclusion of peace brought a temporary check to the whole trade. During the War, the price of pig iron for forge use had ranged between £5 and £7 a ton ; in 1816 it sank to less than £4. Then it rose slowly again till it got back to the war-time level in 1819, and, after some further vicissitudes, reached the unprecedented figure of £7 10s. in 1825.[2] The great boom had begun, and its effects were quickly felt in North Wales. Of the host of newly-floated companies, two at least turned their attention to the ironworks of this region. In 1824 some works which had been started at Coed Talon (in the southern extremity of Flintshire), as soon as trade began to revive after the War, were acquired by the Welsh Iron and Coal Mining Co. One of the directors was John Wilks, the Methodist M.P. for Sudbury, and a prominent advocate of the repeal of the Test and Corporation Acts. The prowess of "Bubble Wilks" (as he came to be called) in finance bears comparison with that of his namesake (with an *e*) in politics, fifty years earlier ; his hold over the credulity of the pious suggests more modern analogies. His frequent visits to Wales cost the Company anything up to £150 apiece, and the shareholders were soon in deep waters. The Coed Talon works were sold, and the new owners long used them to make pig iron for the machinery-manufacturers of Lancashire.[3] Mr. Rowland's furnaces at Acrefair were taken over by the British Iron Company, a firm, owning extensive works at Abersychan in Monmouthshire, with which Richard Cort (son of the inventor of the puddling process) was connected for a time. If Cort's indictments can be trusted, the management and methods of the British Iron Co. were not above

[1] Pigot's *Directory,* 1828–29, pp. 1150, 1161 ; Lewis : *Top. Dict.,* under *Caerwys.* Hammerton, formerly of the Llwyn On mill, failed there in 1829 (*N. W. Chron.,* Jan. I, 1829). Another of the Wrexham wire-drawers tried to restart the industry at Holywell, but went bankrupt in 1822 (*N. W. Gaz.,* Oct. 10, 1822).

[2] Ashton, pp. 153–6 ; *Shrews. Chron.,* Feb. 26, 1819.

[3] *N. W. Gaz.,* Feb. 8, Aug. 3, Sept. 14, 1826, June 14, 1827 ; *Shrewsbury Chron.,* Sept. 8, 1826, Jan. 29, 1830 ; Lewis : *Top. Dict.* (1833 and 1843) under *Tryddin.*

suspicion ; but Cort had a passion for exposing "frauds." The Company at least kept their heads above water, and they spent nearly £140,000 on improvements in their Ruabon works.[1] In the Brymbo region, too, this period saw fresh developments. Mr. John Thompson had come into the district about 1813 to embark, with other members of his family, in the coal and iron industries. One of his ventures was a short lease of the Wilkinson works ; and in 1824, having acquired the Ffrwd colliery (about a mile away), he built a furnace of his own there, and continued smelting at it long after the Brymbo works had passed into other hands.[2]

These long periods of prosperity had spread the new inventions far and wide ; yet the old order died hard. More economical fuel and a source of power not subject, like rivers, to the interruption of dry seasons—these were indeed weighty advantages ; but the new plant was expensive to set up,[3] and in the heart of the country, where communications remained slow, old-established forges like those at Mathrafal in Montgomeryshire or Dolgûn in Merioneth could retain a faithful local *clientèle* without abandoning methods they had followed since the days of George the First. The Mathrafal forge seems to have been still working with charcoal when John Wilkinson died.[4] The one at Dolgûn (near Dolgelley) was offered for sale just before the Peace of Amiens. With it were furnaces for smelting the local ore, and a newly installed blast

---

[1] *Shrewsbury Chron.*, June 18, 1824, March 11, 1825, July 13, 1827 ; Simpson : *Account of Llangollen* (1827), p. 12. The last-mentioned source refers its readers to "Cort's letter" as an authority on the Acrefair works. I have been unable to trace this letter. Miss Edna Bibby, B.A., of Manchester, has kindly looked up for me a pamphlet by Cort entitled *Case in part relative to Frauds practised on the Shareholders of The British Iron Company by some of their agents* (London, 1841), but the only reference to the Ruabon district is the name of the local manager, Mr. Wood. The firm is referred to in Pigot's *Directory* for 1828 under the names of its managing directors —Messrs. Small, Shears, and Taylor.

[2] Palmer : *Wilkinson*, p. 38, *Old Parish of Wrexham*, pp. 115, 128, *Hist. of Wrexham*, p. 79 ; *Brymbo Works Mag.*, II, p. 61 (Sept., 1922).

[3] "In 1812, according to Thomas Attwood, a complete set of ironworks could not be constructed for less than £50,000." (Ashton, p. 163.)

[4] *Bye-gones*, 1891–92, pp. 290, 300 ; *Chester Chron.*, May 8, 1807.

engine, worked by the same river that provided the power for the forge hammers. Here, too, charcoal remained the fuel for both smelting and forging, and the productive capacity of the whole concern was stated to be six tons of bar iron or eight to ten tons of "half-blooms" in the year—perhaps a quarter of what an up-to-date coke furnace in Denbighshire could then make. Another forge near the Mawddach estuary, also worked by water power, was advertised with that at Dolgûn, and recommended as suitable for conversion into a rolling and slitting mill. About the same time we hear of a charcoal furnace at Aberdovey making 150 tons a year. The produce of these little works sufficed for local needs, and some of it was even shipped to other parts from Barmouth.[1]

In the very midst of the coal measures, the victory of coal and steam was still far from complete. There are said to have been charcoal hearths in Ruabon parish as late as 1833 ; water power, too, remained in general use for forges and wire mills, and at Rhuddlan a foundry built just before Waterloo had its bellows worked by a horse engine.[2] All these things belonged to an age that was now passing away. The use of the steam engine spread rapidly after Watt's patent expired in 1800 ; and the number of charcoal furnaces at work in Great Britain sank from fifty-nine in 1788 to eleven in 1806. The circumstances of the time all favoured the concentration of the industry on the more productive coalfields, and in large establishments where mining, smelting, refining, rolling and the manufacture of the finished article could be carried on side by side and under a single control. This, of course, meant the elimination of scattered workshops using antiquated methods and confining themselves to a single process—till at last even the village blacksmith found his custom slipping away from him.[3]

[1] *Salop. Journ.*, June 3, 1795, May 5, 1802 ; Scrivenor : *History of the Iron Trade*, pp. 86–7, 93–5, 359–61 ; *N. W. Gaz.*, shipping returns, 1808 ; *supra*, pp. 19, 23, 24.

[2] Lewis : *Top. Dict.*, under *Ruabon: Chester Chron.*, Dec. 20, 1816.

[3] Ashton, pp. 97–101. During the first half of the nineteenth century North Wales newspapers and directories give many passing glimpses of foundries and forges for agricultural implements in the rural districts. On the decay of smithies in a Welsh village *see* an interesting note in *Bye-gones*, 1909–10, pp. 111-12.

For a time this process of concentration was favourable to East Denbighshire, for it was rich in both coal and ironstone. When the Brymbo Hall estate was put up for auction in 1829, the sale catalogue claimed (on the basis of expert calculations) that at the present rate of consumption there was enough ore there to feed the furnaces for another seventy years, and coal for twice as long. The ironstone of Ruabon Mountain had paid handsome royalties since the days of the Lords Marcher. For special grades of iron, it is true—such as that used in the manufacture of ordnance—an admixture of ores imported from Lancashire or Cumberland was found advisable ; but there were hopes (though these proved delusive) of finding a nearer supply of satisfactory ore in Flintshire.[1]

The scale of production had grown enormously. Here, as elsewhere, "integration" was the order of the day, and there were works equipped for carrying through every stage from the extraction of raw material and fuel to the manufacture of a wide range of cast or malleable iron goods.[2] In the early days of coke-smelting the Bersham furnace could only reach an output of five tons a week ; a century later, the weekly make of the two blast furnaces at Brymbo was estimated at seventy to eighty tons. At the other end of the scale we find little forges like the one at Chirk, which in 1833 was only making twenty tons a week and employing twenty men.[3] According-ing to figures given in a local paper there were in 1827 twelve furnaces in North Wales, producing between them 24,000 tons—something like 3·5 per cent of the total output for England and Wales. So far as can be judged from data which are very incomplete and often contra-dictory, the increase in production since the 'eighties

---

[1] Extracts from sale catalogue in *Brymbo Works Mag.*, I, pp. 190–1 (June–Sept., 1921) ; Palmer : *Ruabon*, pp. 66–77, 142 ; Davies : *General View*, p. 63 ; Evans : *Beauties*, pp. 89, 513, 585.

[2] *See*, e.g., advt. of ironworks at Cefn, *Shrewsbury Chron.*, April 3, 1825. By 1842 the British Iron Co. at Ruabon was employing 1,500 men, women, and children in works and collieries (*C.E.R.*, 1842, XVII, p. 377).

[3] *N. W. Gaz.*, Nov. 9, 1815 ; *Brymbo Works Mag., ut.sup.;* Lewis : *Top. Dict.*, under *Chirk*.

must have been proportionally higher here than in the country as a whole.[1]

By this time, however, the industry was in the throes of that crisis "which," observed a North Wales newspaper of 1828 (wise after the event), "the most ordinary foresight might have anticipated as consequent on the very high prices of 1824."[2] We find the first signs of uneasiness in the summer of 1825 ; from that time onwards the state of the iron trade is a subject of weekly discussion—now gloomy, now sanguine—in the columns of the local press ; until in 1831 the talk is of an "appalling and long-continued depression" which has brought the price of pig iron down to £3 and that of bar iron from £15 to less than £5.[3] The long war of prices and the fierce competition for markets between one iron district and another had their inevitable issue : furnaces were blown out, ironworkers and colliers thrown out of work or forced to accept starvation wages ; and for the ironmaster the only chance of weathering the storm lay in abundance of capital and the economies of large-scale production. The districts which stood in the most favourable position were those where the coalfields were wide enough to hold a number of extensive works, turning out products (such as the puddled iron of South Wales) with an established reputation. The owner of half-a-dozen large iron-works could distribute his orders with a view to maximum economy of plant ; a group of neighbouring ironmasters controlling a large proportion of the national output could do the same in combination ; and so they were able to monopolize such trade as remained, at the expense of the less populous, less developed and less well-known areas.[4]

After 1826 we rarely read of the building of new iron-works in North Wales ; even old-established concerns

[1] N. W. Chron., Oct. 16, 1828 ; cf. estimates in Mushet, p. 44, Scrivenor, pp. 86–7, 93–7, Ashton, p. 98, Smiles (Industrial Biography), p. 117 n, Lord, pp. 144–5.

[2] N. W. Chron., Aug. 7, 1828, et passim.

[3] Shrewsbury Chron., July 15 and Oct. 21, 1825, Oct. 21, 1831, et passim.

[4] On the struggle between Welsh and Scottish ironmasters see N. W. Chron., Nov. 19, 1829 ; and contrast the agreement of the South Wales ironmasters in 1836 for a limitation of output, to which the Staffordshire, Shropshire, Scottish, and North Wales ironmasters acceded on request. (Ashton, p. 178.)

had all their work cut out to keep afloat, and the 'forties proved to be as hungry a time for ironworkers as the 'thirties. Two of the leading Ruabon ironmasters went bankrupt about 1840, and only three furnaces in the parish remained in blast in 1844 : eight had been blown out within the last few years. Soon after this the Hawarden works were closed down, and the district where they stood—a hive of industry for more than seventy years—reverted to rural solitude, undisturbed even by the passing of the mail-coach. In 1847 North Wales had more furnaces out of blast than in.[1]

Yet this was the great age of railway construction. The North Wales Mineral Railway was authorized by Act of Parliament in 1844, and soon both Ruabon and Brymbo were linked up with the chief trunk lines.[2] With improved transport and the new demand for boilers and rails, the ironmasters of North Wales might well hope for the return of better times. The Brymbo works, as we have seen, had already come under new management, and in the 'fifties new capital began to flow into some of the others. Ffrwd furnace, with its collieries, was acquired in 1855 by a Staffordshire man, of a family long connected with the coal industry, and with experience in the iron-works of Wolverhampton ; under the new management it went on working till shortly after the South African War. In the Ruabon district, the British Iron Company gave place to the New British Iron Company, and their works at Acrefair survived till 1888 ; those at Ponkey were "taken over by a large capitalist" in 1850. When George Borrow walked from Wrexham to Ruabon on an inky night in 1854, he found his way by the aid of three immense glares. from three different ironworks. One of them—the Cefn foundry—was producing 200 tons a week in 1859.[3]

The long depression had weeded out the weaker units ; the railway gave a new lease of life to the half-dozen bigger works round Wrexham. But the chief gain went

[1] *Chester Chron.*, Nov. 8, 1844 ; *C.E.R.* (1842, XVII), pp. 371, 397, 413–14, 418 ; Fullarton's *Parl. Gaz.*, II, p. 289 ; *Wrexham Registrar*, 1848, pp. 155–6 ; Clapham : *op. cit.*, p. 430.
[2] *Supra*, pp. 117–18.
[3] *Bye-gones*, 1901–02, pp. 322–3 ; Palmer : *Ruabon*, p. 61 ; *Chester Chron.*, March 30, 1850 ; *Wild Wales*, p. 361 (*cf.* p. 103) ; *Wrexham Advertiser*, May 14, 1859.

to other districts, and the ultimate effect of the railway was to carry the process of concentration a stage further. Between 1830 and 1847 production in South Wales increased by 150 per cent ; in North Wales it remained almost stationary. In 1839 there were twelve furnaces in blast, with a make of about 28,000 tons—a trifle higher than in 1827. In 1848 there were only five in blast, and the output was less than in 1827 ; four years later, with one additional furnace at work, it had reached 30,000 tons. But in Great Britain as a whole the production of iron had meanwhile increased from under 700,000 tons to over two millions. North Wales was now the least productive of all the iron-manufacturing districts. Then came Bessemer's invention of 1856, and the consequent revolutionizing of the steel industry ; the unit of output was still further enlarged, and firms which had not the capital to convert their works to the new processes lagged hopelessly behind. Foreign ores, too, were now imported on a large scale, to the detriment of inland districts which had thriven on their stores of ironstone, and to the great gain of the seaports of South Wales. In the six northern counties the output of iron ore declined rapidly after 1865, and employment in the iron industry, after rising slowly for a couple of decades from 1851 to a maximum of 793, sank again until the opening of the great works by the Dee estuary at the beginning of the twentieth century.[1]

B. Thomas Williams and the Copper Industry.[2]

> Now his hard hands on Mona's rifted crest,
> Bosom'd in rock, her azure ores arrest.
> —Erasmus Darwin : *Economy of Vegetation* (1792),
> Canto I (on "the Giant-Power" of steam).

If ironmasters grew rich on the needs of the army, it was naval demand that made fortunes in the copper and brass industries. The use of copper sheathing for British men-o'-war dates from 1761—the very year when John

---

[1] North : *Coal, and the Coalfields of Wales*, p. 137 ; Mushet, p. 419 ; Scrivenor, p. 292, and second ed. (1852), p. 302 ; Galloway : *Annals of Coal Mining* (second ser.), p. 269 ; Clapham : *Early Railway Age*, pp. 426–7.

[2] Parts of this section have appeared in *Trans. Ang. Ant. Soc.*, 1926, pp. 90–104, where full references are given.

Wilkinson took the Bersham ironworks in hand—and it is then that the continuous history of copper-mining in North Wales may be said to begin. Ever since the beginning of the century Cornish ores, smelted in South Wales and worked up by the manufacturers of Bristol or Birmingham, had been quietly usurping the place hitherto held by German products ; but North Wales had no share in the trade until, somewhere about 1750, the Cheadle Brass Company (which had been founded by Thomas Patten of Warrington in 1719, but proved more stable than most of the flotations of that year of "bubbles") took to smelting some of its copper at Greenfield, near Holywell. Thomas Barker, one of the leading shareholders, was himself a Holywell man, with experience in the iron industry (for some years he worked the tilting mill to which reference was made in the preceding section) ; and we may assume that he was responsible for the choice of site.[1] For Holywell had many advantages to offer. The flocking of pilgrims to St. Winifred's Well—a "superstition" against which Puritanism had 'thundered in vain—first made of it a busy market town ; and when the age of faith declined, more sordid uses were found for the stream that rushes down from the well to empty itself in the Dee estuary at Greenfield. Not long after the Restoration a traveller expressed, in some burlesque verses, his wonderment that "a saint, and a virgin, endu'd with such grace" should yet be so kind to the knavish millers

> As within a few paces to furnish the wheels
> Of I cannot tell how many water mills.[2]

About a century later (in 1774) Dr. Johnson counted nineteen works of various sorts within two miles of the source. Among them were those of the Cheadle Company, The site furnished them with coal as well as water power,

---

[1] Hamilton : *Brass and Copper Industries*, pp. 149–50, *et passim;* Pennant : *Whiteford and Holywell*, pp. 201, 203 ff. On the Pattens, *see* Grant-Francis : *The Smelting of Copper in the Swansea District*, p. 36 and *n*. Barker became a shareholder in 1734 ; in the preceding year we find him leasing coal mines in Shropshire (Victoria County Histories : *Shropshire*, I, p. 464). It is possible that two subsequent partners—Ingleby and Dumbell—were also connected with industrial ventures in Flintshire (*infra*, pp. 174, 296).

[2] Skeel : *The Council in the Marches of Wales.* p. 150 ; Cotton, Charles : *A Voyage to Ireland in Burlesque*, 1670.

and for ten years before Dr. Johnson's visit the Company, attracted by the quality of the local ores of zinc, had been making brass there too. But Wales could not supply the raw copper : that had to be imported from England.[1]

This dependence was soon to pass away ; for at last the rich stores of copper which had so long lain dormant in the rocks of North Wales were yielding to a systematic attack.[2] Already in 1761 we hear of Cornish adventurers at the old workings of Drws y coed, near Nantlle lakes (in the heart of Snowdonia), of prospecting by owners of land on Snowdon itself, and of renewed searching by Scotsmen, Cornishmen, and Welshmen for the elusive copper veins of Anglesey.[3] Near Llanberis a certain Siôn John Robert made a lucky strike which is said to have brought him £300 in three months. On the southern coast of the Lleyn peninsula, far from any town, the old lead mine of Penrhyn Dû was found to contain copper, and was leased in 1764 to a Macclesfield Company in which the leading spirit was Charles Roe, a pioneer of the Macclesfield silk and copper manufactures. The chief interest of this enterprise lies in its connexion with the opening up of Parys Mountain, in Anglesey. Sir Nicholas Bayley, the owner of Penrhyn Dû, was part proprietor here also. Two years earlier he had been induced by a Scottish adventurer to sink shafts, but they were soon flooded out and abandoned. When, however, he granted the lease of Penrhyn Dû, he insisted that the lessees should also take Parys Mountain off his hands for twenty-one years. Very reluctantly they did so ; and after four years of costly and fruitless exploration they sent, as a last resort, for their foreman from Penrhyn Dû—an experienced Derbyshire miner named Jonathan Roose. He adopted the expedient of dividing the workmen into partnerships of three or four apiece, promising a bottle of whiskey to the first who should strike ore ; and before long, as his tombstone still reminds us, he had the satisfaction of hearing the "Miners' first exulting shout." Further discoveries followed. In 1775, just in time for the boom

---

[1] Johnson : *Tour in North Wales*, pp. 71–5.
[2] On the copper of North Wales, *see* Davies : *General View*, pp. 44, 55 ; Hunt : *British Mining*, pp. 121–2, 262–5, 445–6, 895–7.
[3] *Morris Letters*, II, pp. 328, 357–9.

in copper created by the American War, the vein was tapped in another part of the mountain, where Sir Nicholas was co-owner with the Rev. Edward Hughes—an obscure country parson who had got the estate by marriage.

It is at this point that Thomas Williams comes into the story. Mr. Hughes naturally desired to disentangle his share of the property so as to be able to work his ores without encumbrance ;[1] and it was to Williams that the delicate negotiations were entrusted by which, through the services of a London banker named Dawes, Sir Nicholas was induced to grant a lease of his moiety of the joint estate to a partnership consisting of Messrs. Hughes, Dawes and Williams.[2] The Parys Mine Company, as this new concern called itself, was thus enabled to exploit all the western side of the mountain. So successful was the experiment that when the lease of Messrs. Roe and Co. ran out in 1785, the Earl of Uxbridge (successor to Sir Nicholas Bayley's estates), instead of renewing it, followed his neighbour's example by admitting Williams into partnership and forming the Mona Mine Company. Both companies entrusted the entire management of their affairs to Thomas Williams, and he amply justified their choice.

Two years after the Mona Company had been formed, the joint produce of the two mines was estimated at 4,000 tons of pure copper. "Originally," wrote the agent of the Mona Mine some fifty years later ". . . every inch of ground, from the surface downwards, was nearly one unmixed mass of Copper Ore."[3] The ore was mostly quarried in the open. After boring and blasting, it was smashed with sledge hammers and hauled up in baskets by a "whimsey." On top it was broken into smaller pieces by hand—a task which the companies reserved, by way of "charity," for women and children and for the aged and feeble—and then purified by washing and roasting. In addition to this, the sixteenth-century expedient of precipitation from cupreous water by iron

---

[1] There was a long Chancery suit about boundaries, ending in 1776, and disputes cropped up afresh when new veins were tapped in 1832–33 (U.C.N.W. Library : Bangor MS. 405).

[2] Williams sub-let some of his shares to Jonathan Roose, the foreman.

[3] John Sanderson to Stephen Roose, Nov. 26, 1832 (Bangor MS. 405).

bars or plates[1] was revived and improved. Very soon from twelve to fifteen hundred men, women, and children were finding employment in and around the mines.

At first the greater part of the produce was sold in the raw state, but by 1780 the Parys Mine Company had built its own smelting works at Ravenhead and Swansea ; another establishment at Stanley (near Liverpool) was worked by a separate company in which Williams was the leading partner ; and in the village of Amlwch, close to the mines themselves, twenty furnaces were employed by the beginning of the nineteenth century in reducing the inferior ores. Not content with mining and smelting, Williams now began to interest himself in the manufacturing processes. In 1780 he built for the Parys Company a copper forge, wire mill and rolling mill at Holywell, and eight years later he acquired another rolling mill at Bristol. Then he turned to the manufacture of brass. The Cheadle Company's works having been offered for sale, Williams bought them in 1786 under the name of the Greenfield Copper and Brass Company, placing them under the management of an "intelligent and respectable agent" from Warrington, and adding to the original battery mill a melting house for the manufacture of plate brass.

Almost every branch of manufacture could now be carried on in and around Holywell. Copper had fallen into temporary disfavour with the Admiralty, because defective copper bolts were believed to be a contributory cause of our heavy naval losses during the American War ; but Williams perfected at Holywell a bolt which was above suspicion, and by 1785 his forge was supplying bolts, nails, sheathing and rudder-bands to the ex-enemy navies of France, Holland, and Spain as well as to our own. Another mill made copper cylinders for muslin printing ; brassfounders from up and down the country came to the Holywell melting house for their supply of ingots ; the wire mills turned out vast quantities of brass and copper wire ; brass pans used in the manufacture of salt and sugar and the drying of tea were sold to the East and West India merchants, and all manner of cheap and

[1] *Supra*, p. 17.

gaudy brass ornaments to those trading with Africa.[1] Before
the end of the century, nearly forty vessels of thirty to
fifty tons each were constantly employed in carrying raw
material to the Holywell works and exporting the finished
products ; and we have seen how at Amlwch the two companies had to disburse large sums in adapting the harbour
to the needs of their growing fleet.[2] The industry was also
rich in by-products. The preparation of ochre (deposited in
the precipitation process) and of sulphur (collected from the
flues of the roasting kilns) was long carried on at Amlwch,
and later on—when the main industry was falling off—the
Parys Company leased out the site for alkali works, which
they kept supplied with sulphur. Alum was also prepared
for export, and both at Amlwch and at Holywell subsidiary
companies manufactured green vitriol.

A work of such magnitude involved, for the time, a
considerable wage bill, and the owners of the Anglesey
mines found it necessary (like Wilkinson at Bersham)
to coin their own tokens. The first issue of Anglesey
pennies appeared in 1787, bearing the monogram of the
Parys Mine Company, and round the edges the names
of Edward Hughes, Thomas Williams, and John Dawes ;
they soon became popular with connoisseurs for their
artistic finish and with shopkeepers for their weight and
purity. The operations at Holywell were also attracting
the attention of manufacturers elsewhere. Matthew
Boulton tried (but failed) to get admission to the works
in 1781 ; Williams was not the man to give his business
secrets away.[3] By 1800, according to his own account, he
was conducting half the copper industry of Great Britain,
with a capital not far short of a million ; and his various
works consumed nearly a thousand tons of coal every day.
The coal mines of Flintshire developed rapidly under this
stimulus ; in Anglesey, where coal output was negligible,
Parliament was induced to grant the Companies first a
rebate, and then a total remission of the duty on imported
coals. Parys Mountain was not the only source of copper

[1] Pennant : *Whiteford and Holywell*, pp. 133, 203 ff. ; Bingley :
North Wales, I, pp. 50–53 ; Aikin : *Journal*, pp. 174–80 ; Lewis :
Top. Dict., under *Holywell*.
[2] *Supra*, p. 125.
[3] Hamilton : *op. cit.*, p. 221.

for the Holywell brass works ; they were also fed by Cornish ores, smelted in South Wales, and ores from the Duke of Devonshire's mines, smelted in Derbyshire ; and we shall see later how the mining of copper was pushed forward in almost every corner of North Wales.

If English copper came to Holywell, Anglesey ores, *en revanche*, were appearing at the "public ticketings" in England, to pull down prices and to challenge the dictatorship of the Cornish mineowners. For although neither so rich nor so abundant as those of Cornwall they had the great advantage of coming from virgin mines which could be worked with comparative cheapness. The Cornish miners, with their old and powerful organization, could command almost twice the wage that sufficed in Anglesey, when once the cream had been skimmed and the usual crowd of fortune-hunters had come to scramble for the leavings.[1] The fierce competition between these two areas brought down the price of ore from £7 6s. 6d. a hundredweight in 1750 to £5 16s. in 1779, and £3 13s. in 1784, and the principal smelting firms were playing off one set of mines against the other. To meet this situation, Williams sought the co-operation of Matthew Boulton, who was a shareholder in Cornish copper mines as well as in Birmingham brass works. In 1785 Boulton and Williams floated a new company which was to purchase Cornish and Anglesey ores (in proportions determined by the normal output of the respective counties), to get them smelted by such companies as were prepared to enter the "ring," and to sell the product at a common standard price. The principal markets—Liverpool, Bristol, Birmingham, and London—were to be equitably shared, and common warehouses opened ; with the express stipulation, however, that there must be "no mixture of property on any account." Williams was business manager for the whole concern.

For a time Anglesey and Cornwall dominated the world market for copper ; but it was too much to hope that they would work in harmony for long. A price which suited Anglesey was too low for Cornwall ; some of the principal smelting firms remained outside the agreement, and offered tempting baits to disloyal mineowners ; Williams himself was accused of violating the compact by price

[1] *Infra* pp. 337, 341.

cutting. By 1790 the "copper war" had broken out with greater violence than ever, and Williams made one more bid for the control of the whole trade, offering higher terms for Cornish ores and claiming a smaller proportion of the output. He had now, however, to meet the opposition of the Birmingham brass manufacturers, who strove to defend their raw material against price manipulation and limitation of output, by combining to set up smelting works and to purchase mines of their own. Matters were brought to a head by the outbreak of war with France and the consequent disorganization of trade. The Birmingham men asked Parliament to help them by prohibiting the export of copper and abolishing the import duty of eleven guineas a ton, which was keeping the price of English copper higher at home than abroad.

In 1799 a Select Committee of the House of Commons heard both sides, Williams pleading for a "fair profit" for the mineowners, representatives from Birmingham arguing the case for a cheap and abundant supply of raw material for a vital industry. The Committee's Report was discussed in Parliament the next year. Pitt himself spoke in favour of the Birmingham claims, and Hawkesbury (a future Premier) arraigned Mr. Williams as one who "by means of his large capital was the occasion of the rise of copper in 1793"; but Tierney (later to be the ineffective leader of the Whig "rump") spoke in his defence, reminding the House how he "had raised himself from low beginnings to a splendid and well-deserved opulence." Meanwhile the object of Tierney's eulogies (who had purchased for himself the borough of Great Marlow) was busy pulling strings in the background, and between them they procured the defeat of the Birmingham proposals.[1]

Just two years after these debates Thomas Williams died, at the age of 65. As a business man he ranks with John Wilkinson and the other great pioneers of the Industrial Revolution, but he remains a much more shadowy figure. Matthew Boulton described him as "a man of

[1] *Chester Chron.*, March 28 and April 11, 1800. *See* also *Report on Copper*, 1799; Hunt: *British Mining*, pp. 104–6, 116 (where some of the documents are printed); Hamilton: *op. cit.*, chaps. VI to IX; Levy, H.: *Monopoly and Competition* (1911), pp. 142–56.

first-rate abilities," who had "done more in the copper trade than all the other drones in it" (a eulogy which might have been more fortunately phrased !) but he found him as awkward to deal with as he found Wilkinson.[1] The Bishop of Bangor, with whom Williams had a somewhat sordid squabble over the rebuilding of Amlwch church, roundly accused him of impoverishing the whole district to make his own fortune—a charge which he rebutted by pointing to the fact that the firms with which he was connected, besides bearing three-quarters of the burden of the (not excessive) poor rates, spent £700 or £800 a year in doctor's bills and as much again in miscellaneous charities, not counting the provision of "light and easy tasks" (the nature of which we have seen) for those unfitted for heavier work, at a cost of another £3,000. In his own district at any rate he was remembered, a generation after his death, as *Twm Chwareu Têg*—"Tom Fairplay."[2]

The removal of the master mind came at a critical moment for the industries of Amlwch and Holywell. Even when Williams was presenting his case to the Copper Committee, he had to report that the best veins in Parys Mountain were approaching exhaustion, and that his production had sunk to about 1,700 tons of copper in the preceding year. Nor was this a mere piece of special pleading to enlist the sympathy of Parliament. A few months earlier the Parys Company had offered for sale the buildings in which the vitriol and sulphur manufactures were carried on, and as an inducement to purchasers it was pointed out that plenty of cheap labour could be had in the neighbourhood, because "the Mine Companies do not now employ so many hands as they did some time ago."[3] In 1812 the two firms had to dispose of a further slice of their property, and two years later the works at Stanley and Ravenhead came under the hammer. The mines themselves, it was noticed, were not worked "with the same spirit" after Williams' death.[4] This was not

[1] Hamilton : pp. 169, 179, 180. The *D.N.B.* ignores him except for an incidental reference under *Pascoe Grenfell* in the index volume.

[2] "Shôn Gwialan" : *Letter to the Right Reverend Dr. Warren* (privately printed, *c.* 1796) ; Llwyd : *History of the Island of Mona*, pp. 387–9.

[3] *Chester Chron.*, March 8, 1799.

[4] Evans : *Beauties*, p. 232.

wholly the fault of the management. It had now become necessary to sink shafts—sometimes to a great depth—under the old workings, and in the difficult years which followed the Orders in Council these increasing costs were a serious matter.

Before the end of the War, the number employed in the mines had diminished to about 600, their annual output to 600 tons, and their consumption of gunpowder from 15,000 to 6,000 tons. Between the first and the second Census the population of Amlwch dwindled by more than 700, and the decline was attributed to the fact that "many families emigrated to Liverpool, etc., for want of employment."[1] Then came the bad days of the Peace, with the price of copper sinking steadily and demobilized miners flocking home to find their old occupations gone. "I can truly say that we have made every deduction possible in the Mine," writes one of the stewards in 1816, "I scarce know where to go to low [allow] a penny more with propriety."[2] Lord Uxbridge, now Marquis of Anglesey, came home from the Wars, where he had lost a leg, to find Amlwch seething with discontent and breaking out into food riots.

For the time the crisis was tided over. A new Company had taken over the Mona mine on the death of Thomas Williams, but eventually Lord Anglesey resumed control himself. Mr. Hughes, the chief proprietor of the Parys mine, died in the year of Waterloo, and the company was reconstructed under his son Colonel Hughes (afterwards Lord Dinorben).[3] Recovery set in a few years later, marked by an improved price for copper, and between 1811 and 1821 the population of Amlwch increased again by over a thousand—chiefly, says the Census reporter, "because the mines have materially improved." The improvement outlasted the great boom and the collapse which followed. Fresh discoveries were made (on land disputed between the Parys and Mona mines) in 1832, and there were hopes that Parys mine would be "restored

---

[1] *Census: Enumeration Abstracts*, 1801, 1811, 1821.
[2] Quoted in Griffith : *Mynydd Parys*, p. 64.
[3] *N. W. Gaz.*, April 9, 1812 ; Lewis : *Top. Dict.* (1843) ; *Mynydd Parys*, p. 95.

to a productive state."[1]   But before 1840 both mines had
fallen on evil days once more, and this time it was the
beginning of the end.   When a new edition of Bingley's
North Wales was prepared in 1839, the following melancholy
postscript had to be added to the original account of
Parys Mountain, written forty years earlier :—

> The mines are but a wreck of what they formerly were, the
> veins of ore being so exhausted that not more than three
> hundred persons are employed.   The receipts now scarcely do
> more than cover the expenses.[2]

By 1844 the workings were "in great degree abandoned,"[3]
and the Welsh Education Report a few years later tells
of children of seven or eight kept from school to add a
few pence to the family earnings by picking copper out of
the "iron pits."   There was another short-lived revival in
the 'sixties ; but by 1871 mining had been abandoned,
and subsequent efforts to resuscitate it have all proved
abortive, although a few tons have been raised from time
to time by precipitation.   Amlwch, which had over 6,000
inhabitants in 1831, began to decline during the next
decade, till at last its population sank to less than half ;
and in 1921 all the metalliferous mines of Anglesey found
employment for only twenty men.[4]

The death of Thomas Williams, the dwindling output of
Parys Mountain, and the embarrassments of the export
trade all left their mark on the manufacture as well as
on the mining of copper.   The produce of the smelting
houses at Amlwch rose and fell with the output of the
mines.   Up to 1835, nearly 700 tons of copper were turned
out, on an average, every year, the maximum being
reached in 1831 ; but when mining languished, smelting

---

[1] Bangor MS. 405.

[2] Pp. 71–3 ; *cf.* Poole : *Gleanings of the Histories of Holywell,
Flint* [etc.], p. 25, where it is stated that the output "is now believed
to be under average, but whether from low price or exhaustion is
uncertain."

[3] *Parl. Gaz.*, IV, p. 403.

[4] There is a good historical and geological account of Parys
Mountain in Greenly : *Geology of Anglesey*, II, pp. 823–43.   The
ledgers of Parys mine for 1863–71 are preserved in U.C.N.W. Library
(Bangor MS. 406).

was abandoned, and the revival of the 'sixties proved as ephemeral in the one branch as in the other.[1] At Holywell, as well as at Stanley and Ravenhead, the manufacturing activities of the Parys Mine Company seem to have succumbed to the Orders in Council of 1807 ;[2] but the rise of Holywell as an industrial centre had been independent of the discovery of ore in North Wales, and the copper and brass industries were still carried on for some time after the Anglesey mines ceased to be productive.

One of Williams' allies, both in Anglesey and in Cornwall, had been Pascoe Grenfell—Cornish mineowner, financial authority and Whig politician. After Williams' death, his son Owen continued to co-operate with Grenfell, both industrially and politically. For a time they shared the representation of Great Marlow, until Grenfell withdrew to a Cornish constituency.[3] Williams and Grenfell were also partners at the Holywell works (which were almost wrecked in the heavy storms of 1821) and in the Chester and North Wales Bank (of which more later) ; and from 1803 they smelted together near Swansea.[4] Owen Williams is said to have left the firm as early as 1825 or 1826,[5] and his partner died in 1838 ; but the firm of Pascoe Grenfell and Co. was still smelting at Holywell in 1842. This is the last we hear of it there. Soon afterwards

---

[1] Evans : *Beauties*, p. 721 ; Pugh : *Camb. Dep.*, p. 360.

[2] The Company is not mentioned under Holywell in Pigot's 1828 *Directory*, and the references in Lewis' *Top. Dict.* for 1833 (under *Holywell* and *Greenfield*) are ambiguous. The latest definite allusion I have seen is to William Turton, the Company's agent at Holywell (*cf.* Barfoot and Wilkes' *Directory*, 1790, III, pp. 283–5) in *Chester Chron.*, March 28, 1806—the year before the Orders in Council.

[3] *D.N.B.* He returned to Buckinghamshire during the Reform Bill election, when the young Disraeli (just entering political life) claimed to have "frightened . . . old Pascoe Grenfell" from contesting High Wycombe against him (Monypenny and Buckle : *Disraeli*, 1929 ed., I, p. 217).

[4] *N. W. Gaz.*, Sept. 27, 1821 ; Grant-Francis : *Copper Mining in the Swansea District*, p. 122 ; Evans : *Beauties*, p. 273 ; *infra*, p. 316.

[5] Grant-Francis : *loc. cit.*, but Pigot's *Directory* for 1828–29 includes the firm of Williams, Grenfell, Williams and Grenfell as owners of copper and brass works at Holywell. Another family of Williamses, of Cornish origin, has worked in partnership with the Grenfells in the Swansea district since 1823 (Grant-Francis, p. 128 ; Phillips, D. R. : *History of the Vale of Neath*, 1925, p. 269).

(perhaps during the crisis of 1847) the concern was transplanted entirely to South Wales, where the name is still
well known.   Another firm which we first come across in a
Directory of 1828—that of Newton, Lyons and Co.—
outlived the crisis, abandoning the manufacture of brass,
but continuing to work both copper and lead till the
McKinley tariff of 1890–91 forced them to close down.[1]

By this time Holywell had ceased for half a century to
rank among the important centres of copper production.
Water power, its original asset, no longer counted : indeed
it had been supplanted by steam in the Greenfield works
themselves by 1842 ; and the smelting industry passed to
seaports like Swansea, where the ore—no longer procurable
locally—could be cheaply imported in bulk, and coal could
be had in abundance.   By 1853 nearly half the copper
smelting works in Great Britain were at Swansea, and
three-quarters of them were in South Wales.[2]   The manufacture of copper bolts and sheathing for the navy, of which
Holywell once enjoyed the monopoly, was now carried on
in the Admiralty's own works at Portsmouth.   The Royal
Commission on Children's Employment in 1842 thought
the Holywell works barely worth notice beside those of
South Wales.   In 1844 they still employed 600 workpeople
—just about as many as there had been in the copper
wire works alone forty years before—but by 1857 the
number had sunk to less than 50, and only once again
(in 1881) did it exceed a hundred.   By the end of the
century the industry was dead.[3]

Before we leave this subject, something must be said
about the fate of those other copper mines which sprang
into activity at the same time as Parys Mountain.   Outside Anglesey, Caernarvonshire was by far the most
productive county in North Wales.   Messrs. Roe of
Macclesfield made several ventures there.   For some
time they worked the copper veins at Penrhyn Dû in
addition to their major operations on Parys Mountain,

[1] *C.E.R.* (1842, XV), pp. 154–5 ; local information.
[2] Lewis : *Top. Dict.*, under *Holywell;* Cundall and Landman : *op.
cit.*, p. 194 ; Jones, E. J. : *Economic History of Wales*, p. 83 (but
Mr. Jones' total of eighteen works in Great Britain is manifestly
wrong : he names nineteen himself, and he omits Holywell).
[3] *Parl. Gaz.*, II, p. 411 (*cf.* Warner : *Second Walk*, p. 211).

installing a Boulton and Watt engine in 1782 to pump out the water ; but the output proved disappointing, and attempts to get copper there—as in the Lleyn peninsula generally—were abandoned soon afterwards, although Penrhyn Dû continued to yield a little lead till 1839.[1] The copper-bearing rocks of Llanberis, which were taken in hand by Roe and Company after their Anglesey lease had lapsed, were said to yield twenty per cent of pure copper, and further quantities were obtained by precipitation. The ore, after being crushed in a stamping mill by the lake side, was taken across the lake in boats and conveyed by carts to Caernarvon, to be shipped for Swansea. From eighty to a hundred men and boys were employed in 1798, while their womenfolk tended the small grazing farms which still formed the chief household support.[2] Early in the nineteenth century the Macclesfield partnership was dissolved, without having made the Llyn Peris mine a financial success ; but adventurers from Nantwich followed them, and opened new workings as the original veins gave out. The mines were still being "worked with spirit" in 1844 ; forty years later they were only a memory.[3]

Of the workings on Snowdon we hear nothing after Waterloo ;[4] the Drws y coed mine, on the other hand, proved one of the most successful in the county. The first adventurers failed, but the mine was at work again before the wars with Napoleon ended, and it continued to flourish when Parys Mountain declined, providing a refuge for unemployed miners from Anglesey (including a number of women) in the 'thirties ; these *lêdis copor* (copper ladies), as they were known locally, had the reputation of making bad wives![5] The opening of the Nantlle quarry railway gave easy access to Caernarvon for export, and Drws y coed ores, like those of Llanberis, mostly

[1] Pennant : *Tours*, II, p. 368 ; *Chester Chron.*, March 26, 1779 ; Lord, p. 157 ; Lewis : *Top. Dict.* (1843) under *Llanengan*.
[2] Fenton : *Tours*, p. 351 ; Evans : *Tour*, pp. 186–7 ; Bingley : *North Wales*, I, pp. 230–4 ; Census, 1821.
[3] Evans : *Beauties*, p. 424 ; Hamilton : *op. cit.*, p. 158 ; Fullarton's *Parl. Gaz.*, III, p. 162.
[4] Fenton : *Tours*, p. 237.
[5] Evans : *Beauties*, p. 407 *n;* Carlisle : *Top. Dict.*, under *Llanllyfni;* *N. W. Gaz.*, May 28, 1812 ; local traditions.

found their way to Swansea.   As at Llanberis, too, mining was only a secondary employment, subject to interruption during hay harvest ; but the mine remained productive till late in the last century, yielding 200 tons of pure copper in 1879 and 140 in 1881.[1]

Not far away, in the Pass of Aberglaslyn, copper ore reputed to be twice as rich as that of Amlwch was worked with some success during the Napoleonic Wars.   For a time a stamping mill, worked by the river, was in operation, and the produce could be exported from Portmadoc, along with that of the Bron y gadair mine, near Tremadoc.[2] The latter reached its most productive period at the beginning of the nineteenth century.   From 1824–1830 it was worked by Mr. Holland, of Liverpool, whose son, Samuel Holland, had recently taken a lease of one of the Ffestiniog quarries ; and just before Queen Victoria came to the throne it was taken over by the Cambrian Mining Company, which installed a twelve horse-power engine for draining it.   But the water defeated them, and in 1844 work came to a standstill.   Some ore was still procured in the district, however, as late as the middle of the century.[3]   The other workings in the Snowdon district were on a much smaller scale.   In the Pass of Nant Ffrancon trials were being made just before the great discoveries in Anglesey, and mining continued, on and off, for nearly a century ;[4] on the other hand, a promising vein which was discovered at Bangor in 1819 petered out within ten years.[5]

At the eastern end of the county, an attempt to revive the seventeenth-century workings in the Conway valley was among the many undertakings of Messrs. Roe of Macclesfield.   For some years copper was included in the exports of Conway ; after the 'thirties the industry

---

[1] *Antea*, p. 111 ; Lewis : *Top. Dict.*, under *Bethgelart;* Fenton : *Tours*, p. 232.

[2] Evans : *Tour*, p. 153, *Beauties*, p. 404 ; *N. W. Gaz.*, Jan. 5, 1808 ; Pigot's *Directory*, 1828–29, p. 1175.

[3] *Gestiana*, pp. 35–8 ; *postea*, p. 214.   On copper mining near Beddgelert in the 'forties *see* Searell MSS. 2 (U.C.N.W. Library).

[4] *Morris Letters*, II, p. 133 ; Williams : *Observations*, pp. 74–5, 112–3 ; Fullarton's *Parl. Gaz.*, I, p. 368.

[5] *Shrewsbury Chron.*, Nov. 26, 1819 ; *N. W. Chron.*, July 24, 1828, May 28, 1829.

languished.[1] But across the river, on the lower slopes of the Great Orme, copper mining has had a long and profitable history. The original workings were drowned out before 1750, but fresh trials were made in 1782. During the Nap leonic Wars two mines were in full operation— one of them in the hands of a Liverpool company—and Llandudno ore was being regularly sold at Swansea. The annual produce was estimated in 1833 at 3,000 tons of ore, "very pure," and 120 men were said to be at work.[2] During the next decade fresh veins were tapped, and the population of the village increased in consequence by about fifty per cent. But towards 1865 the sea water rushed in once more, and the mines were deserted.[3] Luckily for Llandudno, a more lucrative industry had just been discovered, and the village spread down towards the sea to accommodate the growing crowd of summer visitors.[4] Caernarvonshire as a whole still had an annual output of 8,000 tons of copper ore, yielding five per cent of fine copper, as late as 1860 ; but the Census returns show a drop in the number of miners from 318 in 1851 to 14 in 1891. At the 1921 Census, all the metalliferous mines of the county found work for only 79 men.

Merioneth is the only other county of North Wales where much copper-mining has taken place. A small private company started mining near Trawsfynydd just after the Napoleonic War, and during the boom of 1825 the Welsh Slate, Copper, and Lead Mining Company prospected widely on Crown lands in the north of the county for copper and other minerals, but without any striking result beyond the creation of local feuds.[5] Further south,

[1] *Supra*, p. 18 ; Fenton : *Tours*, p. 173 ; *Chester Chron.*, March 23, 1798 ; Evans : *Tour*, p. 260 ; Lewis : *Top. Dict.*, under *Penmachno*, *Llanbedr-y-cenin*, and *Dwygyvylchi*.

[2] Morris : *Plans of Harbours*, p. 1 ; Aikin : *Journal*, p. 164 ; *Camb. Trav. Guide* (1813), p. 755 ; *N. W. Gaz.*, June 25, 1812, May 10 and 24, June 28, July 19, 1815, Aug. 1, 1822 ; Porth yr aur MSS.

[3] *N. W. Gaz.*, Sept. 18, 1817, May 5, 1821 ; *Shrewsbury Chron.*, June 12, 1829 ; Louis : *Gleanings of a Tour in North Wales*, pp. 6–7 ; Williams : *Aberconway*, p. 141 ; *Wales*, III, p. 295.

[4] Sproule : *Handbook to North Wales* (1859), p. 61. The copper of the neighbouring parishes was leased to Mr. Pennant (afterwards Lord Penrhyn) in 1784 (Porth yr aur MSS.). Llandudno mines inadvertently omitted from "Industrial" Map opp. p. 131.

[5] Amlwch MSS. 4 (xxvi), 8, 9, 10, etc. ; *Shrewsbury Chron.*, Jan. 28, 1825 ; Pigot's *Directory*, 1828–29, p. 1175.

in the neighbourhood of Barmouth and Dolgelley, some old workings became active again towards the end of the eighteenth century, when there was a little export of ore from Barmouth. In addition to what was got by mining, small quantities of "excellent copper" were obtained by burning peat which had become impregnated with the metal, and sending the ashes to Liverpool or Swansea. It was a device known also in the neighbourhood of Parys Mountain.[1] But the great days of mining in Merioneth came after 1850, when the re-discovery in the copper mines of traces of gold—which had been worked there in the days of Charles the First—brought prospectors flocking to the county. Soon there was a chain of gold mines running from north-east to south-west along the high ground north of the Mawddach, bringing fortune or ruin to a succession of mining companies (some of them presided over by John Bright) till quite recently.[2] There was another good vein of copper on the Ynys y maengwyn estate, within a few miles of the Dovey. In 1808 we find the proprietor, Athelstan Corbett, pathetically scouring his lands for coal to smelt it with. The search proved barren, of course, but the copper ore, worked by a London company and smelted elsewhere, continued for some years to yield good results.[3] Copper mining remained an important county industry till the 'sixties, when there were 265 miners at work—more than in Caernarvonshire. After that it declined rapidly.

Little need be said about the rest of North Wales. Denbighshire had a few scattered workings in the early part of the last century, but there were only thirteen miners in 1851, and even these disappeared within the next twenty years.[4] In Montgomeryshire, copper was found in the lead mines of Llan y mynech during the

[1] Morris : *Plans of Harbours,*, p. 9 ; Lewis : *Top. Dict.*, under *Merioneth, Llanelltyd, Dolgelley, Barmouth*, and *Llanvachreth* (*cf.* under *Llanwenllwyvo*) ; 37 Geo. III, cap. 60 ; *N. W. Gaz.*, shipping reports, 1808.
[2] Jones, R. : *History of Barmouth*, pp. 194 ff. ; *Bye-gones*, 1882, p. 10 ; 1887, pp. 472–4; 1889, p. 182 ; 1896, p. 475 ; Cundall and Landman : *op. cit.*, p. 32.
[3] Fenton : *Tours*, p. 121 ; *Shrewsbury Chron.*, July 2, Aug. 8, 1823, Nov. 6, 1829 ; Lewis : *Top. Dict.*, under *Aberdovey* and *Towyn*
[4] Lewis : *Top. Dict.*, under *Abergele, Llangerniew*, and *Llanrhaiadr*.

American War of Independence, and this and a few other veins were worked spasmodically till about 1860 or 1870, after which the industry died out.[1] Foreign competition, against which Thomas Williams had put up so valiant a fight, killed copper-mining in North Wales. Huskisson had reduced by half the duties on imported copper; Russell abolished the residue in 1848. In 1800 the entire output of copper in the world was only about 10,000 tons—hardly more than twice what Parys Mountain alone had produced a few years earlier. By 1845 it had increased more than five-fold; by 1900 fifty-fold; and the increase has continued steadily during the present century. Against such odds the poor and waterlogged mines of Wales could only struggle feebly, and Welsh ores, which had dominated the Swansea copper market at the beginning of the century, provided almost a negligible fraction even of the British copper sold there in the 'sixties. The output of England and Wales was then still as high as 16,000 tons. Now it is barely 500.[2]

C. Lead Mining.

The lead industry of North Wales cannot, like iron and copper, be associated with the name of any one outstanding pioneer. Both mining and smelting were well established long before the period to which the term "industrial revolution" is usually restricted;[3] and their subsequent history has been determined, on the one hand by the general conditions governing the market for lead, on the other by local costs of transport and drainage and the rate at which the ores have become exhausted. In times of brisk demand, not only are new shafts sunk, but adventurers with next to no capital pump out old workings and even rummage abandoned waste-heaps for purposes of re-smelting;[4] though to the sorely-pressed miner it often seems as if the Romans, the ancient

[1] Pennant: *Tours,* III, p. 205; *Bye-gones,* 1916–18, p. 22; *Wales,* III, p. 295.

[2] Cundall and Landman: *op. cit.,* p. 328; Hunt: *op. cit.,* p. 895; Levy: *op. cit.,* pp. 155–6.

[3] *Supra,* pp. 17–22.

[4] E.g. Northop, *c.* 1780 (Carlisle: *Top. Dict.*); Llanfyllin, *c.* 1830 (Lewis: *Top. Dict.*).

Britons or the mediaeval monks—to whom these derelict shafts and levels are impartially attributed—have laid a spell on them for all time. Lewis Morris' Cardiganshire miners keep telling him that "the d - - - l sits cross-legd upon ye ore in ye Roman rake," or that the holy men of Strata Florida have left a curse on the places where they worked, to keep all interlopers at bay.[1] But curse or no curse, work is pushed ahead till the veins become inaccessible or the water can no longer be coped with. Then if prices are still good, a wealthier firm perhaps takes the mine over and installs up-to-date machinery ; but when bad times return, only those concerns survive which can economize on costs, or can afford to await the turn of the tide.

There are two main lead-bearing regions in North Wales. One extends from the northern extremity of Flintshire, in the neighbourhood of Prestatyn and Dyserth, through Whitford, Holywell and Halkin Mountain to Mold, and over the Denbighshire border into Llanarmon, Llanferres and Minera. The other spreads from northern Cardiganshire (a rich district not included in our survey) into southern Merioneth and the south-western regions of Montgomeryshire.[2] In times of good trade other districts, where lead is less abundant, have been stirred into temporary activity. This in Anglesey a peculiar form of ore known as Anglesite was extracted from Parys Mountain when copper declined,[3] and in Caernarvonshire lead has been worked alongside copper in the Conway and Ogwen valleys, on the borders of Merioneth and at Penrhyn Dû in Lleyn.[4] But the most flourishing periods of lead-mining in Caernarvonshire lie outside our scope—in the

---

[1] *Morris Letters*, I, pp. 485, 434 (1756 ff.).

[2] *See* accounts in Pennant : *Tours*, II, pp. 66 ff. ; Davies : *General View*, pp. 55–63 ; *Y Cymmrodor*, VI, pp. 1–52 ; and Hunt : *British Mining*, pp. 261–2, 322–4. All references, unless otherwise stated, are to these sources, the first and third edition of Lewis' *Topographical Dictionary*, and the Census abstracts.

[3] Lewis Morris : *Plans of Harbours*, pp. 2, 3, and 5 ; *Camb. Reg.*, II, p. 417.

[4] Lewis, under *Llanrwst, Penmachno, Trevriw, Bettws y coed, Llanrhychwen, Garthgarmon, Llandegai, Tremadoc, Llanvrothen, Ffestiniog, Llandecwen, Llanengan; Chester Chron.*, Feb. 2, 1781, July 12, 1782, Nov. 7, 1806 ; *N. W. Gaz.*, Jan. 28, 1813 ; Evans : *Tour*, p. 129 ; Fenton : *Tours*, p. 173.

seventeenth century, when the local ores bore a high reputation and were shipped in considerable quantities from Conway and other ports,[1] and again after 1850, when for a short time more than two hundred miners were at work. In 1841 there were only eleven ; in 1921 there were 79.

For the whole of the period now under survey, Flintshire was *facile princeps* in both mining and smelting. Here the ore was found in juxtaposition with coal, and both lay within easy distance of the Dee estuary, so that either crude or refined lead could be exported, without heavy charges for land transport, from one or other of the outlying creeks of the Port of Chester, to manufacturing regions like Bristol or Liverpool ; while Rhuddlan served as an outlet for the mines which lay further west. It was naturally in Flintshire and Denbighshire that the impetus given to the industry by the application of coal to smelting was most strongly felt ; its effects were still apparent in the second half of the eighteenth century. Between 1758 and 1777 the exports of lead, abroad and coastwise, from Chester and its subordinate creeks amounted to nearly 80,000 tons ; those of lead ore to more than 12,000. After 1770, so far as we can judge from the export figures, not much advance was made ;[2] yet new mines were still opening. In Denbighshire, the Minera mines entered on a new phase of activity when in 1761 the Chester Corporation leased out the lands which it held there (under a charitable trust) to one of its own members, a silversmith, who raised more than 10,000 tons of ore during the next twenty years, smelting it at Hawarden.[3] About the same time, the resuscitation of the Llanferres mines gave rise to a famous boundary dispute between their owners, the Grosvenors (later Dukes of Westminster), and the lords of Mold, whose mines lay close by. There were fresh discoveries near Mold at the time of the American Revolt, and to the same period belong the extension of mining to Llanarmon parish and (further north) the opening of the famous

---

[1] Fuller : *Worthies*, III, p. 483.
[2] Pennant : *Tours*, II, p. 69, III, p. 264.
[3] Palmer : *Old Parish of Wrexham*, pp. 45 ff. ; *Memoir of Hawarden*, p. 107.

Holywell Level, which—after involving its proprietors in heavy losses for twenty years—was to become "by much one of the richest works in the county."[1] In the Hundred of Prestatyn, the Crown mines had been sub-let by the lessee to the Mine Adventurers (one of Mackworth's flotations of the post-1688 period) but the Crown surveyor in 1778 reported grave abuses in management.[2] On the Denbighshire coast, some mines near Abergele were productive from early in George the Third's reign till after Waterloo, when flooding and exhaustion compelled them to close down.[3]

The effects of the Napoleonic struggle on the lead industry were very different from its effects on copper. Important as the Flintshire mines might be, they did not, like Parys Mountain in its palmy days, control nearly half the world's supply of a metal indispensable in war-time. There were plenty of mines elsewhere to meet the army's needs, and increased demand at home was more than outweighed by the loss of continental markets (on which Flintshire had come chiefly to depend) and the ruinous freight charges and insurance premiums ; nor could exporters hope to extend their sales, as the copper merchants did, beyond the continent to India and Africa. The export abroad of smelted lead from Flintshire amounted in the third year of War to 270 tons, that of ore to 160 : the one less than a quarter, the other not much more than half what they had been during the preceding quarter of a century ; and the coastwise traffic did not show anything like a countervailing increase.[4]

In the years following the suspension of cash payments work was slack at Llanferres, and in Grosvenor's mine at Llanarmon employment was reduced from 500 to 30. John Wilkinson, who was just beginning to work lead at Minera and Llyn y pandy, had £40,000 worth of pigs and ore lying idle for want of a market ; and the proprietors of the newly-opened Milwr mine at Holywell were in

[1] Pennant : *Whiteford and Holywell*, pp. 249–50 ; *Chester Chron.*, July 20, 1776, Oct. 4, 1782 ; *N. W. Gaz.*, Sept. 10, 1812.

[2] *Chester Chron.*, Dec. 25, 1778.

[3] Williams : *Records of Denbigh*, pp. 223–4 ; *Chester Chron.*, Feb. 26, 1776 ; Lewis : *Top. Dict.*, under *Abergele* and *Kegidock*.

[4] Kay : *Agriculture of North Wales : Flintshire*, p. 24 ; Pennant : *Tours, loc. cit.*

serious financial difficulties.[1] The Orders in Council virtually killed the export trade, and although the home market improved in compensation, the total sales still fell considerably below the average of pre-war years. Attempts had been made to revive the old workings at Nant y ffrith, near Minera, but all work ceased there now—save when an unemployed miner might come and cart away a barrow-load of ore. The disastrous storms of 1807 increased the general distress : hundreds of miners in both Denbigh and Flint were thrown out of work by the flooding of the mines. The years 1811-12 saw further bankruptcies in the Flintshire lead trade, and the Peace, with its inevitable financial troubles, brought no remedy.[2]

Yet the set-back was only temporary, and the war-years had been by no means barren. In particular the organization of the industry was improving. Although several mines had been acquired by wealthy smelting companies from London or Yorkshire when coal was first used,[3] it was still common for petty shop-keepers, farmers or workmen to scrape together in partnership enough money to rent the working of a vein of lead as a profitable subsidiary occupation—much as they might hire an allotment to-day. Even in districts like Holywell and Flint, a directory of 1790 shows that mining was often carried on by farmers, bakers, hucksters, butchers and bacon sellers.[4] But all this was changing. In an advertisement in a local paper for 1797 we can see the process at work. In Cilcen parish the lead had been worked on "take-note bargains" (after the fashion described above) since at any rate the Seven Years' War (one of the mines was named after the Battle of Plassey) ; but now the proprietors announce it as their intention to abandon this practice in the interests of efficiency, and their readiness to treat with "any Company of property."[5]

These more substantial capitalists, who were often owners of coal mines and smelteries, were in a position

[1] Warner : Second Walk, pp. 211 ff., 249 ff. ; Chester Chron., March 24, 1797, June 15, 1798.
[2] Pugh : Camb. Dep., pp. 11, 331, 429 ; Chester Chron., Dec. 11, 1807 ; N. W. Gaz., Feb. 7, 1811, June 18, 1812, May 16, 1816.
[3] Supra, p. 20 ; infra, pp. 309-10.
[4] Barfoot and Wilkes' Directory, III, pp. 113-14, 281-5.
[5] Chester Chron., Oct. 4, 1782, July 21, 1797.

to provide the mines with adequate machinery. This is the period when we begin to hear of the introduction of steam engines to cope with the water. We have already seen[1] how John Wilkinson made lavish use of Boulton and Watt engines both at Minera and at Llyn y pandy. The latter is in a peculiarly troublesome district, where the River Alyn suddenly and inexplicably dives underground ; less than a mile from Wilkinson's mine another proprietor—a member of the local family of Ingleby, who may perhaps be identified with one of the partners in the Cheadle Brass Company[2]—was struggling with the same difficulty. He had started a few years before Wilkinson, and with the most primitive appliances he contrived to raise in some weeks, it is said, as much as a hundred tons of ore at £9 a ton ; and this on an initial outlay of £50 ! But soon the water came flooding in, and forced him to put up a water wheel, and then an old-fashioned steam engine ; and still the flood kept rising. Dissensions with his neighbour did not mend matters, and both mines had to stop working soon after Waterloo.[3] Steam engines were also installed at Holywell, Llanarmon, Llanasa and Cilcen about this time ; at Llanferres a new company drained the mine by driving a level costing several thousands of pounds.[4]

By 1818 the industry was in full swing again. Holywell Level was bringing its proprietors about £130,000 a year ; exploration was taking place as far west as Denbigh and the Vale of Clwyd ; regular markets for the sale of ore were held in alternate fortnights, at Flint and Holywell respectively ; and at Halkin Mr. John Taylor, agent to Lord Grosvenor and one of the most active promoters of the industry, erected in 1823 the first ore-crushing mill in North Wales.[5] Only at Minera were things going badly. There the pugnacious spirit of Wilkinson seemed

---

[1] *Supra*, p. 139.

[2] Hamilton : *Brass and Copper Industries*, p. 247 *n*.

[3] *Cambro-Briton*, I, pp. 257–8.

[4] *Chester Chron.*, Nov. 11, 1802, March 14, Oct. 24 and 31, 1806, Aug. 7, 1807, March 28, 1817.

[5] Aikin : *England Described*, p. 440 ; *Shrewsbury Chron.*, March 20, 1818 ; Lewis : *Top. Dict.*, under *Llanvrothen, Llanynys, Llangerniew*, and *Llanvwrog; N. W. Chron.*, Nov. 13, 1828 ; Hunt, pp. 693–4.

to brood over the mine after his death, and his pumping engines, which had caused such heartburnings while he was alive, now not only failed to cope with their task, but involved his partners, executors, and successors in Chancery proceedings which brought the mines to a standstill in 1824.[1]

Soon after this, the lead industry throughout the country was in the throes of that general mining crisis which came as the penalty for unhealthy speculation. Unemployed miners in Flintshire, it was alleged, were turning poachers, and the owners were petitioning that the duties on foreign ores, which Huskisson had just reduced from twenty to fifteen per cent, should be raised to a prohibitive figure. For Spanish ores were invading the country, and British exports fell from nearly 20,000 tons in 1821 to under 9,000 in 1831.[2] "The question now is," declared a correspondent of the *North Wales Chronicle* in 1828, "whether our mines shall be worked with spirit or abandoned altogether."[3] He had his own remedies to offer: one was that landlords should take longer views, and let their mines on easy terms to substantial *entrepreneurs*, instead of following the practice (which too many of them still clung to) of accepting as tenant any little hole-and-corner speculator who offered a high rent ; the other was that Welsh mineowners, abandoning all hope of competing with foreign ores in ports like Bristol, should concentrate their efforts on capturing the Midland manufacturing districts, which they could now invade by canal.

Economy and machinery did something to tide over the crisis. In 1829 Mr. John Taylor was fêted by a company of Flintshire smelters and mineowners as a leading exponent of the policy of improvements in production instead of reductions in wages.[4] New pumping apparatus was set up at Llanarmon and at Holywell ; the proprietors of Holywell Level, which was formerly approached by water through a tunnel (after the fashion of some of the older Derbyshire mines), replaced this inconvenient adit by a

[1] Palmer : *Old Parish of Wrexham*, pp. 45 ff.
[2] *N. W. Chron.*, Jan. 7, 1830 ; *Shrewsbury Chron.*, Feb. 15, 1828, April 2, 1830 ; Louis : *Sketches of Some Parts of Denbighshire and Flintshire*, p. 33 ; Clapham : *Early Railway Age*, p. 241.
[3] Sept. 18.
[4] *N. W. Chron.*, Sept. 10, 1829.

horse tramway ; its neighbour the Milwr mine, after years of disappointment, was just beginning to pay handsome profits—as much as £17,000 in a year, according to report. But the weaker, more exhausted or more waterlogged mines were already succumbing to foreign competition. In the north of the county the Talar Goch mine, near Dyserth (once the most productive in Flintshire, and still yielding a clear £2,000 a year at the beginning of the century) had begun to decline by 1828, and only employed 34 miners when the 1831 Census was taken.[1] In the neighbouring parishes of Prestatyn and Newmarket and, further south, those of Ysceifiog and Tremeirchion (which had been exploited since James I's time),[2] mining died out ; in Llanasa and Whitford it lasted a little longer, but the population was stationary or declining by the middle of the century. The lead-mining community of Halkin (a mushroom growth of the Industrial Revolution) began to shrink between 1821 and 1831, and found itself smaller in 1851 than it had been even in 1821. The same was happening in Northop and Cilcen, and in the latter parish the Census reporter expressly attributes the decline to emigration induced by slack times in the lead mines. In the Mold district, operations were resumed during the boom period, but there was now a new and ominous obstacle to contend with : in 1826 the employees (between 700 and 800 in number) struck for shorter hours, and stopped the pumps. The issue is unknown, but by 1828 the mines were once more "productive and profitable," and the struggle with the underground river was gamely carried on till about the middle of the century.[3] In Denbighshire work was still brisk at Llanferres, where nearly a hundred men were employed in 1831 and an annual average of a thousand tons was maintained for a time ; but mining was on the down grade at Llanarmon, and by 1841 the industry was declining everywhere.

Before the final collapse came, however, there were two rallies. The first, which took place in the 'forties,

---

[1] *Id.*, Dec. 25, 1828.
[2] Edwards : *Star Chamber Proceedings*, p. 172.
[3] *Shrewsbury Chron.*, March 10, 1826 ; Pigot's *Directory* (1828–29), pp. 1166–7 ; Fullarton's *Parl. Gaz.* III, p. 430; Parry: *Railway Companion* p. 34.

was due largely to the exploitation of the mines for zinc ore ; the second, in the 'seventies, was a ripple on the great wave of speculation which followed the payment of the French war indemnity to Germany. In Denbighshire a new company took over the Llanarmon mines soon after 1840, and set about equipping them with new machinery ; its success inspired a number of individual labourers to re-start small workings on their own account. The Minera mines, after lying idle for a quarter of a century, were revived in 1850 by a company with a capital of £45,000.[1] Even in western Denbighshire fifty or sixty miners were at work for some years on the Hiraethog Hills ; in Flintshire whole cargoes of ore arriving in the Dee estuary were disposed of without difficulty in the Holywell and Flint markets.[2] The decline in the population of mining districts like Cilcen was arrested for a time : the number employed in the Flintshire mines had risen by 1851 from 1,500 to 1,900 (Holywell and Talar Goch accounting for about half of them), and there were 900 in Denbighshire. Fresh discoveries at Minera in 1853 prolonged the boom in this county, and by the next Census over 1,100 men were at work—only 200 less than in Flintshire, where decline had already set in. By 1871 Flintshire had only 800 miners, and Denbighshire 700.

Then came a last spurt. In the winter of 1876 "mining speculation" was a stock jest for the pantomime comedian.[3] How Montgomeryshire was affected by it we shall see shortly ; but Flintshire and Denbighshire were also in the swim. New companies took over the Holywell and Halkin mines between 1875 and 1880.[4] Talar Goch became productive once more ; the Minera mines were working at an average profit of £20,000 a year for thirty years after the discoveries of 1853 ; and Llanarmon and Llanferres both flourished. In 1881 the figures of employment in Flintshire had reached a thousand once again ; in Denbighshire they were even higher. But with the influx of lead ore from the American and Australian

---

[1] Palmer : *Old Parish of Wrexham*, p. 49.
[2] Williams : *Ancient and Modern Denbigh*, p. 261 ; Parry : *Railway Companion*, p. 42.
[3] *History*, XII, p. 226 (Oct., 1927).
[4] *Calendar of Coleman Documents*, No. 1368 ; Edwards : *Flintshire*, pp. 81–2.

silver mines during the following years, all but a few
of the resuscitated workings had to be abandoned. In
Denbighshire the number of miners sank steadily at each
Census, till there were only 23 left. In Flintshire the
new company at Holywell went bankrupt in 1884, and
although the profitable working of Halkin mine led to a
slight increase in employment at the opening of the new
century, there were only just over a hundred miners in
the county in 1921.[1]

The history of the more southerly lead-mining districts
has followed a different course. While Flintshire was
forging ahead, they lay dormant, and their most flourishing
period came when the northern mines were undergoing
eclipse. In the south-western corner of Montgomeryshire
around

Plynlymmon's brow,
Where precious metals dart their purple gleam,[2]

we enter the region of the rich silver-bearing ores of
Cardiganshire. The belt extends northwards towards
the Dovey Valley (where it has been worked on both sides
of the county boundary), and eastwards to Llanidloes ;
and it unexpectedly crops up again in the extreme north of
the county, at Llangynog and Llan y mynech.[3] So fruitful
are the veins that, even after they had made the fortunes
of a long line of adventurers in three successive centuries,
ore was still left in abundance, near the surface and ready
to be worked, without expensive machinery, by any future
speculator. But there were two serious impediments—lack
of coal and difficulties of transport. Once charcoal had
been superseded, the ore could most conveniently be
smelted on the coalfields, and mines which lay at a distance
could not be worked with profit unless the cost of carrying
such an abnormally heavy metal to the smelteries was in
some way kept down. The Cardigan Bay ports formed
the usual outlet for the mines of the west ; lead ore was

[1] *Wales*, III, p. 295 ; *Bye-gones*, 1896, p. 296 ; *Cal. of Coleman
Documents*, Nos. 1367–8 ; Cundall and Landman : *op. cit.*, p. 208.
[2] Dyer : *The Fleece*, Bk. I.
[3] *See* descriptions in Hunt : *British Mining*, pp. 151–60, 253–5 ;
Davies : *General View*, pp. 61–2 ; *Mont. Coll.*, V, pp. 24–33 ; Lewis :
Top. Dict., under *Llangynog, Hirnant, Llanwddyn, Llangadvan,
Llanymynech, Llanvyllin, Llanidloes, Machynlleth, Llanbrynmair,
Darowen* ; *N.L.W. Journ.*, III, p. 148.

among the exports both of Barmouth and of Aberystwyth.[1] But for the produce of land-locked Montgomeryshire there was generally a long and expensive journey—by roads that were notorious, even for North Wales, till the nineteenth century—before it could reach the navigable Dovey in the west or the navigable Severn in the east. Hence mining languished till the railway came.

But if prizes, for a time, ceased to be won, it was not for lack of competitors. The Mine Adventurers, who had caused such storms in Mid-Wales at the end of the seventeenth century, were still raising a little ore near Llanidloes, as well as in Cardiganshire, as late as the middle of the eighteenth.[2] Lewis Morris—antiquary, cartographer, and metallurgist, one of a distinguished trio of brothers from the heart of Anglesey—struggled with the Cardiganshire mines, in his capacity of deputy steward of the Crown manors, for twenty years ; but when he died in 1765 his promised fortune was still unmade. "God help you," his brother had written six years earlier, "you are born to trouble. May I be poor for ever if this is to be the reward of mining."[3] When the industry was booming in Denbigh and Flint, mineowners and smelters from these regions sometimes tried to supplement their resources from the Cardigan and Montgomery mines ;[4] and there were always plenty of local speculators ready to try their hand : shopkeepers, partnerships of working miners, even clergymen and ministers. We hear, for example, of an old minister who, about the middle of the nineteenth century, sank all his little savings in a pathetic attempt to get lead in the neighbourhood of the Mathrafal iron forge.[5] This small-scale method of working persisted in Montgomeryshire when it had long been superseded in Flintshire. During the boom year of 1825, it is true, there was talk of a resuscitation of Sir Hugh Myddleton's old mines by Nathan Meyer Rothschild ; but nothing

[1] Morris : *Plans of Harbours*; Mavor: *Tour*, p. 63; *N. W. Gaz.*, shipping returns, 1808 ff.

[2] Pococke : *Travels*, II, p. 20 ; *Cal. of Crosswood Deeds*, p. 179; *cf. supra*, p. 22.

[3] *Morris Letters*, II, p. 138, *et passim; Y Cymmrodor*, XV, pp. 1–87.

[4] *See*, e.g., Hunt : *op. cit.*, pp. 151 ff. (Flintshire company takes over mines near Aberystwyth) ; other examples follow.

[5] *Bye-gones*, 1893–94, p. 487.

came of it.[1]   Not till after 1850 was the exploitation of the mines once more undertaken on a big scale by wealthy companies.

We may now take a glance at some of the chief mining districts of Montgomeryshire.   A little to the north-east of Plynlimon, the Dylife Hills were worked for lead (by a Flintshire smelting firm, among others) from about 1770, the ore being sent by the new turnpike road to Machynlleth, and then shipped down the Dovey from Derwenlas.[2]   Soon after Waterloo, a new vein was struck by Hugh Williams, a Machynlleth man whose son was later to earn notoriety by his defence of Chartists and Rebecca Rioters in the law courts.   This new mine had completely eclipsed the older ones by the time that Samuel Lewis published the first (1833) edition of his *Topographical Dictionary*, and about a hundred tons of ore were being shipped annually from Derwenlas.   Further north again, near the hamlet of Pennant, miners had been busy, off and on, throughout the latter half of the eighteenth century ;   one of the adventurers came from Wrexham and was possibly related to a future proprietor of Minera, John Burton.   A Flintshire company appeared there shortly before 1810, and new workings were opened by Hugh Williams, whose interests both here and at Dylife were eventually taken over by a firm in which Richard Cobden (now his son-in-law) and John Bright are said to have been shareholders.[3]

A vein of ore was struck at Llanidloes in 1805, but it was worked out before 1833.   The flooded mines of Llangynog were taken in hand at the beginning of the century by a company which drove levels under the old workings ; among the adventurers were John Taylor, the Flintshire lead magnate, and another Halkin mineowner.[4]   Operations seem to have ceased soon after Waterloo, and another revival about the time of the Reform Bill was equally short-lived.   Both here and at Llanidloes one of the main

---

[1] *Shrewsbury Chron.*, Jan. 28, 1825.
[2] *Chester Chron.*, Oct. 29, 1779, Feb. 4, 1780 ;   *N. W. Gaz.*, Dec. 6, 1810.
[3] *Shrewsbury Chron.*, March 6, 1818, Sept. 18, 1829 ;   *N. W. Gaz.*, May 22, 1828 ;   *Mont. Coll.*, XXI, pp. 86 ff., XXVIII, p. 142 ;   *Byegones*, 1882–83, p. 82 ;   *infra*, p. 413.
[4] *Salop. Journ.*, Aug. 7, 1805 ;   *Chester Chron.*, June 20, 1800.

difficulties must have been the long distance from any seaport, and the heavy cost of conveyance by road. But at Llan y mynech the Montgomeryshire canal provided a cheap means of transport to the Midland manufactories, and about 1821 efforts were made to revive the mining of lead and zinc which had been carried on there at intervals during the last quarter of the eighteenth century. Within a few years, however, the enterprise had sunk to nothing—a victim, perhaps, of the great slump.[1]

Across the border of Merioneth there was some mining in the Dolgelley district before 1798 and again towards the middle of the next century ; but the 1851 Census attributes depopulation in the neighbouring parish of Llanfachreth to the stoppage of the mines. Lead was also worked in two parts of the Dovey Valley. Close to the estuary, the Corbetts of Ynys y maengwyn leased out their ore to a London company, which had, however, ceased work by 1833. Further up the valley, near Dinas Mawddwy, a similar course was followed by the owner of the minerals as soon as it became necessary to excavate beyond the superficial outcrops ; but the lessees found them too expensive to work, and their levels were already derelict before 1799.[2] There were hardly more than fifty men at work in the whole county in 1841, and Montgomeryshire itself had only 180—just about an eighth of the number employed in Flintshire. A Parliamentary Report of the next year described the produce of the Plynlimon region as "now of inferior importance," and the Commission of Inquiry into Welsh Education, reporting on the same neighbourhood in 1847, found mines idle and parents too poor to send their children to school.[3]

Then comes a startling change. In 1851 the number of lead miners in Montgomeryshire was reported as 1,100. Most of them were engaged in searching for ore near

---

[1] Pennant : *Tours*, III, p. 205 ; *Camb. Reg.*, I, pp. 265, 272 ; *Shrewsbury Chronicle*, Dec. 7, 1821 ; Cathrall : *History of North Wales*, II, p. 360.

[2] Morris : *Plans of Harbours*, p. 9 ; Davies : *General View*, pp, 61–2 ; Lewis : *Top. Dict.*, under *Merioneth, Llanelltyd, Dolgelley. Towyn*, and *Aberdovey;* Fenton : *Tours*, p. 112 ; *Shrewsbury Chron.*, Aug. 8, 1823, Nov. 6, 1829.

[3] *C.E.R.* (1842, XV), p. 204 ; *Education Report*, 1847, III, App. pp. 143, 146 ; *Camb. Trav. Guide* (1840 ed.), p. 404.

Van Lake, north of Llanidloes. Once again it was from Flintshire that the impetus had come, for the chief prospector, William Williams, used to boast of having worked in the Holywell mines for fourpence a day. It was not till 1865, after nearly £2,000 had been spent in exploration, that the main body of ore was reached. The original proprietors having failed, the Van mine was bought out of Chancery by a London company, under whose direction it produced 150 tons a month for some years. There were fifteen other lead mining companies in the district, and miners flocked in from Cornwall and Devon. In 1871 a branch railway was built to connect the mines with the trunk line completed ten years before.[1]

In the whole county the number of miners had by now risen to nearly 1,500—twice as many as in Flintshire—and it reached the high-water mark of 3,593 in 1881, when Flintshire had not a third of the number. The Van mines accounted for a round thousand ; the rest were absorbed by the renewed activity which the railway had brought into other districts. South of Llanidloes, the old workings of the seventeenth-century Mine Adventurers were re-started. In the Pennant district, beyond Llanbrynmair, a succession of companies from London, Dublin and elsewhere took over the mines, one of which (hitherto a failure) was in 1866 employing nearly a hundred men and producing 120 to 150 tons a month, at an annual profit not far short of £12,000. The Dylife mine, under John Bright and his partners, yielded nearly 200 tons a month ; others in the same district were re-opened by a Holywell man who had worked on Parys Mountain ; and a Birmingham company established itself on the slopes of Plynlimon itself.[2] The produce of this district, instead of going to Derwenlas for transport by river, could now be put on railway waggons at Llanbrynmair station for one or another of the Cardigan Bay ports ; Aberystwyth was at this time doing a regular trade in lead ore with Bristol and the Dee estuary. Even some of the Llangynog workings were re-opened for

[1] Horsfall–Turner : *Llanidloes*, pp. 138–40, 224 ; *Mont. Coll.*, XXXVII, pp. 24–7 ; Hunt : pp. 487–9.

[2] Hamer and Lloyd : *History of the Parish of Llangurig* (1875), pp. 9–10 ; *Mont. Coll.*, XXI, pp. 85 ff. ; *Bye-gones*, 1907–8, p. 246 ; 1916–18, pp. 13–14, 22.

awhile, and in Merioneth employment reached the record figure of 78. George Borrow, visiting Dinas Mawddwy in 1854, found it the headquarters of a squalid, drunken and quarrelsome population of miners—most of them living in lodgings, away from their families, and total strangers to religion, except in so far as Methodism had touched them.[1]

Under the stress of foreign competition, the boom collapsed as suddenly as it had begun. In the single decade 1881–91, employment in Montgomeryshire dropped from over 3,000 to under 400, in Merioneth from 53 to 9 ; and the industry has now become negligible. The Dylife mines were abandoned in 1896, their promoter having long since gone to look for better prospects in Nevada ; the Van mines had about a hundred men at work till the late War ; the last mine at Llangynog was closed in 1916.[2]

D.—The Manufacture of Lead, Zinc and Chemicals.

If the mining of lead was widely diffused, smelting and manufacture were highly concentrated. From the time when coal came into use, Flintshire enjoyed an undisputed pre-eminence in these branches of the industry : it was estimated in 1849 that more than a quarter of the lead of the United Kingdom, including nearly all that of North Wales and some of the coal-less parts of South Wales, of Scotland, Ireland and the Isle of Man, was brought here for smelting. The local ores came in farm waggons or horse-panniers, until the building of mineral railways sent horses back to farm work ; those from a distance were landed at the Dee ports and sold in the Flint and Holywell markets, or else taken direct to the smelteries. Most of these were within easy reach for small vessels unloading the raw material or carrying off the finished product—pig lead or sheets, bars and pipes. At the same works silver and zinc were separated and worked up for the industries that used them, and by-products

---

[1] Morgan : *New Guide to Aberystwyth* (1858), p. 71 ; *Mont. Coll.*, VI, p. 339 ; Borrow : *Wild Wales*, pp. 422–5.
[2] *Mont. Coll.*, XXXVII, p. 26 ; *Bye-gones*, 1916–18, p. 22 ; Roberts and Owen : *Story of Montgomeryshire*, p. 84.

like white and red lead, litharge and sulphur laid the foundations for what was to become a flourishing chemical industry.[1]

The oldest and most important centre of manufacture was Bagillt, near Holywell. The original Governor and Company for Smelting Down Lead was still at work here in 1776, and other big English firms, as well as owners of neighbouring coal and lead mines, were attracted by the obvious advantages of the site ; for it had long been in regular communication with Liverpool by sea, and a steam-packet service was established in 1821.[2] At Flint, smelting works had been built in 1755 for a firm in which the moving spirit was one of the landed proprietors of the district ; these were carried on in the early nine-teenth century by Messrs. Roskell and Tipton, later to become pioneers of the chemical industry. A penny token, issued for paying the workpeople there in 1813, gives us a conventionalized picture of the works as they appeared at that date.[3] The reverberatory furnaces at Llannerch y môr, near Whitford, were built about the same time as those of Flint. They were occupied in 1825 by Richard Kyrke (who had worked with Wilkinson at Minera) in collaboration with a local coalowner named Eyton.[4] But this was a small concern ; Lewis describes it in 1833 as employing 50 men and producing 60 tons a week, "exclusively for the Manchester market." Twice as much was turned out at Flint, where 120 men were employed ; and Bagillt, with 300 employees in three "separate and extensive" works, manufactured 100,000 tons annually.

It was at these three exporting centres that the bulk of the smelting was done ; but sometimes the owners of mines farther inland, if they had coal handy, preferred

[1] Parry : *Railway Companion*, p. 42 ; *Y Cymmrodor*, VI, p. 43 ; *cf. supra*, p. 111.

[2] Pennant : *Whiteford and Holywell*, pp. 261-2, 274-5 ; *Chester Chron.*, March 7, 1776, Oct. 29, 1779 ; *N. W. Gaz.*, Jan. 30, 1812 ; Pigot's *Directory*, 1828-29, p. 1158 ; *supra*, p. 129.

[3] Pennant : *op. cit.*, pp. 281-2 ; Pigot, p. 1155. There is a specimen of this token in the Wrexham Public Museum ; *see* also *Bye-gones*, 1889-90, pp. 388, 407; 1891-92, p. 327.

[4] Pennant : *op. cit.*, p. 156 ; Pigot, p. 1158 ; *cf. N. W. Gaz.*, Dec. 29, 1825, *N. W. Chron.*, April 17, May 29, 1828.

to work up their ores on the spot rather than to hand over the profit to other smelters. Near the Mold mines were two smelting houses and a rolling mill, the produce of which was carried by road to Flint for export ; and John Wilkinson, when he was working there, set up another furnace on Buckley Mountain.[1] There was also some smelting in the neighbourhood of the Minera mines.[2]

At all the furnaces excepting those of Mold and Minera (where the ores are not argentiferous) silver was separated and prepared in refineries for use of the silversmiths of Birmingham and Sheffield. Pennant[3] gives us statistics of a single plant which produced quantities ranging from over 12,000 ounces in 1754 down to 4,000 in 1776 ; Lewis, in his *Topographical Dictionary* of 1833, credits both Bagillt and Flint with an output ten times as high as this later figure. At Greenfield, a mile or two along the coast from Bagillt, works for the manufacture of white and red lead were built about 1754 by Smedleys, a firm which also smelted at Bagillt and raised coal and lead in various parts of Flintshire and Montgomeryshire—till it went bankrupt during the War with America.[4] It was here, too, that Messrs. Newton, Lyons and Co., whom we first encounter in 1828, carried on the manufacture of lead along with that of copper till the closing years of the century. In 1833 about a hundred men were employed at Greenfield in making white and red lead, sheet lead and copper, and patent lead pipes. The produce of the Bagillt smelteries and of Roskell's furnaces at Flint was also manufactured on the spot into bars, sheets and pipes.[5]

It was no mere accident that made the lead and brass industries such close neighbours. For zinc ore, one of the raw materials for the manufacture of brass, is a sort

[1] Warner : *Second Walk*, pp. 251–3 ; Davies : *General View*, p. 57 ; Palmer : *Wilkinson*, p. 18.

[2] *Chester Chron.*, Aug. 14, 1807 ; Pigot's *Directory* (1828–29), p. 1179 ; Palmer : *Old Parish of Wrexham*, p. 77.

[3] *Tours*, II, pp. 67–9.

[4] *Id.*: *Whiteford and Holywell*, p. 201 ; *Chester Chron.*, May 14, June 11, Oct. 29, 1779. Members of the Smedley family continued to be connected with the Flintshire lead industry for some time after the bankruptcy ; Barfoot and Wilkes' *Directory*, III, p. 285 ; *Chester Chron.*, Oct. 3, 1797,

[5] Lewis : *Top. Dict.*, under *Holywell* and *Flint; supra*, p. 164.

of by-product of the lead mines—a by-product which the miner, both here and in Montgomeryshire, used to throw on the rubbish-heap until the knowledge of its use was brought from Somerset (an old zinc-mining county) early in the eighteenth century.[1]   Soon after the middle of the century a Bristol firm began to "engross" the zinc ores of the Holywell district, and set up a plant to prepare them for use in the brass manufacture. But the Bristol monopoly did not remain unchallenged. The Cheadle Company, as we have seen, was making brass at Greenfield from 1765 ; sixteen years later the Birmingham manufacturers sent Matthew Boulton to the district to take precautions against the cornering of calamine, or zinc carbonate (the ore used for brass), with the result that calamine was being calcined at Holywell for the Cheadle and Maccles-field brassworks by 1784, and at Flint for the Smethwick Brass Company from 1794.[2]   At the same time this and other ores of zinc were being shipped at Conway from the Caernarvonshire mines, and at Barmouth and Aber-ystwyth from those of Montgomery, Merioneth and Cardigan ; in the neighbourhood of the Penrhyn slate quarries the preparation of zinc for use in the manufacture of paints was carried on for some years.[3]   The com-petition of German calamine and refined zinc long prevented the industry from expanding in this country, but demand was revived by the invention of galvanized iron in 1837 and of other manufactures in which zinc is involved. New zinc works were built at Bagillt and Greenfield in the 'forties ; and during the second half of the century, decayed mining districts were often explored once more for the purpose of recovering zinc from waste dumps. Flintshire still retains its importance in this branch of production.[4]

[1] Pennant : *Tours*, I, p. 84, II, pp. 69–70 ; *Camb. Reg.*, I, p. 265.
[2] *Id: Whiteford and Holywell*, pp. 273–4 ; Evans : *Beauties*, pp. 848–9 ; Hamilton : *Brass and Copper Industries*, pp. 2 n and 220.
[3] 37 Geo. III, cap. 50 ; Aikin : *Journal*, pp. 44, 126 ; Evans : *Tour*, p. 260 ; Evans : *Walks through Wales*, pp. 118, 166 ; Lewis : *Top. Dict.*, under *Llandegai*.
[4] *Y Cymmrodor*, VI, p. 41 ; Cundall and Landman : *op. cit.*, pp. 201–2, 208 ; Parry : *Railway Companion*, p. 43 ; Lewis : *Guide to Rhyl* (1852), p. 14.   On the mining of zinc and calamine, *see* Lewis : *Top. Dict.*, under *Llanasa, Whitford, Holywell, Trevriw, Llanrwst*, and *Dyserth*.

The mining and preparation of zinc thus provided a fruitful outlet for capital which was ceasing to be productive in the lead industry itself. Another was afforded by the chemical industry, which, developing out of the Flintshire lead works, eventually outstripped them in importance. In 1824 Messrs. Roskell, of Flint, built a tower 140 feet high to collect the waste sulphur from the flues of the works where they manufactured lead and its oxides. This enterprise was gradually extended, and by 1840 the local alkaline deposits were being treated in a separate building adjoining the lead works. During the next decade a still more important alkali manufactory was established by Messrs. Muspratt, and this eventually absorbed the old lead works.[1]

These, although they became the most important, were by no means the earliest chemical works in Flintshire. Farther up the Dee, between Saltney and Hawarden, a Chester button manufacturer built works in 1781 for extracting glauber salts, sal ammoniac and ivory black from his waste bone and horn ; they were subsequently acquired by a neighbouring firm of potters, but only ivory black was made there in 1843.[2] Then there were the vitriol works at Holywell, to which reference has already been made, and towards the middle of the century another establishment, variously described as vitriol works and alkali works, was set up by a Liverpool company near the Gronant lead mines, east of Prestatyn.[3] At Hope the extraction of pyrolignous acid (for the use of cotton dyers and others) from brushwood, was a local industry which dated from the eighteenth century, and lasted well on into the nineteenth.[4] From 1850 onwards these chemical industries, both in Flintshire and in Denbighshire, grew more important as lead-smelting decayed. In 1851, when there were over 400 men in the lead works, the chemical trade only employed 11. Twenty

---

[1] Lewis : *Top. Dict.* ; *C.E.R.* (1842, XVII), p. 445 ; Taylor : *Historic Notices of Flint*, p. 214.
[2] *Memoir of Hawarden*, p. 108 ; Lewis : *Top. Dict.* (1843) under *Hawarden*.
[3] *Education Report*, 1847, III, App. p. 101 ; Parry : *Railway Companion*, p. 53.
[4] Davies : *General View*, p. 415 ; Lewis : *op. cit.*, 1833 and 1843.

years later the alkali works alone accounted for 270, the lead works for only 133. During the next decade, when the lead trade improved for a time, employment in the smelteries doubled, but the alkali works by this time provided for more than 600. This figure, however, was not maintained. In 1911, the number employed was only 207, while there were just 100 in the lead works.[1]

---

[1] The 1921 Census does not give separate figures for lead smelting. All the metal works of Flintshire then employed 4,814, but these would be mostly in the boiler works.

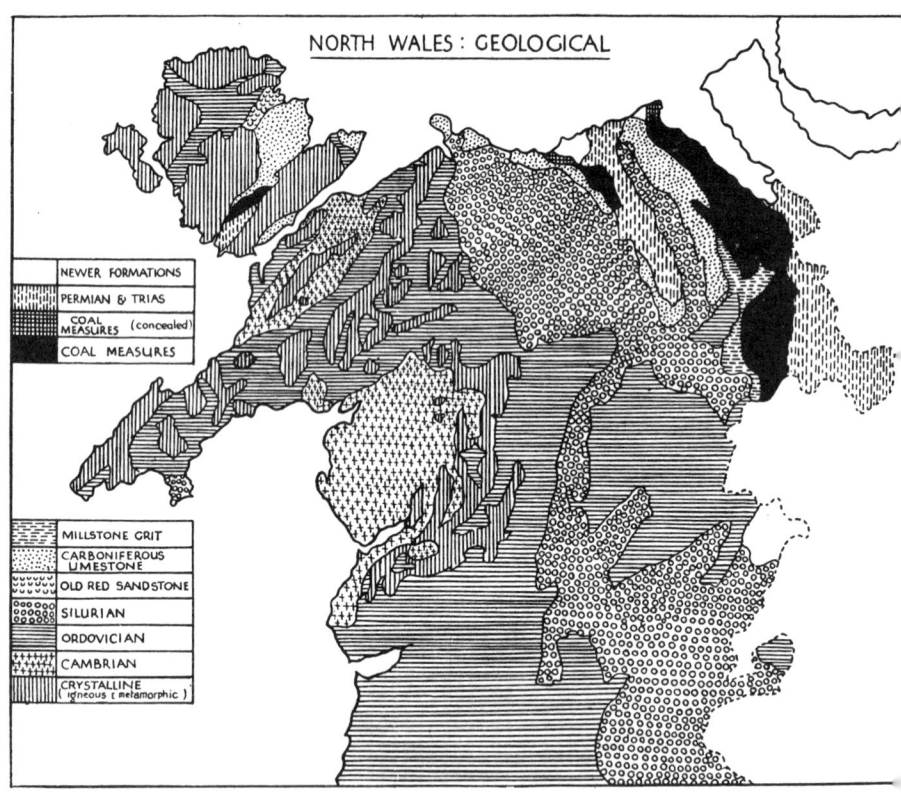

NORTH WALES : GEOLOGICAL

NEWER FORMATIONS
PERMIAN & TRIAS
COAL MEASURES (concealed)
COAL MEASURES

MILLSTONE GRIT
CARBONIFEROUS LIMESTONE
OLD RED SANDSTONE
SILURIAN
ORDOVICIAN
CAMBRIAN
CRYSTALLINE (igneous & metamorphic)

CHAPTER VI.

COLLIERIES AND QUARRIES.

A. Coal.[1]

> " The Coals Com up prety well out of the new Pitt . . . Wee shall sell very little but Sleckes till we have enough to supply your own occasions first."
>
> —Richard Jones (steward) to his master John Meller, June 14, 1721. (Erthig Papers.)

> "I find from . . . an Account of the Coals wanted for the furnace at Brymbo, and the large quantity which must be raised to select a sufficiency from the Furnace supply, that they now begin to stock the Coal, notwithstanding the Season for Sale has been lately at its height, and as my stock must necessarily very much increase unless some means are found to force a Sale—I am under the necessity of giving directions to lower the price to the Country."
>
> —John Wilkinson to his agent Hugh Meredith, Oct. 4, 1799. (Palmer : *Wilkinson*, p. 32.)

In these two passages we have an epitome of the changes that were being wrought in the coal industry by the development of other industries dependent on it. The first introduces us to the old-fashioned type of coal-owner—the landlord who regards the fuel on his estate primarily as a household convenience, and only second-arily as a means of increasing his revenues by sale outside the estate. The second brings us face to face with the industrialist who acquires coal mines as part of his necessary working plant, and exploits them on such a scale that he can only avoid large surplus stocks by entering into cut-throat competition with his neighbours in the general market.

The main coalfield of North Wales extends in a comparatively narrow strip—nine miles across at its widest—from near Oswestry (over the Shropshire border) to the Point of Air, beyond which the seams dip under the Dee estuary to re-appear at Parkgate in the Wirral. In addition, there is the insignificant Anglesey coalfield,

[1] Parts of this section have appeared in *Arch. Camb.* (1929, pp. 197–228), where full references are given.

about nine miles long and scarcely two miles in average width. Not only is the total area much smaller than that of the coal measures of South Wales but the seams are thinner, more deeply buried, and more broken up by faults—drawbacks which have had profound influence on the whole economic development of the country.[1]

In Denbighshire, where lack of good communications, as we have seen,[2] had kept coal-mining more backward than in Flintshire, the chief agents in developing the industry were immigrant ironmasters attracted to the district by its wealth in ironstone and coal. This part of the coalfield has two chief centres : Ruabon in the south and Brymbo in the north. The southern region took the lead. Isaac Wilkinson had been content to get his coal by contract from the owners of existing mines, but as soon as his son John took over the Bersham works he began sinking extensively for himself in various parts of Ruabon parish and as far south as Chirk. Other ironmasters followed suit. In the same neighbourhood William Hazeldine and Thomas Jones had both acquired collieries near to their ironworks by the time of Waterloo, and Edward Lloyd Rowland sank nearly thirty pits before he went bankrupt in 1823 ; these latter passed into the hands of the British Iron Company, which was advertising for 200 miners and colliers in 1829. Farther south still, the old workings of the Myddletons at the Black Park, near Chirk, dating from early in the seventeenth century, were leased in 1805 by Mr. T. E. Ward, who spent £20,000 on developing them, fought a lawsuit to keep them out of the grip of a rival mineowner, and used the produce to displace charcoal in the adjacent ironworks.[3]

Copper, lead, and iron have all played their part in the development of the Brymbo region. Charles Roe of Macclesfield sank for coal there soon after he began mining copper in Anglesey ; after him came Richard Kirk of Chapel-en-le-Frith, who migrated to the district

---

[1] *See* map. opp. p. 189, note on p. 228 (*infra*), and geological description in North : *Coal, and the Coalfields in Wales*, pp. 128–34.
[2] *Supra*, p. 18.
[3] *Shrewsbury Chron.*, July 31, 1829, Dec. 9, 1825 ; *cf. supra*, pp. 134, 144.

about 1775, and used the coal for smelting Minera lead ; but before John Wilkinson bought Brymbo Hall there was still only one pit of any importance in the neighbourhood, and the badness of the roads prevented it from being fully worked. Wilkinson, as we have seen, changed all this. By 1829 there were 41 pits on the Brymbo Hall estate, using up-to-date machinery and competing with Flintshire coals in the Chester market.[1] The exploitation of the pits was continued by Wilkinson's successors, and others were subsequently sunk by neighbouring ironmasters at Ffrwd and Broughton.[2]

The Flintshire coal-field, cut off almost completely from its neighbour by the great Bala Fault, may be similarly divided ; the southern section embraces the parishes of Cilcen, Mold, Hawarden and Northop, and extends down towards the Denbighshire border at Hope, Leeswood, Coed Talon and Treiddyn ; the northern (and narrower) follows the coast to the north-eastern extremity of the county. Both sections had been systematically exploited since Tudor times, the latter depending mainly on the Irish trade, the former on the needs of Chester. But the use of coal in the working of metals opened a new era. First came the demand for the lead works at Llannerch y môr, Bagillt and Flint. By the middle of the eighteenth century a smelting company had acquired coal mines at Bagillt, and was importing skilled miners from Newcastle to work them ; the other principal lead firms followed the example.[3] The extension of the copper and brass industries, starting with the Cheadle Company's works and culminating in Thomas Williams' daily coal-bill of nearly a thousand tons, opened up yet another market. Small wonder that Pennant found the condition of the Deeside collieries in 1796 "the most flourishing I ever remember, inferior only to that in which they were at the latter end of the late and beginning of the present century." Dublin was no longer the principal market ; it had become merely a convenient dumping ground for

[1] *Chester Chron.*, Oct. 4, 1782, Dec. 31, 1802 ; Palmer : *Old Parish of Wrexham*, pp. 21, 104.
[2] *Supra*, pp. 138, 147, 151.
[3] E.g., Smedleys (*Chester Chron.*, Oct. 29, 1779) ; Roscoe and Dixon (*N. W. Gaz.*, Nov. 8, 1810, Jan. 30, 1812) ; Eyton and Kyrke (Pigot's *Directory*, 1828–29).

surplus stocks when the production of coal temporarily outran the needs of local industry.[1]

In the southern part of the county, the mines round Mold—which had been worked since Leland's time, but on a less extensive scale than those nearer the sea coast— also benefited from the demands of the lead industry. John Wilkinson had a pit in the village of Soughton, where he raised fuel for smelting his Llyn y pandy ores ; and twenty years after Wilkinson's death the Soughton Coal Company had a regular contract for supplying coal to a lead-mining company at Mold.[2] At Coed Talon, near the Denbighshire border, it was the establishment of ironworks (soon after Waterloo) that led to the first serious sinking for coal ; and when the works were taken over in 1825 by the Welsh Iron and Coal Company the resident director, a Northumbrian, stirred up a serious riot by going to his own county for experienced colliers.[3] Iron played its part, too, in freeing the Hawarden collieries from their dependence on the Chester consumer. John Rigby's ironworks provided a market on the spot, and by the beginning of the nineteenth century his son was among the largest mineowners in the parish.

A still more important factor in the development of coal-mining at Hawarden was the rise of the Buckley potteries. The quality of the "apparently inexhaustible" supplies of fireclay found in the local coal measures had made the potter a familiar figure in Hawarden parish since the seventeenth century, and in 1757—just two years before Josiah Wedgwood set up as a master potter—Jonathan Catherall began the manufacture of firebricks on Buckley Mountain, between Hawarden and Mold. The business throve, and others sprang up beside it, till in twenty years' time there were fourteen separate establishments in the district, making all manner of articles from tiles and firebricks to flower-pots and mugs.[4]

---

[1] Pennant : *Whiteford and Holywell*, pp. 133, 275–6.
[2] *N. W. Chron.*, June 11, Dec. 10, 1829.
[3] *Supra*, p. 146 ; *infra*, p. 399 ;   Palmer : *History of Wrexham*, p. 97 *n*.
[4] *Trans. Flints. Hist. Soc.*, No. 4, pp. 41 ff. (wills of potters, 1685 ff.) ; *Memoir of Hawarden*, p. 98 ; *N. W. Gaz.*, Feb. 1, 1810 ; Pennant : *Tours*, I, p. 115 ; North : *Coal and the Coalfields*, pp. 69, 131.

Both potters and colliers flocked in from Staffordshire—
"many of them," complained the good folk of Hawarden,
" hackneyed in vicious habits" ; and there,

> Denied the sound of holy bell, and care
> Of sacred pastor,

they formed a straggling, squalid community, neglected
by all but the Methodist preachers, and preserving to
this day, in speech and habits, the marks of its separate
origin.[1] Buckley wares came to be among the chief
cargoes exported from Connah's Quay (the nearest port)
whence they found their way to London, Ireland, and
South Wales.[2]

Potteries, like smelting works, were frequently run in
conjunction with coal mines. Thus Messrs. Rigby,
whom we have already met as ironmasters and coal-
owners, soon afterwards provided themselves with a
market for their surplus coal by setting up as potters also.
Buckley has remained the chief pottery centre of North
Wales, and many of the original firms have continued
to flourish up to our own time ;[3] but the manufacture of
coarse earthenware has contributed to the demand for
mineral fuel in other parts of the coalfield also. From
Buckley it spread to the surrounding regions of Mold and
Northop, and as far north as Bagillt. In Denbighshire,
too, the coal workings were rummaged for fireclay. Coarse
earthenware was made at Cefn mawr, near Ruabon, and
Thomas Jones the ironmaster made bricks at Llwyn
Einion ; but it was not till after 1865 that the
district became noted for terra cotta works in which
the red marl of the upper coal measure was turned into
bricks, tiles, and ornaments, of that glaring hue and
glossy surface which are responsible for so much of the
unloveliness of the newer urban growths.[4] In 1823, after
the opening of the Montgomeryshire Canal had made

[1] *Memoir of Hawarden*, p. 106 ; *cf*. Cary, H. F. : *The Mountain Seat*, 1793 (*Gent. Mag.*, Feb., 1794).

[2] Parry : *Railway Companion*, p. 35 ; *supra*, p. 127.

[3] Pugh : *Camb. Dep.*, p. 10 ; *Wales*, II, pp. 564–5 ; Jones A. M. : *Rural Industries of . . . Wales*, chap. VI.

[4] Davies : *General View*, p. 415 ; *Chester Chron.*, May 1, 1807 ; Pigot's *Directory* (1828), p. 1158 ; Lewis : *Top. Dict.*, under *Ruabon*; *Wales*, II, pp. 257–63, 562–3.

it possible to bring coal cheaply to Mid-Wales, a pottery was established at Newtown by William Tilsley, a local banker and woollen manufacturer whose estate yielded suitable clay.[1]

Agriculture also had its share in the development of coal-mining. On the one hand, the farmer was using more and more lime, and he needed coal to burn it.[2] On the other, the enclosure movement, by diminishing the area from which peat and brushwood could be taken, helped to hasten the adoption of coal as domestic fuel even in the smaller cottages. We find this fact used in 1822 as an argument against the coal duty, in a petition sent from Caernarvonshire—a county where firegrates had not been in general use much more than twenty years. In Anglesey the draining of the Malldraeth Marsh made possible a more vigorous attack on the coal seams lying beneath it, which had kept luring adventurers on to disappointment ever since the fifteenth century—and have continued to do so up to our own time. The principal drawbacks here are the thinness of the seams and the need for expensive pumping plant. Even a local family like the Meyricks of Bodorgan, although some of the coal lay on their estate, had to supplement it from time to time by sending for loads from Bychton, Bagillt, Weppre or Mostyn, or by sea from Liverpool; while for the purposes of an enterprise like copper-smelting at Amlwch, Anglesey coal was not so much as thought of. John Wilkinson, after visiting the pits to see if he could use them for his ironworks, decided that there was no coal worth working. "Had the island been·blessed with stores of iron ore," Gwallter Mechain comments with some asperity, "and that persevering adventurer pro-prietor of them, it is very probable that Mona might be exporting coal instead of importing that valuable fuel."[3]

[1] *Shrewsbury Chron.*, June 13, 27, 1823 ; *infra,* pp. 253, 317.

[2] Pennant (*Whiteford and Holywell,* p 133) gives this as one of the causes of the flourishing conditions of the mines in his district in 1795.

[3] Davies : *General View,* pp. 363–4.   There is a good sketch of the history of the Anglesey mines in Greenly's *Geology of Anglesey,* II, pp. 663–7, 812–22.   But he post-dates the modern re-opening of the mines.   They were working when Lewis Morris drew up his *Plans of Harbours* (1748), and there are frequent references to them in the

In the inland districts it was the improvement of com-munications that made the extension of coal-mining possible. We have seen how mining regions early reaped the benefit of the turnpike system. Soon after 1760 the northern portion of the Flintshire coalfield, and the neighbourhoods of Wrexham and Ruabon, were provided with a good system of roads, which was extended to the Brymbo pits a generation later ; in the Coed Talon region road-making was already in operation (under an Act expressly designed to meet the needs of the collieries) when the boom in coal-mining began. Colliery proprietors were also among the pioneers of the canal movement—another great boon to the Denbighshire mines—and it was they who set the example of railway construction in the pre-locomotive days, and urged the interests of coal transport when the steam engine came.[1]

With the aid of the new markets provided by industry and agriculture, and the cheaper and speedier means of reaching them afforded by turnpike roads, canals and mineral railways, coal-mining made rapid progress throughout North Wales. As in the other mining industries, direct exploitation by the landowner was abandoned in favour of leases to capitalist adventurers, working individually or in companies. These new mine-owners—many of them immigrants, and some also in control of smelting works or potteries—had the capital to enable them to equip their mines with the latest appliances.

First there was the steam engine, which began to oust more primitive pumping devices soon after Watt took out his patent of 1775. It spread rapidly, even in Anglesey, during the last decade of the century, and by 1833 most of the larger pits were employing it. Horse whimseys for winding the coal remained in use a little longer, but in time they too gave way to steam. During the same period, the rough and ready method of sale by traditional measures of capacity, which varied

Meyrick Papers from 1754 onwards (cf. also advt. in Chester Chron., Sept. 24, 1779) ; it is clear, however, from the accounts in Owen's History of Anglesey (1775, p. 54) and Camb. Reg., I, p. 285, II, p. 416 (1795–96), that the workings were still very shallow. We can trace the deepening of the pits from advertisements in N. W. Gaz., 1808–21.

[1] Arch. Camb., 1925., p. 136 ; supra, chap. IV, B and C

from place to place, was superseded by the use of weighing machines. By the beginning of the nineteenth century these had become general in all but remoter regions like Anglesey ; there boys used to bring their donkeys to the pit mouth for a bushel or two, right up to the coming of the railway. The middleman, too, had made his appearance, though with the bigger consumers the colliery proprietors dealt direct. For some time the keen competition between the latter caused prices to fall rapidly. In 1794 the pithead price in Flintshire was 10s. a ton, in Anglesey 16s. By the end of the century John Wilkinson was underselling his neighbours at Brymbo by offering coal at 5s. a ton—a level which had been reached in some of the Flintshire pits a few years earlier. But as demand became brisker, markets wider and working more expensive, prices rose again until they stood at 8s. or 9s. in the 'thirties. When coal was sold by measure to small purchasers the price ranged from 2d. to 7d. a bushel. We shall look in vain, during the period we are considering, for uniformity of prices, even at the pithead ; there were no selling arrangements like the eighteenth-century "vend" at Newcastle, or even like those which ruled the contemporary iron trade.

There was a good deal of improvidence in the early exploitation of the mines. Frequently the most accessible seams were worked at a furious pace, and then left to be drowned out while another shaft was sunk a short distance off ; by this means much good coal has been permanently lost. Nor were human life and its amenities held of much account. Frequent were the accidents caused by leaving derelict shafts unfenced, even by the side of a main highway—mediaeval regulations about the filling in of disused pits having fallen, it would seem, into complete oblivion. In 1833 the new County Hall at Mold was almost destroyed by reckless sinking. And in the pits themselves explosions, floods and defective winding apparatus took their annual toll of life and limb.[1] Firedamp, as we have seen, had made its appearance in some of the Deeside pits as early as the seventeenth century, and they retained a sinister pre-eminence in

[1] For statistics of accidents up to 1840 see *Arch. Camb.*, 1929, pp. 226–8.

frequency of explosions. The Davy lamp made but slow headway, partly through slackness on the managerial side, partly through prejudice on the part of the men. Sir Humphrey himself has left on record how the colliers' wives assembl᷄ ͡ on the bank of one of the Ruabon pits, and tried "with noise and lamentation" to prevent their husbands from taking these new scientific horrors down with them.[1] It should be added that North Wales and Lancashire were the only districts where the men had to buy their own lamps.

Throughout the coalfield, conditions of life were rapidly changing. The old employer might be an autocrat, but his interests were rooted in the district. To the new men the mine and those employed in it were pawns in a bigger game, to the success of which local interests and local feeling must be sacrificed if need arose. The importation of foremen and skilled workers of alien speech and habits, the introduction of methods of work which were novel and therefore suspect, the ruthless discharge of old hands, and the fluctuation of wages in response to trade movements outside, all contributed towards a long-smouldering resentment which only burst into flame when the heyday of prosperity was passing.

The face of the country, too, was undergoing a transformation. In the neighbourhood of the pits, population often doubled itself in the space of twenty years, and the mineowners had to provide some sort of accommodation for the newcomers[2]—unless, indeed, these had already built their own rude shanties on a piece of waste ground before enclosure commissioners came along.[3] The parish church was too far, the parish priest often too indifferènt, to minister to the needs of these turbulent young communities; and when, in the 'forties, mining villages like Bagillt and Mostyn in Flintshire, Brymbo and Rhos Llannerchrugog in Denbighshire, were made into independent parishes, the bulk of the people had long since found their spiritual home and their refuge from sheer barbarism in the Chapel.

[1] Davy : *On the Safety Lamp* (second ed., 1825), pp. 131–2.

[2] *See*, e.g., *Chester Chron.*, Nov. 15, 1832, Aug. 5, 1836. (I am indebted for these references to Mr. Emlyn Rogers).

[3] "Miners usually build their own houses." (Ruabon witness before Children's Employment Commission, 1842, XVII, p. 387.)

Gentlemen were being driven from their country seats by the grime and fumes and the din of machinery. In Holywell an ancient family mansion of the Mostyns is turned into offices for the Parys Mine Company ; Brymbo Hall, a fine old Jacobean relic, is blackened with smoke and lost among blast furnaces and spoil banks. Thomas Pennant abandons and partly demolishes Bagillt Hall, because "the thick smoke of a great smelting mill for lead, and of a great calcining-house for calamine, just beneath, must have ever deterred my descendants from making it their residence" ; and Edward Rowland (brother of the Ruabon ironmaster) has to move from his father's house at Plas Bennion when the coal and iron works encroach on his privacy. A writer in the *Wrexham Recorder* for 1848 tells how during the last quarter of a century Wrexham has been converted from a decayed "genteel" town, where, but lately, many of the neighbouring gentry had kept up town houses, into "something like an improved and improving commercial one." Both here and at Holywell the population grew apace, and at these two principal centres of the coalfield the earliest banks in North Wales had been set up by 1790.[1] Holywell, which had been simply "a little town by the well" in the first edition of Defoe's *Tours* (1724–25), ceased to be "little" by the time the fifth was published (1753), and in the eighth (1778) it was thought worthy of a long paragraph, describing its rapid growth to a population of "upwards of 2,000." The 2,000 had become 5,000 when the first Census was taken, and 10,000 (the high-water mark) by the middle of the century. Similarly the parishes of Mold, Ruabon, and Wrexham all had twice as many inhabitants in 1851 as in 1801.

Of the output of the mines, and the employment they afforded, it is less easy to speak with confidence. The Census gives no trustworthy statistics of occupations until 1841, and in estimates of the numbers employed by individual firms, coal-miners and smelters are frequently lumped together. Experts calculated that 200,000 tons were raised from the Brymbo Hall estate

---

[1] Lewis : *Top. Dict.*, under *Holywell;* Palmer : *Old Parish of Wrexham*, pp. 112–15 ; Pennant : *Whiteford and Holywell*, p. 268 ; Palmer : *Ruabon*, pp. 52–3 ; *infra*, p. 315.

during the twenty years after 1820—by no means its busiest period ; Carlisle's *Topographical Dictionary* credits Hawarden and Northop with an annual output of 70,000 and 25,000 tons respectively in 1811 ; Lewis asserts that Mostyn is producing 300 tons a day and Flint 1,500 a week in 1833. Such were the rough guesses of contemporaries. The export trade, of course, only accounted for a fraction of this output ; but the volume of coal exported from Chester—including its creeks along the Dee estuary—rose from 6,000 chalder (of 26 hundredweight) in 1771, to over 16,000 in 1806, with an intervening lean year (due to war conditions) in 1796 ; by 1834 it had reached 75,000 tons.

This seaborne trade, however, was handicapped by the heavy duty on all coal carried coastwise—an imposition dating back to William the Third's wars with France, and retained by successive Chancellors of the Exchequer for nearly 140 years. Local patriotism saw in it the chief obstacle to economic advancement in North Wales, and an agitation for its repeal was set on foot at the beginning of the American War ; but after that the exigencies of Pitt's finance led to further increases till the duty reached the figure of 4s. a ton on coal sold by weight, and approximately 6s. when it went by measure, with higher rates for the London market. In 1808, Mr. W. A. Madocks introduced into the House of Commons a Bill for the exemption of North Wales, but the Lords threw it out. Nevertheless the agitation continued.[1] The new-born *North Wales Gazette* took up the cudgels, and week after week the arguments against the tax were set forth in angry letters and editorial diatribes, while its news columns were filled with accounts of protest meetings and petitions. Every class in the community, it was claimed, suffered by the iniquitous duty. For a paltry gain of £10,000 to the Exchequer, householders who lived away from the coalfields were having to pay 28s., and even 40s., for coal,[2] cottagers were either ravaging good

---

[1] *Chester Chron.*, Dec. 25, 1775, Feb. 5, 1776, March 31, July 7, 1808.
[2] The prices of imported coal in Anglesey and Caernarvonshire respectively, as given in Kay, 1794 (Anglesey, p. 17, Caernarvonshire, p. 21). *Cf.* these with the pitmouth prices quoted above.

grasslands in search of peat or else shivering for want of fuel, farmers could not afford to burn lime, the roads were torn up by the carting of coal over roundabout land routes. Industry, too, was hard hit ; not only did the collieries suffer from a restricted market, but the burning of bricks, the smelting of metals, the erection of steam pumps in mines and quarries and of steam-driven machinery in textile factories, were all held up by the artificial dearness of coal. As late as 1830, we find the *North Wales Chronicle* roundly declaring : "were it not that the expense of fuel virtually prohibits competition with the English market, it is evident that every copper and iron utensil with which we are supplied by the English might be fabricated in Wales, whereby bread would be given to thousands."[1]   But by this time the tax was on its last legs. It was revised repeatedly after the War, and local pressure contrived to bring about substantial reductions for Wales ; at last, in 1831, Lord Althorp and the Whig cabinet took the plunge and repealed it outright.[2]

The hardships inflicted on North Wales by the coal tax were, of course, exaggerated by those who fought it. As they were ready to point out themselves when they wished to emphasise its unproductiveness,[3] the area directly affected was not large ; many of the regions which suffered from dear coal lay inland and would in any case have to depend on land transport. Anglesey, as we have seen, early secured exemption for coal imported for copper smelting, and the complaint that the local pits suffered from restriction of export need not be taken too seriously.[4] It was in counties like Merioneth—with a good port and no coal—that the burden was most acutely felt. In the Barmouth Harbour Act, special terms had to be granted to imported coal, and the difficulty of obtaining fuel

---

[1] Davies : *General View*, p. 262 ; Warner : *Second Walk*, pp. 300–1 ; *N. W. Gaz.*, 1808–12, *passim* ; *N. W. Chron.*, May 20, 1830.
[2] Dowell, S. : *History of Taxation* (1884), IV, pp. 411–18; Ashton and Sykes : *op. cit.*, pp. 245–6 ; *N. W. Gaz.*, Dec. 15, 1814, Nov. 13, 1817, Jan. 1, 1818, Feb. 14 and 21, March 7, May 30, 1822, May 29, 1823, June 3, 1824, May 4 and 11, 1826 ; *Records of Oswestry*, p. 192 ; *Cambro-Briton*, I, p. 359 ; *Camb. Quart. Mag.*, III, p. 115.
[3] E.g., *N. W. Gaz.*, March 8, 1808, Sept. 3, 1809.
[4] *Id.*, June 14, Aug. 16, 1810.

affords some excuse for the long continuance of primitive methods in farming and quarrying, weaving and spinning.[1] Again, the inhabitants of the Vale of Clwyd, and even of parts of Caernarvonshire, had to fetch their coal by road from Denbighshire pits, instead of utilizing ports like Rhuddlan or Caernarvon, which were thus deprived of a profitable branch of trade.[2]

It is in such regions that money and labour have most often been wasted in the effort to find coal on the spot. It was in the Vale of Clwyd that young Hugh Myddleton, towards the end of Elizabeth's reign, first embarked on a succession of enterprises culminating in the New River by "seekinge of coales" near his native Denbigh ; two centuries later the carboniferous rocks higher up the valley were once more explored in the vain quest for workable coal. Projects for a canal or a railroad to expedite communications with the coalfield likewise ended in smoke ; but farmers of the Vale probably reaped some benefit from the keen rivalry between Brymbo and Mold for their custom.[3] In Montgomeryshire, search was made on the Ystum Colwyn estate in 1759, and in Merioneth on the Ynys y maengwyn estate in 1808. Here Athelstan Corbett, the owner, wanted coal to smelt his lead and copper, and so sure was he of success that he induced the commissioners under a local Enclosure Act to dig their drainage ditches wide enough to serve as navigable cuts for the conveyance of coal. At the other end of the county, near Corwen, the deceptive occurrence of patches of coal dust in the Silurian rocks led to equally fruitless researches in the second half of the century.[4]

The removal of the last relics of the coal tax, so far from producing the promised revival of industry, only served to reveal the hollowness of the hopes—or fears— that North Wales would soon cease to be a rustic backwater. Even before 1820 some of the older workings round Hawarden and Mold were showing signs of exhaustion, and the great slump of 1826 was the beginning of a

[1] 37 Geo. III, cap. 50 ; *supra*, pp. 6, 37, 47, 147-8 ; *infra*, chap. VII.
[2] *N. W. Gaz.*, March 9, 1809.
[3] Davies : *General View*, pp. 488, 385 ; Palmer : *Wilkinson*, p. 32 ; Lewis : *Top. Dict.*, under *Llanbedr*.
[4] *Y Cymmrodor*, XXXVIII, p. 40 ; Fenton : *Tours*, pp. 89, 111-2, 121 ; North : *Coal and the Coalfields*, p. 63.

long spell of lean years throughout the coalfield. Already in 1829 a local paper talks despondingly of the "gradual decline of the coal and iron works" round Wrexham and Ruabon and the following years were marked by the bitterest industrial strife that had yet been known in the neighbourhood.[1] This was the time when one after another of her nascent industries deserted North Wales for the richer coal measures of Glamorgan or of the Black Country. Luckily for the mines of Denbighshire and Flintshire, new uses for coal kept opening up fresh markets on the spot. More and more was wanted for household fuel and for railways and steamships, and coal-gas was coming into general use. A cotton factory at Mold set the fashion in 1812, and another at Llangollen followed suit in 1820 ; the streets of Newtown were lighted with gas from about 1818, those of Holywell from 1824, those of Wrexham from 1827 ; and the practice spread until Flintshire, where seams of good gas coal were tapped in 1858, came to rely chiefly, for its sales of coal, on the local gasworks and those of the neighbouring English towns. In the second half of the century came the development of the chemical and engineering works at the southern end of the Dee estuary, and in Denbighshire the reconstruction of the Brymbo steel works and the new chemical and terra cotta manufactures of Ruabon. With such assistance the collieries were able to hold their own till after the Great War. In 1841 Denbighshire had about 2,000 miners, of whom more than 1,300 were in the single parish of Ruabon ; Flintshire about 300 fewer. During the next twenty years employment was doubled in Denbighshire, while Flintshire showed a slight decline. Then followed a slow but steady increase in both counties, till at the 1911 Census there were 10,500 miners in Denbighshire, and 4,000 in Flintshire. But during the same period the numbers employed in South Wales and Monmouth had risen from 11,000 to 214,000.

The figures are eloquent. The initial handicap to industry had been quite as severe in South Wales as in North ; and up to the Railway Age it was still possible to predict similar lines of development for the two regions. It was coal, more than any other single factor, which

[1] *N. W. Chron.*, Jan. 4, 1829 ; *infra*, pp. 404 ff.

determined that from this time on the industrialization of the South should go forward by leaps and bounds, while in the North whole tracts reverted from industrial to rural pursuits.

B. SLATE.

The quarrying of Welsh slates has developed on different lines from the mining of Welsh coal. The coalfields of North Wales lie close to the border, and at a comparatively early date they attracted both capital and labour from the more advanced mining areas of England. The principal slate rocks, on the other hand, are situated in the very heart of Snowdonia—too remote to tempt the immigrant, even if England had had a sufficient body of skilled quarriers to send there, as she sent Northumbrian coalminers and Staffordshire potters. English labour has therefore been a negligible factor, and nowhere except at Ffestiniog has English capital been of importance ; elsewhere the *entrepreneur* has generally been the owner of the soil. Slate quarrying is, in a sense, the most Welsh of Welsh industries. In the quarries themselves English is a foreign tongue, and those shapeless, monotonous villages which flank them—grey and drab, but clean, in contrast with the dingy red of the colliery districts—are the homes of a vigorous native culture.

Geography, in preserving the Welsh character of the industry, determined also that it should develop late. So long as the roads from the principal quarries to Caernarvon (their nearest convenient outlet) remained little more than horsepaths, anything analogous to the thriving trade between Flintshire coalpits and Ireland during the seventeenth century was out of the question. Slate quarrying did not begin to pass from the stage of superficial working for local needs, by men without capital, to that of systematic exploitation by landowners, until the opening-up of Snowdonia had been seriously taken in hand after 1750[1]—just at the time when in the coalfields the landed proprietor was making way for the industrial adventurer.

The slate rocks of Caernarvonshire form the backbone of the county, both physically and economically. In the

[1] *Supra*, Chapter IVA.

Cambrian formations they are most prolific on the eastern and western slopes of Elidir Fawr, dipping down on the one side to Nant Ffrancon to form the Penrhyn quarries, and on the other to the Llanberis lakes, above which rise the even more productive Dinorwic quarries. Thence we can follow them in a south-westerly direction through the Vale of Nantlle into the Lleyn peninsula, where their produce becomes insignificant. Parallel with this range on the southern side come the Ordovician slate rocks—less tough but finer and smoother than those in the Cambrian series. They have been quarried to some extent in the region of Beddgelert, but it is over the border of Merioneth, at Blaenau Ffestiniog, that they have attained their greatest commercial importance. The range which contains the Ffestiniog quarries stretches north-eastwards towards Dolwyddelan, Penmachno and Bettws y coed, and south-westwards towards Portmadoc, in all of which regions marketable slates have been obtained. In the south of Merioneth we find a further series of parallel slate ranges, also belonging to the Ordovician formations ; they run north and south of the Mawddach valley, south of the Dysynni, and north of the Dovey, the last reaching to the border of Montgomeryshire, where extensive quarrying has been carried on near Corris and Dinas Mawddwy. Finally, slate has been worked in the Ordovician rocks of Denbighshire, both north of the Dee (on Llantysilio Mountain) and south of it on the Berwyns, the slate re-emerging in the neighbourhood of Llangynog, in northern Montgomeryshire.

Local slates, as we have seen,[1] had been used for roofing in parts of North Wales as far back as the Middle Ages, but rarely at any distance from the quarries. By the middle of the eighteenth century, however, they had become an important item in the commerce of Caernarvon. Slate merchants there were supplying the wants of Anglesey[2] and even sending cargoes across to Ireland ; and with the rapid increase of towns and cities there arose a demand for roofing-slates, which promised a fortune to anyone with the means and enterprise to work

---

[1] *Supra*, p. 16.
[2] Meyrick Papers :—1759 : 700 "Ladies" purchased at 14s. from Hugh Williams, Caernarvon ; 1763 : 7,000 "Doubles" at £3 13s. 6d.

them scientifically. It was Richard Pennant, afterwards Baron Penrhyn, who first set the example.[1] On succeeding to the Penrhyn estate in 1765, he found the quarries on what was then known as Cae braich y cafn let out to a number of quarrymen on payment of a portion of the produce to the "slate reeve." Using the most primitive methods, they sent pannier-loads of slate (sixty-four slates to the load) down steep bridle-paths to the nearest creek of the Menai Straits where boats could be loaded—the mouth of the Ogwen or Cegid, or Hirael quay in Bangor. Rather less than a thousand tons was exported annually in this way. They were cut to a variety of standard sizes, from Duchesses, of two feet by one, down through Countesses and Ladies to Doubles, which were only about half the size. This classification, which took the place of an earlier and much rougher one, had only recently been introduced ; and it was almost the only approach towards co-ordinating the work of the various groups of partners.

For a time the old system was continued, save that, instead of paying an eighth of the produce, the quarrymen were given leases of twenty-one years at a fixed annual rental of £1 apiece. But the new owner was soon persuaded that he could make more out of his wide resources than the paltry £80 a year that this arrangement brought in. In 1782, a few years before the expiry of the leases, he bought the lessees out at a cost of £160, and, keeping them on as hired labourers, took the working of the quarries into his own hands. To safeguard his monopoly of quarrying in the district, he also took a lease of the neighbouring Crown wastes—not, it was alleged, for the purpose of working them, but merely to keep off interlopers : a line of policy which led to many complaints and eventually to a Parliamentary enquiry.[2]

[1] On the Penrhyn quarries, see Red Dragon, VII, pp. 319 ff., and early descriptions by Williams (Snowdon Mountains, pp. 127 ff.), Pennant (Tours, III, pp. 82–4), and Davies (General View, pp. 84, 412–3).

[2] Carlisle : Top. Dict. ; Parl. Pap., 1823, XV. ; Shrewsbury Chron., June 13, 1823. Mr. Dawkins Pennant, who succeeded to the estate in 1816, had family influence in the Office of Woods and Forests, which made the renewal of his lease and the Crown support of his claim look rather an ugly "job." He was also accused of deliberately blocking all the neighbouring quays on the Straits which might serve as rivals to his own. See also J.H.C., LXXVI, p. 458.

The way was now clear for systematic exploitation. But first it was necessary to find means for disposing of the produce more rapidly and efficiently. The whole Penrhyn estate, when it came to the Pennants, could not provide more than four wheeled carts; within ten years, the paths leading from the quarry had been turned into negotiable roads, and over a hundred carts were regularly employed in taking slates down to the quay at the mouth of the Cegid, which Lord Penrhyn (as he now was) had enlarged and named after himself. Here they were shipped for Liverpool (whence they could be sent up the Mersey and by canal to the interior of England) and abroad to Ireland, Flanders, and the West Indies. Before the outbreak of war, output had risen to 15,000 tons, and four or five hundred workmen were in regular employment. To house them, Lord Penrhyn had begun building on his estate a model village, in which (as his kinsman, Thomas Pennant, noted with pride)[1] "no corrupting alehouse" was permitted.

The War brought a temporary set-back. Not only was there a cessation of building, but—under colour of avoiding unfair discrimination—Pitt extended to other building materials the taxation which for the last ten years had been borne by bricks and tiles. All cargoes of slate and stone carried coastwise had to pay an *ad valorem* duty of twenty per cent at the port of delivery. This duty (said to amount, on an average, to a third of the prime cost) was a severe blow to the industry; luckily it did not affect the Irish trade, and means were not wanting (it was whispered) to evade it nearer home.[2] But in 1795 the trade had so far declined that Lord Penrhyn was trying to find work on the land for the men he was forced to discharge from the quarry, and by 1798 the number employed at Penrhyn quarry had sunk to 120. The Rev. W. Bingley, who visited it that year, suspected that Lord Penrhyn's neatly whitewashed cottages only served to conceal "the extreme of wretchedness and poverty."[3]

---

[1] *Whiteford and Holywell*, pp. 271–2.
[2] Dowell: *History of Taxation*, IV, pp. 393–5. On effects in Wales *see* Williams : *Snowdon Mountains*, p. 129, Evans : *Beauties*, p. 422 and *n*, *Chester Chron.*, July 1, 1796.
[3] Davies : *General View*, p. 84 ; Bingley : *North Wales*, I, pp. 179–80.

These lean years were used to good purpose in preparing for the future. It was now that the horse tramway was constructed from the quarry to Port Penrhyn,[1] and the port itself was further enlarged. The farmers, deprived of the profits of slate transport, had to turn their horses to farm-work—to the great gain of agriculture. And in the working of the quarry itself Mr. Greenfield, the manager, began a series of improvements of which the effects soon became visible when demand revived. The efforts of the last twelve years had already made a yawning chasm in the rock ; the work was now arranged in terraces, which would provide foothold for the quarrier and a roadway for wheeling off the trucks of slate. The bigger blocks, of course, were removed by gunpowder, which soon began to take its toll of life and limb.[2] A sawing mill was set up, and at the port a factory to prepare slates for the growing needs of schools, which had hitherto been supplied from Holland. It was by means of improved machinery that roofing-slates came to acquire the fine texture, glossy surface, and regular shape which, along with changes in brick-making, must be held accountable for the monotonous line and "machine-like finish" of the modern house ; the day of mass production was already dawning.[3] Another enterprise of Lord Penrhyn, although not directly connected with the slate industry, must have helped to relieve local distress when the market for slates fell off : a mill was erected on the Ogwen to grind chert and quartz from the neighbouring hills for the uses of the Staffordshire potteries.[4]

When the Peace of Amiens was signed, the "spirit of building" began to show signs of revival. Lord Penrhyn's agents were busy signing-on new hands, till the number reached 300 again ; and as many as a hundred tons a day

[1] *Supra*, p. 111.
[2] *N. W. Gaz.*, July 26, Aug. 16, 1810. The number of fatal accidents in Penrhyn quarries between 1784 and 1873, so far as the records go, was only 277—an average of a little over three a year ; but the records are probably incomplete before 1826 (*Red Dragon*, VII, p. 338). The frequency of accidents in other parts of Caernarvonshire is deplored, and the need for benefit clubs emphasised, in Williams : *Tourist's Guide through the County of Carnarvon*, p. 105.
[3] *Cf.* Hughes and North : *The Old Cottages of Snowdonia*, pp. 46–8.
[4] Evans : *Beauties*, p. 454 ; Lewis : *Top. Dict.*, under *Llandegai*.

were taken to Port Penrhyn by the new tramway.[1] This improvement, thanks to the new economies in working, outlasted the brief spell of peace : before Lord Penrhyn's death in 1808 the industry was well on the road towards recovery, and the quarry was bringing in about £7,000 a year.

The development of the Penrhyn quarries gave an impetus to the slate industry all over Caernarvonshire. Before the end of the century the annual revenue brought into the county by this branch of trade was calculated by different observers at sums ranging from £35,000 to twice that figure.[2] In 1793 nearly 250 cargoes of slate were discharged from the port of Caernarvon, and "many thousands" of slates from the neighbouring quarries were being exported.[3] Landowners who had hitherto thought of the slate rock on their estates as so much waste land, worth at the best such trifling rents as could be got by allowing the cottagers to work it on their own account, began to prick up their ears at the news of Lord Penrhyn's success. In the manor of Dinorwic, for example, groups of quarrymen had long made a scanty living by getting slates on the eastern shores of Llyn Padarn. Learning from some of Penrhyn's workmen the use of gunpowder, they were able to extend their operations, and to send whole loads to Caernarvon or Felin Heli for export. But in the year before the French Revolution broke out, Mr. Assheton Smith, lord of the manor, let the largest of the quarries—the one that still goes by the name of Dinorwic—for twenty-one years to two lawyers from Caernarvon. There were then thirty men working on it ; the number was soon doubled, and within a generation ten times as many were employed. When the lease ran out in 1809, Mr. Smith worked the quarry himself, first with three partners to

[1] Williams : *Snowdon Mountains*, pp. 129–30 ; *N. W. Chron.*, Oct. 25, 1827 (report of dispute on the "settlement" of workers taken on in 1802).

[2] Kay (*Agriculture of North Wales :* Caernarvonshire, p. 22) puts it at £35,000 in 1794 ; Williams (*Snowdon Mountains*, p. 129), writing in 1802, reckons it at £60,000, including the freight of coasting vessels, for the period 1782–92 ; Barfoot and Wilkes' *Directory* (1790, II, p. 532) says that Caernarvon alone is making £50,000 by the sale of slates ; Davies (*General View*, 1799–1810, p. 412) puts the county figure at £70,000.

[3] Davies : *op. cit.*, p. 388; Evans : *Cambrian Itinerary*, p. 279.

help, then from 1820 alone. Meanwhile, the adjacent workings had been similarly taken out of the hands of the independent quarrymen (a few of them were prudent enough to sell out their claims beforehand to some wealthy adventurer) ; and, after the Enclosure Acts of 1806 and 1808 had resolved doubts about legal ownership of the commons, new workings were opened in 1810 and 1811.[1]

Here, as in other quarrying areas, transport was one of the main difficulties. Bingley has given us an account of the perilous descent of the loads of slate, in sledges or carts (with a horse behind as well as before, to act as brake), from the heights where they were quarried to the lakeside below. Small boats took them across the lake to a point whence they could be carted to Caernarvon or Felin Heli. The Caernarvon partners who took over Dinorwic quarry in 1788 began to make more practicable roads between the quarry and the lake, and about twenty years later tenders were being invited for a new highway to the "port of shipment"—presumably Felin Heli, which, enlarged and rechristened Port Dinorwic, was soon to become the depôt for the whole district.[2]

The Port of Caernarvon and the neighbouring creeks served as outlets for another quarrying district, stretching westwards from Llyn Padarn towards the Straits. Much of this land was Crown common, and had hitherto been let out to working quarrymen on the usual terms of an eighth or a ninth of the produce ; but from about 1790 the Lords of the Treasury—encouraged, no doubt, by the example of the neighbouring proprietors—began to grant leases to local gentlemen and to slate merchants from Caernarvon, some of whom erected water wheels, pumps and other machinery.[3] Early in the next century, notices were

[1] Parry : *Llanberis*, pp. 68 ff. ; Williams : *Snowdon Mountains*, pp. 62–3 ; Evans : *Beauties*, pp. 421–2 ; advts. in *N. W. Gaz.*, July 26, 1810, May 28, 1812 ; Lewis : *Top. Dict.*, under *Llanddeiniolen;* cf. *supra*, pp. 76–7.

[2] Bingley : *op. cit.*, I, p. 226 ; Parry : *op. cit.*, p. 72 ; Fenton: *Tours*, p. 249 ; *N. W. Gaz.*, Aug. 31, 1809.

[3] *Camb. Reg.*, I, p. 285 ; Porth yr aur MSS. (leases of Hafodlas and Cefn du quarries) ; notices of quarries for sale or to let in *N. W. Gaz.*, April 22, 1813, June 5, 1826 (Cefn du common), July 20, 1809, Sept. 5, 1811, May 28, 1812, May 20, 1813 (near Bettws Garmon), May 11, 1809, May 2, 1811, May 28, 1812 (Hafodlas). *Cf. infra*, pp. 310–11.

posted to warn unauthorized quarrymen off these lands, but portions were still worked in the old way for another generation at least.[1] Above the Vale of Nantlle, the ancient quarry of Cilgwyn (also on Crown land) was revived and let to partnerships which bade fair to make it another Dinorwic, till Smith's superior capital began to tell from 1820.[2] By the beginning of the nineteenth century the exploitation of the south-eastern end of the county had begun, and when Mr. Madocks built his new village of Tremadoc in 1805 he was able to roof the houses with the produce of a quarry which had been opened close by, on Moel y gêst, some twelve years earlier.[3] But it was not till the construction of Portmadoc harbour, in 1824, that this district was provided with a much-needed outlet, which served also the far busier slate traffic of Ffestiniog.[4]

For Ffestiniog slates, too, were now coming into the market. Apart from the casual "digging" for surface slates, which had been carried on from the earliest times (the thatcher's art is said to have been almost unknown in this parish), the resources of the district were hardly touched, till, just about the time when Richard Pennant was succeeding to the Penrhyn estate, a little company of quarrymen came to work, under a local man who was himself a working quarryman, on the rocky wastes in the north of the parish. Many are the tales preserved in local tradition of the exploits of these early adventurers; how one of them walked to Bristol to dispose of a load of slate that had been sent there by sea; how another went on foot all the way to London for the same purpose, and—when some accident delayed the arrival of the ship—was preparing to work his passage back by peddling soap. Apparently they paid no rent: the ground belonged to an estate in the southern part of the county, and its owner placed little value on this piece of barren mountain land.

[1] *See* printed notices in Porth yr aur MSS., 1804, and MS. accounts with quarrymen for 1/9 royalty from various quarries on Cefn du common, Cilgwyn Mountain, etc., 1815–23, in the same collection.

[2] Davies: *General View*, p. 412; Davies: *Slates and Slate Quarrying*, p. 32; *N. W. Gaz.*, April 28, 1814.

[3] *N. W. Gaz.*, Aug. 1, 1811 (Beddgelert), May 28, 1812 (Penmorfa); *Gestiana*, p. 39.

[4] *Supra*, p. 125.

About the beginning of the nineteenth century the property came under the hammer ; the old company went to bid for it, but they were too late. It had been knocked down at £1,000 to a group of Lancashire men. The successful bidders—William Turner and the brothers Casson—had but recently come into the district looking for work. They had no capital to speak of ; they speculated— and events justified them—on inducing moneyed men of the district to take up shares. At first they had to live from hand to mouth, walking back from Bangor or from Holyhead with the proceeds of a lucky sale, by which they were enabled to carry the work a stage further. But henceforward their fortunes were indissolubly bound up with the Ffestiniog quarries, and the one they so adventurously acquired at the dawn of the nineteenth century is still known by the name of Diphwys Casson. Turner, along with one of his Diphwys partners, also took over the Dinorwic quarry for a short spell before Assheton Smith took it in hand himself, and he had for a while another small quarry in Caernarvonshire.[1]

The early years of the Napoleonic War brought distress to this as to the other slate districts, but when recovery began, new quarries were started—some by landowners like Lord Newborough, some by working quarrymen from the neighbourhood. By the end of the War, very considerable inroads had been made on the slate rock, and standardisation after the Penrhyn fashion had been introduced. But the great days of Ffestiniog were still to come ; as yet its name was almost unknown. Travel books of the period rarely mention it ; only more careful investigators like Gwallter Mechain think it worthy of note. Transport was, of course, the main handicap. A little had been done towards improving the roads, but in the upland parts of the parish they remained impassable save for mule convoys, and it was by these that the loads of slate were carried down to the lower ground where Manod station now stands. Here they were taken on carts to Maentwrog quay, where barges conveyed them down the Dwyryd, once a fortnight or so, to meet the ships that came up the Traeth ; it was only at spring tides that ships of any size could anchor at Maentwrog itself.

[1] Parry : *op. cit,*. p. 73 ; advt. in *N. W. Gaz.* Sept. 5, 1811.

These roundabout means of conveyance entailed charges of about 15s. a ton before ever the ships were reached—a heavy handicap on sales.[1] A railway and a port were the crying needs of the industry ; and Mr. Madocks was already planning his harbour at Portmadoc and dreaming of a railway to connect it with the quarries.[2]

Little need be said about the quarries outside Snowdonia. Most of them were at work before Waterloo. From the Conway valley, and from as far south as Dolwyddelan, loads of slate were brought to Trefriw for conveyance by sailing boats to Conway, where they formed a considerable item in the export trade by 1798. Most of these quarries were on the Gwydir estate, and were worked by its proprietor.[3] In Denbighshire the construction of the Ellesmere canal provided a useful outlet for slates quarried on both banks of the Dee. By 1797—a waterway being now open between Chirk and the line of the Montgomeryshire canal—a firm of "slate merchants and undertakers of slating business" at Gobowen had established depôts at various points along the two canals for the produce of their own workings at Glyn Ceiriog and also of those lying north-west of Llangollen.[4] In the former district, which had been exploited at least since the beginning of the seventeenth century, some of the quarries were acquired by William Hazeldine, ironmaster and coalowner, soon after he came from Shrewsbury to work on the Pontcysyllte aqueduct. But here there was a journey of six miles by road (for the Ceiriog is useless for navigation) before the slates could be loaded on canal barges. The Llangollen quarries, on the other hand, were soon to have the benefit of the new "navigable

<hr>

[1] On the Ffestiniog quarries *see Hanes Plwyf Ffestiniog*, pp. 80–113 ; *Salop. Journ.*, Jan. 30, 1799 (the first newspaper reference I have seen) ; *N. W. Gaz.*, Aug. 29, 1811, May 14, 1812 (new road to Maentwrog quay), May 20, 1813 ; Davies : *General View*, p. 412 ; Fenton : *Tours*, p. 43 ; Pugh : *Camb. Dep*,. pp. 167–8 (earliest allusions in books of travel to the Diphwys quarry and its Lancashire owners).

[2] *Gestiana*, p. 178.

[3] Williams : *Aberconwy*, p. 89 ; Evans : *Tour*, p. 261 ; Fenton : *Tour*, p. 188 ; advts. in *N. W. Gaz.*, Dec. 6, 1810, July 18, 1811, Feb. 6, May 6, 1812, Sept. 22, 1814 ; *Chester Chron.*, Jan. 1, 1802.

[4] *Salop. Journ.*, March 22, June 27, 1797 ; *cf.* Davies : *General View*, p. 411 ; *supra*, pp. 103, 106.

feeder" which tapped the Dee just below.[1] The "means of conveyance" as a whole, however, were not "equal to the demand" : transport charges would sometimes add nearly fifty per cent to the price, before the goods had travelled twenty miles from the quarry ; and in consequence the industry had not yet reached the stage where classification by size could profitably be introduced.[2]

Llangynog, where quarrying began about 1775, was even more seriously hampered in this respect. First there was a hair-raising descent in sledges from the quarry face to the road below, then a journey of twenty miles or more before the Severn, the Vyrnwy, or (later) the Montgomeryshire canal could be reached.[3] When the canal was completed, merchants like Hazeldine opened depôts at handy points for the sale of Llangynog slates, and some loads even found their way to Bristol ;[4] but travellers noted that in the southern parts of Montgomeryshire the houses were still roofed with wooden shingles at the opening of the nineteenth century.[5] The southern district of Merioneth did not become important till a later date, but there seems to have been some quarrying there, and also between Bala and Corwen, before 1815 ; the Barmouth Harbour Act of 1797 gives a tariff for the export of slates, and they are frequently named in the *North Wales Gazette* (from 1808 onwards) among the cargoes sent out from the port.[6]

The post-war depression affected quarrying much less than it did the mining industries ; instead of the withdrawal of a factitious war-demand to face, there were

---

[1] *Salop. Journ.*, May 2, 1798 ; *Chester Chron.*, June 19, 1807 ; *Shrewsbury Chron.*, Aug. 13, 1830 ; *Parl. Pap.*, 1823, XV, p. 351 ; *cf. supra*, pp. 16, 104, 109.

[2] Evans : *Beauties*, p. 514 ; *cf.* prices quoted in *Salop. Journ.*, March 22, 1797.

[3] Pennant : *Tours*, III, p. 162 ; Aikin : *Journal*, p. 15.

[4] Davies : *General View*, p. 411 ; *Camb. Reg.*, I (1795–96), p. 265 ; Carlisle : *Top. Dict.* ; Evans : *Beauties*, pp. 93, 805–6 ; advts. in *Salop. Journ.*, May 2, 1798, June 12, 1799, and *Chester Chron.*, Sept. 27, 1799.

[5] Evans : *Tour*, p. 39 ; *cf.* Pennant : *Tours*, III, p. 185.

[6] Davies, D. C. : *op. cit.*, p. 64 (Aberllefeni) ; *Chester Chron.*, Nov. 12, 1802 (Llandrillo) ; *N. W. Gaz.*, May 3, 1810 (Llanuwchllyn),

war-time arrears in building to make up.[1]   After a short
period of acute distress—caused mainly by bad harvests,
and marked by corn riots among the Ffestiniog quarrymen[2]—the industry was soon on its feet again.   In April,
1817, a local paper reported the loading of three large
vessels, two at Felin Heli and one at Port Penrhyn,
with slates for North America.[3]   At the Penrhyn quarries
Mr. Dawkins Pennant, who had succeeded to the estate on
Lady Penrhyn's death in 1816, stated four years later
that he was employing 874 men—the highest number yet
attained.   Since 1803 a Liverpool firm, Messrs. Worthington and Co., had contracted for the whole of the produce,
and under agreement with the proprietor they not only
made themselves responsible for the shipping (on commission), but also took over the manufacture of writing-
slates and chimney pieces and the preparation of the
various by-products—powdered chert for the potteries,
manganese ore for bleaching, and so on.[4]   In the 'twenties
the New Cilgwyn Company acquired a whole group of
quarries in the Cilgwyn area ;[5] new workings were begun
in the Llanberis district and at Pwllheli ;[6] and in Ffestiniog parish, quarrying was extended further west to the
Tan y bwlch estate.   Mr. Oakley (the proprietor) and
Mr. Hugh Williams (of the Machynlleth lead mines)
had both tried to get slates there without much success ;
but in 1819 the land was leased to a Liverpool merchant
named Samuel Holland, and he soon made the Rhiw
quarry (as it was called) a flourishing concern.[7]

Very soon the North Wales quarries were caught on the
crest of the great wave of mining speculation.   Prices
began to soar.   The old small, thick slates of the days
before standardization used to sell, in the seventeenth

[1] *See* evidence of Col. Dawkins Pennant before *Select Committee
on Holyhead Roads*, 1817, pp. 199–200.

[2] *Hanes Plwyf Ffestiniog*, pp. 111–12.

[3] *Chester Chron.*, April 4, 1817.

[4] *Parl. Pap.*, 1823, XV, pp. 381, 416 ; Evans : *Beauties*, pp. 454,
456–9 ; Fenton : *Tours*, pp. 210, 238–9, 254–6 ; *Red Dragon*, VII,
p. 325.

[5] *N. W. Gaz.*, March 13, 1823.

[6] Parry : *Llanberis*, p. 73 ; *N. W. Gaz.*, May 31, Aug. 16, 1821 ;
Camb. Trav. Guide (1840), p. 325.

[7] *Hanes Plwyf Ffestiniog*, pp. 87–8 ; *cf. supra*, p. 42 (Mr. Oakley),
p. 180 (Mr. Hugh Williams).

and eighteenth centuries, at 5s. or 6s. a thousand ;[1] the
same slates were selling in Denbighshire during the
War at 10s. to 20s., according to the distance they had to
travel. Llangynog slates rose from 13s. in the early days
of the War to £1 1s. in 1824.[2] The classified slates of the
more forward districts ranged in price, towards the end
of the eighteenth century, from £3 10s. for Duchesses to
£1 for Ladies and 11s. for Doubles. By 1825 prices were
twice as high, and there was a further rise in the following
year.[3]

So promising an industry could not fail to attract
speculators in days when all the world was sinking its
savings in mines and quarries. Advertisements of
quarries to let or for sale—even in regions which had
been little exploited hitherto—were constantly appearing
in the press, and some were being snapped up by strangers.[4]
But bigger things than this were in the air. Early in
1825, the landowners of the Snowdonian region were
startled by a rumour that a Royal Cambrian Company
was about to receive from the Office of Woods and Forests
the right to explore Crown wastes for minerals. Many of
these wastes were already in the occupation of the neighbouring landowners, and used by them for sheep-walks or
for the exploitation of the minerals ; and a letter to the
North Wales Gazette urged its readers to be on their guard
against "this projected company of strangers of various
persuasions, who can have no regard for the people of
Wales or their customs, manners and habits."[5]

[1] Myddleton, W. M. : *Chirk Castle Accounts* (1908), p. 99 (1661) ;
Bye-gones, 1899, p. 16 (1737). On the Ystum Colwyn estate
(Montgomeryshire), 1,000 slates cost 5s. in 1757, whereas in 1784
twice as much was paid for 100 (*Y Cymmrodor*, XXXVIII,
pp. 40–41).

[2] *Salop. Journ.*, March 22, 1797, June 27, 1798 ; Evans : *Beauties*,
p. 514 (Denbighshire) ; Pennant : *Tours*, III, p. 162 ; Davies :
General View, p. 411 ; *Oswestry Her.*, March 26, 1822 ; *Shrewsbury
Chron.*, June 6, 1823, April 30, 1824 (Llangynog).

[3] Evans : *Tour*, p. 123 ; Davies : *General View*, p. 413 ; Davies :
Slates and Slate Quarrying, p. 172 ; *Hanes Plwyf Ffestiniog*, p. 106.

[4] E.g., *N. W. Gaz.*, June 2, 1825 (Dolwyddelan, etc.) ; July 14,
1825 (Barmouth) ; Feb. 1, 1827 (Harlech) ; June 19, 1828
(Beddgelert).

[5] *N. W. Gaz.*, April 14, 1825 ; cf. *Shrewsbury Chron.*, Jan. 28,
Feb. 4, 1825, and *supra*, p. 58.

The project took shape in the formation of the Welsh Slate, Copper, and Lead Mining Company, of which the chief promoter was Nathan Meyer Rothschild, and which included among its directors Lord Palmerston and the notorious Mr. Wilks. It was soon busy prospecting on "unenclosed sheep walks" on the western side of Ffestiniog parish. The Rhiw quarry was purchased, and some of the adjoining lands which Samuel Holland had leased from the Tan y bwlch estate were claimed as Crown property. A new quarry was also started on the slopes of Moelwyn. Before long the whole district was in an uproar. The dispute between Rothschild and Oakley went before the Merioneth Great Sessions ; then, on the plea of undue local influence, it was called away to Shrewsbury, where Rothschild failed to appear, and lost his case by default.[1] While the suit was pending, Mr. Holland opened a small quarry at Trefriw.

The great financier also obstructed the project for carrying a railroad from the older Ffestiniog quarries to Portmadoc (for which purpose Mr. Madocks and others were trying to secure an Act of Parliament in 1824) so as to make way for his own pet scheme of a railway to start from Moelwyn ; the only result was that Ffestiniog had to wait another nine years for its railway.[2] And on top of all this the directors of the new company quarrelled with each other and with their employees, and pelted each other with angry letters, which were published for the edification of readers of the local press.[3] When Lord Palmerston, on holiday from the War Office, visited the quarries in the summer of 1825, he was met by complaints that the workmen had had no pay for eighteen weeks ; three years later a quarryman was suing the resident agent for arrears of wages to the tune of £29. The Company, indeed, was a typical product of those days of wild speculation. It was widely believed that the only aim of Rothschild and his associates had been to sell out their shares at inflated values. Compelled by the Company Laws to turn quarrymen despite themselves, they worked in a slovenly and half-hearted fashion. Moelwyn was

[1] *N. W. Gaz.*, July 13, 1826.
[2] *Supra*, pp. 111–12.
[3] *N. W. Gaz.*, Aug. 3 and 31, 1826.

disposed of after a few years ; Rhiw was kept on, and after 1840 began to show profits.[1]

The years 1825–8 were a time of turmoil throughout the slate districts. Lawsuits about quarries were frequent. In 1826 there were actions, both at the Shrewsbury Assizes and at the Caernarvonshire Great Sessions, brought by the owners of quarries (one near Llanllyfni, the other near Penmachno) against lessees who were alleged to have failed to carry out the terms of their contract.   In the same year a Denbighshire landowner brought a successful suit before the Great Sessions to prevent a Staffordshire attorney, who had taken a farm on his estate near Cerrig y drudion, from working the slate there ; and actions against defaulting agents and shippers are common during the following years.[2] At Penrhyn there was strife of another kind ; for in 1825 about 150 men in one of the quarries struck for a rise in wages.[3]

The boom period was soon over. In 1826 output at Penrhyn was over 45,000 tons, and more than 500 cargoes were cleared at the port ; but a fall in prices, beginning next year, reduced output by 6,000 tons in two years. There were bad times in Ffestiniog, and unemployed quarrymen were set to navvying on the roads.[4] But the industry as a whole was sound enough, and after prices had resumed their natural level there remained a solid and increasing demand, in the satisfaction of which the Welsh quarries had no serious rival. The time of high profits, too, had seen developments in the industry which continued to bear fruit long after the boom was over. If Ffestiniog had failed to get its railway, Portmadoc harbour was now open to receive the produce of the quarries, and there were better roads and better carts for conveying it there. The Llanberis quarries were linked by a light

[1] *Hanes Plwyf Ffestiniog*, pp. 88–91 ; *N. W. Chron.*, Aug. 21, 1828 ; Guedalla, P. : *Palmerston* (1926), pp. 115, 241, 253.
[2] *N. W. Gaz.*, Aug. 24, 1826, April 19, 1827 ; *Shrewsbury Chron.*, March 24, July 28, 1826, April 13, 1827, Aug. 1, 1828.
[3] *Infra*, p. 402.
[4] *N. W. Chron.*, Jan. 17, 1828 ; Davies. D. C. : *op. cit.*, pp. 170, 172 ; *Hanes Plwyf Ffestiniog*, p. 112; Penrhyn MSS. 2047, 2049.

railway with Port Dinorwic,[1] those of Nant Nantlle with Caernarvon. Everywhere there were better methods of working. At Penrhyn, after the strike, a new manager introduced improvements in tools, transport, drainage and blasting. At Ffestiniog the transition from the primitive method of reckoning by the load, by means of stones or tallies, to that of weighing by the ton—a change which we have seen taking place in the coal mines at an earlier date—gave greater security to the workers ; machinery too, was making headway.[2]

It was during these years that the agitation against the slate duty came to a head. The duty on stone had been removed, thanks to the efforts of the *Edinburgh Review,* in 1823 ; but slate continued to be burdened, and the tax, which had grown apace (after the fashion of its kind) since Pitt first imposed it, was believed to be driving Welsh slate out of the Lancashire market. The *Morning Herald* even declared in 1830 that it was the means of throwing "several thousand workers" out of employ. "I think," wrote "A Quarrier," to the *North Wales Chronicle* in the same year, "we be as honest and willing to work and can live upon as little as any of them, and therefore we ought to have a fair chance." In the following year there were numerous meetings in North Wales to consider "the depressed state of the slate trade," and to petition for repeal. The outcry succeeded, and the slate duty disappeared along with the coal duty in 1831.[3]

With this relief the industry forged rapidly ahead. In one place after another we read of the construction of new tramways or inclined planes, and of experiments with cutting or sawing machines, driven by horses, by water

---

[1] Excepting those on the western side of the lake, which still made use of farmers' carts ten years after the railway was built. The accounts of the Glynrhonwy quarry with the carriers (made up monthly, in great detail) for 1835–6, are preserved in U.C.N.W. Library (Bangor MSS. 419–20).

[2] *Supra*, p. 195; *Red Dragon*, VII, pp. 332–4 ; *Hanes Plwyf Ffestiniog*, pp. 101–2, 106, 108.

[3] Dowell : *History of Taxation*, IV, pp. 394–5 ; *N. W. Gaz.*, Feb. 21, 1822, May 15, 1823, Oct. 26, 1826 ; *N. W. Chron.*, Jan. 21, Feb. 4, April 8, 1830 ; *Camb. Quart. Mag.*, IV, p. 133.

or by steam.[1] At Penrhyn the number of quarrymen had reached 1,200 at the time of the boom ; during the next quarter of a century it grew to about 2,000, and there were almost, if not quite, as many in the quarries round Llanberis. By 1850 the joint tonnage exported annually from the three North Wales slate ports was nearing 200,000.[2] At Ffestiniog the repeal of the slate duty, and the opening of the railway five years later, were followed by a fresh incursion of capitalists from Lancashire and elsewhere, and quarry after quarry was opened up. Over a thousand men were employed in 1843, and the number increased still further during the next decade ; the sales of slate rose from 11,000 tons just before the great boom to over 50,000 in 1854.[3] But work in this region was becoming more expensive. The beds of slate, once the superficial outcrops had become exhausted, had to be followed into the heart of the rock by means of deep shafts and levels. The process had begun about 1830, and in 1856 Samuel Holland had his quarry lighted throughout with gas.[4] Luckily for the trade of the district, the demand for Ffestiniog slates, owing to their fineness of texture, kept pace with these growing expenses. Nant Nantlle is another district where the strata lie deeply buried, and the incursion of water into the workings there made necessary an early recourse to steam engines. Output was slackening off in some of the Nantlle quarries by 1833 ; but Cilgwyn and the bigger concerns continued to flourish, employing between them over 700 men in this same year.[5]

In all the chief quarrying districts the decade following the repeal of the slate duty seems to have been the period of most rapid growth. The population of Caernarvonshire increased during those years by 22 per cent—almost twice as high a rate as in any other county of North Wales ;

[1] E.g., *Hanes Plwyf Ffestiniog*, pp. 86–7, 94, 103 ; Parry : *Llanberis*, p. 73.

[2] *N. W. Gaz.*, Aug. 3, 1826 ; Parry : *Railway Companion*, pp. 97, 111 ; Hicklin : *Excursions in North Wales* (1851), p. 43 ; Parry : *Llanberis*, p. 72 ; Davies, D. C. : *op. cit.*, pp. 170–1.

[3] *Hanes Plwyf Ffestiniog*, pp. 107, 112–13, *et passim*.

[4] *Notes and Queries*, second series, VII (1859), p. 256.

[5] Williams : *Tourist's Guide*, p. 103 ; Lewis : *Top. Dict.* (1833), under *Llanwnda* and *Llanllyvni*.

and most of this growth is directly attributable to slate. The quarrying population was forming its own villages— new Nonconformist parishes, as it were, each clustering round, and many of them named after, the first chapel to be erected. The Penrhyn workmen found Lord Penrhyn's model houses too far away, and they built homes for themselves round Bethesda Chapel, just at the foot of the quarry ; by the 'sixties Bethesda village had five or six thousand inhabitants. In Llanberis parish the old village was left high and dry ; a new Llanberis arose on the southern side of Llyn Padarn, and an Ebenezer farther north, in Llanddeiniolen parish ; and colonies of workmen from Cilgwyn straggled all over the wild mountain lands of Llandwrog and Llanllyfni parishes.[1] Some of the villages and hamlets, as we have seen,[2] had been put up by the quarrymen themselves, on common land, in their spare time. Similar developments were taking place at Ffestiniog. The population of the parish was only 732 when the first Census was taken, and it did not exceed a thousand till 1821. By 1831 it was over 1,600 and in the next ten years it almost doubled itself ; a quarter of the inhabitants were registered in 1841 as born outside the county. Then there was a pause, to be followed by still more striking growth in the 'sixties and 'seventies. But it was not in the existing village that the new houses were run up ; a new village—Blaenau Ffestiniog—built of solid slabs of slate, had come into existence in the north of the parish, close by the principal quarries. Many ·of the houses were built by quarry owners like Mr. Holland, but the formation of a Building Society in 1836 enabled the quarrymen to build for themselves.[3]

[1] The following are some of the figures :—

	1831	1841	
Llandegai	2,600	3,010	due mainly to Penrhyn quarries.
Llanllechid	3,075	4,957	
Bangor	4,751	7,232	
Llanberis	725	1,024	due mainly to Llanberis quarries.
Llanddeiniolen	2,610	4,202	

In the Nantlle region the increases are far less striking.
[2] *Supra*, pp. 77–8.
[3] *Hanes Plwyf Ffestiniog*, pp. 136, 140.

The industry continued to grow during the second half of the century. The opening of a new German market, with Hamburg as its port, inaugurated another period of rapid advance, and at Ffestiniog most of the bigger quarries were taken over by limited companies, formed under the Acts of 1855 and 1862.[1] By the close of the century employment in the quarries had reached its peak of about 15,000—two thousand more than there were in the coal mines ; since then there has been a slight decline. For a time the other quarrying districts continued to expand along with those of Snowdonia, but eventually superior advantages alike in the quantity and quality of the slates, in organization and in transport, gave to the Penrhyn, Llanberis and Ffestiniog quarries almost a complete monopoly.

The decline of quarrying in the Conway valley may be measured by the fact that the exports of slate from Conway port, which reached 27,000 tons in 1858, shrank to 6,000 in less than twenty years.[2] The Corris and Tal y llyn districts, which were in operation by the 'thirties, reached their zenith about forty years later, when light railways were built to connect them up with the trunk lines ; but they have now fallen on evil days. Llangynog has similarly declined, and the other quarries scattered up and down Montgomeryshire have all failed to surmount the fatal obstacle of bad communications. The number of quarrymen in the county increased more than fivefold between 1871 and 1881, reaching a maximum of 265 ; but there were less than 80 at work when the 1921 Census was taken.[3] The quarries of Glyn Ceiriog and Llangollen were still flourishing when Borrow visited them in the middle of the last century, and employed over 600 men in the 'seventies ; now there are only 126.[4] In slate quarrying, as in every

[1] *Id.*, p. 107. Between 1861 and 1881 the number of quarrymen in Caernarvonshire increased from 6,464 to 8,408, in Merioneth from 1,215 to 4,265.

[2] North : *Slates of Wales*, p. 46.

[3] Davies, D. C. : *op. cit.*, p. 64 ; Lewis : *Top. Dict.*, under *Aberdovey, Llanegryn, Mallwyd, Machynlleth, Talyllyn, Llanrhaiadr y Mochnant, Llanwddyn, Llanwrin, Llanidloes* ; *Education Report*, 1847, III, App., p. 156 ; *Mont. Coll.*, XXXVII, pp. 27–8.

[4] Borrow : *Wild Wales*, pp. 71, 389.

other branch of production, improvements in transport were fatal to the less favoured regions ; but for once this meant, not the flight of the industry, but merely its concentration in one district of North Wales.[1]

C. STONE.

The quarrying of stones to build houses is as old an occupation in North Wales as the quarrying of slates to cover them ; but while the unique qualities of Snowdonian slates created a great industry organized to meet a world-demand, the stone quarries have in general been worked on a small scale and to serve a local market. Yet here, too, the quickening effects of the Industrial Revolution were felt, especially in counties like Denbigh and Montgomery (where slate quarrying was of minor importance), and Flint and Anglesey (where it did not exist). In the first place, there was the new demand for lime in farming, building and the iron manufacture to be satisfied. The resources of the country were adequate to meet the need, for limestone is found in a long belt, stretching from the north-western angle of Montgomeryshire, up through the coal measures of Denbigh and Flint and along the north coast to the great Orme, emerging on the other side of the Straits in Anglesey.[2] From these regions the requirements of the rest of the country, and especially of Caernarvonshire, Merioneth and the greater part of Montgomeryshire, had to be supplied. The great Montgomeryshire Turnpike Act of 1769[3] made possible the conveyance of lime over the whole county, as well as in the adjoining parts of Shropshire, from the quarries of Llan y mynech, and increased their activity tenfold. By the end of the century there were about fifty men employed in quarrying

[1] The Porth yr aur MSS. contain abundant material on slate quarrying in Caernarvonshire, of which only very little was available for use in this chapter. Among other documents there are account books of the Cilgwyn Companies, and of many other quarries in the same area, for the early nineteenth century ; the evidence in several Chancery suits, and a number of deeds of partnership, leases, etc. *See* also Nantlle MS. 19 for data on quarries in the Nantlle districts, 1816–24, and Searell MS. 3 on quarries in the Portmadoc district, 1839 ff.

[2] Davies : *General View*, pp. 64 ff. ; *cf.* map VI (opposite p. 189), and *supra*, pp. 18, 48, 109, 194.

[3] *Supra*, p. 92.

all the winter, and three times as many at the kilns during the summer months.[1] Similar works at Minera in Denbighshire and Caergwrle in Flintshire and a host of smaller ones, were doing the same service for the farmers of the more northerly counties and of the Cheshire plain. Wilkinson's ironworks, with their demand for lime as a flux, helped to extend the market in this district ; Wilkinson kept several kilns for his own use.[2]

The enormous growth of towns and cities during George the Third's reign provided the Welsh quarries with customers on the other side of Offa's Dyke. Builders wanted increased supplies, not only of lime with which to mix their mortar, but of good building stone as well. As early as 1775 a Chester builder was advertising in the local paper for stone from the Anglesey quarries.[3] It was not, however, as building stone that the produce of these quarries was chiefly prized. Anglesey had become famous for a species of variegated marble, sometimes streaked with asbestos, and believed by enthusiasts to surpass in brilliancy of surface and variety of colour even the marbles of Italy. It had been worked in some parts of the island since the end of the seventeenth century, and Anglesey quarrymen were familiar with the use of blasting powder from, at any rate, the beginning of George the Third's reign.[4] During the Napoleonic Wars, when foreign supplies were shut off, Anglesey marble became fasionable for chimney pieces. A Beaumaris stone mason sent a specimen to Queen Charlotte ; the Society of Arts became interested ; and a Liverpool man who discovered and worked some of the quarries set up a manufactory for "Mona marble" in the heart of London. Ackermann's *Repository of Arts*, the mirror of contemporary fashion, displayed a plate of a Mona marble mantelpiece in October, 1816, and it was hoped that before long foreign marbles would be completely superseded in the Principality at least, if not in England.

[1] Pennant : *Tours*, III, p. 205 ; *Camb. Reg.*, I, pp. 272–4.
[2] *Imperial and County Register*, 1810, p. 18 ; Palmer : *Wilkinson*, p. 18.
[3] *Chester Chron.*, May 2; 1775.
[4] Greenly : *Geology of Anglesey*, II, pp. 861–2 ; Lhuyd : *Parochialia*, III, p. 115 ; *Morris Letters*, I, pp. 397, 399, 425 ; Morris : *Plans of Harbours*, pp. 4–5 ; Pennant : *Tours*, III, pp. 65–6 ; Meyrick Papers, 1762 ff.

So promising were the prospects that a little quarry at Llanfechell was sold for £1,000.[1]

Such hopes were extravagant, of course. When imports began to come in from abroad once more after Waterloo, the trifling output of the Anglesey quarries soon found itself swamped. Samuel Lewis, in his *Topographical Dictionary* of 1833, could still wax enthusiastic over the qualities of Mona marble, but he had to speak in the past tense of its days of triumph. For less decorative uses, however, Anglesey stone still commanded a wide market. Most of the quarries lay near the coast, and their produce could be exported direct to Liverpool or Ireland with the minimum of cost for land transport. Penmon quarries were particularly active. They are probably the oldest on the island : Edward the First had used them for his castles of Beaumaris and Caernarvon ; and now, more than five hundred years later, they were exploited once more for public works of a more peaceful character. First came Holyhead pier and the column erected to the honour of the Marquis of Anglesey, near Llanfair pwll gwyngyll, on his return from Waterloo ; then the stonework of the new suspension bridge and the rebuilding of Penrhyn castle ; and finally more distant edifices like the new Town Hall at Birmingham—all built or faced with stone from Penmon or from the neighbouring quarries at Red Wharf. And stone that was not good enough for building could always be shipped off to be burned for mortar.[2]

Along the northern coast of Wales, from Abergele to the Orme, was another chain of quarries which helped to supply Liverpool with mortar and building stones. Fifty horses were at one time employed in carting stone from the Abergele quarries to the coast ; those at Llandulas,

---

[1] Pennant : *Tours*, III, p. 65 *n* ; Barfoot and Wilkes' *Directory*, V, p. 9 ; Aikin : *Journal*, pp. 113, 143 ff. ; *N. W. Gaz.*, May 19, 1808, April 20, 1809 ; *Notes and Queries*, fifth series, III (1875), p. 452 ; *cf. Camb. Trav. Guide* (1840), p. 39.

[2] Greenly : *Geology of Anglesey*, II, p. 853 ; *N. W. Gaz.*, Aug. 17, 1815, March 21, 1816 ; *Shrewsbury Chron.*, Dec. 18, 1818 ; Lewis : *Top. Dict.*, under *Holyhead, Llanallgo, Llanbedr Goch, Llanddyfnan, Llanedwen, Llaneugrad, Llanidan, Llangeinwen, Llanfair Pwllgwyngyll, Llanvair Mathavarn Eithav, Llanfair yng Nghornwy, Llanvechell, Llanfihangel din Sylwy, Penmon, Penrhos Llugwy, Pentraeth, Moelvre, Rhoscolyn.*

further west, were provided with a railroad and a pier in 1822.[1] The inland limestone districts were not so well placed for supplying the English market, but the opening of the canals enabled them to serve a wider area at home, and also afforded a temporary demand for stones to build aqueducts and bridges.[2]

For millstones, as we have seen, Wales had hitherto been dependent on foreign countries. There were a few local quarries, it is true. In Henry VIII's time, Leland found "a good quarre of Grinding Stonys in Ruabon paroch" and we know of another, at Caergwrle, which was being worked in the days of James I.[3] Millstones were also dug in Anglesey—on payment of the "tenth stone" as royalty to the landowner—in sufficient quantities to meet the needs of the county and most of Caernarvonshire ; they sold at £16 a pair in 1774.[4] Some were also sent into Flintshire, until a quarry was found near Mold during the War with America.[5] The local product, however, was poor in quality, and unpatriotic millers continued to buy from France—when they could afford it.

In this as in other industries the Napoleonic Wars stimulated the search for home products ; and there was much rejoicing when quarries of millstones, believed to be as good as the French article, were found near Conway and near Welshpool. The Society of Arts gave handsome rewards to the discoverers, and this drew others into the search. At Welshpool the first discoverer had to face the competition of a local ironmonger, who also got his supplies on the spot—a fact which may help to account for the relative cheapness of Welshpool millstones : they

---

[1] Lewis : *Top. Dict.*, under *Abergele, Llandrillo yn Rhos, Llandulas, and Llysvaen.* There was talk of using some of these quarries for the Conway suspension bridge (*N. W. Gaz.*, Aug. 19, 1813).

[2] *Id.*, under *Chirk, Llangollen, Llantisilio, Llanymynech*, and *Ruabon; Report to General Assembly of Ellesmere Canal Proprietors*, 1806.

[3] *Supra*, p. 16 ; Leland : *Itinerary in Wales*, p. 69; Edwards : *Star Chamber Proceedings*, pp. 173, 175.

[4] National Library of Wales : *Cal. of Wynn Papers* (1926), Nos. 1637, 1646 ; Morris : *Plans of Harbours*, p. 2 ; Meyrick Papers : Valuation, 1774 ; Owen : *History of Anglesey*, p. 55; *Camb. Reg.*, II, pp. 416–7.

[5] *Chester Chron.*, March 7, 1776.

sold at fourteen to eighteen guineas a pair, as against
thirty or forty pounds for those from Conway.[1] Another
quarry was found in Nant Ffrancon, and (later in the
War) a Flintshire man qualified for the gold medal of the
Society of Arts by fresh discoveries on Halkin Mountain.
A company was formed to work Halkin quarry, and at the
same time to grind for the use of glass-blowers and potters
the siliceous deposits long known to exist in the neighbourhood, but hitherto neglected.   Lord Penrhyn, we have seen,
had set up a similar plant near his quarries.   The company
was defunct before the middle of the century, but the silica
works still continue.[2] A few years after the conclusion
of peace, we hear of yet another millstone quarry at
Trawsfynydd, in Merioneth.   But in spite of all these
discoveries the hope of dispensing with imported goods
was doomed to disappointment ; demand for the local
product failed to come up to expectations.[3]

It was during the war years, then, that stone-quarrying
began to feel the breath of change.   That was the period
when Welsh stone was finding its way into the English
market, and when capitalists from Liverpool and elsewhere
were coming to work Welsh quarries for themselves.
Messrs. Worthington, whom we have already met as
agents for Penrhyn slate, were at work even earlier on a
quarry of quartz near Caerhûn, in the Conway valley ;
another Liverpool firm was making trials for marble in
the Vale of Clwyd about the time of Trafalgar ; and we
have seen how Liverpool merchants tried to push the sales
of Anglesey marble.[4] Production on a large scale brought
its usual troubles.   At Llandulas the stone quarries
which, lying on unenclosed land, had been worked for
half a century or more by scores of poor quarrymen on
their own account, were leased by the Bishop of Bangor,
early in 1829, for more thorough exploitation by a newly-

---

[1] Davies : *General View*, pp. 70–71 ; *Salop. Journ.*, May 13,
June 24, 1801.
[2] Skinner : *Ten Days' Tour*, p. 89 ; *Shrewsbury Chron.*, April 2,
1819 ; *N. W. Gaz.*, March 14, 1822 ; Pennant : *Tours*, I, p. 27 ;
Parry : *Railway Companion*, pp. 37–8.
[3] *N. W. Gaz.*, Nov. 26, 1818 ; Davies : *General View*, p. 70.
[4] Davies : *loc. cit.*; Pugh : *Camb. Dep.*, p. 442 ; *supra*, pp. 214, 223.

formed company. The episcopal claims rested on a supposed grant of Edward the First to the Bishop who baptized the first Prince of Wales. But the quarrymen cared for none of these things, and when the Sheriff came with the *posse comitatus*, armed with a warrant for their eject- ment, he was met by the resistance of the whole district. It needed a detachment of the 87th Fusiliers from Chester to restore order, and as late as June the *North Wales Chronicle* was indignantly reporting attempts to burn the pier and other acts of *sabotage*—"a system of hostile measures directed by a number of lawless fellows against a company of gentlemen who are devising means for the benefit of those very deluded men."[1]

Most of the stone quarries, however, were small concerns. There was no striking advance during the later years of the century to match that which took place in the slate industry. In some regions the growing habit of importing lime and building stone from England has led to a positive decline. A single quarry near Halkin, in the middle of the century, was believed to be employing 150 men and to be exporting 400 tons of limestone and 30 tons of lime weekly to Liverpool and Manchester ; later on there came a fresh stimulus from the demand for "Halkin marble" for decorative uses ; but since 1901 the whole of Flintshire has not been able to return a single quarryman in the Census tables.[2] In Montgomeryshire, where about 100,000 tons of limestone were exported annually at the end of the last century, the figures of employment at the 1921 Census were the highest yet recorded ; but they did not reach 200. Merioneth could then count about 100 quarrymen ; Anglesey had over 200 (a generation ago the figure was nearer 300), but lime-burning has died out there, and the farmers bring their lime forty miles or more by railway ; the local marble, however, is still occasionally used in a small way for church monuments.[3] The only important developments have been in Denbigh- shire, where large quarries of building stone have been

[1] *N. W. Chron.*, July 7, 1829 ; *Shrewsbury Chron.*, April 24, May 1, 1829.
[2] Anon : *Short Account of Holywell*, p. 14 ; North : *Coal and the Coalfields*, p. 130.
[3] *Wales*, III (1896), p. 295 ; Greenly : *op. cit.*, II, pp. 849–50, 862.

opened at Cefn Mawr and Trevor, and in Caernarvonshire, where, with the rise of the sett-making industry, the figures of employment leapt from under 500 in 1861 to over 2,000 in 1871, since when they have declined again. There has been no "revolution" in stone-quarrying.

[NOTE.—The geological map opposite p. 189, in preparing which I had the benefit of advice from my friend and colleague Professor G. W. Robinson, is intended primarily to illustrate this chapter. Only those regions have been indicated as "coal measures" where coal has actually been proved or worked ; the Vale of Clwyd is (in accordance with general usage) included among these, despite the fact that its coal has never been successfully exploited (*supra*, p. 201). The differentiation of "concealed" coal measures (where the. seams dip deeply below newer strata) is necessarily somewhat arbitrary.]

CHAPTER VII.

WELSH WOOLLENS.

Whilst the harp slept, the Sun of Commerce rose
To bless the arts, and banish Cambria's woes ;
Taught by her power, Llanidloes' sons assayed
To drive the wheel and start the flannel trade.
Check'd in their course, the streams that idly ran,
To gold were turned by this prolific plan . . .
First in his place, with keen attentive eyes,
To part the fleece the patient sorter plies ;
The picker next makes clean each mossy lock,
The pitch cuts off, that mark'd the shepherd's flock ;
Soon through the willow's fangs the fleece is sent,
Here oiled and tossed in countless pieces rent ;
Next through the scribbler's teeth must pass the whole,
And then the carder forms the perfect roll.
The piecer then exerts his infant skill
To join the rolls, and feed the slubbing bill.
The roll half twisted by the slubber's art,
The skilful spinner next performs his part . . .
The winner next in order does appear,
And then the warper forms the lengthened beer ;
The warp in loom, and strengthened well with size,
Quick through its folds the weaver's shuttle flies.
The flannel wove, the motes are plucked away,
And then 'tis cleansed with soap and fuller's clay.
Now washed, perchance, in the same silver tide,
The harmless flock contented fed beside.
Fair seems the web, the work of toiling man,
As the rich plumes that deck the snowy swan.
            —George Thomas, *c.* 1840.[1]

A. Emancipation and Reorganization.

"Our modern system both of manufactures and trade," says the writer of an almost forgotten *History of British Commerce*,[2] "may be regarded as taking its rise from the commencing portion of the reign of George III." Great overseas markets had just been forced open, and manufacturers were working at full pressure to supply them. For

---

[1] *Mont. Coll.*, V, pp. 42–3. Thomas, son of a local millowner, was a prolific writer of light verse (*Mont. Worthies*, 1894, pp. 296–7).
[2] Craik, III, p. 9.

the Welsh woollen industry this meant a new era. The "frize of Cambria" was already in demand among

> . . . those who seek
> Through gulfs and dales of Hudson's winding bay
> The beaver's fur . . ; [1]

Spaniards bought it for the use of their own colonists in South America ; the planters of South Carolina and the West Indies clothed their slaves in it ; some was sold in Africa ; and nearer home, Germany, Holland and Russia (where the Empress Catherine is said to have used it for her soldiers) were all good customers. The Seven Years' War developed the trade in three ways : by extending the empire, by injuring the trade of our European rivals, and by creating a demand for soldiers' uniforms ; for now, as in Charles the First's reign, many of the King's men went into action in Welsh woollens.[2]

A traveller in 1775 found the Dolgelley manufacturers "excessively anxious about affairs in America," which were already producing stagnation in the trade ;[3] but even after the loss of the thirteen colonies, America remained one of the best markets, and during the interval between the War of Independence and the Orders in Council of 1807 the Welsh woollen industry flourished as it had never done before. The sales of the Merioneth webs alone, reckoned at less than £40,000 a year in the middle of the century, were now believed to have reached a figure between £50,000 and £100,000 ; and Montgomeryshire flannels, even in the thick of the French Revolutionary Wars, were bringing in over £64,000, of which £45,000 remained as clear profit to be divided between makers and middlemen. Pennant, quoting figures which probably refer to the years just before the American War, tells us that between 700,000 and 800,000 yards of flannel and a similar quantity of webs were disposed of annually in the big sales. These estimates do not include what was sold locally for home use—a diminishing proportion of the total output.[4]

[1] Dyer : *The Fleece* (1757), IV, 561–5.
[2] Pennant : *Tours*, II, p. 253 ; *Camb. Trav. Guide* (1813), p. 1174 ; *Arch. Camb.*, 1922, p. 252 *n;* Pococke : *Travels*, II, p. 15 ; Aikin : *Journal*, p. 76.
[3] Sir Thos. Cullum's tour (*Y Cymmrodor*, XXXVIII, p. 58).
[4] Morris : *Plans of Harbours* (1748), Addenda ; Pennant : *Tours*, III, pp. 224–5 ; Davies : *General View*, pp. 394–6; *infra*, p. 417.

Such an industry was, of course, a mere minnow beside the tritons of Lancashire and Yorkshire ; yet the prospects of profit were high enough to attract competitors. We have seen in an earlier chapter[1] how long and against what odds the Shrewsbury Drapers' Company had retained its exclusive control over the sale of Welsh woollens. But this monopoly—an anachronism surviving into the Age of Competition from a generation which bowed to the ideal of a "well-ordered" but exclusive trade—was already tottering.[2] In 1746 an attempted prosecution of two Shrewsbury men, not "free of the Company," for buying flannel at Welshpool and Montgomery, had broken down. A generation later the Drapers so far abated their monopoly as to consent to buy Welsh flannels in the open market at Welshpool (they even contributed £100 towards building a new market hall there in 1797), and about 1770 a depôt was opened at Barmouth for the export of Merioneth web cloth direct by sea to the continent.

This latter scheme may have owed something to the growing interest of Liverpool merchants in the industry. Like the London "interlopers" of an earlier age, some of them seem now to have begun the practice of sending agents to Dolgelley to buy webs on the spot and to arrange for their conveyance by sea from Barmouth or Chester. Independent clothsellers from Shrewsbury itself, and even members of the Company, ventured a similar defiance of the time-honoured monopoly—"following the manufacturers into their own country" (where the improvement of communications was daily bringing new customers within reach), and employing "factors" at all the chief centres of the industry. By the 'nineties, when the practice became common, the Drapers' Company was forced to recognize that, in the web trade as well as the flannel trade, its dictatorship was at an end. The weekly sales were attended by dwindling members of Welsh weavers. In 1761 there were still enough of them to give Shrewsbury on a Thursday the aspect of a Welsh town ; as late as 1790 the trade kept three stage waggons plying between Welshpool and Shrewsbury ; but seven years later a

---

[1] *Supra*, pp. 11–12.
[2] On what follows, *see* my article in *Economica*, June, 1929 pp. 197–212, where full references are given.

traveller writes of Shrewsbury : "it was actually the market a few years ago, but now it is little more than nominally so ;"[1] and in 1803 the Drapers' Company gave up its two-centuries' tenancy of the room over the Town Hall, which soon afterwards became an ironmonger's warehouse.

The "interlopers" had won ; but the old economic ties which bound Shrewsbury to the "clothing counties" of North Wales were by no means completely severed. The Shrewsbury wholesalers were still the most important customers the Welshmen had, and their chief means of access to the English market. For some time yet it was they who virtually determined the price lists, and they were strong enough to drive a hard bargain with the unwary weaver from up country. Their warehouses were stocked with Welsh flannels and webs ; they continued to advertise for "assistants accustomed to the Welshpool and Dolgelley markets ;" and as late as 1833 an order for 20,000 yards of Welsh flannel for the East India Company was given through a Shrewsbury Draper.[2] Six years after this, the chief woollen manufacturer of Dolgelley, who gave evidence before the Commissioners on Handloom Weavers, was the resident agent of a Shrewsbury firm.

Even the spirit of monopoly was not yet dead. In 1823 the United Company of Mercers, Grocers, Ironmongers and Goldsmiths in Shrewsbury brought an action to prevent a non-freeman from carrying on business as a mercer in the town, and won their case. This success encouraged the Drapers' Company to make one more bid for its lost privileges—almost exactly two hundred years after its legal monopoly had been abolished by James I. But the Drapers' own fellow-townsmen were against them.

> The whole of the trade of North Wales is in our possession [wrote an indignant reader of the *Shrewsbury Chronicle*]. Do the very respectable, though very limited, Company of Drapers suppose that any prescriptive power which they may exercise can prevent the sale of woollen goods by persons not members of their community, within the town and liberties of Shrewsbury ?[3]

[1] Aikin : *Journal*, p. 72.
[2] Advts. in *Salop. Journ.*, Dec. 10, 1794, March 27, 1805 ; *Camb. Quart. Mag.*, V (1833), p. 617.
[3] *Shrewsbury Chron.*, Aug. 1, 22, 29, Sept. 12, 1823.

Six years later, just when the local paper was lamenting that "the total extinction of the Shrewsbury web trade is fast approaching," a last attempt was made—with the support of some manufacturers from Newtown—to get back the market for flannels from Welshpool. By this time, as we shall see, quantities of Welsh flannels were finding their way to Manchester, and the editor of the *Chronicle* made some prophetic remarks about the danger of depending on trade with a region where cheap imitations could so easily be produced. But his Welsh readers were not slow with retorts about the "monopolistic spirit" which had lost the trade for Shrewsbury, and "the unpleasantness which frequently occurs in the measurement of the goods."[1] When in 1839 there was a brief revival of sales of Welsh flannel in Shrewsbury, the market was no longer a "staple" in the ancient sense, but merely one of many distributing centres, and the Municipal Corporations Act had dealt a final blow at the exclusive privileges of gilds and companies.

Two full and well-informed contemporary descriptions—one "communicated by a friend" to Mr. Arthur Aikin, and published in his *Journal of a Tour through North Wales* in 1797,[2] the other written by Rev. Walter Davies (Gwallter Mechain) in 1799, and published eleven years later in his *General View of the Agriculture and Domestic Economy of North Wales*[3]—together with a number of incidental newspaper and other references, help us to form a tolerably clear idea of the woollen manufactures of North Wales just at the time when they were passing out of the stage of control by an exclusive body of capitalists outside the country, into that of a self-contained industry controlling its own markets.

Manufacture was still widely diffused. Apart from the more highly organized centres of Montgomeryshire, Merioneth and parts of Denbighshire, the spinning wheel and loom were busy in isolated farmhouses and cottages in the remotest parts of the country. In Anglesey and Caernarvonshire, and in outlying villages even of the main

---

[1] *Id.*, June 19 and 26, July 3, Oct. 7, 1829.
[2] Chapter VII.
[3] Chapter XV, Section 6. *See* also Appendix I. (*infra* p. 417 ff).

"clothing counties," cloth-making remained, as we have described it in an earlier chapter, a normal part of the household routine rather than a specialized industry, and even production for the market might be combined with almost any conceivable occupation.[1] Wool could always be bought in small lots from landlords or farmers or at the wool fairs, at prices ranging from 2s. to 5s. a pound according to quality and the state of the market ; and there were few households so poor that they could not afford a pair of hand cards and a spinning wheel. Cheap wheels could be got for a few shillings, and the price of even the better varieties was under a sovereign.[2] A traveller to Montgomeryshire in 1806 describes a house at Llangurig (not far from Llanidloes) where he "heard the wheels going briskly in an inner room and saw some blue yarn still dripping wet from the vat, hanging up against the eaves of the house to dry," and yet was shocked to observe the "miserable state of living and accommodation" of the family.[3]

A loom was a bigger undertaking,[4] and such as could not buy or make one would send their yarn to be made up by a more substantial neighbour—one of those "customer weavers" common in Scotland and the Midlands up to a century ago,[5] and not unknown in the Welsh countryside to-day ; and then, if necessary, have it fulled at a *pandy*. If they did not require all the yarn themselves, there were yarn markets at Machynlleth, Llanidloes and Dolgelley, where it could be sold to the manufacturers.[6]

The "customer weaver" himself might be a considerable farmer, keeping one or two looms in a lean-to building adjoining the farmhouse for use when farm-work slackened off in the winter, hiring his staff of permanent servants with an eye to their spinning or weaving capacities as

---

[1] E.g., "baker and weaver," Bala, 1790 (Barfoot and Wilkes' *Directory*, II, pp. 264–5).
[2] Palmer : *Parish Church*, pp. 171, 164 ; Meyrick Papers. The latter show a striking increase in the purchases of wool by tenants from 1767.
[3] Mavor : *Tour*, p. 74.
[4] In 1879 a loom to weave 1½ yards wide cost £4 (*infra*, p. 263).
[5] Clapham : *Early Railway Age*, pp. 159–60.
[6] *Records of Oswestry*, p. 97 (1625) ; Pennant : *Tour*, III, p. 184 ; Evans : *Tour*, p. 37.

well as their skill in the fields, and in busy seasons employing women by the day to work at the spinning wheel in his house. Very probably he would have a fulling mill too.[1] He would, of course, manufacture his own wool—perhaps even buy some outside the farm—as well as that of his customers. And all over the country there were markets at which he could sell such cloth or flannel as was not directly disposed of to his neighbours. Finally, the spinner and the weaver might be hired by the day in a big country house, like the laundress and the charwoman (indeed, the functions were often combined), to make the woollens needed by the family.[2]

Each district had its own speciality : Anglesey had its so-called "blue" cloth, manufactured from local wool for local use ; Caernarvonshire its *brethyn Sir Fôn*—"a peculiar drab coloured cloth, generally seven-eighths of a yard wide," selling "from 3s. to 5s. per yard of 40 inches," and named from the fact that its chief market was in Anglesey (at Llannerch y medd and Aberffraw fairs), though some went into other counties, and a little was exported to the West Indies.[3] The manufacture of wincey—a mixture of wool and cotton, which was now acquiring the popularity it long retained as a material for women's dresses—was not confined to any particular district, but depended on the accessibility of cotton warp yarn.

All these were of minor importance, however, when compared with the two main products, and the other districts of North Wales were tending to become mere "feeders" for the centres where web and flannel were manufactured. Both wool and yarn were flowing rapidly

[1] *Mont. Coll.*, V, p. 35, XXI, p. 82 ; *N. W. Gaz.*, May 4, 1809 ; *Report on Land*, 1896, pp. 46, 350, 699, etc. One of the *pandai* on the Bodorgan estate was in 1787 in the tenure of a weaver who frequently did work for the Meyrick family. He paid a rent of £6 16s. 0d.—nearly three times what had been paid a generation earlier.

[2] E.g., Meyrick Papers, 1771 : Betty Hughes, 2d. a day for spinning, 3d. a day for charing ; David Evans—account for his work and for his daughter spinning and washing.

[3] Davies : *General View*, p. 391 ; Evans : *Tour*, p. 167 ; *Camb. Reg.*, I (1795), p. 285 ; Williams : *Snowdon Mountains*, p. 25 ; Barfoot and Wilkes' *Directory*, II, p. 7.

into Merioneth and Montgomeryshire, and even into the English clothing districts, from the other counties of Wales. Anglesey seems to have sold its surplus wools chiefly to the Yorkshire clothier, and almost all those of Flintshire (where mining was too profitable to leave much scope for woollen manufacture) went either in this direction or to the neighbouring clothing districts. "Why," asks a Flintshire correspondent of the *North Wales Gazette*, "should English manufacturers be enriched with Welsh wool while hundreds of our own people are unemployed?" The same was largely true of Denbighshire, outside the small district where webs and flannels were made. Caernarvonshire made warp yarn (spun from finer wool than the weft) for Dolgelley; and at Llanidloes yarn market, yarn was collected from up and down the country for the use of what Aikin calls "the grand and most important of Welsh manufactures"—the flannel industry of Montgomeryshire.[1]

Aikin tells us of this industry that

> formerly the Welsh bestowed no pains in sorting the wool; a fleece was broken into two parts, never into more than three: they have now however learnt the economy of a little more trouble, and can make distinctions of sorts to the number of seven or eight: the consequence is a great variation in the texture of flannels, and some have been sold as low as sixpence, while others have been disposed of at four shillings per yard. Coarse goods are at present very scarce, and extravagantly dear, none being to be had under 11 or 12 pence per yard.

Davies (himself a Montgomeryshire man) adds some particulars about the method of manufacture.

> . . . the Montgomeryshire flannels [he says] are from 100 to 120, and some of the finer sort 132 yards long, and seven-eighths of a yard wide. They shrink generally about six inches in width by being milled; and are sold from 1s. to 4s. per yard. Instead of size, a glutinous kind of blueish clay is used in their weaving. They are bleached three times under the hammers of the fulling-mill; the first time with urine,[2] the second with

---

[1] Davies, pp. 391-2; Pennant: *Whiteford and Holywell*, p. 158; Kay: *Agriculture of North Wales: Flintshire*, p. 22, *Denbighshire*, p. 16, *Merionethshire*, p. 16; *N. W. Gaz.*, May 4, 1809, July 30, 1812.

[2] A practice forbidden in London as early as 1376 (*see* Salzman, L. F.: *English Industries of the Middle Ages*, p. 224 *n*). For another account *see* Evans: *Tour*, p. 32.

fuller's earth,[1] and the third with soap. The frize or nap is raised on them, not by carding, but by the adhesion of the several foldings, when the pieces are laid in a particular manner for the purpose. This nappiness gives them a peculiar softness of texture, arising from the quality of the wool ; and renders them exceedingly well adapted to be worn next the skin of the most delicate invalid.

The manufacture of webs was carried on in two districts, each with its own local variety. First there was the "strong cloth" or "high country cloth" made in the neighbourhood of Dolgelley (in Merioneth) and Machynlleth (just over the border of Montgomeryshire). Here, says Aikin,

> . . . almost every little farmer makes webs, and few cottages in these parts are without a loom ; all kinds of wool are used indiscriminately, and a considerable quantity of refuse from the wool-staplers and skinners is collected from all quarters for this purpose. During peace much Kentish wool used to be imported. Many farmers however employ wool of their own growth, and this produces by far the best kind of cloth. The standard width of this article is 7/8th yard ; the length of a piece, or what is emphatically styled a *web*, is about 200 yards : this consists of two ends, each 100 yards, thus divided for the conveniency of carriage. . . . In its rough state, it may at present be purchased of the manufacturer at every price between 11 and 20 pence. . . .
>
> The following [he continues] is the whole process undergone by this article before exportation. The wool is prepared by hand in the usual manner for the loom ; when woven into cloth it is sent to the fulling-mill, where it undergoes the operations of scouring, bleaching and milling ; and is then fit for the market. When purchased by the drapers, it is treated in various ways ; either it is merely committed to the shearmen, who raise the wool on one side with cards, which is called *rowing* ; or it is sent again to the mill, where it is sometimes thickened to a surprising substance, which adds greatly to the price on account of the loss in shrinking ; or it is stretched, and thus made three or four inches wider, an operation that considerably enhances its value ; or, lastly, it is converted into a frieze or napped cloth. It is then put under the packing press. Being formed into bales of different sizes, containing from 500 to 2,000 yards, it is usually sent either to London or Liverpool, whence it is exported to Holland, Germany, and America. A quantity comparatively inconsiderable is used at home for workmen's jackets, ironing-cloths, blankets, &c.

[1] "Fuller's earth is brought by sea from Hampshire, and sold at Machynlleth for about 3s. per cwt. ; which is reckoned sufficient for about 23 pieces" (note by Davies).

The warp [adds Davies] is now made of the fleece wool of the country ; and the woof is a mixture, containing about one-third, and sometimes one half, of lambs wool. The Italian lambs' wool, in 1795, sold at Dolgelleu for 8*l.* a pack of 240 lbs ; but since June 1796, when the French entered Leghorn, none of it has been imported, except some little in neutral vessels. The Kentish lambs' wool sells at Barmouth from 10*l.* to ten guineas a pack.

Next in importance came the "small cloth" of Denbighshire, manufactured principally in the Dee valley, between Corwen and Llangollen. According to Aikin,

small cloth is about ¼ yard narrower than strong cloth ; its length is the same. The best was purchased last year at about 16 or 17 pence per yard, but this was thought a most extravagant price, 14 pence having formerly been deemed its full value. This cloth is used chiefly for dying [*sic*]. Some quantity is indeed sent off in its native or white state. . . . The coarser sort of the high country cloth abounds with long white hairs incapable of taking the dye, called *kemps*. This fabric is made of the coarser part of the very long wool that grows round Oswestry. . . . Instead of lambs' wool [we learn from Davies] these clothiers [the makers of small cloth] mix the woofing of the coarser sort of webs with flocks from the fulling-mills ; and that of the finer sort with combings from Yorkshire and Lancashire, which is bought by the pack of 44 lbs., at from 7*d.* to 9*d.* per lb.

About 22 webs a week were dressed in this district.

It will be observed that the Welsh fabrics were "woollens" in the trade sense of the term : that is to say, they were made from short, carded wool, not from long combed wool, like worsteds. This distinction affected the organization of the industry in more than one way, as we shall see.

Finally, knitting was still a flourishing occupation in the highlands between the upper reaches of the Dee and the Conway, especially in Merioneth, where some women, having learned to knit "as soon as they could talk," were able to finish a whole stocking in a day. The weekly sales of these goods in Bala market had risen, before the end of the century, from £200 to about £350 ; Gwallter Mechain reckoned the annual sales at nearly 200,000 pairs, yielding a clear profit of about £13,000. "In fine stockings," he assures us, "every pennyworth of wool is converted into a shilling." There were critics who said that the wool was spun too fine, and that Shetland stockings, though cheaper, were better ; others argued that an occupation usually carried on while the knitters were "walking, talking and begging, without hardly ever looking at their work," must needs be unprofitable. Yet valetudinarians were known to pay as much as half-a-guinea for a pair of hose made of the soft, warm wool of Merioneth, and eight shillings was quite a common price.[1]

The coming of the stage coach created a market for yet another knitted article. This was the Welsh wig—a sort of woollen cap, greatly favoured (now that the peruke was falling out of fashion) by bald-headed old gentlemen like Dickens' Mr. Fezziwig, especially if they happened to be travelling by coach. It only cost a couple of shillings or so ; and the knitters would congregate at strategic points on the Holyhead coach route to besiege passengers with cries of "D'you want a Welse wig ?—d'you want a wool stockings ?—d'you want a wool gloves ?"[2] Into this branch of the industry also, the factor had obtruded himself by the early years of the nineteenth century. Merchants from Shrewsbury and elsewhere employed agents to buy Welsh stockings for re-sale in London and other English towns, and "Welsh hosiers" travelled through the adjoining English counties to supply shops and warehouses.[3] But some of the middleman's profit was kept at home ; Mr. Davies, the "great stocking merchant," and his son (who also kept a grocery and drapery establishment) were looked up to as men of substance in Bala about the time of Waterloo.[4]

So far as manufacture was concerned, it will be seen, the industry was now almost self-contained. A little wool was imported, but this was partly balanced by what was sold to Yorkshire clothiers in the fairs at Chester, Shrewsbury and Monmouth. Occasionally webs, and more rarely flannels, were sent outside the country to

[1] Pennant : *Tours*, II, p. 204 ; Davies : *Labourers in Husbandry*, pp. 189, 191 ; Kay : *Agriculture of North Wales:* Denbighshire, p. 39 ; Williams : *Hanes Plwyf Ffestiniog*, p. 68.
[2] Mavor : *Tour*, pp. 91–2 ; Smith, J. : *Guide to Bangor, Beaumaris, Snowdonia [etc.]* (Liverpool, 1825), p. 35 ; *Bye-gones*, 1895–96, p. 301 ; 1903–04, pp. 6–7, 26–7 ; *Camb. Quart Mag.*, III, pp. 89–90.
[3] Pugh : *Camb. Dep.*, p. 189 ; Evans : *Beauties*, p. 112.
[4] Fenton : *Tour*, p. 123 ; Pigot's *Directory* (1828–29), p. 1146.

be dyed in Shropshire, Lancashire or Yorkshire; but much was sold undyed, or else—if it was destined for local use—dyed at home, either in the yarn or in the piece. In Merioneth and Snowdonia children used to gather rock-moss (*cenn du y cerrig*, or *lichen omphaloides*) from the slopes of Cader Idris and other mountains, for use as a dye; some of it was exported to Ireland and elsewhere; and it is said to have been used for army uniforms during the Napoleonic Wars.[1] A fulling mill was usually to be found within walking distance of the weaver's house, and even "rowing, double milling and napping" had ceased to be the exclusive preserve of the Shrewsbury shearmen. Only forty of these were left, instead of the 600 of Queen Elizabeth's day, when Pennant wrote his *Tours*. Their hall was turned into a Wesleyan Chapel, and by the time of Waterloo the industry was represented only by a few straggling survivors.[2]

With the disappearance of the Drapers' monopoly, the last stage of all—that of marketing—was now also taking place within the counties where the wares originated. A new market for flannel was built at Welshpool, as we have seen, in 1797. While it was still in process of construction, a conspiracy was set on foot by ten Shrewsbury drapers and 54 flannel manufacturers from Llanidloes and district to get the market removed to Montgomery; but Welshpool managed to keep the trade a little longer.[3] Hither would come, on alternate Mondays, the small farmer from near by, with his bale of cloth on a pack-saddle, or the lumbering wain from further south, bringing the accumulated manufactures of a whole district, which had been brought from the fulling mill by Sabbath-breaking weavers on the Sunday afternoon, and piled under the arches of Llanidloes town hall to await collection.[4]

[1] Pennant : *Tours*, II, p. 325 ; Cradock : *Account of N. Wales*, pp. 22–3 ; Evans, J. : *Circular Tour through N. Wales* (1802), p. 39 ; *N. W. Gaz.*, shipping reports, Jan. 9 and 30, Aug. 11, Sept. 20, 1808 ; Parry : *Llanberis*, p. 210.
[2] Pennant : *Tours*, III, p. 224 ; Phillips : *Shrewsbury*, pp. 135–8 ; Evans : *Tour*, p. 89 *n;* Howell, T. J. : *The Stranger in Shrewsbury* (Shrewsbury, 1816), p. 32.
[3] *Salop. Journ.*, Aug. 30, 1797.
[4] *Shrewsbury Chron.*, May 5, 1826 ; *Mont. Coll.*, XXI, p. 84 ; Horsfall–Turner : *Llanidloes*, pp. 244–5.

"Thousands of pounds' worth," people said, were sold every year at Welshpool in the early nineteenth century at prices ranging from 2s. 6d. to 4s. a yard—either to Shrewsbury drapers for re-sale to London exporters or clothiers from the North and West, or else direct to such wholesalers and retailers of flannel as thought it worth while to come so far. Travellers commented on the "air of opulence" which had so recently come over this little Welsh market town.[1] In 1818 the market day was changed to Thursday—Shrewsbury's old day ; but there still remained an undercurrent of hostility between the Welsh sellers and the Shrewsbury buyers, causing some of the latter in 1832 to support the removal of the staple to Newtown, an old flannel mart now provided (by the generosity of William Pugh, Brynllywarch) with a market hall, where flannel sales were held on alternate Mondays—to the great injury of the trade of Welshpool. Four years later yet another market was established at Llanidloes.[2] In 1838 it was estimated that 400 pieces of flannel were sold fortnightly in Newtown market, and 240 in Llanidloes (which served a more restricted area) ; but the *wagen fawr* travelling with flannel from Llanidloes and Newtown to Welshpool did not stop running till 1859.[3]

Oswestry, which had been ousted by Shrewsbury as the staple for Welsh woollens in the seventeenth century, held up its head again for a few years after the Shrewsbury monopoly had disappeared, serving once more as a depôt for the "small cloth" of Denbighshire. In Aikin's time the goods had to be hunted out in "any garret, stable, parlour or kitchen" for lack of a fixed building ; but in 1807 part of the town hall was set aside for use as a cloth market. By the beginning of Victoria's reign the Oswestry

[1] Carlisle : *Top. Dict.*, under *Welshpool ;* Mavor : *Tour*, p. 141 ; *Camb. Trav. Guide* (1812), p. 1174 ; *Oswestry Her.*, May 7, 1822 ; *Camb. Quart. Mag.*, I, p. 32.

[2] *Shrewsbury Chron.*, April 13, 1818, Dec. 16, 1831 ; Barfoot and Wilkes' *Directory*, IV, p. 68 ; Williams : *Montgomeryshire Worthies* p. 270 ; *Bye-gones*, 1884–85, p. 38 ; *Mont. Coll.*, XXI, p. 84, XXXVI, p. 140, XXXVII, p. 22.

[3] *H.L.W.* (1840, XXIV), pp. 553, 563 ; Horsfall–Turner : *loc. cit.* Nicholson (*Camb. Trav. Guide*, 1840, p. 483) says that 1,500 pieces were sent fortnightly to Newtown.

market had sunk into insignificance again.[1] Wrexham was another mart, but at its great March fairs Welsh woollens were soon to be overshadowed by Manchester, Leeds and Bradford wares.[2] Dolgelley, like Wrexham, was a market town of ancient standing : a traveller in 1775 found it "no despicable little Town for these parts,"[3] for it was rising into prominence as a depôt for the "strong cloth" of Merioneth—though sufficient quantities were still sent direct to Shrewsbury, at the very end of the century, to make it worth while to use a waggon (sometimes with a cart as well) for conveyance, in place of the old pack animals.[4]

Frequently, however, the manufactures were bought direct from loom or *pandy*, even in advance of manufacture, by factors of the Shrewsbury or Liverpool wholesalers. These factors (or "Welsh drapers," as they were called) were coming to play an increasingly important part in the organization of the industry. They usually took up their residence in Wales,[5] travelled from house to house, from farm to farm, from *pandy* to *pandy*, to purchase webs or flannels, and transmitted them to Shrewsbury or Welshpool market, or else direct to those who commissioned them. They demanded a fixed percentage on all transactions, and aimed at disposing of their stock wholesale for ready cash, charging higher rates for retail dealings. With this ready cash they were prepared to make advances to help struggling weavers to buy materials, and this put them in a position to superintend the finishing of the goods for market. The factor was thus well on the way towards becoming a manufacturer in the modern sense, while the "manufacturer" of the old order was sinking into a wage labourer, working by the piece. The Blackwell Hall factors played the same rôle in the woollen industries

[1] Defoe : *Tour* (second ed., 1742), II, p. 342 ; Bingley : *North Wales* (third ed., 1839), p. 16.

[2] Pigot's *Directory* (1828–29), p. 1174 ; Lewis : *Top. Dict.*

[3] Sir Thos. Cullum (*Y Cymmrodor*, XXXVIII, p. 57) ; but contrast Christopher Sykes' "poor miserable town" of 1796 (*Arch. Camb.* 1924, p. 15).

[4] Morris : *Cantref Meirionydd*, p. 115.

[5] A "web merchant" is mentioned among the inhabitants of Bala in Barfoot and Wilkes' *Directory*, II, pp. 264–5 (*c.* 1790).

of the West of England, and the Lancashire cotton industry was going through a similar phase of development.[1] The factors were obviously a novelty when Aikin described them in 1797. He was suspicious of them, dismissing them contemptuously as "a sort of jobbers or forestallers," hinting that their wholesale transactions enabled them to "get rid of many ordinary and damaged articles," and blaming them for the recent rise in the price of flannel. Davies thought differently. He repudiated the "odious name of forestallers" as belonging to a period "before the principles and theory of trade were well understood," and believed the factors to be "a most useful set of men," who "give general satisfaction to the country"; for not only did they "save the indigent manufacturer the trouble, loss of time and expense of coming from 10 to 15 miles to market, for the sake of selling only one piece," but through their means the long and evil reign of monopoly might be brought to an end, and "a more regular and diffusive division of the profit" effected. Even Aikin was of opinion that "owing to the increased demand for Welsh woollens, and the competition between the several drapers in Shrewsbury, the trade is greatly in favour of the Welsh."

This may be doubted. Not only did the wholesale buyer demand his recognized commission of ten per cent, but evidence taken as much as forty years later goes to show that, by virtue of the waiting power which capital can give, he still drove a hard bargain and not always an honest one. The frauds in measurement of which the Drapers' Company used to be accused, and which Davies thought had disappeared with the passing of their monopoly, remained a subject of frequent complaint from the Welsh weavers until, after the removal of the chief market to Newtown, an official measurer and a patent measuring machine were set up there.[2] Reaction from monopoly, indeed, was in danger of landing the trade in the chaos of extreme individualism. Aikin's informant found it difficult to get exact particulars on account of

[1] Evans: *Tour*, p. 88; *cf*. Chapman, S. J.: *Lancashire Cotton Industry* (1904), pp. 63–5, and Daniels, G. W.: *Early English Cotton Industry* (1920), chap. II.
[2] *H.L.W.* pp. 553-5; *cf*. Davies, p. 395.

"the jealousy and shyness of those concerned in the trade . . . Though each draper may know the proportion exported of his own goods, yet no one is acquainted with what his neighbour exports." Further obstacles to advancement were

> . . . the irregular confused manner in which the transactions between the merchant and the manufacturer are conducted, the want of cloth-halls, as in Yorkshire, where to deposit the goods ; of general meetings for those engaged in the business, for the regulation of its concerns ; of accurate public accounts ; and the scarcity of factories, and regular markets.

It was this excessive individualism, combined with the outbreak of war, that brought to an untimely end the interesting experiment of a depôt for export at Barmouth. Pennant tells us that before the American War £40,000 worth of web or flannel was exported from Barmouth to the continent in a single year, together with £10,000 worth of stockings. The trade revived when peace was restored, and during the years 1789–92 the sales from Barmouth warehouse reached an annual average of between 2,500 and 3,000 pieces—nearly 250,000 yards.[1] In 1793, when the war with France began, only 810 pieces were shipped, and in the following year even these exports vanished, and the trade expired. The vessels employed, Davies tells us, had been "from 80 to 100 tons burden, taking upon an average about 300 webs each over a ballast of slate or paving stones." But the Barmouth depôt never recovered from the War. Co-operation proved no easier to establish among weavers and factors then than among farmers to-day. What chance had the ventures of a community where "almost every weaver is a master and . . . no regular entries are kept," against the organized export trade of the English capitalists ?[2]

The War was a severe handicap all round for the budding Welsh woollen industry. It raised the price of wool and other raw materials by about a third, diminished the supply of labour, and cut Wales off from its overseas markets. Even the coastwise traffic to London gave

[1] Lewis (*Top. Dict.*, 1833, under *Dolgelley*) gives 25,000, but this is clearly a slip ; his own data (derived from Davies) contradict the total (*cf. Cantref Meirionydd*, p. 115).
[2] Pennant : *Tours*, II, p. 253.

place to land transport, which cost five times as much—£1 per web instead of 4s.[1] We read of bankruptcies among flannel manufacturers at Newtown in 1798, 1799, 1809, and 1811, at Llanbrynmair in 1810, at Llanidloes in 1811, at Welshpool in 1812, at Pant in 1815.[2] In the general depression of trade after 1815, Merioneth wool was actually sent off to the Yorkshire clothiers, for lack of means to manufacture it at home.[3] But both Aikin and Davies were clear that the set-back was only a temporary one. Davies believed that the drop in sales was already compensated by the higher prices yielded.

> The seeds of opulence [he declares] seem to have taken root in the land, and the baneful effects of imposition and disappointment begin to disappear . . . When peace shall have restored the olive-branch to Britain, our woollen trade will become more brisk than ever. Besides the London market by sea, the manufacturers may find others in the interior of England ; and send their webs and flannels, with a reduction in the expense of carriage by means of the Montgomeryshire Canal, to any quarter, to meet clothiers from the North, the West, or even drapers from Germany, Russia, or America.

All that was needed, in the opinion of both these friendly critics, was the setting up of machinery and factories. If, at a time when man-power was already depleted by the calls of the army, the earnings of weavers were not sufficient to induce even the underpaid farm hand to make it his sole livelihood, the obvious remedy lay in machines which a child could work ; there need no longer then be two or three hundred poor children "without employ" in a district like Dolgelley. Factories would also break down the middleman's control, and attract capital and organizing ability into the processes of manufacture. "With the general adoption of machinery," Aikin prophesies,

> the manufacturers will become large capitalists, as is already the case in Lancashire and Yorkshire ; and the influx of money will enable the farmers to improve their breed of

[1] *Salop. Journ.*, March 27, 1805 ; *N. W. Gaz.*, Feb. 16, 1809 ; Evans : *Tour*, pp. 113–4, *Beauties*, p. 852.
[2] *Salop. Journ.*, Dec. 26, 1798, Aug. 21, 1799 ; *N. W. Gaz.*, March 23, 1809, Oct. 18, 1810, Oct. 24, 1811, Aug. 6, 1812, July 20, 1815.
[3] *Report on Land* (1896), App. A, p. 22.

sheep . . . ; the manufacturers, become rich, will not abandon to the English drapers the advantages of preparing their rough goods for the foreign and domestic markets ; nor to the London and Liverpool merchants, the profits of exporting them . . . ; and thus the whole profits of an extensive national concern will circulate through, and invigorate every part of the province where it originates.

A few tentative experiments in this direction had already been made. The earliest references to machinery in North Wales are provokingly vague, but it is clear that until the closing years of the eighteenth century fulling was the only process not performed solely by hand. At the outbreak of the French War—more than a quarter of a century after James Hargreaves' invention, and almost a decade after it had come into general use in the English woollen industry—spinning was still done on wheels everywhere save in a few Montgomeryshire towns, where 24-spindle jennies had been adopted ; and that at a time when in England the jenny itself was being rapidly ousted by the water-frame. The latter, in turn, was superseded in England before it reached Wales at all, and the mule did not establish itself here for sixty years after Crompton's invention of 1779.[1]

For carding the wool, an invention locally known as *cribau Robin* ("Robin's combs"—named after the in-ventor) was in use in Montgomeryshire towards the end of the eighteenth century. Like the jenny, it was simply an improved hand device, requiring no mechanical power There is also a local tradition (undated) of how a carpenter named John Jerman (or Jarman) pirated a carding machine by getting employment in an English factory and committing the plans to memory ; and then, having sold his copy to pay his way back to Wales, introduced the new machine into factories at Newtown and in Merioneth. The description is vague, but it is possible that the pirated plans were those of Arkwright's patent of 1775.[2] There were precedents going back to the Middle Ages for the use

[1] Kay : *Agriculture of N. Wales : Montgomeryshire*, p. 22 ; *cf.* Mantoux : *Industrial Revolution*, p. 270, Lipson : *English Woollen and Worsted Industries*, p. 184.

[2] *Mont. Coll.*, V, pp. 34–5 ; *Bye-gones*, 1886, p. 73 ; *Cantref Merionydd*, pp. 127–8. We have no record of the date of the introduction of Kay's fly-shuttle into Wales.

of Welsh water power in the service of industry, but the practice had extended so widely of late that in towns like Wrexham and Holywell water wheels were now in use for driving almost every conceivable type of machinery : wire mills, forges and blast furnaces, paper mills,[1] even snuff mills ;[2] and the setting up of a cotton mill at Holywell in 1777[3] gave a still more direct incentive to woollen manufacturers. Ten years after this, there appeared in a Manchester newspaper an advertisement (already referred to in another connection) of a type which was soon to become very familiar. It was a notice "to cotton and other manufacturers" of a mill to be let at Ruthin, of which the proprietor (who, it has been suggested, may have been "fired by the example of Holywell") offered to "advance any sum not exceeding £200 towards fitting up the buildings for the purpose required."[4]

Within two years of the publication of this advertisement the first woollen mill in North Wales appeared near Meifod in Montgomeryshire—a few yards from the ancient iron forge of the Lloyds of Dolobran.[5] Aikin was told that it was "a parish concern" ; Davies believed that at one time it employed 100 weavers—whether on the spot or as outworkers is not clear. In 1807, the manufactory, together with fulling mills and workmen's houses, was offered to be let. It had then two water wheels and "a set of orderly manufacturers," whom the proprietors (owners also of the adjoining forge, which went with it)

[1] On Wrexham paper mills *see* p. 26 (*supra*), and *cf.* Palmer : *Parish Church*, pp. 112 *n*, 114 *n*, *Old Parish of Wrexham*, p. 6. For Holywell *see Cal. of Coleman Documents*, No. 1351, Defoe : *Tour* (1778 ed.), II, pp. 329–30. The industry spread to Caerwys in 1786 (*Bye-gones*, 1893–94, p. 389), and to Hope, Llanrwst, Chirk, and Llanrûg during the Napoleonic Wars (*N. W. Gaz.*, Jan. 17, Nov. 14. 1811, Dec. 1, 1814 ; Evans : *Beauties*, pp. 573, 343).

[2] At Holywell about 1764 (*Chester Chron.*, Sept. 6, 1776) ; at Gresford (near Wrexham) by 1816 (*id.*, Sept. 20, 1816) ; near Machynlleth, *c.* 1795 (*Salop. Journ.*, June 3, 1795). This last was set up by manufacturers from Amlwch, which, with Llannerch y medd, was long famous for snuff-making (*Bye-gones*, 1889–90, p. 289 ; *Rept. on Land*, 1896, p. 45).

[3] *Infra*. p. 283.

[4] *Manchester Mercury*, Feb. 6, 1787 ; *cf. supra*, p. 35.

[5] *Supra*, p. 19 ; not to be confused with another Dolobran— in Mallwyd parish, Merioneth—which was also for many years the seat of a flourishing woollen manufacture (*Bye-gones*, 1874, p. 62).

were willing to keep on till the premises were taken over. The factory seems to have been acquired by a firm of Welshpool bankers, Messrs. Jones & Mytton, who employed a "great number" of men there for a few years, but went bankrupt about the time of Waterloo.[1]

Dolobran was in the flannel district, but there soon followed a factory which served the web industry. It was set up at Machynlleth, about 1794, by Mr. Arthur Williams, timber merchant, ironfounder and woollen manufacturer. Machynlleth had been a seat of the web manufacture for forty years or more ; Aikin thought it had "a more flourishing appearance than any place we have yet seen in Wales," and a little later Edward Pugh, the artist, commented on the "spirit of building" displayed by its inhabitants. But the factory was a small affair, employing only twenty weavers at the end of the century, and Williams himself (if we may trust the precarious evidence of subscription lists) can have been no very substantial capitalist, for half-a-crown was all he could spare towards the local fund for soldiers' clothing.[2]

The example set by these pioneer establishments was soon taken up, not only in Montgomeryshire, but all over the country, and the trade depression of the later war years did not seriously check the movement.

> Carding and spinning machines [Davies adds in a footnote of about 1809] continue to be erected in the most distant parts from the weaving districts, even in Caernarvonshire and Anglesey. Yorkshire manufacturers of carding machinery go about regularly every three months to canvass fresh orders.[3]

[1] *Chester Chron.*, May 8, 1807 ; Pugh : *Camb. Dep.*, p. 253.
[2] Pococke : *Travels*, II, p. 180 ; Kay : *Agriculture of N. Wales* : *Montgomeryshire*, p. 22 ; Barfoot and Wilkes' *Directory* III, p. 867 ; Aikin, pp. 38, 71 ; *Camb. Dep.*, p. 221.
[3] Pp. 390–1 ; *cf.* advt. from Halifax card manufacturer in *N. W. Gaz.*, Dec. 20, 1810.

B. THE EARLY FACTORY AGE (1797–1837).

It was during the forty years between Aikin's tour and Queen Victoria's accession that woollen factories spread most rapidly in North Wales. Suitable premises for woollen factories became a common subject of advertisements in the local press.[1] Denbighshire, Flintshire and Anglesey all had their first factories before the Peninsular War began. In Anglesey there was a carding mill, with dye house and fulling mill, at Bodedern. In Flintshire factories had been built at Bodfari and (probably) Ysceifiog, on the Wheeler ; in Denbighshire at Llanarmon, on the Ceiriog. By the 'twenties the water power of the Dee at Llangollen was being used for manufacturing both cotton and flannel.[2] There were three woollen mills there in 1837, employing 84 hands, and providing work for 56 handlooms ; but although the employment of children "at a very tender age" was hindering education, the quantity of flannel made was still "trifling." By this time Denbighshire had five other water-worked mills : one on the Dee, two on the Ceiriog, and two on tributaries of the Severn, near the Montgomeryshire border ; between them they employed 112 hands. A very imperfect list published a year or two earlier gives three woollen mills for Flintshire, and for Anglesey seven carding mills and six other woollen mills.[3]

In Caernarvonshire, where it was necessary to produce yarn in ever-increasing quantities to meet the demands of the Merioneth web industry, several mills were put up during and immediately after the War. The most interesting, and probably the first, was built by W. A. Madocks, about 1800, to enrich his new village of Tremadoc. He let it to two partners, one of whom was Gwyllym Lloyd Wardle, of Hartsheath in Flintshire, M.P. for Okehampton in Devonshire, and owner (through his wife) of considerable properties in Caernarvonshire. Colonel Wardle had just

[1] E.g. *Shrewsbury Chron.*, Dec. 21, 1803 (Garthbeibio), April 25, 1823 ; *N. W. Gaz.*, May 1, 1808 (Beddgelert), April 25, 1811 (Maentwrog).

[2] *N. W. Gaz.*, May 12, 1808 ; Lewis : *Top. Dict.*, under *Bodedern;* Fenton : *Tours*, pp. 134, 140 ; *Chester Chron.*, June 6, 1806 ; Telford's Report to Holyhead Road Commissioners, May 6, 1824, p. 32 ; *infra*, p. 289.

[3] *Parl. Pap.*, 1839, XLII ; 1840, XXIV, p. 569 ; 1836, XLV, No. 138, pp. 51 ff.

returned from active service with Sir Watkin's militia ; he was soon to be brought more prominently before the public eye by his intrigues with the notorious Mrs. Clarke (the Duke of York's discarded mistress), who joined with him in accusing the Duke of serious misconduct as Commander-in-Chief—an accusation which, despite the enthusiastic backing of his Welsh neighbours, Wardle was unable to substantiate to the satisfaction of Parliament, though it led to the Duke's resignation.[1]   But local tradition brings charges quite as damaging against Wardle himself. Not content with manufacturing yarn for Merioneth, he and his partners (so the story runs) had sixty looms at work in the factory, and on these they produced army cloth which they used to smuggle in boats from Portmadoc to Boney's men, just as Wilkinson was (more credibly) accused of supplying them with guns. It is, of course, a familiar type of war-time rumour ; and men like Wilkinson, Wardle, and Madocks himself—all enthusiastic Foxites—were too outspoken in their criticisms of the Ministry and the War to escape suspicion when men were hunting for the "hidden hand."

When the factory was offered for sale in 1810 (at a price "not to exceed £3,500") it was described as capable of producing 30 "ends" a week of "mixed and medley cloth, kerseymeres, woollen cords, coatings, flannels and woollen goods of every description," and claimed to be "the only manufactory for cloth in the whole Principality." In addition to the handlooms, it had water-worked machinery, presumably for carding, and it continued to turn out coarse army cloth for some years after the War was over.[2]   Before Waterloo, it had found imitators (on a smaller scale) in various parts of the county—for example at Penmachno, Llanrûg, Llanwnda, and Tryfan.[3]   All of them were carding mills, but some contained a few handlooms and jennies, and some also did fulling and dyeing. The jenny was introduced at Llanrûg and Llanwnda before 1812,

---

[1] N. W. Gaz., April 13, Dec. 28, 1809 ; D.N.B.

[2] N. W. Gaz., May 26, 1808, Oct. 18, 1810, May 25, 1815 ; Camb. Trav. Guide (1808), p. 261 ; Camb. Dep., p. 149 ; Lewis : Top. Dict., under Tremadoc ; Y Gestiana, pp. 176-7.

[3] N. W. Gaz., July 25, 1811, March 10, 1814, Oct. 30, 1817 ; Evans : Beauties, p. 343. There are extant two drawings of the Penmachno mill made by George Nicholson in 1809.

and at Dolgarrog (a rather bigger concern, which performed every operation on the spot) by 1818. In the Tryfan factory three "frames" (presumably Arkwright's patent of 1769) had by 1826 been substituted for the three wheels on which all the spinning was done in 1814.[1]

Merioneth, amply fed with yarn by the Caernarvonshire mills, had few of its own, and was thought by travellers in the early nineteenth century to harbour a prejudice against machinery.[2] Dolgelley, long the chief local market, was now becoming also the chief manufacturing centre—especially as the Machynlleth mills came to abandon webs for flannel. Water-driven machinery seems to have been adopted there early in the nineteenth century, and by 1838 there were eight mills, employing 55 hands. The number of independent manufacturers, given as 8 in a directory of 1828, had now risen to 21, each employing from 2 to 13 workpeople. In all, including those outside the factories, the employees at Dolgelley numbered 137, and the output for the preceding two years was estimated at 6,153 "ends."[3]

There were seventeen other water-driven factories in the county, and three lying idle. Three were at Towyn, two at Tal-y-llyn (some ten miles north-eastwards), four on the outskirts of Machynlleth, and three more on the Montgomeryshire border ; all these looked to Machynlleth rather than Dolgelley as their centre, many sending goods in the rough to be finished there. Of the remainder, one (possibly built before 1808)[4] lay south of Harlech, three were in the north-western part of the county, and the last, which had been going since the eighteenth century, was at Corwen—an outpost of the Denbighshire "small cloth" area.[5] Two carding mills at Bala, which had thrown so many old people out of work as to double the rates in thirty years, seem to be ignored in the Parliamentary return from which these statistics are taken.[6] Most of the mills were on a very tiny scale, employing from

---

[1] *Shrewsbury Chron.*, March 20, 1818 ; *N. W. Gaz.*, April 27, 1826.
[2] Mavor : *Tour*, p. 85.
[3] *Cantref Meirionydd*, p. 115 ; *Parl. Pap.*, 1839, XLII, 1840, XXIV, pp. 567–8.
[4] Fenton : *Tours*, p. 118.
[5] Evans : *Tour*, p. 296.
[6] *N. W. Gaz.*, Oct. 23, 1823 ; *M. C. R.* (1837–38, XXXV), p. 229.

one to four hands ; it is significant that, although Merioneth had three times as many mills as Denbighshire, the total number employed in them was considerably smaller. Only in districts like Dolgelley and Towyn, and on the Montgomeryshire border, did the average mill employ as many as seven hands.

It was in the Montgomeryshire flannel industry that machinery and factories made the most rapid progress. Davies estimated that there were about forty carding engines in the county in 1799 ; many of these, however, must have been worked at home by hand, or else—like some of the Lancashire carding engines in the first half of the nineteenth century[1]—by horses ; for the only factories he mentions (apart from those at Dolobran and Machynlleth) are "several" at Newtown, and one each at Berriew and Welshpool. Newtown, indeed, was rapidly changing its character. Up to the middle of the eighteenth century, it had no importance except as a market for corn ; and even when the youthful Robert Owen went off to seek his fortune in England in 1781, what he left behind him was "a very small market town, not containing more than one thousand inhabitants,. . . with . . . no manufactures, except a few flannel looms."[2]   In 1790 the inhabitants included one weaver, one weaver and flannel manufacturer, one cardmaker and one woolstapler, of sufficient standing to be mentioned in a trade directory. Seven years later, Aikin found "infant factories" there, and other contemporary travellers described the manufactures as "extensive" in scale, "masterly" in methods, and "increasing every day."[3]

The rapid advance of machinery at Newtown, and the concentration of the industry in factories, owed much to the efforts of the Rev. G. A. Evors,[4] a very unclerical

[1] Chapman : *Lancashire Cotton Industry*, p. 61.
[2] Pococke : *Travels*, II, p. 19 ; Owen : *Life*, by Himself, p. 2 ; *Bye-gones*, 1886, pp. 82–6.   Actually the population of Newtown did not reach a thousand till the nineteenth century.
[3] Barfoot and Wilkes' *Directory*, IV, pp. 68–70 ; Evans : *Tour*, p. 31 ; Fenton : *Tours*, p. 35.
[4] *See* Rowlands, B. B. : *History of Newtown* (Newtown, 1914), pp. 89 ff. ; *Shrewsbury Chron.*, July 17, 1818 ; *N. W. Gaz.*, March 3, 1825 ; *Bye-gones*, 1891–2, p. 45 ; 1911–12, p. 160 ; *Camb. Quart. Mag.*, III, p. 396.   The name appears variously as Evors, Evars, Evers, and in one place (*H.L.W.*, p. 557) as Evans.

cleric who came to occupy Newtown Hall about 1806, leaving his South Wales parish in charge of a curate. He was long the only resident magistrate in Newtown, where for about forty years he was able to lord it like a petty benevolent despot, though from time to time his policy of "thorough" raised such a storm against him that he had to remember the duties of his cloth, and bury himself in his parish till it had blown over. One of the earliest things remembered about him was that he forced a jenny spinner (the first in Newtown), who had rented part of the Hall as a workshop, to seek more suitable quarters : and Evors himself took a leading part in supplying such quarters. Throughout the district, the makeshift structures which had hitherto housed the industry gave place to commodious factories ; rows of cottages sprang into existence beside them, and the price of building land went up by leaps and bounds. Evors apparently did not work the factories he built, but let them out to manufacturers.[1] For example, the Tudor mill which went by the picturesque name of "Byander," after having been put into repair by Evors, was rented by an *entrepreneur* named John Williams, who, when he went bankrupt in 1826, had two carding engines, a large scribbler, and three slubbing jacks in operation there, and in addition worked two other factories in the neighbourhood and owned a quantity of farming stock.[2]

Another local man—William Tilsley—built in 1809, or earlier, a carding mill at Milford (a little outside the town), where disputes about water power and trespass landed him, some years later, in a lawsuit with the pugnacious Mr. Evors. Tilsley, who belonged to a county family, went in for banking as well as manufacture, and the failure of his bank in 1831 forced him to dispose of his mills, which then included—in addition to the original Milford factory ("with room for ten carding engines") and fulling mill—a second and more recently-built flannel mill

[1] Carlisle : *Top. Dict.* ; *Shrewsbury Chron.*, June 4, 1824. One of the Newtown factories was known as "Mr. Evors' factory" (*id.*, Dec. 31, 1819), but we find Evors in 1836 acting as magistrate in a case under the Factory Act (*Parl. Pap.*, 1837, L, p. 91), which would have been illegal for a manufacturer.

[2] *Mont. Coll.*, XVIII, pp. 65–80, XXIV, pp. 172–5 ; *N. W. Gaz.*, Oct. 12, 1826 ; *Shrewsbury Chron.*, Nov. 3, 1826.

nearer the town.   Both were then in the occupation of
his tenants.[1]

The extension of the Montgomeryshire canal to Newtown
in 1821 helped to confirm its position as the chief centre
of the flannel industry.   Trade directories of 1823 and
1828 show respectively 54 and 66 flannel manufacturers,
instead of the two of 1790.[2]   According to Lewis' *Topographical Dictionary* of 1833, there were then 50 factories
in the town and neighbourhood, working 50,000 spindles,
50 carding machines, and 1,200 looms, turning out 250
pieces (of 160 yards each) every week, and employing
3,000 workmen ;   but this is absurdly exaggerated, unless
by "neighbourhood" Lewis means the whole county.   In
the town itself, population had grown (according to the
Census figures) from under 1,000 in 1801 to 2,000 in 1811,
3,500 in 1821, and 4,500 in 1831, but this last figure was
subsequently questioned, and the 1841 estimate was well
below 4,000 again.   In 1838 it contained six factories,
employing 192 hands ;   including outworkers, there were
672 employees in all, 75 "manufacturers," and 700 looms.
Some employers had only a couple of looms and as many
men to work them ;   others could claim thirty or more
of each.   These figures include the new and rapidly-
growing suburb of Pen y gloddfa (in the parish of Llanllwchaiarn), which contained the biggest factories, and
a population almost half as big as that of the town proper ;
factories had also spread into the adjoining parishes of
Mochdre (Moughtrey) and Llandyssil.[3]

It was small enough foundation for a claim to be called
"the Leeds of Wales" ;   for Leeds in the 'thirties had

---

[1] *Cal. of Coleman Documents*, Nos. 1146–8 ;   *Shrewsbury Chron.*,
Sept, 23, 1831.

[2] *Mont. Worthies*, p. 267 ; Pigot's *Directory* (1828–29),pp. 1169–70.

[3] *Parl. Pap.*, 1839, XLII ; 1840, XXIV, p. 562.   The figures of
employment for the three Pen y gloddfa factories in the third
edition of Lewis' *Top. Dict.* (1843, II, p. 77)—606, 66, and 48
respectively—must surely include outworkers, unless the increase
during the preceding five years was quite phenomenal.   The very
unsatisfactory statistics of employment given in the 1841 Census
only allow 382 woollen workers, all told, for Newtown—but this
again excludes Pen y gloddfa.

already nearly 10,000 inhabitants engaged in manufacture;[1]
yet such was the rate of progress during these transitional
years that a minor bard, revisiting the town after nine
years' absence, found it almost unrecognizable, and was
moved to express his wonderment in stumbling English
verse :

New Bank, New Church, New Halls of great renown,
New House, new Flannel, new gas in brave Newtown . . . ;

who could tell how much further the transformation might
go ?[2]

At the time when the development of factories began,
however, Llanidloes bade fair to be a close rival to Newtown.   An older centre of the industry, it was little if
any later in adopting machinery.   Neither Aikin nor Davies,
it is true, says anything about a factory there ; but by
1810 there were two large establishments, both of a few years'
standing.   The first—Glanclywedog factory—arose from
the nucleus of a fulling mill and dye works which had been
adapted from an old corn mill, about 1790, by one William
Hunt.   His son-in-law, Edward Ingram, went into partnership with an Englishman named Charles Cole, who migrated
to the region in 1797, and they put up machinery
for carding and slubbing.   This was not the first carding
engine in Llanidloes, but probably the first to be successfully
worked by mechanical power.[3]   In 1813 during the
stoppage of cash payments, copper tokens were issued to
pay the workmen at Glanclywedog.[4]   Eight years later
Cole died ; a memorial tablet in Llanidloes Church recites
how, during a twenty-four years' residence, "by his active
exertions he encouraged and extended the manufactures
of the place, and by his liberality he provided employment
for the industrious poor, to whom he was a kind and
constant benefactor."   After his death, Ingram sold the
premises (though Mrs. Cole appears to have retained
an interest in the business), and they were worked for 34

[1] Ure, A. : *Philosophy of Manufactures*, p. 76.
[2] Robyn Ddu Eryri : *An Address to Newtown, Montgomeryshire*
(Oct. 3, 1833), printed in *Bye-gones*, 1901–02, pp. 134–5. (Sad
doggerel, but illustrates well the optimism of the 'thirties.)
[3] Evans : *Beauties*, p. 111 *n* ; *Mont. Coll.*, V, pp. 34–7 ; *N. W.
Gaz.*, March 23, 1815.
[4] Specimen in Powysland Museum, Welshpool (*see Mont. Coll.*,
IV, p. xxxi).

years by David Davies, who became one of the leading manufacturers of the town.[1]   The second, which ultimately came to be known as the Glynhafren factory, and was described in 1810 as "a very large concern," seems to have been built about the same time, by the firm of Herbert and Jones (later Herbert and Britton—Britton being a substantial capitalist from Chester).   The partners, who also kept a bank in the town, went bankrupt in 1813, and had to dispose of their businesses.[2]

The building of factories went on apace during the ensuing years, till in 1838 there were six in the town, employing 180 hands.   One had been built some time after 1806, another in 1823, another in 1834 ; three more were added in the years 1838–40, and another couple in 1850–52. But the bulk of the weaving, as late as 1838, was still done at home.   It was estimated in that year that there were 815 handlooms in the parish, worked by 795 weavers, and making over 8,000 pieces in the year.   These were distributed among 25 manufacturers (excluding the very smallest), each owning between 10 and 60 looms and employing between 10 and 60 journeymen and apprentices.[3] Llanidloes was steadily increasing in population, but at a gentler pace than Newtown, which had outstripped the whole parish of Llanidloes (an exceptionally extensive one) by 1821, though at the beginning of the century it was not half as populous as its rival.   Newtown, by virtue of superior machinery, was turning out goods of far finer texture, selling at higher prices and affording higher wages, and its advantages in situation made it a distributing centre for the whole county at a time when all the flannel sold at Llanidloes market was made within the parish itself.[4]

[1] Shrewsbury Chron., May 18, 1821, Aug. 8, 1823, Aug. 6, 1824, Sept. 22, 1826.

[2] Evans : Beauties, p. 843 ; Shrewsbury Chron., May 14, Aug. 13, 1819, June 2, 1826, April 25, 1828 ; N. W. Chron., May 1, 1828.

[3] Parl. Pap., 1838, XLII ; 1840, XXIV, p. 565 ; Horsfall–Turner : op. cit., pp. 112–6 ; complete list (1872) with dates of foundation, in Mont. Coll., pp. 38–40.   The number of manufacturers is given in 1828 as 28 (Pigot's Directory, p. 1163).   The Census for 1841 gives 343 weavers, 42 flannel manufacturers, and 93 others engaged in the woollen industry.

[4] Lewis : Top. Dict., under Llanidloes and Newtown; H.L.W., pp. 555, 563.

Next to Newtown and Llanidloes, the most important centres were Machynlleth, Llanbrynmair and Welshpool. Machynlleth served as a sort of metropolis to a district extending right up the Dovey Valley, and including the south-eastern parts of Merioneth. The weaving was all done at home, and out-weavers for Machynlleth factories were to be found as far up the river as Dinas Mawddwy. Carding and spinning, on the other hand, had been so completely concentrated in the factories that by 1834 no work was left for women or children in the neighbouring parish of Llanwrin, which had no factories.[1] Flannels had taken the place of webs as the staple commodity of this district by 1828; Machynlleth itself had then fifteen manufacturers, and it was believed that 200 pieces of 150 yards each were sent fortnightly to Welshpool (later Newtown) market. Ten years later there were seven mills in the town (each with its own *pandy*), two more in Penegoes parish, five at Darowen, one at Cemmes, and two at Mallwyd, as well as several on the Merioneth side of the border. But the opening of the Montgomeryshire canal diverted traffic to Newtown, and from the 'twenties Machynlleth was stagnant alike in manufactures and in population.[2] At Llanbrynmair, on a tributary of the Dovey, the first factory was built about 1803, and seven more followed during the next thirty or forty years. Up to the middle of the century, it has been reckoned, at least 1,000 pieces, to the value of £8,000, were manufactured in the parish every year, giving employment to 500 persons.[3] Welshpool had begun to manufacture woollens, as well as distributing them, before the end of the eighteenth century, and by 1828 it had twelve manufacturers and two mills—one for carding only, the other fully equipped for producing finished flannel. There was also a dressing mill belonging to one of the Welshpool manufacturers out at Pool Quay.[4]

[1] *P.L.R.* (1834, XXX), p. 655a.
[2] Pigot's *Directory*, 1828–29 ; Lewis : *Top. Dict.*, 1833 ana 1843 ; *H.L.W.*, p. 565 ; *Shrewsbury Chron.*, June 15, 1821.
[3] *Mont. Coll.*, XXI, pp. 82 ff.
[4] Davies, p. 393 ; Pigot's *Directory*, 1822–23 and 1828–29 ; *Shrewsbury Chron.*, June 4 and 11, 1824, Sept. 26, 1828. I can find no trace of the "dozen factories" referred to in Roberts and Owen's *Story of Montgomeryshire*, p. 82.

North and south of Welshpool, factory after factory sprang up alongside the Severn and its tributaries during these forty years. There was one on the Cain (at Llanfyllin), one on the Vyrnwy (the original Dolobran mill), three on the Banwy (two at Llanfair and one at Garthbeibio), three on the Rhiw (at Berriew, Llanllugan, and Gwallter Mechain's parish of Manafon) ;[1] and outlying factories of the Llanidloes district were to be found in the parishes of Llanwnog (on the Carno), Llandinam (on the Severn), Trefeglwys (on the Tarannon) and—southernmost of all—Llangurig (on the upper waters of the Wye). A list of 1836 gives 52 carding mills and slubbing mills for the whole county, employing 550 hands ; another, two years later, records 61 mills and 723 employees.[2] This makes an average of a little over 11 to each mill. In districts like Llanidloes or Newtown the average was about 36, though some factories (especially at the Pen y gloddfa end of Newtown) considerably exceeded this. Welshpool had an average of 15, Machynlleth of 7 ; and the smallest mill of all employed one boy.

It will be seen that the Montgomeryshire mills were on an appreciably larger scale than those of Merioneth ; but the average English woollen mill then had a staff of about 58, and a big worsted manufacturer in Yorkshire might have as many as 1,000 or 1,500 in his pay, if we include outworkers.[3] Of the numbers employed outside the factories in Montgomeryshire it is hard to form a satisfactory estimate. A traveller in 1798 thought there might be 3,000 in the industry altogether, of whom 500 would be weavers.[4] The Census of 1841 records 866 "woollen manufacturers," 350 "flannel manufacturers," 320 spinners, and 100 or so in other occupations connected with flannel making—about 2,500 in all. The corresponding figures for Merioneth are 186 weavers, 73 spinners, and 67 woollen manufacturers.

---

[1] *Salop. Journ.*, Nov. 29, 1797, Sept. 7, Dec. 21, 1803, March 13, 1805 ; *Shrewsbury Chron.*, May 4, 1827, Oct. 24, 1824.

[2] *Parl. Pap.*, 1838, XLV, pp. 53–4 ; 1839, XLII. But these lists must be incomplete, for the Factory Inspector's Returns for 1836 show 86 factories in Montgomeryshire (*id.*, 1837, L, No. 122, p. 201).

[3] Clapham : *Early Railway Age*, pp. 192–3.

[4] Evans : *Tour*, p. 33.

What was the nature of these early factories ? Their primary purpose was to house the new carding machinery, and for this almost anything with a roof and four walls was good enough—even a mud-walled shed, with holes for windows, such as the first factory at Llanbrynmair is said to have been.[1] This, however, only contained a hand-worked carding engine ; if water power was used, there must be a water-wheel. A new one cost £9 9s. or so,[2] but this expense could be saved if the manufacturer harnessed his machinery to the wheel of an existing corn mill[3] or *pandy*.[4] The common adoption of this plan accounts for the situation of so many factories on farm premises.[5]

When carding and fulling—the initial and final processes of manufacture—were combined in the same building, it was no great step to bring in the intermediate stages as well. The weavers who are mentioned in connection with the Dolobran and Machynlleth mills may have been outworkers, but from early in the nineteenth century the practice of collecting both weavers and spinners into the factories (which had been adopted in the Lancashire cotton industry shortly before the French Revolution)[6] was gradually extending to the woollen mills of Wales. Sometimes the factory owner would simply provide "suitable rooms for spinning and weaving" ;[7] sometimes he would supply looms himself. The 60 looms attributed to the Tremadoc factory in 1800 are an early example, and, if the tradition is to be trusted, they indicate an unusually extensive scale of production for the time. Nineteen years later the Glynhafren factory, at Llanidloes, had only 20 (4 broad and 16 narrow) ; for a tiny concern like that at Tryfan—even after the introduction of spinning frames—3 were

---

[1] *Mont. Coll.*, XXI, pp. 82–3.

[2] *Y Cymmrodor*, XXXVII, p. 41 (Montgomeryshire, 1782).

[3] E.g. Penmachno (1811), Welshpool and Llanfair (1824) ; *cf.* advt. in *N. W. Gaz.*, Jan. 5, 1808 (disused copper mill as factory site).

[4] E.g. Glanclywedog (Llanidloes) and Garthbeibio (*supra*) ; Sycharth (*Bye-gones*, 1905–06, p. 321).

[5] E.g. advts. in *N.W. Gaz.*, June 9, 1808 (Caernarvonshire), Feb. 7, 1811 (Maentwrog), Oct. 23, 1823 (Bala).

[6] Unwin, Hulme, and Taylor : *Samuel Oldknow and the Arkwrights*, p. 110.

[7] *Shrewsbury Chron.*, May 4, 1827.

enough. With the loom came the jenny, which (in the mills at least) had quite ousted the spinning wheel before Queen Victoria's accession. In 1805 a mill at Llanfyllin had 5 jennies (of 50 to 60 spindles each) working alongside 10 looms ; and the same number (with 60 to 80 spindles) sufficed to feed a dozen looms in the larger of the Welshpool factories, twenty-five years later.

Weaving, and (for the most part) spinning, were still handicraft operations, even in the factories ; but there was other machinery besides the carding engine which could be driven by the water wheel : for example, the willow, or willy (for cleansing and disentangling the wool)[1] and the scribbler (for separating the fibres before carding).[2] The slubbing jack (for twisting the carded wool into a loose rope, ready for spinning)[3] and its cousin, the billy,[4] were devices which could be worked either manually or mechanically, and both were also used in many of the Welsh factories for spinning coarse yarn.[5] A well-equipped factory would also have a warping mill (to prepare warp yarn for the loom),[6] a stock of sleys (to keep it in position), bobbins, spindles, reeds, spare cards, oil, logwood, alum, and other accessories.[7] Much of the machinery was now made locally. In 1828 there were seven machine makers at Newtown, one of whom appears to have been also a flannel manufacturer ; three generations of Davieses of Dôl goch (near Llanbrynmair) "supplied machinery to factories in every county of Wales" ; and each centre had its contingent

---

[1] Advertised in factories at Llanfyllin, 1805, Welshpool, 1824, Llandyssil, 1827, Milford, 1831. *See* Ure : *Philosophy of Manufactures*, pp. 160–5.

[2] Welshpool, 1824, Newtown, 1826 ; Ure, p. 165.

[3] Dolgarrog, 1818, Welshpool, 1824, Llandyssil, 1826, Newtown 1826, Llanfyllin, 1827.

[4] Llanrûg, 1833 (Lewis : *Top. Dict.*) ; Ure, pp. 171–81. There is no trace of slubbing by means of a second carding machine with "condenser" (patented 1835, described by Ure, pp. 181–3) before 1865 in North Wales.

[5] *Y Cymmrodor*, XXXIX, pp. 68 ff. ; National Museum of Wales : *Guide to the Collections of Welsh Byegones* (1929), pp. 46–7. (Descriptions by Mr. Iorwerth C. Peate, Assistant Keeper, of machinery taken from factory at Llanrhystyd, Cards.)

[6] Welshpool 1824.

[7] *Shrewsbury Chron.*, Nov. 3, 1826 (Pen y gloddfa).

of millwrights and makers of reeds, sleys, shuttles and bobbins.[1]

The early factory system left almost infinite scope for variety. The manufacturer might perform every process, from wo l-sorting to fulling and dyeing,[2] under his own roof, or he might confine himself to one or two,[3] getting the rest done on commission by domestic spinners and weavers (as at Machynlleth and Llanbrynmair), or taking his stuff to market in the form of yarn or undressed cloth, or sending it to Newtown or Machynlleth for finishing.[4] Again, he might grow his wool, or buy it, or use his customer's ; the latter might be either a humble cottager with his bagful of gleanings from the hedgerows or the sheep-shearing, an independent weaver or hand-knitter, or a farmer substantial enough to be the real *entrepreneur* for the whole transaction.[5] Some millowners simply took toll for their services, like the old-fashioned corn-miller or fuller ; others retained control over the finished product, as a few English fullers had done even in the Middle Ages, and as the typical corn-miller was tending to do after 1770.[6] Often enough the same mill worked in both capacities.[7] A man who owned more than one mill might distribute the different processes of production between them ;[8] but it was also common for a mill to be occupied

[1] Pigot's *Directory*, 1828–29 ;   *Mont. Coll.*, XXI, p. 85 ; *Y Cymmrodor*, *loc. cit.*

[2] In 1831 there were 48 dyers in Montgomeryshire, 12 in Merioneth, and 14 in the other four counties (Census).

[3] Pigot's *Directory*, 1828–29, shows at Newtown 6 who combine the functions of carder and weaver, and 1 who is carder, weaver, fuller and flannel draper ; at Llanidloes 1 carder and weaver, and 1 carder, weaver and fuller ; at Machynlleth 8 carders and flannel manufacturers and 1 who is also a wool merchant.

[4] *H.L.W.*, pp. 555, 565–7.

[5] *Bye-gones*, 1907–08, p. 2 ; 1895–96, p. 301 ; *H.L.W.*, pp. 567–8 ; *Y Cymmrodor*, XXXIX, pp. 74–6.

[6] Salzman: *English Industries of the Middle Ages*, p. 224 ; *infra*, p. 332. The fulling mill which did nothing but fulling for other manufacturers did not, of course, immediately disappear (e.g. *Salop. Journ.*, Oct. 7, 1813—Manafon).

[7] *H.L.W.*, p. 56.

[8] E.g. in 1826 John Williams of Newtown had one factory with jennies, hand-cards, and handlooms, and two others with carding engines. The Glynhafren mill (Llanidloes) and the Byander mill (Newtown) were worked jointly by one manufacturer in 1837 (*Parl. Pap.*, 1837, L, No. 97, p. 91).

jointly by half-a-dozen or more independent carders,[1] and at Newtown the long empty rooms one sees to-day running over a block of dwelling houses were once handloom "factories" occupied by a number of weavers, each working on his own account. Finally, millowners often built or acquired houses for their workmen,[2] and sometimes the whole staff boarded with their employer, receiving yearly wages, after the fashion of farm-servants.[3]

Many of these new "capitalists" must have been men of very slender resources, working from hand to mouth almost as completely as the handicraftsmen whom they superseded. When wool was cheap, humble operatives, who could not even write their names, but had to pay to get bills drawn out for them, would set up as masters—often only to sink back to their former status in a year or two.[4] For, after all, what capital did the small millowner need ? His machinery was the heaviest item ; but landlords, in the early days, were often prepared to help with that,[5] and machine makers like the Davieses of Dôl goch would give him long credits—perhaps even accept farm produce in part payment.[6] The rent of his mill was often as trivial as his wage-bill ;[7] and he did not need to hold heavy stocks, either of raw material or of the finished article[8] : indeed, both might remain throughout the property of his customer.

He could also evade the risks of business (and lose the attendant profits) by selling straight from loom or *pandy* to a factor. For machinery did not at once rob this class of

[1] In Pigot's *Directory*, 1828–9, 6 carders are named at the Byander mill, and 2 at the Mule factory, near Newtown. " Spacious rooms to let, with every convenience for machinery," are advertised at the Milford factory in 1827 ; in 1831 it is in the occupation of Richard Morris and 18 others (*Shrewsbury Chron.* April 6, 1827, Sept. 23, 1831). The mill at Darowen was let to 4 tenants in 1821 (*id.* June 15, 1821). Cf. Lipson : *op. cit.*, p. 196.

[2] E.g. Dolobran (1807), Dolgarrog (1818), Glynhafren (1819), Llanfyllin (1827).

[3] E.g. Price's factory, Towyn (*H.L.W.*, pp. 567–8) ; cf. Mantoux : *Industrial Revolution*, pp. 69–70.

[4] *H.L.W.*, pp. 558–9 ; cf. Mantoux, p. 60.

[5] *Supra*, p. 247.

[6] Through the kindness of Mr. I. C. Peate, I have read his transcripts from the ledgers of this firm, covering the years 1836 to 1893. Many machines are paid for in instalments of 10s. and upwards, spread over two or three years. A small account with

men of their importance in the industry. In the 'twenties and 'thirties we often find commission agents from London or Lancashire offering to introduce the Welsh manufacturer to wholesale firms, and "extensive Manchester houses" seeking commissions from "respectable manufacturers."[9] These middlemen were able to squeeze the bulk of the profit out of the smaller concerns by the simple process of making their purchases early in the year and not selling till summer, when the London buyers came into the market.[10] They even went about among the Newtown manufacturers; but ever since factories began, the more substantial millowners had been "wholesale venders of their own flannels, sending them to their dealers in different parts of the kingdom without the intervening charge of commission or agency,"[11] and advertising for their own

the Dolobran mill is marked in 1848 "settled by meat." The following are a few sample prices of machines :—

Machine.	Date.	Size.	Price.
Carding	1837	26-in. to 30-in. ..	£52
	1843		£42
Jack ..	1836–42	40 spindle	£11 11s. to £12 10s.
	1836–38	50 spindle	£13 to £14
	1838	100 spindle ..	£27
	1879	45 spindle	£10
Scribbler	1843	42-in.	£45
Willow ..	1836–64		£2 10s. to £5 5s.
	1864–84		£6 to £8 10s.
Tucker ..	1836–39		£5 to £6
	1885	(double speed) ..	£10
Condenser	1865–69		£4 to £6
	1887–88		£7 to £7 10s.
Loom ..	1879	to weave 1½ yards ..	£4
Jenny ..	1874	small	10s.

[7] Darowen (1821) £58 ; Llanfair (1824) £35 (newspaper advts.) ; Derwen yn Ial (1833) £7 (Lewis : *Top. Dict.*).

[8] *H.L.W.*, p. 555.

[9] E.g. *Shrewsbury Chron.*, July 23, 1824, Sept. 2, 1825, Aug. 24, 1827, Aug. 21, 1829, June 25, 1830, May 27, 1831.

[10] *H.L.W.*, pp. 553–6, 567.

[11] Davies, p. 394. The chief factory in Llanidloes sent most of its goods direct to London in 1810 (Evans : *Beauties*, p. 843). In 1828 Llanidloes had 7 flannel drapers, none of whom appears to have been a manufacturer ; Welshpool had 2, one of whom was a manufacturer (Pigot's *Directory*, 1828–29, pp. 1163, 1177).

travellers.[1]   One would naturally expect the factor, in the normal course of evolution, to become a millowner himself, but of this there is little evidence outside Dolgelley.[2] Where a factory was on such a scale as to require a greater outlay of capital than a small farmer or weaver could manage, the builder and owner was usually some local landlord (like Evors of Newtown, Tilsley of Milford, or Madocks of Tremadoc), mineowner (like Samuel Howell of Llanbrynmair) or quarryowner (as at one of the Llangollen factories in 1830),[3] or else an immigrant capitalist (like Britton or Cole of Llanidloes).

These immigrants, however, were exceptions.   In general, the woollen industry remained as distinctively Welsh as the slate industry.   Edward Pugh, the artist, writing early in the last century, singled out Montgomeryshire as a county where (in contrast with the mining districts) "manufactures and other commercial works belong to and are conducted by the natives."[4]   Most of the employees also were drawn from local sources.   The sudden increase of population in places like Newtown no doubt owed something to immigration from across the border, but over 89 per cent of the inhabitants of Montgomeryshire in 1841 had been born within the county—a higher proportion than in any other county except Anglesey.   Natural increase (enhanced by a diminishing death-rate), a drift into the towns from the neighbouring countryside, and the conversion of the part-time spinner or weaver into a whole-time mill hand, are sufficient to account for the manning of the factories, which thus entailed comparatively slight disturbance of population.   The time when it was hard to get labourers to desert the plough for the loom was far distant ; more typical of the new age was Borrow's Methodist guide at Llangollen, who (so he alleges) preferred weaving at five shillings a week to serving as a mountain shepherd for three times as much.[5]

Many of the factory hands, of course, were women and children.   Returns of woollen factories in Montgomeryshire

[1] E.g. *Shrewsbury Chron.*, Nov. 30, 1827.
[2] *H.L.W.*, p. 568.
[3] *Mont. Coll.*, XXI, pp. 83, 86–7 ; *Shrewsbury Chron.*, Aug. 13, 1830.
[4] *Camb. Dep.*, pp. 253, 443.
[5] *Wild Wales*, p. 60.

for 1836 and 1838 show that about a quarter of those
employed were females, and nearly three quarters were
under eighteen ; of these "young persons" more than a
quarter were twelve or thirteen years old. In the
Merioneth factories the proportion of female labour was
higher, that of juvenile labour lower. Spinning was
still essentially the women's branch of the industry. In
Montgomeryshire and Merioneth alike, half of those
recorded as spinners in the Census of 1841—both inside
and outside the factories—were women. Female. weavers
were more rare, especially in Merioneth. "Women rarely
weave," a Dolgelley witness told the Commissioners on
Handloom Weavers ; and the Census of 1841 shows that
only five per cent of the female employees in Merioneth
were weavers. In Montgomeryshire, where the Commissioners were informed by a Newtown manufacturer that
"women can weave as well as men," the proportion was
nearer 25 per cent ; in Newtown itself, a third of the
weavers were women and five per cent children.

The other operations performed by women were picking
the wool (which was still usually done at home) and winding the yarn. The younger children were employed in
duties like bobbin-making, the older ones in "willowing"
and in tending the scribbling and carding machines. The
slubbing jack, and generally the loom, were the men's
preserve ; but it was stated that a child of 13 could learn
to weave in nine months, and already there were complaints by adult workers that the competition of child-
labour was lowering their wages. Most of the children
engaged in woollen manufacture must have been in
factories by this time ; in the industry as a whole the
proportion of workers under 20 did not rise above 20 per
cent in either of the two counties investigated.[1]

Up to 1837, the establishment of factories in North
Wales had not produced anything comparable to the
revolution in social life which accompanied the growth
of the factory system in Lancashire or Yorkshire. The
mills were widely scattered and mostly small, and nearly
all of them were worked by water power combined with
hand labour. A steam carding engine had been installed

[1] *Parl. Pap.*, 1836, XLV (No. 138), pp. 51 ff.; 1839, XLII ; 1840,
XXIV, pp. 556, 565–6, 568 ; Census (occupations), 1841.

in one of the Newtown mills by 1822, and another at Welshpool by 1824, but for fourteen years these, and an additional one at Newtown, remained the only steam engines in the county ; their horse power was estimated at 12, 6 and 4 respectively.[1] Newtown and Llanidloes had grown into factory towns without losing their essentially rural character, and without depleting the countryside or squeezing out the diminutive rural mill, or even the domestic worker. The handloom weaver's position—despite some experiments with the power-loom in Montgomeryshire, of which more later—was still unassailed.

For the weaver who valued his independence too highly to seek the comparative security of the factory handlooms, there was still plenty of jobbing work to do at home. Even the half-timer was far from defunct. In the Newtown district, farmers no longer spun and wove their own wool, since it paid better to grow it for the market ; but at Llanbrynmair they still hired labourers to work on the farm in summer and at the loom or jenny in winter, and brought their bundles of flannel to Newtown market once a year. At Machynlleth, only two-thirds of the weavers spent their whole time at the loom, the rest going off to work in the fields at harvest time. George Borrow, touring the country in 1854, found the same absence of specialization at Llangollen, where his guide, John Jones, showed him the path across the mountain along which he used to carry the flannel he wove at home, to the man who "employed" him on the other side.[2] It was different with the carder and spinner ; for machinery killed home carding, and although the jenny could be worked at home (by such as could afford to scrap their spinning wheels and buy one) it displaced the labour of many hand-spinners. The loss of these earnings was already reflected in the poor rates of places like Newtown, Llanidloes, Welshpool and Llanbrynmair before the end of the eighteenth century.[3]

Another penalty of industrialization was the increased sensitiveness of the industry, now that its market had widened so much, to crises and fluctuations originating

[1] Pigot's *Directory* (1822–23), under *Newtown; Shrewsbury Chron.*, June 4 and 11, 1824 ; *Parl. Pap.*, 1839, XLII.
[2] *H.L.W.*, pp. 554–5, 559, 565–6 ; *Wild Wales*, pp. 37, 73, 84–5.
[3] *Infra*, p. 383.

outside the country—each of them bringing its crop of bankruptcies and its aftermath of unemployment. Just when factories were beginning, there came the Napoleonic War, which ruined one of the earliest factory owners at Newtown in 1798 (though by 1833 he had again become a leading figure in the industry).[1] The post-war period was marked by the first strike against a proposed cut in wages and the first noteworthy emigration of weavers to America.[2] But recovery was rapid, for the industry was now making great strides. To many a Montgomeryshire farmer the flannel loom (like the Irishman's pig) was the "gintleman that paid the rint" during the agricultural depression, and in Merioneth, a few years after Waterloo, a single web merchant was reputed to be paying out £1,000 a week to the manufacturers.[3] In both counties the greatest recorded increase in population took place during the decade 1811–21.[4]

The rate of increase was checked during the next decade,[5] when the expense of installing machinery, and the disastrous crisis of 1826, brought many firms to ruin. In 1824, there were two bankruptcies at Newtown and one at Welshpool; in 1825 another at Newtown; two more there, and two at Llanidloes, in 1826; and yet another at Newtown in 1827. Woolstaplers or fellow-manufacturers were generally the principal creditors, but one of the insolvents of 1826, significantly enough, assigned his effects in trust to a Brosely ironfounder and a Leeds cardmaker.[6] The economic troubles which helped to embitter the Reform Bill struggle also left their mark. There were further industrial disputes, further emigrations, and more bankrupts—including a Llanwnog dyer and a Newtown machine-maker in 1829, two flannel manufacturers (at Newtown and Llanidloes) in 1830, and another (at Welshpool) in 1831.[7]

[1] *Salop. Journ.*, March 28, Dec. 26, 1798; *M.C.R.* (1837–38, XXXV), p. 334.
[2] *Infra*, pp. 401, 381.
[3] *N.W.Gaz.*, Aug. 1, 1822; *Bye-gones*, 1882–83, p. 60.
[4] 15 per cent in Montgomeryshire, 11 per cent in Merioneth.
[5] 9 per cent in Montgomeryshire, 3 per cent in Merioneth.
[6] *Shrewsbury Chron.*, March 5, April 2 and 23, 1824, Dec. 2, 1825, March 24, June 2, Sept. 22, Oct. 13, 1826, Aug. 24, 1827.
[7] *Id.*, June 26, Aug. 21, 1829, Feb. 5, May 21, 1830, June 24, 1831; *infra*, pp. 403, 386.

In Montgomeryshire, however, these were only growing
pains, for Welsh flannel was winning a national reputation.
During the cholera epidemic of 1831, the Board of Health
advised the public to wear it as a prophylactic, and a few
years later we find the poet Rogers advising H. F. Cary,
"the Dante man," to carry a roll of it on his Italian travels.
"I do take so much in my time as would reach, you see,
from Welshpool to Shrewsbury," one flannel merchant
would boast to another ; and his rival would cap it with
"Indeed to goodness, I was take so much as would go
from Shrewsbury to London—aye, to Paris for what
I know." So, at least, a Government Commissioner—
forgetting for once the circumspection proper to a blue
book—reported a few years later.[1]

In Merioneth, where little capital was being laid out,
bankruptcies were rarer ; but Welsh webs, so far from
making fresh conquests, were already losing ground.
Since the failure of the Barmouth depôt, the heavy cost
of overland conveyance to London or Liverpool had been
a serious handicap to exports. Machynlleth and Llangollen,
more conveniently placed for the English market, were
already finding that flannel paid better, and in Dolgelley
itself the manufacture (for the home market) of the
twilled fine cloth known as kerseymere had come in to
supplement the deficiencies of the web trade towards the
end of the War.[2] In 1831, when the towns of Dolgelley,
Bala, Barmouth, Towyn and Corwen petitioned for inclusion
among the contributory boroughs of Merioneth in the
new Reform Bill, they mentioned among other proofs of
the increased importance and prosperity of the district,
since Henry VIII fixed the franchise, the fact that
352,000 yards of web were produced every year for export.
They were hardly likely to have underestimated the
figure ; yet it is only half as great as the output calculated
by Gwallter Mechain thirty years earlier. Soon afterwards,

[1] *H.L.W.*, p. 553 ; *Shrewsbury Chron.*, Nov. 25, 1831 ; Davies,
p. 394 ; MS. letter from Rogers to Cary, Jan., 1833 (kindly communicated by my friend Mr. R. W. King, author of *The Translator
of Dante*).

[2] Evans : *Beauties*, p. 917 ; *cf.* Fullarton's *Parl. Gaz.*, IV, p. 400.

it was observed that weavers were beginning to seek other employments.[1]

Just at the opening of Queen Victoria's reign came a crisis in the Welsh woollen industry as serious as that which the mining and smelting industries had undergone a decade earlier. A trade boom in the United States, connected with the paying off of the National Debt in 1835, "fired," as an American writer has unkindly put it, "the imagination of even the dull Europeans," and a period of rash speculation followed in England and Wales. In 1836 a branch of the Bank of Manchester was set up at Newtown, and like many of the new joint-stock banks it promoted a sudden and unhealthy increase in trade by offering too easy terms of credit. Cheap money and cheap wool induced about twenty new manufacturers (many of them workmen with next to no capital) to start in business, and immigrant workmen flocked in to the number of 300 or so. There was a similar boom at Llanidloes; at Welshpool, sixteen tradesmen formed a company for running a flannel mill (after the fashion of Yorkshire "company mills")[2] on a larger scale than had hitherto been attempted; at Machynlleth trade increased in a few months as much as it had declined during several years.[3]

This period of brisk trade was the occasion for important developments, which, however, were checked by the subsequent collapse. The mule and the power loom, which had so swiftly revolutionized the cotton industry, were less easily adapted to the spinning and weaving of wool—especially of the short-staple wool used in the manufacture of woollens proper, as distinct from worsteds. Thus hand-spinning was almost defunct in the manufacture of Yorkshire worsteds by 1810, but in Norfolk— a woollen county—the first yarn factory was not set up till 1834. It was in the following year that David Davies

---

[1] *Shrewsbury Chron.*, June 24, 1831 ; Lewis : *Top. Dict.*, under *Dolgelley*. Estimates of output in the Merioneth web industry differ widely, partly because they are calculated in different units, partly because flannel is sometimes included, sometimes not ; *see* Davies, p. 397 ; *Cantref Meirionydd*, pp. 114–6 ; Fullarton's *Parl. Gaz.*, I, p. 598 ; *Bye-gones*, 1882–83, p. 60 ; *supra*, p. 230.

[2] *Cf.* Lipson : *op. cit.*, pp. 177–9.

[3] Clapham : *Early Railway Age*, pp. 513–6 ; *H.L.W.*, pp. 558–9, 554–5, 569–70.

installed the mule (presumably the self-acting variety patented by Richard Roberts, a Montgomeryshire man, ten years earlier) into the Glanclywedog factory at Llanidloes.[1] So, too, with the power loom. Even in the cotton industry, the violent opposition of the weavers delayed its adoption (except in Scotland) till the early years of the nineteenth century, when a mill at Llangollen (as we shall see[2]) had the distinction of being one of the first to use it successfully, though its success was short-lived. By 1835, when Cartwright's patent had been at work a full generation, the number of power looms in Lancashire had grown to more than a thousand, and in Yorkshire (between the cotton, woollen and worsted industries) to more than four thousand ; but Norfolk still had none, and Gloucestershire only four.[3] Wales also had four ; they had just been set up at Newtown by one who, like the Rev. G. A. Evors, was not himself a manufacturer, but a landed proprietor : William Pugh of Brynllywarch, whom we have already met as a pioneer of canals and turnpikes.[4] Pugh had four more on order ; they were all to be worked by steam power, and let to manufacturers at a rent of £100 a year.

Before Pugh's power looms had woven a single piece, the collapse came. American houses which had borrowed extensively in England failed to meet their obligations ; the Bank of England began to restrict credits in the autumn of 1836 ; the country banks had to follow suit, and there were widespread failures among manufacturers. The new firms at Newtown went under as suddenly as they had sprung up, and the immigrant labourers dispersed. The winter of 1837 was a hard one both here and at Llanidloes, where one of the factories built during the boom passed, on the bankruptcy of its owner, into the hands of the Manchester banking company from whom he had obtained

[1] Lipson : *op. cit.*, p. 184 ; Horsfall–Turner : *op. cit.*, p. 122. The Mule factory, near Newtown (mentioned in *Shrewsbury Chron.*, Nov. 3, 1826, and in Pigot's *Directory* for 1828–29), was doubtless named from its position on the River Mule, not because it contained mules.

[2] *Infra*, p. 289.

[3] *Parl. Pap.*, 1836, XLV, No. 24. Yet Sir Sidney Chapman (*Lancashire Cotton Industry*, p. 47) states that power looms "were not used at all in the woollen industry till after 1839."

[4] *Supra*, pp. 97, 107–8, 241.

too generous credits. The Welshpool company was wound up, the revival at Machynlleth proved a mere flash in the pan, and Pugh of Brynllywarch had to flee abroad, loaded with debts. The Newtown manufacturers began to quibble about the rents of the power looms he had set up, and they were bought by Thomas Jones of Welshpool,[1] who tried them in his factory for nine months there without success. The crisis undoubtedly delayed the adoption of the new machinery in Wales. Although it is commonly stated that David Davies erected power looms in the Glanclywedog factory in 1837,[2] the Assistant Commissioner on Handloom Weavers found none at work in Montgomeryshire in the following year, and neither the power loom nor the mule made any real headway until the second half of the century.[3]

As the home market recovered, trade returned to normal channels, and the Report on Handloom Weavers states emphatically that the flannel trade has not declined. Yet the crisis had left its mark. Although population in the county as a whole continued to increase, at Llandinam, Berriew, Llandyssil and Llanbrynmair—four villages which lived mainly on flannel manufacture—it was already declining in 1841, and the increase of Newtown itself received a serious check. As late as 1846, the highest proportion of paupers in North Wales was to be found in the two main clothing counties.[4]

For Merioneth was also suffering from the effects of the crisis. Indeed, the embarrassments of the American buyer affected the web manufacturer far more directly than the manufacturer of flannel, since his principal custom was among the slave-owners of South Carolina ; and at the

---

[1] The Thomas Joneses in the Welshpool flannel industry are as difficult to sort out as their namesakes in the Wrexham iron industry (*supra*, p. 144 *n*). One had a mill at Pool Quay in 1823 (Pigot's *Directory*) ; another—"a friend to the manufacturing poor"—died in 1828 ; a third (who was also a wine merchant) died in 1831. The Thomas Jones now in question may perhaps be identified with the first.

[2] E.g. Horsfall-Turner (p. 22), followed by Jones, E. J. : *Economic History of Wales*, p. 43.

[3] Clapham : *loc. cit.* ; *H.L.W., loc. cit.* ; *Mont. Coll.*,V, pp. 38–40 ; Lewis : *Top. Dict.* (1843), II, p. 67 ; Roberts and Owen : *Montgomeryshire*, p. 82.

[4] *H.L.W.*, p. 554 ; *infra.* p 397.

same time changing fashions were robbing him of what sales he had at home. "It is seldom," Aikin had written in 1797, "that a Welshman (among the lower classes) wears a coat that is not made in the principality"; within half a century this had ceased to be true, for Yorkshire woollens, sold in fairs and shops, were ousting the native homespun. After 1836 the "little farmers of the hill country" began to desert the loom, leaving the factories of Dolgelley to look after the future of the industry.[1] Here rumours of "an order for Welsh webs amounting in value to £20,000" raised delusive hopes in 1837, but in the following year the Guardians of the Dolgelley Union were inundated with demands for relief from able-bodied men out of work, and had to seek the advice of the Poor Law Commissioners on the proper way to deal with them. Although its manufactories could still be described as "very considerable," Dolgelley was already on the down grade, and for the web industry as a whole the crisis of 1836–7 was the beginning of the end.[2]

C. Steam Power : Concentration and Decline.

The early factory age, with its comparatively cheap machines and its reliance on water power, had lent itself to the wide dispersion of the industry; concentration only came in with the power-loom, the self-acting mule, and their ally the steam engine. This last stage in the evolution of the woollen factory had none of the spectacular swiftness that marked the corresponding stage in the cotton industry. It was a long and painful process, as the handloom weaver knew to his cost. Even in the late 'fifties, not more than half the woollen weavers of Yorkshire itself were in factories, and "more than a third of the power used in the English and Welsh woollen mills was water-power."[3] At Newtown the handloom factories struggled on till 1880–90, and the last of the independent

---

[1] Aikin, p. 81 ; Phillips, Sir T. : *Wales* (1849), pp. 28–9 ; *Cantref Meirionydd*, pp. 114–15 ; Fullarton's *Parl. Gaz.*, I, p. 598.
[2] *Infra*, p. 396 ; Bingley : *North Wales* (third ed., 1839), p. 163 ; Leigh : *Guide to Wales*, p. 143.
[3] Lipson : *op. cit.*, p. 176 ; Clapham : *op. cit.*, p. 442.

weavers did not die till 1911 ; he was followed next year by the last survivor at Welshpool.[1]

It was not at Newtown but at Holywell that the power loom was first successfully used in the Welsh woollen industry, and that not till about 1850, by which time there were between four and five hundred of them at work even in Norfolk.[2] The site of the experiment was a factory employed, up to a few years earlier, in the manufacture of cotton yarn by steam power, and now taken over by a Newtown manufacturer named John Jones, who (according to local tradition) had not been allowed by his workmen to set up weaving machinery at home.[3]

On the strength of this single example (read in the light of tales of machine-wrecking in the English manufacturing districts) the decay of the Welsh woollen industry has been attributed to wholesale obstruction of machinery by the operatives.[4] There is not much evidence for the charge. We have the specific assurance of Thomas Jones that his attempt to work Pugh's power-looms at Welshpool "caused no excitement among the men." The trouble lay with the machines, not with the workers. Water power was too irregular (it caused difficulties at first even with the carding engine) ;[5] steam-power—apart from the cost of fuel—was apt to damage the yarn, thus causing expensive delays and producing a less satisfactory article in the end. This defect of the power loom (which did not affect the more tightly spun worsted yarns) made its adoption later everywhere in the manufacture of woollens than in that of worsteds ; for Welsh flannels, the reputation of which depended so much on the manual skill of the weavers, it was especially serious. Even without the power loom it was observed that the better

---

[1] *Mont. Coll.*, XXXVII, p. 102 *n*, *cf.* XXXIV, p. 139 (Carno) ; local information.

[2] Lipson, p. 250.

[3] *Short Account of Holywell*, p. 3, supplemented by information kindly given by Mr. Thos. Waterhouse, J.P., managing director of Holywell Flannel Works.

[4] E.g. Williams : *Montgomeryshire Worthies*, p. 270 ; "Pearmain" (E. Rowley Morris) in *Bye-gones*, 1893-94, p. 46 ; *Mont. Coll.*, XXXVII, pp. 15–24.

[5] *Mont. Coll.*, V, p. 36.

finish of the flannel turned out by the factories did not by any means indicate a corresponding increase in durability.[1]

It is not surprising, then, that manufacturers hesitated to adopt a machine which could not, like the earlier textile machinery, be obtained at a relatively low cost from a local mechanic,[2] when its effects on the quality of their manufactures was so highly problematical. Pugh of Brynllywarch was gone, and it was hardly worth while for an English capitalist to invest money in setting up steam engines so far from the main coalfields. In Flintshire and Denbighshire the use of steam had been familiar in the mines for fifty years at least; and since the beginning of the nineteenth century it had been extended to corn milling at Ruabon and to cotton weaving at Llangollen, as well as to cotton spinning at Holywell.[3] But here coal was cheap and plentiful, whereas in Montgomeryshire—the only region where the factory system was firmly established—every ton had to be imported; and it was far cheaper to take the wool to the coal than to take the coal to the wool.

It was not, however, the rivalry of other parts of North Wales so much as that of the great northern coalfields, already pre-eminent in other manufactures, that the Montgomeryshire flannel industry had to fear. This rivalry had appeared long before the competition of power looms became serious. At the end of the eighteenth century, Gwallter Mechain found it necessary to correct "an error, lately become prevalent in London and several places, of confounding the Rochdale 'stoved white Welch flannels' with the Montgomeryshire real Welsh flannels," which, as well as being made in pieces more than twice as long, were bleached in the open instead of stoved with brimstone, and in general had a much finer, closer and softer texture than the cheaper imitations. A little later, "a friend to the manufacturers of Montgomeryshire" warned them in the columns of the *North Wales Gazette*

---

[1] *H.L.W.*, pp. 553–5, 557, 560; *Parl. Pap.*, 1837–38, XXXV, p. 229.

[2] The books of the Davieses of Dôl goch do not include a single entry relating to a power loom or a mule.

[3] *Supra*, pp. 165, 174, 195, etc.; *infra*, pp. 333, 290.

against the wiles of the Lancashire manufacturers who were

> sending dyers, &c., into the neighbourhood on pretence of "wanting employ" for the purpose of prying into the secrets of the peculiar mode of dressing which makes Montgomeryshire flannels superior to all others in Great Britain, and of which the Lancashire men are totally ignorant.[1]

By the 'thirties the Montgomeryshire manufacturers were thoroughly on the defensive. The *Cambrian Quarterly Magazine* for 1833 rejoiced that the East India Company, after a year's experiment with Lancashire flannels, found them "so inferior as to be nearly useless," and transferred the order to Montgomeryshire. The Assistant Commissioner on Handloom Weavers was given to understand in 1839 that the Rochdale manufacturers, enabled by their superior capital to hold stocks and to take contracts (which the Welsh could rarely do), were in a position to "impose on the buyer" with an article which cost less only because it contained less weight of material. A body of 394 weavers drew up a petition to him (with the approval of the Rev. G. A. Evors as magistrate), asking that the Lancashire manufacturers should be compelled to put a distinguishing mark on their flannel in order to avoid this confusion.[2] Yet the "imposture" continued, and the more far-seeing manufacturers, realizing that the machine age was begetting a generation that preferred cheapness to durability, resolved to try and fight Rochdale on its own ground. At Llanidloes, both mule and power loom were introduced into one of the leading factories in the early 'fifties, and in 1867 a public presentation was made to Thomas Jones, a manufacturer and an ex-mayor, in recognition of his services in having "stayed the exodus of the Welsh flannel trade" to the North of England by overcoming suspicions of machinery. By this time Newtown, frightened by further defections to Holywell, had also turned over its chief factories to steam power.

---

[1] Davies, p. 393–4 ; Evans : *Tour*, p. 32 ; *N. W. Gaz.*, July 5, 1810.
[2] *Camb. Quart. Mag.*, V, p. 617 ; Fullarton's *Parl. Gaz.*, III pp. 442–3 ; *H.L.W.*, pp. 553–5, 557, 559.

It was largely through collective enterprise that the work was accomplished. Of this there had hitherto been very little in the Welsh flannel trade. The Welshpool company of 1837 soon perished, and only one company appears in a list of manufacturers included in the Hand-loom Weavers' Report. But three years after the Company Act of 1862 the Cambrian Flannel Company, of Newtown and Llanidloes, was founded with a capital of £50,000. Thomas Jones of Llanidloes was managing director, and members of the "aristocracy of Wales" took an active part in promoting the venture. The Company acquired several mills in both towns, installing the latest machinery in some, and keeping handlooms at work (for special branches of production) in others. It was followed by the Welsh Flannel and Tweed Company, of Llanidloes, and in 1874 the Holywell works were taken over by the still existing Welsh Flannel Manufacturing Company.[1]

When economic pressure was forcing the millowners of Newtown and Llanidloes to sell out to joint-stock companies, there was little hope for the small country manufacturer. The Census of 1851 already showed a declining population in Montgomeryshire as a whole, and in particular in nine of the flannel-weaving parishes (including once-important centres like Welshpool, Machynlleth and Llanbrynmair), where the decline was generally attributed to the closing down of factories and the migration of the industry to Newtown. During the next ten years, the number of flannel workers in the county shrank from nearly 4,000 (over half the total for Wales, and 90 per cent of that for North Wales) to a little over 2,000. Welshpool never recovered from the failure of Thomas Jones' experiment with power looms; its trade declined rapidly from the 'forties. An attempt to weave by water power at Llanbrynmair fared no better, and the millowners "one by one . . . gave up in despair the hopeless task of competing with the capitalist manufacturers of Lancashire and Yorkshire"; all but one of the eight factories closed down during the decade 1857–67.

At Machynlleth the inevitable catastrophe was warded off a little longer; there were still 12 flannel manufacturers,

---

[1] *Mont. Coll.*, V, pp. 38–42; Horsfall–Turner: *op. cit.*, pp. 112–13; 127–133; *Red Dragon*, VI, pp. 465–6; *H.L.W.*. p. 562.

5 yarn manufacturers, and 4 wool carders in 1878. Newtown then had 18 flannel manufacturers and Llanidloes 12 ; and in addition new lines like tweeds and shawls had been introduced : there were 6 manufacturers of tweeds and 5 of shawls at Newtown, and 4 of each at Llanidloes. New manufactures, new machines and new companies revived for a moment the hope that Newtown might yet become the Leeds of Wales ; in 1881 its population exceeded 4,000 for the first time in fifty years. But the departure of the flannel industry from its last remaining strongholds was now only a question of time. There was little to distinguish machine-made Montgomeryshire flannels from Rochdale imitations, and the latter had all the advantages of capital, plant, situation, and scale of production.[1]

A letter in the *Herefordshire Times* in 1852, discussing the question of a railway for Mid-Wales, urged that "an ancient and useful manufacture only waits for facilities in reaching the great markets to become still more beneficial" ;[2] but when the railway did come to Montgomeryshire in the following decade, its effect was rather to flood the county with English wares than to open new markets for local manufactures. Even former manufacturers of Welsh flannel found it more paying to stock their warehouses with sham Welsh flannel, bought in Rochdale, than to make their own. On the eve of the Great War, there was only one firm in Newtown that still made real Welsh flannel. The Cambrian Company never rebuilt its Newtown mills after their destruction by fire in 1911 ; at Llanidloes it still employed 200—nearly twice as many as all the other woollen firms put together. The figures of employment in the whole county had sunk below a thousand before the present century opened, and in the 1921 Census only 327 textile workers were recorded : 121 at Llanidloes, 175 at Newtown, and 31 in all the rest of the county. The great majority, including all the weavers, were women.[3]

---

[1] *Mont. Coll.*, XXI, pp. 84–5, XXXVII, pp. 15–24 ; *cf.* XXX, p. 16 (Tregynon).

[2] Quoted in *Letters on Improvement*, p. 35.

[3] *Mont. Coll.*, XXXVII, pp. 15–24 ; Census : enumeration abstracts, 1851–1921.

The web industry went through a similar course of evolution. The field, of course, was much more restricted, for in the middle of the century there was not a single manufacturer of woollen cloth in Wales who employed more than 30 workmen (the majority employed 4 or less), whereas in the flannel manufacture most firms employed between 10 and 100, and one exceeded this limit. By degrees these feebler growths succumbed. The American Civil War, by freeing the negro slaves, deprived Welsh webs of their chief foreign market, and in the 'eighties the annual output of Merioneth was believed to be under 400 pieces (about 48,000 yards)—less than a seventh the output of half a century earlier. At Dolgelley the principal mill (*Y Ffatri Fawr*) was taken over, within living memory, by a limited company which installed steam engines, crushed out its smaller rivals—and then, after a series of misfortunes, gave up the struggle as hopeless. The county population began to dwindle during the decade 1841–51, and that despite the doubling of population at Ffestiniog, whose slate quarries were now completely overshadowing the woollen manufacture in the attention of travellers and topographers. There were still more than 600 workers in the industry in 1851, but year by year the numbers shrank, till now there are only 51 textile workers of any kind in Merioneth—fewer than in any other county of Wales except Anglesey.[1]

In these other counties also the industry has now become negligible. A striking feature of the middle years of the century was the crowding of former textile workers into occupations like teaching and preaching.[2] Others drifted back to the plough, or sought better opportunities at Newtown or Llanidloes, in the English manufacturing centres, or across the Atlantic ; many fell on the rates. There are still lonely spots in the Welsh countryside where the traveller may stumble across a rusty heap of textile machinery—hopelessly antiquated, but once the pride of some humble millowner and the fruit of all his savings—

[1] *Cantref Meirionydd*, pp. 115–16 ; Fullarton's *Parl. Gaz.*, IV, p. 406 ; Census abstracts, 1851 ff. ; local information.
[2] *Education Report*, 1847, Appendices B and D. Biographies of many prominent Anglican and Nonconformist divines bear witness to the same tendency.

buried under the débris of a derelict mill-roof, or lying neglected in a field, not even worth the expense of removal.[1] Flintshire was the only county where the numbers engaged in the industry did not decline during the second half of the century. Starting at the bottom, it had by 1901 become second only to Montgomeryshire, with more than 200 employees, most of them in the Holywell mills. Since then, the artificial silk industry has made it easily the leading textile county in North Wales. In all six counties, the number of woollen workers fell from 4,215 in 1851 to 2,890 in 1861, the most marked decline being in the flannel branch. By the end of the century there were only 1,145—fewer even than in South Wales, which in 1851 had not much more than half as many as the North.

The knitter, who remained in Wales a pure handicraftsman, shared the fate of the weaver. Gwallter Mechain had prophesied that unless a factory for knitting was set up at Bala, the trade would soon depart to more favoured regions. He proved a true prophet. In 1830, the sales of stockings at Bala amounted only to 42,000 pairs (hardly more than a fifth what they had been a generation earlier), together with 5,500 pairs of woollen gloves.[2] There were still wayside knitters at Pentre Foelas, on the Holyhead road, in Borrow's time, and he believed this to be "the general occupation of Welsh females"; but there were few now who made it their principal means of support. In the 1851 Census, only 105 persons in North Wales put themselves down as "knitters," and another 148 as "stocking manufacturers"; all the former, and all but 14 of the latter, were females. Even as a subsidiary occupation knitting was ceasing to pay. Borrow's roadside acquaintances could no longer rely on selling their wares to stage coach travellers, for the coach had not run along the Holyhead road these ten years. The Welsh wig had lost its principal market,

---

[1] Such, e.g. was the fate of the factory Borrow saw at Sycharth (*Wild Wales*, p. 380), after the landlord had taken the building for a sawmill, and of another at Llanfyllin after a disastrous fire. Both were once worked by my wife's grandfather, the late John Owen (1832–1910). Similar scenes may be observed near Dolgelley.

[2] Davies, p. 405 ; *Parl. Pap.*, 1836–37, XXXV, p. 229.

and the locomotive was bringing stocks of cheap machine-made hose from the Midlands to the village shops of Wales. In 1921 the six counties of North Wales could show only eleven women who made their living by hand knitting.[1]

Emancipation from the Shrewsbury Drapers, so far from fulfilling the roseate prophecies of Aikin and Davies, in reality cut the ground from under the feet of the Welsh woollen manufacturer. Even the straitest of free trade theories have allowed that "infant industries" may need some protection against competitors with a long start in the race. In comparison with English industries, the Welsh woollen manufacture was still an "infant industry" when it abandoned its protected market. There remained for it two chances of survival : first, the "natural protection" afforded to it by advantages of situation (whether superior wool, cheap labour or abundance of good water for bleaching and for power), or by the unique character of the product ; secondly, its attractions (largely dependent on these advantages) as a field for economic "penetration" by rich capitalists from outside. But English investors, never numerous, lost interest after the crisis of 1837 ; and geography could give no protection against the power of steam to annihilate distance, to centralize industry, and to standardize products, prices and wages.

The Welsh rural woollen industry has never wholly died out. From time to time, one of the abandoned mills, where the machinery has not rusted away, is taken over at a trifling rent by some local man, either to make yarn for the Rochdale factories to send back as "real Welsh flannel,"[2] or to turn into cloth the wool of a few remote farmsteads still lying off the beat of the railway companies ; for the woollen manufacture proper (unlike the worsted branch) has always been able to make use of scattered factories.[3] Within these last few years there

---

[1] *Wild Wales*, p. 150 ; Hicklin : *Excursions in North Wales* (1851), p. 24 ; *Bye-gones*, 1895–96, p. 301.

[2] The little mill at Cadnant, near Menai Bridge, apparently sent its cloth to Yorkshire for finishing as early as 1852 (*Arch. Camb.*, 1924, p. 36). After the late War it was taken over by a Rochdale firm who used it for producing yarns to be woven in their own mills. It is now idle.

[3] Clapham : *Woollen and Worsted Industries*, pp. 13, 133–4.

have been thirty or forty such mills at work in North Wales, distributed between all six counties, but mostly in Montgomeryshire and Caernarvonshire. By far the majority use water power only ; in a few the handloom is still employed. In South Wales—which the Handloom Weavers' Commission did not think worth the trouble of investigation in 1839, so trifling was its output—there are now three times as many mills as in the North.[1] Whether, with the development of electrical power, these relics of an earlier economic order can be galvanized into fresh activity, so as to bring a much-needed diversity into Welsh rural life, depends largely on the capacity of the Welsh peasant to learn those lessons of co-operation which bitter necessity drove home to the Danish small-holder sixty years ago.[2]

[1] Jones, A. M. : *Rural Industries of . . . Wales,* chap. II ; *H.L.W.,* pp. 571–4.

[2] Some time ago the Welsh Industries Association made a good start in this direction (*Bye-gones,* 1899–1900, p. 151).

CHAPTER VIII.

OTHER TEXTILES.

Mr. Escot (at Tremadoc) : I confess, the sight of those manufactories, which have suddenly sprung up, like fungous excrescences, in the bosom of these wild and desolate scenes, impressed me with . . . much horror and amazement. . . . Twenty years ago, at the door of every cottage sate the good woman with her spinning-wheel. . . . Where is the spinning-wheel now, and every simple and insulated occupation of the industrious cottager ?
　　　—Peacock : *Headlong Hall* (1816), chap. VII.

It was not only old-established industries like woollens that benefited from the general diffusion of manufactures during the earlier stages of the Industrial Revolution ; the abundant water power of North Wales, together with the cheapness of labour and the absence of old vested interests, attracted capitalists to experiment there in novelties like cotton and silk. Both industries found homes by the stream flowing from the well at Holywell.

The establishment of the cotton industry at Holywell is connected with the career of the most typical, and perhaps the best known, of all the pioneers of the Industrial Revolution—Richard Arkwright. One of the many men on whose backs Arkwright climbed to fame was John Smalley, a liquor merchant and house painter of Preston, who, out of his slender capital, helped to finance the original water frame in 1767–8. But Arkwright wanted richer partners, and in 1771 he found them in Need of Nottingham and Strutt of Derby, two prosperous hosiery manufacturers, in partnership with whom he set up the famous Cromford Mill. Smalley's services were no longer needed ; he joined at first in the venture at Cromford, but according to his son's account a "tyrant rival" (presumably Arkwright) compelled him to move elsewhere—carrying with him, however, the secret of the great invention. Coming from Lancashire, a county where Catholicism was strong, Smalley may have heard pilgrims talk of the miracles wrought by the waters of St. Winifred ; at anyrate he now resolved to test their power of performing a new sort of marvel.

With his son Christopher (then aged 23), he took up his quarters at Holywell in 1777, and opened up negotiations with a local man named John Chambers, whose mother held a lease of some buildings on the stream at Greenfield, (on the site of the old corn mill of the monks of Basingwerk) where she worked a coarse paper mill and her son a wire mill. Chambers and Smalley went into partnership ; Mrs. Chambers sub-let part of the buildings to them, and with the aid of stones from the ruined Abbey they put up a three-storeyed cotton mill, with a large water wheel. From the fact that its walls were washed yellow, it came to be known as the Yellow Mill ; it had fallen into ruins before the middle of the last century, and at present not a vestige of it remains.[1] Smalley probably brought spinners from England to work the mill ; at a later date, at any rate, the bulk of the employees were English.[2]

Smalley only lived for five years to enjoy the fruits of his new venture. He died in 1782 ; his colleague Chambers, who must have soon retired from the partnership, had gone bankrupt two years earlier.[3] John's son Christopher took over the works at a propitious moment—just when the first great cotton boom was beginning. Two new mills, known as the Upper and Lower Mills, were built in 1783 and 1785 respectively. Each of them was six storeys high, and it is characteristic of the times that the first (which had nearly 200 windows) was completed within six weeks.[4] The concern was now important enough to cause some uneasiness to Arkwright himself, In 1787 we find Richard Arkwright, junior, asking his fellow-manufacturer, Samuel Oldknow (then on a visit to Wales), to spy out the land. It is unlikely that he was successful, for nearly forty years later the proprietors were distinguished from the Lancashire manufacturers by

---

[1] Mantoux : *The Industrial Revolution*, pp. 227–8 ; Pennant : *Whiteford and Holywell*, p. 203 ; Defoe : *Tour* (eighth ed., 1778), pp. 329–30 ; Jones, A. Seymour : *Roller Leather for Cotton Spinning* (Manchester, 1893), pp. 15–21. The lease (from Alice Chambers to John Chambers and John Smalley, dated July 17, 1779) is summarized in *Cal. of Coleman Documents*, No. 1351.

[2] Louis : *Gleanings*, p. 29.

[3] Pennant : *loc. cit.; Chester Chron.*, March 24, 1780.

[4] Bingley : *North Wales*, I, pp. 50–51.

their unwillingness to admit strangers to the works.[1] The cotton boom was now over, and a spell of bad trade set in. Smalley secured himself by introducing fresh capital (chiefly from Lancashire) into the business. Prominent among the new partners was Mr. John Douglas, and the firm was henceforth known alternatively as Douglas and Co., Douglas, Smalley and Co., or the Cotton Twist Company. It was probably by this new partnership that a fourth mill, the Crescent Mill (also of six storeys), was built in the spring of 1790.

Within a few years work was as brisk as ever. Pennant, who visited the mills in 1795, obtained a full description of the manufacture from Mr. Smalley. Cotton twist of 130 hanks to the pound (each hank 840 yards long) was produced for the manufacturers of England and Scotland to make into ginghams, muslins, dimities, nankeens, fine calicoes and fustians. The total number of employees was 1,225, including 100 men, 500 women and children, 300 or 400 parish apprentices (housed on the spot), and between 200 and 300 outworkers in neighbouring parishes.[2] At Denbigh the firm had hired a defunct woollen mill (the one built by Mostyn, Pigot and Co., in 1749) where 140 hands were engaged in sorting and picking cotton;[3] and there were more outworkers at Ysceifiog and Newmarket. After being picked (we are told in a description by the Rev. R. Warner, a few years later), the cotton was thrice carded and thrice roved preparatory to being spun on an

> improved cotton machine, the first view of which irresistibly impresses the mind with the idea of magic. Here thirty or forty thousand spindles are seen moving in the most rapid manner without any perceptible cause, spontaneously performing operations of the most curious nature in the most systematic manner.

[1] Unwin, Hulme, and Taylor : *Samuel Oldknow and the Arkwrights*, p. 94 ; Louis : *Gleanings*, p. 28.

[2] Barfoot and Wilkes' *Directory*, III, pp. 283 ff. ; Bingley : *loc. cit.;* Pennant : *op. cit.*, pp. 115–6 ; Lewis : *Top. Dict.* There are drawings and a description of the mills in John and Josiah Boydell's *Collection of Views . . . in North Wales* (1792), Plates V and VI.

[3] Williams : *Ancient and Modern Denbigh*, p. 128 ; *cf. supra*, pp. 14–15.

Warner adds that this was "the machine of Sir Richard Arkwright," but it is clear from Pennant's account that the mule was also in use by this time. To keep off other adventurers, Smalley and his partners were said to be paying £5,000 a year for a fall on the stream which they themselves had no immediate intention of using.[1]

By this time England was at war, and the male employees (in the picturesque but inaccurate phrase of a visitor to the works) were deserting the loom for the sword, leaving the women and children to carry on.[2] Smalley was a public-spirited man. He and his father had joined the local Association for the Prosecution of Felons only a few years after the mill was started, and now he took a leading part in organizing the Holywell Volunteers. The firm subscribed a fifth of the necessary funds and promised twenty men. Thomas Pennant, as President of the Loyal Association, put Smalley's name forward for a commission—whereupon "the trading part of the town and some others," out of jealousy, threatened to resign.[3]

The Cotton Twist Company survived both the War and the many trials of the post-war years—including serious damage by floods (the same that wrecked the copper works) in 1821, and an attempt of "some miscreants" to burn down one of the mills in 1822. Christopher Smalley died in 1829, at the age of 75.[4] Towards the end of his life he had extended his operations by opening banks (in partnership with Douglas) at both Holywell and Mold.[5] The banks did not last long ; but the cotton works continued to flourish, attaining in 1833 a production of 26,096 pounds a week. There were now 12,218 spindles at work in the Upper Mill, 7,492 in the Lower, and 8,286 in the Crescent. Some time before 1835, steam engines

[1] Warner : *Second Walk* (1799), pp. 207–8 ; Davies : *General View*, p. 401.

[2] Hucks : *Pedestrian Tour*, p. 51.

[3] *Chester Chron.*, March 31, 1780 ; Thomas Pennant to Lord Kenyon, March 27, 1797 (*Hist. MSS. Com.*, 14th Rept., App. Pt. IV). The Smalleys of the Bodfari wireworks also took up commissions in the Volunteers during the later years of the war (*S lop. Journ.*, May 27, 1805).

[4] *N. W. Gaz.*, Sept. 27, 1821 (*cf. supra*, p. 163) ; *id.*, Feb. 14, 1822 ; *Shrewsbury Chron.*, Jan. 23, 1829.

[5] *Infra*, p. 318.

were installed. There were then five in the cotton mills
of Flintshire, with a total horse power of 258 ; probably
all were at Holywell, though the cotton industry, as we
shall see, had by this time extended to other parts of the
county. In Flintshire as a whole, cotton factories "in which
machinery is worked by mechanical power" now gave employment to 1,151 operatives, including 452 males (202 under
18 and 250 over) and 699 females (241 under 18 and 458
over). No children under 11 were employed. For
Holywell itself we have more exact figures in Parliamentary
returns for 1836 and 1838. In the former year the mills
employed 844 hands, including 343 under 18 ; there
were five steam engines and two water wheels. In 1838 the
number of employees had diminished by 70, and there
were now a few children under 10 in the mills. The total
horse power of the machinery was estimated at 136.[1]

The Holywell cotton industry was clearly declining, and
the decline, once it had begun, was rapid. The slump of
1837 hit the cotton trade as hard as it did the manufacture
of woollens. By 1841 the number employed had sunk to
14, and now or soon afterwards the Cotton Twist Company
went into liquidation.[2] "The closing of some cotton
factories owing to the migration of this branch of business,"
says a guide book of 1859, "for a time threw a shade over
the town, leaving houses empty and hands unemployed ; but
they have gradually been absorbed by the growing demands
of other departments." The chief of these "other departments," of course, was the woollen industry ; for it was
only a few years after the cotton mills closed down that
Mr. John Jones came over from Newtown to use the buildings for power-loom flannel weaving.[3]

The success of the Smalleys encouraged other Lancashire
cotton firms to come to North Wales. In 1792 Messrs.
Samuel and James Knight, of Manchester set up near
Mold, a "handsome and stupendous cotton factory" which,
twenty years later, gave an example to North Wales in
the use of gas for lighting. By 1820, 300 hands were
employed, and the premises were greatly enlarged during

[1] Lewis : *Top. Dict.* ; Ure : *Philosophy of Manufactures*, opp.
p. 467 ; *Parl. Pap.*, 1836, XLV, No. 138, pp. 130–3 ; 1839, XLII.
[2] Census, 1841 ; Lewis : *Top. Dict.* (1843), I, p. 426.
[3] Sproule : *Handbook to North Wales*, p. 78 ; *supra*, p. 273.

the boom of 1825.[1] Like the Smalleys, the Knights combined banking with cotton-spinning ; but their resources do not seem to have been equal to the strain of the years of slack trade which followed the boom. We do not hear of the bank after 1828, and by 1833 operations in the cotton mill were at a standstill.[2] It was re-opened, however, when trade improved ; by 1836, 236 hands were employed, and in 1838 (despite the slump) 60 more. More than half the employees were now women, and more than half were under 18. The increase was partly due to the fact that the new proprietors, Messrs. Inman and Son, had extended their operations by installing thirty power looms, which were worked by a staff of 14 women, under the supervision of two male weavers from Manchester. The Mold factory had long sent its cotton waste to Manchester ; it was now able to send bales of the stout calicoes known as "domestics." It had also ceased to be a mere water mill. One steam engine came in with the power looms, and a second followed soon after, giving the mill (between water and steam) a total capacity of 112 horse power.[3]

Having survived the worst troubles of the early years of the century, the Mold cotton mill was able to maintain itself for another generation. The Census of 1841 shows 246 cotton operatives in Flintshire, and of these, as we have seen, Holywell only accounted for 14. During the next decade, the number fell to 48, but it had risen again to 171 by 1861 ; nearly 70 per cent were females. In 1866, however, the works were completely destroyed by fire, and, as trade had not yet recovered from the cotton famine of 1861–5, they were not rebuilt. At the time of the fire, there were 250 employees and 25,000 spindles ; weaving, however, had apparently been abandoned, and the mill had reverted to water power.[4]

The Mold mill started and ended as a spinning establishment ; those at Holywell were never anything else ; but

---

[1] Pugh : *Camb. Dep.*, pp. 345–6 ; *Cambro-Briton*, II (1820), p. 258 ; Lewis : *Top. Dict.*, under *Mold*.

[2] Lewis : *Top. Dict.*, under *Flintshire*.

[3] *Parl. Papers*, 1836, XLV, No. 138 ; 1839, XLII ; 1840, XXIV, pp. 570–1.

[4] Census, 1841–61 ; Leslie, C. H. : *Rambles round Mold* (Mold, 1869).

the third cotton factory in North Wales—at Llangollen—produced finished goods from the outset. It was probably the fear of seeing their mill burned down by the mob (as the first power loom factory in their own town of Manchester had been in 1791) that induced Messrs. Turner and Comber to go to Wales when they wanted to start power-loom weaving. Steam power, although Cartwright himself had applied it to his invention in 1789, was not yet considered indispensable—the rapid waters of the Dee at Llangollen promised an excellent substitute ; and there were the additional inducements of "the cheapness of Labour, of Provisions, and of Fuel." There were, moreover, no weavers' vested interests to contend with ; but the aesthetic sensibilities of the neighbouring gentry proved at first almost as serious an obstacle, and it was only by means of a strategem that Messrs. Turner and Comber secured a plot of land on which, some time before 1805, they constructed "stately Fabricks" for carrying on an enterprise, popularly believed to be "likely to prove injurious to Manchester," and subsequently claimed as "the first successful attempt to manufacture fancy goods by power looms." It is likely enough that the Llangollen factory was one of the first in South Britain where power looms actually got to work.[1]

The days of the Orders in Council were not friendly to industrial enterprise, but the new firm managed to avoid disaster. Its employees were largely women and children, who, unlike the cotton spinners at Holywell, were drawn from the immediate neighbourhood—to the great benefit of the poor rates.[2] All the heavier was the blow to the district when, in 1814, a fire (believed to have been caused by lightning) "destroyed all the valuable machinery and the interior of the building," leaving only the outer shell intact. The proprietors were well covered ; they had insured with the newly-founded Atlas Insurance Company. For the distressed operatives a subscription list was opened, and the famous Ladies of Llangollen headed it

---

[1] Mavor : *Tour in Wales*, p. 136 ; Carlisle : *Top. Dict.* ; Pugh : *Camb. Dep.*, p. 311 ; Lewis : *Top. Dict.* (1833) ; Mantoux : *Industrial Revolution*, pp. 247–9.

[2] *Chester Chron.*, March 14, 1806 (women advertised for, especially "stretchers" and "cotton batters") ; *Camb. Dep., loc. cit.*

with five guineas each.[1]   In these circumstances work was soon resumed ; but the destroyed looms do not appear to have been replaced.   Henceforth the proprietors called themselves only "cotton spinners," and even in that capacity their days were numbered.   During the slump of 1819 they went bankrupt, and their factory was offered for sale in the following year.   The spinning mill is described in the advertisement as a three-storeyed stone building, 72 feet by 32, heated by steam and lighted by gas ; the outbuildings included warehouses, wheelhouse, mechanics' workshop, oil vault, retort house for the gas plant, and steam boiler house—so that by this time water power must have been supplanted.[2]

Another Manchester firm—Messrs. Gardner, Taylor, and Bell—bought up the concern.   Weaving was resumed, and both coarse cottons and woollen goods were produced.   In 1833 the number employed is given as 120, and the weekly output as 15,000 yards, "chiefly for the home market." But, like the Cotton Twist Company at Holywell, the firm succumbed to the great slump of 1837.   The mill is not included in the Parliamentary returns for 1839, and the 1841 Census shows only five cotton operatives in the county. By 1843 the works (again following the example of Holywell) had been converted into a flannel mill.[3]

In addition to these more ambitious establishments, a few small mills and a number of domestic spinners and weavers were to be found in North Wales during the brief period when the cotton industry was expanding outside Lancashire.   At Denbigh, as well as the building used by the Holywell firm for picking cotton, there were two small mills (on a stream just outside the borough) where spinning was done for Manchester manufacturers ; both had become woollen carding mills by 1843.[4]   Mr. Joseph Ablett, of

---

[1] *N. W. Gaz.*, Dec. 15 and 29, 1814, Feb. 2, 1815.

[2] *Shrewsbury Chron.*, April 30, 1819 ; *Oswestry Her.*, May 16 to June 6, 1820.

[3] Pigot's *Directory*, 1828–29, pp. 1161–2 ; Lewis : *Top. Dict.*, 1833 and 1843.

[4] Barfoot and Wilkes' *Directory*, V, pp. 54–5 ; Lewis, *ut. sup.* ; *Bye-gones*, 1893–94, p. 177.   Evans (*Beauties*, p. 112) and Fullarton's *Parl. Gaz.* (IV, p. 406) speak as if there were cotton factories at Northop and Ysceifiog, but this is probably due to a misreading of Pennant's statement about the outworkers in 1795.

Llanbedr Dyffryn Clwyd, "a gentleman of extensive dealings in the Manchester cotton trade," tried to catch the votes of the Denbigh burgesses, when he stood as parliamentary candidate in 1826, by giving out that he intended to erect a number of cotton mills in Denbigh ; but nothing further was heard of the project after the election.[1] Each successive Census shows a few scattered cotton workers—doubtless outworkers of the Lancashire mills—in almost every quarter of North Wales ; as many as 64 were registered in Montgomeryshire in 1841. But the days of dispersion were over, and the era of concentration had set in, long before this. It is significant that, while during the decade 1786-95 only 13 of the 34 steam engines set up in cotton factories were in Lancashire, the next five years saw 29 erected in Lancashire as against 6 in the rest of the country.[2] The cotton industry in North Wales was only an accidental by-product of a phase of economic evolution that soon passed by.

The same is true of ribbon-weaving, which established itself at Holywell for a period of about fifty years. Here again cheapness of labour was one of the chief attractions of North Wales. The Act of 1773, which set up special machinery for the regulation of Spitalfields silk weavers' wages, caused a considerable migration of the masters to districts where wages were unregulated, and its extension in 1792 to manufactures in which silk was mixed with other materials must have led to a further exodus.[3] Among those who now left was Hugh Roberts of Little Moorfields—a Welshman, to judge by his name. In 1795 he established a colony of ribbon weavers at Pen y maes, near Holywell (opposite the vitriol works), taking a 99 years' lease of land from Thomas Pennant on which to erect a small factory.

Sixteen looms were set up at once, and by 1821 the number had risen to sixty, employing about ninety persons.

[1] *Chester Chron.*, June 9, 1826. I owe this reference to my friend and former pupil Mr. Glyn Roberts, of Swansea.

[2] Lord : *Capital and Steam Power*, pp. 167–71.

[3] Hammond. J. L. and B. : *The Skilled Labourer, 1760–1832* (1920), pp. 209 ff.

The articles turned out were narrow silk goods—"galloons" and "doubles"; Roberts doubtless sent them to London for sale in the silk mercer's shop which he still kept in Aldgate Street.[1] The work must have been done on hand looms, for the power loom had not yet touched the silk industry, and even the so-called "engine-loom" for ribbon weaving (an improved variety of hand loom) did not become common till after 1818. At first, the "throwing" of the silk, preparatory to weaving, was also done by hand—unless indeed Roberts bought it ready thrown; but in 1822 he added to his works a throwing mill—an invention more than a century old, but only recently adopted in the Manchester silk works. By 1833 the throwing mill was believed to give work to another hundred operatives, over and above those engaged in weaving.[2]

Roberts was evidently a man of no great resources. A few years after he built his factory, he had to raise funds by mortgaging the land to a fellow-silkman of London.[3] But, unlike many a wealthier capitalist, he survived all the troubles of the early machine age. During the depression of 1831, his employees struck against a proposed reduction of wages. The strike lasted seven days, and its sole result was the replacement of the male workers (on whom Roberts, in contrast with the cotton manufacturers, had hitherto exclusively relied) by women. In 1838 there were only five men at the works, out of a total which had now sunk to 54, and much of the coarser work was done by "young persons." The relieving officer reported that the operatives were well-fed and contented.[4] It must have been soon after this, however, that the enterprise was abandoned. In 1841 only 12 silk workers were left in Holywell; ten years later these had been reduced to two.[5]

There are a few other small silk works in North Wales of

---

[1] Pennant: *Whiteford and Holywell*, p. 267; *Cal. of Coleman Documents*, No. 1359; Pigot's *Directory*, 1828–29, p. 1159; *H.L.W.*, p. 570.
[2] Lewis: *Top. Dict.;* Clapham: *Early Railway Age*, pp. 196–8; Mantoux: *Industrial Revolution*, p. 245.
[3] *Cal. of Coleman Documents*, 1359.
[4] *H.L.W.*, p. 570.
[5] Census, 1841 and 1851.

which we get passing glimpses,[1] and the Census records a handful of silk manufacturers, silk dyers and ribbon weavers in the counties of Denbigh, Merioneth, and Montgomery before 1861. In 1871 there were seven in all Nor... Wales ; after that the entries cease, and the industry vanished without leaving a ripple on the surface of social life. Its re-establishment in Flintshire in the form of the artificial silk manufacture lies outside our purview.

The linen trade stands on quite a different footing. Instead of planting an exotic industry in North Wales, and then transplanting it back to the regions from which the seeds had spread, the Industrial Revolution had here an ancient and widespread handicraft to deal with. Its initial effects were almost negligible, for the new mechanical processes spread but slowly to the linen industry, and (with a few trifling exceptions) they never reached this district at all. The final result was the elimination of the industry—not through migration to the English industrial centres, for they, too, have had to yield ground to the manufacturers of Ireland and Belgium—but because, in the often-quoted words of William Radcliffe, "cotton, cotton, cotton had become the almost universal material of employment."[2]

The dressing, spinning and weaving of flax had been carried on from early times in every nook and corner of North Wales. It was generally a spare-time domestic occupation, often combined with the making of woollens, but with this far-reaching difference—that, whereas for the latter there were abundant local supplies of raw material, the recognized qualities of which gave Welsh woollens a footing in the English market, the material for the former had mostly to be brought from outside, so that the industry remained far less specialized in scope, and the product rarely travelled far from the place of origin.

[1] E.g. Caerwys (*Chester Chron.*, Sept. 20, 1816) ; near Menai Suspension Bridge (*Bye-gones*, 1913–15, p. 154) ; domestic weavers in Merioneth (Pratt : *Gleanings*, 1800 ed., I, p. 43).

[2] Clapham : *op. cit.*, pp. 245–6, and *Economic Development of France and Germany* (1923), pp. 255–6 ; Radcliffe, W. : *Origins of the New System of Manufactures* (1828), p. 61.

A few coarse linens, and "linsey woolseys" for women's gowns, found their way to the local fairs and markets ; but the ordinary cottager was content with supplying the slender wants of his own family, and earning a few pence by a day's spinning or weaving at the squire's.[1] There had been a time when North Wales grew its own flax. In East Denbighshire flax yards were abundant in the seventeenth century ; flax was not unknown as a farm crop in Merioneth in the eighteenth ; in Caernarvonshire, still later, it was cultivated on the land reclaimed from Traeth Mawr, by the engineer who made the embankment ; and at Llan y mynech, in northern Montgomeryshire, the last farmer did not give it up till 1835.[2] But by the middle of the eighteenth century most of the flax used in North Wales came through Liverpool, from Ireland, Holland, the Baltic or America.   Patriotic attempts to revive home cultivation in time of war met with little response, despite government bounties, for landlords were not prepared to encourage so exhausting a crop.[3]

We have abundant evidence of the wide diffusion of the industry in the eighteenth and early nineteenth centuries, though it is equally clear that, among a population which generally wore flannel shirts and slept between blankets, the number of people who made their living by it was always small.   In Anglesey "coarse linens" were made "in abundance," and some were sold outside the county.[4] Much was also produced in the mountainous parts of Caernarvonshire ; Merioneth made little, but a traveller of 1797 found flax-dressing almost the "only employment" of the villagers of Corwen, and another (in the same year) wrote a harrowing description of a linen weaver's household at Barmouth, where fourteen hours' toil at the loom brought in eightpence to the family exchequer.[5]   In Flint-

---

[1] Meyrick papers (1755–98) *passim;* Evans : *Beauties*, p. 320 ; Defoe : *Tour* (eighth edition, 1778), II, p. 331.

[2] Palmer : *Wrexham*, p. 10 ; Williams : *Hanes Plwyf Ffestiniog*, p. 67 ; *Bye-gones*, 1889–90, p. 192 ; *Mont. Coll.*, XII, pp. 400–2, XXXII, p. 263.

[3] Meyrick papers ; *Camb. Dep.*, p. 259 ; *N. W. Gaz.*, Feb. 18, 1813 ; Davies : *General View*, pp. 210–11.

[4] Morris : *Plans of Harbours* ; Owen : *Hist. of Anglesey*, p. 7 ; Evans : *Beauties*, pp. 156, 320.

[5] Williams : *Snowdon Mountains*, p. 25 ; Wigstead : *Remarks*, p. 21.

shire, too, the industry was unimportant, for mining was too strong a competitor to give the textile industries much chance outside the towns ; but in the two counties of Denbigh and Montgomery it flourished for generations. The Vale of Clwyd and the Wrexham district were the chief centres in Denbighshire ; linens and linsey-woolseys were still extensively sold in the Wrexham March Fair in 1833, and thefts of flax and linen were frequent offences.[1] In Montgomeryshire some was manufactured in the flannel districts, but far more in the small area in the north of the county (round Llan y mynech, Llandisilio and Llansant-ffraid ym Mechain) where flannels did not seriously compete.[2]

The "heckling" or dressing of the flax ready for spinning was the most highly specialized branch of the trade. Up to about 1830, trade directories show one, two or three flax-dressing establishments in each of the principal market towns : Llangefni and Llannerch y medd in Anglesey ; Caernarvon, Conway and Pwllheli in Caernarvonshire ; Holywell, Mold and St. Asaph in Flintshire ; Denbigh (where there were 6 in 1790), Wrexham and Llangollen in Denbighshire ; Welshpool in Montgomeryshire.[3] There is no sign of the introduction here of the heckling machinery which came into use in Leeds during the Napoleonic Wars ;[4] flax-dressing remained a skilled handicraft, to which, up to the end of the eighteenth century, children were regularly apprenticed.[5] One or two attempts were made, however, at spinning by machinery : for example at St. Asaph, where there was talk in 1807 of setting up a machine (made in Liverpool) capable of spinning twenty yards of flax or tow per spindle per minute ; and at the

[1] *Arch. Camb.*, 1906, p. 131 ; Palmer : *Wrexham*, pp. 10, 19 ; Lewis : *Top. Dict.* ; *N. W. Gaz.*, May 3, 1810, Sept. 13, 1821 ; cf. Davies : *Labourers in Husbandry*, p. 189 (Llandegla).

[2] *Mont. Coll.*, XXXVI, p. 140, XII, pp. 401–2, XXXII, p. 263 ; *Bye-gones*, 1907–8, p. 316.

[3] Barfoot and Wilkes' *Directory* ; Pigot's *Directory*, 1822–23 and 1828–29.

[4] Clapham : *Early Railway Age*, p. 146.

[5] The present writer has in his possession the indentures of apprenticeship of his great-grandfather, John Griffiths, to Thomas Jones, flaxdresser, of Wrexham, dated 1798. The apprentice was to live at home and to receive 1s. a week in his second year, 2s. in the third, 3s. the fourth, 4s. the fifth, and 5s. the sixth and seventh.

Hope mill, near Wrexham, where linen yarn was spun by Messrs. Grueber and Grucher till they went bankrupt in 1826.[1]

Bleaching was the subject of a more ambitious experiment, to which reference has already been made. It was about 1780 that the eccentric aristocrat, Thomas Fitzmaurice, erected on his estate at Llewenni a linen bleachery—"the most elegant structure of its kind in Europe"—costing £20,000. It consisted, we are told, of

> an extensive pile of buildings in the form of a crescent, with a beautiful arcade of four hundred feet in length, terminating at each end in a pavilion having five fountains in front, of Dutch ornamental work.

He intended it primarily for the brown linens which his Irish tenants paid him by way of rent, but weavers of the Vale of Clwyd and other parts of Wales also brought their linen there to be whitened at so much a yard. His own linens, amounting for some time to about 4,000 pieces a year, the proprietor sold in person at Chester fair.[2] He was succeeded in 1793 by a son of very different calibre, who bore the courtesy title of Viscount Kirkwall. To get the troublesome bleach works off his hands, he let them to Mr. Dumbell, a Warrington cotton manufacturer (possibly son of one of the partners in the Cheadle Brass Company), who used them for bleaching muslins and ginghams as well as linen. Then they passed into the hands of J. Matthews and Co., who opened depôts for collecting unbleached linen at Chester, Denbigh and Caernarvon.[3]   But in 1809 Lord Kirkwall went bankrupt, and his estate—including the bleach works—was put up for sale. No one seems to have attempted to revive the industry; by 1833 the buildings themselves had disappeared.[4]

---

[1] *Chester Chron.*, July 10, 1807 ; *Shrewsbury Chron.*, March 10, 1826.

[2] *Supra*, pp. 32–3 ; Pennant : *Tours*, II, pp. 143–4 ; Williams : *Ancient and Modern Denbigh*, pp. 128–9.

[3] Davies : *General View*, p. 410 ; *Chester Chron.*, May 5, 1797, May 25, 1798, Feb. 28, 1800, March 12, 1802, April 11, 1806, March 20, 1807 ; Pugh : *Camb. Dep.*, p. 395 ; Hamilton : *Brass and Copper Industries*, p. 247 *n*.

[4] *Imperial and County Register*, 1810, Pt. V, p. 6 ; *N. W. Gaz.*, Oct. 5, 1809, April 12, 1810 ; Evans : *Beauties*, p. 529 ; Lewis : *Top. Dict.*, under *Denbigh*.

No definite date can be given for the decline of the linen industry in North Wales. The Napoleonic Wars, by cutting off foreign supplies of flax, did considerable damage ;[1] but extinction did not come about by a series of spectacular crises and widespread bankruptcies, as in the cotton and woollen industries. What happened was simply that one by one the looms and spinning wheels—ceasing to earn a living for their owners—were stowed away in garrets and lumber rooms, or else used exclusively for wool ; parents, too, ceased to apprentice their children to flax-dressing, so that as the old craftsmen died off, no new ones arose to take their places. At Wrexham the death (in 1837) of Thomas Jones—last of a long dynasty of flax-dressing Joneses—left his former apprentice, John Griffiths, as solitary survivor of a once widespread craft.[2] At last he deserted it to become parish bellman (while his wife kept school), and with his death in 1862 the Wrexham flax-dressing industry became a mere memory. In Montgomeryshire the process of elimination dragged on to the end of the century. An old inhabitant of Llan y mynech, whose family had maintained themselves for generations by weaving for the local gentry, was still making linen on the handloom in 1900.[3]

The available statistics tell us little, for the industry was already on its last legs before the Census began to include details of occupations ; but the following figures help to illustrate the final stages of decline. In 1841 there were 25 flax-dressers and 14 linen weavers in North Wales ; of the latter, ten were in Montgomeryshire and the rest in Denbighshire and Flintshire ; the flax-dressers were distributed between all six counties. By 1851 the whole industry accounted only for 19 workers : 7 in Montgomery, 4 apiece in Denbigh and Flint, two each in Anglesey and Caernarvon. Most of them worked single-handed ; one employed two assistants and another four : no one more than that. The next two Censuses saw a further

[1] *N. W. Gaz.*, Feb. 18, April 7, 1808.
[2] Palmer : *Wrexham*, p. 19 (*cf.* 49, 55, 219), *Older Nonconformity*, pp. 114–15, 127–8, *Parish Church*, p. 104 ; *Chester Chron.*, Sept. 25, 1778, July 13, 1781, April 6, 1798, Feb. 19, 1802.
[3] *Bye-gones.* 1899–1900, p. 403.

shrinkage to 12 and then 9, after which the occupation rarely appears at all. "The period since the 'seventies," says Dr. Clapham,[1] "was the one in which the European linen industry as a whole was contracting, losing ground to cotton, and in which the English—though not the British—industry almost died out." In Wales it was already little more than an antiquarian survival, the period of rapid decline having ended at least a generation earlier—just when the cottager could least afford to lose another subsidiary source of income and to sink a stage further into dependence on the huckster and the shop-keeper.

In the eighteenth century hemp, as well as flax, was grown and manufactured on a small scale in parts of North Wales—mostly in eastern Montgomeryshire, with a few patches in Anglesey and Caernarvonshire. Some of it was manufactured into rough cloth (which was sold at 1s. 6d. to 2s. 6d. a yard in the markets of Cardigan-shire), into fishing nets, or into fine tablecloths for home use.[2] But with the growth of shipping and of mining, the most extensive demand came from the rope-maker and the sail-maker. In 1811 the owners of vessels at Caernarvon complained of the distance they had to go to procure ropes and sails, and promised their patronage to any local manufacturer; a rope-maker soon appeared, but we hear of no response to the appeal for sailmakers, Pwllheli, however, already had a firm engaged in the trade, and the making of hempen nets had been a wide-spread occupation there since the middle of the eighteenth century.[3] A Liverpool firm of sailmakers set up in busi-ness at Bangor in 1825,[4] and there were two sailmakers at Holyhead by 1828. Up to the latter date ropes were made, not only at seaports like Holyhead and Pwllheli and river towns like Llanrwst and Llanelltyd (the port of

---

[1] *Economic Development of France and Germany*, p. 255.

[2] Davies : *General View*, p. 210 ; *Bye-gones*, 1907–08, p. 316. Payments for hemp, hempen cloth and rope yarns, and for spinning hemp and twisting it into fishing nets, frequently appear in the Meyrick papers between 1755 and 1774.

[3] *N. W. Gaz.*, Sept. 5, 1811, April 8, 1813, Aug. 22, 1811 ; Pococke ; *Travels*, II, p. 178.

[4] *N. W. Gaz.*, Nov. 10, 1825.

Dolgelley), but even in high and dry market towns, such as Denbigh and Wrexham ; and at Llan y mynech a man from Chester started a rope-walk at the beginning of Victoria's reign and kept it going for forty years.[1]   But the biggest establishment in North Wales was at Bagillt, in the midst of the coal and lead district of Flintshire. Set up some time before the end of the eighteenth century, it continued for fifty years or more to cater for both the shipping and the mining interests.   The premises, hired at an annual rental of £22, included—in addition to the actual rope-walk of nearly 4,000 yards (partly covered in) —hemp warehouse, dressing room, tarring house and capstan, two houses for clerk and foreman, and cottages for workmen.   But the work seems to have been done entirely by hand, despite the fact that a machine patented by Cartwright (the inventor of the power loom) had been on the market since 1792.[2]

By 1833 the cultivation of hemp in North Wales had almost ceased, and the ropemakers—increasingly dependent on imported material, and faced with the competition of machine-made goods—gradually dropped out of the business.   There were still sixty in the middle of the century (most of them in the counties of Caernarvon, Denbigh and Flint), but the numbers were already declining, and at the 1921 Census not more than half-a-dozen were left.[3]   One tiny and highly localized branch of the rope-making industry, however, has persisted to the present day in a remote corner of Anglesey.   It uses as its material, not hemp, but a peculiarly tough sea-reed—known locally as *moresg*, in English as matweed, marram or staregrass, and to botanists as *ammophila arundinacea*—which grows abundantly on the sand dunes of the west coast of the island, especially near Newborough.   For fully three centuries, and probably for much longer, the inhabitants of Newborough have made a scanty living by plaiting this material into mats and ropes for the farmers' haystacks, barn roofs and cucumber frames, as well as into nets and

---

[1] Pigot's *Directory*, 1822–23 and 1828–29 ; *Mont. Coll.*, X, p. 394.
[2] Davies : *General View*, p. 414 ; *N. W. Gaz.*, Aug. 11, 1808 ; Lewis : *Top. Dict.*, 1833 and 1843.
[3] Lewis : *op. cit.*, under *Montgomeryshire;* Jones, A. M. : *The Rural Industries of . . . Wales*, pp. 82–3.

cordage for the fishermen. In the palmy days of the industry, it gave work to men, women and children, and "every house was a little factory," supplying not only the district around, but even parts of Caernarvonshire, Denbighshire and Flintshire. The competition of commercial products has robbed it of these more distant markets, and production has shrunk since 1800 to about a quarter its former extent ; that it has survived at all is due partly to the remoteness of a region still untouched by the railway, partly to the recent growth of co-operative organization among the makers.[1]

The leather industry does not come strictly within the scope of this chapter, but it may fittingly be treated here, not only as another branch of the clothing trade, but also because of its close connection, through the development of roller spinning, with cotton. Before the nineteenth century, leather goods—boots, shoes, and gloves, saddles and harness—were made for local use in most market towns of North Wales, and "every self-supporting village had its tanner" ;[2] but, as in the woollen industry, a few places had become more specialized centres of production. Denbigh had its gilds of glovers and corvisors from early in the seventeenth century, and during the next 200 years the leather trade was well represented among the aldermen and councillors. The appointment of an inspector of raw hides was still one of the duties of the Corporation in 1799.[3] The branch of the industry in which Denbigh specialized was the manufacture of gloves.[4] From the middle of the eighteenth century, travellers commented on the large quantities sent every year to London, Liverpool and Bristol, some portion for export to the West Indies and elsewhere. At the end of the century the

[1] Pennant: *Tours*, III, p. 5; *Trans. Ang. Ant. Soc.*, 1923, pp. 62–4; Jones, A. M. : *op. cit.*, pp. 75–9 (but the origin of the industry is here post-dated by two centuries at least ; *see* Randall, H. J., and Rees, W. (ed.) : *Storie of the Lower Borowes*, Cardiff, [1932], p. 155).

[2] Jones, A. M. : *op. cit.*, p. 84.

[3] Williams : *Records of Denbigh*, pp. 126, 155, and chap. XIII.

[4] It was also carried on during the seventeenth and eighteenth centuries at Wrexham (*Cal. of Coleman Documents*, 1074, 1088), Newtown (*id.*, 1721), and in parts of Merioneth (*id.*, 1386) ; at Bala and Ruthin (Barfoot and Wilkes' *Directory*, 1790), and at Welshpool (*Mont. Coll.*, XXXVI, p. 18).

annual output was about 7,000 dozen pairs. There was also a manufacture of shoes, far beyond the requirements of the town itself, and of leather breeches for the army. In 1790 Denbigh had 8 master glovers and breeches makers, and 18 boot and shoe makers.[1]

The leather for boots and shoes was tanned on the spot, but the more delicate skins needed by the glover came from Dolgelley, where there was a considerable trade in dressed skins (sheep, lamb, and kid), both native and imported. Besides those sent to Denbigh, some were made into gloves at Dolgelley itself, some were sent to Chester and Worcester, and a few to London ; and during the years when woollen cloth was exported from Barmouth (itself a tanning centre), dressed skins sometimes formed part of the cargo. As many as 100,000 skins a year were dressed at Dolgelley in the early nineteenth century.[2]

Tanning proper was so widespread an occupation that one can only enumerate a few of the places where it attracted the notice of travellers and others. The trade was especially popular in Montgomeryshire—partly, perhaps, owing to the plentifulness of oak bark, partly to the softness of the Severn water ; though Llanfyllin, one of the chief centres, stands not on the Severn, but on one of its tributaries. Here the records of admission to burgess-ship in the seventeeth and eighteenth centuries indicate the supremacy of tanning and glove-making over all other occupations, and the comfortable position of those engaged in it. A tanyard advertised in 1814 had 57 tan pits, 4 lime and 2 waste pits, 9 vats, a copper furnace and a patent bark mill, as well as storehouses, drying sheds (with a capacity of 250 to 300 hides) and bark bays (with room for 60 to 100 tons of bark).[3] Welshpool, Newtown and Llanidloes (which drew many of its mayors from the tanning industry) all had the advantage of Severn water ; Llansantffraid (on another tributary), and

---

[1] Defoe : *Tour* (second ed., 1742), II, p. 329 ; Pennant : *Tours*, II, p. 159 ; Davies : *General View*, p. 414 ; Pugh : *Camb. Dep.*, p. 388 ; Barfoot and Wilkes' *Directory*, V, pp. 53–8.
[2] Davies : *loc. cit.;* Lewis : *Top. Dict.*, 1833 and 1843 ; Meyrick papers, 1770.
[3] *Mont. Coll.*, XXIII, pp. 146–54 ; *N. W. Gaz.*, Jan. 7, 1814.

Machynlleth (on the Dovey) both had many tanneries of long standing.[1]

In Anglesey the tanners and curriers were strong enough to organize a protest against the leather duty in 1813.[2] They were mostly congregated in the little market town of Llannerch y medd—long famous for its boots and shoes, in the manufacture of which 250 men were said to be employed in 1833. Their brethren at Holyhead still celebrated St. Crispin, the patron saint of shoemakers, as late as 1821.[3] Caernarvon, which had exported leather at least since the reign of Henry VIII, could at this time boast a large tannery with 50 tan pits and slaughter house attached.[4] Most important of all was Wrexham, in whose parish registers the names of skinners, tanners and curriers, as well as of glovers and breeches makers, abound from the seventeenth century onwards, and where tanners (necessarily men of substance, since they usually had to wait eighteen months before their goods were ready for market) almost monopolized the office of churchwarden in the eighteenth.[5]

It was the manufacturing branch of the industry that first showed signs of decay. Towards the end of the eighteenth century more and more of the skins produced in Wales were being sent to the English glovers, who "from a superior art in dressing them" were "able to send a much neater article at a lower price into Wales."[6] Huskisson's remission of the duty on imported gloves in 1825 was a further blow to the trade. By 1828 the number of master glovers at Denbigh had been reduced (since 1790) by three-quarters, and the boot and shoe makers by half. The Municipal Corporations Report of 1835 states that the leather trade has "declined greatly." Denbigh was

[1] Lewis : *Top. Dict.*; Horsfall–Turner : *Llanidloes*, pp. 231, etc. ; *Bye-gones*, 1907–08, pp. 299, 306, 315–16 ; 1909–10, pp. 105, 142 ; Pococke : *Travels*, II, p. 180 ; Aikin : *Journal*, p. 38.

[2] *N. W. Gaz.*, March 14, 1813.

[3] Lewis : *Top. Dict.*; *Rept. on Land* (1896), p. 45 ; *N. W. Gaz.*, Nov. 8, 1821.

[4] Lewis : *Mediaeval Boroughs of Snowdonia*, p. 187 ; *N. W. Gaz.*, Oct. 6, 1821.

[5] Palmer : *Wrexham*, p. 9, *et passim*, *Parish Church*, chap. V ; *Camb. Dep.*, p. 324.

[6] Evans : *Tour*, p. 132.

moving in the opposite direction to Wrexham, and becoming (as it was described nine years later) "more a place of genteel retirement than trade." The manufacture of fine gloves (except to order) had almost ceased by the middle of the century ; the only articles still made were heavy gauntlets and the like. The blame for the decline of the boot and shoe industry has been laid at the door of an ill-judged strike of the Society of Operative Cordwainers in 1834.[1] Actually, of course, far wider causes were at work, affecting not only Denbigh but the country at large. For, in this as in other trades, the handiwork of the local craftsman was being swamped (thanks to improvement in transport) by goods sent out from central factories, where improved machinery could be used. There were still nearly 5,000 people engaged in the boot and shoe industry in North Wales in 1851, and about 40 glovers ; in 1921 only one glover was left, and the number of shoe-makers—including those engaged only in repairs and retailing, who form the vast majority—was not much over 1,000.

To compensate for the dwindling demand in home manufactures, Welsh leather found a new and profitable market in the Lancashire cotton factories. In 1770— just a year after Arkwright took out his first patent for roller-spinning—John Peers established at Wrexham what came to be the largest of the local leather works. Seven or eight years later John Smalley of Holywell, visiting Wrexham Fair in search of fresh custom for his cotton twist, met Peers, and got into conversation with him on the subject of leather for the rollers of the spinning machine. The upshot was a regular trade in roller leather between the Wrexham tanneries and the cotton mills, not only of Holywell, but of Lancashire. This trade virtually created a new branch of the leather industry, and added materially to the prosperity of Wrexham. Peers was succeeded in 1822 by Evan Morris, a Montgomeryshire man who had been apprenticed at Oswestry. It was he who, to obtain a softer and more pliable grade of leather, substituted tawing with alum for tanning with bark. The works were

[1] Williams : *Ancient and Modern Denbigh*, pp. 129, 131 ; Pigot's *Directory*, 1828–29 ; *Parl. Pap.*, 1835, XXVI, p. 596 ; Fullarton's *Parl. Gaz.*, I, p. 501. On Wrexham *cf. supra*, p. 198.

purchased in 1858 by Messrs. Jones and Rocke, who have in recent years given place to a limited company.[1]

The manufacture of roller leather spread to many of the other tanneries of North Wales. There are now 16 (out of a total of 24 in all Wales) which confine themselves to treating sheep skins and goat skins, mainly for the Lancashire market. Welsh skins have been found peculiarly suitable for the purpose, since only they can stand being shaved down to the requisite fineness. Had it not been for this, the Welsh tanning industry would be almost defunct. The competition of cheaper leather made by more rapid machine-processes in the English works, the loss of the market provided by the local saddler and shoemaker, and the lack of great industrial centres to create a local demand, have reduced the number of tanneries making strong leather (from cow-hides) for the boot, shoe and harness trades, to about half-a-dozen in the whole of Wales. Much of this decline took place during the last quarter of the nineteenth century. In Montgomeryshire, for example, the industry was still important and extensive in at least four towns in 1878 ; on the eve of the great War only Newtown was left. But since the remaining works, especially those engaged in the roller leather trade, generally employ far more men than the old-fashioned tanneries which have been squeezed out, the number employed in leather-making itself has not suffered nearly so serious a diminution as that of manufacturers of leather goods.[2]

---

[1] Jones, A. Seymour : *Roller Leather*, pp. 29 ff.
[2] Jones, A. M. : *op. cit.*, chap. V ; *Mont. Coll.*, XXXVII, pp. 15 ff. The numbers are 538 in 1851 and 428 in 1921.

CHAPTER IX.

THE NEW CAPITALISTS.

Attolwg Syr, ebr fi, pa ryw o ddynion yw y rhain ? Rhyw *Siôn lygad y geiniog*, eb ynte, yw'r cwbl . . . Marsiandwyr, C[r]ibddeilwyr[,] Llogwyr ; . . . Maelwyr a fydd yn cadw ac yn codi'r Farchnad at eu llaw eu hunain : Siopwyr (neu Siarpwyr) a elwant ar *angen*, neu *anwybodaeth* y prynwyr . . ., Tafarnwyr sy'n *yspeilio* Teuluoedd yr oferwyr o'u *dâ*, a'r Wlâd oi *Haidd* at fara i'r tlodion.[1]

—Gweledigaetheu y Bardd Cwsc, 1703.

The Merchant . . . takes nothing from the industrious Labourer ; he pays the poor Man for his Work ; he communicates his Profit with Mankind ; . . . he furnishes Employment and Subsistence to greater Numbers than the richest Nobleman.

—Spectator, No. 174, Sept. 19, 1711 (Steele).

The new scale and technique of production which we have seen invading one industry after another, called for a heavier outlay on fixed plant, a good stock of fluid capital to meet the swelling wage bills, and new distributive agencies to bridge the widening gulf between the producer and his market. In the English industrial districts these problems had been faced and solved (in a fashion appropriate to the stage of economic evolution) long before the great inventions began ; so that there the Industrial Revolution was simply the logical outcome of a long process of development, and the differentiation between economic groups such as landlords and *entrepreneurs*, producers and dealers, industrial workers and peasants, master craftsmen and wage earners, had come about by gradual stages. North Wales had been disqualified by its history from participating in these earlier steps towards capitalism ; here everything had to be telescoped into the space of two or' three generations ; and the sudden

---

[1] "Prithee, sir, quoth I, what manner of men be these ? A sort of catchpennies, said he, all of them . . . merchants, grabbers, moneylenders, . . . traders who make the market rise and fall for their own ends ; shopmen (or sharpers) who trade on the need or ignorance of the buyers . . ., taverners who spoil wasters' families of their goods, and the land of its barley—the bread of the poor."

emergence of new social classes and new social relationships changed the centre of gravity of society, and gave the movement a significance out of all proportion to its statistical magnitude. With the rank and file of the industrial army we shall deal in the next chapter ; here we are concerned with the personnel and tactics of the higher command.

The first problem was the provision of capital for working minerals and putting up machinery and buildings. In England this capital, the fruit of years of expanding foreign trade, lay ready accumulated in the hands of prosperous merchants, needing only the assurance of profit and the removal of restrictions to bring it to the service of industry. In North Wales, for reasons we have seen,[1] there had been no such accumulation of mercantile capital ; and when once agricultural depression had tightened the purse-strings of the gentry, and confined their activities to a few special industries like slate-quarrying, the Industrial Revolution took on itself more and more the form of an economic "penetration" by the English speculator. Apart from such striking exceptions as Lord Penrhyn or Pugh of Brynllywarch on the one hand, and Thomas Williams of Llanidan on the other, the capitalists who financed the bigger undertakings were almost all Englishmen.

English invasions, of course, were no novelty. Even in the Middle Ages the prospector had followed hard on the warrior ; but the impress he left on the life of the country had been a much feebler one. From the middle of the eighteenth century, however, starting with the Wilkinsons and the Cheadle Brass Company, wave after wave of immigrant capitalists swept over the country, and each wave left behind some permanent deposit. From Cornwall and from Macclesfield they came in quest of copper, from Bristol for calamine, from Derbyshire and Cheshire for lead, from Staffordshire, Yorkshire and Northumberland for coal. The Wilkinsons were followed by other Midland ironmasters ; Manchester manufacturers built cotton mills, and introduced new processes into paper mills ;[2] Liverpool

[1] *Supra*, pp. 25-27.
[2] E.g., Thomas Rostron, at Holywell (*N. W. Chron.*, April 8, 1824).

merchants developed shipping, dabbled in quarries and copper mines, opened shops, and put money into the woollen industry ; potters from the English Potteries worked up the Buckley clay deposits ; Chester, Shrewsbury and Dublin helped with the roads ; and investors from all over the country took shares in canals and railways. The climax came with the rage for Welsh minerals and the booming of Welsh water-power and other resources in 1825–6.[1] Then, as the mines became exhausted or waterlogged, as steam power displaced water power and industry sought the coalfields, the flow of English capital was diverted elsewhere, and the industries of North Wales were left to fight their own battle against the devastating competition of better-equipped regions.

The displacement of the landlord by the new industrial *entrepreneur* meant a real revolution in social life. The relation between the old-fashioned landlord and his employees had always remained essentially feudal in character. When Sir Watkin Williams Wynn's colliers flocked into Wrexham in 1715 to wreck Dissenting meeting houses, they at least felt themselves to be loyally fighting under the banner of their Jacobite lord and master, even though he might feel it incumbent upon himself, as a magistrate, to disown them. Sir Thomas Mostyn's miners in Flintshire, rioting against the machinations of corn dealers in 1740, raised the cry of "A Mostyn," just as their ancestors had done, when (if tradition speaks true) they followed the Mostyn of that day to join the standard of Harry of Richmond on Bosworth field. Both Sir Watkin and Sir Thomas were suspected of collusion ; and more than a century later we find a lingering echo of this old instinctive alliance of the lord and his retainers against the moneyed middle classes, in the sympathy shown by Sir Watkin's grandson towards the coal strike of 1830–31.[2] But by that time Methodism had already slackened the bond, and when these same miners learned to join with others like themselves in the new middle-class Radical

---

[1] *See*, e.g., *Shrewsbury Chron.*, Feb. 4, Aug. 19, 1825 ; *N. W. Gaz.*, Sept. 7, 1826.
[2] Palmer : *Older Nonconformity*, p. 63 ; Ashton and Sykes,: *op. cit.*, pp. 131–2 ; *cf. supra*, pp. 23, 28 ; *infra*, pp. 405–6.

agitations against the Corn Laws, the Game Laws and the rotten boroughs, the last link was severed.[1]

The new capitalist might emulate the wealth of the old aristocracy ; he might settle on their estates, get himself arms from the College of Heralds, take out a game licence, and dub himself esquire ; he might even become High Sheriff of the county ; but if it was hard for a *novus homo*, it was harder still for a stranger in blood and speech to win for himself this sense of tribal loyalty among his dependents. When Christopher Smalley—a mere cotton manufacturer—was put forward for a commission in the Holywell Volunteers, the rank and file sulked ; and it was not with the war-cry of "A Wilkinson" or "A Kyrke" that the colliers of the nineteenth century were roused to revolt !

Even more subversive of old social relationships was the impersonal Company, with scattered shareholders, and undertakings in a dozen different counties. From Elizabeth's time to the Bubble Act of 1719, such companies had occasionally taken in hand operations in North Wales (such as the mining and smelting of metals), which went beyond the vision or the capacities of the local landowners. But the Bubble Act, passed for the protection of investors at the height of the South Sea panic, penalized joint stock enterprise for over a century by making incorporation difficult and expensive, and leaving the legal status of the unincorporated company in a perilous uncertainty.[2] Existing companies, however, were not touched ; we have seen[3] how the Mine Adventurers (for example) remained active in North Wales till late in the century ; and, on a less imposing scale, a capitalist could still privately invite partners to take up shares in a work he was unable to undertake alone—avoiding the expense of formal

[1] The names of local bankers, smelters and flannel manufacturers appear prominently in the Reform agitation of 1830–31 (e.g. *N. W. Chron.*, March 4, 1830, *Shrewsbury Chron.*, Dec. 10, 1830, Jan. 14, 1831). *Cf. infra*, pp. 395, 409 *n.*

[2] 6 Geo. I, cap. 18, § 18 ; Holdsworth, W. S. : *History of English Law*, VIII, pp. 219–21 ; Palmer, Sir F. B. : *Company Law* (ed.Toppam, A. F., 1924), p. 6.

[3] *Supra*, p. 179.

incorporation and the legal pitfalls of the Stock Exchange.[1]
Shares in these private partnerships—usually quoted in
"moieties," quarters, eighths, sixteenths and thirty-
seconds, more rarely in thirds, tenths, twelfths, eighteenths
or twenty-fourths, and occasionally (when mines were in
question) in ounces—were often offered for sale in the
local press on the death or bankruptcy of the shareholder.
Common from time immemorial in the ownership of sailing
vessels, this form of partnership was extended to corn,
paper and wire mills,[2] to metal works, and above all, to
mines.

The Cheadle Brass Company (which, although not
primarily a Welsh concern, had Welsh partners and Welsh
works) will serve as an example of the private company in
the smelting industries. Founded in the very year of the
Bubble Act, it included in 1736 six partners, holding
between them a capital of £3,600 in shares of 1-24 each, of
which Patten (the founder) had 8, Barker (the Flintshire
partner) 9, three others 2 each, and the sixth, 1. By 1780
many of the original partners had disappeared and been
replaced. The capital was now £30,000, held in shares of
1-20 by five partners; Patten, who had been steadily
increasing his control since Barker's death or resignation,
now had 12 shares, and the others from 1 to 3.[3]

Shareholding of this sort was particularly common in
lead mines.[4] A London company had taken over the Talar
Goch mine (near Dyserth) before the Bubble Act, and
notices of meetings of shareholders and of shares for sale
are to be met with in local papers up to a hundred years
later. Here the total number of shares, in 1799, was
2688.[5] On a much smaller scale was the company which
worked the Nant y ffrith mine (near Wrexham) from

[1] Clapham : *op. cit.*, pp. 234, 434 ; Ashton and Sykes : *op. cit.*,
p. 4.
[2] E.g. *N. W. Gaz.*, Feb. 6, 1809, Aug. 2, 1821, April 9, 1829.
[3] Hamilton : *English Brass and Copper Industries*, p. 247 *n.*
[4] E.g. shares advertised in *Chester Chron.* : Pant y mwyn, Mold,
June 20, 1776 ; Erw Mostyn, Llanarmon, Oct. 4, 1782 ; Whitford,
Dec. 26, 1777 ; Holywell Level, Oct. 31, 1806 ; Catch Whimsey,
Halkin, June 20, 1800 ; Llanrwst district, Nov. 7, 1806.
[5] Lhuyd : "Parochialia" (*Arch. Camb.*, Suppt., 1909), p. 56 ;
Chester Chron., Feb. 28, 1776, Oct. 29, 1779, Jan. 11, 1799 ; Pigot's
Directory, 1828–29 ; Lewis : *Top. Dict.*, 1833 and 1843.

1753–7. It started with three partners, all holding equal shares, but one receiving an additional salary of £4 4s. as manager. Three others joined them later, on various terms ; but the total profits to be divided between all six at the end of a year were not much over £100 !¹

In coal mines and slate quarries individual exploitation was more general. A landowner like Lord Penrhyn, possessing at once land, minerals and foreshore, could work his business unaided ; a successful *entrepreneur* like John Wilkinson, with his irons in many fires all over the country, found even a family partnership too cramping. But not all the coal mines were worked by ironmasters or landed proprietors ; in Flintshire at least there were several private partnerships, such as the Yorkshire company which had taken over one of the Hawarden pits by 1790, or the Flintshire Coal Mine Adventurers and the Irish Coal Company, of which we read early in the next century.² Even in Anglesey the Berw colliery was in the hands of a company in 1814.³

Examples of the working of slate quarries at Ffestiniog by private partnerships, when the district was first developing, have been given in another chapter ;⁴ they could be freely supplemented from Caernarvonshire during the same period. The Rev. R. M. Humphreys, who had worked a quarry on his farm at Hafodlas independently for several years with the aid of a steam engine, took into partnership in 1812 a Liverpool merchant, a Caernarvon innkeeper, and a quarryman from Llanllyfni. The terms of partnership were as follows : three-quarters of the rent (£630) were to be paid over to Humphreys by the other partners (as soon as the water was cleared), in proportions of 6/16, 4/16, and 2/16 respectively ; in addition he was to receive 5 per cent on all further moneys he might advance for machinery and the like. When more capital was needed, each of the partners was to pay into the Caernarvon bank such sums as a majority (in value)

¹ Palmer : *Old Parish of Wrexham*, pp. 129–30.
² *Memoir of Hawarden*, pp. 104–5 ; *N. W. Gaz.*, March 17, 1808 ; Lewis : *Top. Dict.*, under *Northop*.
³ *N. W. Gaz.*, Sept. 23, 1814. 9½ shares in it were offered for sale in 1821 (*id.*, Jan. 14).
⁴ *Supra*, pp. 210-11.

might think necessary from time to time. Humphreys was not to be required to take an active part in the management, and he was empowered to transfer his share to another partner whenever it might suit him. Within a few years, however, Humphreys and his Liverpool partner were dead, the quarryman had sold his interest out, and the concern was in Chancery while Mrs. Humphreys and the innkeeper fought out their financial liabilities. The quarries on the Crown commons of Cefn du and Cilgwyn hitherto worked on the usual terms by working quarrymen, were leased in 1800 to a local partnership of four, styled the Cilgwyn and Cefn du Slate Company. During the next 20 years or so, shares changed hands with a speed which shows at least that there was no lack of elasticity about these primitive capitalistic ventures.[1] The partners included illiterate quarrymen, local shopkeepers, slate merchants from Caernarvon and York, a Liverpool architect and several Liverpool and Bristol merchants. A deed of copartnery of 1812 shows similar arrangements to those at Hafodlas : a senior partner, who provides the bulk of the capital, manages (unlike Humphreys) all dealings with merchants and shippers, and draws on the other partners as occasion requires. Here, too, the partnership issued in financial quarrels, non-payment of workpeople, and a harvest for the lawyers ; and towards 1830 the Cilgwyn Company, its output shrunk to a paltry 265 tons, was in serious financial straits.[2]

In copper mining the classic example is the Parys Mine Company, in which Hughes, as owner of the minerals, had the co-operation of Dawes (with his fluid capital) and Williams (with his business ability) ; and even Roose (as technical expert) came in for a part share. The companies in which Thomas Williams himself was the guiding brain

[1] A deed of transfer of a share in 1820 specifically defines the share as including a third of the quarries, engines, cabins, sheds, levels, and all other conveniences, roads, etc.

[2] Porth yr aur MSS : deeds of copartnership, Hafodlas (July 9, 1812), Cefn du (Dec. 31, 1812) ; deeds of transfer, Aug., 1820, etc., and numerous other legal documents ; *N. W. Gaz.*, March 13, 1823 (first reference to Cilgwyn Co.), May 11, 1809 (notice of expiry of lease to Messrs. Jones, Humphreys and Co.), June 15, 1826, Oct. 25, 1827 (shares offered for sale). Shares in a Llanddeiniolen quarry are offered for sale in *id.,* July 26, 1810.

defy enumeration. They culminated in that vast copper cartel, which, without "any mixture of property," for a time controlled the copper trade of the whole kingdom.[1] The textile trades were more individualistic ; the Cotton Twist Company at Holywell found no imitators in the woollen industry (apart from such partial co-operation as the joint occupation of carding mills), until the Bubble Act had gone.[2]

The partners in these collective concerns were drawn from all ranks of society. Imposing structures like the old joint stock companies or the Parys Mine Company had at their backs wealthy men whose investments usually extended far beyond this one concern. Shares in single lead mines were often taken, in earlier days, by landlords as a convenient form of investment near to hand ; later the shareholders were more likely to be smelters who wished to ensure their stock of ore.[3] At the bottom of the scale come partnerships of working miners or quarrymen, shopkeepers or professional men, bargaining with the owner of the soil or with the lessee, sometimes for the entire working of a small mine, sometimes for the exploitation of a single seam. We shall find relics of this "more or less democratic copartnery" in the working of coal, lead and copper mines, as late as the middle of the nineteenth century. By that time the leading partner had become a sort of gang-leader, and the growing volume of capital needed for working the mine had thrown the gang of partners more and more into dependence on the *entrepreneur* who necessarily supplied the bulk of it.[4] The private companies which occupied so much of the field of mining enterprise between 1719 and 1825 therefore provide an important link between the "free" and the wage-earning miner, just as the "customer weaver" serves to bridge the gulf between independent craftsman and factory hand.

[1] *Supra*, pp. 158-9. There were also humbler companies in copper mining, such as the partnership of nine which began working on Sir Watkin Williams Wynn's lands at Tan yr allt, near Trawsfynydd, in 1816–17. The papers of John Matthews the surveyor (*supra*, p. 68 *n* ; Amlwch MS. 4 (xxvi), 8 ff.) record frequent meetings of the proprietors, sales of shares in half-ounces, etc.

[2] *Supra*, chaps. VII and VIII.

[3] *See*, e.g., Palmer : *Old Parish of Wrexham*, p. 230 ; *Chester Chron.*, Oct. 29, 1779.

[4] Ashton and Sykes : *op. cit.*, p. 114 ; *infra*, pp. 365-6.

Both are transitional phases of capitalism which long co-existed with its developed forms.

Developments in transport began a new era in collective enterprise. The construction of canals in North Wales, in the 'nineties, was undertaken under Acts of Parliament by companies with transferable shares (whose prices were regularly quoted in the press), attracting investors from across the border as well as among industrialists on the spot. But the inconvenience and expense of applying for a separate Act of Parliament for each flotation, and the legal insecurity of the investor's position, were serious limitations ; and when 1825 brought a still more formidable crop of joint-stock projects—mining companies, insurance companies, pre-locomotive railway schemes— Canning and Huskisson decided that the time had come for modernizing the law and smoothing the way for collective undertakings. The Bubble Act was repealed,[1] though the principle of limited liability was not recognized for another generation.

In North Wales, as in other parts of the country, first experiences of the new order were not entirely happy. All that came of the ambitious schemes of Rothschild, and of shadier promoters like Wilks, was the flotation of the Welsh Coal and Iron and the Welsh Slate and Copper Companies—neither of much service to the country. The British Iron Company, despite internal dissension, was more fortunate. South Wales was its principal field of operations, but it had got busy in the Ruabon district by 1827, and within fifteen years it had over 1,500 employees in its coal and iron works there.[2] By 1828 there were coal mining companies at all the main colliery centres ; six had headquarters at Mold.[3] The railway age brought a further extension of the investment habit—though, as we have seen, most of the capital for the North Wales lines was subscribed by existing English companies.[4] Eventually joint

[1] 6 Geo. IV, cap. 91.
[2] *C.E.R.* (1840, XVII), p. 377.
[3] Pigot's *Directory*, 1828–29.
[4] For an example of early railway investments on a large scale in North Wales, *see* the ledgers of Mr. J. Ignatius Williams, Pentremawr, Denbigh, 1827 ff. (Bangor MS. 81). In 1839 he had £13,722 in railway shares, £14,059 in shipping, £299 12s. in turnpike bonds, and £11,868 in land. By 1846 his railway investments had come to include the new Chester–Holyhead railway.

stock—freed by the Act of 1862 from the incubus of un-limited liability—captured one field after another, from textile mills to mineral-prospecting, till it came to be accepted as one of the commonplaces of industrial life.[1]

Investments in the fixed plant of industry only solved one of the problems of large-scale production. This capital was locked up ; and frequently the *entrepreneur* had to face bigger wage bills, and heavy disbursements on materials and rents, power and transport—to say nothing of increasing war taxation—before it began to bring in returns ; this, too, at a time when war was producing a serious financial stringency and small change was scarce every-where. He could not afford to keep money idle in his house after the fashion of the old-fashioned landlord or mine prospector ; he must "coin his credit." He might follow the example of tradesmen in the latter half of the seventeenth century (another period of currency famine) by issuing tokens for small payments—the method adopted by Wilkinson and the Parys Mine Company in 1787, and by the Glanclywedog Factory and the Flint Lead Works in 1813. But the circulation of token money was neces-sarily restricted, and, apart from the guinea notes issued by Wilkinson and a few other English ironmasters, its use was confined to small payments.

For bigger transactions there was the bill of exchange, the use of which was greatly extended in North Wales towards the close of the eighteenth century. The glovers and the shoemakers of Denbigh, dealing in a large way with the London exporters, "drew on London in exchange for goods" in order to avoid the inconvenience of frequent cash dealings ; and in Merioneth, during the years when the woollen industry was expanding rapidly and emancipating itself from the Shrewsbury Drapers, it was boasted that "a person may have a bill on London for £100 or much greater sums at the shortest notice."[2] But the bill of exchange was a clumsy instrument, often hard to negotiate in so remote a country as Wales. The credit

[1] *Supra*, pp. 142, 151, 168, 177, 182, 221, 276, 304, etc.

[2] Barfoot and Wilkes' *Directory* , V, p. 54 ; *Camb. Reg.*, I, p. 251. On early banking in North Wales *see Economica*, March, 1926, pp. 16 ff. References, when not otherwise stated, are to this paper.

represented by the tradesman's token was too local ; that which lay behind the bill of exchange was too distant. The need of the age was something to link the two together ; and that was precisely the service of the country banks.

In the chief industrial districts of England these were already familiar. Nottingham claims to have had one before the Bank of England was founded ; for the clothing district of the South West there was Wood's Bank at Gloucester, founded in 1716 ; Bristol Old Bank had appeared by the middle of the century ; and the first in the northern coalfield was established at Newcastle in 1755. But it was after 1760 that the practice spread most rapidly, till in 1808 there were more than 600 country banks. The foundations of Lloyds Bank were laid at Birmingham in 1765 ; the first banks at Manchester and at York followed in 1771 ; even Cornwall had banks by 1778.[1] It was during this period that banking began in Wales. South Wales was little, if any, behind Manchester ; for even if we reject the unverified tradition of a bank at Aberystwyth in 1762, there was one at Merthyr by about 1770, and another at Brecon by 1778.[2] Cardiff remained without one till 1792,[3] by which time North Wales had entered the field.

Here, as elsewhere, the first bankers were almost invariably drawn from the three classes whose operations demanded the greatest turnover of capital : landlords, merchants and industrialists. Wrexham and Holywell, the two chief industrial centres, naturally led the way. In 1785, if not earlier, the first bank at Wrexham was founded by Richard Myddleton Lloyd, a flannel merchant whose father had carried on a business as mercer in the town, and came of good landowning stock. The North Wales Bank at Holywell followed soon after—by the early 'nineties, at any rate. This is probably identical with the

[1] Grindon, L. H. : *Manchester Banks and Bankers* (Manchester, 1872), chap. I ; Easton, H. T. : *The History of a Banking House* (1903) ; Phillips, Maberley : *A History of Banks . . . in Northumberland, Durham and Northern Yorkshire* (1894) ; Ashton : *Iron and Steel*, pp. 227–32. Lord (*Capital and Steam Power*, pp. 68, 114, 126, 229, etc.) appears to post-date the country banks.

[2] *Hist. Soc. of West Wales Transactions*, VI (1916), pp. 135, 153 ; Wilkins, C. : *History of Merthyr Tydfil* (1908), p. 529.

[3] Barfoot and Wilkes' *Directory*, II, p. 640.

Flintshire Bank, which during the currency famine of 1811 issued copper and silver tokens—an unusual practice with banks, though one or two other examples of it are to be found in South Wales during the same year.[1] The most active partner in the Flintshire Bank was Richard Sankey, a local colliery proprietor. Two other partners, Oldfield and Oakley, appear to have been connected with the coal and lead industries. The fourth was John Wilkinson's nephew, Thomas Jones, whose unlucky adventures as an ironmaster have been noticed in an earlier chapter. He had, however, relinquished his partnership before he went bankrupt. Messrs. Sankey had a bank in Denbigh also by 1817.

The Chester and North Wales bank, originating at Chester in 1792, derived its capital from Anglesey copper ; for the founder was Owen Williams, son of the great Thomas Williams, and he was later joined by Pascoe Grenfell (partner in his copper smelting works), and by his brother-in-law, Colonel Hughes (afterwards Lord Dinorben)—son of the "poor curate" who had made his fortune on Parys Mountain. By 1812 a branch had been opened at Caernarvon,[2] where it was used for receiving subscriptions to the Traeth Mawr embankment, and for discounting bills for the customs officials.[3] There was a second branch at Bangor by 1822, and others were subsequently opened at various towns of North Wales, including Amlwch—the *fons et origo* of the wealth on which the bank was built.

Next in order of seniority come Denbigh and Welshpool. In or about 1794, the firm of Clough, Mason and Co. started banking at Denbigh. The partners belonged to

[1] *Hist. Soc. of West Wales Trans.*, VI, p. 132.
[2] This may possibly be identical with the bank of Messrs. Jones, Hughes & Co., mentioned in articles of copartnery relating to a slate quarry in the same year (Porth yr aur MSS.: Hafodlas quarry, July 9, 1812). But there was a still earlier bank there, founded by Richard Roberts, agent to the Coed Helen estate (who died in 1799), and continued by his brother Robert (d. 1809) and his son Richard (d. 1828) (Griffith, J. E. : *Pedigrees of Anglesey and Caernarvonshire Families*, 1914, p. 7 ; *Chester Chron.*, Feb. 1, 1799 ; *N. W. Gaz.*, Dec. 28, 1809).
[3] *Y Gestiana*, p. 174 ; Letters from Customs House collectors at Beaumaris to the Board in London, 1816–17 (substance kindly communicated by Mr. David Thomas.)

the local gentry and clergy, and one of them was an agricultural improver of some note. They were also connected with the woollen industry ; for when they failed in 1816, the sale of bankrupt stock included the Dolgarrog woollen factory, as well as considerable landed estates and the Porth Llwyd paper mill. At Welshpool the "Old Bank" of Messrs. Pugh, Pugh, Turner and Griffiths, who served as bankers to the Montgomeryshire Canal, also began operations in 1794. This was ruined by the crisis of 1816–17, along with another Welshpool bank (that of Mytton, Jones and Mytton), the date of whose foundation is unknown. Their place was at once taken by a branch of the Shrewsbury bank of Messrs. Beck, which had been founded in 1800, and was amalgamated with Lloyds eighty years later.

It was, of course, Welshpool's position as a distributing centre of the flannel industry that led to the establishment of banks there ; but there is no evidence that flannel manufacturers played any part in founding them. The names of the principal partners are those local landowning families. At Newtown and Llanidloes the connection between banking and woollens is more direct. Mr. William Pugh of Brynllywarch carried on in association with his textile enterprises the bank that had been established at Newtown by his father some time before 1807, and one of his partners, William Tilsley, was an owner of flannel mills (which were sold when the bank failed in 1831), as well as of potteries. At Llanidloes Messrs. Herbert and Britton, millowners and bankers, were compelled "under peculiar circumstances" to suspend payment in 1813, though eventually the creditors were paid in full. Dolgelley, the metropolis of the web industry, was served from 1803 by the banking firm of Thomas and Hugh Jones. The second partner is the selfsame Hugh Jones of Hengwrt, Dolgelley, who had recently come to the aid of Messrs. Turner and Casson in their slate-quarrying venture at Ffestiniog, and who subsequently joined Turner in taking a lease of one of Mr. Assheton Smith's quarries at Llanberis.[1]

Most of the banks hitherto mentioned were run by natives ; but immigrant industries sometimes set up banks

---

[1] *Hanes Plwyf Ffestiniog*, pp. 82–3 ; Parry : *Llanberis*, p. 12.

for themselves. An example has already been given in the cotton industry of Flintshire,[1] where, for a few years in the 'twenties, Douglas and Smalley kept banks at Holywell and Mold, and S. and J. Knight another at Mold. Finally we have the shopkeeper as banker. For a typical case of this not uncommon combination we must turn to Wrexham again. In 1800 we read of the theft of some bank bills from the shop of Mr. James Kenrick, grocer and tallow chandler. Soon after this he stopped selling groceries and devoted his whole attention to banking. He was joined in 1824 by a partner from Manchester, and the firm continued to do business till the crash of 1848. A less reputable sample may be found in the career of Mr. J. Pearson of Holyhead. When we first hear of him, in 1806, he is keeping a private school for young gentlemen, while his wife educates their sisters, and he is stoutly denying "malicious reports" that he intends to quit for Dublin. A few years later he reappears as bookseller, keeper of a circulating library, dealer in tea, jewellery, lace, perfumery, and patent medicines—opening and closing shops at Bangor, Caernarvon, Beaumaris, and Holyhead with surprising agility. In 1809 he gives notice that he has "declined the banking business," and that any person holding notes signed "J. Pearson, Holyhead," may have them immediately cashed on application ; once again, too, "malicious rumours which have been circulated to injure his character and credit" have to be refuted. Within two months—as the reader will have anticipated—his name appears in the list of bankrupts.

Here we have the seamier side of the old private banks. It is illustrated on a bigger scale by the operations of Mr. John Dicas, who in 1823 brought an action against the *Manchester Guardian* for calling him "a prison bird and a confessed pauper." The defendants were able to prove that, after serving two years' imprisonment for suing out a fraudulent commission of bankruptcy, he had induced a wealthy gentleman at Holywell to join him in founding the Flintshire New Bank, which issued large quantities of £1 notes, made to resemble as closely as possible those of the Old Bank of Messrs. Sankey. Writs were already out

---

[1] *Supra*, pp. 286, 288.

against the firm for debts of £50 and upwards, and the plaintiff claimed that the *Guardian* article had so discredited the notes that as many as a thousand were tendered for payment within six weeks. The plaintiff won his case, but we hear no more of the Flintshire New Bank.

The spread of banking undoubtedly gave to the budding local industries a buoyancy and confidence which would never have been possible under the old financial order. "What can the Bank of England know of country securities ?" asked a correspondent of a Bangor paper in 1810.[1] London bankers themselves recognized the difficulty, and early in the nineteenth century we find them using the local press as a means of getting into touch with "country banking correspondents." All the more reputable banks that we have been considering availed themselves of such opportunities. The Dolgelley bank announces in 1810 that "the Notes and Drafts of Messrs. THOMAS and HUGH JONES of Dolgelley Merionethshire, drawn on Messrs. BRICKWOODS, and Co. will be paid at the Banking house of the Hon. SIMON FRASER, Sir JOHN PERRING, BART. and Co. Cornhill, London."[2] Mr. R. M. Lloyd, Wrexham, made use of Smith, Payne and Smiths—a house which, originating in Nottingham, always kept in close touch with the textile trades of the North and Midlands. Similarly Messrs. Knight of Mold kept up their Manchester connections by drawing on Jones, Loyd and Co.—originally a Manchester bank which dealt largely in weavers' "checks."

In the flotation of companies the assistance of the London banks was invaluable ; the Montgomeryshire Canal Company, for example, announces in 1796 that the purchase money of shares can be paid either through Messrs. Pugh, of Welshpool, or through their Lombard Street agents, Harcourt and Co. Connections with London also facilitated the discounting of bills, a service for which local banks charged at first 5s. per cent., and later (after the crisis of 1816–17), 7s. 6d., and even 10s. For a short loan, Lloyd of Wrexham charged at the rate of 6 per cent

---

[1] *N. W. Gaz.*, Aug. 16, 1810.

[2] *Id.*, July 19, 1810.

per annum, exclusive of commission and stamp charges.[1]
Of a different nature again was the service performed in
1829 by Sir Richard Carr Glynn and Co., the London agents
of the Newtown bank. A young Newtown flannel merchant
had got into trouble in London through finding his pockets
too heavy after a successful deal ; the magistrates sensibly
asked Glynns to take charge of his purse till he got safely
home again.

By such means as these, the newly-founded banks slowly
won their way into public confidence. Sometimes the
"country correspondent" was even strong enough to
survive the failure of the London house with which he
dealt ; Esdailes, for example, were among the victims of
1837, but the banks at Dolgelley and Chester which had
been doing business with them continued to flourish. On
the other hand, we have seen that public confidence was
sometimes misplaced, and even a bank of good repute might
bring disaster on itself and others by offering credit on too
easy terms. Most perilous of all their services was
the issue of notes of low denomination. Between 1810
and 1826, when provincial joint-stock banking began, we
have references to local issues of £1 notes at Newtown,
Dolgelley, Denbigh, Wrexham, Mold, the Old and New
Flintshire Banks, and the Old Banks at Welshpool and
Chester, in addition to the copper and silver tokens of
the Flintshire Old Bank. The ability of the banks to
withstand the successive financial panics of the age
depended largely on how far they could inspire trust in
these issues.

The first serious shock they had to encounter was in
1810, when twenty provincial banks throughout the
country stopped payment. The Receiver General of Taxes
in Wales gave notice, first that no local notes would be
received except under stringent conditions, then that they
would not be accepted at all. The different towns
concerned adopted varying policies. The gentry and
tradesmen of Caernarvon issued a manifesto in close imitation of the Receiver General's ; those of its rival Bangor
took the opposite side on principle—as they did on all

[1] Foulkes MS., printed in *Bye-gones*, 1905, p. 118 ; Beaumaris
Custom House papers (extract kindly communicated by Mr. David
Thomas).

public questions, from county dispensaries to suspension bridges; Beaumaris followed the lead of Caernarvon, and so on. The local press seethed with recrimination and crude economics.

It does not appear that any of the banks of North Wales succumbed to this crisis; but the next—that which followed the conclusion of the Napoleonic Wars—was more serious. During the three years 1814–16 no fewer than 89 country banks failed, and once again the panic began to undermine confidence in local paper. At Denbigh, gentlemen of influence tried to induce people to accept the notes of Clough, Mason and Co., by a public declaration that they were well covered by the assets of the firm, even without recourse to the valuable private estates of the partners—a statement which was confirmed by the bank's eventually paying 20s. in the pound. It was in vain; there was a run on the bank, and it appeared in the *Gazette* next year. The two Welshpool banks also collapsed; that at Llanidloes had gone under in 1813. Local patriotism has remembered that the Chester Old Bank, with its two Welsh branches, was "a tower of strength" during these troubles. But it was long before North Wales recovered from the shock. War taxation had drained the country of silver and Bank of England notes, and the frequent forgeries of banknotes of all kinds increased the disposition of farmers to eye them askance—with disastrous results to trade and agriculture.

Before the crisis of 1825–6, general confidence in the local banks had grown considerably. This time the stoppages of country banks amounted to eighty in two years. "In the agitated state of the public mind in the last fortnight", boasts the *North Wales Gazette* on December 22nd, 1825, "we feel happy in being enabled to congratulate our readers, that not the smallest rumour or doubt has attached as to [*sic*] the stability and credit of all the banks connected with the Principality"; at Holywell, Mold, Newtown, Welshpool, and doubtless other places as well, meetings of influential inhabitants were passing resolutions expressing "implicit confidence" in the local bankers, and readiness to "take their Notes as usual, to any amount." A slight flutter was caused at Caernarvon in the following spring by the refusal of Williams and Co. to accept the notes of other banks in the district except at a 5 per cent discount, but the alarm proved groundless.

Already, however, the day of private banks and local pound notes was drawing to a close. The Act of 1826, which authorized the formation of local joint-stock banks with power to issue notes of £5 and upwards, at the same time prohibited fresh issues of lower denomination by any of the local banks—to the indignation of the tradesmen of Flintshire, who held a protest meeting at Mold in 1828, when the clause was about to come into operation. Four years later, Lloyd of Wrexham is mentioned in a blue-book as the only banker in North Wales who compounds with the Stamp Office for his notes, and the latest extant specimen from this bank was printed in 1844—the very year of the Bank Charter Act, the ultimate effect of which was to restrict to the Bank of England the issue of paper money of all denominations.

The private banks themselves were also being driven from the field. In Montgomeryshire, where the recent failure of Tilsley's at Newtown had left the county with only one bank (the Welshpool branch of Beck's), a joint-stock project was afoot in 1831, but it came to nothing. It was from Manchester that the new type of bank spread to this district, and the results were far from reassuring. The Bank of Manchester, founded in 1828, set up a branch at Newtown some three years later—in time for the great crash of 1837, which ruined the Newtown branch, though the head office survived for another five years. In 1833 was established another Manchester joint-stock bank—the North and Central Bank of England. Within a few years it had opened branches in forty places, including Caernarvon, Bangor, Wrexham, Denbigh, Holywell, and Mold. But it too foundered in 1837, and had to be formally wound-up two years later. The first successful joint-stock bank in North Wales was the North and South Wales Bank, founded in 1836. By the following year, branches had been opened at Holywell, Bangor, Conway, Tremadoc, Amlwch, and St. Asaph, as well as at Shrewsbury, Ellesmere, and fourteen places in South Wales ; and during the next five years there sprang up four more in Denbighshire, three each in Merioneth and Caernarvonshire, two in Anglesey and Flintshire, and six in Montgomeryshire—though not all of these survived. In 1838 it absorbed the Dolgelley bank, and from that time forward those private banks which survived the successive crises of the century were swallowed up by this and other joint-stock concerns. Williams and Co.—who outlived all the others, and retained their independence till they were absorbed by Lloyds in 1897—are said to have saved their Bangor branch from a "run" during the panic of 1848 by the device of placing behind the counter barrels of sawdust thinly covered with a layer of golden sovereigns ; in the same year both the private banks of Wrexham collapsed, and even the young "Wales Bank" had to suspend payments for three months. The small banker who lived on localized credit was a thing of the past, and the initial difficulties of financing industry were overcome—just when industry itself was migrating to more favoured regions.

Meanwhile, distributive problems were being tackled. Up to the middle of the eighteenth century the producer had generally been both wholesaler and retailer of his own wares. The spinner would bring her basket of yarn to market,[1] the weaver his roll of cloth, the farmer his produce and stock. The lead miner had only to charter horses from the nearest farm to carry his ore a few miles to the smeltery ; the gentry sent their own carts to fetch coal from the pit mouth ;[2] the quarryman could sell direct to the builder ; the tanner to the bootmaker or glover who kept a shop in the next market town ; the worker in iron was content with the custom of the neighbouring farmers and gentry. There were a few industries, it is true, which served a wider market ; here the producer could generally make use of the services of a middleman, who bought the goods outright on speculation—the Shrewsbury draper or the cattle drover. Most of the coal mines engaged in the Irish trade were exploited by prosperous landlords, and the lead works—the only other concerns which entailed distant dealings and the holding of valuable stocks—by wealthy companies.

But as the range of business widened, the producer,

[1] *See*, e.g., *Mont. Coll.*, XXXVI, p. 140.
[2] E.g. Meyrick papers, 1754 (Bychton), 1760 (Bagillt), 1764 (Weppre), 1774 (Mostyn).

cut off from personal contact with the consumer, was finding it increasingly difficult to ascertain beforehand the extent of his wants and the length of his purse, nor could he hope (as in simpler times) to receive, as soon as the goods were finished, the payment which would enable him to get on with the next order. Firms with plenty of capital and an established reputation could keep in touch with their market by means of travelling, correspondence and the use of samples ; and they could afford to keep stocks on hand and to grant long credits. At this higher industrial level, indeed, the tendency of the age was towards the elimination of the middleman rather than the interposition of new agencies between producer and consumer. The packman merchant, buying from factory and selling to shopkeeper or consumer, was disappearing from the textile trades of the North of England just about the time when the bigger millowners of Montgomeryshire, and even the web manufacturers of Merioneth in combination, were learning to get at their customers without the help of the Shrewsbury middlemen. A Wilkinson or a Williams, exporting in bulk and dealing largely with the Government, had no more need of an intermediary in disposing of his goods than Boulton of Soho or Wedgwood of Etruria, who always kept up direct correspondence with continental purchasers ;[1] and the big colliery companies could similarly work on regular contracts with the smelting firms.[2]

For the man in a small way such measures as these were out of the question ; yet he too struggled long to maintain that hold on his market which for him spelt independence. We have seen how, in the heroic age of quarrying at Ffestiniog, quarry owners possessed of more enterprise than capital would accompany their loads of slate to Bangor or Holyhead, and even go afoot as far as Bristol or London, to meet their customers and collect the ready money without which the work could not go on. We have seen, too, how John Smalley, when his mill at Holywell was still an infant enterprise, used to go to Wrexham fair to push the sales of his cotton yarn.[3] But as the volume

---

[1] Clapham : *Early Railway Age*, p. 220.
[2] *Supra*, p. 192.
[3] *Supra*, pp. 210-11, 303.

of business increased, these personal dealings became more and more difficult, and the *entrepreneur* who was not content with serving a limited local market, if he could not afford to keep his own staff of travellers and agents, had no recou..;e but to fall into the grip of the factor of some big business house, who stood to him almost in the relation of an employer.[1] From early in the nineteenth century such commission agents were in the habit of offering their services through the Welsh newspapers.[2]

Retail as well as wholesale agencies were helping to mediate between producer and consumer. In the coal trade, for example, although mineowners long continued to advertise their coal in the local press,[3] and to sell at the pithead—not only in bulk to farmers and other big consumers, but even (in remoter regions) to cottagers by the bushel[4]—selling agencies were becoming common before the end of the eighteenth century. At the bottom of the scale were the poor pedlars whom travellers used to encounter, in the days of the Napoleonic War, on the road between Hawarden and Chester, knitting as they walked beside their donkeys with pannier loads of coal, and "setting a laudable example of industry to the sluggard and the beggar."[5] Then came the skipper in the coasting trade, who would buy a cargo of coal outright from a colliery near the coast and load it at a convenient quay for some big works or country house.[6] Finally, there were the coal merchants who established wharves along the canals and at the principal ports, and opened depôts in the towns. In 1790 Flint had four and Holywell two ; by 1828 they were to be found in all the chief market towns, Newtown having as many as eight.[7]

The sale of slates was similarly organized, though for these, of course, the demand was more specialized. In

---

[1] *Supra*, pp. 231, 239, 242–3, 262–3 ; Clapham : *op. cit.*, p. 223.

[2] E.g. *N. W. Gaz.*, April 5 and 19, 1809.

[3] Advertisements from five different colliery proprietors appear in the *Chester Chron.* for 1802.

[4] *Supra*, p. 196.

[5] *Anon.: Tour from Holyhead to Chester* (*Collection of Welsh Tours*, London and Chester, second ed., 1797), p. 135.

[6] Meyrick papers ; *N. W. Gaz.*, Jan. 15, 1824 ; *cf.* Clapham : *op. cit.*, p. 234.

[7] Barfoot and Wilkes' *Directory* ; Pigot's *Directory*, 1828–29.

1778 a Chester paper announces that " Captain John Rowlands has contracted for a large variety of Caernarvon and Bangor slates, which he will supply at short notice in his own vessels."[1] Slate wharves were established on both the Ellesmere and the Montgomeryshire Canals as soon as the canals were open to traffic, and slate merchants began to appear in towns like Ffestiniog and Bangor. Before 1830, there were copper merchants in the mining districts of Snowdonia, and monthly lead ore markets at Flint and Holywell.[2] Most of the big farmers, too, had taken to selling through professional dealers such corn as they did not dispose of directly to millers and maltsters. A Liverpool Jew who had set up as a corn merchant at Llangefni went bankrupt in 1814, owing money to half the farmers of Anglesey.[3]

The spread of the shopkeeping habit was one of the outstanding features of the period. The parish of Ffestiniog possessed only one shop in the eighteenth century. Its owner used to fetch goods from Wrexham fair twice a year ; he died in 1796, worth £800. With the development of the quarries, shops were opened in various parts of the parish. At first they drew their stores chiefly from the market towns of Llanrwst, Bala and Dolgelley, but afterwards carriers began to supply them from Chester. In the 'twenties Mr. Holland, one of the quarry owners, used to get provisions by sea from Liverpool (his own town), and sell them to his workpeople ; and the growth of a trading connection with Lancashire is illustrated by the fact that a commercial traveller from a Lancashire house, going on horseback to Ffestiniog in 1826, lost his way and perished on the mountains.[4] Llanidloes, which in the middle of the eighteenth century depended for its stores

---

[1] *Chester Chron.*, March 20, 1778 ; *cf.* ledgers of Nantlle quarry, 1816–25 (Nantlle MS. 19), where most of the sales are to sea captains and slate merchants.

[2] Pigot's *Directory*, 1828–29 ; *supra*, p. 174.

[3] *N. W. Gaz.*, Oct. 27, 1814 ; *cf. id.*, Dec. 12, 1812 (Llansantffraid), *N. W. Chron.*, March 14, 1828 (Montgomery), Dec. 14, 1812 (Bangor). The 1831 Census enumerates 9 corn dealers in Anglesey, 16 in Caernarvonshire, 4 in Denbighshire, 5 in Flintshire, 11 in Merioneth, and 10 in Montgomeryshire.

[4] *Hanes Plwyf Ffestiniog*, pp. 72, 135–6 ; *N. W. Gaz.*, March 2, 1826.

on Newtown men who came in on market days, had 36 shopkeepers by 1828 ; its principal tradesman, in the 'fifties, used to visit London and Manchester four times a year to replenish his stock, and had to charter farmers' carts (for the railway had not yet come to Llanidloes) to bring home his purchases.[1]

These examples are taken from regions where industry was making rapid headway, but a similar tale could be told of the rural districts. In the remote south-western corner of Anglesey we find the Meyricks of Bodorgan, just before the French Revolution, buying goods like flannel, cloth, silk, and even tobacco from the village shop at Llangadwaladr, instead of waiting for the visit of the wandering pedlar, or the "Scotchman" travelling in woollen and linen ware, as they would have done twenty years earlier.[2] On the other side of the island, Beaumaris, with its fashionable crowd of summer visitors, was in the early nineteenth century attracting the attention of shop-keepers from Liverpool and Chester. A Liverpool man opened a drapery and lace business there in 1808, making periodic visits to Manchester and Scotland to select his stock ; and a jeweller from Chester, having opened up a connection by visiting Beaumaris, Bangor and Caernarvon every season with a view to interesting "all the fashion of the place in their morning amusements" (a practice commonly adopted by English dealers in rare and costly wares), eventually settled down at Beaumaris in 1810 as general dealer. His stock-in-trade included groceries, hardware (spades ; Staffordshire and Lancashire nails ; bar, bolt, rod, sheet and hoop iron ; pig and sheet lead), and marine stores (sail canvas, sacks, tar, pine baulks and laths).[3]

[1] *Supra*, p. 9 ; Pigot's *Directory*, 1828–29 ; Horsfall-Turner : *Llanidloes*, pp. 116–7.

[2] Meyrick papers, 1757, 1768, 1787. An owner of coasting vessels in the neighbouring parish of Llanynghenedl had also set up as grocer by 1774. On the "Scotchman'" *see* Clapham : *op. cit.*, pp. 221–2. The proprietor of the "bazaar" (as it now called itself) at Llangadwaladr, was a subscriber to the Anglesey Horticultural Society in 1835 (Annual Report).

[3] *N. W. Gaz.*, April 14, July 21, 1808, April 20, 1809, Aug. 16, 1810 ; *cf.* Dec. 27, 1810 (Liverpool watchmaker, jeweller and silversmith at Castle Inn, Caernarvon, for 8 days) and May 4, 1815 (Chester

By 1830 the Welsh housewife could supply most of her daily wants at a shop in the nearest town. A London firm of tea dealers in 1821 announces agencies at three towns in Montgomeryshire, two each in Denbighshire and Caernarvonshire, one in Flintshire and one in Anglesey ; and a comparison between commercial directories of 1790 and 1828 shows an enormous increase, between the two dates, in the number of shopkeepers at almost every place included in both. By 1828 Wrexham had 60 dealers in foodstuffs and drugs, and 32 in clothing ; Holywell had 52 of the one and 32 of the other (as against 22 and 12 in 1790) ; next in order came a group of market towns including Caernarvon, Bangor, Ruthin, Denbigh, Mold and Llanrwst, and then Newtown, Welshpool and Machynlleth, in the woollen district. Merioneth was, as usual, the most backward county : Dolgelley had only 24 shopkeepers ; but even Dinas Mawddwy—the smallest place included in the list— had a couple.[1]

It is likely that many of these dealers did not keep permanent shops, but only stalls in the market. For the weekly, bi-weekly, or fortnightly markets were still the chief means of bringing country produce within the reach of the town dweller, though their share in the distribution of clothing and other commodities was fast diminishing. At these and at the great cattle fairs the local producer continued to meet and bargain with his customers in person, as he had done from time immemorial. The ancient March Fair at Wrexham, too, played an important part in the economic life of North Wales (as that of Carmarthen in South Wales) long after their greater English counterpart, Stourbridge Fair, had been "left sleepy, if still noisy, by its

musical instrument maker visiting Anglesey and Caernarvonshire). Newtown by 1824 a jeweller who also dealt in pianos and built organs (*Shrewsbury Chron.*, April 30). The accounts of a general shop at Penmorfa (in Lleyn) from 1792 to 1800 are preserved in U.C.N.W. Library (Bangor MS. 82). They are surprisingly well kept in comparison with the ledgers of the average country woollen mill of the period—or much later. Groceries, haberdashery and ironmongery, with a few simple medical stores, formed the bulk of the stock-in-trade.

[1] Barfoot and Wilkes' *Directory* ; Pigot's *Directory*, 1828–29. It should be noted, however, that shopkeepers in the outlying districts are included in these lists—e.g. at least one of those in the Wrexham list kept shop at Brymbo, five miles away.

sluggish brook."[1] Yorkshire woollens, Manchester cottons, Irish linens, Birmingham hardware, Coventry ribbons and Spitalfield silks were among the goods brought there for sale. Most of the regular traders erected for themselves, in the course of the eighteenth and early nineteenth centuries, "squares" consisting of rows of shops built round an open quadrangle. A company of "chapmen" from Manchester, Pendleton, Blackley, and Stockport set the fashion in 1743 by taking a lease of an old inn and yard with the right to erect booths or shops on any part of it ; a few years later they built Manchester Square, near the premises, for the sale of cotton goods. Yorkshire Square followed in 1788, then Birmingham Square, the Irish Linen Hall, and Queen's Square (which was built, some time before 1804, for the dealers in calicoes and table linen). It was not till after 1840 that the dealers ceased to frequent the Squares. Some of these developed into slums, while others were roofed in to make permanent produce markets, and one—in 1873—to make a public hall ; and the March Fair degenerated by degrees into a haunt of merry-go-rounds, coconut-shies and cheap-jacks.[2]

The "great proportional increase in the work of trans-portation and dealing,"[3] which inevitably went hand in hand with production on a large scale, was itself at once a product of and a further stimulus to the allied processes of specialization and concentration. The lack of special-ization in Welsh industrial life had long been a theme of travellers and topographers—whether in criticism or in admiration. "It is usual" (so runs a description of Caer-narvonshire published in 1812)[4] "for the head of the family to be skilled in every trade . . . as that of carpenter, smith, wheelwright, shoe-maker, taylor, &c. in which occupa-tions the rest of the family assist him." We have seen how the farmer would supplement his resources by hiring

[1] Clapham : *op. cit.*, p. 223.

[2] Palmer : *Wrexham*, pp. 43, 83, 86–7, 93, 95–6, 157 ; *N. W. Chron.*, March 20, 1828 (advertisement from Cornelius Hardman of Birmingham, button-maker and hardwareman, 27 and 28, Birmingham Square) ; Pugh : *Camb. Dep.*, p. 324.

[3] Meredith, H. O. : *Economic History of England* (n.d.), p. 276.

[4] Evans : *Beauties*, p. 320 ; *cf.* Pugh : *Camb. Dep.*, pp. 75–7.

out horses for the carriage of slates or ores, by mining, weaving, and fulling, and even by selling coal ; how lead mines in Flintshire were worked by bakers, butchers, and bacon sellers ; how copper mines in Caernarvonshire had to close down during the hay harvest as late as Waterloo. The tradition of regarding industrial employment as a means of filling in slack times in the fields hampered even the building of Conway suspension bridge, for the contractor found his navvies melting away when the harvest began.[1] But the tendency of capitalism was to eliminate these debatable belts and scattered *enclaves* from the economic map—just as nationalism was removing them from the political map—and to substitute hard-and-fast functional frontiers.

This process of specialization can be traced, for example, in the brewing industry. Cottage brewing had never been common in Wales, because so little grain was grown ; but farmers habitually made their own mead, and the brewhouse and malthouse were a necessary part of the equipment of a country house. It is, perhaps, a sign of the decay of this immemorial practice that the Meyricks of Bodorgan, who had kept a brewer on their permanent staff in 1754, could by 1792 get all the brewing they needed done by an occasional woman hired at 9*d*. a night.[2] Since the 'sixties they had been in the habit of sending to Caernarvon for an occasional barrel of beer ; but as yet the public brewer—as distinct from the brewing victualler, or the keeper of a temporary drinking booth who sold his own beer at the fair—was a rare figure in North Wales. The Caernarvon brewery failed to pay, and the town was still without one in 1821 ; Bangor had its first in the following year, citizens who scorned the beer-shops having previously had to send to "Liverpool and other distant parts" for their supplies, just as seaside towns like Aberystwyth had to prepare for the bathing season by importing cargoes from Bristol.[3]

[1] *Supra*, pp. 47, 165–6, 173, 234, 259 ; Barfoot and Wilkes' *Directory*, III, pp. 113–4 ; *N. W. Gaz.*, Aug. 5, 1824.

[2] Meyrick papers. Brewing utensils were sold among the family effects at Llantysilio Hall in 1821 (*N. W. Gaz.*, Sept. 13).

[3] *N. W. Gaz.*, May 10, 1821, April 11, 1822, Feb. 22, 1810 ; [Feltham, J.] : *Guide to the Watering and Sea Bathing Places* (1806), p. 3. The N. Wales Port Book for 1730 (Bangor MS. 484) records the export of 2 casks of Welsh ale from Caernarvon in September, but it is an isolated entry. *Cf. History*, XVIII, p. 52.

Even Wrexham, with its 55 alehouses and its ancient and influential body of taverners (strong enough as far back as Charles I's time, tradition says, to procure the dismissal of an over-zealous Puritan curate), had no public brewery till 1799.[1] Holyhead, as the busy port for Ireland, had anticipated Wrexham by several years ; Amlwch, with its thirsty mining population (it had already 60 alehouses in 1793), followed suit before 1812 ; and in 1818 the first public brewery for Flintshire was opened at Kelsterton, near Northop. Several of these new breweries served the whole surrounding district. Amlwch sent supplies across to the mainland (one of its drays had the distinction of being the first vehicle to cross Telford's new bridge), and Kelsterton helped to victual Chester.[2] By the 'thirties the industry was well established in every county of North Wales, and moralists were shaking their heads over the increased facilities for tippling.[3]

Here the effect of specialization was to create a new industry ; more often it only meant the destruction of an ancient vested interest. English wares were usurping more and more space in the Welsh retailer's shop window, and terms like "hosier," "hatter," "shoemaker" and "clothier" were acquiring a new meaning ; for tradesmen so described were selling Nottingham hosiery, London hats, Leicester shoes and Yorkshire woollens, instead of goods of their own manufacture, and the Welsh countryman was finding it (or fancying it) cheaper to buy these at the shop than to make his own or to get his neighbours to make them. This did not happen all at once, of course ; much depended on local feeling and on conditions of transport. The manufacture of felt hats, for example, had been common in all the wool-producing regions from early times (with a few places like Welshpool, Denbigh, Wrexham and Pwllheli as the chief centres), and had produced a thirsty race of journeymen, notorious for their brawling, as well as for their working capacities ; it still had a few

[1] Palmer : *Parish Church*, p. 74, *Wrexham*, p. 223 ; Davies : *General View*, p. 445.

[2] Barfoot and Wilkes' *Directory*, III, p. 387 ; Bangor MS. 31, pp. 51–2 ; *N. W. Gaz.*, March 19, 1812, Jan. 2, 1826 ; Lewis : *Top. Dict.*, under *Amlwch* and *Kelsterton*.

[3] Pigot's *Directory*, 1828–29 ; *P.L.R.* (1834, XXIX), p. 188 a ; Census (occupations).

representatives left in every county but Anglesey and
Merioneth in 1828, and did not become extinct at Welshpool
till about 1880.[1] "Beaver" hats—often made by furriers
who bought up rabbit skins from the neighbourhood[2]—were
driven out of fashion by the silk hat soon after the Napoleonic War; but milliners kept on making their own straw
bonnets till past the middle of the century—there were
seventy straw hat makers in North Wales in 1851.[3] And
in districts of scattered farms the periodic visits of the
itinerant craftsman continued till well on in the second
half of the century.[4]

Corn milling was another local "interest" which put up
a long fight with the tendencies of the age. The English
miller had since early in George III's reign been developing
into a middleman, buying wheat and selling flour on his
own account, instead of a quasi-public official, charging
toll to all comers for the use of his mill.[5] In Wales, on the
other hand, "suit at mill" was a frequent clause in leases
up to the time of Waterloo, and a fine of 2d. a bushel for
grinding corn elsewhere than at the lord's mill was still
imposed at Wrexham in 1827. That the miller retained
his old status in Caernarvonshire is indicated by a resolution of the County Justices in 1829 to put a stop to his
extortions by enforcing the legal obligation to post a list
of tolls in some conspicuous place.[6]

Such were the prevailing conditions when the acceleration of transport brought the Welsh miller up against the
competition of English-made flour. A case before the
Anglesey Great Sessions in this very year, 1829, reveals to
us a shopkeeper at Bodedern, right in the heart of the
county, making purchases of flour from Liverpool,
despite the proximity of a brand-new mill at Beaumaris,
and of another, scarcely more than a dozen years old, at

---

[1] *Supra*, pp. 15, 272 ; *Bye-gones*, 1893–4, p. 177 ; *Mont. Coll.*,
XIV, pp. 219–20 ; Pigot's *Directory*, 1828–29.
[2] *N. W. Gaz.*, Jan. 12, 1808 ; *Mont. Coll.*, XXXVII, p. 30.
[3] Pigot's *Directory*, 1828–29 ; Census, 1851.
[4] *Supra*, p. 9 ; *Mont. Coll.*, XXI, pp. 347 ff.
[5] *Cambridge Historical Review*, I (1923), pp. 85–90.
[6] *Cal. of Crosswood Deeds*, p. 307, *et passim; Shrewsbury Chron.*,
Aug. 24, 1827 ; *N. W. Chron.*, Dec. 2, 1829. Feudal conditions
survived quite as late in the corn mills of the West Riding (Clapham :
op. cit., p. 444).

Amlwch.[1] For Liverpool had up-to-date steam mills (the first had been built in 1817, just before the establishment of steamboat communications with North Wales) ; and although steam had been used in a Ruabon corn mill more than a decade earlier, the new method of grinding did not spread in North Wales till the second half of the century, when the railway was already carrying fine English flour far and wide, and Free Trade had opened the ports to foreign produce.[2] Even in the early part of the century the frequency with which mills changed hands, and the eagerness with which their owners pointed out how well they would serve the purposes of a cotton or woollen manufacturer, are ominous symptoms ;[3] but up to 1851 there were still more than 300 millers in Montgomeryshire, over 200 in Caernarvonshire and Denbighshire, over 100 in Anglesey, and 71 in Flintshire. The effect of improved communications on what still remains the most essentially local of trades—the trade in foodstuffs—is seen in the fact that at the 1921 Census the whole of North Wales could not show as many millers as Denbighshire alone possessed in 1851.[4]

Thus developments in transport and distribution were forcing the domestic craft group, the village workshop and the small working capitalist—all of them still active forces in Welsh life after they had become anachronisms in England—to compete with the large-scale undertakings set up by capitalists, both in Wales itself and over the border. They had now to adapt themselves to the new scale of production, on pain of sinking to the ranks of wage labour. In various ways this complete dependence on an employer's capital might be staved off for a time. In boom years easy credit, in which the local banks assisted, would give the working weaver or the small speculator in mines a precarious footing in the employing class, till the next crisis eliminated all but the exceptionally fortunate or

[1] *N. W. Chron.*, April 3, 1828 ; *N. W. Gaz.*, Feb. 23, 1826, March 4, 1816.
[2] Bennet, R., and Elton, J. : *History of Corn Milling* (1898–1904), II, App. A. ; *Chester Chron.*, April 25, 1806.
[3] E.g. *Salop. Journ.*, March 9, Dec. 21, 1803 (Llanfyllin and Garthbeibio).
[4] Census, 1851–1921. On the decline of corn milling in Montgomeryshire, *see Mont. Coll.*, XXXVII, pp 28–9.

exceptionally capable. The partner in a "take-note bargain," or even the outworker for a factory, owning his own tools, kept at least the outward marks of independence, though the pretence wore thinner and thinner as the proportion of the working capital which he could supply grew steadily smaller. In isolated districts, sheltered by backwardness of transport from the full blast of competition, the relics of an older economic order have often survived to our own times, but with more and more the air of a quaint survival. In industry as in agriculture, the tendencies of the age under review were all against the small concern.

CHAPTER X.
" THE LABOURING POOR."

O ! Dylodion *isel* Fri
Mae'n rhaid i chwi ymprydio,
Cym'rwch *Fara* i chwi yn Drych ;
Ni chewch ond edrych arno.
—John Jones, Glan y gors : *A Welsh Hymn to
be sung on the Fast Day.*[1]

A. WAGES AND PRICES.

"Plenty of workpeople may be had at low wages."
"Workmen are superabundant and wages very low."
These and similar inducements were constantly being held
out to English capitalists, throughout our period, in
advertisements of sites and works in North Wales.[2] Where
statistics of wages are available, they serve to confirm the
impression that the Welsh peasant had been accustomed
to a standard of living considerably below that prevailing
among the "lower orders" in England. When Arthur
Young made his tour through the southern counties in
1768, he found that the rate of wages generally varied in
inverse proportion to the distance from London. Thus
within a twenty-mile radius of the capital, 10s. 9d. a week
was the normal agricultural wage ; but before he had
travelled much more than a hundred miles away, it had
sunk to 6s. 3d. The mean wage for the whole district
he reckoned at 7s. 9d. for farm labourers and 8s. 5d. for
"manufacturers." In Glamorganshire (the only part of
Wales included in his survey) labourers got 1s. a day—a
level which was only just being reached in North Wales,

[1] Printed in *Chester Chron.*, March 4, 1796, where the following
free translation is appended :—

> Ye hapless sons of humble life,
> Who ne'er aspire to feast,
> Now distant view the bread you want
> But must not dare to taste.

[2] *Oswestry Her.*, May 16, 1820 ; *Chester Chron.*, Nov. 15, 1833 ;
cf. *Manchester Mercury*, Aug. 6, 1787 (*supra*, p. 35) ; *Shrewsbury
Chron.*, April 25, 1828.

even in districts bordering on England ; for it was not long since reapers had had to be content with 6 *d.* a day in Anglesey, and 8 *d.* had been the general wage in Flintshire. A few labourers round Wrexham were able to extort 1 *s.* by 1768, but the hard-headed squire of Erthig told his steward emphatically, a couple of years later, "I do think 10 *d.* a day sufficient, and nothing shall induce me to exceed it."[1]

Even when the Napoleonic War broke out, farm labourers in Merioneth were only getting 8 *d.* a day for the winter months and 1 *s.* in summer, those of Caernarvonshire and Anglesey, 10 *d.* for the one and 1 *s.* for the other ; but by this time wages in Montgomeryshire had risen to 1 *s.* and 1 *s.* 2 *d.*, and in Denbighshire as high as 1 *s.* 2 *d.* and 1 *s.* 4 *d.* Rates for corn harvest (which often included victuals) are excluded from these figures. Permanent servants were engaged at rates ranging from five guineas to ten pounds a year.[2]

Industrial wages were generally a little higher than agricultural, but there was not quite the same disparity as in England. Except in the neighbourhood of Parys Mountain (where the general rate of wages in 1794 was fourpence higher than in the rest of the island), the number of workmen employed in industry was as yet so small[3] that their wages tended to be assimilated to those of the surrounding countryside rather than *vice versâ.* The

---

[1] Young : *Southern Counties,* pp. 264–71 ; Meyrick papers, 1755 ff.; Davies : *General View,* p. 423 ; Cust : *Chronicles of Erthig,* II, pp. 20, 77–8, 163. In Anglesey wages can have changed but little during the first half of the century. A Justices' assessment for 4 Geo. I (preserved in the MS. diary of William Bulkeley of Brynddu) gives 6 *d.* for reapers, 9 *d.* for mowers, 5 *d.* to 6 *d.* for labourers, and 5 *d.* for women.

[2] Kay : *Agriculture of N. Wales :* Anglesey, p. 23, Carnarvonshire, pp. 20–21 ; Montgomeryshire, p. 18 ; Merioneth, p. 16 ; Denbighshire, p. 15.

[3] Even after the Census figures begin, they are too imperfect, till a very late date, to make possible a satisfactory estimate of the number of industrial as compared with agricultural labourers. Ure's table (*Philosophy of Manufactures,* p. 77, based on the Census returns for 1831) shows the following ratios ; Montgomery, 1 : 4·5, Flint 1 : 8, Merioneth 1 : 20, Denbigh 1 : 34, Anglesey 1 : 45, Caernarvon 1 : 46. But this only includes "manufacturing labourers," a category which excludes miners, and for most counties is virtually equivalent to "textile workers."

earnings attributed to miners on Parys Mountain during the prosperous years following the discoveries of 1768 are almost fabulous. Davies asserts that for a time they might take anything from 5s. to 15s. a day, and that even after decline began, 1s. 10d. a day was quite usual. In Staffordshire, in 1769, copper miners got 12s. a week.[1] Nothing can be found to match this in the other mines of North Wales. Lead miners at Nant y ffrith (near Wrexham), a decade before Young's tour, were getting 10d. to 1s. a day, though for the driving of levels—a highly skilled job—as much as 10s. or 12s. a week might be paid. A generation earlier the wage of colliers in the same district had ranged from 8d. to 1s. 2d., as against an average of about 1s. to 1s. 6d. in England.[2]

Textile workers were usually on piece wages. The rate for carding (in Anglesey) in the middle of the eighteenth century was 3d. a pound, for spinning 6d. to 1s., or even 1s. 3d. ; for weaving flannel and cloth 1½d. and 2d. a yard respectively, as compared with 3d. or 5d. for heavier materials, like curtain stuffs and carpets, and as much as 1s. 3d. for fine linens. Tasks like dyeing and wool-picking brought in only 3d. a day ; fulling cost 1½d. a yard, or 1s. to 1s. 3d. for a pair of blankets. These rates, it may be noted, differed little from those current at the beginning of the seventeenth century. By the 'seventies, the pay for weaving flannel seems to have gone up to 3d. a yard, but it was still possible for a woman to get as little as 2d. for a day's spinning in a country house—no more than she would have got in Charles I's time.[3] Spinning was still, in most parts of the kingdom, a subsidiary household duty, and poorly paid ; Young gives the general rate

[1] *General View*, p. 47 ; Hamilton : *Brass and Copper Industries*, pp. 312–3.
[2] Wage bill of John Meller of Erthig at Bryn yr Owen colliery, May 9, 1724 (*Wrexham Advertiser*, Feb. 19, 1881) ; accounts of Nant y ffrith Lead Mining Company, 1753–57 (Palmer : *Old Parish of Wrexham*, pp. 129–30) ; Ashton and Sykes : *Coal Industry*, p. 135. The Ystum Colwyn accounts (Montgomeryshire) include under 1759 the record of a payment of 1s. 4d. a day to a collier (presumably a sinker, since no coal can really have been found) for 22 days (*Y Cymmrodor*, XXXVIII, p. 40).
[3] Meyrick papers ; Davies : *General View*, pp. 496–500 ; Lipson : *Woollen and Worsted Industries*, p. 65 ; Myddleton, W. M. : *Chirk Castle Accounts, 1650–66*. p. 15.

in England as 4*d*. to 6*d*. a day.   But weavers, he tells us, got 8*s*. a week in Yorkshire, 9*s*. in the south-east, and even 11*s*. on some special lines ;   and certainly there were no wages in North Wales, before the Napoleonic War, to compare with the English woolcomber's 13*s*. a week.[1]

But if wages were comparatively low, so was the cost of living.   Wales had long been known as a land of cheapness. During the hard times which followed the Civil Wars of the seventeenth century, Englishmen who visited Wales found everything cheaper there than at home—except tobacco pipes.[2]   In 1757—a full century later—butter could be had at Wrexham (right on the English border) for 3½*d*. a pound, beef and mutton for 1½*d*. a pound, and a live goose for 1*s*.   Welshmen in London at the same time were startled to find their butter costing them 5½*d*. to 6*d*. (or even 7*d*. to 10*d*. if it was fresh), beef 4*d*. to 4½*d*., and mutton 4½*d*. to 5*d*. Lack of demand was the chief cause for the low level of Welsh prices ;   on the one hand the Welsh peasant, who rarely touched butcher's meat or wheaten bread, could satisfy most of his simple wants without going to market at all ;   on the other hand, communications were still too bad to enable Welsh produce to reach the big centres of population.[3]

Arthur Young's knowledge of Wales, as we have seen, was limited to Glamorganshire, which was in touch by sea with the Bristol market ;   here prices, though considerably below the London level, were not much lower than the average for the Southern counties.   "Had my private business then suffered me to penetrate further into *Wales*," he says, ". . . where no turnpike road exists, I have no doubt but I should have met with a great change in everything."   Where these new roads were beginning to widen the range of sales, the effect on prices was already visible.   A few years before Young wrote, for example, butter from Wrexham was finding its way to Chester and Liverpool, and consequently the price there had gone up

---

[1] Young : *op. cit.*, pp. 270, etc. ; Mantoux : *Industrial Revolution*, pp. 70, 432.

[2] *Verney Memoirs* ("Silver Library"), II, p. 140 ; Phillips, J. R. : *Civil War in Wales and the Marches* (second ed., 1878), p. 22 *n*.

[3] *Morris Letters*, I, pp. 491-2.   The prices for 1757 are much the same as those shown in the Henblas accounts (Henblas MSS. 11) a quarter of a century earlier.

to 7*d.* a pound—a little above Young's average.[1]   On the eve of the outbreak of war, the extension of turnpikes had made these higher price-levels pretty general ; butter was now 6*d.* to 8*d.*, meat 3*d.* to 3½*d.*, as against 10*d.* to 1*s.* and 4½*d.* to 5*d.* respectively in the South of England.[2]

Corn, owing to the variety of local measures as well as of local prices, is more difficult to bring into comparison. Since most of the wheat consumed in North Wales had to be imported, the tendency was for prices to keep above, rather than below, the average for the whole kingdom ; but Welshmen lived chiefly on cheaper grains.[3]   Potatoes— just coming into vogue—were sold at 2*s.* 4*d.* a bushel in Montgomeryshire in 1763.[4]   For his firing the cottager could still, in many parts of the country, rely on getting brushwood and peat from the common land.   If he had to buy coal, what he had to pay depended entirely on his proximity to the pit mouth.   Young quotes 3½*d.* a bushel as the price for South Wales and Monmouthshire, whereas

[1] Young : *op. cit.*, pp. 251–61 ; *Bye-gones*, 1911, p. 48.
[2] Davies : *Labourers in Husbandry*, pp. 189, 191 ;   Kay : *Agriculture of N. Wales:* Caernarvonshire, p. 21, Denbighshire, p. 15 ; Hasbach : *English Agricultural Labourer*, p. 124.
[3] The following are some sample statistics :—

Year.	Place.	Wheat (N. Wales) Bushel.	Wheat Quarter.	Wheat (Eng. av.)	Barley (Bushel).	Oats (Bushel).	Authority
1763	Gregynog (Mont.)	6*s.*	48*s.*	42*s.* 8*d.*	8*s.* 6*d.*	7*s.* 6*d.*	*Mont. Coll.*, XXV, p. 114.
1767	Hawarden (Flints.)	9*s.*	72*s.*	59*s.* 1*d.*	5*s.* 6*d.*	—	*Bye-gones*, 1905-6, p. 36
1771	Wrexham (Denb.)	6*s.* 6*d.*	52*s.*	48*s.* 7*d.*	—	—	*Chronicles of Erthig*, II, 165
1771	Kerry (Mont.)	6*s.* 6*d.*	—	—	—	7*s.*	*Bye-gones*, 1880–81, pp. 159–60
1794	Denbighshire	6*s.* 6*d.*	52*s.*	52*s.* 3*d.*	4*s.* 4*d.*	2*s.* 6*d.*	Kay : *loc. cit.*

[4] *Mont. Çoll.*, XXV, p. 114.   No estimate of the cost of clothing has been attempted—the subject is far too complex—but the following items of expenditure from the Gwyddelwern (Merioneth) Vestry Book may serve as examples:—1783 : for pare of clocks [clogs], 9*d.*, for betgowne and Pettigot, 5*s.* 4*d.*;—1798 : yard and a half Linen to make Shurt, 1*s.* 7½*d.*, two Blanckets, 3*s.* ; 1800 : for flanen to make 2 wasgot, 3*s.*, for pare of Clocks, 1*s.* 3*d.* ; 1802 : for 3 yards of cloth, 3*s.* 9*d.* ; 1804 : Betgown and Pety Cot to the Girl, 9*s.*, Clocks, 6*d.*, Stockins, 6*d.*   The Caerhûn (Caernarvonshire) Vestry Book shows that a pair of shoes (*c.* 1780) cost from 2*s.* 6*d.* to 5*s.*

in the East of England it cost from 7*d*. to 1*s*. a bushel ; and we have already seen how the coal duty and the high cost of transport inflated prices in parts of North Wales where coal had to be imported.[1]

However much cheaper most things might be in North Wales, it is clear that, even before the War, the cottager found it no easier to make his budget balance here than in many parts of England. David Davies, in his *Case of Labourers in Husbandry*,[2] gives us balance sheets (collected just before the French Revolution) of three families in rural Denbighshire and two in Merioneth. All five, with the utmost economy, found their expenditure in excess of their revenue to the extent of between £4 and £8 in a year.

With the War there began an upward movement in both wages and prices, which was accentuated, as the years went by, by industrialization, movements of population, and improvements in transport. Gwallter Mechain, writing in 1810, reckoned that "in the neighbourhood of manufactories, mine works, collieries, and canals in the making, the price of labour had advanced about 30 per cent between the years 1793 and 1799," and it was still rising. Permanent farm servants had "had their wages advanced about 40 per cent within these last 15 years." Labourers could now earn 1*s*. 6*d*. to 2*s*. on their own victuals (from 2*s*. to 4*s*. in harvest time), and skilled farm servants might get as much as £12 to £15 a year with board and lodging.[3] This was a good deal more than farmers paid in South Wales, and not much less than they paid in the South of England (where wages were already much lower than in the North). If these rates were at all general (which seems unlikely) they must long have remained the high-water mark.[4]

A decade after the War, Montgomeryshire farm labourers only got 1*s*. 2*d*. to 1*s*. 6*d*. in winter, and 1*s*. 4*d*. to 1*s*. 8*d*. in

---

[1] Young : *op. cit.*, p. 262 ; *supra*, pp. 196, 199.

[2] Pp. 188–91. For details *see* Appendix II, pp. 420 ff. (*infra*).

[3] *General View*, p. 353. Eden, writing a few years earlier, gives 1*s*. 2*d*. to 1*s*. 6*d*. as the rate prevailing at Llanferres, and 1*s*. 2*d*. to 1*s*. 4*d*. at Wrexham, with higher rates for harvest work. (*State of the Poor*, III, pp. 887, 891.)

[4] *Cf*. Hasbach : *op. cit.*, pp. 121–3.

summer, and in the year of the Reform Bill the highest rate paid to permanent servants in the same county was £8.[1] According to the Poor Law Report of 1834, married labourers in North Wales then got 8s. a week in winter and 9s. in summer, and single servants £3 to £6 a year with their keep, which was reckoned equivalent to an income of £20 to £21. At the opening of Victoria's reign, labourers on Lord Kenyon's estate in Flintshire were given 10s. to 12s. a week, together with allotments ; but on the Madryn estate in Caernarvonshire the normal rate was 5s. to 7s., only skilled tradesmen and head ploughmen receiving as much as 12s., and women as little as 2s. 6d., which had been their usual wage in George I's reign.[2] An estimate drawn up in 1860 puts the average rate for Wales at 8s. a week in 1824 and 7s. 6d. in 1837, as compared with 9s. 4d. and 10s. 4d. for the whole of England and Wales.[3]

Industrial wages are a more complex problem, both on account of their far more violent fluctuations, and because of the difficulty of interpreting piece-work statistics—and even day rates—where employment and output were so irregular. For example, copper miners at Amlwch, according to Aikin, were earning from 1s. to 1s. 8d. a day (on piece rates) in 1797 ; Davies tells us that in 1799 they got "8s. a week, certain wages," irrespective of output ; but during the bad times after 1815 wages were so much depressed by competition for the best places in the mine that "many scores" (so the stewards reported) were working for 3s. to 5s. a week. With this we may compare the rates earned by Cornish copper miners : 7s. 6d. to 10s. 6d. a week in 1791 and 11s. 3d. to 15s. 3d. in 1799.[4] As the mines became exhausted, wages at Amlwch got worse and worse : in 1846 the framers of the Welsh Education Report found that parents there could not send their children to school for lack of clothing.[5]

---

[1] Mont. Coll., XXXII, p. 266.
[2] P.L.R. (1834, XXIX), pp. 187–8 ; Rept. on Land, 1896, App. A, p. 27 ; Yale MSS. 24.
[3] Hasbach : op. cit., pp. 223–4.
[4] Aikin : Journal, p. 140 ; Davies : General View, p. 47 ; Griffith : Mynydd Parys, p. 64 ; Hamilton : Brass and Copper Industries, p. 315.
[5] Educ. Report, III, App., p. 4.

Miners' wages in general Davies estimates at 1s. to
1s. 6d. a "stem" (or shift) of 6 hours—which meant 2s. to
3s. a day.[1] If the figures are intended to apply to coal
mines, they sound surprisingly high, for even Northumbrian miners (then or a little earlier) were only getting
2s. 6d. to 3s. a day, Scottish miners 3s., and those of South
Wales about 2s. But we have the evidence of a Ruabon
collier before the Children's Employment Commission that
he used to make 3s. a day in 1820, when 3s. 3d. was the
average rate for Scotland. How many days a week the
Welsh miner then worked we do not know. Dr. Clapham
hazards 4½ days as a general average for the kingdom, but
the miners of the Ruabon district declared during the
strike of 1830–31 that, on an average of summer and winter,
they only worked 3½ days a week.[2] So far, it appears that
the coal mines of North Wales could pay a wage which
did not lag far behind the English and Scottish standards ;
for in many of the pits virgin seams were being worked,
and the smelting industries—especially the ironworks, on
which the selling price of coal ultimately depended[3]—were
not yet out of the running for competition with the great
industrial centres. But after the slump of 1826, wages
here came to diverge more and more widely from those
paid in the English coalfields, proportionally with the
growing disparity in scale of production. On the eve of
the great strike of 1830–31, colliers' wages in North Wales
were still, according to one estimate, 1s. 8d. a shift, according to another 2s. a day, or about 8s. or 9s. a week ; whereas
in Scotland they had reached 5s. 3d. a day in 1825 and
had not yet sunk below 4s.[4] After the strike there was a
temporary improvement in wages. In the summer of
1831, the proprietors of Chirk Bank and Ffrwd collieries
advertised for hands at 15s. to 18s. a week and 3s. a day
respectively ; round Holywell, 15s. 6d. was being paid in
1836. This was at a time when Northumbrian miners

[1] *Op. cit.*, p. 355. The figures refer to some date later than 1799,
when Davies began writing his report.
[2] *C.E.R.* (1842, XVII), pp. 413–4 ; Clapham : *Early Railway Age,*
pp. 558–9 ; Ashton and Sykes : *op. cit.*, p. 138 ; *Shrewsbury Chron.*,
Jan. 7, 1831.
[3] *Cf.* Rees : *Industrial Revolution in South Wales*, pp. 22–3.
[4] *Chester Chron.*, Jan. 7, 1831 ; *Bye-gones*, 1876, pp. 171–2 ;
Clapham : *loc. cit.*

earned 3s. 4d. to 4s. 5d. a day (which, however, only worked out at 15s. to 20s. a week), and Staffordshire miners 4s. 3d. a day.[1]

For the first ten years of Victoria's reign, coal miners' wages were low everywhere—not more than about 3s. 6d. a day. In 1847 there was a general rise to the neighbourhood of 5s., then another drop during the next two years. In the middle of the century the South Wales collieries were paying 3s. a day, those of Northumberland and Staffordshire 3s. 6d., Durham 3s. 9d., and Lancashire 20s. a week. Estimates of wages for this period in North Wales vary widely. The proprietors of one of the Flintshire pits claimed to be paying their men 18s. to 25s. a week in 1842 ; but evidence taken by the Assistant Commissioner on Children's Employment in the preceding year tells a different tale. One miner at Brymbo gives his earnings as 2s. 6d. a day, but adds that he is only working three or four days a week—which makes his weekly wage about 7s. 6d. to 10s. ; even in one of the biggest of the Ruabon pits, the manager estimates the average wage at only 13s. to 15s. a week. Another witness declares that 13s. a week is the minimum on which a man can live in the neighbourhood. Many testify to recent reductions and unparalleled distress.[2] According to the Welsh Education Report— which was drawn up in 1846–7, before the great mid-century depression set in—miners' wages round Wrexham had only just reached 2s. 9d. a day, and in Flintshire they averaged 12s. to 14s. a week. By 1849 wages in the Ruabon district were again down to 2s. or so.[3] It seems, then, that from about 1830 to 1850 wages in North Wales coal mines were at best not much more than three-

[1] *Shrewsbury Chron.*, June 10, 1831 ; *Chester Chron.*, Aug. 12, 1831 ; *H.L.W.*, p. 570 ; Clapham : *loc. cit.*

[2] Clapham : *loc. cit.* ; *Chester Chron.*, April 29, 1842 ; *C.E.R.* (1842, XVII), pp. 377, 394, 413–4. The statement in *Shrewsbury Chron.*, Feb. 2, 1844, that Flintshire colliers were getting 4s. and demanding 5s. sounds highly improbable.

[3] *Educ. Report*, III, App., pp. 82, 97 ; *Wrexham Advertizer*, April 23, 1859. Mr. Emlyn Rogers, in his thesis on *Trade Unionism in the Coal Mining Industry of North Wales*, quotes figures from a chalter-master's account book of 1849, showing that wages at Rhos Llannerchrugog ranged from 1s. 3d. to 2s. 5d. a day. I am indebted to him for several references in the foregoing paragraphs.

quarters, and at worst barely half, those paid in England and Scotland.

For lead mining our statistics are more limited. In 1838 miners at Holywell got 10s. to 12s. a week on piece rates, 10s. on time rates ; smelters had 10s. to 15s. a week. Three years later, in evidence before the Children's Employment Commission, miners' wages were given as 10s. to 20s. a week, and smelters' 10s. to 15s. ; but witnesses who had been working between 30 and 40 years could not agree on the question whether conditions had improved or deteriorated during that time.[1]   In the Penrhyn slate quarries, 1s. a day is the rate usually given for the period immediately following Lord Penrhyn's reorganization ; but only a "small and unavoidable" portion of the work (according to a statement made by Lord Penrhyn's successor in 1822) was done at time rates.[2] Piece rates brought with them the usual disparities in earning power. When the Penrhyn quarrymen went on strike in 1825, they declared that it was possible for men working on the same rock face to earn as much as £5 or £6 or as little as 17s. in a month. Seventeen years later the Children's Employment Commissioners put the earnings of children of 12 in the quarries at 13s. or 14s. a week ; this would probably be the full adult wage. At Ffestiniog, in the middle of the nineteenth century, quarrymen at the rock face got 2s. 4½d. a day, miners (in the underground workings) and labourers 1s. 6d. to 1s. 9d.[3]

Probably the best paid work in North Wales during the period was in the iron forges round Ruabon. The manager of the biggest works reported in 1842 that forgemen got from 13s. to 15s. a week ; at another establishment skilled men like head rollers and forge managers, gave their earnings as 20s., 30s., and even 60s. a week, and testified to the great improvement that had taken place during the last quarter of a century. These figures bear comparison

[1] *H.L.W.*, p. 570 ; *C.E.R.* (1842, XVII). pp. 430–1, 445–6, 454, 456, 459.
[2] The rates he quotes are : opening levels, 6s. a yard : quarrying top rock, 1s. a yard ; making slates 6s. 6d. a ton or 4s. 6d. to 20s. a thousand, according to size and quality. (*Parl. Pap.*, 1823, XV, p. 377.)
[3] U.C.N.W. Library : Coetmor papers, 49 ; *C.E.R.* (1842, XVII), pp. 373–4, 377 ; *Hanes Plwyf Ffestiniog*, pp. 112–3.

with the average of 36s. a week (the highest yet attained) paid to Manchester ironmoulders in 1845–46. On the other hand, in one of the smaller works of the Ruabon district a witness spoke of recent reductions from 30s. to 10s. a week.[1]

Textile wages are as complex a problem as mining wages. During the early years of the Napoleonic War, when the revolution in spinning was creating such abundance of cheap yarn that weavers were commonly earning 11s. and 12s. a week, and as much as 18s. in Yorkshire,[2] the rates paid in North Wales were little, if any, higher than they had been 40 years earlier. In Merioneth, weaving seems to have been paid at $1\frac{1}{2}d$. a yard, and the figures given for spinning range from 2d. and $4\frac{1}{2}d$. a pound (including the carding of the wool) to 8d. and 9d. These figures, however, are of little value in the absence of fuller knowledge about relative speeds of work than we now possess.[3] We do not know, for example, at what date Kay's fly-shuttle was introduced, nor how soon the improvements made in the spinning wheel after 1750[4] became general. Each of these would have an incalculable effect on output ; and the jenny might easily make its influence felt on piece-rates even in districts where it was not yet adopted. All we know of daily wages is that Dolgelley weavers in 1799 got 1s. 2d. a day "on their own victuals" (doubtless the agricultural rate for the county), and that spinners a few years later were sometimes paid as little as 1s. a week.[5]

But if Welsh handloom weavers never attained to the high wages earned in England during the "bumper" years, they also avoided the other extreme. At the time of the Handloom Weavers' Commission, the competition of the

[1] C.E.R., pp. 410–13, 415, 418 ; Clapham : op. cit., p. 550.

[2] Mantoux : Industrial Revolution, p. 435.

[3] My wife's grandfather (b. 1832) could weave about 20 yards a day (working 12 to 14 hours) on the spring loom. Cf. Parl. Pap., 1840, XXIII, pp. 439 ff., and (on spinning) infra, p. 390.

[4] Lipson : op. cit., p. 134. The pre-Kay loom is still used in parts of Wales—or was less than a generation ago.

[5] Davies : General View, pp. 398, 402 ; N. W. Gaz., May 4, 1809 ; Arch. Camb., 1924, p. 35 (extracts from old account book). In the account books of a little factory near Abererch, Pwllheli, for the early years of Victoria's reign (a chaotic and almost illegible bundle of old diaries preserved in U.C.N.W. Library), spinning is charged at 4d. to 7d. a yard, carding at $1\frac{1}{2}d$. to $3\frac{1}{2}d$. (Bangor MSS. 444–6.)

power loom had driven down Yorkshire weavers' wages to 5s. 6½d. a week, whereas the rates in North Wales were 7s. at Llanidloes, 7s. to 9s. at Machynlleth, 9s. at Dolgelley, 10s. 6d. at Welshpool, and 11s. at Newtown (though some witnesses there declared that, when all deductions were made, their wages did not come to more than 8s. 6d.). On the other hand, at Norwich (which, like Wales, was still innocent of the power loom) weavers got 14s. 5d. to 16s. a week. Spinners were paid by the piece in most factories, but at Llanidloes their wages were reckoned at 12s. a week. At Towyn, where workers were taken on by the year, a slubber got an annual wage of £10, and a woman spinner of £5, in addition to their keep.[1]   In 1846 the average weekly earnings in Newtown factories were 8s. to 9s. a week, in those of Llanidloes, 7s.[2]

The meagre statistics available, then, show remarkably little variation in textile wages, except in the earnings of women spinning on jennies for the factories, as compared with the old-fashioned domestic wheel-spinner ; we see nothing like the wild fluctuations which took place in England.   But we must remember that the investigations of the Handloom Weavers' Commission took place just after the great slump of 1837 ; we have no figures for the most prosperous period of the Montgomeryshire flannel industry ; nor, on the other hand, can we trace the declining prosperity of the Welsh handloom weaver without embarking upon investigations which would take us far beyond our period.   It will suffice to add a few details of Montgomeryshire factory wages in 1872, after steam had come into general use for both spinning and weaving. Handloom weavers at Newtown then got 10d. to 2s. 6d. a "wall" (4 yards, 3 inches) as against 8d. to 2s. (7d. to 1s. 8d. at Llanidloes) in 1838 ; power loom weavers were paid 10d. to 1s. 6d. a wall at Newtown, 6s. to 15s. a week at Llanidloes.   The weekly rate for handloom weavers can hardly have been a third of this, for even in the 'twenties

[1] Clapham : *op. cit.*, pp. 553–4 ; *H.L.W.*, pp. 556, 563, 567, 569–70 ; *M.C.R.* (1837–38, XXXV), p. 371.
[2] *Educ. Report*, III, App., pp. 154, 161. *Cf.* figures for English woollen mills in 1835, given in Ure, p. 476 : the maximum wage at Leeds is 22s. 6½d., in Gloucestershire 15s. 3½d.   But women's and children's wages are given separately here, whereas they are no doubt included in the Welsh statistics above. · On this *see* later.

a power loom could do the work of three handlooms. The weaver, however—whether by hand or by machine—was the worst paid of all the factory operatives ; woolsorters had 16s. to 18s. in one factory, and 20s. to 25s. in another ; slubbers and spinners from 16s. to 20s., carders 21s. to 30s., fullers 13s. to 20s.[1]

Outside the woollen industry, the Handloom Weavers' Report shows that workers in the cotton factory at Mold (who were engaged on a weekly basis) were paid 5s. 6d. to 8s. a week, and that in the Holywell silk mills, after the substitution of female for male workers in the early 'thirties, wages went down from 14s. to 12s. a week, and subsequently to 9s., with even lower earnings on piece-rates.[2]

In the middle of the nineteenth century it was stated that wages in North Wales, and in the western counties of South Wales, were lower than in any other part of South Britain. It is pretty clear, at any rate, that they had not risen 40 per cent since 1790, as Dr. Clapham believes English wages had done.[3] And what of the cost of living ? At the beginning of the century, war was sending prices up everywhere, and enclosures were driving more and more people to the shops for things like bacon and beef. But Welsh enclosures came later than English, and it took some time (during the struggle with Napoleon, as during the last War) for war-prices to reach some of the remoter parts of Wales. De Quincey declares that when he was living in Merioneth in 1802 (during a lull in the War, be it noted), "so cheap . . . were all provisions, which one had any chance of meeting with in a labouring man's house, that I found it difficult under such a roof to spend sixpence a day."[4] No doubt this was partly due to the number of things—necessities to the English artisan —which could not be got there at all ; but other travellers, while admitting that prices had risen, commented on the relative cheapness of Welsh inn charges. On the other hand, it was manifestly absurd to state, as one of them

---

[1] *Mont. Coll.*, V, p. 41 ; *H.L.W.*, pp. 556, 563.
[2] *H.L.W.*, pp. 570–1.
[3] Phillips : *Wales* (1849), pp. 29, 30 ; Clapham : *op. cit.*, p. 56.
[4] *Opium Eater* ("Everyman" ed.), p. 131.

did, that £100 would go as far in Wales as £300 would in England.[1]

Gwallter Mechain, writing in the early years of the nineteenth century, tells us that "provisions, in general, are a little under the London prices; corn somewhat dearer, but seldom [to the extent of] more than 5d. to 6d. a bushel." This is, on the whole, confirmed by such sample prices as can be obtained. By 1797 butter was fetching 8d. and 9d. a pound, butcher's meat 3d. to 5d. (sometimes 7d.), wheat 13s. to 14s. a bushel, barley 6s. 6d., oats 3s. 6d. to 4s.; and bacon had gone up from 5d. (in 1781) to 1s.[2] Later in the War, butter reached 8d. (in some exceptional places 1s. 4d.), meat 6d. to 8d., and potatoes 3s. a hundred. The average English prices in 1805 were 1s. 1½d. a pound for butter and 8d. to 9½d. for meat.[3] Where wheat prices can be compared, the Welsh price is nearly always in advance of the London average—sometimes far more so than Davies allows.[4] The industrial regions of South Wales must have been still worse off, for a Cowbridge correspondent assured the publisher of the *Cambrian Register* in 1811 that everything except house rents and firing was actually dearer there than in London. But even in North Wales provisions were almost twice the pre-war prices in 1813, and some things were four times as dear as in 1760.[5] Small wonder that, from early in the War, we read of county meetings to discuss the high prices of necessaries,[6] and that the local press rang with declamations against profiteers[7] and demands for the enforcement

---

[1] Warner: *Walk* (1798), pp. 88–9; Pratt: *Gleanings* (1796), I, p. 91, *cf. Camb. Reg.*, II, p. 428, where his price-list is ruthlessly pulled to pieces.

[2] Davies: *General View*, pp. 360–1; Eden: *loc. cit.*; *Chester Chron.*, Aug. 4, 1797.

[3] Williams: *Snowdon Mountains* p. 21; *N.W. Gaz.*, Nov. 14, 1811, June 3, 1813; Hasbach: *op. cit*, p. 124.

[4] E.g. in 1797, when wheat was 13s. to 14s. at Wrexham, the London average had not yet exceeded 9s. 8½d. (Eden: *loc. cit.*)

[5] *Camb. Reg.*, III, pp. 383–4. In England the rise in prices during that period has been reckoned at 100% for bread, 146% for meat, 140% for butter, and 134¾% for provisions in general. (Hasbach, p. 126.)

[6] E.g. Montgomeryshire (*Salop. Journ.*, Nov. 19, 1800), Anglesey (*Chester Chron.*, Oct. 17, 1800).

[7] E.g. *N. W. Gaz.*, Jan. 16, May 28, 1812.

of the Assize of Bread, which, indeed, was regularly observed in some parts of North Wales up to the time of its abolition in 1824.[1]

The slump of 1815–16 brought prices down to the pre-war level, or even lower. At Bala, for example, wheat was 60s. a quarter (less than the London average), barley 22s. 6d. and oats 15s., in 1816 ; in Anglesey oats were down to 9s., beef to 2d. or 4d. a pound. In a single season oats and barley, livestock, butter and cheese, had gone down by half, wheat and milch cows by two-thirds. Yet handicraftsmen, it was said, were worse off than when they paid double the price for bread, so scarce was work.[2] But prices soon recovered. By 1828–9 they stood at much the same level as during the later years of the War,[3] a level which, on the whole, was maintained during the next decade. In England it has been estimated that in 1839 (a time of dear food) prices, excluding meat, had risen 23 per cent since 1790. In Wales the evidence points to an even greater rise, and to a gradual approximation (through improvements in transport) to English prices. The following are a few samples of the prices which prevailed in North Wales in 1838–39 :—[4]

Article.	Llan-idloes.	New-town.	Wales generally.	Do. 1794.
Butcher's meat (lb.)..	4½d. to 6d.	5d. to 6½d.	4d. to 6d.	2d. to 3½d.
Pork (lb.)	5d.	6d.	2d.	—
Bacon (lb.)	10d.	10d.	—	—
Milk (gal.)	—-	8d.	—	8d. (1797)
Potatoes (240 lbs.) ..	12s.	22s. 6d.	—	—
Butter (lb.)	11d.	1s. 2d.	10d.	6d. to 7d.
Cheese (lb.)	6d.	9d.	—	—
Oatmeal (peck) ..	4s. 8d.	2s. 4d.	—	(Oats) 7½d.
Barley (peck) ..	3s. 9d.	1s. 3d.	—	1s. 1d.
Loaf (white)	—	3d.	—	—
Loaf (brown) ..	—	2½d.	—	—
Flour (lb.)	—	—	3½d.	—
Candles (lb.)	8d.	7d.	—	—
Soap (lb.)	5d.	6d.	—	—

[1] *Id.*, Oct. 6, 1809, March 29, 1810, Oct. 3, 1811 ; *Caernarvonshire Advertizer*, Feb. 2, 1822. *Cf.* Pennant's regrets about the disappearance of the law against forestallers (*Whiteford and Holywell*, p. 162).

[2] *Agricultural State of the Kingdom*, 1816, II, pp. 89–98. *Cf.* figures

It is significant that the price lists now include several articles—ale, tea and sugar, vegetables, fish and poultry— which had scarcely appeared in the market at all during the earlier part of our survey. Ale was undoubtedly more widely consumed in the new industrial towns and villages, especially after the repeal of the duty in 1830 brought the price down, than it had formerly been among the scattered peasantry. It cost 1½d. a pint in 1839, as against 1d. a century earlier.[5] Tea was advertised by local grocers, towards the end of the War, at prices ranging from 5s. to 16s. a pound. In the year of Waterloo it cost as much as 24s. in a remote village of Merioneth, and sugar (which had been 6d. a pound in 1771) was now 1s. 6d.[6] In 1836–38, Montgomeryshire weavers had to pay 5s. to 6s. (about a week's wages) for a pound of tea, and 6½d. to 7½d. for a pound of sugar. Cabbages do not appear on any price list before 1797, and little value was set on poultry until improvements in transport brought the country into touch with the great English markets. Before the War, chickens could be had for 4d. a pair, a goose or a turkey for 1s. Then came Enclosure Acts which "stole the common from the goose," and by 1839 the prices were 1s. 8d., 2s. 6d. and 4s. respectively.[7] It seems to have been about the time of the War, too, that fish first came to be commonly sold in places away from coast villages and fishing rivers, where they had always been plentiful and cheap.[8]

in *N. W. Gaz.*, Nov. 27, 1815, Nov. 20, 1817 ; *Rept. on Holyhead Road*, 1817, pp. 199, 200.

[3] E.g. Bangor, 1828–29 : meat 4d. to 7d., butter 9d. to 1s., eggs 6d. a dozen, salmon 1s. a pound, fowls 1s. a couple. (*N. W. Chron.*, Jan. 3, July 31, 1828, Dec. 31, 1829.)

[4] *H.L.W.*, p. 561 ; Leigh : *Guide to Wales and Monmouthshire* (1839), p. 5. The first edition of the latter was published in 1831, so that the statistics may be a little out of date.

[5] *Morris Letters*, I, pp. 50–51.

[6] *N. W. Gaz.*, 1808 ; *Bye-gones*, 1880–81, pp. 159–60 ; *Rept. on Land*, 1896, p. 626 *n*. An Anglesey gentleman paid 6s. 8d. for 2 lbs. of Bohea in 1760 (MS. diary of W. Bulkeley of Brynddu).

[7] The figures for 1838–39 are taken from *H.L.W*. and Leigh, as above.

[8] Salmon cost 6d. a lb. in Montgomeryshire in 1763 (*Mont. Coll.*, XXV, p. 114), 2d. in 1781, 1s. in 1797 and again in 1828 (*Chester Chron.*, Aug. 4, 1797, *N. W. Chron.*, July 31, 1828). At Hawarden it is said to have risen from 2d. in 1782 to 1s. 6d. or even 4s. in 1822

Two important items in the working-class budget remain to be mentioned—fuel and house rents. Both were injuriously affected by enclosures. The loss of the right to gather turf and brushwood forced more people to buy coal; the abolition of the right of building on the wastes (together with the pressure of urban concentration) increased competition for cottages. Even after the coal duty had gone, Caernarvonshire people had to pay 21s. to 27s. a ton for Lancashire coal, and 13s. to 20s. a ton for North Wales coal, as against 8s. or 9s. near the collieries.[1] In 1788 the average rent of a cottage and garden in rural Denbighshire was 25s. a year; half a century later cottage rents ranged from 30s. to £3 in the country, but nearer the towns they sometimes went up to £6. At Dolgelley a three-roomed house could be rented for £2 10s. a year in 1838; at Pwllheli, a little earlier, £3 would rent a house and enough land to keep a pig and plant a few potatoes; and in 1831 colliers at Ruabon declared they were paying 1s. 3d. to 1s. 6d. a week (out of a wage of 8s. or 9s.) for "two rooms without one yard of land with it." A weaver who had migrated from Manchester to Mold told the Assistant Commissioner on Handloom Weavers in 1838 that he found provisions about the same price as in Manchester, but coal 40 per cent and house rents 20 per cent cheaper.[2]

By the middle of the nineteenth century, Wales— even rural Wales—had ceased to be a land of exceptional cheapness. On the one hand the decay of domestic manufactures and subsistence husbandry was forcing more people to buy in shops, markets and fairs; on the other hand greater facilities of communication were tending to standardize everything. From the coming of the railway, economic conditions in North Wales become more and more assimilated to those of the rest of the kingdom.

(Mem. of Hawarden, p. 160). In 1839, 4d. was the general price— just about what country gentlemen had paid a century earlier (Henblas MSS. 11).
[1] M.C.R. (1837–38, XXXV), pp. 245, 348; Shrewsbury Chron. Jan. 7, 1831; Camb. Quart. Mag., IV, p. 351.
[2] Davies: Labourers in Husbandry, pp. 188–91; Parl. Pap., 1834, XXIX, p. 174; 1837–38, XXV, p. 347; 1840, XXIV, pp. 568–71; Shrewsbury Chron., Jan. 7, 1831. In 1789 a cottage could be thatched for 3s. 6d. (Caerhûn Churchwarden's Book).

B. LIFE AND LABOUR.

If the economic gulf between Wales and England was closing up, that which separated rural from industrial Wales was growing wider. The farm labourer, apart from the fact that he had acquired some new tastes, and that he now bought many things that he used to make or grow for himself, changed his general standard of living but little till after the Repeal of the Corn Laws and the opening up of the country by railways.[1] Gwallter Mechain describes rural fare in 1799 (for small farmers, as well as for their labourers) much as Pococke had described it in 1751 ;[2] and the loud talk about increasing luxury during the later war years[3] finds little echo in subsequent investigations, either official or unofficial.[4] The answers to the "rural queries" issued by the Poor Law Commission in 1834 show that in most parts of North Wales, although work was plentiful, the labourer could only just maintain an average family of young children by living on potatoes, oatmeal, milk—and little else ; from four parishes in Montgomeryshire (including Llanidloes) it was roundly asserted that on the wages then current even that was impossible. "The labourer," declared a Flintshire country curate, "feels that he is not remunerated for his labour ; all his efforts are thus paralysed."[5] Rural housing conditions also show little advance, except in a few districts where improving landlords had put up model dwellings for their labourers. According to the Education Report of 1847, labourers' cottages were still, in many parts, "thickly clustered filthy hovels," with one room and a straw bed ; in Merioneth the farmers' houses themselves were little better, though elsewhere the standard of farm buildings showed a great advance.[6]

[1] *Rept. on Land*, 1896, p. 629.
[2] *Supra*, p. 2 ; *cf.* Davies : p. 357, Kay :   *Agriculture of N. Wales:* Merioneth, p. 16, Evans : *Tour*, p. 349.
[3] E.g. *N. W. Gaz.*, May 17, 1810, July 9 and 23, 1812.
[4] E.g. Select Cttes. on Agriculture, 1821 and 1833 (*Rept. on Land*, 1896, App., pp. 26–7) ; *P.L.R.* (1834, XXIX), p. 388*a* ; *M.C.R.* (1837–38, XXXV), p. 229 ; *N. W. Chron.*, Feb. 25, 1830 ; Phillips : *Wales*, pp. 29–30 ; early chapters of *Life and Opinions of Robert Roberts*.
[5] *P.L.R.*, 1834, XXXI, XXXII.
[6] Evans : *Tour*, pp. 31, 86, 115, 160–2 ; Evans : *Walks*, pp. 67–8 ; *N. W. Gaz.*, May 25, 1809 ; *Educ. Report*, 1847, Pt. III, pp. 63–4,

In industrial areas the trouble was not so much a permanently low standard of living as uncertainty both of work and of wages, which discouraged thrift and made life a gamble. In good times, as moralists never wearied of telling,[1] high wages went on drink and other extravagances ; in bad times hundreds of unemployed had to go on the rates or to migrate to other regions. Conditions among the two main classes of industrial workers were the subject of two exhaustive investigations towards the end of our period ; Mr. W. A. Miles reported on Wales for the Handloom Weavers' Commission in 1839, and Mr. H. Herbert Jones, of Edinburgh, collected the Welsh evidence for the Commission on Children's Employment in 1841. Each report was published in the following year.[2] The impression they jointly convey is that of a shifting standard of living—more comfortable, on the whole, than it had been a generation earlier, and easier than that of the farm labourer, but still appreciably below English standards.

Miners and quarrymen lived mostly on bread (of barley or oats as a rule), butter, potatoes, milk or broth, sometimes bacon, in Flintshire at least plenty of vegetables, but little flesh meat, except sometimes for the Sunday dinner. "They call this sufficient food," said the manager of a lead mine, "but an English workman would not." Clocks and table linen were the general badges of respectability, and the first things to vanish from the house when times were hard. It was with obvious pride that a young lad from Halkin (in Flintshire) told Mr. Herbert Jones how at his home the Sunday dinner—meat, potatoes and pudding—was served up on a linen cloth, with knives and forks for all. In contrast with this, we read how a Newtown weaver's Sunday dinner was generally the worst of the week, because by then the money had given out !

and App., pp. 129, 136; *Rept. on Land*, 1896, p. 698. Contrast Fullarton's *Parl. Gaz.* IV, p. 405 : "the squalid huts of North Wales are being substituted by [*sic !*] better though still humble abodes."

[1] E.g. Hucks : *Pedestrian Tour*, pp. 137–43 ; *Educ. Report*, 1847, III, App., pp. 97, etc. ; *H.L.W.*, p. 561 ; *C.E.R.*, 1842, XV, p. 169, XVII, p. 377.

[2] *Parl. Pap.*, 1840, XXIV, 1842, XVII (general results embodied in 1842, XV), 1843, XV. In the rest of this section references, unless otherwise stated, are to these reports.

On workmen's houses there is much conflicting evidence. There had clearly been improvement in some districts— four-roomed cottages, for example, were taking the place of two-roomed—and the miner and artisan were said to be, on the whole, better housed than the peasant.[1] But the industrial districts had special problems of their own, chief of which was the sudden inrush of immigrants for whom accommodation had to be found. When the *entrepreneur* was also a landlord who took pride in keeping his estate free from at least the external marks of squalor, and in playing the benevolent despot over his men—as in some of the quarrying districts[2]—the worst evils were avoided. Owners of woollen mills also frequently built cottages for their employees ; but the chief centres of the woollen industry were old market towns with a decent architectural tradition, and the country mills were too thinly staffed to entail much overcrowding ; so that here, too, conditions were generally tolerable, though the two-roomed hovel was by no means unknown.[3]

The real plague spots were places like Halkin or Rhos Llannerchrugog (in the mining area), Buckley (the potters' colony), and some of the new quarrying villages—mushroom growths, far from any organized centre of population, where cottages had been hastily run up, either by adventurers with no family traditions at their back, or else by the workmen themselves.[4] At Halkin, even the household referred to above, which kept up such a goodly show of high living on Sundays, crammed itself into one single bedroom when the day was over ; and many families ate and slept in the same room. The Education Report of 1847 contains some very black pictures. Rhos is described by its vicar as "worse than Merthyr Tydfil," and this is borne out by a description of the prevailing type of miners' cottage :

> Some . . . consisted of a single room from 9 to 12 feet square ; others have in addition a sort of lean-to, forming a

[1] Cooke : *Topographical and Statistical Description of North Wales*, p. 56.
[2] *Supra*, p. 206.
[3] *Supra*, p. 262. *See* descriptions of Llanidloes, Welshpool, Meifod, Towyn, and Montgomeryshire in Lewis : *Top. Dict.*
[4] *Supra*, pp. 78, 193, 197, 220 ; Pennant : *Tours*, I, p. 96 ; *Camb. Trav. Guide* (1813), pp. 713–14.

separate place to sleep in. They are in general void of furniture, but in some I found a bed which is made to accommodate double numbers by arranging the occupants feet to feet. The roofs are wattled, sometimes plastered over with mortar, sometimes bare ; others are of straw, and full of large holes open to the sky, which are frequently the only means of admitting light. Each of these hovels contains on an average a family of six children, with their parents. If they comprise two rooms the parents sleep in one, and the children in the other ; if there is but one room all sleep together.

Flint was "almost as degraded as Rhos" ; at Bagillt the cottages were "dirty, ill-ventilated, and overcrowded" ; Amlwch was "in the matter of housing more degraded than any place in Anglesey."[1] Even in some of the older towns the general increase in population, from early in the nineteenth century, was giving the speculative builder his chance to put up mean streets of jerry-built houses to be let, if possible, to pauper tenants, whose rates would be paid by the relieving officer ;[2] and although the first half of the century saw numerous improvements in sanitation and water-supply, many places were still very inadequately equipped for the needs of their increasing numbers.[3]

The term "plague spots" has been used advisedly. Scurvy, malaria and ague; the ancient pests of the Welsh countryside, retreated before the draining of marshes and improvements in the cottagers' diet ;[4] but in the squalid and huddled cabins of the new industrial communities new and still more dread diseases broke out. As early as 1779 Sir Watkin Williams Wynn had the poor of Ruabon inoculated against smallpox by Dr. Lancaster of Bala— perhaps the first inoculator in North Wales.[5] There was

[1] *Educ. Rept.*, 1847, III, App., pp. 74–5, 90, 98, 4.

[2] *See*, e.g. advts. of building sites at Bangor and Caernarvon in *N. W. Gaz.*, Jan. 5, 1808, and *cf.* accounts of conditions there in *P. L. R.*, 1834 (summarized in *Rept. on Land*, 1896, App., p. 29), and in *Educ. Rept.*, III, p. 64 and App., p. 21. Over 800 houses were built in Bangor during the 15 years after 1813 (Pigot's *Directory*, 1828–29, p. 1140).

[3] *See*, e.g. *N. W. Gaz.*, Feb. 4, 1813 (Beaumaris), Sept. 13, 1821 (Caernarvon) ; *Records of Denbigh*, p. 156 ; *Ancient and Modern Denbigh*, pp. 335–6 ; *M.C.R.*, 1837–38, XXXV, p. 371 (Welshpool), 1835, XXVI, p. 539 (Caerwys), and descriptions of Amlwch, Holywell, Denbigh, Llanidloes, Machynlleth, Montgomery, Newtown Pwllheli, Rhuddlan, and Wrexham in Lewis : *Top. Dict.*

[4] Roberts : *Welsh Home-spun*, p. 53.

[5] *Chester Chron.*, Aug. 6, 1779 ; Barfoot and Wilkes' *Directory* III, p. 264.

an outbreak at Holywell (where fevers, pleurisy and quinsy were frequent), just before the Napoleonic War,[1] and during and immediately after the War the disease broke out in parts of Montgomeryshire (where inoculation was provided at the Forden House of Industry), Anglesey, and Merioneth, and at Caernarvon and Denbigh. In many places, public dispensaries and private practitioners offered free inoculation or vaccination.[2] Smallpox was raging again at Bangor in 1823 and at Caernarvon in 1827. Indeed, in the narrow alleys of Bangor, where tramps congregated, both smallpox and typhus were endemic in the 'thirties.[3] In the same period typhoid and typhus broke out among the Ffestiniog quarrymen ; and in the 'forties the Commissioners on Welsh Education reported that at both Rhos and Caernarvon the shocking sanitary conditions bred fevers of all sorts and emptied the schools.[4] The first visitation of cholera (in 1831–2) seems to have been limited to Denbigh (though there were many false alarms, and fever was raging in Newtown at the time) ; the second (in 1849) ravaged Welshpool, and the third (1853) Newtown.[5]

If these were the conditions in the labouring man's home, it was perhaps no grave loss that he saw so little of it. Agricultural labourers generally worked 12 to 14 hours in summer, and from dawn to dusk in winter ;[6] in coal mines and factories the normal working day was of 12 hours, in quarries and lead mines, 10 ; one witness stated in 1841 that lead miners were only 6 to 8 hours actually underground. Meal-times occupied anything from half an hour to one and a half hours out of this total—the periods

---

[1] Davies : *General View*, p. 447 ; Pennant : *Holywell*, pp. 278–81.
[2] *Mont. Coll.*, XXXVII, pp. 103, 104, 106, 126 ; XV, p. 29 ; Davies : *op. cit.*, p. 429 ; *N. W. Gaz.*, Nov. 3, 1808, Jan. 16, 1812, Jan. 28, Dec. 9, 1813, Sept. 8, 1814 ; Gwyddelwern Vestry Book, 1796.
[3] *N. W. Gaz.*, July 3, 1823 ; *Shrewsbury Chron.*, March 23, 1827 ; *N. W. Chron.*, Jan. 7, 1830.
[4] *Hanes Plwyf Ffestiniog*, p. 115 ; *Educ. Rept.*, III, p. 66 and App., p. 33.
[5] *P.L.R.*, 1834, XXIX, p. 190a, XXXV, pp. 323–9 ; *Shrewsbury Chron.*, April 2, 1831 ; *Mont. Coll.*, XXIX, p. 286 ; Rowlands : *History of Newtown*, p. 107 ; *Y Drysorfa*, 1832, p. 278 *et passim*.
[6] So Davies (*General View*, p. 355) ; Kay says 12 hours in Anglesey, Caernarvonshire and Denbighshire, and 14 in Merioneth.

were rarely fixed. Normal working hours were from 6 to 6 ; they might be either during the day, or during the night, or both in turn, but night work was rare in the lead mines. Denbighshire colliers used to work an hour less on Saturday, and start at 3 instead of 6, so as to have the afternoon free.[1] Overtime was frequent in some industries, either when work was brisk or when a breakdown occurred ; in the copper and brass works men would sometimes work as much as 24 or even 36 hours at a stretch For this they were usually paid at higher rates : even at the beginning of the century industrial workers who went a couple of hours beyond their twelve each day were often paid a seven-days' wage for six days' work. On the other hand, the day's work would be shortened when times were slack, and there were many days of both voluntary and involuntary idleness. For, in addition to Sundays, public holidays, and other occasions when the works stopped, the day labourer could always take a day off if he chose to lose his pay and risk his job (as well as possibly holding up his fellow-workmen), whereas the permanent servant on an annual wage might land himself in the House of Correction for a month if he stole a few hours to see a cock fight.[2] The domestic spinner or weaver could arrange his hours as he chose, but he was lucky if he could make a living on less than twelve or fourteen hours a day.

The workman was not necessarily separated from his family for the whole of this period ; the family wage-earning group might be transplanted *en bloc* to mine or factory. The novelty of this lay not in the actual employment of women and children, but in the conditions under which they worked. Welsh peasant women were inured to hard toil, but—with a few exceptions like domestic service or apprenticeship to a milliner—it was work that could be done in and around their own homes, in the midst of the family. They had always worked in the harvest, and sometimes at the plough ; and, like the French *paysanne*, they slipped naturally into their husbands' or fathers'

[1] *Bye-gones*, 1876, p. 171.
[2] E.g. *N. W. Gaz.*, May 31, 1810 (Montgomeryshire). The "regulations for setting" adopted in a Caernarvonshire quarry in 1844 impose a fine of 2s. 6d. for failure to work the full 10 hours, and dismissal of the whole gang of partners if it does not turn up in full strength on "setting day" (Searell MSS. 3).

places in the fields when war broke out. For the more
prosperous there were tasks like taking farm produce to
market, bringing back stores with which to keep shop for
the benefit of their neighbours, or brewing beer and keeping
open house for travellers. Eighteenth-century visitors to
Wales remark on the fact that innkeeping and shopkeeping are largely in the hands of women ; sometimes they
even find women serving as barbers.[1] Above all, there
was the universal spinning wheel—a stand-by on winter
evenings for rich and poor alike, and an indispensable
adjunct to whatever earnings were made elsewhere.
  It was the loss of this subsidiary income through the
spread of machine-spinning that made women "more and
more reluctant to undertake field work"[2] (which, for women,
was irregular and ill-paid) and drove them into mining
and manufacture. In the flannel industry they swarmed
into the new factories ; they supplanted men at the Holywell ribbon works, outnumbered them by two to one in the
neighbouring cotton mills, almost monopolized the new
power looms at Mold, and formed (with a few children) the
entire staff of the Turkey paper mill near Wrexham.
Their work at the mines consisted of breaking up copper
ore (as at Parys Mountain and Llanberis)[3] or "banking"
and winding (as in the coal mines round Ruabon)—hard
enough drudgery, but not to be compared with the horrors
of underground life in some of the English mines. In
North Wales women never descended the shafts ; and the
lead mines, smelting works and quarries did not employ
them at all. Statistics of the number of women workers
given in the Census returns of 1841 show that the highest
percentages were in the two textile counties, Montgomery
and Merioneth, where about 20 per cent of the female
population over 20 years old, and about 15 per cent of
those under, were "gainfully employed." Next in order
come Denbighshire, Caernarvonshire and Anglesey. Flintshire (which closed its mines to women) stands last of all,

[1] Meyrick papers ; Evans : Tour, pp. 5, 55, 281, 292 ; N. W. Gaz.,
April 8, 1813. Pigot's Directory for 1828–29 confirms this impression ; women's names are numerous in every occupation, especially
innkeeping and retail trade, and there is one example of a woman
blacksmith.
[2] P.L.R. (1834, XXX), p. 656a.
[3] Aikin : Journal, p. 137 ; Evans : Tour, p. 186.

despite the cotton mills ; there the figures are only 15 and 10 per cent respectively.

Children had always been expected to start working for their living by the time they were ten, and to keep themselves when they were fifteen—or at latest seventeen. But in Wales before the Industrial Revolution the range of available employment, outside agriculture, was very limited. There was much correspondence in the local press, early in the nineteenth century, about enforcing the Elizabethan apprenticeship code ; but the truth was that apprenticeship had already lost whatever vitality it may have possessed in a land where skilled trades were so few, although in England the Children's Employment Commission found it still flourishing in the 'forties.[1] We hear now and then of lads apprenticed to shopkeepers or professional men, or to skilled trades like those of printer, cooper, blacksmith and flax-dresser ;[2] benevolent landlords would sometimes pay the fees for indenturing their tenants' daughters to millinery or mantua making ;[3] and a few parish authorities continued to carry out their duty of apprenticing the children of the poor to a useful trade, under the Elizabethan Act, up to the eve of its demise.[4] But generally all there was for a child to do was to follow his father to the fields or to help the womenfolk with wool-picking, carding or spinning at home.

The extension of large-scale industry brought new opportunities. In the lead and copper mines, children were given the job of preparing the ore for the smelteries by picking, washing and sometimes breaking it ; but in the lead mines the latter task, originally done by hand with hammers (whereby much poisonous dust was inhaled), was mostly taken over by machinery after 1830. For these jobs boys were taken on at the age of 10, more rarely

[1] *N. W. Gaz.*, Dec. 17, 1812, May 20, Dec. 30, 1813 ; *P.L.R.* (1834, XXIX), p. 186 ; Clapham : *Early Railway Age*, p. 571.

[2] E.g. *N. W. Gaz.*, Jan. 5, Feb. 2, July 28, 1808, Nov. 9, 1809, July 19, 1810 ; *Chester Chron.*, Jan. 22, 1802, Sept. 11, 1807, Aug. 7, 1823 ; Amlwch MSS. 4 (xxii) ; *supra*, p. 295n.

[3] "Paid Mary Owen, Mantua Maker, her apprentice money with Mrs. Williams (Llangristiolus) daughter : £7 17s. 6d. ; remaining part towards clothing her : £6 15s. 0d. ; indentures : 7s. 6d." (Meyrick papers, 1763).

[4] *Arch. Camb.*, 1926, pp. 127–8.

at 6, 7 or 8. A few boys—not more than 60 in all Flint-shire—were employed underground, to pump air into the deeper mines ; but generally underground work did not begin till 18 or 20. In the coal mines, on the other hand, lads of 11 and 12, and sometimes as young as 7 when the seams were thin, regularly went below ground with their fathers. In 1828 two boys of 8 and 12 respectively were killed in an explosion at one of the Flintshire collieries.[1] The very youngest children had the light but monotonous task of opening and shutting the air doors, but they were soon put on to heavier work, such as hooking-on the "pyches" (or trams), and dragging them, on all fours, along the narrow passages, with two to four hundred-weight of coal—or even eight to twelve hundredweight where the trams ran on rails. In the few pits where ponies or donkeys were kept it was the children who looked after them. At twelve, or thereabouts, they were considered strong enough to start filling the pyches.

As a result of the enquiry of 1842, children under 10 were, from the following year, completely excluded from the pit-bottoms, and those between 10 and 13 were not allowed to work more than three days a week.[2] But this did not prevent their continued employment on the banks from a tender age. In 1846 it was still usual at Rhos, Flint, Bagillt and Buckley for children to begin work at the pits when they were 8 or 9, and at Amlwch children of the same age were sent by their parents to rummage in the waste heaps of the (now almost derelict) copper mine.

Somewhat older boys were employed in the smelting works of Denbighshire and Flintshire. Probably the biggest number was at the British Iron Company's works at Acrefair, where the Commissioners of 1842 found 380 boys, 25 of them under 18, but none under 11. A few more served as moulders, fillers, lifters or shear-lads in the Company's forges at Ruabon. There were fewer in the Flintshire lead works ; some of these employed no one under 20, and none admitted children under 13. In the copper works they started at 11. A few lads of 12 to 14 were employed in the Buckley brickworks ; and children

[1] *N. W. Chron.*, May 29, 1828.
[2] 5 and 6 Vict., cap. 99.

of 8 sometimes worked in the Caernarvonshire slate
quarries, though 10 was the more usual age for beginning. In all these branches of industry the children
stayed at work till the adults finished—even when there
was a spell of overtime or night work. In the collieries
children were sometimes known to work 18 hours on end,
and in the copper works (on rare occasions) as many as 24.
One manager told the Commissioners that the work could
not go on if the children's hours were restricted, because
the men would be held up for lack of assistants ; and
parents were generally up in arms against any talk of
limiting the highly profitable overtime of these youngsters.[1]

We do not know at what date the employment of children
in the mines and quarries began ; but they came into the
factories almost as soon as factories were built. Smalley
had children in his cotton mills at Holywell probably
from the outset, certainly by 1795 ; and Charles Cole is
said to have brought children into the Glanclywedog
factory at Llanidloes about 1797.[2] In 1839 the number
of employees under 18 in the factories of North Wales
was officially reported as follows :—[3]

	9–13	13–18
Flintshire (cotton) ..	78	395
Denbighshire (wool) ..	27	66
Montgomeryshire (wool)	174	341
Merioneth (wool) ..	18	50

As a result of the Act of 1833, no children under 9 were
employed.

To the weaving districts the admission of children to
factories came as a godsend, for machinery was rapidly
superseding the work they used to do at home. Most of
them, no doubt, came with their parents and remained
under their care, the younger ones performing such simple
services as they had been accustomed to at home, the
older ones helping to tend and feed the machines. But a

---

[1] *Educ. Rept.*, 1847, III, App., pp. 38, 41, 74, 90, 92, 94, 98, 101,
114.

[2] Pennant : *Holywell*, p. 208 ; *Mont. Coll.*, V, p. 37.

[3] *Parl. Pap.*, 1839, XLII.

few apprentices were taken on from the workhouses, as in the English mills. In 1809 David Roberts, manufacturer, of Black Mill, Welshpool, was summoned on a charge of ill-treating an apprentice from Forden House of Industry ; twenty years later the Quarter Sessions of Montgomeryshire turned down a claim from the parish of Llandinam that certain children who had been taken from there by factories at Llanidloes and Llangurig should be regarded as hired servants, and therefore chargeable to the parishes where they were employed. The millowners, indeed, were always chary of giving a "settlement" to any children they might employ from another parish. No formal indentures of apprenticeship were entered into ; the children were simply hired by word of mouth, for periods of one to three years.[1]

Parish apprentices were employed more extensively in the Holywell cotton works. In 1795 there were three or four hundred of them, in addition to children from the neighbourhood. We do not know where Smalley got them from, but he gave Thomas Pennant a very full account of their treatment. They were lodged in two "commodious houses"—one for the boys and one for the girls—which were whitewashed twice a year and fumigated (by tobacco smoke) three times a week. They slept two or three in a bed, but no attempt was made (as in so many English factories) to economize space by using the same beds twice over for successive shifts of apprentices. All the windows in the sleeping rooms were opened while the children were at work, and the rooms were scrubbed out twice a week. Clothing and workhouse fare were supplied by the employers, and a Sunday School was held weekly in each of the houses.[2] If we may trust Smalley's account (and Pennant was in a position to check most of his statements), his treatment of the apprentices avoided the more flagrant abuses against which the Act of 1801 was directed, and anticipated many of its provisions.

The Act of 1833—the first really serious attempt to grapple with factory problems—excluded children under 9 from textile factories, prohibited night work for those

[1] *Mont. Coll.*, XXXVII, p. 128 and *n: Shrewsbury Chron.*, July 24, 1829 ; *H.L.W.*, pp. 557–8.
[2] *Whiteford and Holywell*, pp. 115–16.

under 18, prescribed (in gradual doses) a maximum working week of 48 hours, with a minimum of two hours' schooling a day, for all under 13, and subjected the mills to inspection. The task of enforcing this, and later restrictions on juvenile labour, in the factories of Montgomeryshire and Merioneth was entrusted to Mr. T. Jones Howell, inspector for the West of England factories. Those of the other counties of North Wales were at first placed under the supervision of Mr. R. Rickards, but subsequently (from 1839) included in Howell's district. Howell found that the practical effect of the Act in North Wales was to make the millowners reluctant to employ any child under 13 at all. They were there to help the adults, and if they could not work full adult hours they were useless, for in the little Welsh factories the relay system, in which English millowners often took refuge, was quite unworkable.

Prosecutions for offences under the Act were almost confined to the Newtown and Llanidloes factories, where at first there were "repeated and general infractions of the law" ; convictions at Machynlleth, Pool Quay and Caersws are also reported. The smaller country mills, especially those of Merioneth, were rarely troubled ; indeed, the inspector declared that it was impossible to apply the Act where there was no clock in sight and where the employer could neither read nor write nor speak a word of English. The commonest offences were the employment of children under 13 without vouchers of school attendance, or certificates of age ; more rare were prosecutions for the keeping of young people under 18 at work after 9 p.m. This offence was treated more seriously : one culprit was fined as much as £5 ; generally fines ranged from 5s. to £1.[1]

The earnings of the women and children in mines and factories were important contributions to the family exchequer, which must be borne in mind in any attempt to compare industrial with rural conditions. Women generally earned about 6s. a week, either in factory or on pit bank—at least twice as much as they would get in the

---

[1] Factory Inspectors' Reports, 1835–40 ; *cf. Educ. Rept.*, 1847, III, App. p. 154, on falsification of age. Mr. T. Waterhouse, of Holywell, tells me that a man who retired from service in the flannel works there in 1924, at the age of 78, had started at Llanidloes (in 1853) when he was only 7.

fields. Children of 8 could bring home 1s. 3d. to 2s. 6d. a
week for their work in coal mines or slate quarries. At
9 the factories were open to them, with wages ranging from
1s. 6d. to 5s. a week.[1] By the time they were 10 they
could earn about 2s. by washing ore at the lead mines,
and sometimes as much as 6s. or more in the slate quarries.
At 12, they might get 2s. 6d. in the copper works, 3s. to
4s. 6d. at the lead mines, and 5s. to 6s. 8d. at the brickworks. After they had reached the age of 13 the range
of earnings widened rapidly : in the quarries they could
now get 13s. or 14s. a week ; they might find admission to
ironworks, where their wages, starting at 3s. to 5s., would
reach 9s. or 10s. in a few years ; and as much could be
made in some of the collieries. In the lead mines 9s. 6d.,
in the copper works 6s. to 8s., was the normal wage at 17.
It was usual in the mines, and probably in the factories
too, for the children to pay all their wages to their parents,
as contributions towards their keep; sometimes the
employers did it for them.

These additions to the family earnings of industrial
workers, however, were balanced by many serious drawbacks in the methods of paying wages. The farm labourer
got his money regularly and suffered little from unemployment ;[2] in industry employment was irregular even in
good years (the coal mines were always idle several days
a week in summer, and the textile worker's busy season
only lasted four months in the year),[3] and subject to
periodic crises when works were at a standstill for weeks
or closed down for good. Further, most industrial wages
depended on output. For the factory hand, apart from
occasional stoppages of machinery, output was fairly
constant ; for the miner or quarryman it depended on
incalculable factors like the productivity of the spot where
he happened to be working ; for both classes, piece rates
involved frequent disputes about the unit of output. Thus
the Newtown weavers complained to Mr. Miles in 1838

---

[1] At Leeds (in 1835) children got from 2s. to 4s. 4d., women 7s.
to 7s. 7d. ; in Gloucestershire children got 1s. 8d. to 3s. 1d., women
5s. to 5s. 8d. (Ure, p. 476).
[2] P.L.R. (1834, XXIX), passim (rural queries).
[3] C.E.R. (1842, XV), p. 112 ; H.L.W., p. 557.

that their masters were persistently increasing the length of the "wall" (on which weaving rates were calculated), and reducing the width of the reed.

Sub-contracting prevailed extensively in both mines and quarries. Groups of four to six "bargain-takers" would contract to clear a specified area at fixed tonnage rates, which were paid over to the gang leader. Jonathan Roose introduced the method from Derbyshire into the Parys mine in 1768, and the good luck it brought the owners, after their long fruitless searches for ore, made it generally popular with managers of copper mines—but not with the miners, who soon found, to their cost, that the competition among themselves for good places enabled a tyrannical steward to keep on lowering the tonnage rates at each successive "setting."[1] The agents at Penrhyn quarry, in the early nineteenth century, often made such contracts with groups of quarrymen for a year at a time, and the other quarries followed suit.[2] Another variant was to be found in the working of lead mines : in the early days, lessees of mines would sometimes allow adventurers from outside to work a vein, exacting from them rather higher royalties than they themselves had to pay to the owners of the soil ; and even in the 'forties miners would supplement their wages by "taking ventures," in their spare time, from the owner of an unemployed mine.[3]

The system is seen in its most developed form in the coal mines. Here it was usual for the manager to bargain with a few charter (or chalter) masters to work the whole pit. They were the only employees who received their wages direct from the employer, and out of these earnings they hired and paid their own gangs of assistants,[4] and

[1] *Supra*, pp. 154, 341 ; *Trans. Ang. Ant. Soc.*, 1926, p. 97 ; Sygun mine setting book (Searell MSS. 2).

[2] *N. W Chron.*, Oct. 25, 1827, Aug. 21, 1828. For a sample contract (with "Griffith Williams & Company," 1818–20, Griffith signing the document with his mark) *see Parl. Pap.*, 1823, XV, p. 417. *See* also "regulations for setting" in Searell MSS. 3.

[3] *Supra*, p. 173 ; *C.E.R.* (1842, XVII), p. 459. In the Nant y ffrith mine (1753–57) the lessees paid 25s. a ton to Lord Grosvenor, and received 30s. to 35s. from private adventurers (Palmer : *Old Parish of Wrexham*, pp. 129–30).

[4] The children on the banks of lead mines were sometimes employed by the man who contracted with the manager to prepare the ore (*C.E.R.*, 1842, XV, p. 230).

provided tools, timber, and waggons. Sometimes (as at Coed Talon in 1826),[1] the banksmen were paid by the owner, who also supplied rails and ropes, where necessary. Similar methods of working prevailed in the coalfields of the English Midlands (from which they had doubtless spread to Wales); but not in Scotland or in the North, where the proprietors were wealthier men, able to provide all the capital themselves, and where the methods of working lent themselves more to individual than to gang labour. Originally the chalter masters may have brought only their own families to the pit, but by the 'forties their gangs included other people's children as well, and the way was open to grave abuses both in the allotting of places and in the payment of wages. Frequently the chalter masters only settled their accounts once a month. At the end of the month they might find themselves without enough in hand to .pay what they had promised; and during the course of it, the worker who found himself running short could only apply for *sist*—an advance of wages on account.[2]

In some of the collieries, *sist* took the form of a ticket for goods on the "tommy "shop kept by the owner (or occasionally by the chalter master). For when mines were opened at a distance from any centre of population, the proprietor might find it necessary to turn shopkeeper, as well as house builder, for the benefit—or otherwise—of his men. The shops opened two or three times a week, and supplied the miners' wives with all the commoner sorts of provisions, debiting the purchases against their husbands' wages at the end of the month. Tommy shops were commonest in the Ruabon area—at Plas Madoc, at Chirk, and (most unpopular of all) at the British Iron Company's works at Acrefair ; there was also one at Coed Talon. Some had been opened at the request of the men themselves, but generally they were hated. Miners' wives, it was said, had to waste precious time by waiting in queues for their turn to be served ; in the absence of ready cash they were often forced to trade goods from the shop (at a sacrifice) for things like milk and barm, which were not

[1] Ashton and Sykes : *op. cit.*, p. 111.
[2] I am much indebted to the excellent account of the chalter master system in Mr. Emlyn Rogers' thesis, cited above.

sold there ; worst of all, the tommy shops were accused of extortionate prices and unjust weights and measures. During the strike of 1830–1, the proprietors of the Acrefair shop (where sugar cost 8*d*. a pound instead of 5*d*., and flannel 1*s*. 4*d*. a yard instead of 1*s*.) were publicly convicted of selling short weight. The Truck Act of 1831[1] entirely failed to put down the practice. All the old complaints were brought up again before the Commissioners of 1842 (who were told by colliers from Wrexham and Brymbo that the absence of truck made their wages go 10 per cent further) and before the Education Commissioners in 1846-47.[2]

We do not hear of tommy shops in connection with lead mines, although here, too, monthly payment was frequent ; and the Children's Employment Commission reported that in the slate industry wages were paid regularly, and never in truck. But we know from other sources that the Welsh Slate Company opened a retail flour, butter, and bacon warehouse (to which the *North Wales Gazette* urged the addition of a brewery and bakehouse) for its workmen at Ffestiniog. Another Ffestiniog quarry owner sent regularly to Liverpool by steamboat for provisions for his men, and a third opened an inn.[3] A few of the Montgomeryshire factory owners also kept shops, and although wages were seldom (if ever) paid in tickets for goods, workmen who failed to deal with their employers found their jobs in jeopardy. Checked (but not extinguished) at Llanidloes by the strike of 1830, truck was still rampant ten years later at Newtown, where goods in the tommy shop were marked 5 per cent above current prices ; and at Machynlleth, where improvident weavers would get advances from their employers in flour, butter, or bacon while their flannel was still on the loom.[4]

---

[1] 1 and 2 Gul. IV, cap. 37.

[2] *Bye-gones*, 1876, pp. 171-2 ; *Y Gwyliedydd*, VIII (1830), p. 61 ; *Educ. Rept.*, 1847, III, pp. 64-5. *Cf.* statement of a Barnsley miner in 1842 that he would rather 17*s*. cash (a Monmouthshire miner even said 15*s*.) than 20*s*. in "tommy" (Clapham : *op. cit.*, p. 564).

[3] *N. W. Gaz.*, Sept. 14, 1826 ; *Hanes Plwyf Ffestiniog*, pp. 71, 136. A letter from a quarry manager to his employers in London in 1843 states that "at most other quarries in Wales they pay once a month" (Searell MSS. 3).

[4] *H.L.W.*, pp. 557, 563-6.

The tommy shop was peculiar to the industrial districts, but truck as an institution was also familiar to the agricultural labourer. The account books of a Caernarvonshire estate for 1841–44 show that labourers' services are regularly offset by gifts of coal, flour, meal or butter, remissions of house rent, and tickets on village shops—often enough leaving no cash balance at all.[1] But the farm hand did not, like some industrial workers, have to buy from his employer stores needed for carrying on the work. The Parys Mine Company, for example, sold gunpowder, ropes and candles to its miners, and unscrupulous stewards were believed to make a handsome profit out of the men by these dealings.[2] This, however, is not a general complaint.

On the physical and moral effects of work in the mines and factories it is well not to dogmatize too confidently. Outside critics from among the gentry, farmers and professional classes—ever suspicious of the new industry—were disposed to darken the picture, contrasting an idealized life in the fields with the excessive tasks and the stunted growth of the factory children.[3] Employers and foremen were naturally biassed in the opposite direction ; and even workmen, when they appeared as witnesses before Royal Commissions, walked warily lest Government should put some new restriction on their earning capacities.[4] When evidence was collected for the Children's Employment Commission in 1841, the clerk to the Petty Sessions at Ruabon and Wrexham assured the Assistant Commissioner that colliers were "equal in intellect, character, and physique with any other class." Doctors declared that (leaving aside accidents, on which something has been said in an earlier chapter[5]) work in the mines was healthy and not excessive, and that the diseases from which miners suffered were generally due to their own negligence. Others testified how the children ran off to play, and their fathers hastened to the potato patches which many of the Flintshire and Denbighshire miners

[1] Madryn estate labourers' accounts (Yale MS. 24).
[2] *Trans. Ang. Ant. Soc.*, p. 97.
[3] E.g. "Scotus" in *N. W. Gaz.*, April 8, 1813 ; *cf. supra*, p. 160.
[4] *See*, e.g., C.E.R. (1842, XVII) p. 397.
[5] *Supra*, pp. 196–7, 207.

still possessed (in spite of enclosures), as soon as they had come up the shaft. Managers emphasized the eagerness of children to get into the pits, and declared (what we can well believe, for where is the lad who does not want to be a man as soon as he is breeched ?) that they would gladly start work when they were six if the masters would let them. Magistrates spoke of the orderliness and high moral tone of the mining population, except for a little trouble about poaching and a few petty thefts ; and those who knew them best said they were "better conducted than the English." All save a few incumbents of the Established Church bore witness to the moralizing influence of Methodism and Dissent among a people formerly notorious for drunkenness, brawling and sexual immorality.

Some witnesses, it is true, declared that a miner already looked worn out at 30, became asthmatic by the time he was 40, and developed into an old man at 60 ;[1] several even among the managers deplored the effects of too early employment in the mines ; and a few stoutly denied the existence of any improvement, moral or physical. But there is certainly some significance in the fact that, while farm labourers frequently sought work in the mines, miners rarely, if ever, went off to farming. If work was slack in one pit, they tried another. Of deliberate cruelty to the children, either in mines or in factories, there is little sign ; and the Commissioners on Handloom Weavers bear testimony to the freedom of the Montgomeryshire flannel districts from petty crimes like embezzlement of yarn, so common among English weavers.[2] The quarries were singled out for special praise. The work was said to be healthy, discipline easy, wages regularly paid ; but for the one blot of illiteracy (the result of starting work too young) the picture would be almost an idyllic one.

The Education Report of 1847, which depended more on the testimony of outside observers and less on that of masters and workmen themselves, gives a much more sombre view. It speaks of the bad physical and moral effects of women's work on the pit banks, of the frequency

---

[1] It should be noted, however, that the same sort of thing was said by travellers at an earlier date about the rural population (e.g. Hucks : *Pedestrian Tour*, pp. 137 ff.).
[2] *H.L.W.*, pp. 53–7.

of bastardy among mill girls at Llanidloes, and the "promiscuous debauchery" that prevailed there ; above all, of the universal ignorance of the children.   The trustworthiness of this famous Report—*Brad y Llyfrau Gleision*[1] as it is called among Welsh patriots—has been a subject of constant and acrimonious controversy from the time of its publication to our own day.   It is certainly a prejudiced document : it treats the Welsh language with scorn ; its exaggerated talk about the "profane and seditious character of which [*sic*] the negligence and apathy of the higher classes has reduced the manufacturing population" of Montgomeryshire betrays the panic inspired by Welsh working-class Radicalism—still active even after the Chartist *débâcle* ; and the emphasis laid on industrial evils no doubt owes something to the fact that the more familiar and more docile rural labourers (among whom, according to one contemporary critic of the Report,[2] bastardy was three times as common) presented a less disturbing problem.   But there is no need to doubt such statements as that farm hands left their children longer at school than miners or factory workers, that in many industrial areas parents were honestly unable to afford a penny a week for their children's schooling, or that miners' children left school too early for the lessons they learned there to leave any impression at all.   The prevalence of illiteracy among this class is alleged by other contemporary documents, such as the Children's Employment Report, which also dwells on the unwillingness of Dissenting miners to send their children to Church schools.[3]   But one must remember that the investigators were mostly Englishmen, or Anglophiles, whose standard of literacy was ability to speak and write English.   Some knowledge of Welsh, at least, was being diffused by the Sunday Schools.   One need not, then, take too literally the assertion that at Brymbo only one child out of ten could read, and only one out of twenty write ; but that the standard of education was low—not only among industrial workers, but among farm hands and even farmers themselves—is beyond cavil.[4]

[1] "The Treason of the Blue Books."
[2] *See* correspondence on the Report in *Wrexham Registrar*, Nov. and Dec., 1848.
[3] 1842, XVII, pp. 371, 384, 385.
[4] *Educ. Rept.*, III, App., pp. 53, 67–8, 82, 153–4, etc.

Not much was done by employers of labour towards remedying these evils. Many of them, it is clear from their evidence before Royal Commissions, were frankly suspicious of education, at any rate if it went an inch beyond learning to read the Bible. Some saw no objection to children's attendance at night schools (after 12 hours down the pit) provided the teachers' fees were deducted from wages ; but very few expressed a definite preference for dealing with educated men, and the Commissioners of 1842 pointedly observed that only one mineowner in the Halkin district subscribed to the local school. On the other hand, the owner of one of the Buckley brickworks paid out of his own pocket the expenses of an evening school attended by some of his lads ; and it was Mr. Turner, the quarry proprietor, who had made the first move towards providing elementary education at Ffestiniog in the early years of the century.[1]

Under the Act of 1833, millowners were compelled to make some provision for the education (during two hours in the day) of their juvenile employees. Most of them were content with producing vouchers of their attendance at the nearest British, National, or Dame School, but a few made their own arrangements. The Sunday School at Smalley's mill was in existence before Factory Acts were thought of. Later on, a schoolmaster was employed (at £20 a year) to teach the children at the Mold mill, in a "filthy room" on the premises ; but when the Education Commissioners visited it in 1846 they found, actually under instruction, only three of the children who nominally attended, and they were ragged, dirty and ignorant. Even the proprietors of a tiny woollen mill at Garth, near Machynlleth, hired a woman to teach in the mill rather than waste the children's time by sending them to the National School in the town, a mile away. The Montgomeryshire magistrates, in order to "make the punishment fit the crime," usually paid over fines received for breaches of the educational provisions of the Act, either to the factory teacher, or to the local Sunday Schools.[2]

[1] 1842, XVII, pp. 379, 383, 394, 405, 423–5 ; *N. W. Gaz.*, June 4, 1812.

[2] *Educ. Rept.*, III, App., p. 103 ; *Parl. Pap.*, 1840, XXIII, p. 51 ; Factory Inspectors' Reports.

For adult workers, there was a Mechanics' Institute at Newtown in the 'forties, but the fees were too high to enable many real "mechanics" to join ; nor can we imagine the impoverished Amlwch miners flocking to pay two shillings for the monthly lectures "on literary and scientific subjects" which the Marquis of Anglesey organized for their benefit about the same time. The Society for the Promotion of Useful Knowledge, with its Penny Magazine, and the various local and diocesan Book Societies and Tract Societies, which did what they could to disseminate improving literature, were extensively patronized by the gentry and clergy, but one rarely meets the name of an industrial employer on the local committees.[1]

The workman's physical welfare received rather more attention than his intellectual needs. Long before Parliament had begun to trouble itself about such matters, the proprietors of the Anglesey copper mines (on their own showing at least) were spending large sums on medical aid. If this was given free to the miners, they were more fortunate than those of Denbighshire and Flintshire, who in the 'forties had to pay twopence a week out of their wages for the services of the pit doctor. The same practice was adopted at Ffestiniog, where a doctor was appointed in 1848 to serve four quarries. Both here and (in its later days) at the Parys mine, he was elected by the workmen.[2] Douglas and Smalley, the cotton manufacturers, adopted the alternative plan of subscribing heavily towards a public dispensary, which was set up at Holywell in 1825.[3] Similar institutions had been in existence for some years at Denbigh and Bangor, and Welshpool soon followed suit ; but here the chief contributors were the landed gentry. Fitzmaurice of Llewenni had set the example as early as 1777.[4]

---

[1] *Educ. Rept.*, III, App., pp. 45, 55 *n*, 160 ; Lewis : *Top. Dict.* (1843) under *Amlwch; N. W. Gaz.*, Aug. 15, 1822 ; *Imperial and County Register*, 1810, p. 73 ; list of local committees in *Penny Mag.*, 1832 ff.

[2] *Supra* p. 160 ; *Hanes Plwyf Ffestiniog*, pp. 116–8 ; *Mynydd Parys*, pp. 96–7.

[3] *N. W. Gaz.*, Jan. 13, 1825.

[4] *Chester Chron.*, Oct. 13, Dec. 11, 1807 ; *N. W. Gaz.*, 1808–10, *passim* : *Shrewsbury Chron.*, Feb. 2, 1827 ; *supra*, p. 33. Wrexham infirmary was built in 1838 (Palmer : *Wrexham*, p. 76).

More important in this respect, as also in the struggle against pauperism, was the work of the Friendly Societies, in which employers sometimes interested themselves. In the older industrial centres and market towns, these had made their appearance before the middle of the eighteenth century. Wrexham had its first in 1744, Holywell in 1751, and before the century closed there were six and four in the respective parishes.[1] Whitford followed in 1766, and Welshpool in 1773. By 1775, Machynlleth had three Friendly Societies ; and Lord Penrhyn started one (the first of five in the Bangor district) among his quarrymen—all of whom were "induced" to join—some time before his death in 1808. The usual contribution to these early clubs was 6d. a month *plus* 2d. for ale ; this did not mean, even for the poorest labourer, more than a day's wage every month. With the aid of subscriptions from wealthy patrons some of the societies were able to build up good reserve funds and to keep their members off the rates. Their tone was eminently respectable. They eschewed politics, imposed fines for "speaking ill of the Government," and sometimes excluded Dissenters altogether. In 1824, when Catholic Emancipation and other subversive measures were threatening, Llanfyllin Friendly Society showed its political soundness (in face of the rampant Dissent of the town) by investing in a new banner with the device Y *Llywodraeth mewn Gwlad ac Eglwys* ("The Government in State and Church").[2] Many supported local charities, and most of them subscribed loyally to the funds for national defence and for soldiers' clothing in the early years of the Napoleonic War.[3] But their respectability did not always prevent them from coming to grief, whether through dishonest officials or as a result of

---

[1] Pennant : *Whiteford and Holywell*, pp. 243–4 ; Palmer : *Wrexham*, pp. 207–8 ; Eden : *State of the Poor*, III, pp. 891 ff.

[2] Pennant : *op. cit*, p. 101 ; *Mont. Coll.*, XIV, pp. 194–5 ; *Bye-gones*, 1909–10, p. 293 ; Davies : *General View*, pp. 422–4 ; *N. W. Gaz.*, May 5, 1808 ; *N. W. Chron.*, Dec. 13, 1827 ; *Shrewsbury Chron.*, Jan. 2, 1824. It was in 1824 that the *North Wales Gazette* adopted as its motto "Our King, Constitution and Laws."

[3] E.g. Montgomery, Wrexham, Welshpool (where it was noted that the club "consisted entirely of labourers"), Bangor Iscoed (*Salop. Journ.*, Feb. 12, 1794 ; *Bye-gones*, 1882–83, p. 142 ; *Mont. Coll.*, XI, p. 275 ; *Chester Chron.*, July 13, 1798).

internal dissensions ;[1] and by Gwallter Mechain's time the movement was already declining.

The nineteenth century brought with it a great revival and extension—largely as a result of the encouragement given by Rose's Act of 1793,[2] which conferred many legal privileges on such Friendly Societies as were prepared to submit their rules to the inspection of a magistrate. The mining areas led the way. By 1825 there were two Friendly Societies (both of recent origin) among the copper miners of Amlwch, and three among the colliers of the Hawarden district—including two old foundations with five or six hundred members apiece. Then came the weaving districts : 400 members walked in the St. David's Day procession at Dolgelley in 1830, and the Handloom Weavers' Report tells of five Societies at Newtown and four at Llanidloes—all supported almost exclusively by weavers, of whom there were 250 in one of the Newtown societies alone.[3] Quarrymen, despite the excellent lead given by Lord Penrhyn's men, were slower to join—the need for benefit societies among them is emphasized in a Caernarvonshire guide book of 1821—but several societies were founded in the Llanberis area in the 'thirties. The movement extended in some degree to the agricultural districts : the first Society at Llansilin was founded in 1810, at Llansantffraid in 1831, at Llan y mynech in 1833, at Ysbyty Ifan in 1838.[4] But the members in places like this were mostly drawn from the class of small tradesmen and mechanics, slaters, wheelwrights, smiths, tailors, and so on ; among the farm labourers themselves Friendly Societies have never flourished.[5]

Fees had naturally gone up with rising prices. Monthly payments were now generally about 10*d.*, and entrance fees might be as high as £1. Out of these, most societies provided their members with medical attention and free burial, and some of them added annuities for old age. But the Friendly Societies also conferred other, less tangible,

[1] E.g. Llanferres (Eden, III, pp. 887 ff.).
[2] 33 Geo. III, cap. 54.
[3] *N. W. Gaz.*, Aug. 18, 1825 ; *Memoir of Hawarden*, p. 160 ; *Shrewsbury Chron.*, March 12, 1830 ; *H.L.W.*, pp. 557-8, 565.
[4] *Bye-gones*, 1909-10, pp. 247-8 ; 1911-12, p. 159 ; *Mont. Coll.*, XII, pp. 368 ff. ; *supra*, p. 207 *n*.
[5] *P.L.R.*, 1834, XXIX, p. 188 *a*.

benefits. Their ritual and finery gave a touch of colour to what was rapidly becoming, in town and country alike, a very drab and colourless existence : in some places the annual procession of Friendly Societies took the place of the old *Gwylmabsant* (or Wakes) as the great local festival. And although the honorary members who were still enrolled from among the neighbouring gentry[1] may have helped in the management of the finances, the business experience acquired by the ordinary members (many of them illiterates)[2] was an invaluable training for democratic government. An interesting feature oi the age was the extension of the movement to women. Lady Penrhyn started a Female Friendly Society at Bangor, and other places followed her lead.[3] The bank failures of the first half of the nineteenth century eliminated many of the small local societies, and left the field clear for lodges of those big quasi-federal societies (like the Oddfellows) which sprang into existence in the 'thirties.[4]

More recent in origin than the Friendly Societies, which really carried on the traditions of the ancient gilds, were the Savings Banks. In 1816, when George Rose—the patron saint of Friendly Societies—drew the attention of Parliament to the claims of these other *protégés* of his, they were already fairly common in England, but apparently unknown in North Wales. Their claims were now widely canvassed in the local press, and an English pamphlet on the subject was translated into Welsh by Gwallter Mechain.[5]

[1] *See*, e.g., list of those in Conway Friendly Societies, *Camb. Quart. Mag.*, V, p. 296.

[2] E.g. out of the 13 members of the Llansilin Club who signed a contract with a doctor in 1811, only 5 could write their names.

[3] *N. W. Gaz.*, March 12, 1812 (Bangor) ; *Shrewsbury Chron.*, July 7, 1818 (Newtown), June 18, 1830 (Llangollen).

[4] E.g. most of the Wrexham Friendly Societies were involved in the failure of R. M. Lloyd in 1849 (*supra*, p. 323), leaving only lodges of the Oddfellows, Ancient Britons, and Foresters. The rules of the following Friendly Societies are preserved in U.C.N.W. Library, Bangor : Menai Bridge (1825), Caernarvon Union Society (1829), Nant Padarn (1832), Tegeingl (1833), Machynlleth (1834), Dinorwig (1835), Llanllyfni (1838), Ysbyty Ifan (1838), and others of more recent origin.

[5] *Annerch Caredig at y Diwyd a'r Llafurus; ar Fanteision, neu Fuddioldeb, Banciau Cynhilo . . . gan y Parch. Walter Davies.* Llanfyllin, 1817. The intention of forming a bank at Llanfyllin is announced on the fly-leaf.

Within twelve months of the passing of the Act of 1817,[1] at least six Savings Banks had been founded in North Wales —those of Holywell and Wrexham (always in the van), Caernarvon, Bangor, Ruthin, Mold, Pwllheli, and St. Asaph.[2] There soon followed a bank for Anglesey (with branches at Beaumaris, Amlwch, Llangefni and Holyhead) and a branch of the Chester bank at Hawarden.[3] By the early 'thirties Newtown, Denbigh, Welshpool and Machynlleth had all taken advantage of the Act.[4]

During the early years of the new institution, there was a rapid increase in deposits. The funds of the Anglesey bank grew threefold between 1822 and 1827 (largely through the opening of new branches). Those of the Bangor bank rose from under £500 in 1818 to nearly £11,000 in 1827 (though the number of depositors did not increase in anything like the same ratio, the average deposit being twice as great in 1827 as in 1823).[5] But this rate of progress was not maintained. At Caernarvon deposits were already falling off (owing to bad trade) in 1829 ; and in 1844 the Savings Bank deposits for North Wales, per head of population, were 50·7 per cent below the average for the whole country.[6] The bankruptcies of 1848-9 were a further set-back.[7]

It is not easy to determine how far the· deposits in Savings Banks may be taken as a criterion of increasing prosperity—or of increasing respectability—among the "labouring poor." It is true that deposits were received down to 1s., sometimes even 6d. ; that interest was paid on sums as low as 15s. ; and that no one (except Friendly

[1] 57 Geo. III, cap. 130.
[2] *Shrewsbury Chron.*, Feb. 6, March 13, April 17, 1818 ; *N. W. Gaz.*, Feb. 19, 1818 ; Hughes, Rev. W. : *Life . . . of the Very Rev. J. H. Cotton* (Bangor, 1874), pp. 26–7.
[3] *N. W. Gaz.*, May 22, 1821 ; *N. W. Chron.*, Dec. 31, 1829 ; *Memoir of Hawarden*, p. 160.
[4] *Shrewsbury Chron.*, Dec. 30, 1825 ; *N. W. Gaz.*, Jan. 18, 1827 ; *Bye-gones*, 1895–96, pp. 292–3 ; *H.L.W.*, pp. 565–6.
[5] Balance sheets of Anglesey, Caernarvon, and Bangor banks in *N. W. Gaz.*, 1821–29.
[6] *Educ. Rept.*, III, p. 65 *n.*
[7] R. M. Lloyd, the Wrexham banker who failed in 1849, served as treasurer to the Wrexham bank ; about the same time the trustees of the Bangor bank had to make good the defalcations of the manager. (Hughes : *Life of Cotton*, p. 27 ; *Bye-gones*, 1877, p. 178).

Societies) was allowed to deposit more than £50 (later £30) in any one year after the first, or more than £150 to £200 altogether.[1] It is also true that the actual deposits remained well below these maxima. At Caernarvon the average amount put in annually by any one contributor was about £6 to £8 ; and in most banks of which we have any particulars, half the contributors had less than £20 in all, very few had. more than £100, and the average total deposit was a little under the English mean of £34. There must, therefore, have been a good number whose savings were very considerably less than £20, and it is among these that we must look for the genuine working-class depositors ; for how many working people, in the few years covered by these statistics, could have saved even £20 out of an annual wage which, at worst, would barely reach that figure, and at best would not be more than half as much again ? It is significant that the proportion of the lowest class of depositors tended to diminish, that of depositors of £20 to £30 to increase—which suggests a growing popularity among the middle and lower middle classes.[2] According to Reports of Royal Commissions, farm labourers were as shy of Savings Banks as they were of Friendly Societies ; and not a penny was put in the Machynlleth bank by an operative weaver during the first four years of its existence. On the other hand, the Holywell bank was said to be "much resorted to by miners."[3] The principal working class contribution, it is probable, came through the Friendly Societies, of which five kept their balances in the Bangor Savings Bank in 1827.

Building Societies, with their monthly subscriptions of 10s. or so, were also beyond the reach of all save the "aristocracy of labour" but these, too, became fairly common during the second decade of the nineteenth century : at least three were founded at Caernarvon, and two in the Bangor district, during the years 1825–27. The

[1] *See* rules of Caernarvon and Welshpool banks (*N. W. Chron.*, Oct. 16, 1828 ; *Bye-gones*, 1895–96, pp. 292–3), and of those of Mold (1842) and Pwllheli (1824) in U.C.N.W. Library, Bangor ; *cf.* terms of Acts of 1817 and 1824 (Clapham, p. 299).

[2] Balance sheets of Anglesey, Caernarvon, and Bangor banks (*N. W. Chron*) ; Clapham, pp. 298–300, 592.

[3] *P.L.R.* (1834, XXIX), p. 188a; *H.L.W.*, pp. 565–6 ; *C.E.R* (1842, XVII), p. 376.

Ffestiniog quarrymen, as we have seen, formed one in
1836.[1] A more novel and less fortunate experiment was
made at Newtown in 1832. It was the period when the
Owenite movement for co-operative production was at
its height—some four or five hundred co-operative societies
are said to have been in existence in that year—and the
enthusiasm spread to Owen's old home. Fifty-two flannel
workers paid weekly subscriptions by means of which
they bought groceries wholesale, and rented $3\frac{1}{2}$ acres of
land, selling the former (at current prices) to each other and
the general public, and letting the latter out in allotments
to members. Their ultimate aim was to accumulate
enough capital to enable them to become their own
employers. For a time the stores flourished, and the
weekly cash takings amounted to about £30. But the
Newtown society shared the fate of so many others : the
storekeeper ran off to America with the funds.[2]

Just about the same time there reached Wales another
movement designed to improve both the moral and the
material condition of the workers. In 1832 the temperance
agitation was sweeping Lancashire (where the word
"teetotaller" was coined in the following year). By 1836
it claimed 100,000 adherents in North Wales. The movement flourished among the textile operatives of Montgomeryshire and the miners of Wrexham and Ruabon,
and the resulting diminution of drunkenness in the two
areas is noted with approval in the reports of 1840
and 1842—at the time when the more comfortable folk
who went to Drury Lane Pantomine were listening ruefully
to songs about the good old days, now passing,

When underneath the table you were bound your guest to land,
And no one rose to go—till he was sure he could not stand.[3]

Factory teachers, works doctors and public dispensaries, Friendly Societies, Building Societies and Savings
Banks, Co-operation and Teetotalism—all of these do at

[1] U.C.N.W. Library, Bangor : Rules of Carnarvon (1825), Carnarvon Union (1827), Eryri (1827), Bangor Benefit (1826), and
Pentir (1827) Building Societies ; cf. supra, p. 220.
[2] Aves, E. : Co-operative Industry (1907), p. 8.   H.L.W., pp.
557–8.
[3] Bye-gones, 1889, pp. 200, 220 ; 1907–08, p. 316 ; H.L.W., p.561 ;
C.E.R. (1842, XVII) p. 376 ; History, 1927, pp. 218–19.

least indicate, on the part of the more enlightened among both employers and employed, a desire to mitigate the harsher aspects of industrialism. But such palliatives left untouched the two great organic maladies of the time— intermittent employment among industrial workers, and chronic inability of the worst-paid rural workers to balance their budgets. Even the alleviation of these distresses— still more their prevention or cure—called for organized public assistance, a matter which must be dealt with in a separate section.

C. PAUPERISM AND EMIGRATION.[1]

A millstone dug up in Hawarden parish some years ago was found to bear the following inscription :—

> This Mill was built in A.D. 1767 by Sr John Glynne, Bar., Lord of the Manor . . . Wheat was in this Year at 9s. and Barley at 5s. 6d. a Bushel. Luxury was at a great height and Charity extensive. But the poor were starving, Riotous and Hanged.[2]

Fifteen years after this time of dearth at Hawarden, a county meeting was summoned in Denbighshire to consider the high price of corn and the distress of the poor. It decided (correctly) that wheat was actually cheaper than it had been ten years back, but appointed a sub-committee to investigate the state of the poor—and so to bed.[3]

Such were the problems of poverty that confronted the ruling classes in North Wales before the Napoleonic War. Distress there was plenty, especially after a bad harvest, but private charity could generally keep it within manageable bounds. The standard of living was low everywhere, but there was ground for hoping that the "numerous mines of coal, slates, copper, &c.," which were becoming "a great source of employment to the poor,"[4] would remedy all this, and banish poverty from the land.

These hopes were doomed to disappointment. The inadequacy of old-fashioned methods of haphazard relief was already becoming apparent during the twenty years

---

[1] Parts of this section have appeared in *Arch. Camb.*, 1926, pp. 111 ff, where full references are given.
[2] *Bye-gones*, 1905–06, p. 36.
[3] *Chester Chron.*, Dec. 13, 1782.
[4] Hucks : *Pedestrian Tour*, p. 149.

or so preceding the War. By 1775 all six counties were burdened with poor rates. In Anglesey and Caernarvonshire they were still negligible, but Merioneth was raising £1,000 a year, Flintshire nearly £5,000, Montgomeryshire nearly £6,000, and Denbighshire over £6,000—sums from four to six times as great as were levied in the middle of the century. In the course of the next decade, the rates in each of these four counties were doubled, and even in Anglesey and Caernarvonshire they reached £1,000 and more. These increases may be accounted for partly by the growth of population (through natural causes and by immigration to the neighbourhood of newly-opened mines and other works),[1] partly by a change in the spirit of Poor Law administration. Increasing contact with England was teaching Welsh magistrates English methods and standards ; and in England itself, humanitarian notions were extending public relief far beyond the range originally contemplated in the Elizabethan Act. This tendency was accentuated after 1783 by the operation of Gilbert's Act,[2] which encouraged the granting of relief to persons in receipt of regular wages.

With the Napoleonic War began that series of far-reaching changes in social life which was destined to make the Elizabethan Poor Law, instead of a *deus ex machinâ* invoked in time of grave emergency, a permanent and vital factor in the life of the country. First came the hardships of the War itself—the stoppage of exports and the rise in the price of foodstuffs. Already in 1794, before we had been a year at war, the exports of lead and the manufacture of cotton were suffering, and Welsh woollens were ceasing to go abroad. The French capture of Leghorn in 1796 still further hampered woollen manufacturers by cutting them off from one of their supplies of raw material ; and at the same time machinery was disorganizing the flannel industry.[3] Enclosures and the coal tax intensified the general distress, which came to a head

---

[1] *See* the estimates made by Davies in *General View*, pp. 437–57.

[2] 22 Geo. III, cap. 83. But Poor Law statistics for North Wales in 1783–85 do not suggest that any immediate effect was produced on the rates, unless perhaps in Anglesey.

[3] Kay : *Agriculture of N. Wales :*. Flintshire, p. 24, Carnarvonshire, p. 22 ; *supra*, pp. 172, 238, 244, 266, 286.

with the droughty summer and the late snows of 1798–99, making things even harder for the countryman than for the industrial worker.[1] It was under pressure of these hardships that Welshmen began to turn their thoughts towards America as a land of promise. Many of their ancestors (especially from central Wales) had fled there from the religious persecutions of the seventeenth century, when America was still an English colony. Now it had been a free land for a dozen years or more, and agents of the new Government were going about offering tempting baits to the Welsh emigrant. Welsh patriots like William Jones of Llangadfan and Morgan John Rhys (pioneer of Sunday Schools), dreamed of a Welsh colony there, and in 1795–6 the Cambrian Company was founded at Philadelphia to promote the scheme. Nothing came of it as yet : Jones died brokenhearted at the failure of his hopes ; Rhys went out alone in 1794. But a trickle of emigrants began : 12 from Llanbrynmair (Montgomeryshire), and a few from other parts, in 1795, 14 from Caernarvonshire in 1797.[2]

"How unnatural it is," exclaims Gwallter Mechain, "to permit our peasants to emigrate into the wilds of Kentucky, in quest of that labour which is so much wanted on our own extensive wilds at home."[3] Local newspapers took the same line. The *Chester Chronicle*[4] assured the "great numbers" who were reported to be on the point of emigrating from North Wales to America in 1802 "for want of employ" that there was plenty of work for them in South Wales. The *North Wales Gazette* in 1811[5] tried to frighten off intending emigrants by publishing accounts of life in America which call to mind Dickens' savage picture of Eden City, a generation later. But if the destitute looked for work in industrial centres nearer home, what happened? There were many immigrants from

[1] *See* account of conditions during these years in the neighbourhood of Madocks' embankment in *Gestiana*, p. 169 ; at Dinas Mawddwy in *Rept. on Land*, p. 626 n; at Ffestiniog in *Hanes Plwyf Ffestiniog*, pp. 109–11 ; and at Llanberis in Parry's *Llanberis*, p. 210.
[2] *Rept. on Land*, pp. 51, 54 ; *Camb. Reg.*, I, p. 460, II, p. 247–51 ; *Arch. Camb.*, 1906, p. 162.
[3] Davies : *General View*, pp. 99, 443, 269.
[4] Aug. 20, 1802.
[5] July 25.

North Wales in the Lancashire cotton mills ; after the first decade of war, finding prospects of work no better there than at home, they began to drift back, carrying with them the seeds of city-bred disease, and adding to the calls on the charity of their own country.[1]

These calls were daily growing more urgent. To make the food supply go round (in default of Government rationing) the principal inhabitants of Montgomeryshire decided at a county meeting in 1795 to reduce their consumption of wheat by diluting their bread with rye or barley. A Denbighshire gentleman, attempting similar economies at his home, found that a wag had chalked on his gates :

> A Good House and no Cheer,
> A Large Park and no Deer,
> Large Cellars and no Beer—
> Sir Foster Cunliffe lives here.

Sir Foster's neighbour, the great Sir Watkin, began in 1801 to supply upwards of eighty families of colliers in his employ with mixed grain at reduced prices—a charity which cost him, so people said, £14 a week.[2] Collections for the poor in churches, and distributions of coal and other comforts, had become common in Wales from the second year of our entry into the War, and (later on) the subscriptions raised throughout the country to celebrate King George's jubilee were devoted to the same purpose.[3]

But the chief burden fell on the rates. While Gwallter Mechain was engaged on his report to the Board of Agriculture, conditions changed so rapidly that 5s. in the £, which was an average rate in 1798, had become a minimum by 1800. At Mold the rates had grown from £400 in 1771 to £1,400 in 1796–7 ; and many Flintshire parishes, before the end of the century, were paying "a shilling towards the relief of the poor for every penny they paid

---

[1] *See, e.g., Chester Chron.*, Jan. 30, 1807 (Llansantffraid woman, lately returned from cotton factory in Manchester, escaped from Ruthin House of Correction) ; *N. W. Gaz.*, Jan. 16, 1812 (return of families from Liverpool and Manchester owing to lack of employment) ; Mantoux : *Industrial Revolution*, p. 420 n.

[2] *Mont. Coll.*, XI, p. 395, XIX, pp. 101–2 ; *Bye-gones*, 1893–94, p. 453 ; *Salop. Journ.*, March 11, 1801.

[3] *Hanes Plwyf Ffestiniog*, pp. 109, 111 ; *Salop. Journ,.* 1795, *passim; Mont. Coll.*, XIV, p. 206.

forty years back." In the flannel districts of Montgomery-shire, the displacement of hand labour by the carding machine and the jenny was making matters desperate. The first poor rate in Llanidloes parish had been levied in 1744, at 1s. in the £; during the next generation, the assessment rose steadily to 3s. 3d., then in 1797 it jumped to 11s.; by 1801 it was 28s. An outbreak of pestilence, filling the parish with unprovided orphans, helped to make the burden heavier here, but at Newtown, Welshpool and Llanbrynmair also the first effect of the new machines was a heavy increase in pauperism.[1] For Montgomeryshire as a whole the rates are said to have reached the sum of £37,000 by 1803. If the figure is correct, it means that they were between six and seven times as high as in 1775, amounting to about 15s. 7d. per head of population. During the same period, those of Denbighshire and Flint-shire had increased between threefold and fourfold, bringing the expenditure per head to about 8s. 1d. and 6s. 8d. for the respective counties. In Caernarvonshire they had reached £9,000 (4s. 4d. per head), and even in Anglesey £6,000 (3s. 7d. per head). The contemporary increase for England and Wales as a whole was well under 200 per cent.[2]

Worse was to follow. Robert Owen has left a vivid picture of the intense bewilderment produced on the minds of the ruling classes by the first great crisis of "over-pro-duction," which engulfed the country soon after the conclusion of peace.[3] The crisis was intensified by the terribly wet harvest of 1816. John Matthews, the surveyor, who had a small holding near Mold, records in his diary how some of the corn that year was not got in till late in November.[4] In agriculture, in mining and smelting, in the textile industries, unemployment was rife ; the Caer-narvonshire quarries fared a little better, but Ffestiniog suffered as badly as anywhere. The return of discharged soldiers, and of further bands of unfortunates who had

[1] Davies : General View, pp. 415–37 ; Evans : Beauties, p. 836 ; Mont. Coll., V, pp. 19–20, XXIII, pp. 270–86, XIV, pp. 202–3.
[2] Fullarton's Parl. Gaz. ; Cunningham, Rev. W. : Growth of English Industry and Commerce, III, p. 935.
[3] Life (by Himself), pp. 168 ff.
[4] Amlwch MSS. 8, under Nov. 21 ; cf. supra, pp. 67–8.

failed to get a living in England, intensified the general misery.[1]

In 1817, when distress reached a climax (it was the year of the Blanketeers), relief works—usually maintained by parochial subscriptions, but sometimes at the sole expense of an employer or landlord—were organized at Amlwch, Caernarvon, Bangor, Ruabon, and Welshpool. A Select Committee on the Holyhead Roads reported in favour of pushing ahead with the work, with the double purpose of getting it done more cheaply and at the same time relieving the rates ; for in many districts through which the road passed, men were offering to work for their bare victuals, and the poor rates simply could not be collected from farmers who were little better than paupers themselves. "A few years ago," wrote an Anglesey farmer in 1818, "no one approached our doors for alms but the aged, the infirm, or a neighbour in case of sickness" ; but "the distress of last year broke through every barrier," till "Beaumaris gaol and castle together" would not have held the swarm of tramps and beggars had the Vagrancy Laws been strictly applied. Bangor, too, had to set up a nightly patrol to arrest wandering beggars.[2]

By now prospects were beginning to improve, after "the blessing of a bountiful harvest," and Savings Banks were springing up all over the land ; but habits of pauperization were not so easily shaken off. The rates continued to soar, till by 1819 they had reached £16,000 in Anglesey, £17,000 in Merioneth, over £20,000 in Caernarvonshire and Flintshire, and £40,000 in Denbighshire. Montgomeryshire still remained, in proportion to its population, the most heavily-burdened county, but there the worst was over. The rates went down for a few years after 1803, and even after a subsequent rise they still fell short of £40,000—only a 5 per cent increase among a population which must have grown by nearly 25 per cent. In all the other counties the expenditure on the poor had increased much more rapidly than the people who had to bear it. In no county of North Wales did population go up more than 35 per cent between 1801 and 1821, whereas the increase

---

[1] *See*, e.g., *Mynydd Parys*, p. 95.
[2] *N. W. Gaz.*, Feb. 5 and 19, 1818.

in poor rates from 1803 to 1819 ranged from over 60 per cent in Denbighshire to about 170 in Anglesey.

After this there was a temporary easing of the burden ; but complaints of mendicancy continued,[1] and in the 'twenties—despite such signs of returning prosperity as the boom in Friendly Societies and Building Societies— the tide of emigration began to flow once more, especially from Montgomeryshire and Denbighshire. In April, 1820, the *Oswestry Herald* commented on the number of families from Montgomeryshire passing through the town on their way to Liverpool, bound for America—" that Land of Promise, whence so many thousands of deluded Englishmen have returned to their native country, in a state of wretchedness and beggary." A hundred emigrants from the neighbourhood of Llangollen (where the proprietors of the cotton mill had just gone bankrupt) were said to be preparing to set sail there in 1821, and a party from near Welshpool left in 1822. South Africa was attracting others. Forty-two Welsh families were accepted as prospective colonists for the new Albany Settlement in 1819–20 ; probably they included the party of "artificers and agriculturists" which left Newtown for the Cape in 1820.[2]

Then in 1826 came the second great crisis. The poor rates began to mount again, and by the winter of 1829–30 (the worst since 1813) public and private charities for the relief of distress were almost as general as they had been at the height of the post-war crisis.[3] Once again agriculture, mining and manufacture were all involved ; and by this time enclosures were producing their full effects— depriving the labourer of cheap fuel, driving his cow or his pig from the common, and even evicting him from his cottage. Apart from formal enclosure, too, the pulling down of cottages on some big estates was helping to swell

[1] *Id.*, May 17, 1821.

[2] *Osw. Herald*, April 25, 1820 ; *N. W. Gaz.*, April 26, 1821, May 2, 1822 ; *Rept. on Land*, 1896, p. 55 ; *Cambro-Briton*, I (1820), p. 279.

[3] *See*, e.g., *N. W. Chron.*, Jan. 28, March 4, 1830 (Flintshire), Feb. 18, 1830 (Bangor) ; *Shrewsbury Chron.*, March 12, 1830 (Denbighshire), Jan. 7, 1831 (Llanidloes and Machynlleth).

the volume of surplus labour in the towns.[1] The plague of tramps began to reappear : Bangor, Holyhead and Llanfyllin were specially troubled, and emergency measures to keep them in check had to be adopted at St. Asaph, Llangollen and Welshpool. In the Wrexham district alone 700 paupers were being relieved, and 200 more were provided for by relief works, receiving 3s. to 5s. a week (according to the size of their families) from funds raised by private subscription.[2] There were further emigrations to America from the rural districts of Caernarvonshire, and from Newtown and Dolgelley ;[3] others went to look for work in the mines of Northumberland and Durham, where they were used as blacklegs during the great strike of 1832 ; there was also by now a "numerous Welsh population" in the coal and iron works round Birmingham.[4]

Pauperism had now become one of the great national problems pressing for solution at the hands of the new Whig Ministry which came into power in 1830. Wellington's administration, before it went out, had already done something for the poor by repealing the duties on beer and leather ; Althorp, the new Chancellor of the Exchequer, sent the coal and slate duties after them in 1831 ; and in February, 1832—while the Reform Bill still hung in the balance—he moved for and obtained a Royal Commission to go into the whole question of poor relief. The voluminous reports issued by this Commission in 1834 included one on North Wales by Mr. Stephen Walcott,[5] and from this, with the aid of scattered local records, we can form some impression of the way in which the old Act was administered in this district.

In four of the six counties, the expenditure on the poor

---

[1] *Supra*, pp. 87–8 ; *M.C.R.* (1835, XXVI), p. 596.

[2] *N. W. Chron.*, Jan. 7 and 14, March 11, 1830 ; *Bye-gones*, 1900, pp. 479–80 ; *P.L.R.* (1834, XXIX), pp. 189a–190a.

[3] Census, 1831 (Bryncroes 29, Aber 69, Maenan 96) ; *H.L.W.*, IV, pp. 556 ff. ; *P.L.R.* (1834, XXIX), p. 188a.

[4] Welbourne, E. : *Miners' Unions of Northumberland and Durham* (1923), pp. 38, 46, 74 ; *Camb. Quart. Mag.*, IV (1832), p. 280, V (1833), p. 298.

[5] Appendix A, Part II (*P.L.R.*, 1834, XXIX), pp. 167a–192a.

per head of population was already decreasing,[1] and North Wales was reported to be a district of "comparatively good administration" ; but there was still sufficient cause for disquietude. In the first place, there was the preponderance of outdoor relief. In very few places were the paupers kept under proper supervision, in fewer still was there any attempt to make relief "deterrent." Several workhouses, as we have seen,[2] had been built under the Act of 1723, but most of them had by now either disappeared or ceased to provide any pretence at work. The parish authorities of Wrexham, for example, had put up a workhouse within fourteen years of the passing of the Act. In 1757 they enlarged it, fitted it out with looms and spinning wheels, and allowed the workhouse master to make what he could out of the inmates' earnings (an arrangement generally followed where work was provided).[3] But the new legislation of 1783 soon made its malign influence felt. By Eden's time the institution contained mainly "aged, infants, and infirm" : none were able to work, and the "present of thirty guineas" which the authorities had just voted to the master in view of the dearness of living was doubtless intended also as compensation for the loss of this income.[4] It is to be noticed also that from 1830 the numerous country townships of this extensive parish agreed to maintain their own poor locally, instead of sending them all to town—a retrograde step from the point of view of the 1834 Report.[5]

[1] The figures are as follows :—

			1821		1831	
			s.	*d.*	*s.*	*d.*
Anglesey	..	..	6	3¾	6	9¾
Caernarvon	..	..	5	11¾	6	7
Denbigh ..	..	..	9	6	8	5¼
Flint ..	..	..	8	2¾	6	10
Merioneth	..	..	8	11½	8	4
Montgomery	..	..	12	3¾	10	5½

[2] *Supra*, p. 29.
[3] E.g. Kerry (*Mont. Coll.*, XXVI, p. 94), Overton (Report, pp. 171a–172a).
[4] Eden : *State of the Poor*, III, pp. 891 ff.
[5] *N. W. Chron.*, April 22, 1830, June 17, 1831.

In contrast with this, the inmates of the workhouses at Llansilin and Chirk (the one built in 1756, the other by 1775) had been transferred to a central institution at Oswestry before 1834 ; and those of Meifod, Welshpool and Llanrhaiadr ym Mochnant (dating from the same period) to Forden House of Industry, of which more later. Similarly Holywell parish, which had a poorhouse of its own in the 'eighties, now sent its paupers to Chester.[1] The workhouses which had existed at Newtown and Kerry in the middle of the eighteenth century had disappeared, or else degenerated into "poorhouses" where no work was provided—a category in which the Report also includes the institution established within the walls of Caernarvon Castle about 1794,[2] the Wrexham workhouse, the Holyhead House of Correction (set up in 1741 to deal with Irish vagrants), and a few others.

These poorhouses were intended and used merely as a more economical means of paying the house-rents of paupers. Usually they consisted of a row of cottages where the paupers lived rent-free and looked after themselves without supervision. The Report describes them sweepingly as "places of punishment to the aged and schools of idleness and profligacy to the young." At Wrexham, however, the parish authorities took a little more upon themselves. Here clothing, beds, bedding and the necessary minimum of furniture were provided by the parish, while food, drink, fuel and medical assistance were supplied on contract by a workhouse master. In 1834 the weekly allowance he received from the parish authorities for the inmates' food was 3s. a head. Out of this (unless the rations had been changed, along with the allowances, since Eden's time) he supplied them with a breakfast of broth or milk, a dinner of meat and vegetables three days a week, and of bread and butter (or cheese), the other four, and a supper of bread and milk—fare very

[1] Cf. Chester Chron., March 30, 1781, with Pennant : Whiteford and Holywell, p. 265.
[2] Kay : Agriculture of N. Wales: Carnarvonshire, pp. 10 and 22. Possibly the reference in the Report is to the older institution for Llanbeblig parish (which included Caernarvon) mentioned by Davies (General View, p. 422) ; or again, this may have been transferred to the Castle.

similar to what was provided for the apprentices at Holywell cotton mill, and certainly no worse than what many independent labourers, and even small farmers, had to put up with ; so that in this respect, at least, the institution was far from "deterrent." Similar provisions for "farming out" the paupers are to be met with in several other parishes.[1]

The only establishments which Mr. Walcott would allow to be real "workhouses" were the one at Hawarden (a year older than Wrexham workhouse, and therefore probably the first in North Wales), another—small and little frequented—at Overton in Flintshire, and the Forden House of Industry. This last institution calls for more than a passing notice. It was built in 1792, under a special Act of Parliament which incorporated eighty parishes in eastern Montgomeryshire and the adjacent parts of Shropshire, authorizing them all to send their poor to the new central establishment. The house was to be governed by 21 directors, appointed by the constituent parishes, which were to contribute fixed quotas of the expenditure. The resident officials included steward, matron, dairymaid and kitchenmaid, barber, butcher, chaplain, and (later) schoolmaster and supervisors of industry. The building was completed in 1794 at a cost of £12,000, and a further Act of 1796 gave additional powers to the directors. Similar Acts had been passed for Chester and Oswestry, and great hopes were roused by these new "incorporated unions."

From the beginning, a serious attempt was made to justify the pretensions of the establishment as a real House of Industry. Slubbing and carding, spinning and weaving, tailoring and shoemaking, were among the occupations provided for the inmates, and a small farm was leased at £100 per annum. Stocks of wool, flax and hemp were purchased, and the first piece of flannel made at Forden was sold at Welshpool Fair in March, 1796. Then the directors grew more ambitious. They appointed, at fixed salaries, a resident manufacturer to superintend the woollen industry, a woman to teach jenny-spinning, and a tailor and a shoemaker to give instructions in their

[1] E.g. Welshpool, Kerry, Newtown. Meifod. At Overton workhouse the paupers had meat five times a week.

respective trades. They began to set up the latest carding and spinning machinery. But circumstances were against them. Under war conditions it was difficult to find a sale for the goods, and the tailoring, shoemaking, spinning and weaving businesses were all abandoned in 1805, the machinery being sold. When the War ended, a fresh start was made, this time with straw-plaiting, and in 1819 the woollen industry was revived—machinery and all—only to be given up in despair five or six years later.

The children at first worked 12 hours in summer and from dawn till dark in winter, but from this total must be deducted an hour for meals, an hour for schooling, Saturday evenings, Sundays, and ten whole holidays in the year. The hours of work were later reduced to nine, meal-times increased to an hour and a half, and Thursday and Saturday afternoons given to instruction in "reading, writing and accounts." Women were expected to spin four pounds of yarn in a week. Slackness was punished by public whippings, minor offences by the docking of meals ; the stocks and the scold-bridle were also used to repress disorderly conduct. Occasionally the inmates were allowed out to assist in the harvest at neighbouring farms. The dietary was much the same as at Wrexham ; the weekly cost was about 2s. 4d. a head for those over ten, and less than 2s. for the small children. The house was built to accommodate 500, but it was rarely full. In its early years the numbers generally hovered between 300 and 400, reaching the high-water mark of 459 during the year 1800. Then there was a falling-off until after 1815 : one week in 1817 the unprecedented figure of 556 was reached. By 1828, the general distress had so far abated that the average number provided for was only about 78, and after that it generally ranged round 100.

The Forden House of Industry never fulfilled the extravagant hopes it had aroused. The reluctance of paupers to enter it, and their frequent efforts to escape when once they had been immured, may perhaps be taken as a tribute to its deterrent qualities, and it certainly did succeed in reducing the rates of the incorporated parishes below, though not sensationally below, the country average. But the directors remained in constant financial difficulties. The War, besides intensifying industrial distress, threw on them the burden of maintaining the wives and widows of soldiers, and the difficult years of the peace strained their resources to breaking-point. The whole position was investigated by a committee in 1818, and six years later a fresh Act was obtained, under which each of the constituent parishes was once more made responsible for the maintenance—inside or outside the House of Industry— of its own poor. As a manufacturing centre it had completely failed ; all that remained in 1834 was the farm, on which hay and potatoes were raised, and a few cows kept, at a cost fifteen times greater than the total receipts. Small wonder that the directors were finding it cheaper to give out-relief, and tending more and more to bring only the aged and impotent into an institution which still bore the ironical name of a House of Industry. Yet they protested vigorously against the proposals of 1834, as they had done against Pitt's Bill in 1797.

Of out-relief, by far the biggest item everywhere was the payment of cottagers' rents. Before the last quarter of the eighteenth century this had played a comparatively small part, except in Montgomeryshire, where it already swallowed up about a tenth of the money raised. By 1834, however, the growth of urban population and the increase of enclosures had begun to tell. At Llanidloes 40 per cent, and at Bodedern 30 per cent of the rates were spent in the payment of rent. Small speculators made their fortune by building rows of squalid cottages and letting them at impossible rents, which were recovered from the parish. Sometimes all that was needed was for the overseer, as owner of house property, to transfer the sum from one pocket to another. The mere exemption of cottages from payment of rates—another frequent form of relief—had similar results.

There was one vice, common in England, from which North Wales was comparatively free ; the "Speenhamland" system of supplementing wages out of the rates never became general here. Money doles were never given to single men in employment, except as temporary assistance in time of sickness ; but to the unemployed, and to those with large families dependent on them (which usually meant with more than three young children), regular weekly payments out of the rates had now become a fixed institution, and the balance of local opinion was against risking serious riots by putting a stop to it. Occasionally (though more rarely now) relief was given in the form of food, clothing, fuel and medicine. At Newtown the poor were farmed out *en bloc* to a doctor for medical attention at £20 a year.

One or two parishes still tried to "set the poor on work," without bringing them into workhouses, by giving them materials or implements to work with at home. It was useless to give spinning wheels and stocks of hemp or flax— a common form of relief up to the 'eighties—now that the factories were pressing so hard on the domestic spinner and carder ; but seed potatoes, agricultural implements and the like were sometimes distributed, up to within a few years of the passing of the new Act. Very rarely, however, was work made the condition of relief. Montgomery, St. Asaph and Holywell are commended in the Report as parishes where applicants for relief are set on breaking stones, at wages below the usual rates. The work was done at a loss, but the device was believed to be effective in checking pauperism and keeping the rates down. The pernicious "roundsman" system—common in some parts of England—by which all the farmers of a parish were compelled to employ their quota of paupers in turn, was comparatively rare in North Wales. It was adopted by voluntary agreement among the farmers at Bodedern, and at Ffestiniog this was the normal method of providing for the children of paupers—until the rector objected, and insisted that they should be properly apprenticed.

For, as we saw in the preceding section,[1] the apprenticeship clauses of the Elizabethan Act had not yet fallen wholly into oblivion. We find the directors of the Forden House of Industry, in the very first year of its existence, apprenticing a pauper child to a chimney sweep ; and it remained their regular practice, at least as late as 1817, to place out children between ten and sixteen years of age as apprentices to farming, flannel-weaving, or some such trade, usually with a premium of £5. Legal proceedings were taken against employers who refused to accept the charge. This practice of compelling parishioners of a

[1] *Supra*, p. 359.

certain standing to accept pauper children as apprentices is to be found in many parishes of North Wales right up to the expiry of the old Poor Law. Sometimes, too, without any formal apprenticeship, children for whom their parents could not provide, and even aged paupers, were boarded out with ratepayers (chosen by lot), the parish providing the clothing and a sum of money for their keep. There is little evidence that the expense of giving a decent start in life to the children of the poor formed any considerable part of the increasing burden of the poor rates. At Wrexham it was stated to be still customary, in 1812, to apprentice pauper children by ballot as soon as they reached the age of ten ; but the expenditure on this object had shrunk from a little over £41 in 1790 to £13 in the following year, and nothing at all in 1792.

But if little was spent on rescuing from pauperism the rising generation, the Poor Law authorities of the early nineteenth century made ample amends for this economy by the handsome sums they paid out in litigation. Fifty or sixty years before the Commission of 1834, lawyers' fees already formed a considerable item in the total expenditure, ranging from over a third in Caernarvonshire to less than 1 per cent in Merioneth—the only county where it did not exceed the amount spent in actually "setting the poor on work." Gwallter Mechain records how, a few years before he wrote his *General View*, "two parishes in Anglesey . . . expended 206*l*. in determining the settlement of a pauper, the winner paying 56*l*., the loser 150*l*."[1] During the last decade of the old Poor Law, forensic wars between neighbouring parishes became a regular item of news in the local press. The thorniest question was that of the acquisition of a settlement—with the right to claim relief—by means of apprenticeship or service within the parish. To protect themselves, many local authorities refused to countenance hirings for longer than six months at a time, and Montgomeryshire millowners, as we have seen, refused to enter into any indentures with the children "apprenticed" to them. Much money, too, was spent in the attempt (usually futile) to enforce payment from the reputed fathers of illegitimate children

[1] P. 425.

who had been left to the care of the parish. But in this matter North Wales was reported to have a cleaner bill than most English districts.

Although vagrancy is described in the Report as "a growing evil," the expenditure on checking it was not very heavy. In Wrexham parish it cost £13 in a year; Llangollen, Llanfyllin, Welshpool, Northop and Flint spent between 10s. and £2; Flintshire had reduced this item from £98 in 1821 to £5 14s. in 1831. The vagrants were usually English or Irish—rarely Welsh, and hardly ever Scots! Most parishes refused to relieve them unless they were ill : the money was spent in "passing them on.".

If the Poor Law system had not broken down as completely here as in some parts of England, it was certainly failing to fulfil the purposes for which the wisdom of past ages had designed it. Already the independence of the labourer was being undermined, and farming capital was dwindling under pressure of the overburdened rates. Labourers were marrying young—usually under twenty-four, often under twenty-one—and bringing up families which they relied on the parish to keep. Paupers were being preferred to independent labourers as house-tenants, and overseers were finding means of lining their own pockets. No remedy hitherto tried had proved a complete success. Incorporated unions and large-scale Houses of Industry had failed to avoid the pitfalls of out-relief, and had effected no startling reduction in the rates. The substitution of Select Vestries for the unwieldly body of parishioners which feebly and spasmodically supervised the administration of the Poor Law had been tried here and there (under the Sturges Bourne Act of 1817), but it proved too great a strain alike on the patience and on the rectitude of the selected shopkeepers and farmers. Over 100 parishes, too, had availed themselves of the provision of the same Act enabling them to appoint salaried overseers, thereby introducing some order into parochial finance ; but too much power still lay in the hands of the incompetent amateur overseers, appointed for a year at a time, and anxious only to be quit of the job and to do the best they could for themselves and their friends while it lasted. One or two parishes had adopted the expedient of appointing a permanent overseer ;[1] it had proved a measure both of efficiency and of economy, but the example was not widely followed. And there always remained to aggrieved paupers the recourse of appeal to a distant and ignorant magistrate.

Yet the Report ends on a note of optimism. Habits of industry had not yet been lost, and population was certainly not "redundant." The Assistant Commissioner, whistling to keep his courage up after such a dismal array of evidence, boldly declares that "none need want work who will take it." He belittles the emigration statistics by representing the emigrants as generally small farmers or mechanics who have gone out to escape high rates or to join their friends ; on the whole, the subject "has aroused little interest in Wales." All that was needed to ward off bankruptcy and to root out pauperism was a stern application of the principle of "deterrence," such as was prescribed by the Act of 1834.

It was unfortunate for the fulfilment of these expectations that the Boards of Guardians elected under the new Act were immediately confronted, not with normal poverty, but with the devastating effects of another economic crisis. In the early years of Victoria's reign all the old phenomena of destitution were reappearing. The Children's Employment Commission reported that discharged miners from the Ruabon district had gone off to look for work in Lancashire (where they met with a hostile reception), in South Wales and in Scotland.[2] Relief works again became the order of the day, and miners from Rhos were petitioning, not only the House of Commons, but the young Queen herself, to alleviate their distress by getting rid of the hated Corn Laws. The suggestion came from middle-class advisers, who sought by this means to divert them from more violent courses.[3] "Extensive failures among the manufacturers" had also thrown many out of

---

[1] Wrexham had set the example in 1785, with instantaneous effects on the rates ; later the overseer was reinforced by a committee of twelve, meeting once a fortnight to "attend to the complaints of the poor." (Davies, p. 421 and *n*).

[2] *C.E.R.* (1842, XVII), p. 415.

[3] *Chester Chron.*, June 24, 1842 ; Home Office papers, cited in Mr. Emlyn Rogers' thesis, as above.

work at Llanidloes, and distress was equally severe among the Ffestiniog quarrymen.[1] The Census of 1841 records further emigrations from every county except Merioneth, including twenty from the Ruabon district and nearly a hundred from Montgomeryshire, during the early months of 1841.[2]

In these circumstances the application of the new law to North Wales—especially to Montgomeryshire, with its high percentage of paupers—was slow and painful. In 1837 the relieving officer of Llanfair Caereinion (near Welshpool) was besieged by a howling mob in the hamlet of Heniarth ; he had to call in a troop of the Montgomeryshire Yeomanry, and a collision occurred in which "some few gain'd each a blister'd nose."[3] The Guardians of the new Dolgelley Union did not dare to shut up their unemployed in a workhouse (the course recommended to them by the Commissioners in 1838) ; they stuck to the outdoor labour test—sanctioned by the Commissioners four years later—till past the middle of the century.[4] Those of Llanidloes Union, more venturesome, had to summon the militia to protect their new workhouse at Caersws in the winter of 1838 ; and for some years none but children were immured in it.[5] At Machynlleth, wages were still occasionally made up out of rates at the time of the Handloom Weavers' Commission.[6] The only Unions, apart from Llanidloes, which had built workhouses during the first ten years of the new Act were those of Pwllheli, Ruthin, Holywell, St. Asaph, Corwen and Llanfyllin ; in a few other places (like Wrexham) existing institutions were adapted to the new requirements. By 1847 prohibitory orders against outdoor relief were in force in all these Unions, and also at Bala and Ffestiniog ; but those of Anglesey, Bangor (with Beaumaris), Conway, Llanrwst and Machynlleth, as well as Dolgelley, were content with

[1] Lewis : *Top. Dict.* (1843), II, p. 67 ; *Hanes Plwyf Ffestiniog,* p. 112.

[2] Emigrants during last 5 months : Anglesey 6, Caernarvonshire 38, Denbighshire 39, Flintshire 20, Montgomeryshire 92.

[3] *Bye-gones,* 1907–08, p. 213 ; Jones, E. J. : *Econ. Hist. of Wales,* p. 140 ; Anon. : *History of the Chartists . . . of Montgomeryshire.*

[4] *Bye-gones,* 1880–81, p. 99 ; 1903–04, p. 126 ; Webb : *English Poor Law Policy,* p. 26.

[5] *Mont. Coll.,* XIII, p. 19 ; Lewis : *Top. Dict.,* 1843.

[6] *H.L.W.,* pp. 565–6.

the outdoor labour test. Of these Bangor and Llanrwst built workhouses before 1851.[1] The new Poor Law had certainly saved the rates. The money spent on relieving the poor was less in 1846 than in 1831—despite the continuing increase in population—in every county but Caernarvonshire and Anglesey ; the expenditure per head of population had gone down by half in Anglesey, nearly three-quarters in Montgomeryshire, and by various intermediate fractions in the other counties. Montgomeryshire still had the highest percentage of paupers (13·7) but the expenditure per head of population was highest, curiously enough, in Flintshire, where the percentage of paupers was lowest (only 7·8). In the six counties together, 9·6 of the population were in receipt of poor relief—1·4 per cent more than in South Wales, and 1·2 per cent more than in England and Wales as a whole.[2] Montgomeryshire's bad eminence is partly accounted for by the fact that the flannel industry was now going through the second stage in the transition to machinery : the downfall of the handloom weaver had begun, and steam was crushing out the rural factories, almost depopulating villages like Llanbrynmair. More than 2,000 people from this one district already had relatives in America, and another 70 went to join them in 1852.[3] In every other county of Wales, except Anglesey, the 1851 Census names several parishes in which population has been reduced by

---

[1] Census, 1841 and 1851 ; Webb : *op. cit.*, pp. 321 ff.
[2] Phillips : *Wales*, pp. 580–1. The details are as follows :—

	Expenditure on poor, per head of population.		Percentage of paupers.
	s.	d.	
Anglesey	3	7	12·8
Caernarvon	2	5	10·1
Denbigh	3	5	8·8
Flint	6	6	7·8
Merioneth	3	0	11·0
Montgomery	5	4	13·7

[3] *Letters on Improvements* (1851), pp. 41, 46 ; letter in *Y Cronicl*, July, 1852 ; *Land Rept.*, 1896, p. 52 and App., p. 189.

emigration.[1] The failure of the potato crop in 1846 was felt in Wales as well as in Ireland,[2] and Free Trade had as yet brought no relief. The elimination of pauperism seemed as far off as ever : it was no truer in 1850 than it had been in 1834 that "none need want work who will take it."

D. REVOLT.

Through all these afflictions, in season and out of season, Methodist and other preachers were counselling patience, and their preaching was not without effect. The *North Wales Gazette* in 1812[3] congratulates its readers on their immunity from Luddite disorders. Sixteen years later, the *Cambrian Quarterly Magazine* rejoices that "the morality of the Principality" has saved it from those "degrading scenes of brutalised anarchy which have lately disgraced some parts of the Empire" ; and again in 1831 : "the system of riot and incendiarism that has spread itself in England" (says the same journal) "is regarded by the Welsh peasantry with alarm and religious abhorrence."[4] The Poor Law Report tells the same tale ; and an underground agent at a pit near Ruabon described to the Children's Employment Commissioners how during times of unemployment the chapels were thronged, while ministers (many of whom had probably been in the pits themselves) used all their eloquence to dissuade their hearers from violent courses.[5] The freedom of North Wales (as contrasted even with counties like Glamorgan and Monmouthshire) from crimes of violence, is borne out by criminal statistics for the period.[6]

But it was hardly likely that the Welsh labourer would always suffer in silence, especially when to the ordinary causes of friction between employer and employed were

---

[1] The figures are : 6 parishes in Caernarvonshire (500 emigrants from 5 of them in the last 5 years), 2 in Denbighshire, 3 in Flintshire, 3 in Merioneth, 7 (nearly all flannel parishes) in Montgomeryshire.
[2] *Hanes Plwyf Ffestiniog*, p. 112.
[3] July 23.
[4] I, p. 504, III, p. 130.
[5] *P.L.R.* (1834, XXIX), p. 188 *n;* *C.E.R.* (1842, XVII), p. 415.
[6] *See*, e.g., *N. W. Gaz.*, Sept. 18, 1808, Aug. 10, 1809, April 18, 1811, July 23, 1812 ; *N. W. Chron.*, March 13, 1828 ; *Imperial and County Register*, 1810, p. 10 ; Phillips : *Wales*, p. 72.

added those of racial and sectarian bitterness. For English employers liked to have English foremen, who were often no more kindly disposed towards strange tongues and "fancy religions" than the proverbial Sergeant-Major. It was sometimes alleged that when there was need to discharge hands, an Anglican foreman would see that Dissenters went first.[1] On the other hand, employers complained that attendance at Methodist meetings made men irregular in their work, and Kay in his report of 1794 tells of Methodist farm labourers in Caernarvonshire who were willing to take lower wages in return for leave to go to all their chapel meetings.[2] These difficulties constantly crop up in the history of the Parys mines, as well as in imaginative works like *Rhys Lewis*, which faithfully portrays a state of affairs persisting till well past the middle of the last century.

The colliers, from the very nature of their work, were always a difficult class to handle. Working in gangs out of the light of day, straggling home at night with blackened faces to their grimy and sequestered villages, they lived a life apart—intensely intimate, intensely self-contained alike in its shopkeeping, its amusements and its religion ; and they early developed that exclusive *camaraderie* and that defiant self-consciousness which have left their marks to this day on the coal-mining communities of North Wales. To peaceful town-dwellers the cry of "the colliers are coming to town" was as terrifying in the eighteenth century (or even as late as 1830) as the cry of "the beggars are coming to town" had been in the sixteenth.[3] And the colliers, for their part, were ever resentful of the intrusion of strangers. In 1776 there were riots against the employment of Englishmen in the collieries round Wrexham ;[4] fifty years later the Welsh Iron Company raised a hornets' nest by bringing in Northumbrian colliers to work the new pits at Coed Talon, and the Mold Yeomanry and the Royal Maylor

[1] E.g. *N. W. Gaz.*, May 16, 1816.
[2] *Agriculture of N. Wales :* Carnarvonshire, pp. 20–21.
[3] *See* ballad printed in *Bye-gones*, Aug. 16, 1876, and *cf. supra*, p. 197.
[4] *Chester Chron.*, Oct. 4, 1776.

Cavalry had to be called out to restore order.[1] At one of the Holywell pits in 1819 (a bad year) the introduction of men from as near by as Brymbo was enough to cause a riot.[2] Here, as in England, the miners were in the forefront of most of the frequent food riots.[3] In 1778 Flintshire miners prevented the export of a boat-load of corn from Flint.[4] Eleven years later the general dearth which helped to produce the French Revolution issued in bread riots along the whole length of the North Wales coalfield, as well as in other parts of the country. A little over three weeks after the fall of the Bastille, the High Sheriff and Justices of Denbighshire received an address from the principal inhabitants of Wrexham, thanking them for the military aid (a detachment of dragoons from Manchester) by which the "late seditious spirit" in the neighbourhood had been checked ; but in another three months the colliers were "threatening to rise again" in revolt against the price of bread, and it was feared that the general populace might join them.[5] When war broke out, and corn prices went soaring higher still, disaffection became more general. In 1795 wheat went up to 75s. 2d—higher than it had been since the Civil Wars ; this time it was lead miners from Talar Goch (near Dyserth) who forcibly stopped corn from going out of the county ; and the general spirit of revolt found issue in riots at Bala and other places, and even hindered recruiting for the army and navy.[6] There were several disturbances, from the same cause, at Machynlleth ; in 1800, when corn reached the unprecedented figure of 113s. 10d., a detachment of infantry was moved there from Shrewsbury to prevent any further outbreaks.[7] The conclusion of peace brought no relief,

[1] N. W. Gaz., April 6, 1826 ; Bye-gones, 1903–04, pp. 460–4 ; 1905–06, pp. 41–2.
[2] Cambro-Briton, 1820, p. 198 ; Bye-gones, 1905–06, loc. cit.
[3] Supra, p. 28 ; Ashton and Sykes, chap. VIII.
[4] Chester Chron., March 20, 1778.
[5] Handbill in Wrexham Public Library ; letter from P. W. Davies to Lord Kenyon, Nov. 21, 1789 (Hist. MSS. Com., 14th Rept., App., Pt. IV, No. 1348 a) ; Ashton and Sykes, pp. 127–31.
[6] Chester Chron., March 11, 1796 ; Bye-gones, 1906, p. 245 ; Salop. Journ., April 22 and 29, 1795 ; Bulletin of Board of Celtic Studies, IV, Pt. I, p. 61 (Nov., 1927).
[7] Salop. Journ., March 12, 1800 ; Bye-gones, 1888, pp. 3, 112.

despite the agricultural depression ; further food riots took place at Ffestiniog in 1815, and at Amlwch in 1817.[1]

In the agricultural districts (especially in Caernarvonshire) enclosure was a fruitful source of disorders.[2] Alarms of incendiarism, too, were not infrequent ; but there is no evidence that either the periodic farm fires[3] or the conflagrations which broke out at Wilkinson's lead works at Buckley in 1802, and at the old cotton mill at Holywell twenty years later,[4] were part of any deliberate campaign of destruction.

Soon after the War, we pass into the more familiar atmosphere of disputes about wages. The following quaint notice, which was posted outside the Ffrwd pit, near Brymbo, on May 3, 1817,[5] introduces us at once to the new spirit which was abroad in industry :—

> I, Sam[1]. Davies and Co., do give you notis that we have put the Coal Pit to stand that you may not enter down it No more.
> Sam[1]. Davies.

At the end of June, 1819, the Montgomeryshire Yeomanry, originally raised for war service in 1803, were for the first time embodied to help the civil power. On the score of depression in the flannel trade, the Newtown manufacturers had threatened a "trifling" reduction in wages, whereupon weavers began to collect in menacing groups round their houses at night. Throughout the night of June 30, and again of July 10, the Yeomanry remained on duty. A few windows were broken, and three ringleaders were arrested on a charge of conspiracy ; but they were let off lightly on the ground that this was the "first offence of

[1] *Hanes Plwyf Ffestiniog*, pp. 111–12 ; *Mynydd Parys*, pp. 58–6 ; *Chester Chron.*, Feb. 21, 1817.

[2] *Supra*, pp. 76–9.

[3] E.g. Llandisilio, Montgom. (*Salop. Journ.*, Nov. 25, 1802), Henllan, Denb. (*N. W. Gaz.*, Jan. 26, 1809).

[4] *Chester Chron.*, Dec. 3, 1802 ; *N. W. Gaz.*, March 14, 1822.

[5] This transcript from a written notice in his possession was very kindly sent to me by Alderman Edward Hughes, J.P., Glyndwr, Wrexham. It is not clear whether it is a declaration of a lock-out by the owners or of a strike by a group of "bargain-takers."

the kind in the county" ; and in a few days all was quiet again. Presumably the masters got their way.[1]
It was not long before trouble arose between masters and men in other districts and in other industries. In 1822, the Halkin lead miners "rioted" against an "improved system," introduced by Lord Grosvenor's agent (Mr John Taylor) with the help of three experienced overseers who were strangers to the district.[2] Three years later came a strike among the Penrhyn quarrymen for an advance in wages. The wide divergencies in earning had long been a source of discontent in the quarry, and there had been some friction with the overseers. Soon after the death of James Greenfield (chief overseer under the owner's agent and brother-in-law, James Wyatt), who drowned himself in February, 1825, matters came to a head. About 150 men from the lower quarry struck work, demanding a basic minimum wage of 3s. a day, irrespective of output,[3] and "drove the rest off." They came in a body to demand an interview with the proprietor ; Wyatt met them on his behalf, and offered to put them entirely on day wages instead of piece rates. This offer was rejected, but the discussions were perfectly good-humoured until one quarryman made an incautious reference (interpreted into a threat) to the fate of the late overseer. Henceforth it was war to the knife. Mr. Pennant, the owner, announced in the local paper that all who were unwilling to work under the present system would be paid off at once, and that he would attend to any reasonable complaints of those who stayed at their posts. He is said to have distributed hand-bills to the same effect. This broke the strike. Work was resumed, and the leaders—deserted by their comrades—were dismissed.[4] Next year came the strikes of lead miners at Mold and of coal miners at Coed Talon.[5]

[1] *Shrewsbury Chron.*, July 16 and 30, 1819 ; *Mont. Coll.*, XVIII, pp. 18–19 ; *Bye-gones*, 1907–08, p. 209. This is probably the strike referred to in *H.L.W.*, pp. 556 f., although the dates do not tally.
[2] *N. W. Gaz.*, Dec. 5, 1822.
[3] The manifesto of the quarrymen to Mr. Dawkins Pennant, a somewhat garrulous document printed in Welsh and dated March 24, 1825, may be read in the Coetmor collection (No. 49), U.C.N.W. Library, Bangor.
[4] *Shrewsbury Chron.*, Feb. 4, April 1, 1825 ; *N. W. Gaz.*, March 24, 1825 ; Parry : *Chwareli a Chwarelwyr*, pp. 205, 220–1.
[5] *Supra*, pp. 176, 399.

As we approach the 'thirties, the signs of unrest grow more and more ominous. For one thing, arrests for arson become commoner. A woman was executed in 1827 for setting fire to a Montgomeryshire farmer's haystacks ;[1] there were further conflagrations (of suspicious origin) in Merioneth and Flintshire in 1828 and 1830 ; and in 1831 a farmer near Llanidloes, whose clover stacks had been fired, found letters threatening both him and his neighbours with arson.[2] Before this last outrage, the winter of 1830–31 had brought matters to a crisis in the industrial districts. All over the country, industrial strife was adding daily to the perplexities of the new Whig ministry, and the virus infected both the flannel districts of Montgomeryshire and the coalfield of Denbighshire and Flintshire.

At Llanidloes the textile workers struck for five weeks in 1830, with the object (in which they are said to have had the secret support of the Newtown employers) of bringing wages up to the Newtown standard. On this occasion the masters gave in ; but the trouble seems to have broken out afresh two years later, with sufficient violence to call for the enrolment of fifty special constables.[3] Meanwhile there had been serious disturbances at Newtown itself, and the Montgomeryshire Yeomanry (disembodied since 1828) had to be hastily re-formed and summoned to the scene of action, along with 300 special constables. At Christmas time, 1830, a magistrate living near Newtown was rash enough to arrest six men who had come begging in a body to his house. They were promptly liberated by an angry crowd of weavers, and it needed all the tact of Pugh of Brynllywarch—the popular Radical magistrate— to induce the crowd to disperse and the ringleaders to give themselves up. Four of them were indicted under the Riot Act ; they pleaded that they were in liquor, and got off lightly.[4]

To the same period belong the strike of the Holywell ribbon weavers (to which reference has already been

<hr />

[1] *Shrewsbury Chron.*, Dec. 1, 1826 ; *N. W. Gaz.*, April 12, 1827.

[2] *N. W. Chron.*, Jan. 31, 1828, March 11, 1830 ; *Shrewsbury Chron.*, Nov. 11, 1831.

[3] *H.L.W.*, pp. 563 f. ; *M.C.R.* (1837–38, XXXV), p. 272.

[4] *Shrewsbury Chron.*, Dec. 31, 1830, Jan. 14 and 21, 1831 ; *Y Gwyliedydd*, VIII, pp. 157–8 ; *M.C.R.*, *loc. cit.*, p. 368 ; *Montgomeryshire Worthies*, pp. 268–9.

made)[1] and the beginning of organized resistance among the coal miners. In October, 1830, the Friendly Associated Coalminers' Union had been founded in Lancashire, and the first Welsh lodge was formed next month at Bagillt. The aims of the Union, as published in its rules, were modest enough : to resist reductions in wages, to help the unemployed, and to encourage "honesty, sobriety, industry and peaceful behaviour." As in the old-fashioned Friendly Societies, politics were eschewed, and respect for the Government, the laws, and even the employers and their agents, was strictly enjoined.[2]

The new Union soon captured the Flintshire miners. Times were bad, and when the new members came to compare their wages with those earned by their comrades in Lancashire, it was not likely that they would content themselves with the official aims of the Union—especially after they had heard whispers of a projected general strike soon after Christmas. For some time menacing crowds of them had appeared periodically near the houses of the principal mineowners ; they had levied "voluntary contributions" for the relief of their distress, and held indignation meetings against the tommy shops. It only needed a spark to fire the train, and this was provided by a dispute in one of the collieries near Hawarden. On December 20th the men struck for a wage of 3s. for skilled men and 2s. 6d. for the lowest grade. The owners, taken by surprise, conceded the terms—provided (so, at least, one report has it) that the other employers in the district could be induced to do the same. The men returned to work on Christmas Eve, and set about the task of fulfilling this rash condition. One colliery after another was visited for the purpose of calling out the men, administering the Union oath, and exacting allegiance to what had now become the Union programme.

Meanwhile the magistrates and the mineowners were making their plans of defence, and the Home Office was besieged with warnings and entreaties. On December

---

[1] *Supra,* p. 292.

[2] The records of this Union have been investigated by Mr. Emlyn Rogers (from Home Office papers and elsewhere), and the account which follows is largely based on his thesis. For other authorities, *see* my paper in *Arch. Camb.*, Dec., 1929, where a detailed account of the strike is given.

27th—the day for which, according to reports which had reached the Home Office, the general strike was planned— the Denbighshire Yeomanry were mustered at Wrexham ; and on the following day they made for Rhos, to anticipate a contingent of strikers who had marched there to continue the swearing-in. The strikers, now reinforced by crowds of Rhos men, accordingly found themselves confronted by Yeomanry, special constables, and the Lord Lieutenant himself—Sir Watkin Williams Wynn. They stated their demands, and refused to disperse till after two of their comrades had been arrested and placed in a temporary lock-up. The rest then rushed off to free them, and re-assembled on a slag-heap. Sir Watkin had the Riot Act read, and, after a few cinders had been thrown at the troopers by miners' wives, and a random shot fired, a third arrest was made ; but before the rioters had had a chance to make yet another rescue, Sir Watkin himself released him, and the crowd went peacefully home.

There was no work in the pits next day. The miners all assembled, in driving snow, at the neighbouring village of Acrefair, to demonstrate against the hated tommy shop. Once more the Yeomanry came on the scene, and the Riot Act was read ; and this time the crowd dispersed on a promise by Sir Watkin that he would arrange a meeting between the masters and a deputation from the men on the following morning. On the 30th the meeting duly took place in the Wynnstay Arms Hotel at Ruabon, but Sir Watkin was not present. The body of miners waited outside, but when news came that the masters would make no concession they rushed the building, roughly handled several of the employers, and almost killed Mr. Wood, manager for the British Iron Company, which owned the tommy shop. (It is significant, by the way, that the men's fiercest anger should have been reserved for the agent of an impersonal employer). Sir Watkin arranged another meeting at his own house in the afternoon, got the men's demands in writing, and persuaded most of the employers to sign their names to them.

It only remained to get the same concessions from the owners of the neighbouring pits over the Shropshire border. For this purpose a body of Denbighshire miners set out for Oswestry on January 3rd. They were met at

Chirk bridge by a detachment of the Shropshire Yeomanry, with the usual *posse* of special constables and magistrates. A deputation was allowed to cross the bridge to interview the leading employers : but before they returned (having gained their point) the waiting crowd got restive. Again the Riot Act was read and three more arrests were made. Then at last things settled down : satisfied with their apparent victory, the men went back to work next day.

The employers, smarting under this humiliation, now bent their energies to the triple task of preventing a recurrence of the outbreaks, capturing and punishing the ringleaders, and breaking up the Union. The Yeomanry, who remained under arms till the middle of the month, were kept constantly on the run by false alarms and wild rumours, and special constables remained on duty even longer. But a mere civilian force, with ties in the neighbourhood, was hardly felt to be an adequate protection. Had not Captain Morris, who commanded the Yeomanry under Sir Watkin, made himself so popular with the colliers that they carried him shoulder-high when he made known the terms of settlement ? And was not that settlement—notoriously favourable to the men—largely the work of the Lord Lieutenant himself, whose slackness in searching out the ringleaders now brought on him a sharp rebuke from Lord Melbourne as Home Secretary ? Such suspicious conduct in high quarters was not likely to stimulate the loyal co-operation of the rank and file : an attempt to recruit a "citizen army" in Wrexham, to keep order during the strike, had fallen dismally flat. For these reasons, on the earnest representations of the mineowners, a detachment of infantry was marched from Chester to Wrexham early in February, and three Bow Street runners were sent to superintend the work of bringing the criminals to justice. Even so it proved no easy task. The arch-offender—Samson Jones of Brymbo, "the swearing collier," who had gone about with a Bible under his arm swearing-in new members to the Union—successfully slipped through their fingers ; and the only satisfaction which could be obtained from the March Assizes (where the prisoners were skilfully defended by John Jarvis, later Attorney General in Lord John Russell's administration) was the passing of three sentences of a year's imprisonment each on the men found guilty of assaulting Wood.

Whatever else happened, however, the masters—and
especially the outraged Mr. Wood and the influential
company he served—were determined to smash the Union
and to tear up the settlement it had extorted. They had
only signed the terms—so they claimed—under duress ;
to carry them out to the letter meant increasing the price
of iron to a figure which would preclude competition with
the Midlands and South Wales ; and so they sought
every opportunity for evading them. Even before the
end of January disputes about the exact interpretation of
the settlement had led to fresh turnouts at Ffrwd and Coed
Talon. In July, an attack on some Anglesey blacklegs
("knobsticks," in the local vocabulary) who had been
brought in to supplant Union men at the Bromfield pit,
near Mold, led to the indictment of three men for assault
and riot at the ensuing Assizes, where once more the skill
of Jarvis procured their acquittal, despite an adverse
summing-up from the Bench. The same month the Ffrwd
men were out again. The dispute dragged on till November,
when it spread to the whole Flintshire coalfield, and the
Flintshire Yeomanry had to be called out. At last the
disastrous effects on the lead industry forced the employers
to yield.

In each of these disputes the main efforts of the masters
were directed towards inducing the men to renounce their
Union, and whenever they had occasion to advertise for
hands they took care to insert such warnings as that "no
one need apply who is in any way concerned in the colliers'
Union Club."[1] From the fact that the rates of pay
offered in such advertisements were often identical with
those just refused to Union men, we may fairly conjecture
that the employers were influenced less by the straits of
the iron industry than by resentment at "outside inter-
ference" in domestic disputes—a resentment which found
strong expression in a manifesto sent to the local press by
two Flintshire mineowners in November.[2]

The Union showed surprising power of resistance. During
the early months of 1831 it was daily gaining fresh adherents
throughout the colliery villages of Flintshire, Denbighshire

---

[1] *Shrewsbury Chron.*, June 10, 1831.
[2] *Chester Courant*, Feb. 15, Nov. 29, 1831. I owe these two
references to the kindness of Mr. Emlyn Rogers.

and the adjoining part of Shropshire. By April, headquarters at Bolton had all its work cut out to divert the enthusiasm of the Flintshire lodges—already spoiling for another fight—into financial support for Lancashire. In June, the chief organizer of the Union, William Twiss, was sent down to recruit round Wrexham; and by the end of the month the lodges in Ruabon parish, with a membership of about 2,500, were strong enough to send help to their brethren in South Wales. After this our information trickles out. The parent Union probably exhausted itself with strikes in the course of the next few years. It may have left a few isolated lodges behind in Flintshire—at any rate the Municipal Corporations Commissioners reported in 1834 that "the system of combination and striking for wages" had "prevailed so extensively among the neighbouring collieries as to have called for a permanent station of the military at Mold"[1]—but in Denbighshire no trace of any local organization can be found after 1831. Wages, as we have seen, were as low as ever in the coalfield by the early 'forties, and the general depression of the industry precluded all hope of redress by strikes. Abuses like truck, which the strike had temporarily checked, reappeared in full force, and the only lasting fruits of the great fight were embittered memories and hard-won experience.

By the opening of the new Queen's reign, the mining areas had settled down into sullen quiescence, and it was felt safe to disband the Flintshire and Maylor Yeomanry, and to reduce the Denbighshire Yeomanry from five troops to three. But the same course could not be taken in Montgomeryshire; for there some military force was needed to keep in check the growing disaffection against the new Poor Law—the only remedy the Government had to offer in the severest crisis the flannel trade had yet encountered.[2] This agitation was soon to be merged in a wider movement with a definite programme—political

[1] *M.C.R.* (1835, XXVI), p. 610.
[2] *Supra*, pp. 269 ff., 395–6. It was not the introduction of machinery (as Mr. E. J. Jones states in his *Econ. Hist. of Wales*) that caused the distress which issued in Chartism: for the carding machine and the jenny had established themselves long before, and the power loom and mule (as he himself points out on p. 43) had not yet arrived.

in its immediate aims, but looking ahead to a vaguer economic Utopia. Ever since the disillusionment over Reform in 1832, a group of London working-class Radicals, including Lovett and Hetherington, had been engaged in that intensive propaganda which issued, early in 1837, in the birth of Chartism. Among the many men to be influenced by contact with Hetherington was Thomas Powell, a native of Newtown (of good county descent), who, after serving his apprenticeship with a Welshpool ironmonger, went to practise his trade in London. Returning to Welshpool, Powell soon retired from business and devoted himself to Chartist propaganda. It was from Birmingham (the rival Chartist centre) that the new doctrines were carried to Llanidloes—once again by a local man (Richard Jarvis), who had imbibed revolutionary ideas during a brief stay in England.

The seed fell on receptive soil, and Chartism was spreading rapidly in the flannel districts of Montgomeryshire when it had scarcely begun to sprout in South Wales. In the course of 1838, Political Unions on the Birmingham model were formed at Newtown,[1] Llanidloes, and Welshpool, and by September they had all adopted the Charter. At Welshpool—where industry was not strong enough to counteract the conservative influences emanating from Powis Castle—the movement soon languished, but at Newtown and Llanidloes weekly meetings were held, and the branches were strong enough, in October to organize a county demonstration addressed by delegates from Birmingham. It was a similar monster meeting at Caersws, on Christmas Day—to which

> The Chartist chiefs came in a wain
> That oft had carried pigs and geese,
> The people's charter to obtain
> If hearers would give pence apiece

—that led to military preparations against a supposed intention to attack the new "Bastille" there.

The precautions proved unnecessary, for Montgomeryshire Chartism was still on its good behaviour. Whatever may have been said in the more secret conclaves of the

---

[1] An earlier Political Union at Newtown had procured 5,000 signatures for reform in 1831 (*Shrewsbury Chron.*, Nov. 18, 1831).

initiated, official utterances, at least, were almost fulsome in their respect for law and order.   Early in 1839 the tone begins to change.   At the great Birmingham Convention in February, Charles Jones of Welshpool (about whom little else is known) sat alongside the more notorious Frost of Newport to represent Wales, and took with him £37 as Montgomeryshire's contribution to the National Rent.   At his request, Hetherington was sent down as special missionary to Montgomeryshire early in April. Hetherington found enthusiasm already running so high that (according to his own account) he was more occupied in curbing than in spurring forward.   His reported speeches are certainly less inflammatory in tone than those of the local leaders.   But Hetherington was a staunch Owenite, and the Owenite gospel—in the form in which it reached the hungry and ignorant flannel workers of Owen's old home—seemed to promise the immediate abolition of poverty by an equal sharing of the world's goods.   This crude popular communism, and the exaggerated hopes which it roused among the Chartist rank and file,

> When their learned Solons went
> To light the world in Parliament,

are satirized in George Thomas's mock heroic *History of the Chartists and the Bloodless Wars of Montgomeryshire*, published anonymously at Welshpool in 1840.   The author— a man of education, who sometimes displays quite a pretty wit—tells how the local Chartists

> . . . preached New Harmony[1] was heav'n . . .
> Said work was mixed with hellish leav'n,
> And looms and jennies Tantalus,

and how in their heated imagination

> The lands were shar'd from Rhiew to Rhyddol,
> Havod, Greenfields and Llanerchydol ;
> One Powis Castle longing eyed,
> Another fix'd on Severn Side.

Meanwhile

> Each harmless infant thought it queer
> That since papa became a peer :
> The broth was thin, the tea was weak,
> And brown and butterless the cake.

[1] The community in Indiana built by German Rappists in 1815, and purchased by Owen in 1823 as a site for putting into practice his *New View of Society*. On George Thomas *cf. supra*, p. 229*n*.

> The child wist not the reason why,
> The pig had vanished from the sty . . .
> Why since his father practis'd drilling,
> His mother went without a shilling.

These nocturnal drillings on the neighbouring hills, together with the manufacture of pikes, seem to have begun before Hetherington's visit ; after he had gone they became more general and systematic. Both at Newtown and at Llanidloes ex-militiamen were to be found among the Chartist leaders, and they took a pride in organizing manoeuvres and shooting-matches to prepare their followers—should occasion arise—against an attack by the forces of law and order. A few wilder spirits may even have dreamed of establishing the Owenite Commonwealth by a sudden *coup*. But, whether for defence or for insurrection, arms were first needed. Bands of Llanidloes Chartists began a round of visits to the surrounding farmers to "borrow" muskets for use in their shooting competitions. Few dared refuse, though only one instance is recorded—and that on dubious evidence—where actual force was used.

A report of these proceedings from one of the molested farmers alarmed the Lord Lieutenant (Lord Clive) into appealing to the Home Office for troops. Lord John Russell, the Home Secretary, took a course which combined the maximum of irritation with the minimum of security : he sent down three London policemen, and it was their arrival at Llanidloes on Monday, April 29th, that precipitated the outbreak. To strengthen their hands, the magistrates had sworn-in about 300 special constables from surrounding villages ; a few were also brought in from Welshpool, together with the municipal police officers from there and Newtown ; and warrants were issued for the arrest of the ringleaders. According to local tradition, the Chartists' bugler was warned of these proceedings by maids from the Trewython Arms Hotel, where the policemen were lodged, and early on Tuesday morning he summoned an open-air meeting to discuss the emergency. While the meeting was in progress, the bugler (still on his rounds) and two other leaders were arrested in front of the hotel, handcuffed and taken indoors. At once the waiting crowd rushed to the rescue.

The prisoners were freed, the policemen badly mauled, and the hotel reduced to a wreck. Yet all contemporary accounts agree that there was next to no drunkenness : the contents of the wine cellars were simply poured down the gutters. The magistrate who had ordered the arrests fled from the town (under Chartist colours, it is said) to invoke military aid from Brecon.

From then till the following Saturday the Chartists ruled the town. After hot blood had cooled down, there was little disorder. The Chartist leaders set up a watch, and administered rough justice to any of their own numbers who behaved badly. Thomas Powell came from Welshpool to use his influence on the side of restraint. Apart from the fact that shopkeepers had to accept for their goods such prices as the Chartists thought just, this little experiment in "dictatorship of the proletariat" does not seem to have worked badly. By Thursday the mills (which had not been touched in the outbreak) were able to re-open. But on Friday the county magistrates, meeting at Welshpool, plucked up courage to fix on a plan of compaign. In consequence, the Montgomery-shire Yeomanry marched next day to Llanidloes, under the command of the Right Hon. C. W. Wynn, brother of Sir Watkin of Wynnstay, and famous (in pre-Reform days) as the ineffective leader of the Grenville connection in the Commons. At the same time, the South Salopian Yeomanry were ordered to Newtown. Here, too, there had been some disorder, and tradition has it that when the cavalry arrived the resident magistrate (Mr. Evors) would have had them fire on the mob, but the officer refused.[1]

The Llanidloes Chartists were again forewarned, and about a hundred of them were already on the hills, in full flight for Merthyr—the haven of all discontented spirits—where they could at least find temporary shelter, if not rally forces for a counter-attack. On Sunday, May 5th, the cavalry were reinforced by a detachment of regular infantry—two companies of the 14th Regiment from Brecon.[2] They were all surprised to find the town so

---

[1] *Bye-gones*, 1895–96, pp. 91–2.
[2] Mr. J. E. Samuel's account in *Cymru Fu*, II (1889), pp. 34–5, makes the infantry arrive first, but I have followed the order given in Mr. C. W. Williams Wynn's History of the Montgomeryshire Volunteer Yeomanry in *Mont. Coll.*, XVIII, pp. 19–20.

peaceful ; but their job was to make the arrests which had proved beyond the power of the civil arm. From Monday a regular blockade was instituted, and the hills were combed for fugitives. Altogether 32 arrests were made. On Wednesday or Thursday, the Yeomanry marched off—their work accomplished—and the infantry were relieved by a battalion of the "Holy Twelfth" from Cork, detachments of which were also sent to Newtown and Welshpool.

The Chartist trials took place at Welshpool the following July. Hugh Williams, the solicitor in charge of the defence, was himself a friend of Hetherington and a writer of Chartist songs, and was later to earn notoriety in the Rebecca riots. His father we have already met as an owner of lead mines near Machynlleth ; his sister kept up the Radical traditions of the family by becoming, two years later, the wife of Richard Cobden.[1] An able counsel was called in (probably the same who had served the Denbighshire miners so well[2]) but the sentences were heavy. Three men were transported—one for 15 years, two for 7—and the other penalties ranged from two to twelve years' hard labour.[3]

It would be a great mistake to regard the Llanidloes outbreak as a deliberately planned "rebellion," like its successor at Newport six months later. Heady talk at the Birmingham convention, and the dangerous habit of

---

[1] *Mont. Worthies, loc. cit; supra.* p. 180.

[2] J. E. Samuel, in an otherwise trustworthy account, gives his name as Yardley ; but names easily get confused in oral tradition. Rowlands (*History of Newtown*) says it was Jarvis. Possibly the Newtown rioters had a different counsel. They do not appear to be included in the statistics of penalties given above.

[3] The foregoing account is based chiefly on : *Mont. Coll.*, XIII, pp. 19–20 (account of Montgomeryshire Yeomanry), XVIII, pp. 305–6 (diary of R. Griffiths–Parry, solicitor, Welshpool—an eye-witness) ; *Cymru Fu*, II, pp. 24–39, 125, 179–80 (notes by J. E. Samuel, based on depositions of surviving eye-witnesses) ; *Bye-gones*, 1907–08, pp. 213–14 ; 1890, p. 504 ; Rowlands : *History of Newtown*, pp. 111–14. I have also been able, through the kindness of Miss Myfanwy Williams, to check statements in the text by reference to her thesis on *Welsh Chartism* (based chiefly on local and Chartist periodicals) for which she obtained the degree of M.A. in the University of Wales in 1919. Mark Hovell's *Chartist Movement* (1918) is unreliable for Montgomeryshire, and Mr. E. J. Jones' account in *Econ. Hist. of Wales* is undocumented.

handling firearms, may have created an atmosphere of revolt ; but it is unlikely that any such collision would have taken place but for the folly of the Home Office. It was on the "cockney" policeman that all the fury of the mob was centred, and for years after the outbreak, the property of the magistrate who went to Brecon for soldiers was never safe from popular vengeance. From this point of view the explosion may be regarded as but one more of the long series of "anti-foreign" riots. But its real significance lies deeper. It was not by accident that the agitation seized on Montgomeryshire, the county where dreams of general prosperity—so freely indulged in when the transformation of an ancient handicraft was just beginning[1]—had given place, in little more than a generation, to the waking reality of pauperism on a scale unknown in any other part of North Wales ; nor was it by accident that the actual outbreak took place at Llanidloes, with its persistently low rates of wages. Just before the Chartist movement took root, we read of mass meetings of weavers at Newtown to discuss wages and to consider protective measures against Lancashire imitations.[2] The irruption of Chartism turned these constructive energies into paths which at best were airily Utopian, and at worst purely destructive. In 1846 the Education Commissioners found the working men of Newtown and Llanidloes still addicted to "secret clubs" in which they desecrated the Sabbath by poring over the works of Paine and Owen and other "pernicious tracts and periodicals."[3] It was only in that year that the armed forces were removed ; two years earlier they had been called out again, this time to deal with attacks on the turnpike gates at Llanidloes and Llangurig—a distant eddy of the Rebecca Riots in South Wales.[4]

Workers in other districts were no more forward than those of Montgomeryshire in creating permanent organizations to protect their standard of life. In the Denbighshire and Flintshire coalfield, Martin Jude's Union of Miners of Great Britain and Ireland, which in 1844 attained a local

[1] *Supra*, pp. 245–6.
[2] *H.L.W.*, p. 557.
[3] *Educ. Rept.*, III, p. 67, App., pp. 153, 160–1.
[4] *Rept. on Land*, 1896, App., p. 33.

membership of nearly a thousand, collapsed (after ill-timed strikes) as quickly as its predecessor of 1830 had done ; and until after 1860 the miners had to be content with ephemeral local clubs, which rarely survived a strike, and most of which—from the very secrecy they had to maintain—have left no trace of their existence save in local tradition and the Home Office papers.[1] Similarly with the Penrhyn quarrymen : the strike of 1825 left no lasting organization, nor did a second strike in 1846 ; the Union created after a third strike, in 1865, was given up under pressure from Lord Penrhyn, and it was not till 1874 that the North Wales Quarrymen's Union came into being.[2] Lead miners, we are specifically told in the Children's Employment Report, were not given to Unionism.[3]

It is possible that a closer investigation would reveal the existence, in a few of the old corporate towns, of exclusive aristocratic Unions of skilled men (such as the Society of Operative Cordwainers at Denbigh)[4] whose origins might go back as far as the time when the gilds ceased to give adequate protection to the manual labourer. But on the whole it remains true that there was no native Trade Union movement in North Wales. The first impulse came from English agitators like William Twiss, or gangs of imported English navvies like those who caused so much trouble to the contractors for the Conway tubular bridge in 1848 ;[5] and the movement never flourished until the Acts of 1871 and 1876 had removed the stigma of illegality which frightened off the loyal chapel-goer. For the chapels—and especially the powerful Calvinistic Methodist body—were consistently hostile. In October, 1831, the Calvinistic Methodist Assembly at Tredegar forbade its communicants to join Trade Unions, and the veto was repeated at Mold in the following year.[6]

Not all the religious bodies took so uncompromising a line. Church officials and ministers were sometimes in active

[1] Mr. Emlyn Rogers' thesis, cited above ; S. and B. Webb : *History of Trade Unionism* (1919), pp. 181–2.
[2] *Chwareli a Chwarelwyr*, chap. XXV.
[3] Evidence of Vicar of Halkin, *C.E.R.* (1842, XVII), p. 467.
[4] *Supra*, p. 303.
[5] *Bye-gones*, 1880–81, p. 65.
[6] Thomas : *Labour Unions*, p. 17 ; *Y Drysorfa*, 1832, p. 121.

sympathy ; and even a precisian who deprecated strikes in general might (like the Llanidloes weaver who gave evidence before the Handloom Weavers' Commission) make an exception in favour of "partial strikes against a particular master wishing to encroach upon labour."[1] It was, however, no comfortable "social gospel," but a stern individualist creed, that the chapels of that day placed before the Welsh working man. Their real social service was to show him the way to self-respect and confidence in a squalid and shifting world, and to offer him an escape from that world into realms of spiritual fellowship and ecstatic song—almost his only taste of culture, and his earliest training in self-government.

[1] *H.L.W.*, p. 563.

APPENDIX.

I. SOME STATISTICS RELATING TO THE WELSH WOOLLEN INDUSTRY.

A. COSTS AND PROFITS, 1799.

(1) WEB.[1]

(a) *Cost of manufacturing a Dolgelley web (two pieces of 90 yards × ¾ to ⅞ yard).*
Weaving : 15s. to 18s. (weaver gets 14d. a day on own victuals).
Scouring and milling : 3s. 6d. to 5s.
Carding and spinning : warp 18d. a stone (4 lb.).
           woof 8d. ,, ,, ,,
Total expense of working a pack of wool into web cloth : £3 16s.

(b) *Expenses of material of a piece (95 yards) of Denbighshire small cloth.*

	£	s.	d.
Warp : 36 lbs. of wool, at 10d.	1	10	0
Woof : 37 ,, ,, ,, ,, 9d.	1	7	9
19 ,, ,, combings at 8d.	0	12	8
Blubber oil	0	3	8
Weaving	0	5	6
Milling	0	1	6
Measuring, and house-room for sale	0	0	8
	£4	1	9

(2) FLANNEL.

Estimated annual sales :—

			£	s.	d.
(a)	260 pieces of 132 yards, at 2s. 9d. a yard		4,719	0	0
(b)	1,950 ,, ,, 110 ,, ,, 2s. ,, ,,		21,450	0	0
(c)	5,590 ,, ,, 110 ,, ,, 1s. 3d. ,, ,,		38,431	5	0
	7,800		£64,600	5	0

Expenses :—

			£	s.	d.
Wool	(a) 34 lbs. at 2s. a lb.		884	0	0
	(b) 36 ,, ,, 1s. 6d. ,,		5,265	0	0
	(c) 42 ,, ,, 1s. ,,		11,739	0	0
Oil,	3s. to each piece		1,170	0	0
Soap, 8d. ,, ,, ,,			260	0	0
Fullers earth, 3s. to every 23 pieces			50	17	4
			£19,368	17	4

[1] *Cf.* cost of manufacturing a piece of coarse medley cloth of Gloucestershire wool, 1683, and a piece of superfine broadcloth, 1781–1828 (Lipson : *Woollen and Worsted Industries*, pp. 256–60).

				£	s.	d.
Sale price ..	..	..	..	64,600	5	0
Cost ,, ..	..	..	..	19,368	17	4
Profits	..	..	45,231	7	8
Drapers' commission[1]	..	..	5,872	15	0
Wages of labour	..	£39,358	12	8

(3) KNITTED STOCKINGS.[2]

Estimated annual sales:—				£	s.	d.
12,000 pairs at 5s.	a pair	..	3,000	0	0
60,000 ,, ,, 3s.	,, ..	..	9,000	0	0
60,000 ,, ,, 1s. 4d.	,, ..	..	4,000	0	0
60,000 ,, socks at 8d. a pair	..	2,000	0	0
192,000		£18,000	0	0

Expenses:—				£	s.	d.
(a) wool : 72,000 pairs at 8d.	..	..	2,400	0	0
60,000 ,, ,, 7d.	..	..	1,750	0	0
60,000 ,, ,, 3d.	..	..	750	0	0
192,000		4,900	0	0
(b) dyeing : 1s. a dozen pairs	..	..	800	0	0
		£5,700	0	0

						£	s.	d.
Sale price ..	..	..	..	..	..	18,000	0	0
Cost of materials	..	..	..	..	..	4,900	0	0
Surplus ..	..	..	..	..	..	13,100	0	0
Cost of dyeing	..	..	..	..	..	800	0	0
Knitters' profits	..	..	..	..	12,300	0	0

[1] "In a piece of 132 yards they pay but for 120, and in a piece of 110 yards they account only for 100."

[2] *Cf.* the prices of stockings of "good Welsh cotton" worn by Cromwell's soldiers in Ireland, 1645–49 : 1s. to 1s. 1½d. (Firth, C. H. : *Cromwell's Army*, 1921, p. 236).

(4) SUMMARY.

Article.	Sales.	Costs.	Profits.
	£	£	£
Denbighshire small cloth ..	12,679	8,475	4,204
Dolgelley strong cloth ..	47,923	30,656	17,267
Bala stockings	18,000	4,900	13,100[1]
Montgomeryshire flannels	64,600	19,368	45,232
	£143,202	£63,399	£79,803

(Davies, pp. 395–6, 398, 402, 406.)

B. MERIONETH WEBS, 1809.

(a) *Expenses:*—
    (1) Spinning : woof, 2*d.* a lb. (wool 9*d.* to 12*d.* a lb.).
               warp bought in Caernarvonshire.
    (2) Weaving piece of 110 yards :—
          warp, 32 lbs. at 13*d.* to 24*d.* per lb.
          woof, 80 ,, ,, 12*d.* ,, 13*d.* ,, ,,
          weaving, 10*s.*
          fulling and scouring, 2*s.* 6*d.*

(b) *Sale price:*—
    18*d.* to 24*d.* per yard.

(c) *Sizes:*—
    1 web=2 pieces, each 100 to 120 yards long × ¾ yard to 1 yard
    wide.

(*N. W. Gaz*, May 4, 1809.)

¹ Including dyers' wages.

II. LABOURERS' BUDGETS.

A. LLANDEGLA AND LLANARMON.

(Contributed by Mr. John Edwards, 1788.)

1. Man, wife, and six children (eldest 13, youngest 3, five too young to earn).
2. Widow and five children (eldest 10, youngest 2).
3. Man, wife, and four children (eldest under 8, youngest baby).

	No. 1 (8 persons)			No 2. (7 persons)			No. 3 (6 persons)		
	£	s.	d.	£	s.	d.	£	s.	d.
Weekly expenses.									
Barley or oat meal	0	5	0	0	4	2	0	3	8
Butter	0	1	9	0	1	4	0	1	3
Milk	0	0	7	0	0	6	0	0	5
Potatoes	0	0	6	0	0	5	0	0	5
Salt, soap, and tallow ..	0	0	4½	0	0	4	0	0	4
Bread	0	0	1½	0	0	1	0	0	1
Total	0	8	4	0	6	10	0	6	2
Per annum	£21	13	4	£17	15	4	£16	0	8
Annual expenses.									
Rent of cottage and garden	1	5	0						
Clothing	1	10	0						
Fuel (3 cart loads coal) ..	1	1	0						
Shoes, hats, etc.	0	15	0						
Lying-in, etc.	1	10	0						
	6	1	0	5	10	0	5	0	0
	21	13	4	17	15	4	16	0	8
Total	£27	14	4	£23	5	4	£21	0	8
Weekly earnings.									
Man	0	6	0	—			0	6	0
Woman	0	1	0	0	4	0	0	0	6
				(parish) pay)					
Children	0	0	9				—		
	0	7	9	0	4	0	0	6	6
Per annum	20	3	0	10	8	0	16	18	0
Total annual expenses ..	£27	14	4	£23	5	4	£21	0	8
Total annual receipts ..	£20	3	0	£10	8	0	£16	18	0
Annual deficit	£7	11	4	£12	17	4	£4	2	8

B. Llanfawr and Llangeil (Llanycil)

(Communicated by Rev. S. Lloyd, Curate of Bala, 1788.)

1. Man, wife, and four children (eldest 10).
2. Man, wife, and six children (eldest 9).

			No. 1 (6 persons)			No. 2 (8 persons)		
Weekly expenses.			£	s.	d.	£	s.	d.
Barley or oat meal	..	..	0	4	6	0	5	0
Butter	..	..	0	1	8	0	1	6
Sugar	..	..	0	0	1		—	
Salt	..	..	0	0	1	0	0	1½
Milk	..	..	0	0	6	0	0	6
Potatoes ..	..	..	0	0	5	0	0	6
Soap, etc.	..	..	0	0	1	0	0	2
Tallow	..	..	0	0	2½	0	0	2
Total	..	..	0	7	6½	0	7	11½
Per annum	..	..	19	12	2	20	13	10
Clothes, rent, fuel, etc...	..	..	4	10	0	5	0	0
Total annual expenses ..	..	..	£24	2	2	£25	13	10
Weekly earnings.								
Man	..	..	0	6	6	0	6	0
Woman ..	..	..	0	0	9	0	1	0
Children ..	..	..	0	0	3	0	1	0
Total	..	..	0	7	6	0	8	0
Per annum	..	..	19	10	0	20	16	0
Total annual expenses	..	..	£24	2	2	£25	13	10
Total annual receipts	..	..	£19	10	0	£20	16	0
Annual deficit	..	..	£4	12	2	£4	17	10

(Davies : *Labourers in Husbandry*, pp. 188–91.)

C. LLANFERRES, 1797.

		s. d.
JANUARY (one week).		
Earnings.		
Father	.. ..	7 0
Eldest son	.. ..	2 6
		9 6
Expenses.		
Barley (1 measure) ..	.. ..	7 0
Butter (1 lb.).. ..	.. ..	0 9½
Potatoes (½ measure)	.. ..	1 0
Milk	.. ..	0 3
House and firing ..	.. ..	1 0
		10 0½
Deficit	.. ..	0 6½
HARVEST (one week).		
Earnings.		
Father	.. ..	10 6
Mother	.. ..	6 0
Eldest son ..	.. ..	2 6
Two girls (15 and 11)	.. ..	4 0
		23 0
Expenses.		
Barley (1 measure)	.. ..	7 0
Butter (1½ lb.) ..	.. ..	1 0
Potatoes ..	.. ..	1 0
Milk	.. ..	0 4
House and firing ..	.. ..	0 10
Butcher's meat ..	.. ..	1 0
Salt, etc.	.. ..	0 2
		11 4
Savings	.. ..	11 8
Rent (paid half-yearly) omitted.		

(Eden : *State of the Poor*, III, p. 887.)

INDEX OF PLACES.

A

Abenbury, 19, 24, 144.
Aber, 386n.
Aberdaron, 88n.
Aberdovey, 23n., 98, 148.
Abererch, 345n.
Aberffraw, 235.
Abergele, 34, 172, 224.
Aberglaslyn, 43, 93, 166.
Aberllefeni, 213n.
Abersychan, 146.
Aberystwyth, 34, 98f., 101, 122, 179 and n., 182, 186, 315, 330.
Acrefair, 145f., 151, 366f., 405. See also Ruabon.
Africa, 13, 157, 172, 230, 385.
Air, Point of. See Point of Air.
Alyn (Alun), R., 62, 174.
America (N.), 121, 136, 177, 214, 230, 237, 245, 267, 269ff., 278, 294, 378, 381, 385f., 397. See also Indies, New York, Nevada, Pennsylvania, South Carolina.
——(S.), 121, 131, 230.
Amlwch, 120, 124f., 127, 130, 156–62, 247n., 316, 322, 331, 333, 341, 355, 372, 374, 376, 384, 401.
Archangel 13.
Arustley (Arwystli), 83.
Australia, 177.

B

Bagillt, 20, 62, 126, 129, 184ff., 191, 193f., 197f., 299, 355, 360, 404.
Bala, 15, 113, 118, 213, 238f., 251, 268, 279, 300n., 326, 349, 355, 396, 400.
——Lake, 105.
——fault, 191.
Baltic, 294.
Bangor, 91, 93, 95, 99f., 116, 128f., 166, 205, 211, 220n., 298, 316, 318, 320–30 passim, 350n., 355n., 372f., 375ff., 384ff., 396f.

Bangor Iscoed, 373n.
Bardsey Is., 123.
Barmouth, 34, 98, 105, 120ff., 124, 128, 148, 168, 179, 186, 200, 213, 215n., 231, 238, 244, 294, 301.
Barnsley, 367n.
Basingwerk, 284.
Bath, 98.
Beaumaris, 25, 43f., 63, 95, 119ff., 126, 128f., 223f., 318, 320f., 327, 332, 355n., 376, 396.
Beddgelert, 112, 166n., 204, 210n., 215n.
Belfast, 130.
Belgium, 293.
Berriew, 54, 106, 252, 258, 271.
Bersham, 23f., 102f., 133–41, 144f., 149. See also Esclusham.
Berw, 310.
Berwyns, 16, 204.
Bethesda, 47, 220. See also Penrhyn quarry
Bettws Abergele, 81n.
——Garmon, 209 n.
——y coed, 204.
Birmingham, 22, 97, 115, 131, 153, 158f., 182, 185f., 224, 315, 329 and n., 386, 409f., 413. See also Smethwick, Soho.
——and Liverpool Railway, 115.
Blackwell Hall. See London.
Blaenau Ffestiniog, 204, 220. See also Ffestiniog.
Bodedern, 249, 332, 391f.
Bodfari, 55n., 249.
Bodorgan. See Meyrick.
Bolton, 408.
Boston, 42.
Bradford, 242.
Brecon, 315, 412, 414.
Brecknockshire, 39.
Bretton, 101.
Bristol, 23, 98, 120ff., 153, 156, 158, 171, 175, 182, 186, 210, 213, 300, 306, 311, 315, 330.

London, 7, 8, 14, 98ff., 108, 115, 120, 122f., 127, 130, 158, 168, 173, 181f., 193, 199, 210, 237, 239, 241, 244ff., 263 and *n*., 292, 300f., 314, 319f., 327f., 331, 335, 338, 367*n*., 409.
——and Birmingham Railway, 115.
——, Blackwell Hall, 13, 242.
——, Moorfields, 291.
——, New River, 42, 201.
——, Paddington, 108.
——, Smithfield, 26.
——, Spitalfields, 291, 329.
——, Welsh Hall, 13.
Long Mountain, 63.
Ludlow, 114, 118.

Ll

Llanaber, 66*n*., 67, 73*n*.
Llanaelhaiarn, 73.
Llanarmon Dyffryn Ceiriog, 249.
—— yn Ial, 170–2, 174–7, 309*n*., 420.
Llanasa, 174, 176.
Llanbeblig, 88*n*., 388.
Llanbedrog, 75.
Llanberis, 47, 93, 111, 154, 165, 210, 214, 217, 219ff., 358, 374, 381*n*.
Llanbrynmair, 182, 245, 257, 259ff., 264, 266, 271, 276, 381, 383, 397.
Llandanwg, 69, 88*n*.
Llanddeiniolen, 73*n*., 74*n*., 76–8, 80, 88*n*., 220 and *n*., 311*n*.
Llanddona, 56*n*.
Llandegai, 68, 220*n*.
Llandegla, 420.
Llandinam, 271, 362.
Llandisilio, 295.
Llandudno, 167.
Llandulas, 224, 226.
Llandwrog, 78, 88*n*., 220.
Llandyssil, 254, 260*n*., 271.
Llaneilian, 65*n*.
Llanelltyd, 122, 128, 298.
Llanerful, 85*n*.
Llanfachreth, 181.
Llanfair Caereinion, 98, 258, 259*n*., 263*n*., 396.
——pwll gwyngyll, 224.

Llanfawr, 56*n*., 421.
Llanfechell, 224.
Llanferres, 170ff., 174, 176f., 340, 374*n*., 422.
Llanfihangel y traethau, 88*n*.
Llanfwrog, 82.
Llanfyllin, 84, 258, 260 and *n*., 262*n*., 279*n*., 301, 333*n*., 373, 375*n*., 386, 394, 396.
Llangadfan, 381.
Llangadwaladr, 327 and *n*.
Llangefni, 66*n*., 74*u*., 295, 326, 376.
Llangollen, 41, 54, 104, 108, 117, 202, 212, 221, 238, 249, 264, 266, 268, 274, 289f., 295, 375*n*., 385f., 394.
Llangurig, 234, 258, 362.
Llangynog, 22, 122, 178, 180, 182f., 204, 213ff., 221.
Llanidan, 37, 306.
Llanidloes, 9, 83, 98, 119, 178–82, 236, 240f., 245, 255f., 258f., 261*n*., 263*n*., 266f., 269ff., 275f., 301, 317, 321, 326f., 346, 349*n*., 352, 361f., 363*n*., 367, 374, 383, 385*n*., 391, 396, 403, 409, 411–14, 416.
Llanllechid, 88*n*., 220*n*.
Llanllugan, 258.
Llanllwchaiarn. *See* Newtown.
Llanllyfni, 75, 217, 220, 310, 375*n*.
Llannerchrugog Hall, 142, 144.
Llannerch y medd (Llanerchy-medd), 56*n*., 235, 247*n*., 295, 302.
——y môr (Llanerchymor), 184, 191.
Llanrhaiadr ym Mochnant, 388.
Llanrûg, 88*n*., 247*n*., 250, 260*n*.
Llanrwst, 15, 69*n*., 92, 122, 247*n*., 298, 309*n*., 326, 328, 396f.
Llansannan, 16.
Llansantffraid ym Mechain, 295, 301, 326*n*., 374.
Llansilin, 374, 375*n*., 388.
Llantysilio Mountain, 204.
——Hall, 330*n*.
Llanuwchllyn, 213*n*.
Llanwnda, 78, 88*n*., 250.
Llanwnog, 258, 267.

INDEX OF PERSONS AND SUBJECTS.